5.6e $\frac{1}{125}$
4e $\frac{1}{125}$

Structured and Object-Oriented Techniques

Structured and Object-Oriented Techniques

An Introduction Using C++

SECOND EDITION

Andrew C. Staugaard, Jr.
College of the Ozarks

An Alan R. Apt Book

Prentice Hall, Upper Saddle River, New Jersey 07458

Library of Congress Cataloging-in-Publication Data
Staugaard, Andrew C.
    Structured and object-oriented techniques : an introduction using
  C++ / Andrew C. Staugaard, Jr. -- 2nd ed.
      p.   cm.
    "An Alan R. Apt book."
    Includes index.
    ISBN 0-13-488736-0
    1. C++ (Computer program language) 2. Structured programming.
  3. Object-Oriented Programming I. Title.
  QA76.73.C153S717   1996
  005.13'3–dc20   96-22095
                                                   CIP

Publisher: Alan Apt
Production Editor: Mona Pompili
Managing Editor: Laura Steele
Cover Designer: Bruce Kenselaar
Copy Editor: Shirley Michaels
Production Coordinator: Donna Sullivan
Editorial Assistant: Shirley McGuire

© 1997 by Prentice-Hall, Inc.
Simon & Schuster / A Viacom Company
Upper Saddle River, New Jersey 07458

The author and publisher of this book have used their best efforts in preparing this book. These efforts include the development, research, and testing of the theories and programs to determine their effectiveness. The author and publisher shall not be liable in any event for incidental or consequential damages in connection with, or arising out of, the furnishing, performance, or use of these programs.

Printed in the United States of America

10 9 8 7 6 5 4 3 2 1

ISBN 0-13-488736-0

PRENTICE-HALL INTERNATIONAL (UK) LIMITED, *London*
PRENTICE-HALL OF AUSTRALIA PTY. LIMITED, *Sydney*
PRENTICE-HALL CANADA, INC., *Toronto*
PRENTICE-HALL HISPANOAMERICANA, S.A., *Mexico*
PRENTICE-HALL OF INDIA PRIVATE LIMITED, *New Delhi*
PRENTICE-HALL OF JAPAN, INC., *Tokyo*
SIMON & SCHUSTER ASIA PTE. LTD., *Singapore*
EDITORA PRENTICE-HALL DO BRASIL, LTDA., *Rio de Janeiro*

PREFACE

This book has been written to provide an introduction to both structured and object-oriented programming techniques using the C++ language. Because of its hybrid nature, C++ is ideal for learning both the structured and object-oriented paradigms. It is no harder learning good program structuring techniques using C++ than it is using a traditional teaching language such as Pascal. Because C++ has taken the commercial software development industry by storm, an added benefit is that of learning a language that is widely accepted in the industrial world. This text starts from the beginning, assuming no previous knowledge of C, or any other programming language. The text is appropriate for any introductory programming (CS1) course using the C++ language as well as experienced programmers wanting an introduction to structured and object-oriented programming techniques using the C++ language.

Approach

The text emphasizes problem solving techniques using the C++ language. In fact, problem solving is the essential theme throughout the text. The student begins mastering the art of problem solving in Chapter 1, using problem abstraction and stepwise refinement via the "Programmer's Algorithm." Emphasis is first based on the structured (procedural) paradigm building gradually to the object-oriented paradigm. Traditional data types are presented as classes early, with constants and variables treated as objects of those classes. This approach gradually prepares the student for in-depth coverage of classes and objects later in the text, while building essential structured programming concepts.

This second edition is based on the highly successful first edition that has been widely used in CS1 courses since 1993. The first edition has been adopted at large and small institutions alike. One of the many reasons for the success of the first edition is that the text is highly readable and student oriented, with a teachable pedagogy and excellent features. The text provides sufficient material for a fast-paced one semester course or slower paced two semester course sequence.

Features

- Highly readable and student oriented.
- Thoroughly instructor and student tested via first edition adoptions at large and small institutions alike.
- Presentation and coverage of C++, adhering to the most current draft of the ANSI C++ standard.
- Early introduction to problem abstraction and stepwise refinement in Chapter 1 and used as a theme throughout the text with 19 "Problem Solving In Action" case studies.
- A gentle introduction to classes and objects, beginning in Chapter 2. In-depth coverage of C++ classes and objects in Chapter 9.
- The "Programmer's Algorithm": A step-by-step process used to get students started on the right programming tract by considering problem definition, solution planning via algorithms, and good documentation. Problem solving using problem abstraction and stepwise refinement, prior to coding, is stressed throughout the text. All "Problem Solving in Action" case studies follow these proven software engineering techniques.
- Early introduction to C++ functions for top-down design in Chapter 2.
- Discussion of a class at both the abstract and implementation levels provides the student the bigger software design picture as well as the coding details.
- Comprehensive development of the stack, queue, and linked list ADTs using C++ classes to ensure encapsulation and information hiding.
- ADTs viewed as black boxes, thus illustrating the importance of the function interfaces over the implementation details at the software design level.
- Over 70 tip and note boxes for students throughout, including
  - Programming Tips
  - Programming Notes
  - Style Tips
  - Debugging Tips
  - Debugging Results
  - Caution Boxes
  - Compiler Notes
- Over 350 section-by-section quick-check exercises for students to check their progress with all answers in an appendix.
- Over 70 examples that pose problems and then give solutions immediately.

- Over 270 chapter questions.
- Over 175 chapter programming problems with solutions in an instructor's manual and accompanying disk.
- Important terms and concepts are boxed throughout the text.
- Entire chapter on class inheritance, including a real-world "Problem Solving in Action" exercise for using inheritance via a banking example.
- All C++ syntax formatting is shown throughout within shaded boxes
- Comprehensive glossary of general computer science as well as object-oriented programming terms.
- Comprehensive index.

To the Instructor

This text has been written to teach structured and object-oriented programming techniques using the C++ language at the freshman level in a CS1 type of course. In today's market, it is imperative that students know both paradigms. Students understand the roles of and relationship between classes and objects early-on by treating the standard data types as classes and variables as objects of those classes, while at the same time learning structured programming techniques. I have found that there is *no* "paradigm shift" when class and object concepts are integrated into the structured paradigm. Structured, or procedural, programming is built around functions, and object-oriented programming is built around classes. Do the two have any relationship whatsoever? Yes! The classes that we build are constructed using elements of structured programming, namely functions. As a result, the structured paradigm is embedded within the object-oriented paradigm. This is why we need to study structured programming first, integrating object-oriented conepts where the oportunity arises, and gradually move into object-oriented programming.

Some will say that you can't teach programming using C++, because the language is too complicated. I disagree. There is no need to teach every detail of the language in a beginning course. I have used a subset of C++ to teach fundamental structuring and object-oriented concepts and have found that beginning students do not have any more difficulty using C++ than Pascal with this approach. In addition, learning C++ has the added benefit for the student of learning a very widely used industry standard.

The text can be taught in one or two terms, depending on the ability of the students. In a two term sequence, I would suggest coverage through the topic of functions (Chapters 1–7). Then, begin the second term with arrays and finish out the book (Chapters 8–14).

The text begins with problem solving using problem abstraction and stepwise refinement in Chapter 1. These concepts are presented in detail here and used as a theme throughout the text. The chapter discusses problem solving using what I call "The Programmer's Algorithm" and should be covered thoroughly. The programmer's algorithm is a step-by-step process that I have used to get students started on the right programming track by considering problem definition, step-by-step solution planning via algorithms, and good documentation. I have employed a pseudocode algorithmic language for problem solution that is generic, simple, and allows for easy translation to the coded C++ program.

Chapter 2 introduces the concepts of data abstraction and ADTs. Traditional data types are treated as classes with constants and variables treated as objects of those classes. Here is where we begin integrating the structured and object-oriented paradigms to prevent any possible "paradigm shift" for the student when object-oriented programming is covered in-depth in Chapter 9. I suggest that you emphasize the concepts of classes, objects, and ADTs here to get students accustomed to object-oriented concepts. Discussing traditional data typing in terms of classes and objects provides an ideal opportunity to introduce object-orientation. In addition, Chapter 2 introduces students to C++ functions, the common denominator of both paradigms.

In Chapters 3–6, students learn about program I/O, decision making, and iteration. These chapters provide the "nuts and bolts" required to write workable C++ programs. The sequence, decision, and iteration control structures available in C++ are covered thoroughly, emphasizing program logic and the required C++ syntax. The common pitfalls of program logic design are pointed out throughout this material via program debugging tips and caution boxes. Again, I have integrated object-oriented techniques within these traditional structured programming topics, especially in Chapter 3 when using the C++ I/O classes and objects. Chapter 3 also introduces files so that students can begin reading and writing their own files early. Again, this opportunity is used to integrate object-oriented techniques into the discussion through the use of C++ file stream classes and objects. Detailed file manipulation is covered later, in Chapter 13.

At this point, your students have a solid knowledge of the important role of functions for both the structure and object-oriented paradigms. Since Chapter 2, they have been designing structured programs using functional decomposition and have observed the role of functions relative to object behavior. In Chapter 7, functions are covered in-depth. This chapter has been greatly improved over the previous edition, based on my experience of teaching C++ functions. I have incorporated easy to follow guidelines for building function interfaces relative to the topics of return values and parameter passing. It is critical that students understand this material in order to become successful C++ programmers and understand the object-oriented concepts presented in later chapters. The last section of this chapter discusses the important topic of problem solving with recursion. Recursion is introduced via a simple compound interest example, followed by and in-depth discussion of how recursion works and when it should be applied.

Students get their first exposure to data structures in Chapter 8, which discusses one-dimensional arrays. Again, I feel it is important that students have a solid knowledge of arrays and their manipulation. As result, this chapter covers traditional C-type arrays and not some array class built by the author to hide the details and pitfalls associated with arrays. I have also used this topic to present several classic searching and sorting algorithms which are essential at this level.

At this point, the student is prepared to learn about classes and objects in-depth. Again, there will be *no* paradigm shift here, because we have integrated these topics into the course since Chapter 1. In-depth coverage of classes and objects is provided in Chapter 9 and a solid introduction to class inheritance is provided in Chapter 10. Chapter 9 begins with a discussion of C++ structures (records). Structures are discussed in detail as an introduction to C++ classes, which are essentially structures with function members. In the remaining sections of Chapter 9, students learn how to create their own classes and objects, using them in object-oriented programs. Chapter 10 expands on the material in Chapter 9 by discussing inheritance. Many texts avoid the topic of inheritance. However, inheritance is one of the cornerstones of OOP and is relatively easy to cover at this point. Chapter 10 provides the student with solid understanding of inheritance through a comprehensive banking example. The chapter closes with a discussion of polymorphism and dynamic binding.

The important topic of pointers is "addressed" in Chapter 11. This material, combined with the material on classes and objects in the previous two chapters, prepares the student to learn about the classic stack, queue, and linked-list ADTs in Chapter 12. Pointers are fundamental to programming in C++ and should be covered thoroughly. Furthermore, subsequent chapters employ pointers throughout so that the student becomes comfortable with their use.

Chapter 13 provides an introduction to ADTs in preparation for an advanced course in data structures. The classic stack, queue, and linked list ADTs are covered thoroughly. In this chapter, ADTs are covered at two levels: The purely abstract level using the black box interface approach, and at the implementation level using C++ classes. Here is where the student really appreciates object-oriented programming, because ADTs are naturally implemented using C++ classes.

Files manipulation is discussed in-depth in Chapter 13. Here, the student learns how to read, write, append, and change disk files using C++. The topic of files in C++ provides a great opportunity to show how C++ employs inheritance to create reusable code. Here, the student learns how to employ inheritance through the C++ file stream class hierarchy to implement files.

The text closes with a chapter on multidimensional arrays. This chapter focuses primarily on the manipulation of two-dimensional arrays. The chapter closes with a comprehensive case study which applies two-dimensional arrays to simultaneous equation solution using Cramer's rule. If you wish, you can cover this chapter immediately after covering one-dimensional arrays in Chapter 8 without any loss in continuity.

The code in the text is portable and meets the new ANSI C++ standard as close as possible at this time. New features of the language, such as the **bool** class, are covered even though current compilers might not implement these features. When this is the case, the text shows how to implement these new features using the pre-ANSI C++ language definition.

Finally, the following supplements are available to support this text:

- A student laboratory manual and workbook that provides over 30 laboratory exercises that guide the student through program development with minimal instructor involvement. (ISBN 0-13-193061-3)
- A solutions manual that provides solutions to all the chapter questions and problems.
- An instructor's disk that provides source code to all the chapter programming problems.
- "Problem Solving in Action" source code as well as the text figures for making transparencies can be downloaded using ftp from

  ftp.prenhall.com

  login as anonymous

  use your e-mail address as the password

  change directory to: pub/esm/the_apt_series.s-042/staugaard/struct.00.tech

To the Student

The market demands that computing professionals know the latest programming and software engineering techniques. This book has been written to provide you with an introduction to both structured and object-oriented programming techniques—two of the most important and widely used techniques within the industry. The text emphasizes problem solution through the use of problem abstraction and stepwise refinement throughout. You will learn to attack problems using a "divide and conquer" strategy. By the end of the text you will have the knowledge required to solve complicated problems using this modular top-down structured approach that today's computer solutions require. In addition, you will get a solid introduction to *object-oriented programming (OOP)* and *abstract data types (ADTs)* to prepare you for further study of these topics.

Make sure that you go through all the examples and "Problem Solving in Action" case studies. These have been written in short, understandable modules that stress the fundamental concepts being discussed. These problems are integrated into the text at key points in an effort to tie things together and present a structured design approach to problem solving using the C++ language.

Finally, above all, get your hands dirty! You cannot become a competent programmer by just reading this book and listening to your instructor's lectures. You must get your hands dirty at the machine by developing *your own* C++ programs. Get started early by sitting down at a computer, getting acquainted with your C++ compiler, and writing *your own* C++ programs.

To the Professional

The C++ programming language has taken the commercial software development industry by storm. Most of today's window-based software is being developed using C++ because of its object-orientation. Whether you are an experienced programmer or a novice, you will find that this book provides the "nuts and bolts" required to get you writing C++ programs quickly. In fact, this book is all that you will need to begin learning the C++ language. The text provides comprehensive coverage of structured programming using the C++ language and a sound introduction to object-oriented programming, both of which are essential in today's programming market.

Acknowledgments

Contributions to this text have come from many circles. From the academic world I would like to thank Buster Dunsmore of Purdue University, George Luger of the University of New Mexico, Keith Pierce of the University of Minnesota, and Bob Holloway of the University of Wisconsin, at Madison. All have reviewed the manuscript and have made valuable contributions. Special thanks to Bob Holloway who made many excellent suggestions for this second edition.

From the industrial world, I would like to thank Bjarne Stroustrup of Bell Labs who reviewed the first edition manuscript and made many valuable suggestions relative to teaching C++ to beginning students as well as the language philosophy and details.

From the student world, I would like to thank my own students who, over that past five years, have inspired the creation of this text and have made many valuable suggestions. In particular I would like to thank Brenda Snider, a former student and now colleague, who developed the appendix material and reviewed the text from a student's perspective.

From the publishing world of Prentice Hall, I would like to thank my managing editor, Alan Apt, who has created one of the best series of textbooks in the business. I also thank my development editor, Laura Steele, for her guidance during the preparation of this revision. Special thanks go to Mona Pompili, one of the best production editors in the business.

Finally, I would like to thank my youngest son, Andrew III, for his help in the production phase of this text.

Please direct all correspondence to e-mail address **staug@cofo.edu**. I strongly encourage any comments or suggestions that you might have, pro or con.

Enjoy!

Andrew C. Staugaard, Jr.

BRIEF CONTENTS

CHAPTER 1: PROBLEM SOLVING, ABSTRACTION,
AND STEPWISE REFINEMENT   1

CHAPTER 2: DATA ABSTRACTION, CLASSES,
AND OBJECTS   28

CHAPTER 3: INPUT AND OUTPUT OBJECTS   96

CHAPTER 4: STANDARD OPERATIONS IN C++   162

CHAPTER 5: MAKING DECISIONS   210

CHAPTER 6: LOOPING OPERATIONS: ITERATION   250

CHAPTER 7: FUNCTIONS IN-DEPTH   303

CHAPTER 8: ARRAYS   377

CHAPTER 9: CLASSES AND OBJECTS IN-DEPTH   428

CHAPTER 10: CLASS INHERITANCE   504

CHAPTER 11: POINTERS   529

CHAPTER 12: ADTs   580

CHAPTER 13: FILE STREAM I/O: A CASE FOR
INHERITANCE   641

CHAPTER 14: MULTIDIMENSIONAL ARRAYS   670

APPENDIX A: QUICK CHECK SOLUTIONS   710

APPENDIX B: ASCII CHARACTER TABLE   744

GLOSSARY   746

INDEX   756

CONTENTS

CHAPTER 1: PROBLEM SOLVING, ABSTRACTION, AND STEPWISE REFINEMENT

INTRODUCTION   2
1-1 THE PROGRAMMER'S ALGORITHM   2
   Defining the Problem   3
   Planning the Solution   4
   Coding the Program   5
   Testing and Debugging the Program   5
      Desk-Checking the Program   6
      Compiling and Linking the Program   7
      Running the Program   8
      Using a Debugger   8
   Documentation   9
1-2 PROBLEM SOLVING USING ALGORITHMS   10
1-3 PROBLEM ABSTRACTION AND STEPWISE REFINEMENT   13
PROBLEM SOLVING IN ACTION: PYTHAGOREAN THEOREM   16
PROBLEM SOLVING IN ACTION: SALES TAX   20
PROBLEM SOLVING IN ACTION: CREDIT CARD INTEREST   22
CHAPTER SUMMARY   24
QUESTIONS AND PROBLEMS   25
   Questions   25
   Problems   26

CHAPTER 2: DATA ABSTRACTION, CLASSES, AND OBJECTS

INTRODUCTION   29
2-1 SOFTWARE   30
   Machine Language   31
   Assembly Language   32
   High-Level Language   32
   Why C++?   35
2-2 THE IDEA OF DATA ABSTRACTION AND CLASSES   36
2-3 THE STANDARD DATA CLASSES IN C++   41
   The Integer Class   41
   The Floating-Point Class   44
   The Character Class   48
      Strings   51
   The Boolean Class   52

2-4 CONSTANT AND VARIABLE OBJECTS   54
    Declaring Constant Objects   55
        Constant String Objects   57
    Defining Variable Objects   58
        Variable String Objects   62
        Boolean Objects   64
2-5 ENUMERATED CLASSES AND OBJECTS   65
    Declaring Enumerated Classes and Objects   66
        The Ordering of Enumerated Data   67
2-6 THE STRUCTURE OF A C++ PROGRAM   70
    The Preprocessor Section   70
        The *#include* Directive   71
    The Main Function Section   72
2-7 TOP-DOWN DESIGN USING C++ FUNCTIONS   76
PROBLEM SOLVING IN ACTION: BANK ACCOUNT PROCESSING   79
CHAPTER SUMMARY   86
QUESTIONS AND PROBLEMS   87
    Questions   87
    Problems   90

CHAPTER 3: INPUT AND OUTPUT OBJECTS

INTRODUCTION   97
3-1 GETTING THINGS OUT ⇒ *cout*   97
    Using the *cout* Object   97
        Getting Out Fixed Numeric Informaion   98
        Getting Out Fixed Character Information   99
        Getting Out Variable Information   100
        Monitor versus Printer Output   105
    Formatting the Output   107
        Formatting Floating-Point Output   114
3-2 GETTING THINGS IN: ⇒ *cin*   118
    Reading Mixed Data Classes   122
    Reading Single-Character Data   125
        Using *get()* To Read Single Character Data   128
    Reading String Data   130
        Using *getline()* to Read Strings   132
        Using *gets()* and *fgets()* to Read Strings   138
3-3 READING AND WRITING DISK FILES   142
    File Streams   142
    Classes: the Basis for C++ Files   142
    Reading and Writing a Disk File   145
        Using Loops to Read and Process Files   148
PROBLEM SOLVING IN ACTION: USER-FRIENDLY PROGRAMS   150
CHAPTER SUMMARY   155
QUESTIONS AND PROBLEMS   157
    Questions   157
    Problems   159

CHAPTER 4: STANDARD OPERATIONS IN C++

INTRODUCTION	163
4-1 ARITHMETIC OPERATIONS	163
Increment and Decrement Operators	167
4-2 ASSIGNMENT OPERATIONS	169
PROBLEM SOLVING IN ACTION: INVENTORY CONTROL	171
4-3 BOOLEAN OPERATIONS	179
Relational Operators	179
Logical Operators	181
PROBLEM SOLVING IN ACTION: BOOLEAN LOGIC	184
4-4 SOME STANDARD FUNCTIONS IN C++	188
Conversion Functions	188
Mathematical Functions	188
String Functions	189
PROBLEM SOLVING IN ACTION: DATA COMMUNICATIONS	192
A TECHNICAL CHALLENGE: POLAR AND RECTANGULAR COORDINATES	197
CHAPTER SUMMARY	202
QUESTIONS AND PROBLEMS	203
Questions	203
Problems	206

CHAPTER 5: MAKING DECISIONS

INTRODUCTION	211
5-1 THE **if** STATEMENT	212
5-2 THE **if/else** STATEMENT	217
5-3 NESTED **if**'s	221
5-4 THE switch STATEMENT	227
The **default** Option	232
PROBLEM SOLVING IN ACTION: MENU-DRIVEN PROGRAMS	234
CHAPTER SUMMARY	243
QUESTIONS AND PROBLEMS	244
Questions	244
Problems	247

CHAPTER 6: LOOPING OPERATIONS: ITERATION

INTRODUCTION	251
6-1 THE **while** LOOP	251
Data Entry Using **while**	258
6-2 THE **do/while** LOOP	262
PROBLEM SOLVING IN ACTION: LOOP-CONTROLLED MENU-DRIVEN PROGRAMS	267
6-3 THE **for** LOOP	274
Nested Loops	281
Down-to **for** Loops	283

6-4 THE **break** AND **continue** OPTIONS 284
   The **break** Statement 284
   The **continue** Statement 286
PROBLEM SOLVING IN ACTION: PARALLEL RESISTOR CIRCUIT ANALYSIS 288
CHAPTER SUMMARY 296
QUESTIONS AND PROBLEMS 297
   Questions 297
   Problems 300

CHAPTER 7: FUNCTIONS IN-DEPTH

INTRODUCTION 304
7-1 FUNCTIONS THAT RETURN A SINGLE VALUE: NON-VOID FUNCTIONS 305
   The Function Header 306
      The Return Data Class 307
      The Function Name 307
      The Parameter Listing 308
   The Statement Section 310
   Calling Non-Void Functions 312
   Actual Arguments versus Formal Parameters 314
7-2 VOID FUNCTIONS 316
   Value versus Reference Parameters 318
      Value Parameters 318
      Reference Parameters 320
   Locating Functions Within Your Program 324
7-3 FUNCTION PROTOTYPES 326
   Default Parameters 329
   Function Overloading 331
PROBLEM SOLVING IN ACTION: STRUCTURED PROGRAMMING 334
7-4 SCOPING-OUT VARIABLES AND CONSTANTS $\Rightarrow$ BLOCK STRUCTURE 347
   The Scope of Variables 349
   The Scope of Constants 351
   Static Variables 351
7-5 RECURSION 353
PROBLEM SOLVING IN ACTION: STRUCTURED PROGRAMMING 361
CHAPTER SUMMARY 369
QUESTIONS AND PROBLEMS 371
   Questions 371
   Problems 373

CHAPTER 8: ARRAYS

INTRODUCTION 378
8-1 THE STRUCTURE OF AN ARRAY 378
   The Array Elements 380
   The Array Indices 380
8-2 DEFINING ONE-DIMENSIONAL ARRAYS IN C++ 381
8-3 ACCESSING ARRAYS 382

Inserting Elements into One-Dimensional Arrays   383
  Direct Assignment   383
  Reading Elements into the Array   384
  Inserting Array Elements Using Loops   384
Extracting Elements from One-Dimensional Arrays   386
  Direct Assignment   386
  Writing Array Elements   387
  Extracting Array Elements Using Loops   388
8-4 PASSING ARRAYS AND ARRAY ELEMENTS TO FUNCTIONS   390
PROBLEM SOLVING IN ACTION: SEARCHING AN ARRAY USING ITERATION (SEQUENTIAL
SEARCH)   400
PROBLEM SOLVING IN ACTION: SORTING AN ARRAY USING ITERATION (INSERTION
SORT)   403
PROBLEM SOLVING IN ACTION: SEARCHING AN ARRAY USING RECURSION (BINARY
SEARCH)   409
8-5 INITIALIZING ARRAYS   416
  Default Initialization of Global and Static Arrays   420
CHAPTER SUMMARY   422
QUESTIONS AND PROBLEMS   423
  Questions   423
  Problems   425

CHAPTER 9: CLASSES AND OBJECTS IN-DEPTH

INTRODUCTION   429
9-1 STRUCTURES   430
  Declaring Structures   431
  Defining Structure Objects   432
  Initializing Structures When They Are Defined   435
  Storing Information into Structures   437
    Direct Assignment   437
    Reading Information into a Structure   438
  Retrieving Information from Structures   439
  Nested Structures   445
9-2 CLASSES AND OBJECTS   452
  The Idea of Classes and Objects   452
  Classes   454
    The Abstract Level   454
    The Implementation Level   456
  Encapsulation   458
  Information Hiding   458
  Objects   467
    Defining Objects   468
9-3 MEMBER FUNCTIONS   470
  Constructors   472
    Default Parameters for Constructors   474
    Overloaded Constructors   475
  Scoping Inside of Functions   478

The Scoping Operator Revisited   479
The "this" Pointer   479
Access Functions   482
Messages   483
Putting Everything Together in a Complete Program   485
9-4 MULTIFILE PROGRAM CONSTRUCTION   488
PROBLEM SOLVING IN ACTION: BUILDING A MULTIFILE C++ PROGRAM   490
CHAPTER SUMMARY   494
QUESTIONS AND PROBLEMS   496
Questions   496
Problems   500

CHAPTER 10: CLASS INHERITANCE

INTRODUCTION   505
10-1 WHY USE INHERITANCE?   505
10-2 DECLARING AND USING DERIVED CLASSES   508
Single versus Multiple Inheritance   521
Using #ifndef : An Implementation Detail   522
10-3 POLYMORPHISM AND DYNAMIC BINDING   523
Polymorphism   523
Dynamic versus Static Binding   524
CHAPTER SUMMARY   526
QUESTIONS AND PROBLEMS   526
Questions   526
Problems   527

CHAPTER 11: POINTERS

INTRODUCTION   530
11-1 THE IDEA OF POINTERS   530
11-2 DEFINING POINTERS AND INITIALIZING POINTER DATA   533
Static Pointers   534
Dynamic Pointers   535
11-3 ACCESSING POINTER DATA AND POINTER ARITHMETIC   538
Pointer Arithmetic   540
11-4 ARRAYS OF POINTERS ⇒ INDIRECTION   544
11-5 USING POINTERS AS FUNCTION ARGUMENTS AND PARAMETERS   547
11-6 POINTERS TO FUNCTIONS   552
11-7 STRUCTURE AND OBJECT POINTERS   555
Defining Structure Pointers   555
Using the Pointer Operator to Access Structure Data   557
Reading Information into a Structure   558
Retrieving Information from Structures   558
Defining Class Object Pointers   564
Using the Pointer Operator to Send Messages to Objects   565
Destructors   567
CHAPTER SUMMARY   573

QUESTIONS AND PROBLEMS   574
   Questions   574
   Problems   576

CHAPTER 12: ADTs

INTRODUCTION   581
12-1 THE CONCEPT OF DATA ABSTRACTION REVISITED   581
12-2 ADT STACK   585
   Implementing the Stack ADT   588
     Creating a Stack Using an Array   588
     Pushing Elements onto a Stack   589
     Popping Elements from a Stack   591
     Inspecting the Top Element of a Stack   593
     Coding the Stack ADT   594
12-3 ADT QUEUE   601
   Implementing the Queue ADT   603
     Creating a Queue Using a Circular Array   603
     Inserting Elements into a Queue   604
     Removing Elements from a Queue   607
     Inspecting the Front Element of a Queue   609
     Coding the Queue ADT   610
12-4 ADT LIST   616
   Linked Lists   617
   Implementing the Linked List ADT   620
     Creating an Empty Linked List   620
     Inserting Data into a Linked List   621
     Deleting Data from a Linked List   624
     Traversing a Linked List   628
     Checking for an Empty List   628
     Coding the Linked List ADT   629
CHAPTER SUMMARY   636
QUESTIONS AND PROBLEMS   637
   Questions   637
   Problems   638

CHAPTER 13: FILE STREAM I/O: A CASE FOR INHERITANCE

INTRODUCTION   642
13-1 FUNDAMENTAL CONCEPTS AND IDEAS   642
   Classes Provide the Basis for C++ Files   643
   Creating File Streams in C++: The File Stream Definition   644
13-2 ACCESSING FILE INFORMATION   648
   The File Window   648
   File Operations   649
     Getting A Disk File Name from the User   651
     Writing, or Creating, a New File   651
     Reading and Displaying an Existing File   654

Appending an Existing File   656
Changing an Existing File   658
The Application Program   664
CHAPTER SUMMARY   666
QUESTIONS AND PROBLEMS   667
Questions   667
Problems   668

CHAPTER 14: MULTIDIMENSIONAL ARRAYS

INTRODUCTION   671
14-1 TWO-DIMENSIONAL ARRAYS   671
Defining Two-Dimensional Arrays in C++   672
Accessing Two-Dimensional Array Elements   675
Direct Assignment of Two-Dimensional Array Elements   675
Reading and Writing Two-Dimensional Array Elements   677
Using Loops to Access Two-Dimensional Arrays   677
14-2 ARRAYS OF MORE THAN TWO DIMENSIONS   688
PROBLEM SOLVING IN ACTION: SIMULTANEOUS EQUATION SOLUTION   692
Determinants   692
Expansion of a Determinant   693
An Order 2 Determinant Expansion Function   695
Cramer's Rule   696
Implementing Cramer's Rule in C++   697
CHAPTER SUMMARY   703
QUESTIONS AND PROBLEMS   704
Questions   704
Problems   705
                                                                                   748

APPENDIX A: QUICK-CHECK SOLUTIONS

CHAPTER 1   710
CHAPTER 2   711
CHAPTER 3   715
CHAPTER 4   717
CHAPTER 5   719
CHAPTER 6   721
CHAPTER 7   723
CHAPTER 8   725
CHAPTER 9   727
CHAPTER 10   731
CHAPTER 11   732
CHAPTER 12   737
CHAPTER 13   740
CHAPTER 14   741

APPENDIX B: ASCII CHARACTER TABLE   744

GLOSSARY   746

INDEX   756

Structured and Object-Oriented Techniques

1

PROBLEM SOLVING, ABSTRACTION, AND STEPWISE REFINEMENT

INTRODUCTION
1-1 THE PROGRAMMER'S ALGORITHM
    Defining the Problem
    Planning the Solution
    Coding the Program
    Testing and Debugging the Program
    Documentation
1-2 PROBLEM SOLVING USING ALGORITHMS
1-3 PROBLEM ABSTRACTION AND STEPWISE REFINEMENT
PROBLEM SOLVING IN ACTION: PYTHAGOREAN THEOREM
PROBLEM SOLVING IN ACTION: SALES TAX
PROBLEM SOLVING IN ACTION: CREDIT CARD INTEREST
CHAPTER SUMMARY
QUESTIONS AND PROBLEMS
    Questions
    Problems

INTRODUCTION

Programming reduces to the art and science of problem solving. To be a good programmer, you must be a good problem solver. To be a good problem solver, you must attack a problem in a methodical way, from initial problem inspection and definition to final solution, testing, and documentation. In the beginning, when confronted with a programming problem, you will be tempted to get to the computer and start coding as soon as you get an idea of how to solve it. However, you *must* resist this temptation. Such an approach might work for simple problems, but will *not* work when you are confronted with the complex problems found in today's real world. A good carpenter might attempt to build a dog house without a plan, but would never attempt to build your "dream house" without a good set of blueprints.

In this chapter, you will learn about a systematic method that will make you a good problem solver, and therefore a good programmer—I call it the ***programmer's algorithm***. In particular, you will study the steps required to solve just about any programming problem using a *top-down structured* approach. You will be introduced to the concept of ***abstraction***, which allows problems to be viewed in general terms without agonizing over the implementation details required by a computer language. From an initial abstract solution, you will refine the solution step-by-step until it reaches a level that can be coded directly into a computer program. Make sure you understand this material and work the related problems at the end of the chapter. As you become more experienced in programming, you will find that the "secret" to successful programming is good planning through abstract analysis and stepwise refinement, which results in top-down structured software designs. Such designs are supported by languages like C++. In the chapters that follow, you will build on this knowledge to create workable C++ programs.

1-1 THE PROGRAMMER'S ALGORITHM

Before we look at the programmer's algorithm, it might be helpful to define what is meant by an algorithm. In technical terms, it is as follows:

An ***algorithm*** is a series of step-by-step instructions that produces a solution to a problem.

Algorithms are not unique to the computer industry. Any set of instructions, such as those you might find in a recipe or a kit assembly guide, can be considered an algorithm. The programmer's algorithm is a recipe for you, the programmer, to follow when developing programs. The algorithm is as follows:

THE PROGRAMMER'S ALGORITHM

- Define the problem.
- Plan the problem solution.
- Code the program.
- Test and debug the program.
- Document the program.

Defining the Problem

You might suggest that defining the problem is an obvious step in solving any problem. However, it often is the most overlooked step, especially in computer programming. The lack of good problem definition often results in "spinning your wheels," especially in more complex computer programming applications.

Think of a typical computer programming problem, such as controlling the inventory of a large department store. What must be considered as part of the problem definition? The first consideration probably is what you want to get out of the system. Will the output information consist of printed inventory reports or, in addition, will the system automatically generate product orders based on sales? Must any information generated by a customer transaction be saved permanently on disk, or can it be discarded? What type of data is the output information to consist of? Is it numerical data, character data, or both? How must the output data be formatted? All of these questions must be answered in order to define the output requirements.

Careful consideration of the output requirements usually leads to deciding what must be put into the system in order to obtain the desired system output. For instance, in our department store inventory example, a desired output would be most likely a summary of customer transactions. How are these transactions to be entered into the system? Is the data to be obtained from a keyboard, or is product information to be entered automatically via an optical character recognition (OCR) system that reads the bar code on the product price tags? Does the input consist of all numerical data, character data, or a combination of both? What is the format of the data?

The next consideration is processing. Will most of the customer processing be done at the cash register terminal, or will it be handled by a central store computer? What about credit card verification and inventory records? Will this processing be done by a local microcomputer, a minicomputer located within the store, or a central mainframe computer located in a different part of the country? What kind of programs will be written to do the processing, and who will write them? What sort of calculations and decisions must be made on the data within individual programs to achieve the desired output?

All of these questions must be answered when defining any computer programming problem. In summary, you could say that problem definition must consider the application requirements of output, input, and processing. The department store inventory problem clearly requires precise definition. However, even with small application programs, you must still consider the type of output, input, and processing that the problem requires.

When defining a problem, look for the nouns and verbs within a problem statement. The nouns often suggest input and output information, and the verbs suggest processing steps. The application will always dictate the problem definition. I will discuss problem definition further, as we begin to develop computer programs to solve real problems.

PROBLEM-SOLVING TIP

Look for the nouns and verbs within a problem statement; they often provide clues to the required output, input, and processing. The nouns suggest output and input, and the verbs suggest processing steps.

Planning the Solution

The planning stage associated with any problem is probably the most important part of the solution, and computer programming is no exception. Imagine trying to build a house without a good set of blueprints. The results could be catastrophic! The same is true of trying to develop computer software without a good plan. When developing computer software, the planning stage is implemented using a collection of algorithms. As you already know, an algorithm is a series of step-by-step instructions that produce results to solve problems. When planning computer programs, algorithms are used to outline the solution steps using English-like statements, called ***pseudocode***, that require less precision than a formal programming language. A good pseudocode algorithm should be independent of, but easily translated into, *any* formal programming language.

Pseudocode is an informal set of English-like statements that are generally accepted within the computer industry to denote common computer programming operations. Pseudocode statements are used to describe the steps in a computer algorithm.

Coding the Program

Coding the program should be one of the simplest tasks in the whole programming process, provided you have done a good job of defining the problem and planning its solution. Coding involves the actual writing of the program in a formal programming language. The computer language you use will be determined by the nature of the problem, the programming languages available to you, and the limits of the computer system. Once a language is chosen, the program is written, or coded, by translating your algorithm steps into the formal language code.

I should caution you, however, that coding is really a mechanical process and should be considered secondary to algorithm development. In the future, computers will generate their own program code from well-constructed algorithms. Research in the field of artificial intelligence has resulted in "code-generation" software. The thing to keep in mind is that computers might someday generate their own programming code from algorithms, but it takes the creativity and common sense of a human being to plan the solution and develop the algorithm.

Testing and Debugging the Program

You will soon find out that it is a rare and joyous occasion when a coded program actually "runs" the first time without any errors. Of course, good problem definition and planning will avoid many program mistakes, or "bugs." However, there always are a few bugs that manage to go undetected, regardless of how much planning you do. Getting rid of the program bugs (*debugging*) often is the most time-consuming job in the whole programming process. Industrial statistics show that often over 50 percent of a programmer's time is often spent on program debugging.

There is no absolute correct procedure for debugging a program, but a systematic approach can help make the process easier. The basic steps of debugging are as follows:

- Realizing that you have an error.
- Locating and determining the cause of the error.
- Fixing the error.

First of all, you have to realize that you have an error. Sometimes, this is obvious when your computer freezes up or crashes. At other times, the program might work fine until certain unexpected information is entered by someone using the program. The most subtle errors occur when the program is running fine and the results look correct, but when you examine the results closely, they are not quite right.

The next step in the debugging process is locating and determining the cause of the errors—sometimes the most difficult part of debugging. This is where a good programming tool, called a ***debugger***, comes into play.

Fixing the error is the final step in debugging. Your knowledge of the C++ language, this book, C++ on-line help, a C++ debugger, and your C++ reference manuals are all valuable tools in fixing the error and removing the "bug" from your program.

When programming in C++, there are four things that you can do to test and debug your program: ***desk-check*** the program, ***compile/link*** the program, ***run*** the program, and ***debug*** the program.

Desk-Checking the Program

Desk-checking a program is similar to proofreading a letter or manuscript. The idea is to trace through the program mentally to make sure that the program logic is workable. You must consider various input possibilities, and write down any results generated during program execution. In particular, try to determine what the program will do with unusual data by considering input possibilities that "shouldn't" happen. Always keep Murphy's law in mind when desk-checking a program: If a given condition can't or shouldn't happen, it will!

For example, suppose a program requires the user to enter a value whose square root must be found. Of course, the user "shouldn't" enter a negative value, because the square root of a negative number is imaginary. However, what will the program do if he or she does? Another input possibility that should always be considered is an input of zero, especially when used as part of an arithmetic operation, such as division.

When you first begin programming, you will be tempted to skip the desk-checking phase, because you can't wait to run the program once it is written. However, as you gain experience, you soon will realize the time-saving value of desk-checking.

Compiling and Linking the Program

At this point, you are ready to enter the program into the computer system. Once entered, the program must be compiled, or translated, into machine code. Fortunately, the compiler is designed to check for certain program errors. These usually are *syntax* errors that you have made when coding the program. A syntax error is any violation of the rules of the programming language, such as using a period instead of a semicolon. There might also be type errors. A *type error* occurs when you attempt to mix different types of data, such as numeric and character data. It is like trying to add apples to oranges.

A *syntax error* is any violation of the rules of the programming language, and a *type error* occurs when you attempt to mix different types of data.

During the compiling process, many C++ compilers will generate error and warning messages as well as position the display monitor cursor to the point in the program where the error was detected. The program will not compile beyond the point of the error until it is corrected. Once an error is corrected, you must attempt to compile the program again. If other errors are detected, you must correct them, recompile the program, and so on, until the entire program is successfully compiled.

After the program is successfully compiled, it must be linked to other routines that might be required for its execution. Linking errors will occur when such routines are not available or cannot be located in the designated system directory.

A *link* error will occur when any required routines cannot be located by the compiler.

Running the Program

Once the program has been compiled and linked, you must execute, or run, it. However, just because the program has been compiled and linked successfully doesn't mean that it will run successfully under all possible conditions. Common bugs that occur at this stage include *logic errors* and *run-time* errors. These are the most difficult kinds of errors to detect. A logic error will occur when a loop tells the computer to repeat an operation, but does not tell it when to stop repeating. This is called an *infinite loop*. Such a bug will not cause an error message to be generated, because the computer is simply doing what it was told to do. The program execution must be stopped and debugged before it can run successfully.

A *logic error* occurs when the compiler does what you tell it to do, but is not doing what you meant it to do. A *run-time* error occurs when the program attempts to perform an illegal operation as defined by the laws of mathematics or the particular compiler in use.

A run-time error occurs when the program attempts to perform an illegal operation, as defined by the laws of mathematics or the particular compiler in use. Two common mathematical run-time errors are division by zero and attempting to take the square root of a negative number. A common error imposed by the compiler is an integer value out of range. Most C++ compilers limit integers to a range of −32,768 to +32,767. Unpredictable results can occur if an integer value exceeds this range.

Sometimes, the program is automatically aborted and an error message is displayed when a run-time error occurs. Other times, the program seems to execute properly, but generates incorrect results, commonly called *garbage*. Again, you should consult your compiler reference manual to determine the exact nature of the problem. The error must be located and corrected before another attempt is made to run the program.

Using a Debugger

One of the most important programming tools that you can have is a debugger. A debugger provides a microscopic view of what is going on in your program. Many C++ compilers include a built-in, or *integrated*, debugger that allows you to single-step program statements and view the execution results in the CPU and memory.

DEBUGGING TIP

A word from experience: Always go about debugging your programs in a systematic, commonsense manner. Don't be tempted to change something just because you "hope" it will work and don't know what else to do. Use your resources to isolate and correct the problem. Such resources include your algorithm, a program listing, your integrated C++ debugger, your reference manuals, this textbook, and your instructor, just to mention a few. Logic and run-time errors usually are the result of a serious flaw in your program. They will not go away and cannot be corrected by blindly making changes to your program. One good way to locate errors is to have your program print out preliminary results as well as messages that tell when a particular part of the program is running.

Documentation

This final step in the programmer's algorithm often is overlooked, but it probably is one of the more important steps, especially in commercial programming. Documentation is easy if you have done a good job of defining the problem, planning the solution, coding, testing, and debugging the program. The final program documentation is simply the recorded result of these programming steps. At a minimum, good documentation should include the following:

- A narrative description of the problem definition, which includes the type of input, output, and processing employed by the program.
- An algorithm.
- A program listing that includes a clear commenting scheme. Commenting within the program is an important part of the overall documentation process. Each program should include comments at the beginning to explain what it does, any special algorithms that are employed, and a summary of the problem definition. In addition, the name of the programmer and the date the program was written and last modified should be included.
- Samples of input and output data.

- Testing and debugging results.
- User instructions.

The documentation must be neat and well-organized. It must be easily understood by you as well as any other person who might have a need to use or modify your program in the future. What good is an ingenious program if no one can determine what it does, how to use it, or how to maintain it?

One final point: Documentation should always be an ongoing process. Whenever you work with the program or modify it, make sure the documentation is updated to reflect your experiences and modifications.

 Quick Check

1. English-like statements that require less precision than a formal programming language are called _____.

2. What questions must be answered when defining a computer programming problem?

3. What can be done to test and debug a program?

4. Why is commenting important within a program?

1-2 PROBLEM SOLVING USING ALGORITHMS

In the previous section, you learned that an algorithm is a sequence of step-by-step instructions that will produce a solution to a problem.

For instance, consider the following series of instructions:

> Apply to wet hair.
> Gently massage lather through hair.
> Rinse, keeping lather out of eyes.
> Repeat.

Look familiar? Of course, this is a series of instructions that might be found on the back of a shampoo bottle. But does it fit the technical definition of an algorithm? In other words, does it produce a result? You might say "yes," but look closer. The algorithm requires that you keep repeating the procedure an infinite number of times, so theoretically you would never stop shampooing your hair! A good computer algorithm must terminate in a finite amount of time. The repeat instruction could be altered easily to make the shampooing algorithm technically correct:

> Repeat until hair is clean.

Now the shampooing process can be terminated. Of course, you must be the one to decide when your hair is clean.

The foregoing shampoo analogy might seem a bit trivial. You probably are thinking that any intelligent person would not keep on repeating the shampooing process an infinite number of times, right? This obviously is the case when we humans are executing the algorithm, because we have some commonsense judgment. But what about a computer? Most computers do exactly what they are told to do via the computer program. As a result, a computer would repeat the original shampooing algorithm over and over an infinite number of times. This is why the algorithms that you write for computer programs must be precise.

Now, let's develop an algorithm for a process that is common to all of us—mailing a letter. Think of the steps that are involved in this simple process. You must first address an envelope, fold the letter, insert the letter in the envelope, and seal the envelope. Next, you need a stamp. If you don't have a stamp, you have to buy one. Once a stamp is obtained, you must place it on the envelope and mail the letter. The following algorithm summarizes the steps in this process:

> Obtain an envelope.
> Address the envelope.
> Fold the letter.
> Insert the letter in the envelope.
> Seal the envelope.
> If you don't have a stamp, then buy one.
> Place the stamp on the envelope.
> Mail the letter.

Does this sequence of instructions fit our definition of a good algorithm? In other words, does the sequence of instructions produce a result in a finite amount of time? Yes, assuming that each operation can be understood and carried out by the person mailing the letter. This brings up two additional characteristics of good algorithms: Each operation within the algorithm must be ***well-defined*** and ***effective***. By well-defined, I mean that each of the steps must be clearly understood by people in the computer industry. By effective, I mean that some means must exist in order to carry out the operation. In other words, the person mailing the letter must be able to perform each of the algorithm steps. In the case of a computer program algorithm, the compiler must have the means of executing each operation in the algorithm.

In summary, a good computer algorithm must possess the following three attributes:

1. Employ well-defined instructions that are generally understood by people in the computer industry.

2. Employ instructions that can be carried out effectively by the compiler executing the algorithm.

3. Produce a solution to the problem in a finite amount of time.

In order to write computer program algorithms, we need to establish a set of well-defined, effective operations. The set of pseudocode operations listed in Table 1-1 will make up our algorithmic language. We will use these operations from now on, whenever we write computer algorithms.

TABLE 1-1 PSEUDOCODE OPERATIONS USED IN THIS TEXT

Sequence	Decision	Iteration
Add (+)	If/Then	While
Calculate	If/Else	Do/While
Decrement	Switch/Case	For
Divide (/)		
Increment		
Multiply (*)		
Print		
Read		
Set or assign (=)		
Square		
Subtract (−)		
Write		

Notice that the operations in Table 1-1 are grouped into three major categories: *sequence*, *decision*, and *iteration*. These categories are called *control structures*. The sequence control structure includes those operations that produce a single action or result. Only a partial list of sequence operations is provided here. This list will be expanded as additional operations are needed. As its name implies, the decision control structure includes the operations that allow the computer to make decisions. Finally, the iteration control structure includes those operations that are used for looping, or repeating, operations within the algorithm. Many of the operations listed in Table 1-1 are self-explanatory. Those that are not will be discussed in detail as we begin to develop more complex algorithms.

 Quick Check

1. Why is it important to develop an algorithm prior to coding a program?

2. What are the three major categories of algorithmic-language operations?

3. List three decision operations.

4. List three iteration operations.

1-3 PROBLEM ABSTRACTION AND STEPWISE REFINEMENT

At this time, we need to introduce a very important concept in programming—*abstraction*. Abstraction allows us to view a problem in general terms, without worrying about the details. As a result, abstraction provides for generalization in problem solving.

> *Abstraction* provides for generalization in problem solving by allowing you to view a problem in general terms, without worrying about the details of the problem solution.

You might have heard the old saying "You can't see the forest for the trees." This means that it is very easy to get lost within the trees of the forest without seeing the big picture of the entire forest. This saying also applies to problem solving and programming. When starting out to solve a program, you need to get the "big picture" first. Once you have the big picture of the problem solution, the "forest," you can gradually *refine* the solution by providing more detail until you have a solution, the "trees," that is easily coded in a computer language. The process of gradually adding more detail to a general problem solution is called ***stepwise refinement***.

> ***Stepwise refinement*** is the process of gradually adding detail to a general problem solution until it can be easily coded in a computer language.

As an example, consider the problem of designing your own "dream house." Would you begin by drafting out the detailed plans of the house? Not likely, because you would most likely get lost in detail. A better approach would be to first make a general perspective artist's rendition of the house. Then make a general floor plan diagram, and finally make detailed drawings of the house construction that could be followed by the builders.

The concepts of problem abstraction and stepwise refinement allow you to *divide-and-conquer* the problem and solve it from the *top down*. This strategy has been proven to conquer all types of problems, especially programming problems. In programming, we generate a general problem solution, or algorithm, and gradually refine it, producing more detailed algorithms, until we get to a level that can be easily coded using a programming language. This idea is illustrated in Figure 1-1.

In summary, when attacking a problem, always start with the big picture and begin with a very general, or *abstract*, model of the solution. This allows you to concentrate on the problem at hand without getting lost in the "trees" by worrying about the implementation details of a particular programming language. You then gradually refine the solution until you reach a level that can be easily coded using a structured programming language, like C++. The *Problem Solving in Action* examples that follow illustrate this process.

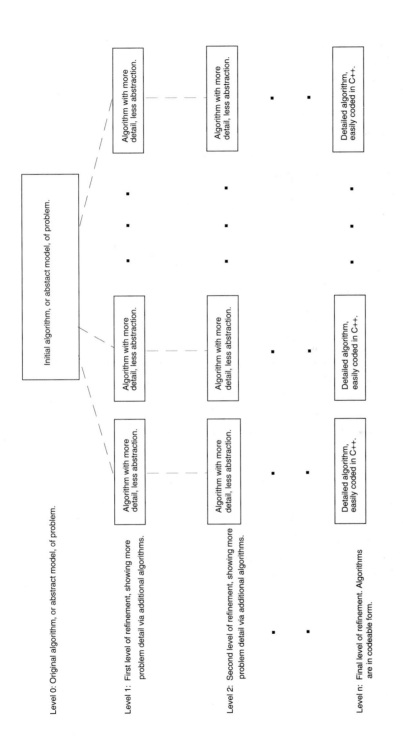

Figure 1-1 Problem solution begins with general, abstract model of the problem, which is stepwise refined, producing more and more detail, until a codeable level of algorithms is reached.

Quick Check

1. Explain why abstraction is important when solving problems.
2. Explain the process of stepwise refinement.
3. How do you know when you have reached a codeable level of an algorithm when using stepwise refinement?

PROBLEM SOLVING IN ACTION: PYTHAGOREAN THEOREM

Problem

Develop a set of algorithms to find the hypotenuse of a right triangle, given its two right angle sides, using the Pythagorean theorem depicted in Figure 1-2. Construct the final algorithms using the algorithmic instructions listed in Table 1-1.

$$H^2 = A^2 + B^2$$

Figure 1-2 Solving the hypotenuse of a right triangle using the Pythagorean theorem.

Defining the Problem

When defining the problem, you must consider three things: *output*, *input*, and *processing* as related to the problem statement. Let's label the two sides *A* and *B*, and the hypotenuse *H*. The problem requires us to find the hypotenuse (*H*), given the two sides (*A* and *B*). So the output must be the hypotenuse (*H*). We will display the hypotenuse value on the system monitor. In order to obtain this output, the two sides (*A* and *B*) must be received by the program. Let's assume that the user must enter these values via the system keyboard.

The Pythagorean theorem states that the hypotenuse squared is equal to the sum of the squares of the two sides. In symbols,

$$H^2 = A^2 + B^2$$

This equation represents the processing that must be performed by the computer. In summary, the problem definition is as follows:

Output: The hypotenuse (*H*) of a right triangle displayed on the system monitor.

Input: The two sides (*A* and *B*) of a right triangle to be entered by the user via the system keyboard.

Processing: Employ the Pythagorean theorem: $H^2 = A^2 + B^2$.

Now that the problem has been defined in terms of output, input, and processing, it is time to plan the solution by developing the required algorithms.

Planning the Solution

We will begin with an abstract model of the problem. This will be our initial algorithm, which we will refer to as *main()*. At this level, we are only concerned about addressing the major operations required to solve the problem. These are derived directly from the problem definition. As a result, our initial algorithm is as follows:

Initial Algorithm

    main()
    BEGIN
        Obtain the two sides (*A* and *B*) of a right triangle from the user.
        Calculate the hypotenuse of the triangle using the Pythagorean theorem.
        Display the results on the system monitor.
    END.

Notice that, at this level, you are not concerned with how to perform the foregoing operations in a computer language. You are only concerned about the major program operations, without agonizing over the language implementation details. This is problem abstraction!

The next step is to refine repeatedly the initial algorithm until we obtain one or more algorithms that can be coded directly in a computer language. This is a relatively simple problem, so we can employ the pseudocode operations listed in Table 1-1 at this first level of refinement. Three major operations are identified by the preceding algorithm: getting data from the user, calculating the hypotenuse, and displaying the results to the user. As a result, we will create three additional algorithms that implement these operations. First, getting the data from the user. We will call this algorithm *GetData( )*.

First Level of Refinement

GetData( )
BEGIN
    Write a program description message to the user.
    Write a user prompt message to enter the first side of the triangle (*A*).
    Read (*A*).
    Write a user prompt message to enter the second side of the triangle (*B*).
    Read (*B*).
END.

STYLE TIP

The *GetData( )* algorithm illustrates some operations that result in good programming style. Notice that the first *Write* operation is to write a program description message to the person running the program—the user. It is good practice always to include such a message so that the user understands what the program will do. In addition, the second *Write* operation will display a message to tell the user to "Enter the first side of the triangle (*A*)." Without such a prompt, the user will not know what to do. You must write a user prompt message anytime the user must enter data via the keyboard. Such a message should tell the user what is to be entered and in what format the information is to be entered. (More about this later.)

In Table 1-1, you will find two sequence operations called **Read** and **Write**. The *Read* operation is an input operation. We will assume that this operation will obtain data entered via the system keyboard. The *Write* operation is an output operation. We will assume that this operation causes information to be displayed on the system monitor. The *GetData()* algorithm uses the *Write* operation to display a **prompt** to the user and a corresponding *Read* operation to obtain the user input and assign it to the respective variable.

The next task is to develop an algorithm to calculate the hypotenuse of the triangle. We will call this algorithm *CalculateHypot()* and employ the required pseudocode operations from Table 1-1, as follows:

CalculateHypot()
BEGIN
   Square(A).
   Square(B).
   Assign $(A^2 + B^2)$ to H^2.
   Assign square root of H^2 to H.
END.

The operations in this algorithm should be self-explanatory. Notice how the *Assign* operation works. For example, the statement *Assign square root of H^2 to H* sets the variable H to the value obtained from taking the square root of H^2. We could also express this operation as *Set H^2 to $(A^2 + B^2)$*. The *Assign* and *Set* operations are equivalent; however, the verb objects within the respective phrases are reversed.

The final task is to develop an algorithm to display the results. We will call this algorithm *DisplayResults()*. All we need here is a *Write* operation as follows:

DisplayResults()
BEGIN
   Write(H).
END.

That's all there is to it. The illustration in Figure 1-3 is called a **structure diagram**, because it shows the overall structure of our problem solution. The structure diagram shows how the problem has been divided into a series of subproblems, whose collective solution will solve the initial problem. By using the above algorithms and structure diagram, this problem can be coded easily in any structured language, such as C++. You have just witnessed a very simple example of structured top-down design using stepwise refinement.

When you begin coding in C++, you will translate the preceding algorithms directly into C++ code. Each of the algorithms will be coded as a C++ *function*. Functions in C++ are subprograms designed to perform specific tasks, such as those performed by each of our algorithms. Thus, we will code a function called *GetData()* to get the data from the user, another function called *CalculateHypot()* to calculate the hypotenuse, and a third function called *DisplayResults()* to display the final results to the user. In addition, we will code a function called *main()* to sequentially *call* these functions as needed to produce the desired result.

A *function* in C++ is a subprogram designed to perform specific tasks, such as those performed by an algorithm.

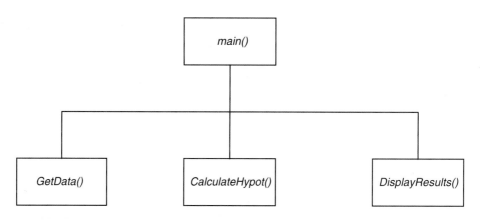

Figure 1-3   A structure diagram for the Pythagorean theorem problem shows the top-down structured design required to solve the problem using a structured language like C++.

PROBLEM SOLVING IN ACTION: SALES TAX

Problem

Develop a set of algorithms to calculate the amount of sales tax and the total cost of a sales item, including tax. Assume the sales tax rate is 7 percent and the user will enter the cost of the sales item.

Defining the Problem

Look for the nouns and verbs within the problem statement, as they often provide clues to the required output, input, and processing. The nouns suggest output and input, and the verbs suggest processing steps. The nouns relating to output and input are *sales tax*, *total cost*, and *cost*. The total cost is the required output, and the sales tax and item cost are needed as input to calculate the total cost of the item. However, the sales tax rate is given (7 percent), so the only data required for the algorithm is a user entry of the item cost.

The verb *calculate* requires us to process two things: the amount of sales tax, and the total cost of the item, including sales tax. Therefore, the processing must calculate the amount of sales tax and add this value to the item cost to obtain the total cost of the item. In summary, the problem definition in terms of output, input, and processing is as follows:

Output: The total cost of the sales item, including sales tax to be displayed on the system monitor.

Input: The cost of the sales item to be entered by the user on the system keyboard.

Processing: $Tax = 0.07 \times Cost$
$TotalCost = Cost + Tax$

Planning the Solution

Using the foregoing problem definition, we are now ready to write the initial algorithm as follows:

Initial Algorithm

```
main()
BEGIN
    Obtain the cost of the sales item from the user.
    Calculate the sales tax and total cost of the sales item.
    Display the total cost of the sales item, including sales tax.
END.
```

Again, we have divided the problem into three major tasks relating to input, processing, and output. The next task is to write a pseudocode algorithm for each task. We will refer to these algorithms as *GetData()*, *CalculateCost()*, and *DisplayResults()*. Due to the simplicity of this problem, we need only one level of refinement as follows:

First Level of Refinement

GetData()
BEGIN
    Write a program description message to the user.
    Write a user prompt to enter the cost of the item (*Cost*).
    Read (*Cost*).
END.

CalculateCost()
BEGIN
    Assign ($0.07 \times Cost$) to *Tax*.
    Assign (*Cost* + *Tax*) to *TotalCost*.
END.

DisplayCost()
BEGIN
    Write (*TotalCost*).
END.

Can you develop a structure diagram for this solution?

PROBLEM SOLVING IN ACTION: CREDIT CARD INTEREST

Problem

The interest charged on a credit card account depends on the remaining balance according to the following criteria: Interest charged is 18 percent up to $500 and 15 percent for any amount over $500. Develop the algorithms required to find the total amount of interest due on any given account balance.

Let's begin by defining the problem in terms of output, input, and processing.

Defining the Problem

Output: According to the problem statement, the obvious output must be the total amount of interest due. We will display this information on the system monitor.

Input: We will assume that the user will enter the account balance via the system keyboard.

Processing: Here is an application in which a decision-making operation must be included in the algorithm. There are two possibilities as follows:

1. *If* the balance is less than or equal to $500, *then* the interest is 18 percent of the balance, or

$$Interest = 0.18 \times Balance$$

2. *If* the balance is over $500, *then* the interest is 18 percent of the first $500 plus 15 percent of any amount over $500. In the form of an equation,

$$Interest = (0.18 \times 500) + [0.15 \times (Balance - 500)]$$

Notice the use of the two **if/then** statements in these two possibilities.

Planning the Solution

Our problem solution begins with the initial algorithm we have been calling *main()*. Again, this algorithm will simply reflect the problem definition as follows:

Initial Algorithm

```
main()
BEGIN
    Obtain the account balance from the user.
    Calculate the interest on the account balance.
    Display the calculated interest.
END.
```

Due to the simplicity of the problem, only one level of refinement is needed, as follows:

First Level of Refinement

GetData()
BEGIN
    Write a program description message to the user.
    Write a user prompt to enter the account balance (*Balance*).
    Read (*Balance*).
END.

CalculateInterest()
BEGIN
    If *Balance* <= 500 Then
        Assign ($0.18 \times Balance$) to *Interest.*
    If *Balance* > 500 Then
        Assign (0.18×500) + [$0.15 \times (Balance - 500)$] to *Interest.*
END.

DisplayResults()
BEGIN
    Write(*Interest*).
END.

As you can see, the two decision-making operations stated in the problem definition have been incorporated into our *CalculateInterest()* algorithm. Notice the use of indentation to show which calculation goes with which **if/then** operation. The use of indentation is an important part of pseudocode, because it shows the algorithm structure at a glance.

How might you replace the two **if/then** operations in this algorithm with a single **if/else** operation? Think about it, as it will be left as a problem at the end of the chapter!

CHAPTER SUMMARY

The five major steps that must be performed when developing software are (1) define the problem, (2) plan the problem solution, (3) code the program, (4) test and debug the program, and (5) document the program. When defining the problem, you must consider the output, input, and processing requirements of the application. Planning the problem solution requires that you specify the problem solution steps via an algorithm. An algorithm is a series of step-by-step instructions that provides a solution to the problem in a finite amount of time.

Abstraction and stepwise refinement are powerful tools for problem solving. Abstraction allows you to view the problem in general terms, without agonizing over the implementation details of a computer language. Stepwise refinement is applied to an initial abstract problem solution to develop gradually a set of related algorithms that can be directly coded using a structured computer language, such as C++.

Once a codeable algorithm is developed, it must be coded into some formal language that the computer system can understand. The language used in this text is C++. Once coded, the program must be tested and debugged through desk-checking, compiling, and execution. Finally, the entire programming process, from problem definition to testing and debugging, must be documented so that it can be easily understood by you or anyone else working with it.

Your C++ debugger is one of the best tools that you can use to deal with bugs that creep into your programs. It allows you to do source-level debugging and helps with the two hardest parts of debugging: finding the error and finding the cause of the error. It does this by allowing you to trace into your programs and their functions one step at a time. This slows down the program execution so that you can examine the contents of the individual data elements and program output at any given point in the program.

QUESTIONS AND PROBLEMS

Questions

1. Define an algorithm.
2. List the five steps of the programmer's algorithm.
3. What three things must be considered during the problem-definition phase of programming?
4. What tools are employed for planning the solutions to a programming problem?
5. Explain how problem abstraction aids in solving problems.
6. Explain the process of stepwise refinement.
7. The writing of a program is called _____.

8.   State three things that you can do to test and debug your programs.

9.   List the minimum items required for good documentation.

10. What three characteristics must a good computer algorithm possess?

11. The three major control structures of a structured programming language are
     _____, _____, and _____.

12. Explain why a single **if/then** operation in the credit card interest problem
     won't work. If you know the balance is not less than or equal to $500, the
     balance must be greater than $500, right? So, why can't the second **if/then**
     operation be deleted?

Problems

Least Difficult

1.   Develop a set of algorithms to compute the sum, difference, product, and
     quotient of any two integers entered by the user.

2.   Revise the solution you obtained in problem 1 to protect it from a divide-by-
     zero run-time error.

More Difficult

3.   Develop a set of algorithms to read in an employee's total weekly hours
     worked and rate of pay. Determine the gross weekly pay using "time-and-a-
     half" for anything over 40 hours.

4.   Revise the solution generated in the credit card problem to employ a single
     if/else operation in place of the two **if/then** operations.

5.   A dimension on a part drawing indicates that the length of the part is 3.00
     ± 0.25 inches. This means that the minimum acceptable length of the part is
     $3.0 - 0.25 = 2.75$ inches and the maximum acceptable length of the part is
     $3.00 + 0.25 = 3.25$ inches. Develop a set of algorithms that will display
     "ACCEPTABLE" if the part is within tolerance and "UNACCEPTABLE" if
     the part is out of tolerance. Also, show your problem definition in terms of
     output, input, and processing.

6.   Employ Ohm's law to develop a set of algorithms to calculate voltage from
     current and resistor values entered by the user. Ohm's law states that voltage
     is equal to the product of current and resistance.

7. The resistance of a conductor can be calculated based on its material composition and size using the following equation:

$$R = \rho\,\frac{l}{A}$$

where

   R is the conductor resistance, in ohms.

   ρ is the resistivity of the conductor.

   l is the length of the conductor, in meters.

   A is the cross-sectional area of the conductor, in square meters.

Develop a set of algorithms to calculate the resistance of any size copper conductor, assuming that the user enters the conductor length and cross-sectional area. (*Note:* The resistivity factor for copper is 1.72×10^{-8}.)

8. Revise the solution you obtained to problem 7, assuming that the user enters the conductor length in inches and the cross-sectional area in square inches.

9. Develop a set of algorithms that will allow the entry of three integer coefficients of a quadratic equation and generate the roots of the equation. Provide for an error message if complex roots exist.

10. Develop structure diagrams for the sales tax and credit card problem solutions developed in this chapter.

DATA ABSTRACTION, CLASSES, AND OBJECTS

2

INTRODUCTION
2-1 SOFTWARE
    Machine Language
    Assembly Language
    High-Level Language
    Why C++?
2-2 THE IDEA OF DATA ABSTRACTION
    AND CLASSES
2-3 THE STANDARD DATA CLASSES IN
    C++
    The Integer Class
    The Floating-Point Class
    The Character Class
    The Boolean Class
2-4 CONSTANT AND VARIABLE OBJECTS
    Declaring Constant Objects

    Defining Variable Objects
2-5 ENUMERATED CLASSES AND
    OBJECTS
    Declaring Enumerated Classes and Objects
2-6 THE STRUCTURE OF A C++ PROGRAM
    The Preprocessor Section
    The Main Function Section
2-7 TOP-DOWN DESIGN USING C++
    FUNCTIONS
PROBLEM SOLVING IN ACTION: BANK
    ACCOUNT PROCESSING
CHAPTER SUMMARY
QUESTIONS AND PROBLEMS
    Questions
    Problems

INTRODUCTION

You are now ready to begin learning the building blocks of the C++ language. The C++ language is a structured as well as an object-oriented language. Structured programming, sometimes called *procedural programming*, is built around functions that perform various tasks, or actions. A program is constructed using a top-down, modular, divide-and-conquer approach. Functions are written to perform various tasks and then called upon when needed to perform their respective tasks. Thus, the program consists of a collection of functions, whose combined execution solve the particular application problem at hand.

On the other hand, object-oriented programming is built around *classes* and *objects* that model real-world entities in a more natural way. By natural I mean that object-oriented programming allows you to construct programs the way we humans tend to think about things. For example, we tend to classify real-world entities such as vehicles, airplanes, ATM machines, and so on. We learn about such things by studying their characteristics and *behavior*. Take a class of vehicles, for example. All vehicles have certain characteristics, or attributes, such as engines, wheels, transmissions, and so on. Furthermore, all vehicles exhibit behavior, like acceleration, deceleration (braking), and turning. In other words, we have a general abstract impression of a vehicle through its attributes and behavior. This abstract model of a vehicle hides all the "nuts and bolts" that are contained in the vehicle. As a result, we think of the vehicle in terms of its attributes and behavior rather than its nuts and bolts, although without the nuts and bolts, a real-world vehicle could not exist. How do objects relate to classes? Well, your car is an example, or instance, of the vehicle class. It possesses all the attributes and behavior of any vehicle, but is a specific example of a vehicle. Likewise, in object-oriented programming, we create an abstract class that describes the general attributes and behavior of a programming entity, then create objects of the class that will be actually manipulated within the program, just as your car is the thing that you actually drive, not your general abstract notion of a vehicle.

So, structured, or procedural, programming is build around functions, and object-oriented programming is built around classes. Do the two have any relationship whatsoever? Yes! The classes that we build are constructed using elements of structured programming, namely functions. This is why we need to study structured programming first and gradually move into object-oriented programming. In the next few chapters you will learn how to build structured programs. In addition, you will start thinking of things in terms of classes and objects. Once you have mastered these fundamental concepts, you will be ready to learn about object-oriented programming in later chapters.

You will get your first exposure to the structure of C++ in this chapter as you learn about the various classes of data contained in the C++ language. Data are any information that must be processed by the C++ program. However, before C++ can process any information, it must know what class of data it is dealing with. As a result, any information processed by C++ must be categorized into one of the legal data classes defined for C++.

The simple data classes that you will learn about in this chapter are the *integer*, *floating-point*, *character*, and *Boolean* data classes. It is important that you understand this idea of data classification, because it is one of the most important concepts in any language. Once you learn the general characteristics and behavior of each data class, you will learn how to create different data objects for use in a C++ program. The data objects that you create will be the constants and variables that are actually manipulated within your program.

In addition to the simple data classes employed by C++, this chapter will introduce you to complex data classes called **structs** and **classes**. The class construct is particularly important for you to learn, because it allows you to create your own classes for developing object-oriented programs.

Finally, you will be introduced to the overall structure of a C++ program in general, and C++ **functions** in particular, because functions are the basic building blocks used to construct C++ programs, whether they are procedural programs or object-oriented programs.

At the end of this chapter, you will be asked to write, enter, and execute your first C++ programs. If you have not already done so, it's probably a good idea for you to familiarize yourself with the operation of your system at this time. You should know how to load the C++ compiler, enter and edit programs, compile programs, debug programs, and run programs.

Now, before getting into the finer details of the C++ language, we need to take a look at computer software in general.

2-1 SOFTWARE

If computer hardware can be likened to an automobile, computer software can be likened to the driver of the automobile. Without the driver, nothing happens. In other words, the computer hardware by itself can do nothing. The hardware system requires software that provides step-by-step instructions to tell the system what to do. A set of software instructions that tells the computer what to do is called a **computer program**. To communicate instructions to the computer,

computer programs are written in different languages. In general, computer languages can be grouped into three major categories: *machine language*, *assembly language*, and *high-level language*.

A *computer program* is a set of software instructions that tells the computer what to do.

Machine Language

All of the hardware components in a computer system, including the *central processing unit*, or *CPU*, operate on a language made up of binary 1s and 0s. A CPU does not understand any other language. When a computer is designed, the CPU is designed to interpret a given set of instructions, called its *instruction set*. Each instruction within the instruction set has a unique binary code that can be translated directly by the CPU. This binary code is called *machine code*, and the set of all machine-coded instructions is called the *machine language*.

A typical machine-language program is provided in Figure 2-1a. To write such a program, you must determine the operation to be performed, and then translate the operation into the required binary machine code from a list of instruction set machine codes provided by the CPU manufacturer. As you might imagine, this is an extremely inefficient process. It is time-consuming, tedious, and subject to a tremendous amount of error. In addition, simple operations, such as multiplication and division, often require several lines of machine code. For these reasons, machine-language programming is rarely used. However, remember that high-level language programs are always translated to machine language to enable the CPU to execute the program instructions.

01001100	mov bx, offset value	x = 2;
11101001	mov ax, [bx]	if (x<=y)
10101010	add ax, 5	x = x + 1;
10001110	add bx, 2	else
00001111	add ax, [bx]	x = x − 1;
(a)	(b)	(c)

Figure 2-1 (a) Machine language, (b) assembly language, and (c) high-level language.

Assembly Language

Assembly language is a step up from machine language. Rather than using 1s and 0s, assembly language employs alphabetic abbreviations called **mnemonics** that are easily remembered by you, the programmer. For instance, the mnemonic for addition is ADD, the mnemonic for move is MOV, and so forth. A typical assembly-language program is listed in Figure 2-1b.

The assembly-language mnemonics provide us with an easier means of writing and interpreting programs. Although assembly-language programs are more easily understood by us humans, they cannot be directly understood by the CPU. As a result, assembly-language programs must be translated into machine code. This is the job of another program, called an **assembler**. The assembler program translates assembly-language programs into binary machine code that can be executed by the CPU.

Although programming in assembly language is easier than machine-language programming, it is not the most efficient means of programming. Assembly-language programming is also tedious and prone to error, because there is usually a one-to-one relationship between the mnemonics and corresponding machine code. The solution to these inherent problems of assembly-language programming is found in high-level languages.

This does not mean that assembly language is not useful. Because of its one-to-one relationship with machine language, assembly-language programs are very efficient relative to execution speed and memory utilization. In fact, many high-level-language programs include assembly-language routines, especially for those tasks requiring high-speed software performance.

High-Level Language

A high-level language consists of instructions, or statements, that are similar to English and common mathematical notation. A typical series of high-level statements is shown in Figure 2-1c. High-level-language statements are very powerful. A typical high-level-language statement is equivalent to many machine-code instructions.

High-level languages were developed in the early 1950s to take some of the work out of programming. When programming in a high-level language, you do not have to concern yourself with the specific instruction set of the CPU. Rather, you can concentrate on solving the problem at hand.

You must be aware that even when programming in a high-level language, the system must still translate your instructions into machine code that can be understood by the CPU. There are two types of system programs that can be employed for this purpose: a **compiler** and an **interpreter**. A compiler is a program that accepts a high-level–language program and translates the entire program into machine code all at one time, before it is executed by the CPU. On the other hand, an interpreter translates and executes one high-level statement at a time. Once a given statement has been executed, the interpreter then translates and executes the next statement, and so on, until the entire program has been executed. Although interpreters do have their advantages, especially during the debugging stage, C++ employs a compiler. For this reason, let's look more closely at the operation of a compiler.

Figure 2-2 illustrates the basic functions of a compiler. The compiler acts as the interface between your program and the machine. Here's how a typical C++ compiler works. Once you have entered a C++ program into the system using your C++ editor, the program must be translated into machine code by the compiler. Your C++ program is referred to as a **source program**, and the machine-language program that is generated by the compiler is called an **object program**. C++ source programs usually have a *.cpp* file-name extension, and the corresponding object program has a *.obj* extension.

A **source program** is the one that you write in the C++ language and that normally has a file extension of *.cpp*. An **object program** is the binary machine language program generated by the compiler, which always has a file extension of *.obj*.

As the program is being translated, the compiler checks for errors. After the program is compiled, the compiler displays a list of error messages and warnings. In addition, many C++ compilers will place the cursor on the display monitor at the point in your program where a given error was detected. After you correct all the errors, you must execute the compiler again until you get a successful compilation.

Once compiled, your program must be **linked**. As mentioned in Chapter 1, the linking step integrates your program with any additional routines that are required for proper program execution. These routines can be other high-level programs, assembly-language programs, or operating-system routines. The linking step produces an executable file with an *.exe* file-name extension. Errors can also occur during the linking step, especially if any required routines are not available or cannot be located. Your C++ software will also report any linking errors.

Finally, when the entire program has been successfully compiled and linked, you can execute, or run, your program. When you run your program, the CPU is actually executing the machine-language program generated by the compiler/linker.

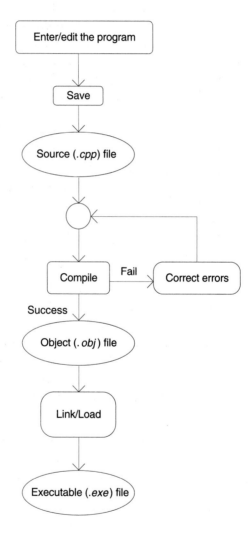

Figure 2-2 The C++ compiler and linker translate source code into machine code that can be executed by the CPU.

Why C++?

As you are probably aware, there are several popular high-level languages, including COBOL, Pascal, FORTRAN, BASIC, LISP, Ada, and C++, among others. Each has been developed with a particular application in mind. For instance, COBOL, which stands for COmmon Business-Oriented Language, was developed for business programming. FORTRAN, which means FORmula TRANslator, was developed for scientific programming. LISP was developed for artificial-intelligence programming, and Pascal was developed primarily for education to teach the principles of structured programming. C++ was developed for efficient implementation of complex high-level structures that are required for software solution of today's complex problems. Let's take a closer look at the C++ language in general.

First, there was the B language, then C, and then C++. All were developed at Bell Telephone Laboratories and, like all high-level structured languages, have their roots in ALGOL. The B language was developed by Ken Thompson at Bell Labs in an effort to develop an operating system using a high-level language. Prior to B, operating systems were developed using the assembly language of the particular CPU on which the operating system was to run. Using the B language as a basis, Dennis Ritchie developed the C language at Bell Labs. The main purpose for the C language was to develop an operating system for the DEC PDP-11 minicomputer. The resulting operating system became known as UNIX. In fact, most versions of UNIX today are written almost entirely in C. The C language was originally defined in the classic text *The C Programming Language*, written by Brian Kernighan and Dennis Ritchie (1977). In fact, the C language became such a popular commercial language that an ANSI (American National Standards Institute) standard for C was released in 1989. A programming language standard is a document that describes the details of a programming language so that programs written to the standard specifications are "portable" between systems.

> ***Portability*** is that feature of a language that allows programs written for one type of computer to be used on another type of computer with few or no changes to the program source code.

The C++ language is an extension of the C language. Bjarne Stroustrup of Bell Labs enhanced the C language in the early 1980s by adding ***object-oriented programming (OOP)*** capability. Object-oriented programming allows complex programs to be developed using simpler constructs, called *objects*, that can communicate by exchanging messages. More about this later. The obvious goal of Dr. Stroustrup was to maintain the efficiency of C while providing the power of OOP to the language. The resulting language became known as C++. You will realize where the ++ came from when you learn about the C++ *increment* operator. Because C++ is an enhancement of C, any C program is also a C++ program; however, the opposite is not true.

Like C, C++ is taking the software development industry by storm because both languages offer all the advantages of a high-level language, but also provide low-level access to system hardware and software, just like assembly language. For this reason, C and C++ are often referred to as *midlevel* languages. In fact, most of the commercial software developed today is written using C or C++. As a result, an ANSI standard for C++ will soon be released.

 Quick Check

1. Why is C++ often referred to as a midlevel language?

2. List the steps that must be performed to translate a C++ source code program to an executable program.

3. What type of file is produced by the compile step?

4. What type of file is produced by the linking step?

5. What is the purpose of the linking step?

6. What is the major difference between the C language and the C++ language?

2-2 THE IDEA OF DATA ABSTRACTION AND CLASSES

Just as C++ programs are highly structured and modular, so are the data that the programs operate upon. You might be thinking: "Data are data, how can there be different *classes* of data?" First, you must think of data as any information that the computer might perform operations on or manipulate. So, let's define a *data object* to be any item of information that is manipulated or operated on by the computer. Many different classes of data objects exist during the execution of a program. Some of these data objects will be programmer-defined, such as constants and variable objects, while others, such as system stacks, will be system-defined.

Now, think about the types of information, or data objects, that the computer manipulates. Of course, a computer manipulates numbers, or **numeric data**. One of the primary uses of a computer is to perform calculations on numeric data, right? But what about **character** data? Isn't the computer operating with character data when it prints out your name? Thus, numeric data and character data comprise two different **classes** of data. What makes them different? Well, numeric data consist of numbers, whereas character data consist of alphanumeric symbols. In addition, the operations defined for these two classes of data will be different. Thus, a **class** describes the data characteristics, or attributes, as well as legal operations, or behavior, of its objects. Remember the vehicle analogy cited in the chapter introduction. The notion of a vehicle describes things such as engines and transmissions (the attributes), as well as acceleration and deceleration (the behavior), for any actual vehicle objects such as your own car.

A **class** describes the data attributes and behavior of its objects.

Take the integers as an example of a data class. The integers include all the whole number data values between minus infinity and plus infinity. Furthermore, there is a set of operations specifically defined for the integers. These operations include addition, subtraction, multiplication, and division, among others, as illustrated in Figure 2-3. Thus, the set of whole numbers from minus infinity to plus infinity, along with their related operations, form a class. Any object created for this integer class, such as an integer variable, can only be a whole number value and only be used in an operation specifically defined for integers. In fact, we say that the integer class forms an **abstract data type**, or **ADT**.

An **abstract data type (ADT)** is a class that describes the data attributes and behavior of its objects.

You were introduced to the idea of abstraction in the last chapter. You found that abstraction, as applied to problem solving, allowed you to concentrate on the problem solution, without worrying about the implementation details. The same is true with ADTs. Abstract data types allow you to work with data objects without concern for how the data objects are stored inside the computer or how the data operations are performed inside the computer. This is referred to as ***data abstraction***. Let's take the addition operation as an example. Integer addition, by definition, dictates that you must supply two integer arguments to be added, and it will return the integer sum of the two. Do you care about the details of how the computer implements addition or how the computer represents integers in memory? Of course not! All you care about is what information needs to be supplied to the addition operation to perform its job and what information is returned by the operation. In other words, all you care about is *what* must be supplied to the addition operation and *how* the operation will respond. This is called ***behavior***—how the ADT, or class, will act and react for a given operation.

> The term ***behavior***, as associated with classes and ADTs, has to do with how the ADT, or class, will act and react for a given operation.

You will learn more about ADTs and behavior later in the text. For now, it is only important that you understand the concept as applied to C++ classes.

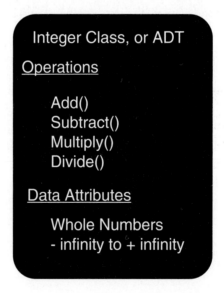

Figure 2-3   The class of integers can be considered an abstract data type, or class of data, where the arithmetic operations on the integers define the behavior of any objects defined for the integer class.

Now for the big surprise: There are more than just numeric and character classes defined for C++. Figure 2-4 shows all of the various classes that can be used in C++ programming. First, observe that there are three major class categories: *scalar, structured*, and *pointer*.

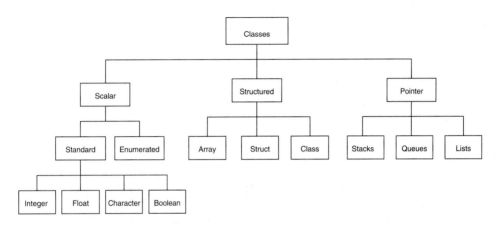

Figure 2-4 Class hierarchy in the C++ language.

Scalar classes are those whose data objects are ordered. By ordering, we mean that given two objects defined for the class, one object is either equal (=), greater than (>), or less than (<) the other object. Numeric data, such as integer and real, or floating-point, numbers, are clearly scalar because all numbers have this ordering property. You will soon find out that characters are also ordered, and thus considered a scalar class.

Observe also from the diagram that scalar classes can be *standard* or *enumerated*. Standard classes are those that are predefined to, or "built into," the C++ language. These consist of integer numbers and floating-point numbers, as well as character data. The enumerated class is one that you, the user of C++, must define to meet a given application problem. In other words, an enumerated class describes data values that you will create within your C++ program for a specific purpose. For example, you might want to define the set of all the days of the week (Sun, Mon, Tue, Wed, Thur, Fri, Sat) as an enumerated data class in your program. Here, the data values are the individual days and are ordered from Sun through Sat. As a result, these values can be manipulated within your program in a similar way as the standard classes. At first, the idea of creating your own set of data values might seem foreign to you, but you will soon see how this can be a powerful tool when programming in C++. You will learn more about enumerated data classes shortly.

The structured class category consists of classes called ***arrays***, ***structs***, and ***classes***. These classes are complex data classes, in the sense that they are made up of other simpler data classes. As an example, your name, address, and telephone number can be combined to form a ***struct***, also referred to as a ***record***. This struct obviously consists of integers and characters, both of which are simple data classes. In other words, structured classes are formed using combinations of the simpler scalar classes as building blocks.

The **class** category provides the foundation for object-oriented programming (OOP) in C++. You now know that the C++ language includes *standard* classes, such as the integer and character class. Well, the C++ **class** allows you, the programmer, to create your own data classes, or ADTs. For example, suppose that you have been hired to write an application program to control an ATM machine. The ATM machine is required to handle various data objects with specific operations defined for those objects, such as deposit and withdrawal. Doesn't this sound like an ideal application for a class, because a class is a collection of data objects along with a set of operations defined for those objects? Obviously, there is no standard ATM machine class built into the C++ language. However, the C++ **class** construct allows you to build your own ATM class, which will define all the data attributes and behavior associated with an ATM machine.

Like a **struct**, a **class** is comprised of simpler data classes. In addition, a **class** includes functions that operate on the **class** data. These functions define the behavior of the class. Thus, the C++ class is ideal for implementing ADTs, because it can be used to define the data attributes of the ADT as well as the behavior of the ADT.

Finally, pointer classes are used to form ADTs called stacks, queues, linked lists, and binary trees. The use of pointers is fundamental to the C and C++ languages, and you will learn about them, as well as stacks, queues, and lists, later in the text.

 Quick Check

1. A _____ describes the data attributes and behavior of its objects.

2. Classes that are predefined within a programming language are called _____ classes.

3. A set of data elements created by you, the programmer, to meet a given application is called a(n) _____ data class.

4. The three major class categories in the C++ programming language are the_____, _____, and _____ categories.

5. What is meant by the term behavior as applied to classes and ADTs.

6. Another name for a struct is a _____.

7. Why is the C++ class ideal for implementing your own ADTs?

2-3 THE STANDARD DATA CLASSES IN C++

Recall that standard data classes are built into the C++ compiler. This built-in feature simply means that the C++ compiler recognizes any legal data values contained in a standard class. There are four standard classes of data that we need to discuss: *integer*, *floating-point*, *character* and *Boolean*.

The Integer Class

As you know, integers are the whole numbers. They may be positive, negative, or 0. In an algebra course, you most likely learned that there are no theoretical limits to the integers. They can range from minus infinity ($-\infty$) to plus infinity ($+\infty$). However, there are practical limits in the real world of computers. In C++, the largest and smallest possible integer values depend on the particular type of integer and compiler that is being used. In most C++ compilers, standard integers range from -32768 to $+32767$. However, there are different classes of integers.

So, you're thinking that integers are integers; how can there be different "classes" of integers? Well, the C++ language defines five separate integer classes that define five separate ranges for integer objects. They are **short int**, **int**, **unsigned int**, **long int**, and **unsigned long**. As you can see from Table 2-1, each integer class defines a legal range of integer values for an object of a given integer class.

You might be wondering why there are different classes of integers. Why not just define one class that will provide enough range for most applications? For instance, why not use the **long int** class all the time, because it provides the largest range of values? Well, recall that an advantage of C++ is its efficiency relative to execution speed and memory utilization. Each of the preceding integer classes employs a predefined number of memory bytes to represent an integer value. For example, **int** requires 2 bytes of memory to represent a value, and **long int** requires twice as many, or 4 bytes, to represent a value. Thus, it takes twice as much memory space to represent **long int** integers as it does **int** integers. In addition, it would take twice as long to fetch a **long int** as an **int**, using a 16-bit CPU. So, the idea is to use the type of integer that has enough range to satisfy a given application. For most applications, **int** will do the job and provide for efficient execution and memory utilization.

COMPILER NOTE

Be aware that the ANSI C++ standard acknowledges that the ranges of the standard data classes usually derive from the architecture of the host computer. As a result, the range of the various data classes within the C++ language might differ from compiler to compiler. For example, your compiler might specify the range of **int** to be from −32768 to +32767, whereas another compiler might define this range to be from −2147483648 to +2147483647.

TABLE 2-1 INTEGER CLASSES AND CORRESPONDING RANGES IN A TYPICAL C++ COMPILER

Integer Class	Range	Bytes
short int, or **short**	−128 to +127	1
int	−32768 to +32767	2
unsigned int	0 to +65535	2
long int, or **long**	−2147483648 to +2147483647	4
unsigned long	0 to 4294967295	4

Example 2-1

Which of the following are *not* legal **int** class values according to Table 2-1?

a. +35
b. 35
c. −247
d. 0
e. 3.14
f. 32,767
g. 32768

Solution

The values in a, b, c, and d are all legal **int** values in C++, because they are all whole numbers within the defined range of **int**. Notice that +35 and 35 are both legal representations of the integer value 35.

   The values in e, f, and g are not legal **int** values in C++. The value 3.14 is not an integer because it is not a whole number. The value 32,767 is an integer within the predefined range, but is not legal in C++, because it contains a comma. Commas are not allowed as part of numeric values in C++. Finally, the value 32768 is not a legal **int** value in C++, because it is outside of the predefined **int** range.

DEBUGGING TIP

You must be especially aware of the integer range limits imposed by C++ when performing integer calculations within your C++ programs. For example, multiplying two integers could easily produce an integer result beyond this range, resulting in an incorrect result. This is called an *overflow* condition. Depending on where it occurs, an overflow condition might or might not generate an error message during program compiling or execution. Even if no overflow error message is generated, the operation will always produce an incorrect result.

Example 2-2

Which of the following **int** operations will generate an overflow condition in C++? (Use Table 2-1 to determine the legal **int** range, and assume that the * symbol means multiplication and the / symbol means division.)

a. 32 * 1000
b. 100 * 1000
c. (100 * 1000)/5

Solution

a. 32 * 1000 = 32000, which is within the predefined **int** range. No overflow condition exists.
b. 100 * 1000 = 100000, which is outside of the predefined **int** range. The overflow condition will result in an incorrect integer result.
c. (100 * 1000)/5 = 100000/5 = 20000. Although the final result is within the predefined **int** range, an overflow condition will occur, thereby generating an incorrect result. Why? Because the multiplication operation in the numerator results in a value outside of the **int** range.

One final point: You probably have noticed that the word **int**, for example, is set in bold type. Such a word in C++ is called a ***keyword***. Keywords have a specific meaning to the C++ compiler and are used to perform a specific task. You cannot use a keyword for anything other than the specific operation for which it is defined. C++ contains about 70 keywords, including **int**. You will learn about other keywords in subsequent chapters. In any event, from now on all keywords will be printed in bold type so that you can easily recognize them.

The Floating-Point Class

Floating-point data values include all of the whole number integers as well as any value between two whole numbers that must be represented using a decimal point. Examples include the following:

$$-2.56$$
$$1.414$$
$$-3.0$$

All of the foregoing values have been written using ***fixed decimal-point*** notation. Fixed decimal-point notation requires a sign, followed by an unsigned integer, followed by a decimal point, followed by another unsigned integer. This format is as follows:

FIXED DECIMAL FORMAT FOR A FLOATING-POINT VALUE

(+ or – sign)(integer).(integer)

Another way to represent a very large or a very small floating-point value is with scientific notation, called ***exponential format***. With this notation, the floating-point value is written as a decimal-point value multiplied by a power of 10. The general format is as follows:

EXPONENTIAL FORMAT FOR A FLOATING-POINT VALUE

(+ or – sign)(decimal-point value)**e**(integer exponent value)

In both the foregoing formats, the leading + sign is optional if the value is positive. Examples of floating-point values using exponential format include

$$1.32e3$$
$$0.45e-6$$
$$-35.02e-4$$

Here, the letter *e* means "times 10 to the power of." The letter *e* is used because there is no provision on a standard computer keyboard to type above a line to show exponential values. Again, the + sign is optional for both the decimal-point value and the exponential value when they are positive.

Example 2-3

Convert the following exponential values to fixed decimal values.

a. 1.32e3
b. 0.45e-6
c. -35.02e-4
d. -1.333e7

Solution

a. $1.32e3 = 1.32 \times 10^3 = 1320.0$
b. $0.45e-6 = 0.45 \times 10^{-6} = 0.00000045$
c. $-35.02e-4 = -35.02 \times 10^{-4} = -0.003502$
d. $-1.333e7 = -1.333 \times 10^7 = -13330000.0$

You might be wondering if there is any practical limit to the range of floating-point values that can be used in C++. As with integers, C++ defines different classes of floating-point data that dictate different legal value ranges. Again, the value range is determined by the C++ compiler that you are using. As an example, Table 2-2 summarizes the floating-point classes defined for a typical C++ compiler.

TABLE 2-2 FLOATING-POINT CLASSES AND CORRESPONDING RANGES IN A TYPCIAL C++ COMPILER

Float class	Range	Bytes
float	3.4×10^{-38} to 3.4×10^{38}	4
double	1.7×10^{-308} to 1.7×10^{308}	8
long double	3.4×10^{-4932} to 1.1×10^{4932}	10

The greater the value range, the greater precision you will get when using floating-point values. However, as you can see from Table 2-2, it costs you more memory space to achieve greater precision when using a floating-point class. Again, the application will dictate the required precision, which, in turn, dictates which floating-point class to use. For most applications, the **float** class will provide the required precision. However, many programmers prefer to use the **double** class to assure adequate precision.

Example 2-4

In data communications, you often see quantities expressed using the prefixes in Table 2-3.

TABLE 2-3 COMMON PREFIXES USED IN DATA COMMUNICATIONS

Prefix	Symbol	Meaning
pico	p	10^{-12}
nano	n	10^{-9}
micro	μ	10^{-6}
milli	m	10^{-3}
kilo	k	10^{3}
mega	M	10^{6}
giga	G	10^{9}

Given the following quantities

220 picoseconds (ps)
1 kilohertz (kHz)
10 megahertz (MHz)
1.25 milliseconds (ms)
25.3 microseconds (μs)
300 nanoseconds (ns)

a. Express each of the listed quantities in exponential form.
b. Express each of the listed quantities in fixed decimal form.

Solution

a. To express in exponential form, you simply convert the prefix to its respective power of 10 using Table 2-3. Then, use exponential notation to write the value, like this:

220 ps = 220e−12 second
1 kHz = 1e3 hertz
10 MHz = 10e6 hertz
1.25 ms = 1.25e−3 second
25.3 μs = 25.3e−6 second
300 ns = 300e−9 second

b. To express each in its fixed decimal form, simply move the decimal point according to the exponent value.

220 ps = 220e−12 second = 0.000000000220 second
1 kHz = 1e3 hertz = 1000.0 hertz
10 MHz = 10e6 hertz = 10000000.0 hertz
1.25 ms = 1.25e−3 second = 0.00125 second
25.3 μs = 25.3e−6 second = 0.0000253 second
300 ns = 300e−9 second = 0.000000300 second

Example 2-5

C++ includes several **standard functions** that you can call upon to perform specific operations.

A **standard function** is a predefined operation that the C++ compiler will recognize and evaluate to return a result.

One such function is the *sqrt()* function. The *sqrt()* function is used to find the square root of a floating-point number. As an example, execution of *sqrt(2)* will return the value 1.414. On the other hand, an operation *not* included as a standard function is the square function. You must write your own *user-defined function* to perform the square operation. More about this later. Now, given the standard *sqrt()* function, determine the result of the following operations:

a. sqrt(3.5)
b. sqrt(−25)
c. sqrt(4e−20)

Solution

a. sqrt(3.5) = 1.87
b. sqrt(−25) is imaginary and will generate a run-time error when encountered during a program execution.
c. sqrt(4e−20) = 2e−10

The Character Class

All of the symbols on your computer keyboard are characters. This includes all the upper- and lowercase alphabetic characters as well as the punctuation, numbers, control keys, and special symbols. Most C++ compilers employ the American Standard Code for Information Interchange (ASCII) character set shown in Table 2-4.

As you can see from the table, each character has a unique numeric representation code because, in order for the CPU to work with character data, the individual characters must be converted to a numeric (actually, binary) code. When you press a character on the keyboard, the CPU "sees" the numeric representation of that character, not the character itself. Table 2-4 provides decimal equivalents of the ASCII characters.

Example 2-6

C++ includes a standard function called *toascii()*. This function is used to generate, or return, the decimal representation for any character. Determine the result of the following operations using Table 2-4.

a. toascii('A')
b. toascii('Z')
c. toascii('a')
d. toascii('z')
e. toascii('#')

Solution

Using Table 2-4, you get the following:

a. toascii('A') = 65
b. toascii('Z') = 90
c. toascii('a') = 97
d. toascii('z') = 122
e. toascii('#') = 35

The foregoing example points out several characteristics of character data. First, each character has a unique numeric representation inside the computer. Because each character has a unique numeric representation, the characters are ordered. This is why they are classified as scalar. For instance, 'A' < 'Z', because the numeric representation for 'A' (65) is less than the numeric representation for 'Z' (90). Likewise, '#' < 'a' < 'z', because 35 < 97 < 122. Next, notice that whenever a character is specified, it is always enclosed in single quotes like this: 'a'. This is a requirement of the C++ compiler.

TABLE 2-4 ASCII CHARACTER CODE TABLE

Dec	Char	Dec	Char	Dec	Char	Dec	Char
0	^@ NUL	32	SPC	64	@	96	`
1	^A SOH	33	!	65	A	97	a
2	^B STX	34	"	66	B	98	b
3	^C ETX	35	#	67	C	99	c
4	^D EOT	36	$	68	D	100	d
5	^E ENQ	37	%	69	E	101	e
6	^F ACK	38	&	70	F	102	f
7	^G BEL	39	'	71	G	103	g
8	^H BS	40	(	72	H	104	h
9	^I HT	41	)	73	I	105	i
10	^J LF	42	*	74	J	106	j
11	^K VT	43	+	75	K	107	k
12	^L FF	44	,	76	L	108	l
13	^M CR	45	-	77	M	109	m
14	^N SO	46	.	78	N	110	n
15	^O SI	47	/	79	O	111	o
16	^P DLE	48	0	80	P	112	p
17	^Q DC1	49	1	81	Q	113	q
18	^R DC2	50	2	82	R	114	r
19	^S DC3	51	3	83	S	115	s
20	^T DC4	52	4	84	T	116	t
21	^U NAK	53	5	85	U	117	u
22	^V SYN	54	6	86	V	118	v
23	^W ETB	55	7	87	W	119	w
24	^X CAN	56	8	88	X	120	x
25	^Y EM	57	9	89	Y	121	y
26	^Z SUB	58	:	90	Z	122	z
27	^[ESC	59	;	91	[	123	{
28	^\ FS	60	<	92	\	124		
29	^] GS	61	=	93	]	125	}
30	^^ RS	62	>	94	^	126	~
31	^-- US	63	?	95	--	127	DEL

Recall that there were different classes of integer and floating-point values defined by the C++ compiler. These different classes define the range of values that are legal for a given class. Well, the same is true of characters. There are two different classes of characters defined for C++: *char* and ***unsigned char***, both shown in Table 2-5.

TABLE 2-5 CHARACTER CLASSES AND CORRESPONDING RANGES IN C++

Character Class	Range	Bytes
char	−128 to +127	1
unsigned char	0 to +255	1

The **char** class allows for all the ASCII characters shown in Table 2-4. The **unsigned char** class also allows for all the ASCII characters shown in Table 2-4 but, in addition, allows for an extended character set as defined for the IBM PC. (See your PC documentation for this extended character set.) Again, the application will dictate which character type to use. The **char** class will satisfy most of the applications in this text.

Characters are stored in the machine as integer values, so you can perform arithmetic operations on character data. For instance, you can add 1 to the character 'A' and get the character 'B'. This is an example of the flexibility built into the C++ language; however, with this flexibility comes responsibility. You must be able to predict the results you will get. Other languages, like Pascal, will not allow you to perform arithmetic operations on characters.

CAUTION

C++ will allow you to perform arithmetic operations on character data; however, be careful because the results can be sometimes difficult to predict. What do you get when you add the character 'A' to the character 'B' or when you multiply these two characters?

Strings

A string is simply a collection of characters. Examples of strings include your name, address, and phone number, as well as the sentence you are now reading. When operating on strings, you must keep in mind that you are still operating with individual characters.

Figure 2-5 illustrates how strings are stored in memory by C++. As you can see, each individual character is placed in a 1-byte memory cell. The collection of cells holding the string is called an ***array***. We will discuss arrays in more detail later, but for now it is only important that you understand how they are used to store string data.

The individual cells in the array are referenced via a position number, beginning with position [0]. The last position in the string array always contains the character '\0' to terminate the string. This '\0' character is referred to as a ***null terminator*** character. The null terminator tells C++ where the string ends in memory.

As you see from Figure 2-5, the character 'C' is located at position [0] of the array, and the null terminator is located at position [3] of the array. Notice that the array requires four cells to store a three character string because of the null-terminator requirement.

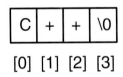

[0] [1] [2] [3]

Figure 2-5 C++ stores character strings in memory arrays that are terminated by a null terminator.

One final point: Strings in C++ are always enclosed in double quotes, like this: "C++". Recall that individual characters are enclosed in single quotes. Thus, 'a' denotes an individual character, whereas "a" denotes a string of one character.

Example 2-7

Given the following strings, determine how many bytes of storage are required to store each string, and show how the strings appear in memory.

a. "This text is great!"
b. "x"
c. "1234"

Solution

a. This string requires 20 bytes of storage. The corresponding string array is shown in Figure 2-6a.
b. This string requires 2 bytes of storage. The corresponding string array is shown in Figure 2-6b.
c. This string requires 5 bytes of storage. The corresponding string array is shown in Figure 2-6c.

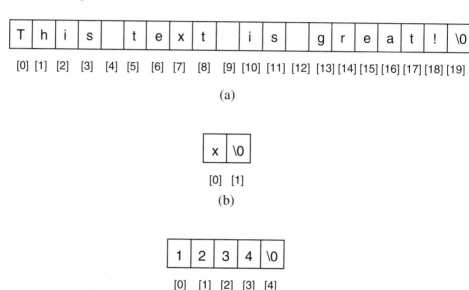

Figure 2-6 cells:

| T | h | i | s | | t | e | x | t | | i | s | | g | r | e | a | t | ! | \0 |

[0] [1] [2] [3] [4] [5] [6] [7] [8] [9] [10] [11] [12] [13] [14] [15] [16] [17] [18] [19]

(a)

| x | \0 |

[0] [1]

(b)

| 1 | 2 | 3 | 4 | \0 |

[0] [1] [2] [3] [4]

(c)

Figure 2-6   Solutions for Example 2-7.

PROGRAMMING TIP

Double quotes around a number, such as "1234", indicate a string of characters and *not* numeric data. In fact, the string "1234" requires 5 bytes of storage, whereas the **int** 1234 requires only 2 bytes of storage. In addition, arithmetic operations cannot be performed on the string "1234". For these reasons, numeric data should be represented using a numeric class and not the character class.

The Boolean Class

Boolean data, consisting solely of the values **true** and **false**, is the simplest form of data that can be employed in a program. Boolean data play an important role in a program's ability to make decisions, because all program decisions are Boolean decisions, based on whether a given condition is true or false. You will learn this later when we discuss program decision-making and iteration.

The ANSI C++ standard specifies a Boolean data class called **bool**. This class contains two elements, **true** and **false**. The **bool** class is a scalar class, because **false** is defined to be less that **true**. The words **bool**, **true**, and **false** are specified as keywords by the standard and, therefore, cannot be used for any other purpose. The **bool** class is the newest data class utilized by C++. As a result, older compilers will not include the **bool** class and its corresponding elements of **true** and **false**. When using a compiler that does not meet the standard, you will have to create your own Boolean class using an enumerated class (to be discussed presently).

Quick Check

1. What range of values can be provided via the standard **int** class?

2. What type of error occurs when, as a result of a calculation, a value exceeds its predefined range?

3. The two ways that floating-point values can be represented in a C++ program are using either _____ or _____ format.

4. What will be returned when the following functions are executed?

    toascii('B')

    toascii('?')

5. What characters must employ the unsigned char class?

6. A character string is stored in a class called a(n) _____.

7. How many bytes of storage are required by the string "The United States of America"?

8. The ANSI C++ standard specifies a Boolean class called _____ that includes the elements _____ and _____.

2-4 CONSTANT AND VARIABLE OBJECTS

Recall that a data object contains data that will be manipulated by your program. There are two different general categories for such objects: constant objects and variable objects. From mathematics, you know that a constant is a value that never changes, thereby remaining a fixed value. A common example is the constant pi (π). Here, the Greek symbol π is used to represent a floating-point value of approximately 3.14159. This value of π never changes, thus remaining constant regardless of where and how it might be used in a calculation.

On the other hand, a variable is something that can take on different values. In mathematics, the symbols x and y are often used to denote variables. Using the equation $y = 3x + 2$, you can substitute different values of x to generate different values of y. Thus, the values of x and y in the equation are variable.

The values of variable objects are stored in main working memory for later use within a program. Each variable object has a symbolic name that locates its value in memory. This idea is illustrated in Figure 2-7. The memory contents located by the symbols x, y, and *Count* might change during the execution of the program. As a result, these symbols are called variable objects.

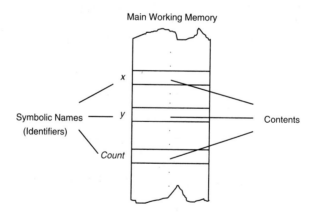

Figure 2-7   Each variable object has a symbolic name, or identifier, that locates its value in memory.

All constant and variable objects to be used in a C++ program must be declared/defined prior to their use in the program. The reason that we must declare constants and define variables in a language is twofold. First, the compiler must know the value of a constant before it is used and must reserve memory locations to store variables. Second, the compiler must know the class of the constants and variables so that it knows the attributes and behavior of such objects. Now, let's see how constants are declared and variables are defined in C++.

DECLARATIONS VERSUS DEFINITIONS

The words *define* and *declare* are often used interchangeably in connection with programming languages. Actually, a declaration specifies the name and attributes of a value, but does not reserve storage. On the other hand, a definition is a declaration that also reserves storage. This is why we declare constant objects and define variable objects in C++.

Declaring Constant Objects

To declare a constant object, you must use the keyword **const**, like this:

> ### CONSTANT DECLARATION FORMAT
>
> **const** <class> <object identifier > = <constant value>;

Notice the syntax: The keyword **const** is followed by the data class of the constant. The compiler must know what class the constant object is to belong. The constant class is followed by the constant object identifier. The identifier is the name of the constant that will be replaced by the constant value during compile time. To identify constants easily within your program, I suggest that your constant identifiers always be in all capital letters. This way, it makes it much more clear that no statement should attempt to alter the constant value. An equals sign (=) is used to separate the constant identifier from its declared value. Finally, each constant declaration must end with a semicolon.

Example 2-8

Suppose you wish to use the price of 32 cents for a first-class postage stamp in your C++ program. In addition, your program must calculate the sales tax required for a given sales item based on a sales tax rate of 7 percent. Declare appropriate constant objects to represent the price of a stamp and the sales tax rate.

Solution

By using the format given before, the postage price and sales tax rate could be declared as follows:

const float POSTAGE = 0.32;
const float TAX_RATE = 0.07;

With these declarations, you would simply use the words *POSTAGE* and *TAX_RATE* when performing calculations within the program. For instance, to find the tax on an item that costs $100, you would write the expression

SalesTax = 100 * TAX_RATE;

When the program is compiled, the compiler simply substitutes the constant value 0.07 for the *TAX_RATE* identifier.

What about the word *SalesTax* in this expression? Is it a constant object or a variable object? You're right—it's a variable object, because its value will change, depending on the sale price of the item. What data class must *SalesTax* be? In other words, what class of data is generated as a result of the operation: integer, floating-point, or character? Right again—floating-point, because the *SalesTax* might often result in a decimal value. Thus, *SalesTax* must be defined as a variable floating-point object. You will find out how to do this shortly.

 STYLE TIP

Always code your constant identifiers in all caps so that they are easily identified as constants within your program. Always code variable identifiers in lowercase, capitalizing the first letter of each word in the identifier.

Notice in Example 2-8 that the constant identifier *TAX_RATE* is made up of two words, *TAX* and *RATE*. The C++ compiler will not allow you to separate multiword identifiers using spaces. Thus, I have chosen to separate the two words with the underscore symbol (_). Also, notice that the variable object identifier *SalesTax* is made up of two words. Here, the two words are run together with the first letter of each word capitalized. These two techniques will be used throughout the text when using multiword identifiers. How long can an identifier be? This depends on the particular C++ compiler that you are using. In a typical C++ compiler, identifiers can be any length, where the first 32 characters are significant. Here are some other rules that govern the use of identifiers in any C++ compiler:

- Identifiers can contain the letters *a* to *z*, *A* to *Z*, the digits *0* to *9*, and the underscore, _, symbol.
- No spaces or punctuation, except the underscore, _, symbol, are allowed.
- Identifiers in C++ are *case-sensitive*. Thus, the identifiers *Tax* and *TAX* are seen as two different identifiers by the compiler.

You are probably wondering why we should declare constants using identifiers. Why not just insert the constant value into the expression whenever it is needed, like this:

SalesTax = 100 ∗ 0.07;

Have you ever known postage or sales tax rates to change? Of course you have! You might say that these types of "constants" are not constant forever. So, when using constants such as these, which might be subject to change in the future, it is much easier to declare them in one single place at the beginning of the program. Then if they need to be changed, you only have to make a single change in your program. Otherwise, a change must be made in each place that you use the constant within the program.

Constant String Objects

Recall that a string in C++ is formed using an array of characters. Thus, to declare a constant string object, you must apply the **char** class to a string identifier, using the following format:

> ### *CONSTANT STRING OBJECT DECLARATION FORMAT*
>
> **const char** <string object identifier>[ ] = "string value";

As you can see, the two key words **const** and **char** are followed by the string identifier. A set of *empty* square brackets must follow the identifier to denote an array. The square brackets are followed by an equals sign, which is followed by the string value enclosed within double quotes. Finally, a semicolon must be used to terminate the declaration. Let's look at an example to illustrate this idea.

Example 2-9

Define three constants that can be used to represent your name, address, and phone number.

Solution

Using the keyword **const**, the appropriate declarations might be

```
const char Name[] = "Andrew C. Staugaard, Jr.";
const char Address[] = "Box 999, C++ City, USA";
const char PhoneNumber[] = "(012)345-6789";
```

When a string constant is compiled, an array is created that contains 1 byte for each character in the array, plus a final byte for the null terminator. Thus, the *NAME* constant in Example 2-9 will occupy 25 bytes of program code each place it appears in the program. Count the characters and add one for the null terminator to see if you agree. Remember that spaces and punctuation must be counted as characters.

You probably are wondering how and where string constants are used. One common use of a string constant is to represent information that must be printed often, such as header information. For instance, each time you need to print your name in a report, you would simply insert an instruction into the program to print the constant identifier *NAME*. The value of *NAME* is your name, so the computer will print your name. You will see how this works when you learn about input and output operations in Chapter 3.

Defining Variable Objects

Before you can use a variable in a C++ program, it must be defined. When you define a variable object, the compiler reserves a location inside the computer memory for the variable value. For program readability and clarity, variable objects should be defined at the beginning of your C++ programs. However, C++ allows you to define a variable anyplace within a program as long as it is defined *before* it is used. To define a variable object, you must specify its class, its name, and an optional initializing value. Here's the format:

VARIABLE OBJECT DEFINITION FORMAT

<class> <variable object identifier> = <optional initializing value>;

The foregoing format requires that the variable class be listed first, followed by the variable object identifier, or name. You can terminate the definition at this point with a semicolon, or you can add an optional equals symbol, =, followed by an initializing value, and then the semicolon to terminate the definition.

PROGRAMMING NOTE

It is good practice to initialize variables when they are defined. When a variable is not initialized, its initial value will be some arbitrary value from memory. Generally, numeric variables will be initialized to the value 0 or 1, and character variables will be initialized with a blank or null terminator. Strings (character arrays) should be initialized with null terminators.

Example 2-10

There is a simple relationship in electronics, called *Ohm's law*, that allows you to find either voltage, current, or resistance, given the other two quantities. Ohm's law states that voltage is equal to the product of current times resistance. In symbols,

$$V = I \times R$$

where

V is voltage, in volts.
I is current, in amperes.
R is resistance, in ohms.

Suppose that you must write a C++ program to calculate voltage from current and resistance values using Ohm's law. Define the three variable objects (V, I, and R) that will be used in the program for the calculation.

Solution

The variable object identifiers are given to be V, I, and R. Now, the question is: What class must these variable objects belong to? You know that V, I, and R will be used to represent numeric data, so your decision as to their class reduces to integer or floating-point. If you define V, I, and R as integers, you will be limited to using whole number values for these variables within your program; however, this might create a problem because voltage, current, and resistance values often are decimal values. So, let's define them as floating-point objects, like this:

```
float V = 0.0;
float I = 0.0;
float R = 0.0;
```

Notice that each variable is defined as a floating-point object and initialized to the value 0. Of course, because these are variable objects, their values will change during the execution of a program.

Example 2-11

You must write a program to calculate the sales tax of a sales item using a sales tax rate of 7 percent. Declare the appropriate constant objects and define the required variable objects.

Solution

First, you must decide what identifiers to use. Always use word identifiers that best describe the related constant or variable. Let's use the word *SalesTax* to identify the resulting calculation, the word *Price* to identify the cost of the item, and the word *TAX_RATE* to identify the sales tax rate. So, using these identifiers, the sales tax calculation would be

SalesTax = Price * TAX_RATE;

Now, the question is: Which objects are variables and which are constants? Obviously, the *SalesTax* and *Price* objects are variables, because they will change depending on the cost of the item. However, the *TAX_RATE* will be a constant object, regardless of the cost of the item. So, we will define *SalesTax* and *Price* as variable objects and *TAX_RATE* as a constant object, like this:

const float TAX_RATE = 0.07;
float SalesTax = 0.0;
float Price = 0.0;

Notice that both the variable objects are defined as floating-point, because both will be decimal values. Suppose that you were to define the tax rate as a variable object rather than a constant object and initialize it to the value 0.07, like this:

float TaxRate = 0.07;

There is no problem with this definition. The compiler will reserve storage for the variable object *TaxRate* and place the initial value of 0.07 at this storage location. However, the value of *TaxRate* could be changed by the program, whereas it could not be changed if declared as a constant object.

STYLE TIP

Most C++ compilers allow identifiers, or names, to be any length, where the first 32 characters are significant. Thus, your programs will become much more readable and self-documenting if you use words, rather than letters and symbols, to represent variable objects. For instance, the variable definition in Example 2-10 would be much more readable to a nontechnical user if you were to define voltage, current, and resistance like this:

```
float Voltage = 0.0;
float Current = 0.0;
float Resistance = 0.0;
```

By using this definition, the actual words (*Voltage*, *Current*, and *Resistance*) would be used within your program when applying Ohm's law. So, the statement required to calculate voltage would appear in your program as follows:

```
Voltage = Current * Resistance;
```

Notice the use of the equals symbol, =, in this equation. This is the way that you must *assign* quantities in C++. Also, notice the use of the star symbol, *, for multiplication.

A word of caution: When using names as variable identifiers, you cannot use any punctuation within the name. For instance, the variable identifier *Total(Sales)* to represent total sales is an illegal identifier in C++ because of the parentheses. Two legal identifiers would be *TotalSales* or *Total_Sales*. In the first case, the two words are connected, with the first letter of each word capitalized. In the second case, the underscore symbol, _, is used to separate the two words instead of a space. This symbol is okay to use within C++ identifiers. You will see both of these techniques employed for identifiers throughout the remainder of this text.

Example 2-12

Choose an appropriate name and define a variable object that could be used to represent the days of the week. Assume that the days of the week are represented by the first letter of each day.

Solution

Let's pick a meaningful variable identifier, such as *DaysOfWeek*. Now, because the days of the week will be represented by the first letter of each day, the object must be of the character class. When defining character objects, you must use the keyword **char** in the object definition, as follows:

```
char DaysOfWeek;
```

Do you see any problems with the definition in Example 2-12? There are no syntax errors, and it is perfectly legal as far as C++ is concerned. But are there any problems associated with the usage of this object? A character object is limited to representing a single character at any given time. This is why each day of the week must be represented by a single letter. However, using the first letter of each day creates a problem. Does an 'S' represent Saturday or Sunday? Likewise, does a 'T' mean Tuesday or Thursday? The solution to this dilemma is found in variable string objects.

Variable String Objects

In C or C++, a string must be stored in an array of characters. So, to define a variable string object, you must define a character array. There are two ways to do this: defining a string object without an initializing value or with an initializing value. Here are the required formats:

> ### VARIABLE STRING OBJECT DEFINITION FORMAT WITHOUT AN INITIALIZING VALUE
>
> **char** <object identifier>[<maximum size of string + 1>];
>
> ### VARIABLE STRING OBJECT DEFINITION FORMAT WITH AN INITIALIZING VALUE
>
> **char** <object identifier>[] = "string value";

In the first case, the compiler must know the maximum size of the string, plus 1. The size must be specified so that the compiler knows how much memory to set aside to store the string. You must specify a size that is one greater than the maximum string size to allow room for the null terminator character.

In the second case, you do not need to specify a string size, because the compiler can determine how much memory to set aside from the initializing string value. A maximum string size can be specified; however, it must be at least as large as the length of the initializing value, plus 1. Initializing a string object to a value is basically the same as defining a constant string value; however, the keyword **const** is not employed. Remember, a constant string object can never be changed within the program, whereas a variable string object can be changed at any time during the program execution. You will learn how to change the value of a variable string object later in the text.

Example 2-13

Using the character object definition in Example 2-12 presents a usage problem when representing the days of the week, because a character object can only represent a single character at a time. Solve this problem by using a string object definition. Define an appropriate string object without an initializing value, and then rewrite the definition to initialize it with the value "Wednesday".

Solution

A string object can be used to represent any number of consecutive characters. So why not define *DaysOfWeek* as a string object, like this:

```
char DaysOfWeek[10];
```

With this definition, the object *DaysOfWeek* can be used to represent the entire day of the week word (Sunday, Monday, Tuesday, etc.). Why did I choose 10 as the maximum length of the string? Because the longest day of the week word is Wednesday, which has 9 characters. However, you must leave room for the null terminator character, making the size of the string 10.

You can initialize the string object to Wednesday with the following definition:

```
char DaysOfWeek[] = "Wednesday";
```

With this definition, the string "Wednesday" is stored in memory and located by the identifier *DaysOfWeek*. The compiler automatically inserts the null terminator character after the last character, 'y'.

Example 2-14

Suppose that you must write a C++ program to instruct the user of the program to enter his/her name, address, and telephone number. Choose appropriate string identifiers and define three string objects to represent this information.

Solution

Let's call the objects *Name, Address*, and *PhoneNumber*, respectively. Now, you must decide the maximum length of each string object. Don't forget to include spaces, special symbols, and the null terminator character. A length of 31 should be sufficient for *Name*, 31 for *Address*, and 14 for *PhoneNumber*. If you are not sure, it is better to overestimate, rather than underestimate its length. By using the foregoing object identifiers and string lengths, the proper definitions are

```
char Name[31] = "\0";
char Address[31] = "\0";
char PhoneNumber[14] = "\0";
```

Notice that each string object is initialized with a null terminator string. This will prevent output of random memory data, and a likely program crash, should the string values not be changed within the program and subsequently displayed on the monitor.

Boolean Objects

As mentioned earlier, Boolean variables are often used within a program for decision-making purposes. A compiler that meets the ANSI C++ standard contains the standard Boolean class, called **bool**, containing the elements **true** and **false**. As a result, Boolean objects can be defined for the **bool** class just as you define any other object—by listing its class followed by the object identifier. Here's an example that illustrates this idea.

Example 2-15

Define a Boolean object called *Flag* for use in a decision-making operation. Initialize the object with a Boolean value of **false**.

Solution

Boolean variables are often used in a program for decision-making operations. A Boolean variable, called *Flag*, can be defined for such a purpose as follows:

```
bool Flag = false;
```

With this definition, the variable *Flag* can be used in a program, taking on the values of **true** or **false** as required by the program logic. If your compiler does not meet the ANSI C++ standard, you must define Boolean objects using an enumerated class. Enumerated classes and objects are the topic of the next section.

 Quick Check

1. What are the two reasons for declaring/defining constant and variable objects in a C++ program?

2. Declare a constant object called *PERIOD* that will insert a period wherever it is referenced in a program.

3. Declare a constant object called *BOOK* that will insert the string "Structured and Object-Oriented Techniques" wherever it appears in a program.

4. Given a string object that must store a string of up to 25 characters, what array size must be specified in the object definition?

5. Define a string object called *Course* that will be initialized to a string value of "Data Structures".

2-5 ENUMERATED CLASSES AND OBJECTS

One distinct advantage of using C++ is that it allows you, the programmer, to create your own classes of data. Up to this point, you have been using the standard data classes of integer, floating-point, character, and Boolean. As you have seen, these classes have been adequate for many programming applications. Although these predefined classes can be used for just about any programming task, they often are insufficient to describe a problem clearly. You will soon discover that enumerated data classes enhance the readability of your program by making it clearer and application-oriented, something we are especially concerned about in problem solving. The more clearly we can express a problem as related to its application, the easier it is for us and others to understand and solve the problem.

Enumerated data classes consist of a set of data values that you, the programmer, define for a particular application. The idea of defining your own data classes might seem awkward to you at first, but you will soon discover that it provides a convenient means of working with real-world problems. There will be times when none of the standard data classes will work conveniently for certain applications. For example, suppose an application problem required the manipulation of the days of the week. Because none of the standard classes include the days of the week as values within their predefined range, you might suggest that each day of the week be set to an integer value using the **const** declaration like this:

```
const int SUN = 0;
const int MON = 1;
const int TUE = 2;
const int WED = 3;
const int THU = 4;
const int FRI = 5;
const int SAT = 6;
```

Then, using this declaration, you could actually manipulate the days within your program. For instance, assuming the variable object *Day* is defined as an integer, a program might include the following pseudocode operations:

If *Day* = FRI Then
    Write ("It's pay day!")

Because you have set the days of the week to integer values, the above **if** statement is simply comparing the value of *Day* to the integer value assigned to *FRI* (5). If *Day* equals 5, then the message is generated.

C++ allows a more convenient way to work with nonstandard data objects through the use of enumerated classes and objects. Rather than using numeric assignments as before, you can declare the set of days using the keyword **enum** like this:

enum DaysOfWeek {Sun, Mon, Tue, Wed, Thur, Fri, Sat};

Here, the keyword **enum** declares the class *DaysOfWeek* to include the set of seven values, *Sun*, *Mon*, *Tue*, *Wed*, *Thur*, *Fri*, and *Sat*. *DaysOfWeek* is called a user-defined class because you, the user, have declared it.

Declaring Enumerated Classes and Objects

The general format and syntax for declaring enumerated data is as follows:

ENUMERATED DATA DECLARTION FORMAT

enum <class identifier> {value #1, value #2, ⋯, value #n};
<class identifier> <object identifier>;

As you can see, enumerated data require a two-part declaration/definition. First, you must declare the data values using the keyword **enum** followed by a class identifier and a list of the values that make up the class. Notice that the value list is enclosed within curly braces, { }, and a semicolon terminates the declaration. Second, one or more variable objects are defined for the enumerated class. The objects provide access to the class values. The object identifier, or name, is listed after the same class identifier used in the **enum** declaration. For instance, let's go back to our days of the week class. The days in the week are first declared as an enumerated class, like this:

enum DaysOfWeek {Sun, Mon, Tue, Wed, Thur, Fri, Sat};

Then, an object must be defined for the class, like this:

DaysOfWeek Day;

Any operations with the enumerated data in your program will then use the object identifier (*Day*), as follows:

> If *Day* = Fri Then
>   Write ("It's pay day!")

The Ordering of Enumerated Data

An enumerated class is also a scalar, or ordered, class. In fact, the word *enumerated* means "numbered with order." As a result, the C++ compiler assigns an order to the enumerated values such that value #1 < value #2 < $\cdots$ < value *#n*. This means that in the *DaysOfWeek* class, *Sun < Mon < Tue < Wed < Thur < Fri < Sat*. As a result, relational operations involving the enumerated class are perfectly legitimate. For instance, consider the following pseudocode:

> If (*Day* > Sun) AND (*Day* < Sat) Then
>   Write ("It's a weekday")

Here, the value of *Day* is compared to *Sun* and *Sat*. Using the above enumerated declaration for *DaysOfWeek*, *Day* must be a weekday if it's between *Sun* and *Sat*, right? How does it work? The C++ compiler actually assigns integer values to the enumerated data values in the order that they are listed, beginning with the value 0. Thus, in the previous example, *Sun* is assigned the value 0, *Mon* the value 1, *Tue* the value 2, and so on. Therefore, the previous **if** statement reduces to a comparison of integer values.

Example 2-16

Declare the following as enumerated classes. Define an appropriate object to go along with the class declaration.

a. *MonthsOfYear*, consisting of the 12 months of the year.
b. *TestGrades*, consisting of the five common letter grades.
c. *ArmyRanks*, consisting of the eight common ranks found in the army.

Solution

a.
enum MonthsOfYear {Jan, Feb, Mar, Apr, May, Jun, Jul, Aug, Sep, Oct,
                              Nov, Dec};
MonthsOfYear Month;
b.
enum TestGrades {F, D, C, B, A};
TestGrades Test;
c.
enum ArmyRanks {Private, Corporal, Sergeant, Lieutenant, Captain,
                        Major, Colonel, General};
ArmyRanks Rank;

Observe the syntax in the foregoing code. First, the class name must be all one word. No space nor punctuation is allowed. Also, notice that individual words within the class name begin with a capital letter. This is not a requirement of C++, but has been done for clarity. Next, you see that the values are listed inside of curly braces and separated by commas. Finally, a semicolon is required at the end of the value listing to mark the end of a given class declaration.

Look at the *TestGrade* class a little closer. Notice that there are no quotes around the character symbols. A common mistake when defining character symbols as enumerated data is to enclose the data symbols in quotes as you would characters. In an enumerated class declaration, the character symbols are not treated as characters, but as unique values of the enumerated class.

You should also note the ordering of each declaration. The *TestGrade* class is ordered such that an $F < D < C < B < A$. This represents a natural ordering, when you consider the application of grading. If the test grades were declared as characters, the ordering would be the opposite, because of the relative ASCII values of the given characters. In addition, the *ArmyRanks* class is ordered according to the natural order of ranks from the lowest rank (*Private*) to the highest rank (*General*). Finally, notice that an appropriate object has been defined for each class.

Example 2-17

In C++, the Boolean value **true** is represented with the integer 1, and the Boolean value **false** is represented with the integer 0. Declare a Boolean class and define a corresponding variable object called *Flag* that will allow the programmer to use the Boolean values of true and false in a program. Initialize *Flag* to **false** as part of the object definition.

Solution

If you are using a compiler that meets the ANSI C++ standard, you do not need to create your own Boolean class because it is specified as part of the standard and, therefore, is already available as a standard class in your compiler. All you need to do is create a variable object for the **bool** class, like this:

bool Flag = false;

If you are using an older compiler that does not meet the ANSI C++ standard, you must create your own Boolean enumerated class, as follows:

enum Boolean {FALSE, TRUE};
Boolean Flag = FALSE;

Here, the Boolean value FALSE is assigned the integer 0, and the Boolean value TRUE is assigned the integer 1 by the C++ compiler. As a result, the programmer can employ the identifiers of TRUE and FALSE in a program in lieu of 1 and 0, respectively, when working with Boolean values. This makes the program much more readable. Remember this example, because we will use the idea when working with Boolean values in our programs.

DEBUGGING TIP

It is important to realize that the enumerated class values are *not* variables or strings. Thus, using the data value *Sat*, for example, as a variable in a program will cause an error. An enumerated data value must never appear on the left side of an assignment operator, like this:

Sat = Fri + 1;

Another common source of error is to inadvertently declare the enumerated data values as strings, like this:

enum DaysOfWeek {"Sun", "Mon", "Tue", "Wed", "Thur", "Fri", "Sat"};

This will always cause a compile error. Again, the individual data values are *not* strings; they are actually constant identifiers.

Quick Check

1. Why would you want to create an enumerated class in your program if a standard class could be used to do the job?

2. Declare an enumerated class called *Automobiles* which consists of at least 10 popular automobile brands.

3. What numeric value does the compiler assign to the first value in an enumerated class?

2-6 THE STRUCTURE OF A C++ PROGRAM

You now have some of the basic ingredients to begin writing C++ programs. You will be doing this shortly. However, before we leave this chapter, let's put things into some perspective and take an initial look at the overall structure of a C++ program.

Recall that the C++ language is a modular, structured language. This idea is evident from the overall appearance, or structure, of a C++ program. Look at Figure 2-8. Observe that any C++ program consists of two sections: a *preprocessor* section and a *main function* section.

First, you should always include a comment at the top of your program to explain the purpose of the program. Notice that comments in C++ are inserted into a program using a double *forward* slash (//). The double forward slash tells the compiler to ignore the rest of that particular line. Thus, a comment on any given line must begin with the double forward slash. The double forward slash can appear anyplace on a given line, but anything after // on a given line is ignored by the compiler. I will be making extensive use of comments within programs in this text to *self-document* the C++ code. I suggest that you do the same in your programs. Comments within your programs make them much easier to read and maintain.

The Preprocessor Section

The *preprocessor* in a C++ program can be viewed as a smart text editor that consists of *directives* that always begin with a pound (#) symbol. Although there are others, the preprocessor directive that you will use the most is the *#include* directive.

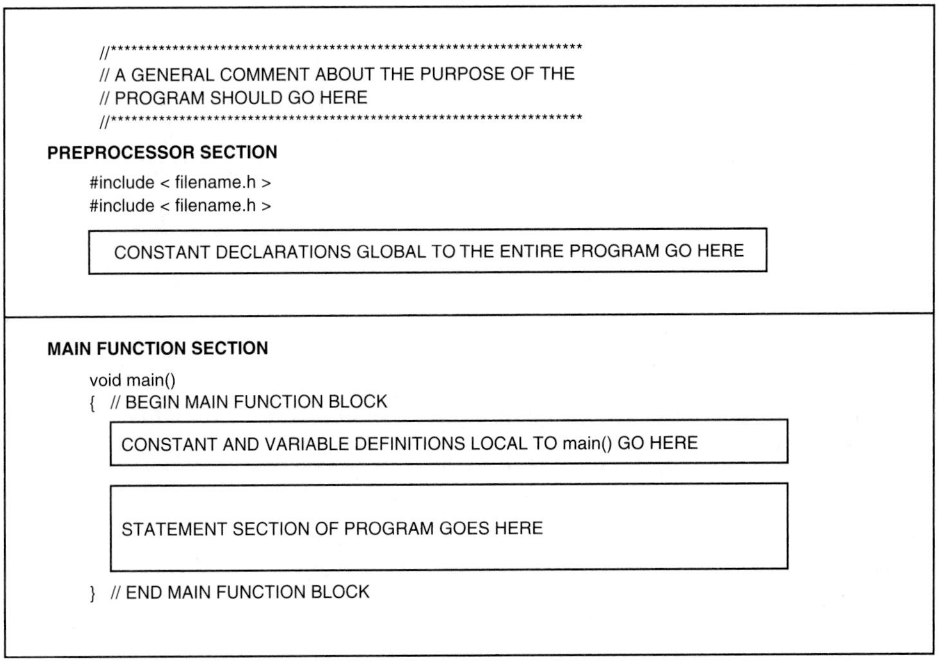

```
//*************************************************************
// A GENERAL COMMENT ABOUT THE PURPOSE OF THE
// PROGRAM SHOULD GO HERE
//*************************************************************
PREPROCESSOR SECTION
   #include < filename.h >
   #include < filename.h >

   CONSTANT DECLARATIONS GLOBAL TO THE ENTIRE PROGRAM GO HERE


MAIN FUNCTION SECTION
   void main()
   {   // BEGIN MAIN FUNCTION BLOCK

      CONSTANT AND VARIABLE DEFINITIONS LOCAL TO main() GO HERE


      STATEMENT SECTION OF PROGRAM GOES HERE


   }   // END MAIN FUNCTION BLOCK
```

Figure 2-8   The general structure of a C++ program.

The #include Directive

The *#include* directive tells the compiler to copy, or include, a given file name into the C++ program at the point where the directive is found. You will see later that C++ programs are *built* by merging several files into one. A file referenced in the *#include* directive is called an **include file** or a **header file**. I will refer to them as header files in this text. In C++, it is common practice to indicate a header file by using a *.h* file-name extension, as shown in Figure 2-8. Header files are employed when a given set of routines might be common to many different C++ programs. Rather than typing the routines into each program in which they must appear, you simply create a header file containing the common code and include that header file in each program, using the *#include* directive. A C++ compiler will contain several standard header files that contain routines that are common to many programs. Consult your compiler reference manual for a complete listing of these files and the routines that they contain. Standard header files that we will use extensively are the *stdio.h*, *stdlib.h*, *math.h*, *string.h*, and *iostream.h* files. We will also be creating our own header files, especially when we work with object-oriented programming.

There are two ways to tell the C++ compiler how to locate a header file: by enclosing the header file name within double angle brackets, < >, or double quotes, " ". When angle brackets are used, the preprocessor looks in the primary system default directory and not the current working directory. The *system default directory* is where the standard header files included with your compiler will be located. On the other hand, the use of double quotes will tell the preprocessor to look for the indicated header file *first* in the same directory where your C++ program is located. This directory is often referred to as the *working directory*. So, whenever we include a standard header file in our program, we will specify the include file name within double angle brackets, like this: *<filename.h>*. Later on, when we write our own header files and place them in the working directory, we will specify the include file name within double quotes, like this: *"filename.h"*.

PROGRAMMING TIP

Whenever you include a standard header file in your program, you must specify the header file name within double angle brackets, like this: *<filename.h>*. When you write your own header files and place them in the working directory, you must specify the header file name within double quotes, like this: *"filename.h"*.

One final point: You *do not* terminate a preprocessor directive with a semicolon, because a preprocessor directive is not an executable C++ statement. Remember, a directive simply acts as a smart substitution editor for the compiler.

The Main Function Section

The main function section of the program is where access to all the executable C++ code resides. As you will see soon, a C++ program is simply a collection of *function* blocks.

A *function* in C++ is a subprogram that returns a single value, a set of values, or performs some specific task, such as I/O.

Notice the syntax shown in Figure 2-8. The main function identifier is *main()*. The main function identifier is preceded by the keyword **void**. The reason for this will become apparent shortly. A left curly brace, {, must follow the main function identifier prior to any other statements. This brace defines the beginning of the main function block and normally appears directly below *main()*. At the bottom of Figure 2-8, you see a right curly brace, }. This brace is used to define the end of the main function block. You must always use a set of curly braces, { }, to define a block of code in C++. Thus, the set of curly braces in Figure 2-8 defines the main function block.

You must declare any ***global*** constants prior to *main()*. ***Global*** constants are those that are accessible to the entire program, versus ***local*** constants, which are accessible only to a localized block within the program. Local constant and variable objects can be declared/defined anywhere in a program block as long as they are declared/defined prior to their use. Always declare your constant objects as globally as possible and your variable objects as locally as possible. The reason for this should become apparent as you learn more about structured programming.

The statement section of *main()* is the main executable body of the program. The program instructions, or statements, go here. Each statement must be terminated with a semicolon. Because C++ is a modular language, the statement section of the program often consists of calls to additional function blocks, whose combined execution performs the overall program task.

Example 2-18

Using the program structure shown in Figure 2-8 and the definitions in Example 2-11, write a program that will calculate the sales tax of a sales item. Assume that you must include a system file named *iostream.h* for the program to perform some future I/O task.

Solution

In Example 2-11, we used the following statement to calculate the sales tax:

SalesTax = Price ∗ TAX_RATE;

where *SalesTax* and *Price* were defined as variable floating-point objects and *TAX_RATE* was declared as a constant object with a value of 0.07.

Putting this information into the required C++ program structure shown in Figure 2-8, you get the following:

```
//******************************************************************
//
//THIS PROGRAM WILL CALCULATE THE SALES TAX  OF A SALES ITEM
//
//******************************************************************
```

```
#include <iostream.h>     //FOR cout

const float TAX_RATE = 0.07;        //SALES TAX RATE, IN DECIMAL

void main()
{
//DEFINE LOCAL VARIABLES
   float Price = 0.0;                //PRICE OF A SALES ITEM
   float SalesTax = 0.0;            //CALCULATED TAX FOR A SALES ITEM

//CALCULATE SALES TAX
   Price = 1.95;                    //ASSIGN $1.95 TO Price
   SalesTax = Price * TAX_RATE;

//DISPLAY SALES TAX
   cout << SalesTax << endl;
} //END main()
```

This program will calculate the sales tax of an item, given the item price of $1.95. The program is very readable, and everything used within the program is clearly defined. The program begins with a brief comment about its purpose. Observe the structure: A preprocessor directive appears first, followed by a global constant, followed by function *main()*. The preprocessor directive includes the *iostream.h* header file that contains the *cout* object employed at the end of the program to display the sales tax. Function *main()* begins by defining the variable objects that are to be used within the main block. A value is assigned to *Price*, followed by the calculation of the sales tax amount. Once the calculation is performed, the resulting sales tax value (*SalesTax*) is displayed on the monitor using a *cout* object. This output object is discussed in the next chapter.

Note that the program statements are indented about three spaces within the main function block. Such indentation is permissible, because C++ ignores spaces. In addition, the indentation clearly shows that the statements are part of the function block *main()*. Indentation is used to "set off" a block of code so that it is not confused with other blocks of code. We will make extensive use of indentation within our C++ programs to make them easier to read and understand. Also, notice the use of commenting within the program. You always want to make liberal use of meaningful comments in order to self-document the program.

That's all there is to it! We have just written our first C++ program!

DEBUGGING TIP

Program comments in C++ are inserted using double forward slashes, //. When the C++ compiler encounters double forward slashes, it ignores the remainder of the line in which the slashes appear. In this text, program comments will appear in all caps so that they can be readily distinguished from the program code.

Program comments are an important part of the program documentation and should be used liberally. At a minimum, the program should include the following comments:

- The beginning of the program should be commented with the programmer's name, date the program was written, date the program was last revised, and the name of the person doing the revision. In other words, a brief ongoing maintenance log should be commented at the beginning of the program.

- The beginning of the program should be commented to explain the purpose of the program, which includes the problem definition and program algorithms. This provides an overall perspective by which anyone, including you, the programmer, can begin debugging or maintaining the program.

- Preprocessor directives should be commented as to their purpose.

- Constant and variable objects should be commented as to their purpose.

- Major sections of the program should be commented to explain the overall purpose of the respective section.

- Individual program lines should be commented when the purpose of the code is not obvious relative to the application.

- All major subprograms (functions in C++) should be commented just like the main program function.

- The end of each program block (right curly brace) should be commented to indicate what the brace is ending.

Remember, someone (including you) might have to debug or maintain the program in the future. A good commenting scheme makes these tasks a much more efficient and pleasant process.

Quick Check

1. Any C++ program consists of two sections, called the _____ and _____ sections.

2. Write a *#include* directive to include a standard header file called *stdlib.h* into a program. Assume that the header file is located in the system default directory.

3. A subprogram that returns a single value, a set of values, or performs some specific task in C++ is called a _____.

4. Where must global constants be declared in a C++ program?

5. Where must local variable objects be defined in a C++ program?

6. True or false: Constant objects should be declared as globally as possible, whereas variable objects should be declared as locally as possible.

7. Comments are inserted into a C++ program using
   a. left and right curly braces like this {COMMENT}.
   b. a semicolon like this ;COMMENT.
   c. a star like this *COMMENT.
   d. double forward slashes like this //COMMENT.

8. State at least four places where your program should include comments.

2-7 TOP-DOWN DESIGN USING C++ FUNCTIONS

The design of C++ lends itself to the use of ***structured design*** and ***structured programming***.

> ***Structured design*** is a methodology that requires software to be designed using a top-down modular approach, and ***structured programming*** allows programs to be written using well-defined control structures and independent program modules.

As you will soon find out, the rules that apply to C++ encourage you to write well-organized, modular programs that are easy to read, understand, modify, and maintain. Structured, modular programs allow you to "divide-and-conquer" a large complex programming problem using a *top-down* approach. The idea is to divide the complex problem into a group of simpler subproblems, or modules. Individual program modules, called **functions**, are then written to solve the simpler subproblems. The function modules then can be easily combined to solve the overall complex problem. This idea is illustrated by Figure 2-9. A nonstructured language, such as BASIC, provides simple solutions to simple problems. However, nonstructured languages require complex solutions to complex problems, because of the lack of modularity, or structure.

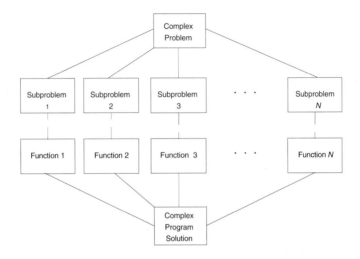

Figure 2-9 The "divide-and-conquer" idea behind a structured programming language like C++.

Functions that you create for your own use in a program are called **user-defined functions**. In this sense, the "user" is you, the programmer.

A **user-defined function** is a block of statements, or subprogram, that are written to perform a specific task required by you, the programmer.

A function is given a name and **called**, or **invoked**, using its name each time the task is to be performed within the program. The program that calls, or invokes, a function is often referred to as the **calling program**.

Functions eliminate the need for duplicate statements within a program. Given a task to be performed more than once, the statements are written just once for the function. Then, the function is called each time the task must be performed. In addition, the use of functions enhances the program listing clarity and readability. And most important, the use of functions within a structured language such as C++ allows you to solve very large complex problems using a top-down program design approach as discussed in the previous chapter.

    The structure of a C++ program that employs user-defined functions is shown in Figure 2-10.

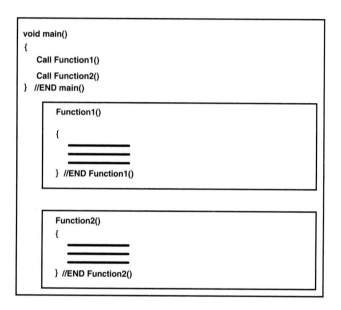

Figure 2-10   The structure of a C++ program that employs user-defined functions.

    Here, you see two user-defined functions that have been added to function *main()*. The user-defined functions are written to perform a specific task required by the program. When the respective task must be performed, a *call* is made within *main()* to the required function.

    Notice the block structure. Function *main()* is the main program module, and *Function1()* and *Function2()* are program submodules that are called, or invoked, by *main()* when needed. You will learn how to write your own functions in Chapter 7. For now, it is important only that you understand the top-down structuring idea employed by the C++ language, or any other structured language for that matter.

Quick Check

1. A methodology that requires software to be designed using a top-down modular approach is called _____.

2. In C++, individual program modules are implemented using _____.

3. In C++, user-defined function code is placed
   a. before *main()*.
   b. inside of *main()*.
   c. after *main()*.
   d. none of the above.

PROBLEM SOLVING IN ACTION: BANK ACCOUNT PROCESSING

Problem

Your local bank has contracted you to design a structured program that will process savings account data. Develop a set of related algorithms using the top-down structured program design method that could be coded using a structured programming language.

Defining the Problem

Output: The program must generate a report showing the account transactions and balance for a given savings account in a given month.

Input: We will assume that the user will enter the monthly transaction information, which will include the previous month's balance, current month's deposits, and current month's withdrawals.

Processing: The program must process deposits and withdrawals and calculate interest to determine the monthly balance.

Using structured program design, we will divide the problem into individual subproblems to solve the overall banking problem. Now, try to identify the separate tasks that must be performed to solve the problem. First, the user must enter the required transaction data, which will include the previous month's balance, current month's deposits, and current month's withdrawals. Once the transaction data are entered, the program must add the deposits to the account balance, subtract the withdrawals from the account balance, calculate the interest, and generate the required report. As a result, we can identify five program tasks as follows:

- Obtain the transaction data entered by the program user.
- Add the deposits to the account balance.
- Subtract the withdrawals from the account balance.
- Calculate the account interest.
- Generate the monthly account report.

The structure diagram in Figure 2-11 shows the block structure required for the program.

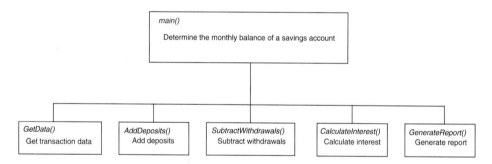

Figure 2-11   A structure diagram for the banking problem.

Planning the Solution

Because we are using the block structured technique to design the program, we must employ stepwise refinement to develop the algorithm. The initial algorithm level, *main()*, will reflect the problem definition and call the individual subprogram, or function, modules as follows:

Initial Algorithm

main()
BEGIN
    Call the function to get the transaction data.
    Call the function to add the account deposits.
    Call the function to subtract the account withdrawals.
    Call the function to calculate the account interest.
    Call the function to generate the account report.
END.

The first level of refinement requires that we show a detailed algorithm for each subprogram module, or function. They are as follows:

First Level of Refinement

GetData()
BEGIN
    Write a prompt to enter the current account balance.
    Read(*Balance*).
    Write a prompt to enter the monthly deposits.
    Read(*Deposits*).
    Write a prompt to enter the monthly withdrawals.
    Read(*Withdrawals*).
END.

AddDeposits()
BEGIN
    Calculate *Balance* = *Balance* + *Deposits*.
END.

SubtractWithdrawals()
BEGIN
    Calculate *Balance* = *Balance* − *Withdrawals*.
END.

AddInterest( )
BEGIN
   Calculate *Balance = Balance + (Balance * Interest)*.
END.

GenerateReport( )
BEGIN
   Write(*Balance*).
   Write(*Deposits*).
   Write(*Withdrawals*).
END.

Coding the Program

The foregoing problem solution can be coded easily in any structured programming language. Here is how the foregoing algorithms are translated into C++ code:

```
//THIS PROGRAM SHOWS THE BLOCK-STRUCTURED NATURE OF C++
//TAKE A GENERAL LOOK AT ITS OVERALL STRUCTURE

#include <iostream.h>   //FOR cin AND cout

//DEFINE GLOBAL INTEREST CONSTANT
const float INTEREST = 0.01; //CURRENT MONTHLY INTEREST RATE

//FUNCTION PROTOTYPES
void GetData(float &Balance, float &Deposits, float &Withdrawals);
void AddDeposits(float &Balance, float Deposits);
void SubtractWithdrawals (float &Balance, float Withdrawals);
void AddInterest(float &Balance);
void GenerateReport(float Balance, float Deposits, float Withdrawals);

void main()
{
//DEFINE FUNCTION ARGUMENT VARIABLES
  float Balance = 0.0;        //ACCOUNT BALANCE
  float Deposits = 0.0;       //MONTHLY DEPOSITS
  float Withdrawals = 0.0;    //MONTHLY WITHDRAWALS

//DISPLAY PROGRAM DESCRIPTION MESSAGE
  cout << "This program will generate a banking account report based"
          "on information entered by the user" << endl << endl;
```

```
    //CALL FUNCTIONS
    GetData(Balance,Deposits,Withdrawals);
    AddDeposits(Balance,Deposits);
    SubtractWithdrawals(Balance,Withdrawals);
    AddInterest(Balance);
    GenerateReport(Balance,Deposits,Withdrawals);
} //END main()

//THIS FUNCTION GETS THE MONTHLY ACCOUNT
//INFORMATION FROM THE USER
void GetData (float &Balance, float &Deposits, float &Withdrawals)
{
    cout << "Enter the account balance:  $";
    cin  >> Balance;
    cout << "Enter the deposits this month:  $";
    cin >> Deposits;
    cout << "Enter the withdrawals this month:  $";
    cin >> Withdrawals;
} //END GetData()

//THIS FUNCTION ADDS THE MONTHLY DEPOSITS
//TO THE ACCOUNT BALANCE
void AddDeposits(float &Balance, float Deposits)
{
    Balance = Balance + Deposits;
} //END AddDeposits()

//THIS FUNCTION SUBTRACTS THE MONTHLY WITHDRAWALS
//FROM THE ACCOUNT BALANCE
void SubtractWithdrawals (float &Balance, float Withdrawals)
{
    Balance = Balance – Withdrawals;
} //END SubtractWithdrawals()

//THIS FUNCTION ADDS MONTHLY INTEREST
//TO THE ACCOUNT BALANCE
void AddInterest(float &Balance)
{
    Balance = Balance + (Balance * INTEREST);
} //END AddInterest()

//THIS FUNCTION DISPLAYS THE MONTHLY ACCOUNT REPORT
void GenerateReport(float Balance, float Deposits, float Withdrawals)
```

```
{
  cout << "The account balance is currently:  $" << Balance << endl;
  cout << "Deposits were  $" << Deposits << endl;
  cout << "Withdrawals were  $" << Withdrawals << endl;
} //END GenerateReport()
```

At this point, the code might look a little overwhelming. However, don't agonize over the coding details; just observe the things that relate to what we discussed in this chapter. First, notice the overall structure of the program. A general program comment is at the top of the program, followed by the preprocessor directives, followed by function *main()*, which is followed by the individual function code. Notice that the only purpose of *main()* is to call the individual functions in the order they are needed to solve the problem. The individual functions simply implement their respective algorithms using C++ code.

Second, notice the object declarations/definitions. The constant object *INTEREST* is declared prior to *main()* to make it a global constant and accessible to the entire program. This means that it will be accessible to *main()* as well as to all the other functions defined in the program. The varaible objects *Balance*, *Deposits*, and *Withdrawals* are defined at the beginning of *main()*. These objects are listed as **arguments** in the function calls. A function argument is a data value that the function requires to perform its defined task. More about this later.

Finally, notice the extensive use of comments. The purpose of the program is commented, as well as the purpose of each function. Furthermore, a comment is placed with each constant declaration and variable definition to specify its purpose in the program. The comments are easily identified from the executable code, because they are coded in uppercase characters.

The foregoing C++ code involved the use of functions to implement the various program modules. It won't be long before you are writing structured C++ programs like this. However, we can implement simple problems like this using a *flat* or *inline* approach. The term *flat* comes from the idea that we will flatten the hierarchical structure of the program by coding all the program steps as one long *inline* sequence of statements as part of function *main()*. Here is the *flat* solution:

```
//ACTION 2-1 (ACT02-01.CPP)
//THIS PROGRAM REPRESENTS THE FLAT SOLUTION TO THE BANKING
//PROBLEM

#include <iostream.h>   //FOR cin AND cout

//DEFINE GLOBAL INTEREST CONSTANT
const float INTEREST = 0.01;        //CURRENT MONTHLY INTEREST RATE
                                    //IN DECIMAL FORM
```

```
void main()
{
  float Balance = 0.0;        //ACCOUNT BALANCE
  float Deposits = 0.0;       //MONTHLY DEPOSITS
  float Withdrawals = 0.0;    //MONTHLY WITHDRAWALS

  cout << "This program will generate a banking account report based"
       << "on information entered by the user" << endl << endl;

  //GET THE MONTHLY ACCOUNT INFORMATION FROM THE USER
  cout << "Enter the account balance:  $";
  cin  >> Balance;
  cout << "Enter the deposits this month:  $";
  cin >> Deposits;
  cout << "Enter the withdrawals this month:  $";
  cin >> Withdrawals;
  //ADD THE MONTHLY DEPOSITS TO THE ACCOUNT BALANCE
  Balance = Balance + Deposits;

  //SUBTRACT THE MONTHLY WITHDRAWALS
  Balance = Balance – Withdrawals;

  //ADD MONTHLY INTEREST
  Balance = Balance + (Balance * INTEREST);
  //DISPLAYS THE MONTHLY ACCOUNT REPORT
  cout << "The account balance is currently:  $" << Balance << endl;
  cout << "Deposits were  $" << Deposits << endl;
  cout << "Withdrawals were  $" << Withdrawals << endl;
} //END main()
```

As you can see, each of the former function statements has been coded inline as part of *main()*. This type of implementation is adequate for simple problems such as this. The program code is clear and easy to understand, given the appropriate program comments. For the next few chapters, we will employ flat implementations. Then, as the problems get more complex, we will need to implement the program modules as C++ functions and replace the inline program statements with calls to those functions as we did in the first program. However, before you can do this, you need to learn the basic implementation details of the C++ language. The next three chapters are devoted to this purpose. We will get back to highly structured C++ programs in Chapter 7, where functions are discussed in detail.

CHAPTER SUMMARY

A data object is any item of information that is manipulated or operated upon by a computer. The simplest types of data objects are numeric and character objects. A class describes the data attributes and behavior of its objects. Data abstraction allows us to work with a class without agonizing over the internal implementation details of the class; this gives rise to the term abstract data type, or ADT. The term behavior has to do with how an ADT, or class, will act and react for a given operation. As a result, all classes (ADTs) exhibit a given behavior, which is determined by the operations defined for the ADT.

C++ is a typed language. This means that all of the data processed by a C++ program must be part of a given class that is defined within the program. There are three major class categories: scalar, structured, and pointer.

Scalar data objects are ordered and consist of standard and enumerated data. Standard scalar classes include the integer, floating-point, character, and Boolean classes. The integer classes in C++ include the **short**, **int**, **unsigned int**, **long**, and **unsigned long** classes, each of which defines a given range of integers that depend on the particular C++ compiler that you are using.

The floating-point class consists of decimal values that can be represented in either fixed decimal or exponential form. Floating-point constant and variable objects can be declared/defined as **float**, **double**, or **long double** classes, each of which defines a given range of floating-point values that depend on the particular C++ compiler that you are using.

Character data include all of the symbols on your computer keyboard. Characters are ordered, because they are represented internally using a numeric ASCII code. In C++, there are two character classes: **char** and **unsigned char**. The former is used to represent the standard ASCII character set. The latter is used to represent the standard ASCII character set as well as the extended PC character set.

A string is a series of characters. C++ implements strings as character arrays, where each element in the array contains a character in the string, with the last string element being the character '\0', called a null terminator.

The Boolean class, **bool**, consists of only two data elements, **true** and **false**. Boolean values are used in programs to make decisions.

Enumerated classes are those that you, the programmer, declare when constructing a program. Enumerated classes can be employed in your C++ programs to make them more understandable and application-oriented. These data classes are declared using the keyword **enum**. Because enumerated classes are scalar, the values declared as part of a given class are ordered in ascending order from the first value in the value listing to the last value in the listing.

All constants and variables used in a C++ program must be declared/defined as class objects prior to their use in the program. Constant objects are declared using the keyword **const**. The constant identifier is set equal to its constant value. Variable objects are defined by listing the variable class followed by the variable object identifier. An optional initializing value can be included in the definition. Like string constants, string variables must be defined as character arrays.

C++ programs consist of two sections: the preprocessor section and the main function section. The preprocessor section contains preprocessor directives that provide smart editing tasks on the program. The *#include* directive is used to copy C++ header files into the source program.

The statement section of the program is the main executable body of the program and is called the *main function block*. This section begins with *main()*, followed by a left curly brace, and closes with a right curly brace. The main function block of the program is where access to all the executable C++ code resides. Global constant declarations must be made prior to *main()*. Local variable objects can be defined anyplace in the program prior to their use, but good style dictates that they be defined at the beginning of the function block where they are used. Constant objects should be declared as globally as possible, whereas variable objects should be defined as locally as possible.

Structured design is a methodology that requires software to be designed using a top-down modular approach, and structured programming allows programs to be written using well-defined control structures and independent program modules. The C++ language facilitates structured programming using user-defined functions. These functions are coded after *main()* and are written to perform specific tasks required by the program. User-defined functions are called when needed within other functions, such as *main()*.

QUESTIONS AND PROBLEMS

Questions

1. Name the three levels of software and describe the general characteristics of each.

2. Explain the operational difference between a compiler and an interpreter.

3. A compiler translates a source program into a(n) _____ program.

4. True or false: A C program is also a C++ program.

5. Explain what happens and the action you must take when your C++ compiler encounters an error in your program.

6. What is the purpose of a linker?

7. Explain why C and C++ are sometimes referred to as midlevel languages.

8. What is the major difference between the C and C++ languages?

9. The file generated by your C++ compiler has an extension of _____.

10. The file generated by the your C++ linker has an extension of _____.

11. What is an abstract data type, or ADT?

12. Give an example of an ADT.

13. What is meant by the term *behavior*, as related to ADTs?

14. Why is the C++ class ideal for implementing ADTs?

15. Name the four standard classes defined in C++.

16. What feature does a scalar class have over a nonscalar class?

17. Which of the following are *not* legal integer values in C++? Explain why they are not valid. Assume the **int** class.
    a. −32.0
    b. +256
    c. 256
    d. 3,240
    e. 32000
    f. 40000

18. What is an integer overflow condition, and when will it generate incorrect results in C++?

19. Which of the following are not legal floating-point values in C++? Explain why they are not valid. Assume the **float** class.
    a. 35.7
    b. −35.7
    c. 0.456
    d. 1.25e−9
    e. −2.5−e3
    f. −0.375e−3
    g. 25

20. Convert the following decimal numbers to exponential notation.
    a. −0.0000123
    b. 57892345.45
    c. 1.00004536

d. +012.345

21. Convert the following exponential values to fixed decimal notation.
   a. 3.45e–7
   b. –2.25e–5
   c. 2.22e6
   d. –3.45e4

22. Three values in a data communications problem are 15.3 kHz, 2.2 MHz, and 10 ps.
   a. Express each as a floating-point value in fixed decimal form.
   b. Express each as a floating-point value in exponential form.
   c. Express each as an integer value.

23. The following current and voltage values are measured in a circuit: 1 milliampere, 32 millivolts, 100 microvolts, and 125 nanoamperes.
   a. Express each current and voltage value in fixed decimal form.
   b. Express each current and voltage value in exponential form.

24. What is the class of each of the following?
   a. 250
   b. –250.0
   c. –16
   d. –3.5e–4
   e. 'x'
   f. '$'
   g. "2"
   h. "175"
   i. "1.25e–3"

25. Enumerated classes are declared using the keyword _____.

26. Given an enumerated class declaration, how are the values ordered within the class?

27. Write declarations for the following enumerated classes. Make sure to define an appropriate object to go along with each class.
   a. *This_Semester_Courses*, consisting of the courses you are taking this semester.
   b. *Major_Courses*, consisting of the courses required in your major program.
   c. *My_Family*, consisting of all the members of your immediate family.
   d. *Weekdays* and *Weekends*, consisting of those respective days of the week that occur in these subranges.
   e. *Spring*, *Summer*, *Fall*, and *Winter*, consisting of those respective months that make up these seasons.

28. Given the following definition
   ```
   enum Colors {Blue, Green, Yellow, Red, Orange};
   Colors Color;
   ```

which of the following are true, and which are false?

a. Blue < Yellow

b. Red > Orange

c. (Green < Yellow) AND (Yellow > Blue)

d. (Yellow > Orange) OR (Yellow > Blue)

29. Using the declarations in question 28, which of the following are valid statements? Explain why a particular statement is not valid.

a. Color = Black;

b. Colors = Red;

c. Color = Blue + Green;

d. Color = "Yellow";

30. Explain how C++ employs functions to allow for structured top-down program design.

31. Where is the code for user-defined functions placed in a C++ program?

32. List at least three places where comments should occur in your C++ program.

33. State the difference between a character and a string object.

Problems

Least Difficult

1. Choose appropriate names and declare constant objects to represent each of the following.

a. A maximum value of 100.

b. The value required to represent the prefix milli.

c. The value required to represent the prefix kilo.

d. Your age.

e. A period.

f. Your birth date.

g. Your school.

2. Declare a series of constant objects that would represent the months of the year.

3. Choose appropriate names and define variable objects for each of the following.

a. Grade point average (GPA).

b. Grade for a course.

c. Gross pay on a paycheck.

d. Student name, course name, and course number. Assume that the student and course names require 25 characters and the course number is a seven-position alphanumeric number such as ENG-103.

4. The = symbol is used in C++ to denote an assignment operation. For now, you can think of it as an equals operation, but you will find out later that it actually has a different meaning than just equals. Given the following,

```
//PROBLEM 2-4

#include <math.h> //FOR sqrt()

//DECLARE CONSTANT
const float VALUE = 2.5;

void main()
{
//DEFINE VARIABLES
   int x = 0;
   int y = 0;
   float a = 0.0;
   float b = 0.0;
}//END main()
```

determine the results of each of the following program segments:
a. x = 25;
   b = sqrt(x);
b. y = 5;
   a = sqrt(sqrt(y));
c. x = 1;
   x = x + 1;
   y = sqrt(x);
d. x = 2;
   y = x + x;
   a = (y + 1) * VALUE;
e. x = 2;
   y = x + x;
   a = y + 1 * VALUE;

More Difficult

5. The *cout* object is used in C++ to display a value on the display monitor. The format for this operation is

cout << variable object or value to displayed << endl;

Notice that the << symbols direct the variable object or value to the *cout* object. The *endl* command creates a carriage return, line feed (CRLF) and flushes the output stream buffer. Thus, to display the value of the object *x* in a program, use the following statement:

```
cout << x << endl;
```

Code the program given in problem 4, including the program segments given in part a through part e of the problem. Add a *cout* statement to each of these segments to display the resulting variable object value. To use the *cout* object you must include the *iostream.h* header file. Compile, link, and run the program. Verify that the output generated by the program is correct according to the respective program calculations.

6. Design and code a C++ program that will find the sum of three variable decimal values and display the sum on the system monitor. Call the variables *A*, *B*, and *C*, and assume that they have initial values of 95.3, 78.5, and 85.2, respectively. Use the program structure given in Figure 2-8. (*Note:* You must include the *iostream.h* header file to use the *cout* object.) Compile, link, and run your program using your C++ compiler.

7. Expand the program you wrote in problem 6 to calculate and display the average of the three values. (*Note:* The / symbol is used for division in C++.) Compile, link, and run your program.

8. Design and code a C++ program that will find the total resistance of three series resistors whose values are 3.3k, 2.2k, and 1M. (*Note:* The prefix k stands for the quantity 1000, and the prefix M stands for 1,000,000. The total resistance of resistors in series is the sum of the individual resistances.) Display the total resistance on the display monitor using a *cout* statement. You must include the *iostream.h* file in your program to use the *cout* object. Use the program structure given in Figure 2-8. Compile, link, and run your program.

9. Use your C++ compiler to find and correct the syntax errors in the following program:

```
//PROBLEM 9 (P02-09.CPP)

#include <iostream.h>        //FOR cout

void main()
{
//DEFINE AND INITIALIZE VARIABLES
    float Voltage = 0.0;            //VOLTAGE IN VOLTS
    Current = 0.001;            //CURRENT IN AMPERES
    float Resistance = 4700.0;    //RESISTANCE IN OHMS
```

```
/ GENERATE PROGRAM DESCRIPTION MESSAGE
  cout << "This program will calculate voltage "
          "given a current value of 0.001 amp \n"
          "and a resistance value of 4700 ohms. " << endl << endl;

//CALCULATE VOLTAGE
  Voltage = Current * Resistance

//DISPLAY RESULTS
  cout.setf(ios::fixed);
  cout.precision(3);
  cout << "Given a current value of " << Current << " amperes "
          "and a resistance value of " << Resistance << " ohms,\n"
          "the resulting voltage is " << Voltage << " volts." << endl;
} //END main()
```

10. Enter, compile, and run the following program. Does the output generated by the program make sense, especially if you were the customer? Of course not! There is a logic error in the program. Use your C++ debugger to locate and correct the logic error. (*Hint:* Watch the variable *Tax* as you single-step the program.)

```
//PROBLEM 10 (P02-10.CPP)

#include <iostream.h>      //FOR cin AND cout

//DECLARE CONSTANT
  const float RATE = 7.0;    //RATE OF INTEREST IN PERCENT FORM

void main()
{
//DEFINE VARIABLES

  float Cost = 0.0;              //COST OF ITEM
  float Tax = 0.0;              //SALES TAX
  float TotalCost = 0.0;        //TOTAL COST OF ITEM

//DISPLAY PROGRAM DESCRIPTION MESSAGE
  cout << "This program will calculate total cost of a sales item. " << endl;

//GET COST FROM USER
  cout << "Enter the cost of the sales item:  $";
  cin >> Cost;
```

```
//CALCULATE INTEREST
  Tax = RATE * Cost;
  TotalCost = Cost + Tax;

//DISPLAY RESULT TABLE
  cout.setf(ios::fixed);
  cout.setf(ios::showpoint);
  cout.precision(2);
  cout << "The total cost of the sales item is:  $" << TotalCost << endl;
} //END main()
```

11. What is the purpose of the *cin* >> statement in the program given in problem 10?

12. The following is an enhanced version of the program given in problem 9. Enter, compile, link, and run this program using your C++ compiler.

```
//PROBLEM 12 (P02-12.CPP)

#include <iostream.h>     //FOR cout
#include <iomanip.h>      //FOR setw()

void main()
{
//DEFINE AND INITIALIZE VARIABLES
  float Voltage = 0.0;          //VOLTAGE IN VOLTS
  float Current = 0.001;        //CURRENT IN AMPERES
  float Resistance = 4700.0;    //RESISTANCE IN OHMS

//GENERATE PROGRAM DESCRIPTION MESSAGE
cout << "This program will calculate voltage "
         "given a current value of 0.001 amp \n"
         "and a resistance value of 4700 ohms. " << endl << endl;

//CALCULATE VOLTAGE
  Voltage = Current * Resistance;

//DISPLAY HEADINGS
  cout  << "\n\n\n\n"
        << setw(20) << "RESISTANCE"
        << setw(20) << "CURRENT"
        << setw(20) << "VOLTAGE\n"
        << setw(20) << "----------"
        << setw(20) << "-------"
        << setw(20) << "-------" << endl;
```

```
//DISPLAY VALUES
  cout.setf(ios::fixed);
  cout.precision(3);
  cout  << '\n'
        << setw(20) << Resistance
        << setw(20) << Current
        << setw(20) << Voltage << endl;

} //END main()
```

13. Look closely at the *cout* statements in the program in problem 12. Try to answer the following questions:

    a. What is the purpose of the '\n' character in these statements?

    b. What is the purpose of the *endl* command in these statements?

    c. What is the purpose of the *setw()* function in these statements?

    d. What is the purpose of the *cout.setf(ios::fixed)* statement in this program?

    e. What is the purpose of the *cout.precision(3)* statement in this program?

14. How does the output generated by the program in problem 12 differ from the output generated by the program in problem 9?

3

INPUT AND OUTPUT OBJECTS

INTRODUCTION
3-1 GETTING THINGS OUT ⇒ *cout*
    Using the *cout* Object
    Formatting the Output
3-2 GETTING THINGS IN: ⇒ *cin*
    Reading Mixed Data Classes
    Reading Single-Character Data
    Reading String Data

3-3 READING AND WRITING DISK FILES
    File Streams
    Classes: the Basis for C++ Files
    Reading and Writing a Disk File
PROBLEM SOLVING IN ACTION: USER-
    FRIENDLY PROGRAMS
CHAPTER SUMMARY
QUESTIONS AND PROBLEMS
    Questions
    Problems

INTRODUCTION

In Chapters 1 and 2, you learned the general concepts of problem solving, data abstraction, and C++ program design. In this chapter, you will begin learning the implementation details of the C++ language. In particular, you will learn how to get information into and out of your system via C++ objects. Getting data into the system is called **reading**, and generating data from the system is called **writing**. You will discover how to write information to your display monitor, printer, and a disk file. Then, you will learn how to read information from your keyboard and a disk file. Armed with this knowledge, you will be ready to write some *interactive* C++ programs. By interactive, I mean programs that will interact with the user—writing user prompts and reading user input data. Make sure that you do the programming problems at the end of the chapter. You *must* get your hands dirty with some actual programming experience to learn how to program in C++.

3-1 GETTING THINGS OUT ⇒ *cout*

When executing your C++ programs, you usually will want to generate information to one of three hardware devices: a monitor, a printer, or a disk file. In fact, there will be occasions when you will need to generate information to all three of these devices during the execution of a program.

You can write information to a display monitor using a *cout* (pronounced "c-out") statement. The word *cout* is not considered a keyword within C++ and, therefore, is not set in bold type. Rather, *cout* is part of the *iostream.h* header file that invokes predefined routines to accomplish the output task. In fact, *cout* is actually an object defined in the *iostream.h* header file for a standard class called *iostream*. Objects are at the core of object-oriented programming, and you will learn how to define and apply your own objects in C++ programs later in the text. For now, let's learn how to use the predefined *cout* object to write data to the display monitor.

Using the *cout* Object

The general format for a *cout* statement is as follows:

> **cout FORMAT**
>
> cout << item #1 << item #2 << item #3 << ⋯ << item #n;

As you can see, *cout* is followed by a list of the items to be written, which are separated by the << **stream insertion operator**. We refer to *cout* as an **output stream object** that is attached, or connected, to your system monitor. A **stream** is simply a sequence of data. Thus, a *cout* statement represents a sequence of data, or stream, flowing to the system monitor. Items are inserted into the output stream using the << stream insertion operator. As items are inserted into the stream, they flow to your system monitor, as illustrated in Figure 3-1.

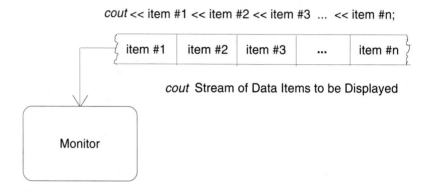

cout << item #1 << item #2 << item #3 ... << item #n;

cout Stream of Data Items to be Displayed

Figure 3-1   Items to be displayed are inserted into the *cout* output stream using the << stream insertion operator.

The best way to understand how *cout* works is to look at the output generated by several different *cout* statements. Probably the simplest use of the *cout* statement is to write fixed, or constant, information. There are two types of fixed information that can be written: numeric and character.

Getting Out Fixed Numeric Informaion

When you want to write fixed numeric information, you simply insert the numeric values into the *cout* output stream using the << operator. Thus, the statement

cout << 250;

generates an output of

250

The statement

cout << –365;

generates an output of

−365

The statement

cout << 1 << 2 << 3 << 4;

generates an output of

1234

The statement

cout << 2.75;

generates an output of

2.75

When several individual items are inserted into the stream, the output does not generate any spacing between the items. This is why the statement

cout << 1 << 2 << 3 << 4;

generates an output of

1234

Next, notice that when a fixed floating-point value is inserted, you get its fixed decimal equivalent on the output, not the exponential equivalent. Both of these conditions (item spacing and decimal output) can be altered using special formatting options within the *cout* statement. Output formatting will be discussed shortly.

Getting Out Fixed Character Information

To write character information, you must enclose the output information in quotes—single quotes for single characters and double quotes for strings. Consequently, the statement

cout << 'A';

generates an output of

A

The statement

cout << "This text is great!";

produces an output of

This text is great!

Example 3-1

Construct *cout* statements to generate the following outputs:

a. 3.14
b. 1 2 3 4

Solution:

a. cout << 3.14;
b. cout << 1 << ' ' << 2 << ' ' << 3 << ' ' << 4;

To get spacing in the output, use blank characters between the output values. Remember that blanks are also characters. As a result, the preceding statement generates blanks, or spaces, where they are inserted using single quotation marks.

Getting Out Variable Information

The next thing you must learn is how to write variable information. Again, this is a simple chore using the *cout* object: You simply insert the variable identifier(s) into the *cout* stream using the << insertion operator. For instance, if your program has defined *Voltage*, *Current*, and *Resistance* as variable objects, you would write their respective values by inserting them into the *cout* stream, like this:

cout << Voltage << Current << Resistance;

The foregoing statement would write the values stored in memory for *Voltage*, *Current*, and *Resistance*, in that order. The order of the output will be the same as the listing order within the *cout* statement. However, there would be no spacing between the values. Blank characters must be inserted separately to provide spacing. Let's see how this statement might be used within a complete program.

Example 3-2

Remember Ohm's law from the last chapter? Ohm's law states that voltage is equal to the product of current and resistance. Write a C++ program that will write a voltage value, given a current value of 0.001 ampere and a resistance value of 4700 ohms.

Solution

Let's define three variable objects to represent voltage, current, and resistance. We will initialize the given current and resistance values and use Ohm's law to calculate the voltage. The resulting voltage will then be written using the *cout* object. Here's the program:

```
//THIS PROGRAM CALCULATES AND DISPLAYS VOLTAGE USING OHMS LAW
#include <iostream.h>   //FOR cout

void main()
{
  float Voltage = 0.0;                //VOLTAGE IN VOLTS
  float Current = 0.001;              //CURRENT IN AMPERES
  float Resistance = 4700.0;          //RESISTANCE IN OHMS
  Voltage = Current * Resistance;     //CALCULATE VOLTAGE
  cout << Voltage;                    //DISPLAY VOLTAGE
} //END main()
```

The output produced by the program is

4.7

STYLE TIP

The output generated in Example 3-2 is simply the number 4.7. What a bore! You need to "dress up" your program outputs so that the user of the program understands what's going on. First, you should always use a *cout* statement at the beginning of your program that tells the user what the program is going to do. This is called a ***program description message***. A program description message does two things:

1. It tells the user (the person running the program) what the program will do.

2. It provides documentation within the program listing as to what the program will do. As a result, the program listing becomes self-documenting.

A program description message for the program in Example 3-2 might be coded something like this:

```
cout << "This program will calculate voltage, given a current of 0.001 ampere \n"
        "and a resistance of 4700 ohms. " << endl;
```

This one *cout* statement will generate the following output:

```
This program will calculate voltage, given a current of 0.001 ampere
and a resistance of 4700 ohms.
```

Observe that one *cout* statement is used to write two lines of character information. The trick is to divide the output sentence into two strings on two separate lines. Notice that each string item must be enclosed within double quotes. Also, notice the symbol '\n' (a backslash followed by the character *n*) at the end of the first line. The '\n' symbol is treated like a single character and is called an **escape sequence**. When inserted into the output stream, a carriage return/line feed (CRLF) is generated wherever it appears. Thus, in the foregoing *cout* statement, the first string item is written on one line, a CRLF is generated to move the cursor to the beginning of the next line, and the second string item is written. The final item inserted into the stream is the *endl* (end-of-line) **manipulator**. The *endl* manipulator does two things: First, like the '\n' escape sequence, it generates a CRLF, and second, unlike the '\n' escape sequence, it flushes the output stream buffer. Some systems accumulate output information in a buffer until there is enough information to justify writing to the screen. The *endl* manipulator forces any accumulated buffer information to be written immediately when it is executed. In the code that follows, you will notice the '\n' escape sequence being used within a *cout* statement for cursor control, whereas the *endl* manipulator will be employed at the end of a *cout* statement to flush the stream buffer. Figure 3-2 illustrates how the '\n' escape sequence and *endl* manipulator control the location of the cursor when used in the *cout* statement.

Good style would dictate that output information should be descriptive. In other words, the output information should be self-documenting. In Example 3-2, the voltage output statement could be modified, like this:

```
cout << "Given a current value of " << Current << " ampere and a \n"
        "resistance value of " << Resistance << " ohms, the \n"
        "resulting voltage is " << Voltage << " volts." << endl;
```

This one *cout* statement will generate the following output:

Given a current value of 0.001 ampere and a
resistance value of 4700 ohms, the
resulting voltage is 4.7 volts.

Let's analyze this output. First, observe that a '\n' escape sequence has been placed at the end of the first two lines in the *cout* statement. This generates a CRLF after the first two lines, thereby creating a single-line spacing effect on the screen. Next, look at the output lines themselves. See how an output sentence is constructed using separate string items. The sentence is formed by separate character strings enclosed within double quotation marks. The current, resistance, and voltage values are inserted into the stream, between the string items, by listing the variables (*Current*, *Resistance*, and *Voltage*) when they are needed as part of the output. Notice that the character strings and variable items are separated from each other using the << insertion operator. It is important that you see that the quotation marks are around the string information and *not* around the variables. Finally, the *endl* manipulator is inserted into the stream to place the cursor on the next line to prepare for any subsequent output and flush the stream buffer to assure that the information is displayed immediately.

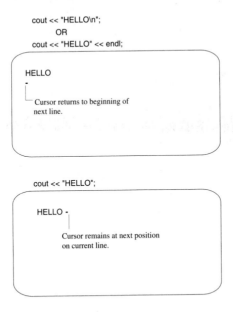

```
cout << "HELLO\n";
        OR
cout << "HELLO" << endl;
```

HELLO

Cursor returns to beginning of
next line.

```
cout << "HELLO";
```

HELLO ‑

Cursor remains at next position
on current line.

Figure 3-2 Using the '\n' escape sequence, or *endl* manipulator, forces the cursor to the next line.

Example 3-3

Insert the *cout* statements given in the previous style tips into the program developed in Example 3-2 to form a complete program.

Solution

```
//THIS PROGRAM CALCULATES AND DISPLAYS VOLTAGE USING OHMS LAW
#include <iostream.h>          //FOR cout

void main()
{
//DEFINE AND INITIALIZE VARIABLES
  float Voltage = 0.0;                //VOLTAGE IN VOLTS
  float Current = 0.001;              //CURRENT IN AMPERES
  float Resistance = 4700.0;          //RESISTANCE IN OHMS

//GENERATE PROGRAM DESCRIPTION MESSAGE
cout << "This program will calculate voltage, given a current of 0.001 ampere \n"
          "and a resistance of 4700 ohms. " << endl;

//CALCULATE VOLTAGE
  Voltage = Current * Resistance;

//DISPLAY RESULTS
  cout << "Given a current value of " << Current << " ampere and a \n"
          "resistance value of " << Resistance << " ohms, the \n"
          "resulting voltage is " << Voltage << " volts. " << endl;
} //END main()
```

As you can see from Example 3-3, the general idea of using the *cout* statement is simple: You place the *cout* statement in your program whenever you want to display information on your system monitor.

Up to this point, you have seen the use of the '\n' escape sequence (CRLF) to control cursor positioning. There are other escape sequences that you might need to use from time to time, some of which are listed in Table 3-1.

To use any of these escape sequences, simply include them as part of a string or insert them as single characters (using single quotes) into the output stream via the << operator. The purpose of each should be obvious from the action described in the table.

TABLE 3-1 ESCAPE SEQUENCES DEFINED FOR C++

Sequence	Action
\a	Bell
\b	Backspace
\f	Formfeed
\n	CRLF
\r	CR
\t	Horizontal tab
\v	Vertical tab
\\	Backslash
\'	Single quote
\"	Double quote
\?	Question mark

Monitor versus Printer Output

All of the output operations that you have seen up to this point will cause the information to be displayed on your system monitor. So how can you get the information to be printed by your system printer? Well, to perform printer output in C++, we must write code to create our own object, a *print* object. Here is a *print* object that I developed for the DOS platform:

```
//*******************************************************************
//THIS SEGMENT OF CODE DEFINES "PRINT" AS AN OUTPUT FILE
//                POINTING TO YOUR PRINTER PORT (PRN)
//                (DOS ONLY)
//*******************************************************************
   ofstream print;            //DEFINE PRINT AS AN OUTPUT FILE STREAM
   print.open("PRN");         //OPEN PRINTER FILE AND POINT TO PRN
   if (!print)                //MAKE SURE PRINTER IS READY
   {
      cout << "There is a problem with the printer." << endl;
      exit(1);
   }//END IF
```

This code will work only on DOS platforms because of the specific reference to the printer file, PRN. However, a similar object could be created for other platforms and used in the same way. Check with your instructor on how to obtain printed outputs if you are not using a DOS platform. At this point, it is not important that you understand the foregoing object-oriented code. This will come in time. The code simply creates a *print* stream object and attaches the stream to your system printer. You will use the *print* stream as an output stream just as you used the *cout* stream. Thus, the *print* statement format is as follows:

---

print FORMAT

print << item #1 << item #2 << item #3 << ⋯ << item #n;

As you can see, the items to be printed are inserted into the *print* stream using the << insertion operator the same way they are inserted into a *cout* stream. Here's an example to illustrate the use of *print*:

Example 3-4

Revise the program in Example 3-3 so that the output information is printed on your system printer rather than to the monitor.

Solution

Here's the revised program:

```
//THIS PROGRAM CALCULATES AND PRINTS VOLTAGE USING OHMS LAW
#include <iostream.h>        //FOR cout
#include <fstream.h>         //FOR print OBJECT
#include <process.h>         //FOR exit()

void main()
{
//*************************************************************
//THIS SEGMENT OF CODE DEFINES "PRINT" AS AN OUTPUT FILE
//          POINTING TO YOUR PRINTER PORT (PRN)
//                      (DOS  ONLY)
//*************************************************************
  ofstream print;              //DEFINE PRINT AS AN OUTPUT FILE STREAM
  print.open("PRN");           //OPEN PRINT FILE AND POINT TO PRN
  if (!print)                  //MAKE SURE PRINTER IS READY
  {
    cout << "There is a problem with the printer.\n";
    exit(1);
  }//END IF
```

```
//DEFINE VARIABLES
  float Voltage = 0.0;              //VOLTAGE IN VOLTS
  float Current = 0.001;           //CURRENT IN AMPERES
  float Resistance = 4700.0;       //RESISTANCE IN OHMS

//GENERATE PROGRAM DESCRIPTION MESSAGE
  cout << "This program will calculate voltage, given a current of\n"
          " 0.001 ampere and a resistance of 4700 ohms." << endl;

//CALCULATE VOLTAGE
  Voltage = Current * Resistance;

//PRINT RESULTS
  print <<  "Given a current value of " << Current << " ampere and a \n"
            "resistance value of " << Resistance << " ohms, the \n"
            "resulting voltage is " << Voltage << " volts." << endl;

  print.close();        //CLOSE PRINT FILE
} //END main()
```

Now the program output will be generated on your system printer rather than on the monitor. Notice that the *print* stream definition code has been integrated into function *main( )* of the program. In addition, for this code to compile properly, we must include the *fstream.h* and *process.h* header files. Once the *print* stream object is created, you simply use it like *cout* to write information to the printer. At the end of *main( )* you find the statement *print.close( )*. This statement is required to close the print file.

Notice how *cout* and *print* are being used to perform the display and printer output, respectively, in Example 3-4. Actually, we could have reattached the *cout* stream to the system printer. By default, the *cout* stream is attached to the system monitor. However, there will be times when you will want to write to the monitor and the printer simultaneously. As a result, we will employ the predefined *cout* stream for display output and our own *print* stream for printer output. Our *print* object is used exactly like the *cout* object to direct information to the printer. This is because our *print* object has **inherited** the same characteristics and behavior possessed by the *cout* object. Both are objects of the standard *iostream* class. More about the important concept of class inheritance later.

Formatting the Output

By formatting an output, I mean structuring it to meet a given application. C++ allows output formatting using special commands within the output statements.

These commands are referred to as *escape sequences* and *I/O manipulators*. You have already seen the use of each, but there are others that we need to discuss. However, before discussing the details, let's learn how the computer "sees" a display screen or printed page.

Many systems divide a page of output into 25 rows and 80 columns as shown by the layout chart in Figure 3-3. Layout charts are used to lay out, or format, your output. The layout chart allows you to align output information so that the following happens:

- Proper margins are provided for header information.
- Numeric and character data are properly aligned under column headings and evenly spaced across the page.
- The output looks professional.

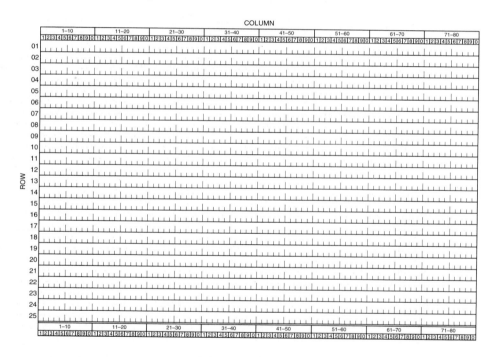

Figure 3-3 A typical layout chart.

The first thing to do when using a layout chart is to fill in the chart with the information to be written. For instance, suppose you must create three columns of output: the first for a person's name, the second for the person's address, and the

third for a person's phone number. Figure 3-4 shows how these three columns
might be laid out on a layout chart. Looking at the figure, you can make the
following observations:

- There are three headings located on row 4.
- There are dashes in row 5 to underscore each column heading.
- The NAME heading has a field width of 15.
- The ADDRESS heading has a field width of 22.
- The PHONE heading has a field width of 23.

The *field width* of an output item is the number of columns on the monitor
or printer that the item will occupy.

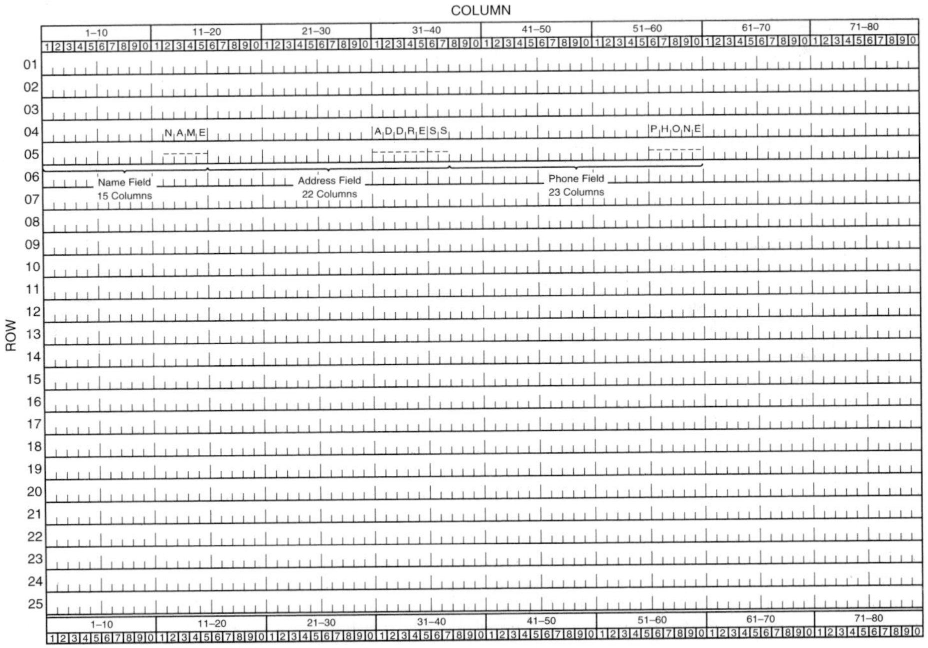

Figure 3-4 Laying out an output using a layout chart.

Using this information, let's write a program that will display the headings
just as they appear on the layout chart. Here it is:

```
//PROGRAM TO GENERATE OUTPUT SHOWN IN FIGURE 3-4
#include <iostream.h>   //FOR cout
#include <iomanip.h>    //FOR setw()

void main()
{

//SKIP THREE LINES AND DISPLAY HEADINGS
 cout  <<"\n\n\n"
       << setw(15) << "NAME"
       << setw(22) << "ADDRESS"
       << setw(23) << "PHONE" << endl;
 cout  << setw(15) << "----"
       << setw(22) << "-------"
       << setw(23) << "-----"
       << endl;
}//END main()
```

The first item inserted into *cout* stream is a string of three CRLF escape sequences. Assuming that the cursor is located in the upper left-hand corner of a clear screen, these three escape sequences generate the three blank lines in rows 1, 2, and 3, respectively. Now, looking at the layout chart in Figure 3-4, you see that each heading is designated by a field width that indicates the number of columns that a given output item will occupy. To communicate the field width to the *cout* object, you must use the *setw()* **I/O manipulator** contained in the *iomanip.h* header file. A list of several I/O manipulators is provided in Table 3-2.

TABLE 3-2 I/O STREAM MANIPULATORS FOR C++

Manipulator	Action
setw(n)	Sets field width to n
setprecision(n)	Sets floating-point precision to n
setfill(n)	Sets fill character to n
dec	Decimal output
hex	Hexadecimal output
oct	Octal output
ws	Extracts whitespace characters
endl	Inserts a new line in the output stream, then flushes the output stream
flush	Flushes the output stream

Notice that I/O manipulators allow you to manipulate the output stream to obtain some desired effect, in our case using the *setw()* manipulator to set the field width of a given output item. Consult your compiler reference manual for more information on these and other I/O manipulators. Remember that in order to use some of these manipulators, such as *setw()*, you must include the *iomanip.h* header file in your program.

Any of the manipulators in Table 3-2 can be inserted in the *cout* stream just like any other item using the << insertion operator. The following format shows how the *setw()* manipulator will set the field width for an item to be output.

FIELD WIDTH FORMAT

```
cout << setw(field width) << output item;
```

In Figure 3-4, observe that the first output, "NAME", has a field width of 15. Thus, *setw(15)* tells C++ to assign a field width of 15 columns to the *next* item to be written, which, as you can see from the program, is "NAME". When "NAME" is written, it will be right justified, by default, within this field width. Because it is right justified, "NAME" is positioned at the extreme right-hand side of the field. And, because the word "NAME" requires only four columns of output, C++ generates 15 − 4, or 11, spaces prior to "NAME".

Next, count the number of columns from the "NAME" field in Figure 3-4 to the last 'S' in the "ADDRESS" field. You get 22, right? Thus, the "ADDRESS" field width is 22. Therefore, *setw(22)* is inserted into the *cout* stream prior to inserting the item "ADDRESS".

Finally, counting the number of columns from the "ADDRESS" field to the last letter ('E') in "PHONE" field, you get 23. Consequently, the "PHONE" field width is set to 23. Notice that the *endl* manipulator is inserted into the stream at the end of the "PHONE" item so that the cursor will be positioned at the beginning of the next output line and the stream buffer is flushed. The same basic idea is then repeated within the next *cout* statement to produce row 5. This statement generates the dashes that provide underscoring for the headings.

Example 3-5

Write a program segment that will format a three-column table for *CURRENT, RESISTANCE,* and *VOLTAGE.* Underscore each column heading.

Solution

Using a layout chart, you must first lay out the output headings. Such a layout is shown in Figure 3-5. Here, the table headings are located in row 5, and each heading has a field width of 20. In addition, each heading is underscored by using dashes in row 6. The dashes must also have a field width of 20 to locate them under their respective headings.

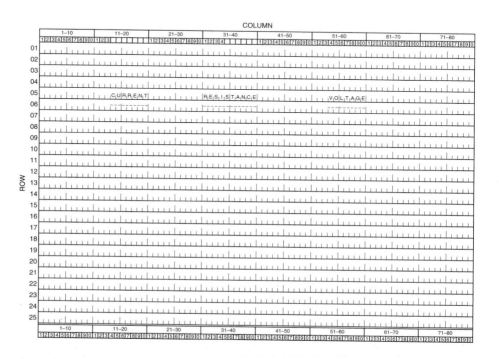

Figure 3-5   Layout chart for Example 3-5.

The resulting program is as follows:

```
//THIS PROGRAM DISPLAYS TABLE HEADINGS FOR OHM'S LAW VALUES
#include <iostream.h>        //FOR cout
#include <iomanip.h>         //FOR setw()

void main()
{
//SKIP FOUR LINES AND DISPLAY HEADINGS
    cout  <<"\n\n\n\n"                           //SKIP FIRST FOUR LINES
          << setw(20) << "CURRENT"               //DISPLAY HEADINGS
          << setw(20) << "RESISTANCE"
          << setw(20) << "VOLTAGE" << endl;
```

```
cout    << setw(20) << "-------"
        << setw(20) << "----------"
        << setw(20) << "-------"
        << endl;
} //END main()
```

Example 3-6

Given a current value of 0.001 ampere and a resistance value of 4700 ohms, write a program to calculate voltage using Ohm's law. Write the current, resistance, and voltage values using the format developed in Example 3-5.

Solution

The following program will do the job:

```
//THIS PROGRAM DISPLAYS A TABLE OF OHM'S LAW VALUES
#include <iostream.h>        //FOR cout
#include <iomanip.h>         //FOR setw()

void main()
{
//DEFINE AND INITIALIZE VARIABLES
  float Voltage = 0.0;            //VOLTAGE IN VOLTS
  float Current = 0.001;          //CURRENT IN AMPERES
  float Resistance = 4700.0;      //RESISTANCE IN OHMS

//CALCULATE VOLTAGE
  Voltage = Current * Resistance;

//DISPLAY HEADINGS
  cout  <<"\n\n\n\n"
        << setw(20) << "CURRENT"
        << setw(20) << "RESISTANCE"
        << setw(20) << "VOLTAGE" << endl;
  cout  << setw(20) << "-------"
        << setw(20) << "----------"
        << setw(20) << "-------"
        << endl;

//DISPLAY VALUES
  cout  << setw(20) << Current
        << setw(20) << Resistance
        << setw(20) << Voltage
        << endl;
} //END main()
```

Here, I have simply combined several things that we have done previously. The headings program segment from Example 3-5 was inserted to generate the required CURRENT, RESISTANCE, and VOLTAGE headings. Notice that the last *cout* statement in the program writes the actual values of current, resistance, and voltage, respectively. Here, the variable identifier is listed after the field-width specifier required to locate the value under the respective heading. You might note that three *cout* statements are used for clarity: one to write the header information, another to underscore the headings, and another to write the variable information.

COMPILER NOTE

To obtain the output required in these formatting examples, you must start with a clear screen. Most C++ compilers provide a standard function to clear the screen. For example, DOS compilers provide the *clrscr()* function as part of the *conio.h* header file. Check your compiler reference manual, or ask your instructor about such a function if you are not using a DOS-compatible platform.

Formatting Floating-Point Output

Many application programs require you to display floating-point data. Recall that C++ employs two methods for representing such data: fixed decimal point notation or exponential notation. The way your compiler displays such data depends on several factors, including the size of the data item to be displayed as well as the compiler design itself. In most cases you will want to avoid any exponential output and force the compiler to generate a fixed decimal point display. The C++ compiler provides two functions in the *iostream.h* header file to accomplish this task. They are *setf()* and *precision()*. The *setf()* function is used to set various formatting flags for the compiler. The only flags that we are concerned about at this time are the *fixed, right,* and *left* flags.

Setting the *fixed* flag using the *setf()* function forces the compiler to display a floating-point value using fixed decimal point notation to a number of decimal places specified by the *precision()* function. Both functions must be called by the *cout* object, as follows:

GENERATING DECIMAL POINT VALUES

cout.setf(ios::fixed);

cout.precision(n);

Notice that a dot, *.*, is used by the object to call the function. This "dot notation" is employed whenever an object calls one of its ***member functions***. A member function of an object is simply a function that is part of the object class. More about this later. The statement *cout.setf(ios::fixed)* directs the compiler to generate a fixed decimal output, and the *cout.precision(n)* statement dictates the number of decimal places to the right of the decimal point to generate. Recall our Ohm's law program from Example 3-6. Suppose that we altered the display part of the program as follows:

```
//DISPLAY VALUES
   cout.setf(ios::fixed);
   cout.precision(2);
   cout   << setw(20) << Current
          << setw(20) << Resistance
          << setw(20) << Voltage << endl;
```

Here, using the *setf()* and *precision()* functions forces the following decimal output:

CURRENT	RESISTANCE	VOLTAGE
--------------	--------------------	----------------
0.00	4700.00	4.70

Notice that the compiler was forced to generate a fixed decimal output with two places to the right of the decimal point. The problem here is that there is not enough precision to display the current value. So, let's change the precision value to 3, like this:

```
//DISPLAY VALUES
   cout.setf(ios::fixed);
   cout.precision(3);
   cout   << setw(20) << Current
          << setw(20) << Resistance
          << setw(20) << Voltage << endl;
```

The resulting display is as follows:

CURRENT	RESISTANCE	VOLTAGE
--------------	--------------------	--------------
0.001	4700.000	4.700

Now we have generated enough precision to display all the values in fixed decimal format.

You can change the precision at any time in the program by calling the *precision()* function as needed, as long as the *setf()* function has been called someplace previously in the program. To place the compiler back in its default display mode, you must use the *unsetf()* function, as follows:

```
//DISPLAY VALUES
  cout.unsetf(ios::fixed);
  cout   << setw(20) << Current
         << setw(20) << Resistance
         << setw(20) << Voltage << endl;
```

Now the output becomes

CURRENT	RESISTANCE	VOLTAGE
---------------	--------------------	---------------
0.001	4.7e+03	4.7

As you can see, the compiler has chosen to display the resistance in exponential form.

You control the justification of a value within a field by using the *right* and *left* flags. By setting the *left* flag, the output value will be left-justified within its field. To right justify a value, you set the *right* flag. Of course, output values are right-justified by default. For example, suppose that you want to left justify the table headings and Ohm's law values in the foregoing program. To do this, we will set both the *fixed* and *left* flags using the *setf()* function. Here's the required syntax:

GENERATING LEFT-JUSTIFIED VALUES

```
cout.setf(ios::fixed ¦ ios::left);
```

Notice that *setf()* is now setting two flags: the *fixed* and the *left* flag. To set more than one flag, you must use the double vertical bar, ¦, between each flag to be set. Here's the Ohm's law code for left justifying the table headings and corresponding values:

```
//DISPLAY HEADINGS
  cout.setf(ios::fixed ¦ ios::left);
  cout.precision(3);
  cout  <<"\n\n\n\n"
        << setw(20) << "CURRENT"
        << setw(20) << "RESISTANCE"
        << setw(20) << "VOLTAGE" << endl;
  cout  << setw(20) << "-------"
        << setw(20) << "----------"
        << setw(20) << "-------"
        << endl;

//DISPLAY VALUES
  cout  << setw(20) << Current
        << setw(20) << Resistance
        << setw(20) << Voltage << endl;
```

Here, the *left* flag has been set prior to writing both the headings and values so that both will be left justified within their respective output fields. This code generates the following output:

```
CURRENT         RESISTANCE          VOLTAGE
--------------  --------------------  --------------
0.001           4700.000            4.700
```

The formatting functions and flags just discussed are summarized in Table 3-3.

TABLE 3-3 FORMATTING FUNCTIONS AND FLAGS

Function/Flag	Description
setf()	Sets an ios flag.
unsetf()	Unsets an ios flag.
precision(n)	Sets decimal output to *n* decimal places.
ios::fixed	Forces fixed decimal point output.
ios::left	Forces left justification within field.
ios::right	Forces right justification within field.
ios::showpoint	Forces a decimal point to be displayed. (Use for currency outputs)

Quick Check

1. The file that must be included to use *cout* is the _____ header file.

2. The operator that must be employed to insert information into the *cout* stream is the _____ operator.

3. Write a *cout* statement to display your name as a fixed string of information.

4. Write a *cout* statement to display your name when it is stored in a string variable called *Name*.

5. The escape sequence that must be used to generate a CRLF is the _____.

6. The file that must be included to use the *setw()* field-width manipulator is the _____ header file.

7. Write a *cout* statement that will display the value of a floating-point variable called *Number* left-justified within a field width of 10 columns and a precision of 3 decimal places.

8. Explain the difference between using a '\n' versus an *endl* within a *cout* statement.

3-2 GETTING THINGS IN: ⇒ *cin*

Getting information into a program for processing is called *reading*. In most present-day systems, information is read from one of two sources: from a keyboard or from a disk file. In this section, you will learn how to read information that is being entered via a keyboard by the system user.

The primary C++ statement that we will use for reading keyboard data is the *cin* (pronounced "c-in") statement. Like *cout, cin* is a predefined stream object in C++ and is part of the *iostream.h* header file. The *cin* stream is an input stream attached, by default, to your system keyboard. Thus, as you enter information via the keyboard, it will flow into the *cin* stream.

Before you can understand how this statement works, you must know a little bit about how C++ "sees" a line of data. Suppose you enter two lines of data as follows:

74 92 88⏎

23 45 16⏎

When typing in the foregoing data on a keyboard, you would type each number consecutively, separating the numbers with one or more spaces. As you enter the values, they are stored in the *cin* stream buffer. At the end of a line, you will press the **ENTER** (⏎) key. How do you suppose the system knows where one data item ends and another begins? You're right—the *whitespace* (blanks) between the data items separate one item from another. Next, how do you suppose the system knows where the line of data ends? Right again—by pressing the ⏎ key you are defining the end of the line and entering a CRLF into the stream buffer. The stream buffer and its contents after this data entry operation are illustrated in Figure 3-6.

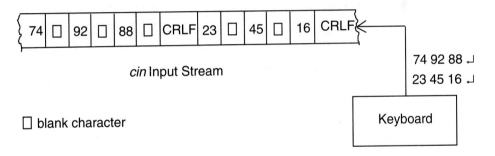

Figure 3-6   The input stream buffer after entering two lines of data.

Now back to the *cin* stream. The general format for using *cin* is as follows:

cin FORMAT

cin >> variable to be read;

Notice that the word *cin* is followed by the double right-angle bracket *stream extraction operator*, >>, which is followed by the variable to be read. We say that the >> operator *extracts* the data to be read from the input data stream buffer. The input data item is then *assigned* to the variable object listed in the *cin* statement. Of course, the variable object must be defined using a legal data class prior to using it in the *cin* statement.

DEBUGGING TIP

A common source of error when first writing *cout* and *cin* statements is to use the wrong operator. Remember that the << insertion operator is used to insert items in the *cout* stream, and the >> extraction operator is used to extract items from the *cin* stream.

Suppose, for example, that you have defined three integer variable objects called *Score1*, *Score2*, and *Score3*. To read three scores into the system, you would insert three *cin* statements into your program, like this:

```
cin >> Score1;
cin >> Score2;
cin >> Score3;
```

When C++ encounters the foregoing statements in your program, it halts execution until the user enters the required data. Now suppose the user enters the following via the system keyboard:

74 ↵

92 ↵

88 ↵

What do you suppose happens? You're right again—the value 74 is extracted from the *cin* stream and assigned to *Score1*, the value 92 is extracted and assigned to *Score2*, and the value 88 is extracted and assigned to *Score3*. Thus, you can think of the *cin* operation as an assignment operation. A value entered on the keyboard is extracted from the input stream using the >> operator and assigned to the variable listed in the *cin* statement. The contents of the stream buffer for these entries are shown in Figure 3-7(a).

The user might also have entered these same values on a single line, like this:

74 92 88↵

The contents of the buffer for these entries are shown in Figure 3-7(b). If the same three *cin* statements were to read these entries, the same variable assignments would occur. Look at the two streams in Figure 3-7 again. Notice that the first stream contains three CRLF characters, whereas the second stream contains two blanks and one CRLF character. If the same variable assignments are made for both streams, what does this tell you about the >> extraction operator? The only possible conclusion is that the >> extraction operator has totally ignored both the blank and CRLF whitespace characters—it is only extracting non-whitespace character data.

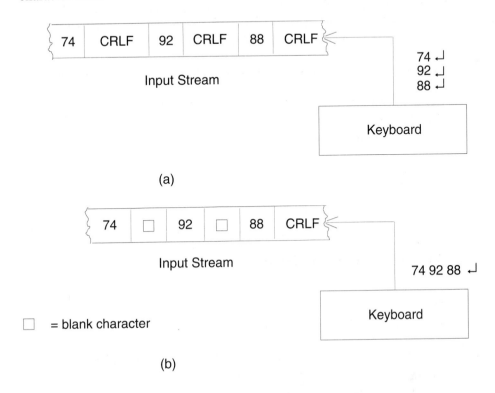

(a)

(b)

□ = blank character

Figure 3-7   The same variable assignments will occur for both of these two user entries, because the >> stream extraction operator ignores all whitespace, including CRLFs.

PROGRAMMING NOTE

You can use the *cin* stream with the >> operator to read several variables as part of a single statement. For example, the statement

cin >> Score1 >> Score2 >> Score3;

would allow you to read three user entries using a single *cin* statement. The values entered on the keyboard are assigned on a one-to-one basis to the variables listed in the *cin* statement. The assignment order is the order of the respective input data and variable listings.

Although this technique is acceptable, I suggest that, to prevent possible entry errors and confusion, you read only one variable at a time.

One other point: You should always generate a ***prompt*** to the screen using a *cout* statement prior to reading *each* variable, like this:

```
cout << "Enter an integer value for Score 1: " << endl;
cin >> Score1;
cout << "Enter an integer value for Score 2: " << endl;
cin >> Score2;
cout << "Enter an integer value for Score 3: " << endl;
cin >> Score3;
```

Prompting for and reading one variable at a time also provides for better program readability and documentation.

Reading Mixed Data Classes

The two cardinal rules that apply when reading any data are as follows:

1. All variable objects listed within the *cin* statement must be defined prior to their use in the statement.
2. The class of data entered for a given variable should match the data class defined for that variable.

By now, the first rule should be obvious. You cannot use a variable in a C++ program unless it has been previously defined in the program. The second rule needs to be explored a bit further. Consider the following program:

```
//THIS PROGRAM DEMONSTRATES THE cin OPERATION.

#include <iostream.h>   //FOR cin AND cout

void main()
{
//DEFINE INPUT VARIABLES
  int Score1 = 0;
  float Score2 = 0.0;
```

```
//PROMPT AND READ USER DATA
  cout << "Enter a number: " << endl;
  cin >> Score1;
  cout << "Enter a number: " << endl;
  cin >> Score2;
}//END main()
```

Now, suppose the user enters the following data when the *cin* statements are encountered:

Enter a number:
98.5↵
Enter a number:
78↵

What happens? Notice that the program defines *Score1* as an integer and *Score2* as a floating-point variable. However, the user has entered a decimal value for *Score1* and an integer value for *Score2*. Thus, C++ attempts to assign a decimal value (98.5) to an integer variable (*Score1*). This is called a **type mismatch** and will result in an error in many strongly typed languages, like Pascal. However, recall that C++ is not as strongly typed as some other structured languages. C++ actually assigns the integer portion of the first value to *Score1* and the decimal portion of the first value to *Score2*. Thus, *Score1* takes on the value 98 and *Score2* takes the value 0.5. The input value of 78 is not extracted from the stream and, therefore, remains in the stream buffer. This value would be read by any subsequent *cin* statement in the program. This clearly illustrates the reason you should define a variable object so that it is the same data class as the data that are expected to be entered for that variable. In addition, the prompt should clearly state the type of data the user must enter. In this case, the first prompt should have directed the user to enter an integer value, and the second prompt should have directed the user to enter a decimal value. Otherwise, you are likely to obtain invalid data. Such a bug is often very difficult to track down.

Next, using the same program, suppose the user enters the following line of data:

98↵
78↵

Now there is no problem. But, how can this be, because the compiler assigns an integer value (78) to a floating-point variable (*Score2*)? This is okay, because the integers are a subset of the real numbers. The compiler simply converts the integer value to the floating-point format. Thus, the integer value 78 is converted to the floating-point value 78.0 for storage within main working memory.

DEBUGGING TIP

When you initially code a program, it is always wise to echo an input value to the display. This assures you that the program has performed the read operation and made the correct variable assignment. To echo an input value to the display, you simply insert a *cout* statement after the *cin* statement. Within the *cout* statement, you list the same variables that are listed within the *cin* statement. For instance, to echo the test scores in the foregoing program, you would add a *cout* statement, like this:

```
//THIS PROGRAM DEMONSTRATES HOW TO ECHO
//INPUT VARIABLES DURING PROGRAM DEVELOPMENT

#include <iostream.h>   //FOR cin AND cout

void main()
{
//DEFINE INPUT VARIABLES
  int Score1 = 0;
  float Score2 = 0.0;

//PROMPT AND READ/WRITE USER DATA
  cout << "Enter an integer value: " << endl;
  cin >> Score1;
  cout << Score1 << endl;
  cout << "Enter a decimal value: " << endl;
  cin >> Score2;
  cout << Score2 << endl;
}//END main()
```

Once the program has been debugged and is completely operational, you can remove the echoing *cout* statements.

Reading Single-Character Data

Reading numeric data is straightforward, as long as you adhere to the two rules for reading data. However, there are several things that you will want to keep in mind when reading character data using *cin*.

1. Only one character is read at a time.
2. *Whitespace* (blanks, tabs, new lines, carriage returns, etc.) are ignored by *cin* when using the >> operator. However, whitespace can be read using different *cin* functions.
3. Numeric values can be read as characters, but each digit is read as a separate character.

Let's look at a simple program that illustrates most of these concepts. Consider the following:

```
//THIS PROGRAM DEMONSTRATES READING
//OF CHARACTER DATA

#include <iostream.h>   //FOR cin AND cout

void main()
{
//DEFINE INPUT VARIABLES AND INITIALIZE WITH BLANKS
  char Grade1 = ' ';
  char Grade2 = ' ';
  char Grade3 = ' ';

//READ/WRITE USER DATA
  cin >> Grade1;
  cout << Grade1 << endl;
  cin >> Grade2;
  cout << Grade2 << endl;
  cin >> Grade3;
  cout << Grade3 << endl;
}//END main()
```

The foregoing program defines three variables (*Grade1*, *Grade2*, *Grade3*) as character objects, which are initialized with blanks. The program then reads the three character variables from the system keyboard and echoes the variables to the system display. Now, let's see what the program will do for several input cases.

Case 1:

User types in: **A.**⌟
System displays: A

User types in: **B.**⌟
System displays: B

User types in: **C.**⌟
System displays: C

You see the output that you would expect. The compiler assigns a single input character to the respective character variable listed in the *cin* statement.

Case 2:

User types in: **ABC.**⌟
System displays: A
                 B
                 C

Here, the user has entered the input characters 'A', 'B', and 'C', on a single line. Thus, all three characters are placed into the input stream buffer. The compiler still assigns the character 'A' to *Score1*, the character 'B' is to *Score2*, and the character 'C' to *Score3*. Here's how it works: The user has placed three characters in the input stream. The first *cin* statement extracts only the first character ('A'), and the subsequent *cout* statement echoes the character to the display. As result, the character 'A' is extracted from the stream, but the characters 'B' and 'C' remain. The second *cin* statement extracts the second character ('B') from the stream, leaving the character 'C' in the stream. The subsequent *cout* statement echoes 'B' to the display. Finally, the third *cin* statement extracts the last character ('C') from the stream. This character is then echoed to the display. Although the input assignments have worked as expected, a prompt prior to each *cin* statement to instruct the user to enter a single character would clarify how to enter the data and prevent any possible assignment errors.

Case 3:

User types in: **A B C↵**
System displays: A
            B
            C

Notice here that there are blanks between the 'A' and 'B' and the 'B' and 'C' characters. This whitespace is ignored by the >> operator. Thus, the compiler still makes the correct assignments to the respective variables.

Case 4:

User types in: **75 92 88↵**
System displays: 7
            5
            9

In this case, the user has typed in three numeric test grades on a single line rather than letter grades. However, because the variables are defined as character objects, the system treats the digits as characters during the read operation. Each digit within a number is seen as a separate character. Thus, the character '7' is assigned to *Score1*, the character '5' is assigned to *Score2*, and the character '9' is assigned to *Score3*. The remaining data (2 88) are not extracted from the stream by the three *cin* statements, but still remain in the stream buffer. Of course, any subsequent *cin* statements would extract all or part of the remaining data. The lesson to be learned here is to always use numeric variables (integer or floating-point) to read numeric data. As you can see, data can easily be corrupted when using character variables to read numeric data.

Case 5:

User types in: **97.5 73 84↵**
System displays: 9
            7
            .

Again, the user has typed in three numeric test scores, which are treated as character data by the program. Thus, the first three characters are assigned, and the remaining information is left in the input stream buffer. As you can see from the echo, the character '9' is assigned to *Score1*, the character '7' is assigned to

Score2, and the decimal point is assigned to *Score3*. Again, generating a prompt prior to each *cin* statement clearly stating how much and what type of data to be entered would prevent many of the problems encountered here.

Using *get()* To Read Single Character Data

From the previous discussion, it is quite obvious that the >> operator ignores whitespace characters. There will be times, however, when you will need to read and store non-whitespace as well as whitespace characters. The *iostream* class includes a function called *get()* for this purpose. The *get()* function will extract any single character, including whitespace, from the input stream. It is called using the *cin* object via the following statement format:

---

get() **FORMAT**

cin.get(character variable);

To call the *get()* function, you follow *cin* with a dot, **.**, which is followed by the *get()* function using a character variable as its argument. When called, *get()* extracts a single character from the input stream and assigns it to the character variable listed as its argument.

In one of the cases we considered earlier using the >> operator, the user entered three grades separated by blanks, like this:

A B C⏎

How many total characters does this place in the stream buffer? You're right if you thought six characters. There are three non-whitespace characters and three whitespace characters. To read all these characters would require six calls to *get()*, as follows:

```
cin.get(Char1);
cin.get(Char2);
cin.get(Char3);
cin.get(Char4);
cin.get(Char5);
cin.get(Char6);
```

Of course, this assumes that the six variables, *Char1–Char6*, have been defined as character objects. What do you suppose the variable assignments would be? Well, let's use a *cout* member function called *put()* to write these character variables. The *put()* function inserts a single character into the output stream and is called by the *cout* object, like this:

---

put() FORMAT

cout.put(character variable);

To display the six characters just read by *get()*, we would call *put()* six times, as follows:

```
cout.put(Char1);
cout.put(Char2);
cout.put(Char3);
cout.put(Char4);
cout.put(Char5);
cout.put(Char6);
```

This would display the six characters just as they were entered by the user. Thus, the output would be

A B C↵

Of course, you would not see the CRLF character, but it would force the cursor to the next line of the display. This should be proof enough that *get()* reads whitespace as well as non-whitespace characters.

Example 3-7

There will be times when you want to "freeze" the display for the user until he/she takes some action, such as pressing the **ENTER** key. This can be accomplished by inserting a call to the *get()* function into your program, along with an appropriate prompt, at the point you want to freeze the output. Write the C++ code required to accomplish this task.

Solution

```
cout << "HELLO THERE! Press the ENTER key to continue" << endl;;
cin.get();
cout << "GOOD LOOKING!" << endl;
```

With this code, the message "HELLO THERE! Press the ENTER key to continue" is displayed, and program execution is halted by the *cin.get()* statement until the user presses the **ENTER** key. The *cin.get()* statement reads the CRLF produced by the **ENTER** key, and program execution continues, displaying the message "GOOD LOOKING!". Notice that there is no argument provided for *get()*. This is okay, because we do not need to store the CRLF entry.

As you can see, reading only one character at a time imposes a severe limitation on entering character data. A separate variable is required for each individual character to be read. Because most real-world character information appears in the form of strings, we need a way to read string data.

Reading String Data

You will have difficulties when trying to use the *cin* object with the >> operator to read string data. Let's see what happens when we try to do it via the following program:

```
//THIS PROGRAM SHOWS HOW cin READS STRING DATA
//USING THE >> OPERATOR

#include <iostream.h>   //FOR cin AND cout

const int SIZE = 31;                      //DECLARE ARRAY SIZE CONSTANT

void main()
{
  char Name[SIZE] = "\0";                 //DEFINE CHARACTER ARRAY
  cout << "Enter your name: " << endl;    //PROMPT FOR NAME
  cin >> Name;                            //READ STRING
  cout << Name << endl;                   //WRITE STRING
  }//END main()
```

This program defines *Name* as a character array whose size is specified by the constant *SIZE*. The constant *SIZE* has a value of 31, allowing the user to enter a name of up to 30 characters, leaving room for the '\0' null terminator character. After the definition, a prompt is generated via a *cout* statement, and *Name* is read via a *cin* statement. The user input is then echoed to the display via a *cout* statement. Here's how the program works:

User types in: **Jane Doe.**↵
System displays: Jane

What happened to Jane's last name? Well, when reading *string data*, the >>
operator *terminates* the read operation whenever any whitespace is encountered.
So, the *Name* character array includes only the string "Jane". Here is what you
would see if you were to inspect the *Name* character array in memory using your
C++ debugger.

DEBUGGER RESULTS

     Name

[0]	'J'
[1]	'a'
[2]	'n'
[3]	'e'
[4]	'\0'
[5]	'\0'
.	
.	(null terminators left from array initialization)
.	
[30]	

As you can see, array positions [0] through [3] contain the string "Jane"
formed by the individual characters 'J', 'a', 'n', and 'e'. Array position [4]
contains the null terminator character, '\0'. The >> operator inserts the null
terminator in the array and terminates the read operation when it encounters the
blank character (whitespace). Thus, the remaining input characters are not
extracted from the stream, as reflected by the remaining array positions containing
the initializing null terminators. In fact, if another *cin* statement were to follow
this one, it would read Jane's last name ("Doe"), because the user has already
typed in the full name, thereby placing "Doe" in the stream buffer.

There are several ways around this dilemma. One way is to define a separate
character array variable for each whole word to be entered. In this case, you could
create a *FirstName* character array and a *LastName* character array and use two
cin >> statements to read in the first and last names, respectively.

Using *getline()* to Read Strings

Another, more preferred, solution to the whitespace dilemma is to use a member function of the standard *iostream* class called *getline()*. The *getline()* function is used in conjunction with *cin* rather than the >> operator. This function will allow *cin* to read the entire string, including any whitespace. Recall that *cin* is an object of the *iostream* class. Because *getline()* is a member function of the *iostream* class, *cin* can call upon *getline()* to read an entire line, including any whitespace. Here's the general format:

> ### *READING STRINGS WITH* cin
>
> *cin.getline*(<string var.>, <array size>, <'delimiting character'>);

The *getline()* function uses three arguments. The first argument is the string variable identifier. This is the name of the character array defined to store the string. The second argument is the size of the array into which the string will be read. Remember, the size of the largest string that can be read into this array is actually one less than the array size to leave room for the '\0' null terminator character. The *getline()* function automatically inserts the null terminator as the last string character. Finally, the delimiting character tells the *getline()* function when to terminate the read operation. The delimiting character terminates the string entry and is *not* stored as part of the string.

The *getline()* function reads characters into the array, one at a time, until the specified delimiter is encountered. Once the delimiter is encountered, the function extracts it from the input stream and discards it so that it is not stored as part of the string. If no delimiting character is specified, its value defaults to the '\n' (CRLF) escape sequence character. Let's look at an example program:

```
//THIS PROGRAM SHOWS HOW TO USE getline() TO READ
//STRING DATA

#include <iostream.h>   //FOR cin AND cout

const int SIZE = 31;                        //DECLARE ARRAY SIZE CONSTANT

void main()
{
```

```
char Name[SIZE] = "\0";              //DEFINE CHARACTER ARRAY
cout << "Enter your name: " << endl;  //PROMPT FOR NAME
cin.getline(Name,SIZE);              //READ THE NAME STRING
cout << Name << endl;                //DISPLAY THE NAME STRING
}//END main()
```

The program works like this:

User types in: **Jane Doe**⏎
System displays: Jane Doe

If you were to use your C++ debugger to display the *Name* array, you would see this:

DEBUGGER RESULTS

Name

[0]	'J'
[1]	'a'
[2]	'n'
[3]	'e'
[4]	' '
[5]	'D'
[6]	'o'
[7]	'e'
[8]	'\0'
[9]	'\0'
[10]	'\0'

.

.   (null terminators left from array initialization)

.

[30]

You see here that the array now holds the entire string, including the blank between the first and last names. Also notice that no delimiting character is specified for the *getline()* function. As a result, the **ENTER** key (CRLF) terminates the operation. However, the CRLF ('*\n*') character is not stored as part of the string in the array. This character was extracted from the stream and discarded by the *getline()* function.

Example 3-8

Write a program that will read and write the user's name and address.

Solution

Obviously, the data to be entered will be string data. So, you must define several character arrays to accommodate the input strings. How must the input information be partitioned? Should you define one character array for the user's name and another for his/her address? But, what if our program needs to access just the user's zip code? It might make more sense to break up the address into several character arrays that could be individually accessed. So, let's define one character array to store the user's name and then define five character arrays to store the user's street, city, address, state, and zip code, respectively. Then we will insert individual *cin* and *cout* statements to read and write the required information. Here's the program:

```
//THIS PROGRAM WILL READ AND WRITE THE USER'S
//NAME, ADDRESS, AND PHONE NUMBER

#include <iostream.h>        //FOR cin AND cout

const int SIZE = 31;         //DECLARE Name AND Street SIZE

void main()
{
//DEFINE CHARACTER ARRAYS
    char Name[SIZE] = "\0";          //USER NAME
    char Street[SIZE] = "\0";        //USER STREET
    char City[21] = "\0";            //USER CITY
    char State[3] = "\0";            //USER STATE ABBREVIATION
    char Zip[11] = "\0";             //USER ZIP
    char Phone[14] = "\0";           //USER PHONE

//PROMPT USER AND READ/DISPLAY NAME AND ADDRESS STRINGS
    cout << "Enter your name: " << endl;
    cin.getline(Name,SIZE);
    cout << "Enter your street address: " << endl;
    cin.getline(Street,SIZE);
    cout << "Enter your city: " << endl;
    cin.getline(City,21);
    cout << "Enter your state: " << endl;
    cin.getline(State,3);
    cout << "Enter your zip code: " << endl;
    cin.getline(Zip,11);
    cout << "Enter your phone number: " << endl;
    cin.getline(Phone,14);
```

```
//DISPLAY NAME AND ADDRESS STRINGS
  cout << Name << endl;
  cout << Street << endl;
  cout << City << endl;
  cout << State << endl;
  cout << Zip << endl;
  cout << Phone << endl;
} //END main()
```

First, notice that each of the required strings has been defined as a character array. I have defined each array length to be *one* character longer than need be. This is to leave room for the '\0' null terminator character. For instance, the *State* array is 3 bytes long to provide for a two-character state abbreviation along with the null terminator character. Once the character arrays are properly defined, the program reads each string with a separate *cin* statement and then writes each string with a separate *cout* statement.

Here is what will happen when the program is executed:

User types in:

Jane M. Doe.⏎
999 Programmer's Lane.⏎
C++ City.⏎
WY.⏎
12345.⏎
(000)123-4567.⏎

System displays:

Jane M. Doe
999 Programmer's Lane
C++ City
WY
12345
(000)123-4567

A Problem When Using getline()

Although *getline( )* will work when reading consecutive string data, you will have trouble trying to use it to read a string variable after you have used *cin* to read a character variable or a numeric variable. For instance, suppose that you read the string variable *Name* after you read the integer variable *Number*, like this:

```
//THIS PROGRAM DEMONSTRATES THE PROBLEM OF
//USING cin.getline() TO READ A STRING AFTER YOU
//HAVE READ A NUMERIC VARIABLE

#include <iostream.h>   //FOR cin AND cout

const int SIZE = 31;                        //DECLARE ARRAY SIZE CONSTANT

void main()
{
//DEFINE INPUT VARIABLES
  int Number = 0;                           //INTEGER VARIABLE
  char Name[SIZE] = "\0";                   //STRING VARIABLE

//PROMPT USER AND READ/DISPLAY INPUT DATA
  cout << "Enter an integer:  ";            //PROMPT USER FOR INTEGER
  cin >> Number;                            //READ INTEGER
  cout << Number << endl;                   //DISPLAY INTEGER

  cout << "Enter a name:  ";                //PROMPT USER FOR STRING
  cin.getline(Name,SIZE);                   //READ STRING
  cout << Name << endl;                     //DISPLAY STRING
}//END main()
```

When this program is executed, it seems as if C++ skips over the *cin.getline()* statement. How could this be? Well, if you use your debugger to look at *Number* and *Name*, here is what you see after the program is executed. Assume you entered the integer 123 for *Number*.

DEBUGGER RESULTS

	Number	
int		123

	Name	
[0]		'\0'
[1]		'\0'

Notice that the string variable *Name* contains the null terminator at position [0] of the array because when you enter the number 123, you must press the **ENTER** key. This places a CRLF character in the input stream buffer. However, the *cin >> Number* statement does not extract the CRLF character (because it is whitespace), and it remains in the buffer. When the *cin.getline(Name,SIZE)* statement is executed, it reads the buffer and sees the CRLF character. By default, this is the delimiting character, so it stops reading and inserts the null terminator character in the array. Thus, the user never gets an opportunity to enter a name.

There are basically three ways around this problem. One way is to specify a different delimiting character in the *getline()* function. However, the user must enter this character to terminate the operation.

A second way is to clear the buffer by reading the CRLF character into a *trash* variable after reading any numeric or character data and prior to reading any string data. To do this, you must define a *trash variable* as a two-character array, like this: char Trash[2];

After using *cin* to read any numeric or single-character data, we will use the statement *cin.getline(Trash,2)* to read the remaining CRLF character in the keyboard buffer, thus clearing the buffer. Here's how the preceding program would be modified to employ this trash operation:

```
//THIS PROGRAM SHOWS HOW TO USE A TRASH
//VARIABLE TO CLEAR THE KEYBOARD BUFFER
//AFTER YOU HAVE READ A NUMERIC VARIABLE

#include <iostream.h>   //FOR cin AND cout

const int SIZE = 31;                    //DECLARE ARRAY SIZE CONSTANT

void main()
{
//DEFINE INPUT VARIABLES
 int Number = 0;                        //INTEGER VARIABLE
 char Trash[2] = "\0";                  //TRASH VARIABLE
 char Name[SIZE] = "\0";                //STRING VARIABLE

//PROMPT USER AND READ/DISPLAY INPUT DATA
 cout << "Enter an integer:  ";         //PROMPT USER FOR INTEGER
 cin >> Number;                         //READ INTEGER
 cout << Number << endl;                //DISPLAY INTEGER

 cin.getline(Trash,2);                  //CLEAR KEYBOARD BUFFER
 cout << "Enter a name:  ";             //PROMPT USER FOR STRING
 cin.getline(Name,SIZE);                //READ STRING
 cout << Name << endl;                  //DISPLAY STRING
}//END main()
```

A third method is to employ the *ws* (whitespace) I/O manipulator to read any whitespace prior to using *getline()*. The *ws* manipulator extracts any leading whitespace from the input stream. To use it, simply place a *cin >> ws* statement prior to the *cin.getline()* statement in your program, like this:

```
//THIS PROGRAM DEMONSTRATES THE USE OF ws
//TO CLEAR THE KEYBOARD BUFFER OF WHITESPACE
//PRIOR TO USING getline() TO READ STRING DATA

#include <iostream.h>   //FOR cin AND cout

const int SIZE = 31;                //DECLARE ARRAY SIZE CONSTANT

void main()
{
//DEFINE INPUT VARIABLES
 int Number = 0;                    //INTEGER VARIABLE
 char Name[SIZE] = "\0";            //STRING VARIABLE

//PROMPT USER AND READ/DISPLAY INPUT DATA
   cout << "Enter an integer:  ";   //PROMPT USER FOR INTEGER
   cin >> Number;                   //READ INTEGER
   cout << Number << endl;          //DISPLAY INTEGER
   cout << "Enter a name:  ";       //PROMPT USER FOR STRING
   cin >> ws;                       //EXTRACT WHITESPACE
   cin.getline(Name,SIZE);          //READ STRING
   cout << Name << endl;            //DISPLAY STRING
}//END main()
```

The statement *cin >> ws* extracts any leading CRLF whitespace from the input stream buffer so that the *getline()* function does not terminate its execution prior to reading the string. The *ws* manipulator is included as part of the *iostream.h* header file.

Using *gets()* and *fgets()* to Read Strings

There is a collection of string I/O functions defined in both C and C++ for reading and writing string data. Two of these functions are listed in Table 3-4. These functions are provided in the *stdio.h* header file. In fact, there are many other I/O functions in this header file, but we will need to employ only the string I/O functions in this text. The *gets()* or *fgets()* functions will solve the problem we have with *getline()*.

TABLE 3-4 STRING I/O FUNCTIONS IN C AND C++

Function	Description
gets()	Reads the input string.
	CRLF converted to a null terminator.
fgets()	Reads the input string.
	CRLF is read and a null terminator is added.

To use *gets()* or *fgets()*, you must include the *stdio.h* header file and pass one or more arguments to the respective function. Here's the format for both functions:

---

gets() FORMAT

gets(<string variable>);

fgets() FORMAT

fgets(<string variable>,<array size>, stdin)

The *gets()* function requires only that the string variable identifier be passed to the function. The *fgets()* function requires the string identifier, the character array size, and the word "stdin".

From Table 3-4, you see that *gets()* will convert the CRLF character (produced by the **ENTER** key) to a null terminator. Thus, no CRLF is stored in the string with *gets()*. However, *fgets()* reads the CRLF character, stores it in the character array, and adds the null terminator. As a result, the CRLF and null terminator characters will always occupy the last 2 bytes of the string.

As an example, suppose you use *gets()* and *fgets()* in a program, like this:

```
//THIS PROGRAM DEMONSTRATES THE USE OF gets() AND fgets()
#include <iostream.h>        //FOR cout
#include <stdio.h>           //FOR gets() AND fgets()

const int SIZE = 31;              //DECLARE ARRAY SIZE CONSTANT

void main()
{
```

```
//DEFINE STRING ARRAYS
  char Name[SIZE] = "\0";              //USER NAME
  char Address[SIZE] = "\0";           //USER ADDRESS

//PROMPT FOR AND READ USER DATA
  cout << "Enter your name:  ";        //PROMPT FOR USER NAME
  gets(Name);                          //READ NAME
  cout << "Enter your address:  ";     //PROMPT FOR USER ADDRESS
  fgets(Address,SIZE,stdin);           //READ ADDRESS
}//END main()
```

Suppose that you make the following entries when executing the program:

Enter your name: **Jane Doe**⏎
Enter your address: **C++ City**⏎

If you use your debugger to inspect *Name* and *Address*, you will see the following:

DEBUGGER RESULTS

Name

[0]	'J'
[1]	'a'
[2]	'n'
[3]	'e'
[4]	' '
[5]	'D'
[6]	'o'
[7]	'e'
[8]	'\0'

Address

[0]	'C'
[1]	'+'
[2]	'+'
[3]	' '
[4]	'C'
[5]	'i'
[6]	't'

[7]	'y'
[8]	'\n'
[9]	'\0'

You see that *Name* does not include the CRLF character, whereas *Address* does. You can always use *cout* to write string data. The *cout* object will write all the characters stored in the string until it encounters the null terminator. Thus, no CRLF is generated if a string is read using *gets()* and subsequently written using *cout*. However, the same string read using *fgets()* will generate a CRLF when subsequently written with *cout*.

Quick Check

1. The operator that must be employed to extract data from the *cin* input stream is the _____ operator.

2. Write statements to prompt the user to enter a value for an integer variable called *Number.* Use *cin* to read the user entry.

3. Provide some examples of whitespace.

4. Write a statement to read a single whitespace character and store it in a variable called *Whitespace.*

5. Write a statement to display the single whitespace character read in question 4.

6. True or false: When reading single-character data, *cin* >>will read only one character at a time.

7. When does the *cin* statement terminate when using the >> operator to read string data?

8. What function can be employed with *cin* to read string data, including whitespace?

9. When should you use *gets()* or *fgets()* in lieu of *cin* to read string data?

10. Employ the *gets()* function to read a string of up to 25 characters and store it in a variable called *Name.*

11. How is the CRLF character treated with *gets()*?

12. How is the CRLF character treated with *fgets()*?

3-3 READING AND WRITING DISK FILES

To complete our discussion of I/O, we must discuss the basics of reading and writing disk files. At this time, it is only important that you understand how to read information into your program from a disk file and write program data to a disk file. You will learn more about manipulating disk files later, in Chapter 13.

File Streams

In C++, all I/O is based on the concept of file streams.

> A *file stream* provides a channel for data to flow between your program and the outside world.

In particular, a file stream provides a channel for the flow of data from some source to some destination. Think about what happens when you are typing characters on the keyboard when prompted by a program. You think of the characters as flowing, or streaming, from the keyboard into the program through the input stream buffer. Likewise, when your program generates a character display, you visualize the characters streaming from the program to the display via the output stream buffer.

Classes: the Basis for C++ Files

The familiar *cin* and *cout* stream objects that you have been using in your programs for keyboard input and display output are objects of the *iostream* file class. As you are aware, the *cin* and *cout* objects invoke predefined file streams. Thus, we say that *standard input* is read from the *cin stream* and *standard output* is written to the *cout stream*. When you include the *iostream.h* header file in your program, the *cin* and *cout* file streams are defined automatically. Of course, the only files that you can access conveniently with *cin* and *cout* are the keyboard and display files that are attached to these file streams.

When you create your own file stream for reading/writing disk files, the first thing you must do is define an object for one of the file classes. File stream objects that are used exclusively for input are defined as objects of the *ifstream* class. Thus, the statement

ifstream Input;

defines *Input* as an input file stream object. You use the *ofstream* class to define file stream objects that are used exclusively for output. Thus, the statement

ofstream Output;

defines *Output* as an output file stream object. Finally, you must use the *fstream* class when defining objects that will be used for both file input and output. The statement

fstream InputOutput;

defines *InputOutput* as both an input and output file stream object.

Next, you must attach, or connect, the file stream object to a physical disk file. When a file stream object is attached to a physical disk file, the disk file is opened for access. This requires the use of the *open()* function, which is *inherited* by all the file stream classes. Here is the format required to call this function:

FORMAT TO OPEN A DISK FILE

<file stream object>.**open** (<disk file name>, <file open mode>);

The first thing that must be specified is the file stream object. The object name is followed by a dot, which is followed by the *open()* function and its required arguments. This statement simply calls the *open()* function defined in the respective file stream class.

The *open()* function has two arguments: a disk file name and an open-mode designator. The disk file name must adhere to the requirements of the operating system. For DOS systems, the file name cannot exceed eight characters. A three-character extension, separated from the file name by a dot, is optional. Thus, DOS file names such as *sample*, *sample.dat*, and *sample12.dat* are all legal file names. The physical disk file name can be specified directly within double quotes (i.e., "*sample.dat*") or indirectly as a string variable.

The open-mode designator argument defines what type of file access is to be performed. Although there are more, we are concerned only with the *ios::in* and *ios::out* designators at this time.

Suppose that we want to open a file stream called *InputOutput*. The file stream is defined for the *fstream* class and is to be attached to a disk file called *test.dat*. In addition, the program will both read and write the file. The appropriate open statement would be

InputOutput.open("test.dat", ios :: in ¦ ios :: out);

As you can see, the file stream object calls the *open()* function using the dot operator. The physical disk file to be opened is placed within double quotes as the first argument in the function call. The first argument could also be a string (character array) variable that holds the disk file name. The second argument provides the file-mode designators. Here, two designators are ORed together using the double vertical bar, |, operator to tell the compiler that the file can be both read from (*ios :: in*) or written to (*ios :: out*).

The read/write mode(s) must always be specified when a file stream object is defined for the *fstream* class, because, by definition, this class is used for both input and output (reading/writing) file access. Read/write modes do not need to be specified when opening files defined for the *ifstream* or *ofstream* classes, because such files are input and output files, respectively, by default. For instance, if *Output* is defined as a file stream object of the *ofstream* class, the open statement simply would be

Output.open("test.dat");

On the other hand, if *Input* is defined as a file stream object of the *ifstream* class, the open statement would be

Input.open("test.dat");

Example 3-9

Write statements to create the following disk files:

a. A file stream called *Read* that will read from a disk file called *sample.doc*.
b. A file stream called *Write* that will write to a disk file called *sample.doc*.
c. A file stream called *ReadWrite* that will read and write a disk file called *sample.doc*.

Solution

a. ifstream Read;
   Read.open("sample.doc");
b. ofstream Write;
   Write.open("sample.doc");
c. fstream ReadWrite;
   ReadWrite.open("sample.doc", ios :: in ¦ ios :: out);

Again, notice that the *ios :: in* and *ios :: out* file modes are ORed together to create a read/write file when the *fstream* class is specified.

Once a file is opened, it is ready for processing. After the file processing is complete, you must always close the file. This is accomplished with the *close()*

function. To close a file, all you need to do is call the *close()* function with your file stream object using the dot operator. As a result, the statements *InputOutput.close()*, *Output.close()* and *Input.close()* would close the files that we opened in the foregoing discussion.

Reading and Writing a Disk File

You read from a disk file using your input file stream object and the >> extraction operator, just as you do using the standard *cin* file stream object and the >> operator. For example, suppose that we have opened an input file, like this:

```
ifstream Input;
Input.open("test.dat");
```

Here, the file stream object that we have created is called *Input*. To obtain a string of data from this file, all we need to do is apply the >> operator to our *Input* object, like this:

```
Input >> String;
```

Of course, this statement assumes that *String* has be defined as a character array.

You write to a disk file using your output file stream object and the << insertion operator, just as you do using the standard *cout* file stream object and the << operator. Thus, if we open an output file object, like this:

```
ofstream Output;
Output.open("test.dat");
```

we could write a string of data to this file using the statement

```
Output << String << endl;
```

Again, this assumes that the variable *String* has been defined as a string variable, or character array.

Example 3-10

Code a program to copy three strings of data from a disk file called *input.dat* to a file called *output.dat*.

Solution

A file copy operation requires that we read one file and echo that input information to a second file. We will read the *input.dat* file and write to the *output.dat* file. First, we need to open two file objects. Let's call them *Input* and *Output*. Then, we will read using the *Input* file object and write using the *Output* file object. Finally, we must close both files. Here's the required code:

```
//THIS PROGRAM COPIES THREE STRINGS FROM ONE FILE TO ANOTHER
#include <fstream.h>    //FOR FILE I/O

const int SIZE = 25;    //STRING SIZE

void main()
{
//DEFINE STRING VARIABLE
  char String[SIZE] = "\0";

//DEFINE FILE OBJECTS AND OPEN FILES
    ifstream Input;              //DEFINE INPUT OBJECT
    ofstream Output;             //DEFINE OUTPUT OBJECT

    Input.open("input.dat");     //OPEN INPUT FILE
    Output.open("output.dat");   //OPEN OUTPUT FILE

//COPY FILE DATA FROM INPUT FILE TO OUTPUT FILE
    Input >> String;             //READ FIRST STRING
    Output << String << endl;    //WRITE FIRST STRING
    Input >> String;             //READ SECOND STRING
    Output << String << endl;    //WRITE SECOND STRING
    Input >> String;             //READ THIRD STRING
    Output << String << endl;    //WRITE THIRD STRING
    Input.close();               //CLOSE INPUT FILE
    Output.close();              //CLOSE OUTPUT FILE
} //END main()
```

The first thing you should notice in this program is that the *fstream.h* header file is included using the *#include* preprocessor directive. This header file must be included in order to use the *ifstream* and *ofstream* classes, required for file I/O. Next, two file objects are defined for their respective classes and the files are opened using the *open()* function. The *Input >> String* statement reads a string of data from the *input.dat* disk file and places it in the character array called *String*. Remember that the >> operator terminates when whitespace is encountered. As a result, no blanks will be read as part of a given string. How can you read whitespace as part of a string? By using the *getline()* function in lieu of the >> operator with your input file object. The statement would be *Input.getline(String,SIZE)*. The same rules apply when reading strings from a disk file using your own object as when reading strings from the keyboard using the *cin* object.

Once a string is read, the *Output << String << endl* statement copies the string to the *output.dat* disk file. Notice that each output statement includes an *endl* manipulator to place a CRLF at the end of each line in the output file.

Finally, both files are closed by calling the *close()* function with each file object.

Example 3-11

Code a program that will read two integers from a file called *integers* and write their sum to a file called *sum*.

Solution

The major difference here is that we will be reading integer data rather than string data. Here's the solution:

```
//THIS PROGRAM READS TWO INTEGERS FROM ONE FILE AND WRITES
//THEIR SUM TO ANOTHER FILE

#include <fstream.h>          //FOR FILE I/O

void main()
{
//DEFINE STRING VARIABLE
int Integer1 = 0;            //FIRST INTEGER VARIABLE
int Integer2 = 0;            //SECOND INTEGER VARIABLE
int Sum = 0;                 //SUM VARIABLE

//DEFINE FILE OBJECTS AND OPEN FILES
    ifstream Input;          //DEFINE INPUT OBJECT
    ofstream Output;         //DEFINE OUTPUT OBJECT

    Input.open("integers");  //OPEN INPUT FILE
    Output.open("sum");      //OPEN OUTPUT FILE

    Input >> Integer1;       //READ FIRST INTEGER
    Input >> Integer2;       //READ SECOND INTEGER
    Sum = Integer1 + Integer2; //CALCULATE SUM

    Output << Sum;           //WRITE SUM
    Input.close();           //CLOSE INPUT FILE
    Output.close();          //CLOSE OUTPUT FILE
} //END main()
```

Here, we have defined three integer variables: two variables to hold the two integer values to be read and a third variable to calculate their sum. The file objects are first defined, and the two disk files are opened. The two integers are read from the *integers* file by the *Input* object using the >> operator. The sum is calculated and then written to the *sum* file by the *Output* object and the << operator. Finally, the two files are closed. That's all there is to it! Remember, once you create your own file objects for input or output and open the disk files, you simply apply all that you have learned about the standard *cin* and *cout* objects to your own input and output file objects, respectively.

Using Loops to Read and Process Files

Although you have not studied loops yet, it is often advantageous to use a loop to read an input file so that you do not have to have to repeat the input statement for each data item in the file. At this point, I will provide you with the code to use until Chapter 6, where you will study loops in detail.

Here's the general format for such a loop:

```
<read first input file data item>
while (!Input.eof())
{ //BEGIN LOOP

    <process data item>
    <read input file data item>

} //END LOOP
```

A statement must precede the *while* loop to read the first data item in the input file. Then the loop is coded to read the remaining data in the file. The loop says "while not (!) end-of-file marker (*eof()*), process the current data item and read another data item." So, when the loop is executed, it will repeatedly process and read the file data items, one at a time, until an end-of-file marker is detected. All disk files contain an **end-of-file marker**, called EOF, to mark the end of a given file on the disk. When reading a disk file, we instruct the compiler to look for the EOF marker and terminate the reading operations when it is detected. This is accomplished by using the foregoing *while* loop and testing for the EOF marker using the standard *eof()* function.

Notice that our file processing and read statements are placed within the body of the loop, which is *framed* using curly baces, { }.

Example 3-12

Rewrite the program given in Example 3-10 to employ a loop to copy the *input.dat* file to the *output.dat* file.

Solution

Here's the revised code using a loop:

```
//THIS PROGRAM COPIES ONE FILE TO ANOTHER

#include <fstream.h>   //FOR FILE I/O

const int SIZE = 25;    //STRING SIZE

void main()
{
//DEFINE STRING VARIABLE
char String[SIZE] = "\0";

//DEFINE FILE OBJECTS AND OPEN FILES
   ifstream Input;                      //DEFINE INPUT OBJECT
   ofstream Output;                     //DEFINE OUTPUT OBJECT
   Input.open("input.dat");             //OPEN INPUT FILE
   Output.open("output.dat");   //OPEN OUTPUT FILE

//READ FIRST STRING
   Input >> String;

//COPY FILE DATA FROM INPUT FILE TO OUTPUT FILE USING A LOOP
while (!Input.eof())
{ //BEGIN LOOP
     Output << String << endl; //WRITE A STRING TO OUTPUT FILE
     Input >> String;               //READ A STRING FROM INPUT FILE
} //END LOOP

//CLOSE THE FILES
   Input.close();               //CLOSE INPUT FILE
   Output.close();              //CLOSE OUTPUT FILE
} //END main()
```

Notice that the file read operation is placed within the loop as well as the file write operation. This is because we are simply reading a data item from the input file and echoing it to the output file as our processing operation. The loop will repeatedly read a string from the input file, then write the string to the output file until an end-of-file marker is detected within the input file.

Another advantage to using such a loop to read a file is that you often do not know how many data items a file contains. By using a loop and testing for the EOF marker, you do not need to know how many data items are in the file, because the loop will continue to read the file until the end of the file is reached.

Quick Check

1. Which header file must be included to read/write disk files?

2. The class used to define input file objects is the _____ class.

3. The class used to define output file objects is the _____ class.

4. What three tasks must always be executed to read or write any disk file?

5. Define an object called *MyInput* as an input file object and an object called *MyOutput* as an output file object.

6. Write statements to open a disk file called *data* for processing by your input file object from question 5 and a disk file called *results* for processing by your output file object from question 5.

7. Assume that the file called *data* in question 6 contains an unknown number of integers. Write the code required to read each integer in the file, multiply it by 10, and write the product to the *results* file in question 6.

8. Combine all your answers to the preceding questions into a single C++ program that will accomplish the file processing tasks indicated.

PROBLEM SOLVING IN ACTION: USER-FRIENDLY PROGRAMS

Problem

As an overall program summary to the material presented in this chapter, let's write a user-friendly program that will calculate voltage from different values of current and resistance entered by the user. We will format a three-column table for current, resistance, and voltage and underscore each column heading. The final program output will be a table showing the current, resistance, and voltage values. In addition, we will display the program user's name and the date the program was run.

Let's first define the problem in terms of output, input, and processing as follows:

Defining the Problem

Output: The final program output must be a table showing the calculated voltage value along with the current and resistance values used in the calculation. The user's name and date the program was run will be displayed above the table. In addition, user prompts should be provided on the monitor to direct the user to enter the required values.

Input: The input must be the user's name, date the program was run, a value for current, and a value for resistance.

Processing: Ohm's Law: *Voltage = Current × Resistance.*

PROGRAMMING TIP

You must always strive to make your programs as user-friendly as possible. By a user-friendly program, I mean a program that is easy to use and does not confuse the user. Such a program should always include the following (at a minimum):

1. A program description message that tells the user what the program is going to do.
2. Prompting messages prior to any read operations. These user prompts must tell the user what information to enter and how to enter it in clear, unconfusing terms.
3. Output information that is well-formatted and whose meaning is easily understood by the user.

Planning the Solution

The next step is to construct a set of algorithms from the problem definition. Using structured program design, we will divide the problem into individual subproblems to solve the overall problem. Now, try to identify the separate tasks that must be performed to solve the problem. First, the program must get the required data from the user. Once the data are entered, the program must multiply the current and resistance to get the voltage. Finally, the program must display the results. Thus, we can identify three program tasks, or functions, as follows:

- Get the user's name, date of program run, current value, and resistance value from the user.
- Multiply current and resistance to get voltage.
- Display the user's name, date the program was run, and table of results.

The structure diagram in Figure 3-8 shows the block structure required for the program.

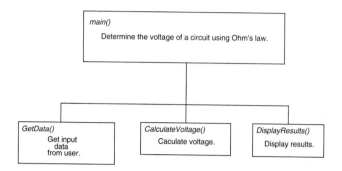

Figure 3-8   A structure diagram for the Ohm's law problem.

Because we are using the block-structured technique to design the program, we must employ stepwise refinement to develop the algorithms. The initial algorithm level, *main()*, will simply reflect the problem definition and call the individual subprogram functions, as follows:

Initial Algorithm

main()
BEGIN
    Call function to get the input data from the user.
    Call function to calculate the circuit voltage using Ohm's law.
    Call function to display the results.
END.

The first level of refinement requires that we show a detailed algorithm for each subprogram module, or function. They are as follows:

First Level of Refinement

GetData()
BEGIN
    Write a user prompt to enter the user's name.
    Read(*Name*).
    Write a user prompt to enter the date.
    Read(*Date*).

Write a user prompt to enter the current value.
Read(*Current*).
Write a user prompt to enter the resistance value.
Read (*Resistance*).
END.

CalculateVoltage( )
BEGIN
Calculate the voltage: *Voltage = Current × Resistance.*
END.

DisplayResults( )
BEGIN
Display user's name and date of program run.
Display table headings for current, resistance, and voltage.
Display the current, resistance, and voltage values under the respective headings.
END.

Coding the Program

Here is how the foregoing algorithms are translated into C++ code using a flat implementation:

```
//ACTION 3-1 (ACT03-01.CPP)

//OUTPUT:
//THE PROGRAM OUTPUT MUST BE A TABLE
//SHOWING THE CALCULATED VOLTAGE VALUE ALONG
//WITH THE CURRENT  AND RESISTANCE VALUES USED
//IN THE CALCULATION. THE USER'S NAME AND DATE OF
//PROGRAM RUN WILL APPEAR AT THE TOP OF THE DISPLAY

//INPUT:
//THE INPUT MUST BE THE USER'S NAME AND DATE,
//A VALUE FOR CURRENT AND A VALUE FOR RESISTANCE.

//PROCESSING:
//OHM'S LAW:  VOLTAGE = CURRENT * RESISTANCE
```

```
#include <iostream.h>   //FOR cin AND cout
#include <iomanip.h>    //FOR setw()

//DECLARE CONSTANTS
const int NAME_SIZE = 31;    //SIZE OF USER NAME ARRAY
const int DATE_SIZE = 9;     //SIZE OF DATE ARRAY

void main()
{
//DEFINE VARIABLES
  char Name[NAME_SIZE] = "\0";    //USER'S NAME
  char Date[DATE_SIZE] = "\0";    //DATE OF PROGRAM RUN
  float Voltage = 0.0;            //VOLTAGE IN VOLTS
  float Current = 0.0;            //CURRENT IN AMPERES
  float Resistance = 0.0;         //RESISTANCE IN OHMS

//DISPLAY PROGRAM DESCRIPTION MESSAGE
  cout << "This program will calculate voltage from current"
          "and resistance values that you enter." << endl << endl;

//GET INPUT DATA FROM USER
  cout << "Please enter your name:" << endl;
  cin.getline(Name,NAME_SIZE);
  cout << "Enter the date in XX/XX/XX format:" << endl;
  cin.getline(Date,DATE_SIZE);
  cout << "Enter a current value in amperes:" << endl;
  cin >> Current;
  cout << "Enter a resistance value in ohms:" << endl;
  cin >> Resistance;

//CALCULATE VOLTAGE USING OHM'S LAW
  Voltage = Current * Resistance;

//DISPLAY NAME, DATE, AND OUTPUT TABLE
  cout.setf(ios::fixed);
  cout.precision(3);
  cout << "\n\n" << Name << endl;
  cout << Date;
  cout    <<"\n\n\n\n"
          << setw(20) << "RESISTANCE"
          << setw(20) << "CURRENT"
          << setw(20) << "VOLTAGE\n"
          << setw(20) << "----------"
```

```
                 << setw(20) << "-------"
                 << setw(20) << "-------"
                 << endl;
      cout    << setw(20) << Resistance
                 << setw(20) << Current
                 << setw(20) << Voltage
                 << endl;
} //END main()
```

You now should have no trouble understanding this program with the material presented in this chapter.

Now, make a serious effort to complete all of the questions and problems that follow. It is time to get your hands dirty and program your system to apply the program exercises that follow. This is where you will really begin learning how to program in C++.

CHAPTER SUMMARY

Getting information into your system is called *reading*, and getting information out of your system is called *writing*. The C++ statement used for reading is the *cin* statement, and the statement used for writing is the *cout* statement.

Each *cout* statement must include a listing of the items to be written. The items in the listing must be separated by the << stream insertion operator. The *cout* statement can be used to write either fixed or variable information. Fixed numeric information is written by simply listing the numeric values within the *cout* item listing. When writing fixed character information, the information to be written must be enclosed within single quotes for single characters and double quotes for strings. When writing variable information, the variable object identifier must be listed within the *cout* statement. Information can be written to the system monitor or printer. You use the built-in *cout* output stream object for writing to the monitor, but you must define your own *print* stream object for writing to the printer. To format an output, you must often include an I/O manipulator in the item listing. As an example, the *setw()* field-width manipulator must be included prior to the item to be written to adjust the item field width. The field-width manipulator value specifies the number of columns of output that will be allocated to the item being written. You must include the *iomanip.h* file when using the *setw()* I/O manipulator. In addition, always use a layout chart to lay out your output and determine the correct field-width values.

For reading data in C++ you employ the *cin* input stream object. Like *cout*, *cin* is a predefined file stream object in C++. The *cin* statement must include a variable(s) to be read. Any variable listed within the *cin* statement must be defined prior to its use in the program. Moreover, the class of data entered for a given variable should match the data class defined for that variable. The >> stream extraction operator is used within the *cin* statement to extract data from the input stream and assign these data to the variable(s) listed in the *cin* statement. When reading single-character data, the >> operator ignores whitespace. However, you can use the *get()* function with *cin* to read single-character whitespace data.

When reading string data, the >> operator will terminate on whitespace. As a result, you should use the *getline()* function along with *cin* when reading character arrays, or strings. When using *getline()*, you must discard the '\n' character remaining in the keyboard buffer from a prior read operation. To accomplish this, you can use a different delimiting character for *getline()*, a trash variable, or the *ws* manipulator. The *gets()* and *fgets()* functions contained in the *stdio.h* header file are also used for reading strings. The *gets()* function converts CRLF to a null terminator when the string is stored, and *fgets()* reads and stores CRLF while adding the null terminator at the end of the string.

All program I/O is supported by files that operate on predefined classes in C++. For accessing disk files, you must use one of three classes: *ifstream*, *ofstream*, or *fstream*. The *ifstream* class is used to perform input, or read, operations from disk files, the *ofstream* class is used to perform output, or write, operations to disk files, and the *fstream* class can be used to perform both read and write operations on disk files. All three of these classes are declared in the *fstream.h* header file.

There are three tasks that always must be executed to manipulate disk files in C++:

1. Define a file stream object for one of the *fstream.h* file classes.
2. Attach the file stream object to a particular disk file to open the file.
3. Close the file.

All disk files contain an *end-of-file marker*, called EOF, to mark the end of a given file on the disk. When reading a disk file, we instruct the compiler to look for the EOF marker and terminate the reading operations when it is detected. This is accomplished by using a loop and testing for the EOF marker using a standard function called *eof()*.

User-friendly programs require interaction between the program and the user. At a minimum, a user-friendly program must do the following:

- Write a program description message to the user.
- Prompt the user prior to any read operations.
- Generate well-formatted outputs whose meanings are easily understood by the user.

QUESTIONS AND PROBLEMS

Questions

1. Indicate the output for each of the following:
   a. cout << "\n\n" << endl;
   b. cout << setw(40) << "HELLO" << endl;
   c. cout << setw(12) << –36.2 << endl;
   d. cout << 3.75 << endl;
   e. cout << '\n' << 1 << '\t' << 2 << '\t' << 3 << '\t' << 4 << endl;
   f. cout << setw(20) << "My test score is: 97.6/n/n " << endl;
   g. cout <<"\n\t\tTEST SCORE\t\t97.5" << endl;
   h. cout <<"\n\t\tTEST SCORE\n\t\t97.5" << endl;
   i. print <<"\t\tTEST SCORE\n\t\t97.5\f";

2. Suppose that you define a constant as follows:
   const char SPACE = ' ';
   What will the following statement do?
   cout << '\n' << setw(20) << SPACE << "HELLO" << endl;

3. What will the following statement do?
   cout << '\n' << setw(20) << ' ' << "HELLO" << endl;

4. What is the difference between the output produced by the following two statements?
   cout << "\n#\n#\n#" << endl;
   cout << "\n###" << endl;

5. Consider the following program segment:
   char A = ' ';
   char B = ' ';
   cin >> A;
   cin >> B;
   cout << A << B << endl;
   What will be displayed for each of the following user entries?
   a. A
      B
   b. AB
   c. 3.14
   d. A B (*Note:* There is a space between the 'A' and the 'B'.)

6. What header file must be included in order to use the *setw()* field-width specifier?

7. What function must be used with *cin* to obtain string data?

8. Define an appropriate variable object and write statements to read and then display your school name.

9. Suppose that you must generate two separate pages of output on a printer. How do you make the printer advance to the second page once the first page is printed?

10. True or false: The *getline()* function stores the delimiting character as part of the string array.

11. The default delimiting character for the *getline()* function is the _____ character.

12. What arguments must be provided when using *getline()* to read string data?

13. What is the relationship between *iostream, cin*, and *getline()*?

14. Why should you define a string 1 byte longer than the maximum string length if you are using *cin.getline()* to read the string?

15. Explain the difference between an escape sequence and an I/O manipulator.

16. When should *gets()* or *fgets()* be used in lieu of *cin.getline*?

17. What header file must be included to use *gets()* or *fgets()*?

18. Explain how the operation of *gets()* differs from that of *fgets()*.

19. Why is *getline()* unsafe for reading string data after it is used to read numeric or single character data?

20. Describe three methods for solving the *getline()* problem referred to in question 19.

21. Write the code necessary to obtain a decimal output with three decimal places to the right of the decimal point.

22. What is a file stream?

23. Write statements to create the following disk file streams:

    a. A file stream called *FileIn* that will read a disk file called *mydata.txt*.

    b. A file stream called *FileOut* that will write to a file whose name is stored in a character array called *Name*.

24. Why is it advantageous to use loops when reading and processing a disk file?

25. What should you do in order to make a program more user-friendly?

Problems

Least Difficult

1. Using the layout chart in Figure 3-3, write a program to display your first name in the middle of the monitor screen.

2. Using the layout chart in Figure 3-3, write a program to display your first name in the upper left-hand corner of the display using characters that are six lines high.

3. Write a program that will generate a rectangle whose center is located in the middle of the display. Construct the rectangle 8 lines high and 20 columns wide using X's.

4. Write a program that will generate the following output in the middle of the display:

STUDENT	SEMESTER AVERAGE
--------------	-----------------------------------
1	84.5
2	67.2
3	77.4
4	86.8
5	94.7

More Difficult

In the problems that follow, you will need to employ several arithmetic operations. In C++, a plus symbol (+) is used for addition, a minus symbol (−) is used for subtraction, a star symbol (∗) is used for multiplication, and a slash symbol (/) is used for division.

5. Write a program to calculate simple interest on a $2000 loan for 2 years at a rate of 12.5 percent. Format your output appropriately, showing the amount of the loan, time period, interest rate, and interest amount. (*Note*: Set the *ios::showpoint* flag to assure proper dollars and cents format for currency output.)

6. Write a program that will prompt the user to enter any four-letter word. Then display the word backwards. (Keep it clean!)

7. Electrical power in a direct-current (dc) circuit is defined as the product of voltage and current. In symbols, *Power = Voltage × Current*. Write a program to calculate dc power from a voltage value of 12 volts and a current value of 0.00125 ampere. Generate a tabular display of input and output values in decimal form.

8. Write a program that employs a loop to read character file called *lowcase* consisting of all lowercase characters. Convert the lowercase characters to uppercase by subtracting 32 from each character, and write the uppercase characters to a file called *upcase*. (*Note*: You must create the *lowcase* file using your ASCII text editor.)

9. Write a user-friendly program that will calculate power from voltage and current values entered by the user. Generate a tabular display of input and output values in decimal form.

Most Difficult

10. Write a user-friendly program that will calculate the weekly gross pay amount for an employee, given his/her rate of pay and number of hours worked. Assume the employee is part-time and, therefore, works less than 40 hours per week. Generate a display showing the employee's name, rate of pay, hours worked, and gross pay. Provide the appropriate display headings. (*Note*: Set the *ios::showpoint* flag to assure proper dollars and cents format for currency output.)

11. Write a user-friendly program to calculate the circumference and area of a circle from a user's entry of its radius. Generate a tabular display showing the circle's radius, circumference, and area. (*Note:* Circumference of a circle = 2 × pi × r. Area of a circle = pi × r^2.)

12. Write a user-friendly program that will allow a student to calculate his/her test average from four test scores. Generate a display of the student's name, course name, individual test scores, and test average.

13. The "4 Squares" bowling team has four bowlers. On a given bowling night, each team member bowls three games. Write a program that will read the date, each bowler's name, and the individual game scores for each bowler. Using the input information, display a bowling report. The report should show the date at the top of the screen, and then a table showing each bowler's scores, total, and integer average.

14. Write a user-friendly program that will calculate the equivalent resistance of a series circuit from five resistances entered by the user. Generate a tabular display of input and output values in decimal form. (*Note:* The equivalent resistance of a series circuit is found by summing the individual resistances.)

15. Write a user-friendly program that will calculate the equivalent resistance from two parallel resistances entered by the user. Generate a tabular display of input and output values in decimal form. Use the following product over sum rule to calculate the equivalent resistance value:

$$R_{equiv} = (R_1 \times R_2) / (R_1 + R_2)$$

Observe the use of parentheses to group the quantities in this equation. Why do you suppose this is necessary?

4

STANDARD OPERATIONS
IN C++

INTRODUCTION
4-1 ARITHMETIC OPERATIONS
    Increment and Decrement Operators
4-2 ASSIGNMENT OPERATIONS
PROBLEM SOLVING IN ACTION:
    INVENTORY CONTROL
4-3 BOOLEAN OPERATIONS
    Relational Operators
    Logical Operators
PROBLEM SOLVING IN ACTION:
    BOOLEAN LOGIC

4-4 SOME STANDARD FUNCTIONS IN C++
    Mathematical Functions
    Conversion Functions
    String Functions
PROBLEM SOLVING IN ACTION: DATA
    COMMUNICATIONS
A TECHNICAL CHALLENGE: POLAR AND
    RECTANGULAR COORDINATES
CHAPTER SUMMARY
QUESTIONS AND PROBLEMS
    Questions
    Problems

INTRODUCTION

You are now ready to begin learning how to write simple straight-line programs in C++. By a straight-line program, I mean a program that does not alter its flow; it simply executes a series of statements in a straight line, from beginning to end.

In order for your programs to perform meaningful tasks, you must be familiar with several standard, or built-in, operations available to you in C++. The simplest of these are the standard arithmetic operations. By definition, an arithmetic operation generates a numeric result. Such operations are the topic of the first section of this chapter.

The second section deals with the C++ assignment operators. Assignment operators assign a value to a variable object in memory. There are compound assignment operators in C++ that allow you to combine an arithmetic operation with the assignment operation.

In addition to arithmetic operations, there are logical operations available in C++ that generate a true or false result. These operations are covered in the third section.

In order to simplify the programming task, C++ employs several standard functions. These functions allow you to easily implement many common operations, such as square root, sine, and cosine, without writing special routines. Standard functions are discussed in the fourth section.

4-1 ARITHMETIC OPERATIONS

Arithmetic operations in C++ include the common add, subtract, multiply, and divide operations, as well as increment/decrement operations. The basic add, subtract, multiply, and divide operations can be performed on any numeric data class. Recall that the standard numeric data classes in C++ are the integers and reals (floating-point). In addition, you can perform arithmetic operations on character data in C++, because characters are represented as integers (ASCII) within the computer.

Table 4-1 lists the five basic arithmetic operations and the C++ symbols used to represent those operations. The addition (+), subtraction (−), and multiplication (∗) operators are straightforward and do not need any further explanation. However, you might note that an asterisk (∗) is used for multiplication rather than a times symbol (×) so that the computer does not get multiplication confused with the character 'x'.

TABLE 4-1 ARITHMETIC OPERATORS
DEFINED IN C++

Operation	Symbol
Add	+
Subtract	−
Multiply	*
Remainder (modulus)	%

The division operator needs some special attention. This operator will generate a result that is the same data class of the operands used in the operation. Thus, if you divide two integers, you will get an integer result. If you divide one or more decimal floating-point values, you get a decimal result. Thus, 10 / 3 = 3 and 10.0 / 3 = 3.333333. Here, the former is integer division and generates an integer result. The latter is floating-point division and generates a floating-point result.

Finally, the remainder, or modulus, operator is defined only for integer operands. You will get a compile error if you try to apply it to floating-point values. The modulus operator (%) simply generates the remainder that occurs when you divide two integers. For example, the result of 5 % 3 is 2, 5 % 4 is 1, and 5 % 5 is 0.

Let's look at a couple of examples that illustrate these operations. Example 4-1 shows several arithmetic operations on integers, and Example 4-2 deals with arithmetic operations on floating-point values.

Example 4-1

What value will be computed as the result of each of the following operations?

a. 3 * (−5)
b. 4 * 5 − 10
c. 10 / 3
d. 9 % 3
e. −21 / (−2)
f. −21 % (−2)
g. 4 * 5 / 2 + 5 % 2

Solution

a. 3 * (−5) computes the value −15.
b. 4 * 5 − 10 computes the value 10. Note that the multiplication operation is performed before the subtraction operation.

    c. 10 / 3 computes the value 3, because this is integer division.

    d. 9 % 3 computes the value 0, because there is no remainder.

    e. −21 / (−2) computes the integer quotient, 10.

    f. −21 % (−2) computes the remainder, −1.

    g. 4 ∗ 5 / 2 + 5 % 2 = (4 ∗ 5) / 2 + (5 % 2) = 20 / 2 + (5 % 2) = 10 + 1 = 11.
       Notice that the multiplication, ∗, division, /, and remainder, %, operators are performed first, from left to right. The addition operation is performed last.

Aside from showing how the individual operators work, the foregoing example illustrates the priority, or ordering, of the operators. When more than one operation is performed in an expression, you must know the order in which they will be performed to determine the result. C++ performs operations in the following order:

- All operators within parentheses are performed first.

- If there are nested parentheses (parentheses within parentheses) the inner-most operators are performed first, from the inside out.

- The ∗, /, and % operators are performed next, from left to right within the expression.

- The + and − operators are performed last, from left to right within the expression.

Arithmetic operations on floating-point values are basically the same as those on integers, with the exception of division. Remember that the / operator will return a floating-point value if *either* of its operands is floating-point. The remainder operation (%) is defined only for integers and will generate a compiler error if you attempt to apply it to floating-point values.

When performing several floating-point operations within an arithmetic expression, division and multiplication have the same priority. Thus, operators within parentheses are performed first, followed by multiplication and division, followed by addition and subtraction.

Example 4-2

    Evaluate each of the following expressions:

    a. 4.6 − 2.0 + 3.2

    b. 4.6 − 2.0 ∗ 3.2

    c. 4.6 − 2.0 / 2 ∗ 3.2

    d. −3.0 ∗ ((4.3 + 2.5) ∗ 2.0) − 1.0

    e. −21 / −2

    f. −21.0 % −2

   g. 10.0 / 3

   h. ((4 * 12) / (4 + 12))

   i. 4 * 12 / 4 + 12

Solution

   a. 4.6 − 2.0 + 3.2 = (4.6 − 2.0) + 3.2 = 2.6 + 3.2 = 5.8

   b. 4.6 − 2.0 * 3.2 = 4.6 − (2.0 * 3.2) = 4.6 − 6.4 = −1.8

   c. 4.6 − 2.0 / 2 * 3.2 = 4.6 − ((2.0 / 2) * 3.2) = 4.6 − (1.0 * 3.2) = 4.6 − 3.2 = 1.4

   d. −3.0 * ((4.3 + 2.5) * 2.0) − 1.0 = −3.0 * (6.8 * 2.0) − 1.0 = −3.0 * 13.6 − 1.0 = −40.8 − 1.0 = −41.8

   e. −21.0 / −2 = 10.5

   f. −21.0 % −2 = "Illegal use of floating-point error" because % is defined only for integer values.

   g. 10.0 / 3 = 3.333333

   h. ((4 * 12) / (4 + 12)) = 48 / 16 = 3

   i. 4 * 12 / 4 + 12 = 48 / 4 + 12 = 12 + 12 = 24

DEBUGGING TIP

When using parentheses within an arithmetic expression, the number of left parentheses must equal the number of right parentheses. When coding your programs, always count each to make sure that this equality holds.

   Notice that I have used parentheses in the solutions for the preceding examples to indicate the order of the operations. As you can see, the parentheses clarify the expression. For this reason, I suggest that you always use parentheses when writing arithmetic expressions. This way, you will always be sure of the order in which the compiler will execute the operators within the expression. Keep in mind, however, that the compiler will always perform the operators within parentheses from inside out, as shown in part d of Example 4-2. In particular, notice how the evaluation of part h of Example 4-2 differs from part i. The parentheses in part h force C++ to perform the division operation last, after the addition operation. In part i, the division operation is performed prior to the addition operation, generating a completely different result. This is why you should always use parentheses when writing expressions. It is better to be safe then sorry!

Increment and Decrement Operators

There are many times in a program when you will need to increment (add 1) or decrement (subtract 1) a variable. The increment and decrement operators shown in Table 4-2 are provided for this purpose.

TABLE 4-2 INCREMENT AND DECREMENT OPERATORS

Operation	Symbol
Increment	++
Decrement	−−

Increment/decrement can be applied to both integer and floating-point variables, as well as character variables. An increment operation adds 1 to the value of a variable. Thus, $++x$ is equivalent to the statement $x = x + 1$. Conversely, a decrement operation subtracts 1 from the value of a variable. As a result, $--x$ is equivalent to the statement $x = x - 1$. Here's a short example to illustrate increment/decrement:

Example 4-3

Determine the output generated by the following program:

```cpp
#include <iostream.h>  //FOR cout

void main()
{
  int x = 5;
  int y = 10;
  cout << " x = " << ++x << endl;
  cout << " x = " << --x << endl;
  cout << " y = " << (y = ++x - 2) << endl;
  x = 5;
  cout << " y = " << (y = x++ - 2) << endl;
  cout << " x = " << x << endl;
  x = 0;
  cout << " y = " << (y = x-- - 2) << endl;
  cout << " x = " << x << endl;
}//END main()
```

Solution

Here is the output that you will see on the monitor:

```
x = 6
x = 5
y = 4
y = 3
x = 6
y = -2
x = -1
```

Notice that the variable x is initialized with the value 5 at the start of the program. The first *cout* statement simply increments x to the value 6. The second *cout* statement then decrements x back to the value 5. Next, the third *cout* statement **preincrements** the value of x and then subtracts 2 from its value. We say that x is preincremented because the increment symbol appears before x and the increment operation is performed *before* x is used in the expression. Thus, the expression reduces to $y = x + 1 - 2 = 5 + 1 - 2 = 4$. Observe that the arithmetic operations are performed first, and then the result is assigned to y via the assignment operator. Thus, the value displayed by the *cout* object is the value of y, or 4.

Finally, the fourth *cout* statement involves a *postincrement* operation on x. A postincrement operation is indicated by the increment symbol following x. So, what's the difference between a preincrement and a postincrement operation? Well, a preincrement operation increments the variable *before any expression involving the variable is evaluated*. On the other hand, a postincrement operation increments the variable *after any expression involving the variable is evaluated*. Now, looking at the fourth *cout* statement in the program, you find that x starts out with the value 5. Thus, the expression reduces to $y = x - 2 = 5 - 2 = 3$. *After* the expression is evaluated, x is incremented to the value 6, as shown by the next *cout* statement. Finally, the last two *cout* statements show the result of a postdecrement operation. Here, x is assigned the value 0 to be used in the expression. Thus, $y = 0 - 2 = -2$. *After* the expression is evaluated, the value of x is decremented to -1, as shown by the last output value.

From Example 4-3, you see that a variable can be preincremented or postincremented. Likewise, a variable can be predecremented or postdecremented. If a variable is preincremented or predecremented within an expression, the variable is incremented/decremented *before* the expression is evaluated. On the other hand, if a variable is postincremented or postdecremented within an expression, the variable is incremented/decremented *after* the expression is evaluated.

Quick Check

1. List the order in which C++ performs arithmetic operations. Be sure to mention how parentheses are handled.

2. Write a statement using the decrement operator that is equivalent to the statement $x = x - 1$.

3. True or false: The division operator will produce an integer result when either of the operands is an integer.

4. True or false: The modulus operator is defined only for integers.

5. What is the difference between using the preincrement operator versus the postincrement operator on a variable, especially when the variable is used as part of a compound expression?

6. What is the result of 10 / 100?

4-2 ASSIGNMENT OPERATIONS

An assignment operation stores a value in memory. The value is stored at a location in memory that is accessed by the variable on the left-hand side of the assignment operator. As a result, a C++ assignment operator *assigns* the value on the right side of the operator to the variable appearing on the left side of the operator. Another way to say this is that the variable on the left side of the operator is *set* to the value on the right side of the operator. The C++ assignment operators are listed in Table 4-3.

TABLE 4-3 ASSIGNMENT OPERATORS USED IN C++

Operation	Symbol
Simple assignment	=
Compound addition assignment	+=
Compound subtraction assignment	−=
Compound multiplication assignment	*=
Compound division assignment	/=
Compound remainder assignment (integers only)	%=

First, let's say a word about the simple assignment operator, =. Although an equals symbol is used for this operator, you cannot think of it as equals. Here's why: Consider the statement $x = x + 1$. If you put this expression in an algebra exam, your professor would mark it wrong, because x cannot be equal to itself plus 1, right? However, in C++, this expression means to add 1 to x, and then assigns the resulting value to x. In other words, set x to the value $x + 1$. This is a perfectly legitimate operation. As you will soon find out, equals is a Boolean operator and uses two equals symbols, ==, in C++.

The compound assignment operators shown in Table 4-3 simply combine the assignment operator with an arithmetic operator. Suppose that we define x and y as integers; then the following holds:

$x \mathrel{+}= y$ is equivalent to $x = x + y$

$x \mathrel{-}= y$ is equivalent to $x = x - y$

$x \mathrel{*}= y$ is equivalent to $x = x * y$

$x \mathrel{/}= y$ is equivalent to $x = x / y$

$x \mathrel{\%}= y$ is equivalent to $x = x \% y$

As you can see, both the increment/decrement operators and the compound assignment operators provide a shorthand notation for writing arithmetic expressions. Get used to this notation, because it will be used extensively in programs throughout the rest of this text.

 Quick Check

1. Write a statement using the compound addition assignment operator that is equivalent to the statement $x = x + 5$.

2. Write a statement using the compound division assignment operator that is equivalent to the statement $x = x / y$.

PROBLEM SOLVING IN ACTION: INVENTORY CONTROL

Problem

Following is a partial inventory listing of items in the sporting goods department of Ma and Pa's General Store:

Item	Quantity	Units Sold This Month
Fishing line	132 spools	24 spools
Fish hooks	97 packages	45 packages
Sinkers	123 packages	37 packages
Fish nets	12 ea.	5 ea.

Write a program that will print a monthly report showing the item name, beginning quantity, units sold this month, ending quantity, and percent of quantity sold.

The problem solution begins with the problem-definition phase.

Defining the Problem

Output: The program must generate a printed monthly report of the item name, beginning quantity, units sold this month, ending quantity, and percent of quantity sold. Now is a good time to develop the output format. Suppose we use a tabular format, like this:

MONTH:

ITEM BEGIN QTY UNITS SOLD ENDING QTY % SOLD

Input: Ma or Pa must enter the month of the report and inventory data shown in the above table. Therefore, the program must be *very* user-friendly.

Processing: Because the item, beginning quantity, and units sold are entered by Ma or Pa, the program must use this information to calculate two things: the ending quantity and the percent sold. The ending quantity is found by simply subtracting the units sold from the beginning quantity, like this:

$$Ending\ Qty\ =\ Begin\ Qty\ -\ Units\ Sold$$

The percent sold is found by dividing the units sold by the beginning quantity and multiplying by 100%, like this:

$$\%\ Sold\ =\ (Units\ Sold\ /\ Begin\ Qty)\ \times\ 100\%$$

Planning the Solution

We must now construct a set of algorithms from the problem definition. Using structured program design, we will divide the problem into individual subproblems to solve the overall problem. There are four major tasks that follow directly from the problem definition:

- Print the report header information.
- Get the inventory data for a given item from the user.
- Calculate the ending quantity and percent sold for the given item.
- Print the item report.

Because we are going to print the report, item by item, the last three tasks must be repeated for each item in the inventory. The diagram in Figure 4-1 shows the block structure required for the program.

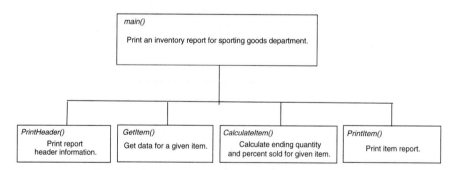

Figure 4-1   A structure diagram for the inventory problem.

The initial algorithm level, *main()*, will reflect the foregoing analysis and call the individual subprogram modules.

Initial Algorithm

> *main( )*
> BEGIN
>   Call function to print report header information.
>   Call function to get the inventory data for a given item from the user.
>   Call function to calculate the ending quantity and percent sold.
>   Call function to print the item report.
>   Repeat last three tasks for each inventory item.
> END.

In developing the algorithm, you would quickly realize that the processing is the same for each sales item. As a result, a single *repeat* statement is added at the end of the algorithm, rather than actually repeating all of the algorithm statements three more times. This has been done to make the algorithm more efficient.

The first level of refinement requires that we show a detailed algorithm for each task, or function, that we have identified. They are as follows:

First Level of Refinement

> *PrintHeader( )*
> BEGIN
>   Write a user prompt to enter the month.
>   Read (*Month*).
>   Print the header information.
> END.

> *GetItem( )*
> BEGIN
>   Write a user prompt to enter the item name.
>   Read (*Item*).
>   Write a user prompt to enter the beginning quantity.
>   Read (*Begin Qty*).
>   Write a user prompt to enter the number of units sold.
>   Read (*Units Sold*).
> END.

CaculateItem()
BEGIN
   Calculate *Ending Qty = Begin Qty − Units Sold.*
   Calculate *% Sold = (Units Sold / Begin Qty) × 100 %.*
END.

PrintItem()
BEGIN
   Print *Item, Begin Qty, Units Sold, Ending Qty*, and *% Sold.*
END.

Given our problem definition, the foregoing collection of algorithms is straightforward. Ma or Pa must enter the month for the inventory report. The *PrintHeader()* function will then print the report header information, including the report table headings. The next three functions must then be executed for each of the items in the inventory. The *GetItem()* function prompts and reads the item information from the user. The *CalculateItem()* function will make the required calculations. Finally, the *PrintItem()* function will print the item report.

Now the job is to code this algorithm in C++. With your present knowledge of C++, coding most of the algorithm should not present a problem. But what about the repeat statement at the end of the *main()* function algorithm? Well, notice that this statement requires that you go back and repeat many of the previous statements over and over until all the items are processed. Such a repeating operation is called an **iteration**, or **looping**, operation. To date, you do not have the C++ tools to perform such an operation. So, we will have to repeat all of the processing steps for each of the sales items in the inventory. In Chapter 6, you will learn how to perform iterative operations in C++, thus making the code much more efficient.

Here's the flat implementation of the foregoing algorithms:

Coding the Program

```
//ACTION 4-1 (ACT04-01.CPP)

//OUTPUT:      A PRINTED MONTHLY REPORT OF THE
//             ITEM NAME, BEGINNING QUANTITY,
//             UNITS SOLD THIS MONTH, ENDING
//             QUANTITY, AND PERCENT OF QUANTITY
//             SOLD
//INPUT:       MA OR PA ENTER THE INVENTORY DATA
```

```
//PROCESSING:      THE PROGRAM MUST CALCULATE TWO THINGS:
//                 ENDING QUANTITY AND THE PERCENT SOLD

#include <iostream.h>      //FOR cin AND cout
#include <iomanip.h>       //FOR setw()
#include <fstream.h>       //FOR print OBJECT
#include <process.h>       //FOR exit()

//DECLARE CONSTANTS
const int MONTH_SIZE = 9;      //SIZE OF MONTH ARRAY
const int ITEM_SIZE = 21;      //SIZE OF ITEM NAME ARRAY

void main()
{
  char Month[MONTH_SIZE] = "\0";        //MONTH OF REPORT
  char Item[ITEM_SIZE] = "\0";          //SALES ITEM NAME
  float BeginQty = 1.0;                 //BEGINNING QUANTITY
  float UnitsSold = 0.0;                //NUMBER OF UNITS SOLD
  int EndQty = 0;                       //ENDING QUANTITY
  float PercentSold = 0.0;              //PERCENT OF SALES

//*******************************************************************************
//
//THIS SEGMENT OF CODE DEFINES "print" AS AN OUTPUT
//FILE POINTING TO YOUR PRINTER PORT (PRN)
//                     (DOS ONLY)
//
//*******************************************************************************
  ofstream print;              //DEFINE PRINT AS AN OUTPUT FILE STREAM
  print.open("PRN");           //OPEN PRINT FILE AND POINT TO PRN
  if (!print)                  //MAKE SURE PRINTER IS READY
  {
    cout << "There is a problem with the printer." << endl;
    exit(1);
  }//END IF

//DISPLAY PROGRAM DESCRIPTION MESSAGE
  cout << "Dear Ma or Pa\n\n"
          "You will be asked to enter four sales items, one at\n"
          "a time.  With each item you will be asked to enter\n"
          "the item name, the beginning quantity, and the quantity\n"
          "sold this month.  The computer will then print a monthly\n"
          "inventory report for the sales items." << endl << endl;
```

```
//PRINT REPORT HEADER INFORMATION
  cout << "Please enter the month in XX/XX/XX format:  ";
  cin >> Month;
  print << "\n\nMONTH:  " << Month << endl;
  print << "\n\n\n" << setw(15) << "ITEM" << setw(15) << "BEGIN QTY"
       << setw(15) << "UNITS SOLD" << setw(15) << "ENDING QTY"
       << setw(10) << "% SOLD" << endl;
  print << setw(15) << "----" << setw(15) << "---------"
       << setw(15) << "----------" << setw(15) << "----------"
       << setw(10) << "------" << endl;

//GET ITEM DATA FROM USER
  cout << "Please enter the item name:" << endl;
  cin >> ws;
  cin.getline(Item,ITEM_SIZE);
  cout << "Please enter the beginning quantity of " << Item <<  endl;
  cin >> BeginQty;
  cout  << "Please enter the number of units of " << Item
       << " sold in " << Month  << endl ;
  cin >> UnitsSold;

//CALCULATE ENDING QUANTITY AND PERCENT SOLD FOR ITEM
  EndQty = BeginQty - UnitsSold;
  PercentSold = (UnitsSold / BeginQty) * 100;

//PRINT ITEM REPORT
  print.setf(ios::fixed);
  print.precision(2);
  print << setw(15) << Item << setw(15) << BeginQty
       << setw(15) << UnitsSold << setw(15) << EndQty
       << setw(10) << PercentSold << endl;

//GET ITEM DATA FROM USER
  cout << "Please enter the item name:" << endl;
  cin >> ws;
  cin.getline(Item,ITEM_SIZE);
  cout << "Please enter the beginning quantity of " << Item <<  endl;
  cin >> BeginQty;
  cout << "Please enter the number of units of " << Item
       << " sold in " << Month  << endl ;
  cin >> UnitsSold;
```

```
//CALCULATE ENDING QUANTITY AND PERCENT SOLD FOR ITEM
  EndQty = BeginQty - UnitsSold;
  PercentSold = (UnitsSold / BeginQty) * 100;

//PRINT ITEM REPORT
  print << setw(15) << Item << setw(15) << BeginQty
      << setw(15) << UnitsSold << setw(15) << EndQty
      << setw(10) << PercentSold << endl;

//GET ITEM DATA FROM USER
  cout << "Please enter the item name:" << endl;
  cin >> ws;
  cin.getline(Item,ITEM_SIZE);
  cout << "Please enter the beginning quantity of " << Item <<  endl;
  cin >> BeginQty;
  cout << "Please enter the number of units of " << Item
      << " sold in " << Month  << endl ;
  cin >> UnitsSold;

//CALCULATE ENDING QUANTITY AND PERCENT SOLD FOR ITEM
  EndQty = BeginQty - UnitsSold;
  PercentSold = (UnitsSold / BeginQty) * 100;

//PRINT ITEM REPORT
  print  << setw(15) << Item << setw(15) << BeginQty
      << setw(15) << UnitsSold << setw(15) << EndQty
      << setw(10) << PercentSold << endl;

//GET ITEM DATA FROM USER
  cout << "Please enter the item name:" << endl;
  cin >> ws;
  cin.getline(Item,ITEM_SIZE);
  cout << "Please enter the beginning quantity of " << Item <<  endl;
  cin >> BeginQty;
  cout  << "Please enter the number of units of " << Item
      << " sold in " << Month  << endl ;
  cin >> UnitsSold;

//CALCULATE ENDING QUANTITY AND PERCENT SOLD FOR ITEM
  EndQty = BeginQty - UnitsSold;
  PercentSold = (UnitsSold / BeginQty) * 100;
```

```
//PRINT ITEM REPORT
  print << setw(15) << Item << setw(15) << BeginQty
        << setw(15) << UnitsSold << setw(15) << EndQty
        << setw(10) << PercentSold << endl;

//CLOSE PRINT FILE
print.close();
} //END main()
```

Using the sales data provided, this program will print the following inventory report:

MONTH: May

ITEM	BEGIN QTY	UNITS SOLD	ENDING QTY	%SOLD
Fishing Line	132	24	108	18.18
Fish Hooks	97	45	52	46.39
Sinkers	123	37	86	30.08
Fish Nets	12	5	7	41.67

Again, notice how a whole block of C++ code is repeated four times to process the four sales items. Wouldn't it be nice to simply code the processing steps once and then tell the computer to repeat these steps the required number of times? Such a repeating operation would make our coding much more efficient, wouldn't it?

You should be able to understand the above C++ code, given the material presented up to this point in the text. However, there is one small, but important, point that needs some discussion. Look at the *PercentSold* calculation in the program. Notice that it is obtained by dividing the *UnitsSold* by the *BeginQty* and multiplying by 100. Now, you see that in the definition section at the top of the program that both *UnitsSold* and *BeginQty* are defined as floating-point values. Well, why couldn't they be defined as integers, because both will always be whole-number values, right? The reason that you can't define them as integers is that if you divide two integers using the / operator, you will get an integer result. Thus, if the units sold were 10 and the beginning quantity were 100, the *integer* quotient would be 10 / 100 = 0. As a result, the *PercentSold* would be 0, which is obviously incorrect. So, the solution is to define *UnitsSold* and *BeginQty* as floating-point values. Then dividing the two will yield a floating-point result. Using the preceding values, you would get 10 / 100 = 0.1, resulting in a correct value of 10% sold.

```
#include <iostream.h>  //FOR cout

void main()
{
   cout << (3 + 4) << endl;
   cout << ('J' > 'K') << endl;
   cout << (3 * 10 % 3 – 2 > 20 / 6 + 4) << endl;
}//END main()
```

Solution

The output generated by the above program is

7
0
0

      The first output line is obvious, because $3 + 4 = 7$. The remaining output lines are logical values based on the evaluation of the respective relational operations. Remember that a logical false is represented by a 0 and a logical true by a 1 in C++. Thus, the result of 'J' > 'K' is 0 (false) because the ASCII value for 'J' is not greater than the ASCII value for 'K'. Finally, the result of the last expression is 0 (false). Here, the evaluation process goes like this:

$$(((3 * 10) \% 3) - 2) > ((20 / 6) + 4) =$$
$$((30 \% 3) - 2) > (3 + 4) =$$
$$0 - 2 > 7 =$$
$$-2 > 7 =$$
$$0 \text{ (false)}$$

Notice that the multiplication operation is performed first, followed by the % and / operations, from left to right. Then the addition/subtraction operations are performed, and finally the greater-than operation is performed.

Logical Operators

Logical operations also generate Boolean results. The three logical operations used in C++ are given in Table 4-5. The C++ ANSI standard allows you to use the operation names when performing logic operations. As an alternative (and a necessity when using old compilers), you see from the table that the exclamation symbol (!) is used for **NOT**, the double vertical bar symbols (¦¦) for **OR**, and the double ampersand symbols (&&) for **AND**.

TABLE 4-5 LOGICAL
OPERATORS USED IN C++

Operation Name	Symbol
NOT	!
OR	¦¦
AND	&&

The **NOT** operator is used to negate, or invert, a Boolean value. Because there are only two possible Boolean values (true and false), the negation of one results in the other. For example, suppose we define a Boolean variable object A. Then the variable A can take on only two values, true or false. If A is true, then **NOT** A is false. Conversely, if A is false, then **NOT** A is true. This operation can be shown using a ***truth table***. A truth table simply shows the result of a logic operation on a Boolean value. Here is the truth table for the simple **NOT** operation:

A	**NOT** A $(!A)$
true	false
false	true

The **OR** operation is applied to multiple Boolean values. For instance, suppose that A and B are both defined as Boolean variables. Then A and B can be either true (nonzero) or false (zero). The **OR** operator dictates that if either A or B is true, the result of the operation is true. Another way to say this is that "*any* true results in true." In terms of a truth table,

A	B	A **OR** B $(A$ ¦¦ $B)$
true	true	true
true	false	true
false	true	true
false	false	false

Notice from the table that A **OR** B is true whenever A is true or B is true. Of course, if both A and B are true, the result is true.

The **AND** operator also operates on multiple Boolean values. Here, if A and B are Boolean variables, then the expression A **AND** B is true only when both A

and *B* are both true. Another way to say this is that "*any* false results in false." In terms of a truth table

A	*B*	*A* **AND** *B* (*A* && *B*)
true	true	true
true	false	false
false	true	false
false	false	false

The Boolean logical operators can also be applied to logical expressions. For example, consider the following:

$$(-6 < 0) \text{ AND } (12 > = 10)$$

Is this expression true or false? Well, −6 < 0 is true and 12 > = 10 is true. Consequently, the expression must be true. How about this one?

$$((3 - 6) == 3) \text{ OR } (\text{ NOT}(2 == 4))$$

You must evaluate both sides of the expression. If either side is true, then the result is true. On the left side, 3 − 6 is equal to −3, which is not equal to 3. Thus, the left side is false. On the right side, 2 == 4 is false, but **NOT**(2 == 4) must be true. Consequently, the right side of the expression is true. This makes the result of the **OR**ing operation true.

Observe in the two foregoing expressions that parentheses are used to define the expressions being operated upon. Remember to do this whenever you use a logical operator to evaluate two or more expressions. In other words, *always* enclose the things you are **OR**ing and **AND**ing within parentheses.

You will see in Chapter 5 how these logical operators are used to make decisions that control the flow of a program. For example, using the **AND** operator, you can test to see if two conditions are true. If both conditions are true, the program will execute a series of statements, while skipping those statements if one of the test conditions is false.

Finally, you should be aware that C++ also includes *bitwise* logical operators that perform the respective logical operations on the individual bits of one or more operands. These operators will not be discussed here, but can be found in your C++ compiler reference materials.

Quick Check

1. Operators that allow two values to be compared are called _____ operators.

2. In C++, a logical false is equated to the value _____.

3. What is the difference between the = operator and the == operator in C++.

4. What value is generated as a result of the following operation?
   4 > 5 − 2

5. What value is generated as a result of the following operation?
   (5 != 5) **AND** (3 == 3)

PROBLEM SOLVING IN ACTION: BOOLEAN LOGIC

Problem

A common Boolean logic operator that is not available in C++ is the NAND (**NOT AND**) operation. Given two variables, *A* and *B*, the NAND operation is defined as follows:

A	*B*	*A* NAND *B*
true	true	false
true	false	true
false	true	true
false	false	true

Notice that the NAND operation is simply the opposite of the AND operation. In symbols, *A* NAND *B* = **NOT**(*A* **AND** *B*). Write a C++ program that will display the NAND result of two logical values entered by the user. Let's begin by defining the problem in terms of output, input, and processing.

Defining the Problem

Output: The program must display the logical result of the NAND operation as defined by its truth table.

Input: The user must enter logical values for the input variables, A and B.

Processing: Although the NAND operation is not available in C++, you can implement it by using the **NOT** and **AND** operators, like this:

$$A \text{ NAND } B = \mathbf{NOT}(A \ \mathbf{AND} \ B)$$

Or, by using alternative syntax

$$A \text{ NAND } B = ! \ (A \ \&\& \ B)$$

Because this is a relatively simple problem, we do not need to divide the problem into smaller subproblems. Rather, we will develop a single algorithm from the problem definition. Now, the problem definition requires us to prompt the user to enter two Boolean values for A and B and apply the foregoing relationship to generate a Boolean result. However, there is one minor difficulty. You cannot read Boolean values from the keyboard. Instead, you must read character information, test the information for true or false, and then make an assignment to the variables, A and B. Here's an algorithm that will do the job:

Planning the Solution

BEGIN
    Write a program-description message.
    Write a prompt to enter a logical value of 'T' for true or 'F' for false.
    Read (*Entry*).
    If *Entry* is 'T' then
       Assign true to A.
    Else
       Assign false to A.
    Write a prompt to enter a logical value of 'T' for true or 'F' for false.
    Read (*Entry*).
    If *Entry* is 'T' then
       Assign true to B.
    Else
       Assign false to B.
    Assign NOT(A AND B) to NAND.
    Write NAND.
END.

The algorithm shows that a character ('T' or 'F') is read in and then tested to see if it is a 'T' or 'F'. An assignment is then made to the Boolean variable, depending on the test. If the character is a 'T', then true is assigned to the Boolean variable; else false is assigned to the variable. This testing operation is called an **if/else** operation, for obvious reasons. You will learn more about this in Chapter 5. Once the proper Boolean values have been assigned, the NAND operation is performed, and the result is displayed. Here's the program:

Coding the Program

```
// ACTION 4-2 (ACT044-02.CPP)

// OUTPUT: THE PROGRAM MUST DISPLAY THE
// LOGICAL RESULT OF THE NAND OPERATION

// INPUT: THE USER MUST ENTER BOOLEAN VALUES FOR
// THE INPUT VARIABLES, A AND B.

// PROCESSING: A NAND B = NOT (A AND B) = ! (A && B)

#include <iostream.h>      //FOR cin AND cout

void main()
{
//DECLARE BOOLEAN ENUMERATED CLASS
  enum Boolean {FALSE,TRUE};

//DEFINE VARIABLES
  char Entry = ' ';                    // USER ENTRY
  Boolean NAND = FALSE;                // RESULT OF NAND OPERATION
  Boolean A = FALSE;                   // BOOLEAN VALUE
  Boolean B = FALSE;                   // BOOLEAN VALUE

//DISPLAY PROGRAM DESCRIPTION MESSAGE
  cout <<   "This program will generate a NAND (not AND) result\n"
            "from two Boolean values that you must enter. " << endl << endl;

//GET USER INPUT FOR FIRST BOOLEAN VARIABLE
  cout << "Enter a Boolean value (T for TRUE or F for FALSE)" << endl;
  cin >>  Entry;
```

```
//TEST USER INPUT FOR TRUE OR FALSE AND
//MAKE BOOLEAN ASSIGNMENT
  if ((Entry == 'T') || (Entry == 't'))
     A = TRUE;
  else
     A = FALSE;

//GET USER INPUT FOR SECOND BOOLEAN VARIABLE
  cout << "Enter a Boolean value (T for TRUE or F for FALSE)" << endl;
  cin >>  Entry;

//TEST USER INPUT FOR TRUE OR FALSE AND
//MAKE BOOLEAN ASSIGNMENT
  if ((Entry == 'T') || (Entry == 't'))
     B = TRUE;
  else
     B = FALSE;

//DETERMINE NAND RESULT
  NAND = !(A && B);

//TEST NAND RESULT FOR TRUE OR FALSE AND DISPLAY RESULT
  if (NAND == TRUE)
     cout << "\n\nThe NAND result is:  TRUE" << endl;
  else
     cout << "\n\nThe NAND result is:  FALSE" << endl;
} //END main()
```

This program will generate the NAND (NOT AND) result, given two Boolean values entered by the user. One thing you will notice is that the variables (*A* and *B*) are defined as objects of an enumerated class called *Boolean*. You see that the variables (*A* and *B*) are assigned TRUE *if* the user enters a 'T' or 't'; *else* the variables are assigned FALSE. Notice also that the logical OR operator, ||, is employed to test for either a 't' or 'T' input character in order to make the appropriate assignment. Once the variable assignments are made, the NAND expression is evaluated and assigned to the Boolean variable *NAND*. Finally, *NAND* is tested using an **if/else** statement to produce the correct output. Don't worry about the **if/else** statement syntax now, because it is covered in the next chapter. At this time, it is only important that you understand the program logic.

4-4 SOME STANDARD FUNCTIONS IN C++

In Chapter 3, you were introduced to several standard functions, such as *sqrt()*, *getline()*, *get()*, and so on. Standard operations such as these are so common in programming that C++ includes them as built-in functions. There are hundreds of standard functions available in the various C++ header files. The tables that follow list some of the more commonly used functions. I should caution you, however, that different versions of C++ have different standard functions available.

As you progress through this text, you will be using some of these functions; they will be discussed in more detail at that time. As a result, do not worry about learning them now. Simply scan each table to get an idea of what functions are available. The tables that follow list the function, its header file, and a short description of its operation. Space does not permit a detailed discussion of each function. Check your compiler reference manual and/or on-line help feature for a listing and explanation of additional standard functions.

Conversion Functions

The conversion functions listed in Table 4-6 convert one class of data to another class, usually between integer and character data classes.

TABLE 4-6 SOME STANDARD CONVERSION FUNCTIONS
AVAILABLE IN TURBO C++

Function Name	Header File	Operation
atoi()	stdlib.h	Converts a string to an integer.
itoa()	stdlib.h	Converts an integer to a string.
toascii()	ctype.h	Converts a character to its ASCII value.
tolower()	ctype.h	Converts a character to lowercase.

Mathematical Functions

Mathematical functions perform an arithmetic operation. As a result, these functions require a numeric argument and return a numeric result; then, they are sometimes called numeric functions. Some standard mathematical functions are listed in Table 4-7. Most these operations should be familiar to you from your background in mathematics. When using any of these functions in C++, you must make sure that the argument is the correct data class as specified by the function definition. In addition, any variable to which the function is assigned must be defined the same data class returned by the function.

TABLE 4-7 SOME STANDARD MATHEMATICAL FUNCTIONS AVAILABLE IN TURBO C++

Function Name	Header File	Operation
abs()	math.h	Returns the absolute value of the argument.
acos()	math.h	Returns the arc cosine of the argument (radians).
asin()	math.h	Returns the arc sine of the argument (radians).
atan()	math.h	Returns the arc tangent of the argument (radians).
cos()	math.h	Returns the cosine of the argument (radians).
hypot()	math.h	Returns the hypotenuse of a right triangle.
log()	math.h	Returns the natural log of the argument.
log10()	math.h	Returns the base 10 log of the argument.
pow()	math.h	Returns x raised to the power of y.
pow10()	math.h	Returns 10 raised to the power of y.
rand()	stdlib.h	Generates a random number between 0 and $2^{15} - 1$.
srand()	stdlib.h	Initializes the random-number generator and should be used prior to *rand()*.
sin()	math.h	Returns the sine of the argument (radians).
sqrt()	math.h	Returns the square root of the argument.
tan()	math.h	Returns the tangent of the argument (radians).

String Functions

The standard C++ string functions are used to manipulate strings. String processing is a large part of many application programs, so these functions are often very useful. The functions listed in Table 4-8 provide some of the more common string manipulation routines.

A string function of special interest is the *strcpy()* function. This function should be used when assigning strings to string variables. As an example, consider the following string variable definition:

```
char Name[31] = "\0";
```

Now, suppose that you wish to assign a string value to the *Name* string. The following statements *will not* compile:

Name[] = "Brenda";   or   Name = "Brenda";

The reason that these assignments will not work is that the string variable *Name* is actually a memory address. Thus, you are attempting to assign a character string value to an address value. This is called a **type mismatch** and will not compile. To assign string data, you *must* use the *strcpy()* function to copy the string value into the string storage area, like this:

strcpy(Name,"Brenda");

Of course, you must include the *string.h* header file in the program for this statement to compile.

TABLE 4-8 SOME STRING FUNCTIONS AVAILABLE IN
TURBO C++

Function Name	Header File	Operation
strcat()	string.h	Appends one string to another.
strcmp()	string.h	Compares two strings.
strlen()	string.h	Returns length of a string.
strcpy()	string.h	Copies a string.

Example 4-6

The string compare function, *strcmp()*, should be used when comparing strings rather than Boolean relational operators because Boolean relational operators are not reliable when comparing strings. Let's see what happens when the following program is executed:

```
#include <iostream.h>  //FOR cout
#include <string.h>      //FOR strcmp()

void main()
{
  cout << strcmp("Janet","Janet") << endl;
  cout << ("Janet" == "Janet") << endl;
  cout << strcmp("JANET","Janet") << endl;;
  cout << strcmp("Janet","JANET") << endl;
}//END main()
```

Solution

The foregoing program first uses the *strcmp()* function to compare the string "Janet" to the string "Janet". The second line of the program also compares "Janet" to "Janet" using the == relational operator. If you look up the operation of *strcmp()*, you will find that it returns a 0 if the two strings are equal, a negative value if the first string argument is less than the second string argument, and a positive value if the first string is greater than the second string. How are the two strings compared? Well, recall that each character in the string is represented by an ASCII value. The *strcmp()* function actually subtracts the individual ASCII values one character at a time from left to right until an unequal condition occurs or it runs out of characters. If all the characters in the two strings are the same, the result of subtracting character-by-character is zero. If a given character in the first string is larger than the corresponding character in the second string, the subtraction result is positive. If a given character in the first string is smaller than the corresponding character in the second string, the subtraction result is negative. Here is the output produced by the program:

```
0
0
-32
 32
```

Notice that the output of the first statement is 0, correctly indicating that according to the *strcmp()* function, the two strings are equal. However, the output of the second statement, which uses the Boolean relational operator == , is also 0. As you know, this means false, thereby erroneously indicating that the two strings are unequal. In the third statement, the *strcmp()* function generates a negative value of −32, correctly indicating that "JANET" is less than "Janet", according to the ASCII code. Finally, in the last statement, the *strcmp()* function generates a positive value of 32, correctly indicating that "Janet" is greater than "JANET".

 Quick Check

1. In order to use a standard function in your program, you must include its
   _____.

2. Explain how you can get an on-line description of a standard function using your compiler.

3. What function must be employed to assign string data to a string variable in your program?

4. Write a statement that will assign the string "C++" to a string variable called *Compiler*.

5. Why should the *strcmp()* function be used instead of Boolean relational operators when comparing string values?

PROBLEM SOLVING IN ACTION: DATA COMMUNICATIONS

Problem

In the field of data communications, binary digital computer data are converted to analog sine wave data for transmission over long distances via the telephone network. This idea is illustrated in Figure 4-2. Here, a binary 1 is represented by a sine wave of a high amplitude, and a binary 0 is represented by another sine wave of a lower amplitude. This is called **amplitude modulation**. Binary data are represented using a sine wave, so the study of data communications often requires the analysis of a sine wave. One such analysis is to find the amplitude, in volts, of a sine wave at any given point in time. This is called the **instantaneous value** of the sine wave and is found using the equation

$$v = V_{peak} \sin(2\pi ft)$$

where
v is the instantaneous voltage at any point in time t on the waveform, in volts.

V_{peak} is the peak amplitude of the waveform, in volts.

π is the constant 3.14159.

f is the frequency of the waveform, in hertz.

t is the time, in seconds, for v.

Write a program to find the instantaneous voltage value of the sine wave in Figure 4-2. Have the user enter the peak voltage in volts, the frequency in kilohertz, and the time in milliseconds.

Defining the Problem

Output: The program must display the instantaneous voltage value, v, resulting from the previous equation.

Input: The user must enter the following information:

- The peak amplitude of the waveform, V_{peak}, in volts.
- The frequency of the waveform, f, in kilohertz.
- The point in time, t, in milliseconds for which the instantaneous voltage must be calculated.

Processing: The program must calculate the instantaneous voltage value using the given equation.

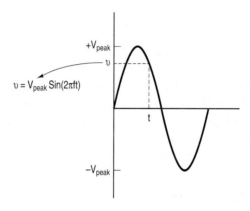

Figure 4-2   A sine wave for the data communications problem.

Planning the Solution

Using the structured approach to solving this problem, we will divide the problem into three subproblems that reflect the problem definition. The three major tasks that follow directly from the problem definition are

- Get the user entries for V_{peak}, f, and t.
- Calculate the instantaneous voltage.
- Display the instantaneous voltage value, v, resulting from the calculation.

Here are the respective algorithms:

Initial Algorithm

> *main()*
> BEGIN
>> Call function to get the user entries for V_{peak}, f, and t.
>> Call function to calculate the instantaneous voltage.
>> Call function to display the instantaneous voltage value, v.
> END.

First Level of Refinement

> *GetData()*
> BEGIN
>> Write a user prompt to enter the peak amplitude of the waveform, V_{peak}, in volts.
>> Read (V_{peak}).
>> Write a user prompt to enter the frequency of the waveform, f, in kilohertz.
>> Read (f).
>> Write a user prompt to enter the time, t, in milliseconds.
>> Read (t).
> END.

> *CalculateVoltage()*
> BEGIN
>> Calculate $v = V_{peak} \sin(2\pi f t)$.
> END.

> *DisplayVoltage()*
> BEGIN
>> Write the instantaneous voltage value, v.
> END.

Coding the Program

The flat implemention of the above set of algorithms follows:

```
//ACTION 4-3 (ACT04-03.CPP)

//OUTPUT:           THE PROGRAM MUST DISPLAY
//                  THE INSTANTANEOUS VOLTAGE VALUE, V,
//                  RESULTING FROM THE ABOVE EQUATION.

//INPUT:            THE USER MUST ENTER THE FOLLOWING:
//                  THE PEAK AMPLITUDE OF THE WAVEFORM, Vpeak,
//                  IN VOLTS.
//                  THE FREQUENCY OF THE WAVEFORM, F,
//                  IN KILOHERTZ.
//                  THE POINT IN TIME, T, IN MILLISECONDS FOR WHICH
//                  THE INSTANTANEOUS VOLTAGE MUST
//                  BE CALCULATED.

//PROCESSING:       THE PROGRAM MUST CALCULATE THE
//                  INSTANTANEOUS VOLTAGE VALUE.

#include <iostream.h>      //FOR cin AND cout
#include <math.h>          //FOR sin()

//DECLARE CONSTANT
  const float PI = 3.14159;

void main()
{
//DEFINE VARIABLES
  float V_Peak = 0.0;           //PEAK VOLTAGE IN VOLTS
  float f = 0.0;                //FREQUENCY IN KILOHERTZ
  float t = 0.0;                //TIME IN MILLISECONDS
  float v = 0.0;                //INSTANTANEOUS VOLTAGE IN VOLTS

//DISPLAY PROGRAM DESCRIPTION MESSAGE
  cout <<   "This program will display the instantaneous voltage\n"
            "value of an AC signal.  You must enter the following\n"
            "three quantities: " << endl << endl;
  cout <<   "\tPeak voltage of the signal, V_Peak.\n\n"
            "\tFrequency of the signal, f.\n\n"
            "\tThe point in time, t, for which the voltage\n"
            "\tmust be calculated. " << endl << endl;
```

```
//GET USER ENTRIES
   cout << "Enter the peak signal voltage in volts:  V_Peak = ";
   cin >> V_Peak;
   cout << "Enter the signal frequency in kilohertz:  f = ";
   cin >> f;
   cout << "Enter the time in milliseconds:  t = ";
   cin >> t;

//CALCULATE INSTANTANEOUS VOLTAGE VALUE
   v = V_Peak * sin(2 * PI * f * t);

//DISPLAY INSTANTANEOUS VOLTAGE VALUE
   cout.setf(ios::fixed);
   cout.precision(4);
   cout << "\n\nThe instantaneous voltage at " << t << " milliseconds is\n"
        << v << " volts." << endl;
} //END main()
```

It's probably a good idea to take a closer look at some of the features of this program. Here is what you will see on the display after the program has been run:

This program will display the instantaneous voltage
value of an AC signal. You must enter the following
three quantities:

   Peak voltage of the signal, V_Peak.

   Frequency of the signal, f.

   The point in time, t, for which the voltage
   must be calculated.

Enter the peak signal voltage in volts: V_Peak = **10**↵

Enter the signal frequency in kilohertz: f = **1**↵

Enter the time in milliseconds: t = **.125**↵

The instantaneous voltage at 0.1250 milliseconds is
7.0711 volts.

As you can see, the program description message describes the purpose of the program. In addition, it tells the user what values must be entered and identifies the variables to be used for the entered values. Another observation from the above program output is that the user must enter the waveform frequency in kilohertz and the time in milliseconds. These are typical units found in data communications. Notice that the user prompts indicate this entry requirement.

The calculation of the output voltage, *v*, is performed with the following program statement:

```
v = V_Peak * sin(2 * PI * f * t);
```

The equation does not have to be altered to accommodate *f* in kilohertz and *t* in milliseconds, because the product of these two units cancel each other out (10^{+3} cancels 10^{-3}). Another thing you see from the program statement is the use of the word *PI* to represent the value 3.14159. As you can see, this identifier is declared as a constant at the beginning of the program. One final point: The *sin()* function in C++ is defined to evaluate angles in *radians*. Fortunately, the quantity (2 * *PI* * *f* * *t*) produces radians and not degrees. If the value to be evaluated by the *sin()* function is in degrees, it must be converted to radians to obtain a correct result. You will see this shortly. To use the *sin()* function, you see that the *math.h* header file has been included at the beginning of the program.

A TECHNICAL CHALLENGE: POLAR AND RECTANGULAR COORDINATES

Problem

Many times in physics and engineering problems, you are required to convert between rectangular and polar coordinates. This is especially true in vector analysis. The vector diagram in Figure 4-3 summarizes the conversion process.

As you can see, a vector can be represented in one of two ways.

1. Polar coordinate:

$$M \angle \theta$$

where
M is the magnitude, or length, of the vector.
θ is the angle the vector makes with the horizontal axis.

2. Rectangular coordinate:

$$x + jy$$

where

x is the real axis, or horizontal coordinate, for the tip of the vector.
y is the imaginary axis, or vertical coordinate, for the tip of the vector.
$j = \sqrt{-1}$, an imaginary number.

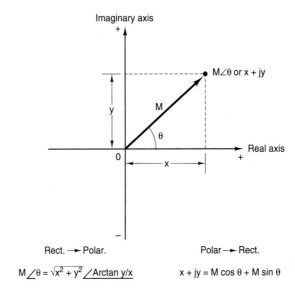

Rect. → Polar.

$$M \angle \theta = \sqrt{x^2 + y^2} \angle \text{Arctan } y/x$$

Polar → Rect.

$$x + jy = M \cos \theta + M \sin \theta$$

Figure 4-3   Polar/rectangular conversion.

Using right-angle trigonometry, you can convert between polar and rectangular coordinates. The conversion equations are shown in the figure. Let's write a C++ program that will convert from polar to rectangular coordinates using values supplied by the user. (A program to convert from rectangular to polar is left as a problem for you at the end of the chapter.)

Defining the Problem

Output: The output will be in tabular form, showing the input polar coordinate and the corresponding rectangular coordinate. The polar coordinate will be displayed in the format M @ θ. The values of M and θ will be displayed as variables, and the @ symbol will be displayed as a fixed character. The rectangular coordinate will be displayed using the format $x + jy$. The values of x and y will be displayed as variables using two decimal places. The + symbol and j character will be displayed as fixed character information.

Input: The user must enter the magnitude of the vector and the angle it makes with the horizontal axis, in degrees.

Processing: The program must calculate x and y as follows:

$$x = M \cos \theta$$
$$y = M \sin \theta$$

Planning the Solution

Using the foregoing problem definition, an appropriate set of algorithms is as follows:

Initial Algorithm

main( )
BEGIN
    Call function to get the user entries for the polar coordinate.
    Call function to calculate the rectangular coordinate.
    Call function to display the input polar coordinate and calculated rectangular coordinate.
END.

First Level of Refinement

GetData( )
BEGIN
    Write a user prompt to enter the vector magnitude, M.
    Read (M).
    Write a user prompt to enter the vector angle, *Angle*, in degrees.
    Read (*Angle*).
END.

CalculateRectangular( )
BEGIN
    Calculate $x = M \cos (Angle)$.
    Calculate $y = M \sin (Angle)$.
END.

DisplayResults( )
BEGIN
    Write the table headings.
    Write the polar coordinate, M @ *Angle*.
    Write the rectangular coordinate $x + jy$.
END.

Coding the Program

Following this set of algorithms, the flat program implementation is as follows:

```
//ACTION 4-4 (ACT04-04.CPP)
// OUTPUT:      THE OUTPUT WILL BE IN TABULAR FORM, SHOWING
//              THE INPUT POLAR COORDINATE AND THE
//              CORRESPONDING RECTANGULAR COORDINATE.
//              THE POLAR COORDINATE WILL BE DISPLAYED
//              IN THE FORMAT M @ ANGLE.
//              THE VALUES OF M AND ANGLE WILL BE DISPLAYED
//              AS VARIABLES AND THE @ SYMBOL WILL
//              BE DISPLAYED AS A FIXED CHARACTER.
//              THE RECTANGULAR COORDINATE WILL
//              BE DISPLAYED USING THE FORMAT X + JY.
//              X AND Y WILL BE DISPLAYED AS VARIABLES USING
//              TWO DECIMAL PLACES.  THE + SYMBOL AND
//              J CHARACTER WILL BE DISPLAYED AS
//              FIXED CHARACTER INFORMATION.

//INPUT:       THE USER MUST ENTER THE MAGNITUDE, M,
//             OF THE VECTOR AND ITS ANGLE.

//PROCESSING:  THE PROGRAM MUST CALCULATE X AND Y AS
//             FOLLOWS:
//             X = M * COS (ANGLE)
//             Y = M * SIN (ANGLE)
//             THE ANGLE MUST BE CONVERTED
//             TO RADIANS DURING THE CALCULATION.
```

```
#include <iostream.h>      //FOR cin AND cout
#include <iomanip.h>       //FOR setw()
#include <math.h>          //FOR sin(), cos()

//DECLARE CONSTANT
 const  float PI = 3.14159;

void main()
{
//DEFINE VARIABLES
   float x = 0.0;                   //RECTANGULAR X-COORDINATE
   float y = 0.0;                   //RECTANGULAR Y-COORDINATE
   float M = 0.0;                   //POLAR MAGNITUDE
   float Angle = 0.0;               //POLAR ANGLE

//DISPLAY PROGRAM DESCRIPTION MESSAGE
cout <<  "This program will convert polar vector coordinates\n"
          "to rectangular vector coordinates. " << endl << endl;

//GET POLAR COORDINATE
   cout << "Enter the magnitude of the vector:  M = ";
   cin >> M;
   cout << "Enter the vector angle in degrees:  Angle = ";
   cin >> Angle;

//CALCULATE RECTANGULAR COORDINATE
   x = M * cos(PI/180 * Angle);         //(PI/180 * Angle) CONVERTS
                                        //DEGREES TO RADIANS
   y = M * sin(PI/180 * Angle);

//DISPLAY POLAR AND RECTANGULAR VALUES TO USER
   cout << "\n\n\n" << setw (25) << "POLAR COORDINATE"
        << setw(40) << "RECTANGULAR COORDINATE " << endl;
   cout << setw(25) << "----------------"
        << setw(40) << "---------------------- " << endl << endl;
   cout.setf(ios::fixed);
   cout.precision(2);
   cout << setw(10) << M << " @ " << setw(6) << Angle << " degrees"
        << setw(23) << x << " + j" << y << endl;

}//END main()
```

This program will generate the following display when executed:

This program will convert polar vector coordinates
to rectangular vector coordinates.

Enter the magnitude of the vector: M = **5**⏎

Enter the vector angle in degrees: Angle = **53.13**⏎

<u>POLAR COORDINATE</u>   <u>RECTANGULAR COORDINATE</u>

5 @ 53.13 degrees   3 + j4

You should now have the knowledge required to write such a program. One thing that you should note is the conversion from degrees to radians within the *cos()* and *sin()* functions. You must multiply the *Angle* by the quantity ($PI/180$) to get radians. Remember that the *cos()* and *sin()* functions will only evaluate radians, not degrees.

CHAPTER SUMMARY

Arithmetic operations in C++ include the common add, subtract, multiply, and divide operations that can be performed on any numeric data type. Addition, subtraction, multiplication, and division are basically the same for both the integer and floating-point data types. However, when you divide two integers, you will get an integer result. If you need a floating-point result, at least one of the operands must be defined as a floating-point value. The remainder (%) operator is defined for integers only and will generate a compile error if used with floating-point values.

There are increment/decrement operators defined in C++. The increment operator, ++, adds one to a variable, and the decrement operator, − −, subtracts one from a variable. You can preincrement/decrement a variable or postincrement/decrement a variable. There's a big difference when the increment/decrement is used as part of an expression to be evaluated by C++. A preincrement/decrement operation on a variable is performed *before* the expression is evaluated, and a postincrement/decrement operation is performed on the variable *after* the expression is evaluated.

The simple assignment operator in C++ is the = operator. A value on the right side of the = operator is assigned to a variable on the left side of the operator. There are compound assignment operators, such as +=, *=, and so on, that combine an arithmetic operation with the assignment operation. These operators are used as a form of shorthand notation within a C++ program.

Boolean operators are those that generate a logical result of true or false. The two categories of Boolean operators in C++ are relational and logical operators. Relational operators allow two quantities to be compared. These operators include ==, != , > , < , <=, and >=. Logical operators perform logic operations on Boolean values to generate a Boolean result. The standard logical operators available in C++ are **NOT** (!), **OR** ($\vdots$), and **AND** (&&).

Finally, the C++ header files include several standard functions that can be used to perform common tasks. There are mathematical functions, conversion functions, and string functions, just to mention a few categories.

QUESTIONS AND PROBLEMS

Questions

1. What value will be returned for each of the following integer operations:
   a. 4 − 2 * 3
   b. −35 / 6
   c. −35 % 6
   d. −25 * 14 % 7 * −25 / −5
   e. −5 * 3 + 9 − 2 * 7
   f. (−13 / 2) % 6

2. Evaluate each of the following expressions:
   a. 0.5 + 3.75 / 0.25 * 2
   b. 2.5 − (1.2 + (4.0 − 3.0) * 2.0) + 1.0
   c. 6.0E−4 * 3.0E + 3
   d. 6.0E−4 / 3.0E + 3

3. Evaluate each of the following expressions:
   a. 5.0 − (6.0 / 3)
   b. 200 * 200
   c. 5 − 6 / 3
   d. (5 − 6) / 3
   e. 1 + 25 % 5
   f. −33000 + 2000

4. Evaluate each of the following expressions:

    a. int i = 0;
        int j = 10;
        ++i + j++;
    b. float k = 2.5;
        k-- * 2;
    c. char Character = 'a';
        ++Character;
    d. int x = 1;
        int y = -1;
        int z = 25;
        ++x + ++y - --z;

5. Evaluate each of the following relational operations:

    a. 7 != 7
    b. -0.75 <= -0.5
    c. 'm' > 'n'
    d. 2 * 5 % 3 - 7 < 16 / 4 + 2
    e. "Andy" == "Andy"
    f. strcmp("Andy","Andy")

6. Determine the output generated by the following:

    a. cout << ((2 % 5) / (5 % 2)) << endl;
    b. cout << (3 * 6 / 3 + 6) << endl;
    c. cout << ((3 * 6) / (3 + 6)) << endl;
    d. cout << (**NOT**(1 **OR** 0)) << endl;
    e. cout << ((2 - 5/2 * 3) <= (8 % 2 - 6)) << endl;
    f. int x = -7;
        int y = 3;
        cout << (**NOT**(3*x < 4*y) **AND** (5*x >= y)) << endl;
    g. cout << (3.5 **AND** 0) << endl;
    h. cout << (3.5 **OR** 2.0) << endl;

7. The ANSI C++ standard specifies the *exclusive OR*, **XOR** logic operation. The standard provides for the keyword **XOR** or an alternative caret, ^, symbol to be used as syntax for this operation. Given any two Boolean variables, *A* and *B*, here is how the **XOR** operation is defined:

A	*B*	*A* **XOR** *B*
true	true	false
true	false	true
false	true	true
false	false	false

Do you see a pattern in the table that gives a hint to how **XOR** works? Well, the **XOR** operation will always produce a true result if there is an odd number of true variables. Now for the question: Which of the following logical expressions will produce the **XOR** operation?

a. **NOT** *A* **OR NOT** *B*

b. (*A* **AND NOT** *B*) **OR** (**NOT** *A* **AND** *B*)

c. **NOT**(*A* **AND NOT** *B*) **OR** (**NOT** *A* **AND** *B*)

d. **NOT**(**NOT** *A* **AND NOT** *B*)

8. What standard logical operation is performed by the expression in question 7d?

9. Develop a truth table for the following logical expression:

NOT *A* **OR NOT** *B*

10. Which of the following is equivalent to the logic operation in question 9?

a. !(A && B)

b. !(A ¦¦ B)

c. !A && !B

d. None of these

11. Explain how to get information on how to use a standard function available in your compiler.

12. Determine the value returned by the following functions. Use your compiler reference manual or on-line help feature to make sure that you understand how the function operates.

a. abs(−5)

b. sin(1.57)

c. log(2.73)

d. log10(100)

e. pow(2,5)

f. pow10(3)

g. cos(0)

h. toascii(' ')

i. tolower('A')

j. strlen("C++")

13. Explain what happens as the result of executing the following functions:

a. strcpy(Name,"Brenda");

b. strcmp(Name1,Name2)

14. Prove or disprove via truth tables that

NOT A **AND NOT** B == **NOT**(A **AND** B)

Problems

Least Difficult

1. Write a program that will allow a user to convert a temperature in degrees Fahrenheit to degrees Centigrade using the following relationship:

$$C = 5/9 \times (F - 32)$$

2. Write a program that will allow a user to convert a measurement in inches to centimeters.

3. Write a simple test program that will demonstrate what happens when you use an illegal argument within a function. For example, what happens when you use a character argument in an arithmetic function?

4. Write a program that will allow a user to find the hypotenuse of a right triangle using the Pythagorean theorem. (*Hint:* Try using the *hypot()* function in the *math.h* header file.)

5. Write a program to solve the following equation for *x*:

$$3x - 5y + 2 = 35$$

Assume that values for *y* will be entered by the user.

6. Write a program to generate a truth table for a NOR operation. A NOR operation is a **NOT OR** operation. Thus,

$$A \text{ NOR } B = \textbf{NOT}(A \textbf{ OR } B)$$

Assume that logical values for *A* and *B* will be entered by the user.

More Difficult

7. Write a program to convert from rectangular to polar coordinates. Generate a tabular output of the rectangular versus polar coordinate.

8. The kinetic energy of a moving object is found using the equation

$$K = (1/2)(mv^2)$$

where

        K is the kinetic energy, in kgm/s.
        m is the mass, in kilograms.
        v is the velocity, in meters per second.

Write a program that accepts inputs of mass and velocity of an object and determines its kinetic energy.

9. Here is the inventory and price list of the Health and Beauty Aids department in Ma and Pa's General Store.

Item	Price
Grandma's Lye Soap	0.49
Bag Bahm	1.29
Chicken Soup	0.29
Liniment	2.35
Baking Soda	0.63

    Ma and Pa want to run a "big" sale and reduce all Health and Beauty Aid items by 5 percent. Write Ma and Pa a program that will print a listing of all the Health and Beauty Aid items showing the regular and sale price. Assume that Ma or Pa will enter the preceding price list.

10. Revise the program in problem 9 to allow Ma or Pa to enter any percentage sales discount.

Most Difficult

11. Revise the program in problem 9 to read the item names and prices from a disk file called "prices". Generate the report on your system monitor. (*Note*: You must create a "prices" text file with your editor that contains the item names and prices given in the table in problem 9.

12. Ma and Pa were so elated with the programs you have written so far that they want to expand their computer operations to the payroll department. Write Ma and Pa a payroll program that will calculate Herb's (their only employee) net pay given the following information:

    > Employee's name
    > Number of weekly hours worked
    > Hourly rate of pay
    > FICA (7.15%)
    > Federal withholding (16%)
    > State withholding (4.75%)

    Assume that Ma or Pa will only be required to enter the first three items when running the program. Generate a report using the following format:

Employee Name: XXXXXXXXXXXXXXXXXXXXXXX

Rate of Pay: $XXX.XX

Hours Worked: XX.XX

Gross Pay: $XXXX.XX

Deductions:

    FICA: $XXX.XX

    Fed. Withholding: XXX.XX

    State Withholding: XXX.XX

    Total Deductions: $XXX.XX

Net Pay: $XXXX.XX

13. The diagram in Figure 4-4 illustrates how triangulation is used to find the distance to an object. Here's the idea: Two triangulating devices are positioned a certain distance apart, and both devices get a "fix" on an object as shown in the figure. The two triangulating devices and the object form a triangle whose one leg, d, and two angles $\theta 1$ and $\theta 2$ are known. The third angle is easily found by subtracting the two known angles from 180 degrees. The distance from each triangulating device to the object is then found using the Law of Sines, which states

$$r_1 / \sin\theta_1 = r_2 / \sin\theta_2 = d / \sin[180 - (\theta_1 + \theta_2)]$$

Write a program to find the distance that the object is from each triangulation device. Assume that the user will enter the distance (d) between the devices and the two angles (θ_1 and θ_2) that the object makes with the triangulating devices.

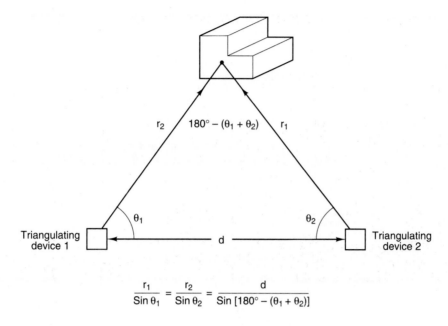

$$\frac{r_1}{Sin\ \theta_1} = \frac{r_2}{Sin\ \theta_2} = \frac{d}{Sin\ [180° - (\theta_1 + \theta_2)]}$$

Figure 4-4   A triangulation diagram for problem 12.

5

MAKING DECISIONS

INTRODUCTION
5-1 THE **if** STATEMENT
5-2 THE **if/else** STATEMENT
5-3 NESTED if's
5-4 THE **switch** STATEMENT
    The **default** Option
PROBLEM SOLVING IN ACTION: MENU-DRIVEN PROGRAMS
CHAPTER SUMMARY
QUESTIONS AND PROBLEMS
    Questions
    Problems

INTRODUCTION

As stated earlier, C++ is a structured programming language. As you will find out, structured programming languages, such as C++, make programs easier to write, check, read, document, and maintain. A major reason for this is the modularity feature of a structured programming language. *Program modularity* means that any program, no matter how complex, can be divided into simpler independent program modules. In fact, any complex program can be divided into modules that conform to one of three fundamental patterns called *control structures*. A control structure is simply a pattern for controlling the flow of a program module.

The three fundamental control structures of a structured programming language are *sequence*, *selection*, and *iteration*. The sequence control structure is illustrated in Figure 5-1. As you can see, there is nothing fancy about this control structure, because program statements are executed sequentially, one after another, in a straight-line fashion. This is called *straight-line programming* and is what you have been doing in C++ up to this point.

A *control structure* is a pattern for controlling the flow of a program module. The three fundamental control structures of a structured programming language are *sequence*, *selection*, and *iteration*.

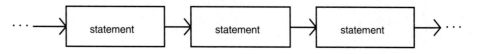

Figure 5-1 The sequence control structure is a series of sequential step-by-step statements.

The second two control structures, selection and iteration, allow the flow of the program to be altered, depending on one or more conditions. The selection control structure is a decision-making control structure. It is implemented in C++ using the **if**, **if/else**, and **switch** statements. These are the topics of this chapter. The iteration control structure is a looping control structure. It is implemented in C++ using the **while**, **do/while**, and **for** statements. These operations are discussed in the next chapter. Now, let's explore the selection control statements available in C++.

5-1 THE if STATEMENT

The operation of the **if** statement is illustrated by the diagram in Figure 5-2.

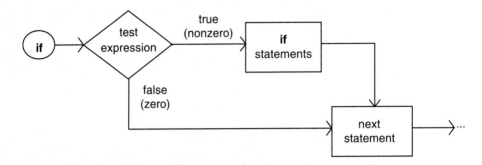

Figure 5-2   The flow of the **if** operation.

Observe that the flow of the program is altered, depending on the result of a test expression. The **if** test can be true (nonzero) or false (zero). Remember that C++ equates a nonzero value to true and a zero value to false during a test operation. If the test expression is true (nonzero), the **if** statements are executed. However, if the result of the test is false (zero), the **if** statements are bypassed and the program flow continues. This is known as a *selection*, or *decision-making*, operation, because the program selects, or decides, between one of two possible routes, depending on the conditions that are tested. In summary, the **if** operation can be stated in words like this: "If the test is true, execute the **if** statements." Of course, this implies that if the test is false, the **if** statements are not executed and are then bypassed.

Before we look at the C++ format for the **if** statement, let's take a closer look at the test expression. The test expression is a conditional test. This means that one or more conditions are tested to generate a true or false result. To test a single condition, you will use the relational Boolean operators of $==$, $!=$, $<$, $>$, $<=$, and $>=$. For instance, a typical test might be if ($x == y$). Here, the single condition, $x == y$, is tested. If x does in fact equal y, the result of the test is true, and the **if** statements will be executed. If x does not equal y, the **if** statements are bypassed, and the next sequential statement is executed.

To test multiple conditions, you must use the Boolean logical operators of **OR** and **AND**. For example, a test such as if (($x != y$) && ($a < b$)) tests two conditions. If x does not equal y *and* if a is less than b, the test result is true, and the **if** statements will be executed. On the other hand, if x equals y *or* if a is *greater than or equal to b*, then the **if** statements are bypassed.

DEBUGGING TIP

A common error when coding an "equals" test in an **if** statement is to use the assignment symbol, =, rather than the Boolean equals test symbol, ==. Thus, the statement **if** (x = y) will always cause a compiler error and must be corrected to **if** (x == y).

The C++ format for the **if** statement is as follows:

if STATEMENT FORMAT

```
if (test expression)
{
    statement 1;
    statement 2;
        •                        //COMPOUND STATEMENT
        •
        •
    statement n;
} //END IF
```

First, notice the overall structure of this format. The word **if** and its associated test expression are written on the first line of the statement. The word **if** is a keyword in C++. The test expression follows the **if** keyword and *must* be enclosed within parentheses. The first line is followed by the statements that will be executed if the test is true. This statement block is "framed" by curly braces. A left curly brace, {, signals the beginning of the statement block, and a right curly brace, }, denotes the end of the block. Notice that the beginning curly brace is placed on a separate line, directly below the keyword **if**. The ending curly brace is placed on a separate line, immediately after the last statement in the block and in the same column as the beginning brace. In addition, you should always indent all the block statements two or three spaces in from the curly braces for readability. When this structure is part of a complex program, there is no question which statements belong to the **if** operation.

If there is more than one statement to be executed within this block, the entire group of statements is referred to as a ***compound statement***. When a compound statement is encountered within a C++ program, the entire group of

statements is treated like a single statement. Compound statements must always be
framed with curly braces. However, framing is optional when there is only a single
statement within the block.

Finally, look at the punctuation syntax of the **if** statement. Notice that there
is no semicolon after the test expression in the first line. However, each statement
within the statement block is terminated by a semicolon.

It's probably a good idea to look at some example exercises and programs at
this time to get a "feel" for the **if** operation.

Example 5-1

Determine the output for each of the following program segments. Assume that *x*
and *y* have the following assignments prior to the execution of each **if** operation:

```
x = 2;
y = 3;
```

a. if (x < y)
    {
       cout << "x = " << x << endl;
       cout << "y = " << y << endl;
    }//END IF

b. if (x)
         cout << "The value of x is nonzero." << endl;

c. if (x < y)
    {
       Temp = y;
       y = x;
       x = Temp;
       cout << "x = " << x << endl;
       cout << "y = " << y << endl;
    }//END IF

d. if ((x < y) && (y != 10))
    {
       Sum = x + y;
       cout << "x = " << x << endl;
       cout << "y = " << y << endl;
       cout << "Sum = " << Sum << endl;
    }//END IF

e. if ((x > y) || (x - y < 0))
    {
       ++x;
       --y;
       cout << "x = " << x << endl;
       cout << "y = " << y << endl;
    }//END IF

f. if ((x > y) ¦¦ (x * y < 0))
    {
        ++x;
        --y;
        cout << "x = " << x << endl;
        cout << "y = " << y << endl;
    }//END IF
    cout << "x = " << x << endl;
    cout << "y = " << y << endl;
g. if (x % y == 0)
        cout << "x is divisible by y." << endl;
        cout << "x is not divisible by y." << endl;

Solution

a. The value of *x* is less than the value of *y*. Thus, the output is

    x = 2
    y = 3

b. Here, the test is on the value of *x*. If *x* is zero, the test is false, If *x* is nonzero, the test is true. Because *x* is a nonzero value, the test is true and the *cout* statement is executed, producing an output of

    The value of x is nonzero.

c. The value of *x* is less than *y*, so the compound statement is executed and the output is

    x = 3
    y = 2

    Notice that the values of *x* and *y* have been swapped using a temporary variable called *Temp*. Why is this temporary variable required?

d. The value of *x* is less than *y* *and* the value of *y* is not equal to 10. As a result, the two values are added and the output is

    x = 2
    y = 3
    Sum = 5

e. Here, the value of *x* is not greater than the value of *y*, but *x* − *y* is less than 0. Thus, the test result due to the **OR** operator is true, and the compound statement is executed, resulting in an output of

    x = 3
    y = 2

    Notice that the compound statement increments *x* and decrements *y*.

f. This time the test is false. Thus, the compound statement is bypassed. As a result, the values of *x* and *y* remain unchanged, and the output is

```
x = 2
y = 3
```

g. This is a tricky one. Here, the test is false, because *y* does not divide evenly into *x*. So, what happens? There are no curly braces framing the block, so the compiler takes only the first *cout* statement to be the **if** statement. As a result, the first *cout* statement is bypassed, and the second one is executed to produce an output of

```
x is not divisible by y.
```

   What would happen if the test expression were true? In this case, both *cout* statements would be executed, generating an output of

```
x is divisible by y.
x is not divisible by y.
```

But, this logic doesn't make sense. You want only one of the *cout* statements executed, not both. To solve this dilemma, we need a different decision control structure called the **if/else** control structure. The **if/else** control structure is discussed next.

 Quick Check

1. True or false: A test expression that evaluates to any nonzero value is considered true.

2. True or false: When a test expression in an **if** statement evaluates to zero, the related **if** statements are bypassed.

3. What is wrong with the following **if** statement?
   ```
   if (x = y)
       cout << "There is a problem here" << endl;
   ```

4. What Boolean operator must be employed to test if two conditions are true?

5. What Boolean operator(s) must be employed to test if one of two conditions is false?

6. What Boolean operator must be employed to test if one of two conditions is true?

7. For what values of *x* will the *cout* statement in the following code be executed?

```
if(!x)
    cout << "Hello" << endl;
```

5-2 THE if/else STATEMENT

The operation of the **if/else** statement is illustrated by the diagram in Figure 5-3. Here, you see that there are two sets of statements that can be executed, depending on whether the test expression is true or false. If the test result is true, the **if** statements are executed. Conversely, if the test result is false, the **else** statements are executed. In words, "If the test expression is true, then execute the **if** statements; otherwise, execute the **else** statements." In C++, an equivalent statement would be "If the test expression evaluates to a nonzero value (true), execute the **if** statements; otherwise, execute the **else** statements." As compared to the **if** operation, you could say **if/else** is a two-way selection process, and **if** is a one-way selection process.

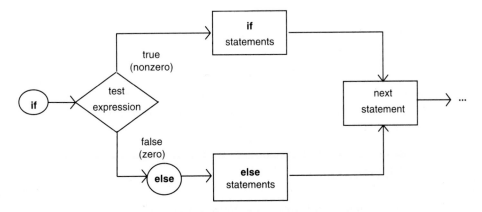

Figure 5-3 The flow of the **if/else** operation.

The C++ format for the **if/else** operation is as follows:

if/else *STATEMENT FORMAT*

```
if (test expression)
{
   statement 1;
   statement 2;
       •
       •
       •
   statement n;
} //END IF
else
{
   statement 1;
   statement 2;
       •
       •
       •
   statement n;
} //END ELSE
```

As you can see, the **else** option is included after the **if** option. If the test expression is true, the **if** statements are executed, and the **else** statements are ignored. However, if the test expression is false, the **if** statements are ignored, and the **else** statements are executed.

A few words about syntax: First, observe that both the **if** and **else** statements are "framed" using curly braces. However, you can eliminate the curly braces in either section when only a single statement is required. Second, notice the indentation scheme. Again, such a scheme makes your programs self-documenting and readable.

DEBUGGING TIP

Always remember to frame your **if/else** statements with curly braces, { }, when you have more than one statement to execute. If the braces are missing, only the first statement will execute. This could cause a logic error that is very difficult to find. For example, consider the following:

```
if (x < y)
    --x;
    cout << "x is less than y" << endl;
else
    cout << "x is greater than or equal to y" << endl;
```

Here, the compiler "sees" three separate statements, one of them illegal. The first statement is the **if** statement that decrements the value of *x* if the test is true. The second statement is a *cout* statement. Even though this statement is indented under the **if**, the compiler does *not* consider it to be part of the **if** statement, because it is not framed as part of the **if**. The only statement that the compiler recognizes as part of the **if** is the −−*x* statement. This is a logic error and would not be caught by the compiler. Finally, the **else** is all by itself and, therefore, is referred to as a *dangling*, or *misplaced*, **else**. An **else** must *always* be associated with a corresponding **if**. This is a syntax error and would be caught by the compiler.

Example 5-2

Determine when the **if** statements will be executed and when the **else** statements will be executed in each of the following program segments.

```
a.  if (x < y)
        Sum = x + y;
    else
        Difference = x - y;
b.  if (x)
        Sum = x + y;
    else
        Difference = x - y;
c.  if (!x)
        Sum = x + y;
    else
        Difference = x - y;
d.  if ((x < y) && (2*x - y == 0))
        Sum = x + y;
    else
        Difference = x - y;
e.  if ((x < y) || (2*x - y == 0))
        Sum = x + y;
    else
        Difference = x - y;
```

f. if (x > 2*y)
        Sum = x + y;
        Product = x * y;
    else
        Difference = x – y;

Solution

a. The **if** statement is executed when *x* is less than *y*, and the **else** statement is executed when *x* is greater than or equal to *y*. Remember, the opposite of less than is greater than *or equal to*.

b. The **if** statement is executed when *x* is nonzero, because a nonzero value in C++ is interpreted as true when tested for a Boolean condition. The **else** statement is executed when the value of *x* is zero, because a value of zero is interpreted as false.

c. This segment uses the opposite logic of the segment in part b, because of the ! (**NOT**) operator. As a result, the **if** statement is executed when *x* is zero, or false, and the **else** statement is executed when *x* is nonzero, or true.

d. This segment employs the Boolean **AND** (&&) operator. Here, the **if** statement is executed when the value of *x* is less than the value of *y and* the value of $2x - y$ is equal to zero. The **else** statement is executed when the value of *x* is *greater than or equal to* the value of *y or* the value of $2x - y$ is not equal to zero.

e. This segment employs the Boolean **OR** (¦¦) operator. Here, the **if** statement is executed when the value of *x* is less than the value of *y or* the value of $2x - y$ is equal to zero. The **else** statement is executed when the value of *x* is *greater than or equal to* the value of *y and* the value of $2x - y$ is not equal to zero.

f. This segment of code will not compile because of a dangling, or misplaced, **else**. The **if** statements must be framed in order for the segment to compile. When the **if** statements are framed, they will be executed when the value of *x* is greater than the value of 2*y*. The **else** statement will execute when the value of *x* is *less than or equal to* the value of 2*y*.

 Quick Check

1. True or false: When the test expression in an **if/else** operation evaluates to zero, the **else** statements are executed.

2. Why does the following pseudocode need an **else** statement?
   If Day == Friday
       Write("It's pay day")
   Write("It's not pay day")
3. True or false: Framing with curly braces can be eliminated when an **if** or **else** statement section only has a single statement.

5-3 NESTED if's

Up to this point, you have witnessed one-way and two-way decisions using the **if** and **if/else** statements, respectively. You can achieve additional selection options by using nested **if** statements. A nested **if** statement is simply an **if** statement within an **if** statement. To illustrate this idea, consider the diagram in Figure 5-4.

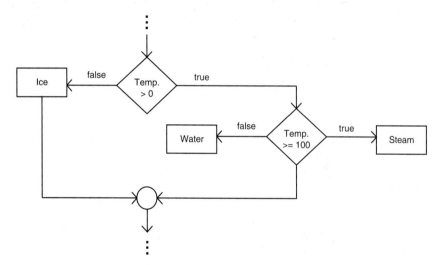

Figure 5-4 A nested **if** operation.

Here, a temperature is being tested to see if it is within a range of 0 to 100 degrees Celsius. If it is within this range, you get water. However, if it is outside the range, you get steam or ice, depending on whether it is above or below the range, respectively.

Let's follow through the diagram. The first test-expression operation checks to see if the temperature is greater than 0 degrees. If the test result is false, the temperature must be less than or equal to 0 degrees, resulting in ice. However, if the test result is true, a second test is made to see if the temperature is greater than or equal to 100 degrees. If this test result is true, you get steam. However, if this second test result is false, you know that the temperature must be somewhere between 0 degrees and 100 degrees, resulting in water. Notice how the second test is "nested" within the first test. The first test result must be true before the second test is performed.

Let's develop a program to implement the nested decision-making operation illustrated in Figure 5-4. We begin with the problem definition.

Defining the Problem

Output: The word "WATER", "STEAM", or "ICE".

Input: Temperature in degrees Celsius from the user keyboard.

Processing: Determine if the temperature constitutes water, steam, or ice.

Now for the algorithm. Here is one that will work:

Planning the Solution

```
BEGIN
    Write a program description message.
    Write a user prompt to enter the Temperature in degrees Celsius.
    Read (Temperature).
    If Temperature  >  0
      If Temperature  >= 100
         Write "STEAM."
      Else
         Write "WATER."
    Else
      Write "ICE."
END.
```

This algorithm is constructed by simply following the diagram in Figure 5-4. Notice how the second **if/else** operation is nested within the first **if/else** operation. If the *Temperature* is not greater than 0 degrees, the nested **if** operation is not performed. However, if the *Temperature* is greater than 0, the nested **if** operation is performed to see if the *Temperature* results in steam or water.

To code the program, you simply follow the algorithm, like this:

Coding the Program

```
//OUTPUT:            DISPLAY THE WORD "STEAM", "ICE", OR "WATER",
//                   DEPENDING ON TEMPERATURE TO BE ENTERED
//                   BY THE USER.

//INPUT:             A CELSIUS TEMPERATURE FROM THE USER.

//PROCESSING:        TEST TEMPERATURE VALUE AGAINST
//                   A RANGE OF 0 TO 100 DEGREES CELSIUS.

#include <iostream.h>   //FOR cin AND cout

void main()
{
//DEFINE VARIABLE
   float Temperature = 0.0;       //TEMPERATURE VALUE FROM USER

//DISPLAY PROGRAM DESCRIPTION MESSAGE TO USER
   cout <<  "This program will evaluate a temperature to see if\n"
            "it produces ice, water, or steam. " << endl << endl;

//GET THE TEMPERATURE FROM USER
   cout << "Enter a temperature in degrees Celsius:" << endl;
   cin >> Temperature;

//TEST IF TEMPERATURE IS  WATER, STEAM, OR ICE
   if (Temperature > 0)
        if (Temperature >= 100)
                cout << "STEAM" << endl;
        else
                cout << "WATER" << endl;
   else
        cout << "ICE" << endl;
} //END main()
```

Notice how the program flow can be seen by the indentation scheme. However, you do not see any curly brace pairs framing the **if** or **else** blocks. Remember that you do not need to frame a code block when it consists of only a single statement. But, you say that the first **if** block looks as if it consists of several statements. Well, the first **if** block contains a single **if/else** statement. Because the compiler sees this as a single statement, it does not need to be framed. Of course, if you are in doubt, it does no harm to frame the block, like this:

```
if (Temperature > 0)
{
    if (Temperature >= 100)
        cout << "STEAM" << endl;
    else
        cout << "WATER" << endl;
} //END IF TEMP > 0
else
    cout << "ICE" << endl;
```

PROGRAMMING NOTE

There are different ways to construct nested **if/else** logic. For example, some might see the algorithm logic as follows:

```
If Temperature <= 0
    Write "ICE"
Else
    If Temperature >= 100
        Write "STEAM."
    Else
        Write "WATER."
```

Here you see the inner **if/else** operation nested inside of the outer **else** operation. This logic will also accomplish the required decision task. Both methods are correct and adhere to good programming style. We will refer to this method as the **if-else-if-else** form and the earlier method as the **if-if-else-else** form. It's simply a matter of personal choice and how you view the logic of the problem. In general, the **if-else-if-else** form should be used when a number of *different* conditions need to be satisfied before a given action can occur, and the **if-if-else-else** form should be used when the *same* variable is being tested for different values and a different action is taken for each value. This latter reason is why I first chose to use the **if-if-else-else** form. Notice also that indentation is extremely important to determine the nested logic.

Example 5-3

Determine when "Red", "White", and "Blue" will be written in each of the following program segments.

```
a.  if (x < y)
        if (x == 0)
            cout << "Red" << endl;
        else
            cout << "White" << endl;
    else
        cout << "Blue" << endl;


b.  if (x >= y)
        cout << "Blue" << endl;
    else
        if (x == 0)
            cout << "Red" << endl;
        else
            cout << "White" << endl;


c.  if ((x < y) && (x == 0))
        cout << "Red" << endl;
    if ((x < y) && (x != 0))
        cout << "White" << endl;
    if (x >= y)
        cout << "Blue" << endl;
```

Solution

All three segments of code will produce the same results. "Red" will be written when the value of *x* is less than the value of *y* and the value of *x* is zero. "White" will be written when the value of *x* is less than the value of *y* and the value of *x* is not equal to zero. "Blue" will be written when the value of *x* is greater than or equal to the value of *y*, regardless of whether or not the value of *x* is zero. Desk-check the logic of each code segment to verify that they all produce the same results.

Example 5-4

Convert the following series of **if** statements to nested **if/else** statements using the **if-else-if-else** form and the **if-if-else-else** form.

```
if (Year == 1)
    cout << "Freshman" << endl;
if (Year == 2)
    cout << "Sophomore" << endl;
if (Year == 3)
    cout << "Junior" << endl;
```

```
if (Year == 4)
   cout << "Senior" << endl;
if (Year > 4)
   cout << "Graduate" << endl;
```

Solution

a. To convert to the **if-else-if-else** form, we use the logic that if the year is greater than 4, then we know to write "Graduate"; else we test to see if the year is greater than 3. If the year was not greater than 4 but is greater than 3, its value must be 4, so we write "Senior"; else we test to see if the year is greater than 2. If it passes this test, you know that the year was not greater than 4 and not greater than 3 but is greater than 2, so its value must be 3, and we write "Junior". We continue this logic to produce "Sophomore" and "Freshman" for year values of 2 and 1, respectively. Here's the resulting code:

```
if (Year > 4)
   cout << "Graduate" << endl;
else
   if (Year > 3)
      cout << "Senior" << endl;
   else
      if (Year > 2)
         cout << "Junior" << endl;
      else
         if (Year > 1)
            cout << "Sophomore" << endl;
         else
            cout << "Freshman" << endl;
```

b. To convert to the **if-if-else-else** form, we use the logic that if the year is greater than 1, we test to see if the year is greater than 2, then 3, then 4. If it passes all of these tests, we know to write "Graduate". However, if the year was not greater than 1 in the first test, we know to write "Freshman", which forms the **else** part of the first **if** test. Next, if the year is greater than 1, but fails the second **if** test (>2), we know to write "Sophomore", which forms the **else** part of the second **if** test. This logic continues to produce "Junior" and "Senior" for year values of 3 and 4, respectively. Here's the resulting code:

```
if (Year > 1)
   if (Year > 2)
      if (Year > 3)
         if (Year > 4)
            cout << "Graduate" << endl;
         else
            cout << "Senior" << endl;
      else
```

```
        cout << "Junior" << endl;
    else
        cout << "Sophomore" << endl;
    else
        cout << "Freshman" << endl;
```

 Quick Check

1. Explain why indentation is important when operations are nested.

2. True or False: Any given **else** always goes with the closest **if**.

Consider the following pseudocode to answer questions 3 – 6:

```
    If Value < 50
        If Value > –50
            Write ("Red")
        else
            Write ("White")
    else
        Write ("Blue")
```

3. What range of values will cause "Red" to be written?

4. What range of values will cause "White" to be written?

5. What range of values will cause "Blue" to be written?

6. Convert the **if-if-else-else** logic to **if-else-if-else** logic.

5-4 THE switch STATEMENT

This last category of selection enables the program to select one of many options, or *cases*. The operation of the **switch** statement is illustrated by the diagram in Figure 5-5. The selection of a particular case is controlled by a matching process. A *selector* variable is first evaluated to produce a value. The selector value is then compared to a series of cases. If the selector value matches one of the case values, the corresponding case statements are executed. If no match is made, the program simply continues in a straight-line fashion, with the first statement following the **switch** statement.

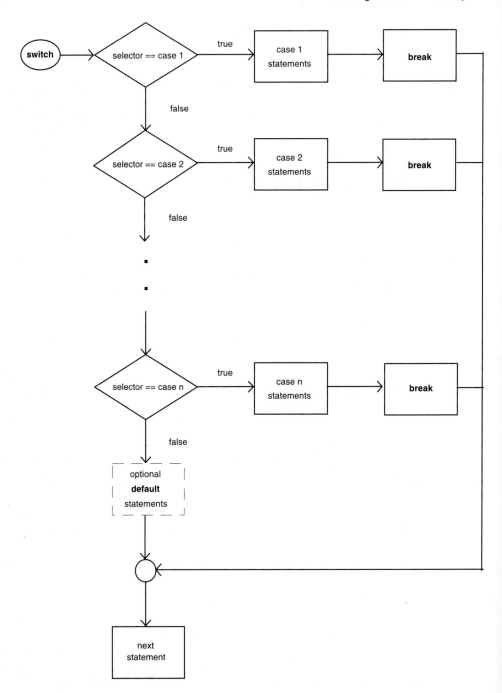

Figure 5-5   The flow of the **switch** operation.

Here's the C++ format for **switch**:

---

switch *STATEMENT FORMAT*

switch (selector variable)
{
   case case 1 value : case 1 statements;
                            break;
   case case 2 value : case 2 statements;
                            break;
                    •
                    •
                    •
   case case n value : case n statements;
                            break;
} //END SWITCH

The format requires the selector variable to follow the keyword **switch.** The selector variable must be enclosed within parentheses and must be an integral data class. By an *integral data class*, I mean a data class that is stored as an integer. This basically means that the selector variable must be defined as either an integer or a character object. Defining the selector variable as a floating-point or character string object will cause a compile error.

DEBUGGING TIP

When coding a **switch** statement, the selector variable and case values must be the same data class. Only the integral data classes (integer or character) are allowed. Any other data class will cause a compiler error.

The **switch** syntax requires the use of curly braces to open and close the **switch** block of **case** statements as shown. The **switch** block is comprised of several cases that are identified using the keyword **case**. An integral case value must be supplied with each case for matching purposes. The **switch** statement attempts to match the value of the selector variable to a given case value. If a match occurs, the corresponding **case** statements are executed. Note that a colon separates the case value from the **case** statements. A given **case** statement block can be any number of statements in length and does not require framing with curly braces. However, the keyword **break** is often inserted as the last statement in a given **case** statement block. If **break** is not used, any subsequent **cases** will be executed after a given **case** match has occurred until a **break** is encountered. This may be desirable at times, especially when multiple **case** values are to "fire" a given set of **case** statements. Again, the idea behind the **switch** statement is easy, if you simply think of it as a matching operation. Some examples should demonstrate this idea.

Suppose the selector variable is the letter grade you made on your last quiz. Assuming that the variable *LetterGrade* is defined as a character variable, a typical **switch** statement might go something like this:

```
switch (LetterGrade)
{
   case 'A' :  cout << "Excellent" << endl;
            break;
   case 'B' :  cout << "Superior" << endl;
            break;
   case 'C' :  cout << "Average" << endl;
            break;
   case 'D' :  cout << "Poor" << endl;
            break;
   case 'F' :  cout << "Try again" << endl;
            break;
} //END SWITCH
```

Here, the selector variable is *LetterGrade*. The case values are 'A', 'B', 'C', 'D', and 'F'. The value of the selector variable is compared to the list of case values. If a match is found, the corresponding **case** statements are executed. For instance, if the value of *LetterGrade* is 'B', the code generates an output of

Superior

Now, suppose you leave out the keyword **break** in each of the previous cases, like this:

```
switch (LetterGrade)
{
   case 'A' : cout << "Excellent" << endl;
   case 'B' : cout << "Superior" << endl;
   case 'C' : cout << "Average" << endl;
   case 'D' : cout << "Poor" << endl;
   case 'F' : cout << "Try again" << endl;
} //END SWITCH
```

This time, assuming that *LetterGrade* has the value 'B', the code generates an output of

Superior
Average
Poor
Try Again

As you can see from the output, case 'B' was matched and its **case** statement executed. However, all of the **case** statements subsequent to case 'B' were also executed. Surely, you can see the value of using **break** in this application.

Are there times where you might want to eliminate the **break** command? Of course! Consider the following **switch** statement:

```
switch (LetterGrade)
{
  case 'a' :
  case 'A' : cout << "Excellent" << endl;
          break;
  case 'b' :
  case 'B' : cout << "Superior" << endl;
          break;
  case 'c' :
  case 'C' : cout << "Average" << endl;
          break;
  case 'd' :
  case 'D' : cout << "Poor" << endl;
          break;
  case 'f' :
  case 'F' : cout << "Try again" << endl;
          break;
} //END SWITCH
```

Here, multiple case values need to fire the same **case** statement. So, if *LetterGrade* has the value 'b', then a match is made with case 'b'. No **break** is part of this case, so the next sequential case is executed, which will write the word "Superior". Because case 'B' contains a **break**, the **switch** statement is terminated after the output is generated.

What happens if no match occurs? As you might suspect, all the cases are bypassed, and the next sequential statement appearing after the **switch** closing brace is executed.

The default Option

The last thing we need to discuss is the use of the **default** option within a **switch** statement. The **default** option is normally employed at the end of a **switch** statement, like this:

default *OPTION FORMAT*

```
switch (selector variable)
{
    case  case 1 value : case 1 statements;
                        break;
    case  case 2 value : case 2 statements;
                        break;
                    •
                    •
                    •
    case  case n value : case n statements;
                        break;
    default: default statements;

} //END SWITCH
```

The **default** option allows a series of statements to be executed if no match occurs within the **switch**. On the other hand, if a match does occur, the **default** statements are skipped. This provides a valuable protection feature within your program. For instance, suppose that you ask the user to enter a letter grade to be used in a **switch** statement. But, what if the user presses the wrong key and enters a character that is not a valid case value. Well, you can use the **default** option to protect against such invalid entries, like this:

```
switch (LetterGrade)
{
    case 'a' :
    case 'A' : cout << "Excellent" << endl;
            break;
    case 'b' :
    case 'B' : cout << "Superior" << endl;
            break;
    case 'c' :
```

```
      case 'C' : cout << "Average" << endl;
               break;
      case 'd' :
      case 'D' : cout << "Poor" << endl;
               break;
      case 'f' :
      case 'F' : cout << "Try again" << endl;
               break;
      default  : cout << "No match was found for the ENTRY "
                      << LetterGrade << endl;
} //END SWITCH
```

Here, the **default** statement is executed if *LetterGrade* is anything other than the listed case characters. For example, if the user entered the character 'x' for *LetterGrade*, the foregoing **switch** statement would produce an output of

No match was found for the ENTRY x

You will find that the **default** option in the **switch** statement is extremely useful when displaying menus for user entries.

Example 5-5

A **switch** statement is simply a convenient way to code a series of **if** statements. Convert the following series of **if** statements to a single **switch** statement that employs the **default** option.

```
if (Year == 1)
   cout << "Freshman" << endl;
if (Year == 2)
   cout << "Sophomore" << endl;
if (Year == 3)
   cout << "Junior" << endl;
if (Year == 4)
   cout << "Senior" << endl;
else
   cout << "Graduate" << endl;
```

Solution

All that needs to be done to convert a series of **if** statements to a single **switch** statement is to use the **if** test variable as the selector variable and the **if** test values as cases within the **switch**. Here's the converted code:

```
switch (Year)
{
   case 1: cout << "Freshman" << endl;
         break;
```

```
    case 2: cout << "Sophomore" << endl;
            break;
    case 3: cout << "Junior" << endl;
            break;
    case 4: cout << "Senior" << endl;
            break;
    default: cout << "Graduate" << endl;
}//END SWITCH
```

Notice how the **default** option is used to write "Graduate". You know to write "Graduate" if no match is made to the previous four cases, right? So, the **else** part of the last **if** test is converted to the **default** in the **switch** statement.

Quick Check

1. The selection of a particular case in a **switch** statement is controlled by a _____ process.

2. Suppose that you have *n* cases in a switch statement and there are no **break** statements in any of the cases. What will happen when a match is made on the first case?

3. True or false: There are never any times when a case should not contain a break statement.

4. A statement that can be inserted at the end of a **switch** statement to protect against invalid entries is the _____ statement.

5. A common application for a **switch** statement is _____.

PROBLEM SOLVING IN ACTION: MENU-DRIVEN PROGRAMS

Problem

The **switch** statement is often used to create menu-driven programs. I'm sure you have seen a menu-driven program. It's one that asks you to select different options during the execution of the program. For instance, suppose you must write a menu-driven program that will allow the user to calculate dc voltage, current, or resistance. By Ohm's law (*Voltage = Current × Resistance*), you know that any one of these can be found by knowing the other two.

Defining the Problem

Output: A program menu that prompts the user to select a voltage, current, or resistance calculation option.
Invalid entry messages as required.
A voltage, current, or resistance value, depending on the program option that the user selects.

Input: A user response to the menu (V, I, R, or Q).
If V is selected: User enters values for current and resistance.
If I is selected: User enters values for voltage and resistance.
If R is selected: User enters values for voltage and current.
If Q is selected: Terminate program.

Processing: Calculate the selected option.
Case V: *Voltage = Current × Resistance*.
Case I: *Current = Voltage / Resistance*.
Case R: *Resistance = Voltage / Current*.
Case Q: Terminate program.

Planning the Solution

Using structured program design, we will divide the problem into individual subproblems to solve the overall problem. There are two major tasks that follow directly from the problem definition:

- Display the menu and read the user choice.
- Perform the chosen calculation and display the results.

First, the program must display a menu of choices to the user. The user will enter his/her choice from the menu, and, depending on this choice, one of three calculations will be made to determine the required quantity. The structure diagram in Figure 5-6 illustrates the top/down design.

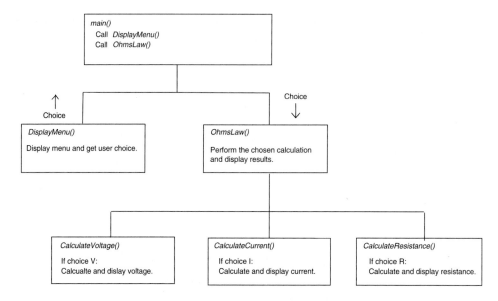

Figure 5-6   A structure diagram for the Ohm's law problem.

Notice that there are now three levels to solving the problem. At the first level, *main()*, a function is called to display the menu and get the user choice. The *DiplayMenu()* function accomplishes this task and *sends* the user choice back to *main()* as indicated on the diagram. Function *main()* will then send the choice to a function called *OhmsLaw()*, which will call one of three functions, depending on the choice, to perform the required calculation. This is the first time you have seen the *passing* of data between functions. This concept is central to structured program design. From the structure diagram you see that the user choice, *Choice*, is *passed* from the *DisplayMenu()* function back to its calling function, *main()*. Then, when *main()* calls the *OhmsLaw()* function, *Choice* is passed from *main()* to *OhmsLaw()*. The *OhmsLaw()* function will then use *Choice* to determine which calculation function to call. The initial algorithm reflects *main()*, which is used to call the *DisplayMenu()* and *OhmsLaw()* functions, as follows:

Initial Algorithm

    main()
    BEGIN
        Call *DisplayMenu()* function.
        Call *OhmsLaw()* function.
    END.

The first level of refinement shows the contents of the *DisplayMenu( )* and *OhmsLaw( )* functions, as follows:

First Level of Refinement

DiplayMenu( )
BEGIN
    Display a program menu that prompts the user to choose a voltage (V), current (I), resistance (R), or quit (Q) option.
    Read (*Choice*).
END.

OhmsLaw( )
BEGIN
    Case V: Call function *CalculateVoltage( )*.
    Case I: Call function *CalculateCurrent( )*.
    Case R: Call function *CalculateResistance( )*.
    Case Q: Terminate program.
    Default: Write an invalid entry message and ask the user to select again.
END.

Notice that the *DisplayMenu( )* function simply diplays the menu and gets the user's choice. The *OhmLaw( )* function calls the required calculation function, depending on the user's choice. In addition, the *OhmsLaw( )* function terminates the program if the user chooses to quit and writes an invalid entry message if the user's choice does not reflect one of the choice options.

Now, we need a second level of refinement to show the contents of the calculation functions. Here it is:

Second Level of Refinement

CalculateVoltage( )
BEGIN
    Write a user prompt to enter a current value.
    Read (*Current*).
    Write a user prompt to enter a resistance value.
    Read (*Resistance*).
    If *Resistance* < 0
        Write an invalid entry message and ask the user to run the program again.

  Else
    Calculate *Voltage = Current × Resistance.*
    Write *(Voltage)*.
 END.

CalculateCurrent( )
BEGIN
 Write a user prompt to enter a voltage value.
 Read *(Voltage)*.
 Write a user prompt to enter a resistance value.
 Read *(Resistance)*.
 If *Resistance* < = 0 then
    Write an invalid entry message and ask the user to run the program
    again.
 Else
    Calculate *Current = Voltage / Resistance.*
    Write *(Current)*.
 END.

CalculateResistance( )
BEGIN
 Write a user prompt to enter a voltage value.
 Read *(Voltage)*.
 Write a user prompt to enter a current value.
 Read *(Current)*.
 If *Current* == 0
    Write an invalid entry message and ask the user to run the program
    again.
 Else
    Calculate *Resistance = Voltage / Current.*
    Write *(Resistance)*.
 END.

   Each calculation function obtains the data required for the respective calculation by Ohm's law. The function makes the calculation and displays the result. Taking a closer look at these algorithms, you find several protection features. The **if/else** statements within each function protect against invalid data entries. A negative resistance value is invalid, because there is no such thing as negative resistance. In addition, you cannot divide by 0. As a result, the

CalculateCurrent() and *CalculateResistance()* functions each check for zero entries for the value to be used as the divisor in the Ohm's law calculation.

Coding the Program

At this time, we will code the solution using a flat implementation. However, remember what you have learned here, because in Chapter 7 we will employ structured programming to modularize the coded solution into the functions. Here is the flat implementation of the foregoing program design:

```
//ACTION 5-1 (ACT05-01.CPP)

//OUTPUT:      A PROGRAM MENU THAT PROMPTS THE USER
//             TO SELECT A VOLTAGE, CURRENT,
//             OR RESISTANCE CALCULATION OPTION.
//             INVALID ENTRY MESSAGES AS REQUIRED.
//             A VOLTAGE, CURRENT, OR RESISTANCE
//             VALUE, DEPENDING ON THE PROGRAM OPTION THAT
//             THE USER SELECTS.

//INPUT:       A USER RESPONSE TO THE MENU (V, I, R, OR Q).
//             IF V IS SELECTED: USER ENTERS VALUES
//             FOR CURRENT AND RESISTANCE.
//             IF I IS SELECTED: USER ENTERS VALUES
//             FOR VOLTAGE AND RESISTANCE.
//             IF R IS SELECTED: USER ENTERS VALUES
//             FOR VOLTAGE AND CURRENT.
//             IF Q IS SELECTED: TERMINATE PROGRAM

//PROCESSING: CALCULATE THE SELECTED OPTION.
//                 CASE V:    VOLTAGE = CURRENT X RESISTANCE.
//                 CASE I:    CURRENT = VOLTAGE / RESISTANCE.
//                 CASE R:    RESISTANCE = VOLTAGE / CURRENT.
//                 CASE Q:    TERMINATE THE PROGRAM

#include <iostream.h>   //FOR cin AND cout

void main()
{
//DEFINE VARIABLES
  char Choice = 'Q';              //USER MENU ENTRY
  float Voltage = 0.0;           //VOLTAGE IN VOLTS
```

```
      float Current = 0.0;              //CURRENT IN MILLIAMPERES
      float Resistance = 0.0;           //RESISTANCE IN KILOHMS

   //DISPLAY PROGRAM DESCRIPTION MESSAGE
      cout << "This program will calculate dc voltage, current, or\n"
              "resistance given the other two values. " << endl << endl;

   //DisplayMenu() FUNCTION
      cout  << "\n\n\t\t\tEnter V to find voltage" << endl << endl
            << "\t\t\tEnter I to find current" << endl << endl
            << "\t\t\tEnter R to find resistance" << endl << endl
            << "\t\t\tEnter Q to quit" << endl << endl
            << "\tPlease enter your choice:  ";
      cin >> Choice;

   //SET OUTPUT PRECISION
      cout.setf(ios::fixed);
      cout.precision(2);

   //OhmsLaw() FUNCTION
      switch (Choice)
      {
        case 'v':  //CalculateVoltage() FUNCTION
        case 'V' : cout << "\nEnter the current value in milliamperes\tI = ";
                   cin >> Current;
                   cout << "\nEnter the resistance value in kilohms\tR = ";
                   cin >> Resistance;
                   if (Resistance < 0)
                      cout << "\n\nThis is an invalid entry. Please
                              " run the program again." << endl;
                   else
                   {
                      Voltage = Current * Resistance;
                      cout << "\n\nThe voltage value is  " << Voltage
                           << " volts." << endl;
                   }//END ELSE
                   break;

        case 'i':  //CalculateCurrent() FUNCTION
        case 'I' : cout << "\nEnter the voltage value in volts\tV = ";
                   cin >> Voltage;
                   cout << "\nEnter the resistance value in kilohms\tR = ";
                   cin >> Resistance;
```

```
                    if (Resistance <= 0)
                       cout << "\n\nThis is an invalid entry. Please"
                                  " run the program again." << endl;
                    else
                    {
                       Current = Voltage / Resistance;
                       cout << "\n\nThe current value is  "
                            << Current<< " milliamperes." << endl;
                    }//END ELSE
                    break;

        case 'r':   //CalculateResistance() FUNCTION
        case 'R' :  cout << "\nEnter the voltage value in volts\tV = ";
                    cin >> Voltage;
                    cout << "\nEnter the current value in milliamperes\tI = ";
                    cin >> Current;
                    if (Current == 0)
                       cout << "\n\nThis is an invalid entry. Please"
                                  " run the program again." << endl;
                    else
                    {
                       Resistance = Voltage / Current;
                       cout << "\n\nThe resistance value is  " << Resistance
                            << " kilohms." << endl;
                    }//END ELSE
                    break;

        case 'q':   //TERMINATE PROGRAM
        case 'Q':   cout << "Program terminated" << endl;
                    break;
                    //DISPLAY INVALID ENTRY MESSAGE
        default :   cout << "\n\nThis is an invalid entry. Please"
                                  " run the program again." << endl;

   } //END SWITCH
} //END main()
```

First, notice how the functions from our structured design are embedded into this flat implementation. The comments show the location of our functions. Now look at the program closely, and you will find that it incorporates most of the things that you have learned in this chapter. In general, you will find a **switch** statement that contains a **default** option. In addition, notice the **if/else** statements embedded within each **case**. In particular, you should observe the beginnings and endings of the various sections, along with the associated indentation and commenting scheme. As you can see, the program is very readable and self-documenting.

Now for the details. There are eight cases, two for each user-selected option. Notice that the first case in each option allows the user to enter a lowercase character. These cases do not have a **break** statement and, therefore, permit the program to fall through to the uppercase character case. This is done to allow the user to enter either a lower- or an uppercase character for each option. Notice that there is a **break** statement at the end of each uppercase case to terminate the **switch** once the case statements are executed.

If the user enters an invalid character from the main menu, the **default** statement is executed, which displays an error message and asks the user to run the program again. Likewise, if the user enters an invalid value within a given case, it is caught by the **if/else** statement, which displays an error message and asks the user to run the program again. As you can see, I have used the **if** part of the **if/else** to catch the invalid entry and the **else** part to proceed with the calculation if the entry is valid. This is typical of the way that many programs are written.

The following output shows the menu generated by the program as well as a sample case execution.

This program will calculate dc voltage, current, or
resistance given the other two values.

                     Enter V to find voltage

                     Enter I to find current

                     Enter R to find resistance

                     Enter Q to quit

        Please enter your choice: **V**↵

Enter the current value in milliamperes I = **10**↵

Enter the resistance value in kilohms R = **5**↵

The voltage value is 50.00 volts.

STYLE TIP

As you begin to frame more operations using curly braces, it often becomes difficult to determine what a closing curly brace is closing. The indentation scheme helps, but a commenting technique is also used. When several closing curly braces appear in succession, you should insert a comment after the brace, as shown at the end of the foregoing program, to indicate what a given brace is closing. Commenting helps both you and anyone reading your program to readily see the program framing.

CHAPTER SUMMARY

In this chapter, you learned about the selection, or decision-making, operations available in C++. These include the **if**, **if/else**, and **switch** statements. Each of these operations alters the flow of a program, depending on the result of a test expression or matching condition.

The **if** statement executes its statements, or clause, "if" its test expression is true (nonzero). If the test result is false (zero), the program continues in a straight-line fashion. The **if** clause can be a single-line statement or a compound statement composed of a series of single-line statements. When using a compound statement, you must frame the entire statement block within curly braces.

The **if/else** statement consists of two separate clauses: an **if** clause and an **else** clause. If the associated test expression is true (nonzero), the **if** clause is executed; otherwise, the **else** clause is executed when the test result is false (zero). Thus, you could say that **if/else** is a two-way selection operation. Again, compound statements can be used within the **if** or **else** clauses; however, they must be framed within curly braces. Additional selection options can be achieved using nested **if** or **if/else** statements.

The **switch** statement achieves selection using a matching process. Here, the value of an integral selector variable is compared to a series of case values. If the selector value matches one of the case values, the corresponding case statements are executed until a **break** statement is encountered or the **switch** statement terminates. If no match is made, the program simply continues in a straight-line fashion. In addition, C++ provides a **default** option with the **switch** statement. When using the **default** option, the **default** statements are executed if no match is made. However, if a match does occur, the corresponding **case** statements are executed, and the **default** statements are skipped. Remember, you must always frame the body of the **switch** statement using curly braces.

QUESTIONS AND PROBLEMS

Questions

1. When will *x* be written as a result of the following **if** statement?
```
if ((x <= 0) && (x % 5))
   cout << x << endl;
```

2. Convert the single **if** statement in question 1 into two nested **if** statements.

3. Consider the following program segment:
```
cout << "Enter a value for x ";
cin >> x;
cout << "Enter a value for y ";
cin >> y;
if x > 0
{
  if y > 0
    --y;
}//END IF x > 0
else
  ++x;
```
   a. Are there any syntax errors in this code? If so, where are they?
   b. Assuming any syntax errors are corrected, when will *y* be decremented?
   c. Assuming any syntax errors are corrected, when will *x* be incremented?

4. Consider the following segment of code:
```
cout << "Enter a value for x ";
cin >> x;
cout << "Enter a value for y ";
cin >> y;
if (x > 0)
{
  if (y > 0)
   --y;
else
  ++x;
}//END IF x > 0
```
   a. Are there any syntax errors in this code? If so, where are they?
   b. Assuming any syntax errors are corrected, when will *y* be decremented?
   c. Assuming any syntax errors are corrected, when will *x* be incremented?

5. True or false: You must always frame the body of a **switch** statement.

6. Which **if** does the **else** belong to in the following code segment?
```
if (x > 0)
  if (y > 0)
   --y;
else
  ++x;
```

7. True or false: When using a **switch** statement in C++, a no-match condition results in an error.

8. Consider the following segment of code:

```
if (x >= 0)
  if (x < 10)
  {
    y = x * x;
    if (x <= 5)
      x = sqrt(x);
  }//END IF x < 10
  else
      y = 10 * x;
else
    y = x * x * x;
cout << "x = " << x << endl;
cout << "y = " << y << endl;
```

What will be displayed by the program for each of the following initial values of *x*?

a. x = 0;
b. x = 4;
c. x = –5;
d. x = 10;

9. Consider the following **switch** statement:

```
x = 2;
switch (Power)
{
  case 0 :  cout << '1' << endl;
            break;
  case 1 :  cout << x << endl;
            break;
  case 2 :  cout << x * x << endl;
            break;
  case 3 :  cout << x * x * x << endl;
            break;
  case 4 :  cout << x * x * x * x << endl;
            break;
  default : cout << "No match exists for this Power." << endl;
} //END SWITCH
```

What will be displayed by the code for each of the following values of *Power*?

a. Power = 0;
b. Power = 1;
c. Power = 2;

d. Power = 3;

e. Power = 4;

10. Consider the following nested **switch** statements:

```
switch (x)
{
  case 2 :
  case 4 :
  case 6 : switch (y)
           {
               case 1 :
               case 2 :
               case 3 :  x = x + y;
                         break;
               case -1 :
               case -2 :
               case -3 : x = x - y;
                         break;
           }//END SWITCH(y)
           break;
  case 1 :
  case 3 :
  case 5 : switch (y)
           {
               case 2 :
               case 4 :
               case 6 : x = x * y;
                         break;
               case -1 :
               case -4 :
               case -6 : x = y * y;
                         break;
           }//END SWITCH(y)
           break;
} //END SWITCH(x)
cout << "x = " << x << endl;
cout << "y = " << y << endl;
```

What will be displayed by the code for each of the following values of *x* and *y*?

a. x = 4;

    y = -2;

b. x = 3;

    y = 6;

c. x = 1;

    y = -4;

d. x = 7;
    y = -2;
e. x = 2;
    y = 5;

Problems

Least Difficult

1. A dimension on a part drawing indicates that the length of the part is 3.00 ±0.25 inch. This means that the minimum acceptable length of the part is 2.75 inches and the maximum acceptable length of the part is 3.25 inches. Write a program to display "ACCEPTABLE" if the part is within tolerance or "UNACCEPTABLE" if the part is out of tolerance. (Note: In Chapter 1, problem 5, you developed an algorithm for this problem. Why not use this algorithm to code the C++ program?)

2. Use your algorithm from problem 9 in Chapter 1 to code a program that will find the roots of a quadratic equation.

3. Write a program that will display two integer values in numerical order, regardless of the order in which they are entered.

4. Write a program that will display the corresponding name of a month for an integer entry from 1 to 12. Protect for invalid entries.

More Difficult

5. Employ nested **if/else** statements to convert a numerical grade to a letter grade according to the following scale:

    90–100 : A

    80–89   : B

    70–79   : C

    60–69   : D

    Below 60 : F

6. Electrical power, in watts, of a direct-current (dc) circuit is defined as the product of voltage and current. In symbols,

$$P = V \times I$$

where

P is power, in watts.
V is voltage, in volts.
I is current, in amperes.

Write a menu-driven program that will allow a technician to find dc power, voltage, or current, given the other two values. Protect against invalid entries.

Most Difficult

7. Ma and Pa are at it again. This time they need a program that will project the profit of their Sporting Goods department. The items in the department are coded with a 1, 2, or 3, depending on the amount of profit for the item. An item with a profit code of 1 produces a 10-percent profit, a code of 2 produces a 12-percent profit, and a code of 3 generates a 15-percent profit. Write a program that will project the profit of the following inventory:

Item	Quantity	Price	Profit Code
Fishing Line	132 spools	$3.95	1
Fish Hooks	97 packages	$0.89	2
Sinkers	123 packages	$0.49	2
Fish Nets	12 ea.	$8.75	1
Spinner Baits	256 ea.	$2.49	3
Jigs	49 ea.	$0.29	3

The program should generate a report of the item, quantity, expected profit in dollars per item, and total expected profit for all items.

8. Besides getting a regular salary, Herb also receives a commission on what he sells at Ma and Pa's General Store. His commission is based on the total dollar sales he makes in one week according to the following schedule:

Sales	Commission (%)
Below $250	0
$250–$499	5
$500–$1000	7.5
Over $1000	10

Write Ma and Pa a program that will determine Herb's sales commission from a user entry of his weekly sales. The program should display the total sales dollars and corresponding sales commission in dollars.

9. The value of y is defined as follows:

$y = x^2 + 2x - 3$ if $-3 <= x <= 2$

$y = 5x + 7$ if $2 < x <= 10$

$y = 0$ if $x < -3$ or $x > 10$

Write a program that will find y, given a user entry for x.

10. Write a menu-driven program that will allow the user to convert between the following units.

1. Degrees Fahrenheit to degrees Centigrade.
2. Degrees Centigrade to degrees Fahrenheit.
3. Inches to centimeters.
4. Centimeters to inches.
5. Pounds to kilograms.
6. Kilograms to pounds.

Provide for invalid user entries.

6

LOOPING OPERATIONS: ITERATION

INTRODUCTION
6-1 THE **while** LOOP
    Data Entry Using **while**
6-2 THE **do/while** LOOP
PROBLEM SOLVING IN ACTION: LOOP-
    CONTROLLED MENU-DRIVEN
    PROGRAMS
6-3 THE **for** LOOP
    Nested Loops
    Down-to **for** Loops

6-4 THE **break** AND **continue** OPTIONS
    The **break** Statement
    The **continue** Statement
PROBLEM SOLVING IN ACTION:
    PARALLEL RESISTOR CIRCUIT
    ANALYSIS
CHAPTER SUMMARY
QUESTIONS AND PROBLEMS
    Questions
    Problems

INTRODUCTION

In Chapter 5, you learned about the selection control structure. It is now time to explore the third and final control structure employed by C++: *iteration*. Iteration simply means doing something repeatedly. In programming, this is called *looping* because the iteration control structure causes the program flow to go around in a loop. Of course, there must be a way to get out of the loop, or the computer would loop forever! Such a situation is called an *infinite loop*, for obvious reasons. To prevent infinite looping, all iteration control structures test a condition to determine when to exit the loop. *Pretest* loops test a condition before each loop is executed. *Posttest* loops test a condition after each loop execution. And, finally, *fixed repetition* loops cause the loop to be executed a predetermined number of times.

The three iteration control structures employed by C++ are the **while**, **do/while**, and **for**. As you will learn in this chapter, each provides a means for you to perform repetitive operations. The difference between them is found in the means by which they control the exiting of the loop. The **while** is a pretest loop, the **do/while** is a posttest loop, and the **for** is a fixed repetition loop. Let's begin our discussion with the **while** loop.

6-1 THE while LOOP

You can see from Figure 6-1 that the **while** loop is a pretest loop because a test is made before the loop statements can ever be executed. If the test expression is true (nonzero), the loop statements are executed. If the test expression is false (zero), the loop statements are bypassed, and the next sequential statement after the loop is executed. As long as the test expression is true, the program continues to go around the loop. In other words, the loop is repeated "while" the test expression is true. To get out of the loop, something must change within the loop that makes the test expression false. If such a change does not take place, you have an infinite loop. In addition, the diagram shows that *if the test expression is false the first time it is encountered, the loop statements will never be executed*. This is an important characteristic of the **while** control structure.

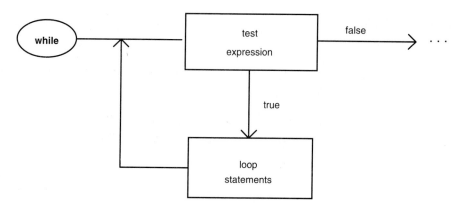

Figure 6-1   The **while** loop operation.

The C++ format for the **while** statement is as follows:

---

while *STATEMENT FORMAT*

while (test expression)
{
    statement 1;
    statement 2;
        •
        •   //LOOP STATEMENTS
        •
    statement n;
} //END WHILE

The first line of the statement contains the keyword **while** followed by a test expression within parentheses. To test a single condition, you will often use the Boolean operators of ==, !=, <, >, <=, >=, and !. To test multiple conditions, you must use the logical operators of **OR** (¦¦) and **AND** (&&). Remember, however, that any expression that reduces to zero will be considered false and any expression that reduces to a nonzero value will be considered true. Notice that the loop statements are framed using curly braces. This forms a compound statement, which consists of the individual loop statements. An indentation scheme is also used so that the loop portion of the statement can be easily identified. Finally, you should be aware that the loop does not have to be framed if it consists of only a single statement. However, the CPU will execute just this single statement during the loop. Any additional statements are considered to be outside the loop structure. Let's see how the **while** loop works by looking at a few simple examples.

DEBUGGING TIP

Always remember to frame the body of a loop with curly braces, { }, if it contains more than one statement. For example, consider the following:

```
Count = 0;
while (Count < 10)
  cout << Count << endl;
  ++Count;
```

The body of this loop obviously consists of two statements, as shown by the indentation. However, the multiple loop statements are not framed. As a result, you have an infinite loop. (Why?)

Example 6-1

What will be displayed by the following segments of code? Assume that the variables employed in each segment have been appropriately defined.

a.

```
Number = 5;
Sum = 0;
while (Number > 0)
{
  Sum += Number;
  --Number;
} //END WHILE
cout << "The sum is " << Sum << endl;
```

Here, the *loop control variable*, *Number*, is first assigned the value 5, and the variable *Sum* is assigned the value 0. The **while** loop statements will be executed as long as *Number* is greater than 0. Observe that each time the loop is executed, the value of *Number* is added to *Sum*. In addition, the value of *Number* is decremented by 1. Let's desk-check the code by tracing through each iteration to see what is happening, keeping track of the values of *Number* and *Sum* after each iteration:

1st Iteration: *Sum* is 5
                   Number is 4

| 2nd Iteration: | *Sum* is 9 |
| | *Number* is 3 |

| 3rd Iteration: | *Sum* is 12 |
| | *Number* is 2 |

| 4th Iteration: | *Sum* is 14 |
| | *Number* is 1 |

| 5th and Final Iteration: | *Sum* is 15 |
| | *Number* is 0 |

The looping stops here because the value of *Number* is zero. As a result, the loop statements are bypassed and the *cout* statement is executed, producing a display of

The sum is 15

In summary, you could say that the program segment computes the sum of integers from 1 through 5.

This same loop could be coded as follows:

```
Number = 5;
Sum = 0;
while (Number)
{
  Sum += Number;
  --Number;
} //END WHILE
cout << "The sum is " << Sum << endl;
```

Here, you see that the greater-than zero (> 0) test has been eliminated. But, has it? You might be thinking that there is no test expression in the **while** statement. However, recall that C++ interprets nonzero values to be true and a value of 0 to be false. Thus, as long as *Number* is greater than zero, the loop statements will be executed to produce the same result.

DEBUGGING TIP

Always initialize a variable that is accumulating a sum to 0; otherwise, you will start with garbage and end with garbage. On the other hand, always initialize a variable that is accumulating a product to 1 *not* 0. What will be the result if such a variable is initialized to 0?

b.

```
Sum = 0;
while (Number > 0)
{
  Sum += Number;
  --Number;
} //END WHILE
cout << "The sum is " << Sum << endl;
```

What has been changed in this segment of code versus the previous segment in part a? Well, notice that the loop control variable, *Number*, has not been initialized prior to the loop test. As a result, *Number* will initially have some arbitrary value from memory. This condition will result in an indeterminate number of looping iterations, often producing an infinite loop for all practical purposes.

DEBUGGING TIP

Make sure the loop control variable always has a meaningful value prior to entering the **while** loop statement. The **while** loop is a pretest loop and, therefore, must have a legitimate value to test the first time the loop test is executed.

c.

```
Number = 5;
Sum = 0;
while (Number > 0)
{
  if (Number % 2)
     Sum += Number;
  --Number;
} //END WHILE
cout << "The sum is " << Sum << endl;
```

Here, an **if** statement has been included within the loop so that *Number* is added to *Sum* only if *Number* is odd. Why will the calculation be performed when *Number* is odd? Well, the remainder of any odd number divided by 2 is 1, right? In a Boolean test situation, this 1 is interpreted as a true result. Thus, the calculation is made. If *Number* is even, the remainder operation generates a 0 result, which is interpreted as a false test expression. As a result, the calculation statement is bypassed. This program segment computes the sum of odd integers from 1 through 5, resulting in a display of

The sum is 9

---

d.

```
Number = 5;
Sum = 0;
while (Number > 0)
{
  if (!(Number % 2))
     Sum += Number;
  --Number;
} //END WHILE
cout << "The sum is " << Sum << endl;
```

This time, the program computes the sum of even integers from 1 through 5, because *Number* is added to *Sum* only if *Number* is not odd. (Why?) As a result, the display is

The sum is 6

---

e.

```
MaxNumber = 5;
Number = 0;
Sum = 0;
while (Number != MaxNumber)
    Sum += Number;
cout << "The average of the first " << MaxNumber
     << "positive integers is :  " << Sum/MaxNumber << endl;
```

This is an infinite loop. Notice that the loop is executed as long as *Number* and *MaxNumber* are not equal. The initial value of *Number* is 0, and the initial value of *MaxNumber* is 5. However, these values are never changed within the loop. Thus, *Number* is always not equal to *MaxNumber*, resulting in an infinite loop. No display is generated, and with many systems you must turn off the computer in order to get out of the loop. To correct this problem, you must change the loop control variable somewhere within the loop so that the loop test will eventually become false. In this segement of code, you need to increment *Number* within the body of the loop, like this:

```
MaxNumber = 5;
Number = 0;
Sum = 0;
```

```
while (Number != MaxNumber)
{
  ++Number;
  Sum += Number;
} //END WHILE
cout << "The average of the first " << MaxNumber
     << " positive integers is:  " << Sum/MaxNumber << endl;
```

The loop will now produce a result of

The average of the first 5 positive integers is: 3

---

f.

What would happen if *Number* were incremented by 2 in part e? This modification would also result in an infinite loop, because the value of *Number* would skip over the value of *MaxNumber* and the two would always be unequal.

DEBUGGING TIP

Remember, an infinite loop is the result of a logical error in your program. ***The compiler will not detect an infinite loop condition***. For this reason, you should always desk-check your loop structures very closely prior to coding and execution.

---

g.

```
enum Boolean {FALSE,TRUE};      //DECLARE BOOLEAN DATA CLASS
Boolean Flag;                   //DEFINE BOOLEAN VARIABLE

int Number;                     //INPUT VARIABLE
int Sum;                        //SUM VARIABLE

Flag = TRUE;                    //INITIALIZE BOOLEAN FLAG TO TRUE
Sum = 0;                        //INITIALIZE Sum TO 0

while (Flag == TRUE)
{
  cout << "Enter an integer number:" << endl;    //GET A NUMBER
  cin >> Number;
  if (Number < 0)               //SET FLAG TO FALSE IF NUMBER < 0
  {
    Flag = FALSE;
    cout << "Loop terminated" << endl;
  }//END IF
```

```
   else                      //ADD NUMBER TO SUM AND DISPLAY
   {
     Sum = Sum + Number;
     cout << "The sum is now: " << Sum << endl << endl;
   }//END ELSE
 }//END WHILE
```

This is an example of a *flag controlled loop*. A *flag* is a Boolean variable that is used to control the flow of a program. We initialize the flag to TRUE, then change it to FALSE when a given event has occurred within the program. Here, we have started out by declaring a Boolean data class called *Boolean* and defining a variable object for that class called *Flag*. The variable *Flag* is then initialized to the value TRUE. The loop will continue to execute as long as the value of *Flag* remains TRUE. With each iteration, the program will display the sum of the integers entered by the user. However, when the user enters a negative number, *Flag* is set to FALSE, and the loop will terminate. The foregoing loop test could also be coded as *while (Flag)*. Why? Here is a typical output produced by the loop:

```
Enter an integer number:
1⏎
The sum is now 1

Enter an integer number:
2⏎
The sum is now 3

Enter an integer number:
3⏎
The sum is now 6

Enter an integer number:
-1⏎
Loop terminated
```

Data Entry Using while

There are many situations in which you will want to use a looping operation to read data. One common example is to read strings of data. The idea is to read a single data element, such as a character, each time the loop is executed. Then break out of the loop when the data string is terminated. For instance, consider the following program:

```
//COUNT THE CHARACTERS

#include <iostream.h>   //FOR cin AND cout

//DECLARE PERIOD CONSTANT
const char PERIOD = '.';

void main()
{
  char InChar = ' ';              //USER ENTRY
  int Count = 0;                  //LOOP COUNTER
  cout  << "Enter a string of characters and terminate the input\n"
           "with a period.  Press ENTER when finished." << endl;
  cin >> InChar;
  while (InChar != PERIOD)
  {
    ++Count;
    cin >> InChar;
  } //END WHILE
  cout << "The number of characters entered was:  " << Count << endl;
} //END main()
```

The general idea of this program is to read a string of characters until a period, '.', is encountered. The period is called a ***sentinel value***, because it ends the input string but is not part of that string. The input variable is *InChar*. The **while** loop is executed as long as *InChar* is not equal to a period. With each iteration, a counter (*Count*) is incremented to count the number of characters that were entered before the period. Here is what you will see when the program is executed:

Enter a string of characters and terminate the input
with a period. Press ENTER when finished.

abcd.⏎

The number of characters entered was: 4

Here the user has entered six characters, including the sentinel value and the CRLF character generated by the **ENTER** key. The program counts the number of characters entered, excluding the sentinel value and the CRLF character.

Now, let's look at the program a bit closer. First, notice that a character is read just prior to the **while** statement because the **while** statement tests the variable *InChar* to see that it is not a period. Without the first read operation, *InChar* would not have a value and, therefore, could not be tested. Remember that the variable being tested in the **while** statement must always have a value prior to the first test. This is a common source of error when writing **while** loops. Why didn't the program count the period or the CRLF character? Well, the loop is broken and *Count* is not incremented for the period character, and the >> operator ignores the CRLF whitespace character.

Now, let's look at another program that employs a **while** loop to read data. This time, we will use the CRLF character as our sentinel value. Here it is:

```
//COUNT THE CHARACTERS

#include <iostream.h>   //FOR cin AND cout

//DECLARE CRLF CONSTANT
const char CRLF = '\n';

void main()
{
  char InChar = ' ';                //DEFINE USER ENTRY VARIABLE
  int Count = 0;                    //DEFINE LOOP COUNTER VARIABLE

cout << "Enter a string of characters and press"
        " ENTER when finished. " << endl;
  cin.get(InChar);
  while (InChar != CRLF)
  {
    ++Count;
    cin.get(InChar);
  } //END WHILE
  cout << "The number of characters entered was:  " << Count << endl;
} //END main()
```

The logic of this program is the same as the previous program. However, this time we have used the *get()* function in lieu of the >> operator to read the character data. Because we are testing a whitespace character (CRLF), we need a function that will read it. In our program, the character read by *get()* is assigned to the variable *InChar*. The *InChar* variable is tested by the **while** statement to see if it is the CRLF character. When the CRLF character is present, the loop is broken and the value of *Count* is not incremented again. Here is what the user will see when the program is executed:

Enter a string of characters and press ENTER when finished.

abcd.⏎

The number of characters entered was: 5

Notice that the period was counted but not the CRLF character. (Why?)

PROGRAMMING TIP

When using a sentinel-controlled loop, always provide a prompt that instructs the user what to enter as the sentinel value. Never use a sentinel value that the user could confuse with the normal data items being entered.

 Quick Check

1. True or false: A **while** loop breaks when the test expression evaluates to zero.

2. True or false: The **while** loop is a posttest loop.

3. What is wrong with the following code?

    ```
    x = 10;
    while (x > 0)
       cout << "This is a while loop" << endl;
       - -x;
    ```

4. Correct the code in question 3.

5. How many times will the following loop execute?

    ```
    x = 1;
    while (x <= 0)
       cout << "How many times will this loop execute?" << endl;
    ```

6. How many times will the following loop execute?

```
x = 1
while (x >=0)
{
    cout << "How many times will this loop execute?" << endl;
    ++x;
}//END WHILE
```

6-2 THE do/while LOOP

The flow of the **do/while** loop can be seen in Figure 6-2.

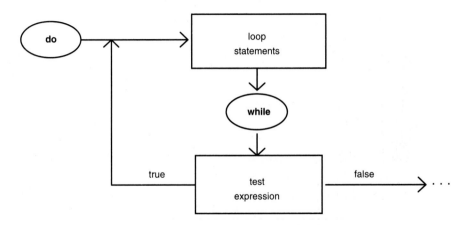

Figure 6-2   The **do/while** loop operation.

If you compare Figure 6-2 to the flow of **while** in Figure 6-1, you will find that the test is made at the end of the loop, rather than the beginning of the loop. This is the main difference between the **while** and the **do/while.** Because the **do/while** is a posttest loop, *the loop statements will always be executed at least once.* To break the loop, the test expression must become false (zero). Thus, if the test condition is initially true, something must happen within the loop to change the condition to false; otherwise, you have an infinite loop. Here's the required C++ syntax:

> **do/while** *STATEMENT FORMAT*
>
> ```
> do
> {
>   statement 1;
>   statement 2;
>       •
>       •              //LOOP STATEMENTS
>       •
>   statement n;
> }//END DO/WHILE
> while  (test expression);
> ```

This format shows that the operation must begin with the single keyword **do**. This is followed by the actual loop statements, which are followed by the keyword **while** and the test expression enclosed within parentheses. You must always frame multiple loop statements with curly braces. However, no framing is required when there is only a single loop statement. In addition, notice that there is no semicolon after the keyword **do** in the first line, but a semicolon is required after the test expression in the last line. Look at the program segments in Example 6-2, and see if you can predict their results.

Example 6-2

What will be displayed by the following segments of code? Assume that the variables employed in each segment have been appropriately defined.

a.

```
Number = 5;
Sum = 0;
do
{
  Sum += Number;
  --Number;
}//END DO/WHILE
while (Number > 0);
cout << "The sum is " << Sum << endl;
```

In this segment, the value of *Number* is initially set to 5, and the value of *Sum* to 0. Each time the loop is executed, the value of *Number* is added to *Sum*. In addition, the value of *Number* is decremented by 1. The looping will end when *Number* has been decremented to 0. The resulting display is

The sum is 15

Notice that this **do/while** loop computes the sum of integers 1 through 5, as did the **while** loop in Example 6-1a.

---

b.

```
Number = 0;
Sum = 0;
do
{
  Sum += Number;
  ++Number;
}//END DO/WHILE
while (Number != 5);
cout << "The sum is " << Sum << endl;
```

In this segment, both *Number* and *Sum* are initially 0. Again, you might suspect that the loop computes the sum of the integers 1 through 5. But, it actually computes the sum of integers 1 through 4. Why? Notice that *Number* is incremented after the *Sum* is calculated. Thus, when *Number* increments to 5, the loop is broken, and the value 5 is never added to *Sum*. The resulting display is

The sum is 10

How would you change the loop to sum the integers 1 through 5? One way is to change the test expression to *while(Number != 6)*. Another, more preferred, way is to reverse the two loop statements so that *Number* is incremented prior to the *Sum* calculation.

---

c.

```
MaxNumber = 5;
Number = 0;
Sum = 0;
do
{
  --Number;
  Sum += Number;
}//END DO/WHILE
while (Number != MaxNumber);
cout << "The average of the first " << MaxNumber
     << " positive integers is :  " << Sum/MaxNumber << endl;
```

In this segment, *MaxNumber* begins with the value 5, and both *Number* and *Sum* are initialized to 0. The loop is broken when the value of *Number* equals the value of *MaxNumber*. How many times will the loop execute? If you said "five," you are wrong! Notice that *Number* is decremented each time the loop is executed. Theoretically, the loop will execute an infinite number of times. However, because the range of integers in C++ is normally from –32,768 to 32,767, the loop will execute 65,531 times. How did I get this figure? Well, 32,768 loops will have executed when *Number* reaches –32,768. The next looping operation will decrement *Number* to 32,767. It then takes 32,762 loops to decrement *Number* to 5. Notice that 32,768 + 1 + 32,762 = 65,531. Of course, this is infinite for all practical purposes.

---

d.

```
MaxNumber = 5;
Number = 0;
Sum = 0;
do
{
  ++Number;
  Sum += Number;
}//END DO/WHILE
while (Number != MaxNumber);
cout << "The average of the first " << MaxNumber
     << " positive integers is:  " << Sum/MaxNumber << endl;
```

Here, the loop in part c has been corrected so that the value of *Number* is incremented by 1 with each iteration. When *Number* reaches 5, it equals the value of *MaxNumber*, and the loop is broken. The resulting display is

The average of the first 5 positive integers is: 3

---

e.

```
const char PERIOD = '.';        //DECLARE PERIOD CONSTANT
char InChar = ' ';              //DEFINE USER ENTRY VARIABLE
int Count = 0;                  //DEFINE LOOP COUNTER VARIABLE
cout  << "Enter a string of characters and terminate the input\n"
         "with a period.  Press ENTER when finished." << endl;
do
{
  ++Count;
  cin >> InChar;
}//END DO/WHILE
while (InChar != PERIOD);
cout << "The number of characters entered was:  " << Count – 1 << endl;
```

This program segment shows how a sentinel value can be employed to break a **do/while** loop. Notice that each iteration reads a single character from the terminal keyboard until the period key is entered. When this operation was performed using a **while** loop, you had to read the first character prior to the loop structure, so there was an initial value to test. This is because the Boolean test is made at the beginning of **while**. On the other hand, a **do/while** loop performs the Boolean test at the end of the loop. As a result, you do not have to read the first character prior to the loop structure, because the loop statements will always be executed at least once and *InChar* will have a legitimate value before the loop test is made.

Now, look at the *cout* statement. You see that the value to be displayed is *Count* – 1. Why? Observe that *Count* will be incremented, even for the last loop iteration that reads the period sentinel value. Therefore, 1 must be subtracted from the value of *Count* to get the correct number of characters entered, excluding the sentinel value. This is required because of the posttest nature of **do/while**.

Assuming the user enters the string "abcd.", the display would be

Enter a string of characters and terminate the input
with a period. Press ENTER when finished.

abcd. ⌐

The number of characters entered was: 4

---

f.

```
const char CRLF = '\n';      //DECLARE CRLF CONSTANT
char InChar = ' ';           //DEFINE USER ENTRY VARIABLE
int Count = 0;               //DEFINE LOOP COUNTER VARIABLE

cout << "Enter a string of characters and press "
        "ENTER when finished." << endl;
do
{
  ++Count;
  cin.get(InChar);
}//END DO/WHILE
while (InChar != CRLF);
cout << "The number of characters entered was:  " << Count – 1 << endl;
```

This segment illustrates how the CRLF character can be used to terminate a **do/while** loop. The loop will continue to read in characters until the CRLF character is generated by pressing the **ENTER** key. Given a user input of "xyz", the output would look like this:

Enter a string of characters and press ENTER when finished.

xyz.⏎

The number of characters entered was: 3

PROBLEM SOLVING IN ACTION: LOOP-CONTROLLED MENU-DRIVEN PROGRAMS

Problem

In the last chapter, you saw that the **switch** statement is used to create menu-driven programs. It is often desirable to allow the user to select a menu option, perform the task associated with that option, then return to the menu to select another option, without terminating the program until a quit option is chosen. Such a program would require the menu to be displayed repeatedly until the quit option is chosen. This is an ideal application for looping. We will encase our menu within a loop so that the menu and associated tasks will keep repeating until the user chooses to terminate the program. We will apply this technique to the menu-driven Ohm's law solution developed in the last chapter. Let's revisit the problem through the problem definition.

Defining the Problem

Output:	A program menu that prompts the user to select a voltage, current, or resistance calculation option.
	Invalid entry messages as required.
	A voltage, current, or resistance value, depending on the program option that the user selects.
Input:	A user response to the menu (V, I, R, or Q).
	If V is selected: User enters values for current and resistance.
	If I is selected: User enters values for voltage and resistance.
	If R is selected: User enters values for voltage and current.
	If Q is selected: Terminate the program.
Processing:	Calculate the selected option.
	Case V: *Voltage = Current × Resistance.*
	Case I: *Current = Voltage / Resistance.*
	Case R: *Resistance = Voltage / Current.*
	Case Q: Terminate the program.
	Repeat the menu until the user chooses to terminate the program.

Planning the Solution

Using the structured program design developed in the last chapter, we divided the problem into two subproblems to solve the overall problem. They were:

- Display the menu and read user choice.
- Perform the chosen calculation and display results.

The structure diagram developed for this solution is shown again in Figure 6-3.

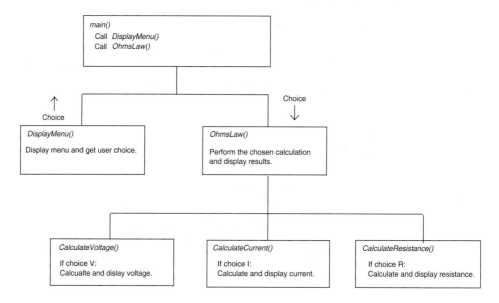

Figure 6-3   A structure diagram for the Ohm's law problem.

Recall that there were three levels to solving the problem. At the first level, *main()*, a function is called to display the menu and get the user choice. The *DisplayMenu()* function accomplishes this task and sends the user choice back to *main()*, as indicated on the diagram. Function *main()* will then send the choice to a function called *OhmsLaw()*, which will call one of three functions, depending on the choice, to perform the required calculation. Now, the process description requires that we add a loop control feature to the program. Here is the revised set of algorithms through the fist level of refinement:

Initial Algorithm

> *main( )*
> BEGIN
>   do
>   Call *DisplayMenu( )* function.
>   Call *OhmsLaw( )* function.
>   while *Choice* ≠ 'q' AND *Choice* ≠ 'Q'
> END.

First Level of Refinement

> *DisplayMenu( )*
> BEGIN
>   Display a program menu that prompts the user to choose a voltage (V),
>   current (I), resistance (R), or quit (Q) option.
>   Read (*Choice*).
> END.

> *OhmsLaw( )*
> BEGIN
>   Case V: Call function *CalculateVoltage( )*.
>   Case I: Call function *CalculateCurrent( )*.
>   Case R: Call function *CalculateResistance( )*.
>   Case Q: Terminate program.
>   Default: Write an invalid entry message and ask the user to select again.
>   END.

Notice that the loop control feature is added to the initial algorithm level, *main( )*. The *DisplayMenu( )* and *OhmsLaw( )* algorithms at the first level of refinement have not changed much from our earlier solution. So, let's focus on the loop control in *main( )*. Now, recall that the *DisplayMenu( )* function obtains the user's menu choice. If the user enters a 'q' or 'Q' to quit the program, the loop will break, and the program terminates. But, is there something wrong here? I said if the "user enters a 'q' *or* 'Q' to quit the program ..."; however, the loop test employs the **AND** operation. So, why have I used the Boolean **AND** operation rather than the **OR** operation to perform this test? This is a classic candidate for desk-checking the algorithm logic *before* coding the program. Ask yourself: "When will the loop break?" A **while/do** loop breaks when the condition tested is false, right? Remember that the result of an **AND** operation is false when any one of its conditions is false. As a result, the loop will break when *Choice* is a 'q' *or* a 'Q'. The loop will continue when both sides of the **AND** operation are true. Therefore, the loop will continue as long as *Choice* is not a 'q' *and Choice* is not 'Q'. Isn't this what we want to do? What would happen if you mistakenly used the **OR** operation in the foregoing loop test? An **OR** operation produces a true result when any one of its conditions is true. One of these conditions would always be true, because *Choice* cannot be both a 'q' and a 'Q'. The result of this oversight would be an infinite loop.

Another point needs to be made here. This application is a classic candidate for a **do/while** loop rather than a **while** loop, because you always want the menu to be displayed at least once to allow for a user choice.

DEBUGGING TIP

A common mistake when developing loop control logic is to use an **OR** operation rather than an **AND** operation, or vice versa. This mistake almost always results in an infinite loop. The lesson to be learned here is to *always* desk-check your loop control logic before coding the program.

We will not repeat the second level of refinement, because it has not changed from the solution developed in the last chapter. Now that we have desk-checked our loop control logic, we are ready to code the program.

Coding the Program

Here is the flat implementation of the foregoing program design:

```
//ACTION 6-1 (ACT06-01.CPP)

//OUTPUT:     A PROGRAM MENU THAT PROMPTS THE USER
//            TO SELECT A VOLTAGE, CURRENT,
//            OR RESISTANCE CALCULATION OPTION.
//            INVALID ENTRY MESSAGES AS REQUIRED.
//            A VOLTAGE, CURRENT, OR RESISTANCE
//            VALUE, DEPENDING ON THE PROGRAM OPTION THAT
//            THE USER SELECTS.

//INPUT:      A USER RESPONSE TO THE MENU (V, I, R, OR Q).
```

```
//              IF V IS SELECTED: USER ENTERS VALUES
//              FOR CURRENT AND RESISTANCE.
//              IF I IS SELECTED: USER ENTERS VALUES
//              FOR VOLTAGE AND RESISTANCE.
//              IF R IS SELECTED: USER ENTERS VALUES
//              FOR VOLTAGE AND CURRENT.
//              IF Q IS SELECTED: TERMINATE PROGRAM

//PROCESSING: CALCULATE THE SELECTED OPTION.
//              CASE V:    VOLTAGE = CURRENT X RESISTANCE.
//              CASE I:    CURRENT = VOLTAGE / RESISTANCE.
//              CASE R:    RESISTANCE = VOLTAGE / CURRENT.
//              CASE Q:    TERMINATE THE PROGRAM
//       REPEAT THE MENU UNTIL THE USER CHOOSES TO TERMINATE

#include <iostream.h>          //FOR cin AND cout

void main()
{
//DEFINE VARIABLES
  char Choice = 'Q';           //USER MENU ENTRY
  float Voltage = 0.0;         //VOLTAGE IN VOLTS
  float Current = 0.0;         //CURRENT IN MILLIAMPERES
  float Resistance = 0.0;      //RESISTANCE IN KILOHMS

//DISPLAY PROGRAM DESCRIPTION MESSAGE AND MENU
  cout << "This program will calculate dc voltage, current, or\n"
          "resistance given the other two values. " << endl << endl;

do                 //BEGIN MENU CONTROL LOOP
{
//DisplayMenu()FUNCTION
  cout << "\n\n\t\t\tEnter V to find voltage" << endl << endl
       << "\t\t\tEnter I to find current" << endl << endl
       << "\t\t\tEnter R to find resistance" << endl << endl
       << "\t\t\tEnter Q to quit" << endl << endl
       << "\tPlease enter your choice:  ";
  cin >> Choice;

//SET OUTPUT PRECISION
  cout.setf(ios::fixed);
  cout.precision(2);
```

```
//OhmsLaw() FUNCTION
  switch (Choice)
  {
    case 'v':   //CalculateVoltage() FUNCTION
    case 'V' :  cout << "\nEnter the current value in milliamperes\tI = ";
                cin >> Current;
                cout << "\nEnter the resistance value in kilohms\tR = ";
                cin >> Resistance;
                if (Resistance < 0)
                  cout << "\n\nThis is an invalid entry. Please"
                          " choose again." << endl;
                else
                {
                  Voltage = Current * Resistance;
                  cout << "\n\nThe voltage value is:  " << Voltage
                       << " volts." << endl;
                }//END ELSE
                break;

    case 'i':   //CalculateCurrent() FUNCTION
    case 'I' :  cout << "\nEnter the voltage value in volts\tV = ";
                cin >> Voltage;
                cout << "\nEnter the resistance value in kilohms\tR = ";
                cin >> Resistance;
                if (Resistance <= 0)
                  cout << "\n\nThis is an invalid entry. Please"
                          " choose again." << endl;
                else
                {
                  Current = Voltage / Resistance;
                  cout << "\n\nThe current value is:  "
                       << Current<< " milliamperes." << endl;
                }//END ELSE
                break;

    case 'r':   //CalculateResistance() FUNCTION
    case 'R' :  cout << "\nEnter the voltage value in volts\tV = ";
                cin >> Voltage;
                cout << "\nEnter the current value in milliamperes\tI = ";
                cin >> Current;
                if (Current == 0)
                  cout << "\n\nThis is an invalid entry. Please"
                          " choose again." << endl;
```

```
                else
                {
                  Resistance = Voltage / Current;
                  cout << "\n\nThe resistance value is:  " << Resistance
                      << " kilohms." << endl;
                }//END ELSE
                break;

        case 'q':  //TERMINATE PROGRAM
        case 'Q':  cout << "Program terminated" << endl;
                   break;

      //DISPLAY INVALID ENTRY MESSAGE
       default :   cout << "\n\nThis is an invalid entry. Please"
                          " run the program again." << endl;
      } //END SWITCH
    } //END DO/WHILE
   while ((Choice != 'q') && (Choice != 'Q'));
} //END main()
```

The major change here is the **do/while** loop control feature that we added in our solution planning. Notice how the conditional loop test is coded at the end of the program. The entire test must be within parentheses. The variable *Choice* is tested twice; both tests must be enclosed within parentheses. The results of both tests are combined via the Boolean **AND** (&&) operation.

DEBUGGING TIP

A common mistake when coding a compound Boolean test on a variable is to forget to code it so that each side of the compound test produces a Boolean result. For example, suppose that we coded the foregoing loop test as

```
while (Choice != 'q' && 'Q');
```

This code will always produce a compiler error, because the right side of the **AND** operation does not produce a Boolean result. It might make sense for you to code it this way, but it doesn't make sense to the compiler!

Quick Check

1. True or false: A **do/while** loop breaks when the test expression is zero.

2. True or false: The **do/while** loop is a posttest loop.

3. What is wrong with the following code?
   ```
   x = 10;
   do
      cout << "This is a do/while loop" << endl;
   while (x > 0);
   ```

4. Correct the code in question 3.

5. How many times will the following loop execute?
   ```
   x = 1;
   do
      cout << "This is a do/while loop" << endl;
   while (x <= 0);
   ```

6. How many times will the following loop execute?
   ```
   x = 1
   do
   {
      cout << "This is a do/while loop" << endl;
      ++x;
   }//END DO/WHILE
   while (x >=0);
   ```

6-3 THE for LOOP

The flow of this final iteration control structure is illustrated in Figure 6-4. The **for** loop is called a *fixed repetition* loop because the loop is repeated a fixed number of times. As you can see, the first thing that takes place before the loop statements are executed is the *initialization* of a loop counter. Initialization means setting a counter variable to some initial, or beginning, value. A test expression is then executed to test the counter value. If the result of this test is true (nonzero), the loop statements are executed. Each time the loop statements are executed, the counter value must be incremented or decremented. The test expression is evaluated again before the loop statements are executed another time. The loop is repeated as long as the result of the test expression is true. In other words, the counter is incremented/decremented, tested, and the loop is repeated *until* the test expression is false. When this occurs, the loop statements are not executed again, and the loop is broken. Control of the program then goes to the next sequential statement following the loop.

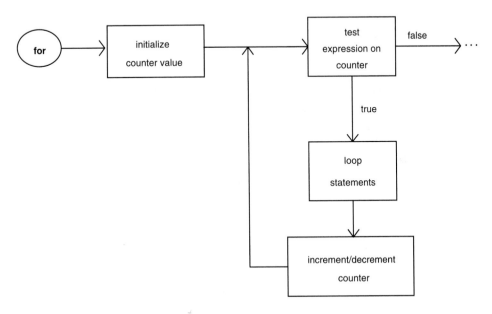

Figure 6-4   The **for** loop operation.

Here's the C++ syntax:

for *STATEMENT FORMAT*

for (<data class> *Counter* = initial value; *Counter* test expression;
      Increment/Decrement *Counter*)
{
   statement 1;
   statement 2;
            •
            •   //LOOP STATEMENTS
            •
   statement n;
} //END FOR

The statement begins with the keyword **for**. This is followed by three separate statements: an *initialization* statement, a *test expression*, and an *increment/decrement* statement, all enclosed within a single set of parentheses. The loop counter is initialized by assigning an initial value to the counter variable. The counter variable can be any simple data class, *except* float. The counter variable can be defined before the **for** statement or within the **for** statement as part of the initialization step, like this:

for (int *Count* = 1; ...

If defined within the **for** statement, it is only valid for the function in which it is defined. Thus, as far as C++ is concerned, the counter variable doesn't exist outside of the function in which the **for** loop appears.

The test expression is used to test the value of the loop counter against some predetermined value. The loop statements will be executed until the result of the test expression becomes false (zero).

The increment/decrement statement is used to change the value of the loop counter so that the test expression becomes false after a fixed number of iterations. If the value of the loop counter is never changed, you have an infinite loop. It is important to note that the increment/decrement statement is not executed until *after* the loop statements are executed in a given iteration. Thus, *if the initial test expression is true, the loop statements will be executed at least once.* However, *if the initial test expression is false, the loop statements are never executed.* This means that the **for** loop acts very much like the **while** loop. In fact, a **for** loop and a **while** loop are really one and the same looping structure, just coded differently. Think about it!

One last point about the loop counter variable: *Never* alter the counter variable within the body of the loop. The counter variable can be used within the body of the loop, but its value should not be altered. In other words, never use the counter variable on the left side of the assignment symbol (=) within the loop.

Finally, notice from the above format that the loop statements are framed within the curly braces. This is always required when there is more than one loop statement. The framing can be eliminated when there is only a single loop statement. Here are a few examples; see if you can predict the results.

Example 6-3

What will be displayed by the following segments of code?

a.

```
for (int Count = 1; Count != 11; ++Count)
    cout << Count << endl;
```

The loop counter variable, *Count*, ranges from 1 to 11. How many iterations will there be? Eleven, right? Wrong! The *++Count* statement increments the value of *Count* <u>after</u> each loop iteration. When the value of *Count* reaches 11, the test expression is false (zero) and the loop is broken. As a result, there is no 11th iteration. With each loop iteration, the *cout* statement displays the value of *Count*, like this:

```
1
2
3
4
5
6
7
8
9
10
```

b.

```
for (int Count = 10; Count; --Count)
    cout << Count << endl;
```

Here, the value of *Count* ranges from 10 to 0. The *--Count* statement decrements the value of *Count* after each loop iteration. When the value of *Count* reaches zero, the loop is broken. Why? Notice that the test expression is simply *Count*. No Boolean relational test operation is needed, because when *Count* reaches zero, C++ interprets the expression to be false. Remember this little trick, because it saves some coding. The output generated by this loop is

```
10
9
8
7
6
5
4
3
2
1
```

---

c.

```
for (int Count = 0; Count != 5; ++Count)
   {
     Sum = Sum + Count;
     cout << "The sum in the first iteration is " << Sum << endl;
     ++Count;
   }//END FOR
```

This is an infinite loop! Notice that the loop counter is incremented within the body of the loop. What actually happens is that the loop counter is incremented twice, once within the body of the loop by the increment statement and then automatically by the **for** statement. As a result, the value of *Count* skips over the value 5, creating an infinite loop. The lesson to be learned here is this: *Never change a* **for** *loop counter within the body of the loop.*

---

d.

```
for (int Count = -5; Count < 6; ++Count)
     cout << Count << endl;
```

Here, *Count* ranges from –5 to 6. Because the loop is broken when *Count* reaches 6, the *cout* loop statement is executed for values of *Count* from –5 to 5. How many times will the loop be executed? Ten, right? Wrong! There are 11 integers in the range of –5 to 5, including 0. As a result, the loop is executed eleven times to produce an output of

```
-5
-4
-3
-2
-1
0
1
2
3
4
5
```

---

e.

```
cout << "\n\tNumber\tSquare\tCube" << endl;
cout << "\t------\t------\t----" << endl;
for (int Count = 1; Count < 11; ++Count)
```

```
cout << '\t' << Count << '\t' << Count * Count
    << '\t' << Count * Count * Count << endl;
```

This **for** loop is being used to generate a table of squares and cubes for the integers 1 through 10. Notice how the counter variable *Count* is squared and cubed within the *cout* loop statement. However, observe that at no time is the value of *Count* altered within the loop. The resulting display is

Number	Square	Cube
1	1	1
2	4	8
3	9	27
4	16	64
5	25	125
6	36	216
7	49	343
8	64	512
9	81	729
10	100	1000

f.

```
for (char Character = 'A'; Character < 'Z'+ 1; ++Character)
    cout << Character;
```

The counter variable in this loop is the character variable *Character*. Recall that the character data class is ordered so that 'A' is smaller than 'Z'. Notice that the test expression, *Character* < 'Z' + 1 forces the loop to execute for the last time when the value of *Character* is 'Z'. Consequently, the loop is executed 26 times as *Character* ranges from 'A' to 'Z'. The value of *Character* is displayed each time using a *cout* statement to produce an output of

ABCDEFGHIJKLMNOPQRSTUVWXYZ

g.

```
const int MAXCOUNT = 100;
float Sum = 0.0;
float Average = 0.0;
cout.setf(ios::fixed);
cout.precision(2);
for (int Count = 1; Count < MAXCOUNT + 1; ++Count)
    Sum +=Count;
Average = Sum / MAXCOUNT;
cout << "The average of the first " << MAXCOUNT
    << " positive integers is:  " << Average << endl;
```

Here, the counter value is being added to the floating-point variable *Sum* each time through the loop. Thus, the loop adds all the positive integers within the defined range of the counter variable. The range of *Count* is from 1 to *MAXCOUNT* + 1. Notice that *MAXCOUNT* has been declared a constant with a value of 100. Therefore, *Count* will range from 1 to 100 + 1, or 101. However, because the loop is broken when *Count* reaches the value 101, this value is never added to *Sum*. This results in a summing of all integers within the range of 1 to *MAXCOUNT*. After the loop is broken, the value of *Sum* is divided by *MAXCOUNT* to calculate the *Average* of all integers from 1 to 100. Here's what you would see:

The average of the first 100 positive integers is: 50.5

Notice that the variable *Sum* was defined as a floating-point object, so that the division operator, /, produces a floating-point quotient. If both *Sum* and *MAXCOUNT* were defined as integer objects, the division operator would produce an erroneous integer result of 50. Also, you should be aware that constants like *MAXCOUNT* are often used as shown here for the initial or final counter values in a **for** loop. The reason is this: If the constant value needs to be changed for some reason, you need to change it in only one place, at the beginning of the program within the **const** declaration. This changes its value any place it is used within the program.

---

h.

```
const int MAXCOUNT = 100;
for (int i = 1; i < MAXCOUNT + 1; ++i)
{
    if (!(i % 17))
        cout << "The value " << i << " is divisible by 17." << endl;
} //END FOR
```

An **if** statement is used in this loop to determine when the counter value, *i*, is divisible by 17. Thus, the loop displays all the values between 1 and *MAXCOUNT* (100) that are divisible by 17. Do you understand how the test expression is working in the **if** statement? Here is what you would see when it is executed:

The value 17 is divisible by 17.
The value 34 is divisible by 17.
The value 51 is divisible by 17.
The value 68 is divisible by 17.
The value 85 is divisible by 17.

PROGRAMMING TIP

Suppose that a loop must execute *n* times and you create a loop control variable called *Count*. In C++, if the loop control variable begins with the value 0, the loop test would use the *less than* (<) operator, like this: *Count* < *n*. If the application requires you to begin the loop control variable with the value 1, the test would use the *less than or equal to* (<=) operator, like this: *Count* <= *n*. When the application does not require otherwise, it is standard practice to initialize C++ loop control variables with the value 0 and use the *less than* test.

Nested Loops

Many applications require looping operations within loops. This is called ***nested looping***. To get the idea, think about the seconds, minutes, and hours of a 12-hour digital timer. Isn't each a simple counter? The seconds count from 0 to 59, the minutes from 0 to 59, and the hours from 0 to 11. For every 60 seconds, the minutes counter is incremented. Likewise, for every 60 minutes, the hours counter is incremented. Thus, the seconds count is "nested" within the minutes count, and the minutes count is "nested" within the hours count. Here's how a digital timer might be coded in a C++ program using nested **for** loops:

```
//DIGITAL TIMER
#include <iostream.h>   //FOR cout
void main()
{
//DISPLAY HEADINGS
   cout << " \t\t\tHours\tMinutes\tSeconds" << endl;
//START TIMER
   for (int Hours = 0; Hours < 12; ++Hours)
     for (int Minutes = 0; Minutes < 60; ++Minutes)
         for (int Seconds = 0; Seconds < 60; ++Seconds)
         {
            cout << "\t\t\t\t\t\r";                    //BLANK DISPLAY
            cout << "\t\t\t" << Hours << '\t'
                  << Minutes                           //DISPLAY TIME
                  << '\t' << Seconds << '\r';
         } //END SECONDS LOOP
} //END main()
```

As you can see, the seconds **for** loop is part of the minutes loop, which is part of the hours loop. The *outer* **for** loop begins by initializing the *Hours* counter to 0. The statement within this loop is another **for** loop that begins by initializing the *Minutes* counter to 0. This leads to the seconds loop, where the *Seconds* counter is initialized to 0. Once the *Seconds* counter is initialized, the seconds loop is executed 60 times, as *Seconds* ranges from 0 to 59. Each time the seconds loop is executed, the *Hours, Minutes*, and *Seconds* count values are displayed. After the seconds loop is executed 60 times, the *Minutes* count is incremented, and the seconds loop is entered again and executed 60 more times.

So, the seconds loop is executed 60 times for each iteration of the minutes loop. Likewise, because the minutes loop is nested within the hours loop, the minutes loop is executed 60 times for each iteration of the hours loop. After 60 iterations of the minutes loop (3600 iterations of the seconds loop), the *Hours* count is incremented and displayed. The hours loop is not broken until it has been executed 12 times, from 0 to 11. Of course, this requires $12 \times 60 = 720$ iterations of the minutes loop and $12 \times 60 \times 60 = 43,200$ iterations of the seconds loop. We say that the seconds loop is the *innermost* loop, and the hours loop is the *outermost* loop.

Notice that *no* framing is required for the hours and minutes loops because the hours loop consists of a single **for** statement, which is the minutes loop, and the minutes loop consists of a single **for** statement, which is the seconds loop. An indentation scheme becomes important here, because it is the indentation that really shows the nesting. The seconds loop requires framing because it consists of two *cout* statements. The first *cout* statement "blanks" the output values prior to displaying the time values in the second *cout* statement. Blanking is required so that the time values appear correctly on the screen. Notice that the '\r' escape sequence is employed in both *cout* statements so that a given output overwrites the previous output.

To make the digital timer work, the seconds counter must be incremented precisely once every second. This requires a time delay routine within the seconds loop to slow down the seconds count accordingly. This will be left as an exercise at the end of the chapter.

Before we leave the topic of nested loops, you should be aware that **while** and **do/while** loops can also be nested. You will find examples of this in the questions at the end of the chapter.

Down-to for Loops

In most of the **for** loops you have seen so far, the loop counter has been incremented from some initial value to some final value. In C++, it is often more convenient to decrement the loop counter down to zero and simply test the counter value, rather than increment the counter and use a relational test. This is because C++ interprets the test expression to be false when its value is zero. Using this idea, the digital timer program segment could be easily revised to employ down-to loops, like this:

```
//DIGITAL TIMER
#include <iostream.h>   //FOR cout
void main()
{
//DISPLAY HEADINGS
   cout << "\t\t\tHours\tMinutes\tSeconds" << endl;
//START TIMER
   for (int Hours = 12; Hours; --Hours)
     for (int Minutes = 60; Minutes; --Minutes)
        for (int Seconds = 60; Seconds; --Seconds)
        {
          cout << "\t\t\t\t\t\r";                   //BLANK DISPLAY
          cout << "\t\t\t" << Hours << '\t'
               << Minutes                            //DISPLAY TIME
               << '\t' << Seconds << '\r';
        } //END SECONDS LOOP
} //END main()
```

The differences here are that the initial and final values of the respective loop counters have been changed so that the timer counts down from 12:60:60 and times out when the count reaches 00:00:00. The test expressions are simply the counter values, and the counters are being decremented rather than incremented. When a given counter value reaches zero, the loop test becomes false and the respective loop is broken. The net effect is still the same: There are 60 iterations of the seconds loop for each iteration of the minutes loop and 60 iterations of the minutes loop for each iteration of the hours loop. Of course, the timer counts down rather than counting up as in the previous program.

Quick Check

1. List the three things that must appear in the first line of a **for** loop structure.

2. True or false: The loop counter in a **for** loop is altered after the loop statements are executed in a given iteration.

3. True or false: A **for** loop can always be replaced by a **while** loop, because both are basically the same looping structure, just coded differently.

4. How many times is the following loop executed?

   ```
   for (int x = 0; x; ++x)
       cout << "How many times will this loop execute?" << endl;
   ```

5. How many times is the following loop executed?

   ```
   for (int x = 0; x <= 10; ++x)
       cout << "How many times will this loop execute?" << endl;
   ```

6. When must the **for** loop statements be framed?

7. Suppose that you have two nested loops. The inner loop executes 5 times and the outer loop executes 10 times. How many total iterations are there within the nested loop structure?

8. In a down-to loop, the loop counter is always _____.

6-4 THE break AND continue OPTIONS

The **break** and **continue** statements can be used to alter the execution of predefined control structures, such as loops, when certain conditions occur. In general, the **break** statement is used to immediately terminate a loop, and the **continue** statement is used to skip over a loop iteration.

The break Statement

You observed the use of the **break** statement within the **switch** statement in the last chapter. Recall that the **break** statement forced the **switch** statement to terminate. The same is true when you use the **break** statement inside a loop structure. When C++ executes the **break** statement within a loop, the loop is immediately terminated, and control is passed to the next statement following the loop. The **break** statement is usually used as part of an **if** statement within the loop to terminate the loop structure if a certain condition occurs. The action of the **break** statement within a **while** loop can be illustrated like this:

THE **break** *OPTION*

```
while  (test expression)
{
   statement 1;
   statement 2;
      •
      •
      •
   if (test expression)
      break;
      •
      •
      •
   statement n;
} //END WHILE
Next statement after while;
```

Consider the following program segment:

```
int Number = 1;                 //LOOP CONTROL VARIABLE
while (Number < 11)
{
   if (Number == 5)
      break;
   cout << "In the while loop, Number is now:  " << Number << endl;
   ++Number;
} //END WHILE

cout << "The loop is now terminated and the value of Number is:  "
      << Number << endl;
```

This **while** loop employs a **break** statement to terminate the loop when *Number* reaches the value of 5. Here is what you would see as a result of the loop execution:

In the while loop, Number is now: 1
In the while loop, Number is now: 2
In the while loop, Number is now: 3
In the while loop, Number is now: 4
The loop is now terminated and the value of Number is: 5

As you can see, even though the final value of *Number* is 5, the *cout* statement within the loop is not executed when *Number* reaches 5 because the **break** statement forces the loop to terminate for this value. Normally, you would not break out of a loop as a result of a natural loop counter value. Doing so would indicate that you have coded your loop test incorrectly. This was done only to illustrate how the **break** statement works. You will use the **break** statement primarily to break out of a loop when the potential for an infinite loop exists. Such an application could be to interrupt the digital timer loops given in the last section as the result of a user entry to stop the timer.

The continue Statement

You have not seen the use of the **continue** statement before this, because it is used primarily to skip an iteration within a loop if a certain condition occurs. Like the **break** statement, the **continue** statement is normally employed within a loop as part of an **if** statement. We can illustrate the operation of **continue** within a **for** loop, like this:

THE **continue** *OPTION*

```
for (Counter = initial value; Counter test expression;
      Increment/Decrement Counter)
{
    statement 1;
    statement 2;
          •
          •
    if (test expression)
       continue;
          •
          •
    statement n;
} //END FOR
Next statement after for;
```

Here you see that when the **if** statement test expression is true (nonzero), the **continue** statement is executed, forcing the current iteration to terminate. It is important to remember that *only the current iteration is terminated* as the result of **continue**. All subsequent iterations will be executed, unless, of course, they are terminated by executing a **break** or **continue**. The following program segment demonstrates how **continue** works:

```
for(int Number = 1;Number < 11; ++Number)
 {
    if (Number == 5)
        continue;
    cout << "In the for loop, Number is now:  " << Number << endl;
 } //END FOR

cout << "The loop is now terminated and the value of Number is:  "
        << Number << endl;
```

Here is the result of executing the program segment:

```
In the for loop, Number is now:  1
In the for loop, Number is now:  2
In the for loop, Number is now:  3
In the for loop, Number is now:  4
In the for loop, Number is now:  6
In the for loop, Number is now:  7
In the for loop, Number is now:  8
In the for loop, Number is now:  9
In the for loop, Number is now:  10
The loop is now terminated and the value of Number is:  11
```

You see here that the fifth iteration is skipped because of the execution of the **continue** statement. All subsequent iterations are performed, and the loop is broken naturally when *Number* reaches the value of 11.

 Quick Check

1. The statement that will cause only the current iteration of a loop to be aborted is the _____ statement.

2. The **break** and **continue** statements are normally used as part of a(n) _____ statement within a loop structure.

3. How many times will the following loop execute?

```
x = 0;
while (x <10)
{
   cout << "How many times will this loop execute?" << endl;
   if (x)
     break;
   ++x;
} //END WHILE
```

PROBLEM SOLVING IN ACTION: PARALLEL RESISTOR CIRCUIT ANALYSIS

Problem

Let's close this chapter by writing several programs that will allow a user to find the total resistance of a circuit for any number of resistors in parallel, as shown in Figure 6-5. We will solve the problem three different ways, using each of the three iteration control structures discussed in this chapter. First, let's define the problem in terms of output, input, and processing. Suppose you are working for an industrial firm and you are assigned to write a program that will allow an engineer to find the total equivalent electrical resistance of a resistive circuit for any number of resistors in parallel.

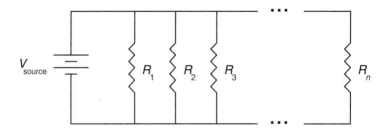

Figure 6-5 The solution of a general parallel resistor circuit is a candidate for iteration.

A simple way to find the equivalent resistance of the circuit is to use the *product-over-sum rule*. To use this rule, you start with the first two resistor values (R_1 and R_2) and calculate an equivalent resistance, like this:

$$R_{equiv} = (R_1 \times R_2) / (R_1 + R_2)$$

Notice that the equivalent resistance for the two resistances is found by dividing their product by their sum. Thus, the rule is called the "product-over-sum" rule.

Next, the equivalent value obtained from this calculation is used with the third resistor value (R_3) to find a new equivalent, like this:

$$R_{equiv} = (R_{equiv} \times R_3) / (R_{equiv} + R_3)$$

Then, this equivalent value is used with the fourth resistor value (R_4) to calculate a new equivalent value, as follows:

$$R_{equiv} = (R_{equiv} \times R_4) / (R_{equiv} + R_4)$$

This process of calculating a new equivalent resistance value from the old one continues until all the resistor values in the circuit have been used. Notice that the same basic calculation must be *repeated* several times. Such a repetition operation would always suggest a loop structure in your program.

Now, do you suppose that you can develop a program to perform the required task? Remember that the program must find the equivalent resistance of any number of resistors in parallel. Let's first define the task at hand in terms of output, input, and processing.

Defining the Problem

Output: The program must first prompt the user to enter the number of resistors in the parallel circuit. A prompt will then be generated to enter each resistor value separately. The final output will be a display of the equivalent parallel resistance.

Input: The number of resistors in the circuit and the individual resistor values.

Processing: Each time a resistor value (R) is entered, the equivalent parallel resistance (R_{equiv}) will be recalculated using the "product-over-sum" rule, as follows:

$$R_{equiv} = (R_{equiv} \times R) / (R_{equiv} + R)$$

Now, using this problem definition, we are ready for the algorithm. Let's first employ the **while** iteration control structure to repeatedly calculate the equivalent parallel resistance each time a resistor value is entered.

Planning the Solution

So as not to distract from concentrating on iteration, we will not step-wise refine the problem solution. Rather, we will employ a flat solution to the problem.

BEGIN
    Write a program-description message.
    Write a user prompt to enter the number of resistors in the circuit.
    Read (*Number*).
    Set *Count* = 0.
    While (*Count* < *Number*)
        Set *Count* = *Count* + 1.
        Write prompt to enter resistor #(*Count*).
        Read (*R*).
        If *Count* == 1 Then
          Set R_{equiv} = *R*.
        Else
          Calculate $R_{equiv} = (R_{equiv} \times R) / (R_{equiv} + R)$.
    Write (R_{equiv}).
END.

As you can see, this is a rather simple algorithm employing the **while** control structure. Each time the loop is executed, an additional resistor value is entered, and the equivalent resistance of the circuit is calculated. You probably are wondering why the **if/else** statement is used within the loop. Well, the first resistor value is entered the first time through the loop. Because *Count* = 1 during this first iteration, the **if** clause of the **if/else** statement is executed, and R_{equiv} is set to this first resistor value. In subsequent iterations, the **else** clause is executed to calculate R_{equiv} using the product-over-sum rule. Without setting R_{equiv} to the first resistor value the first time through the loop, R_{equiv} would have no beginning value for subsequent calculations, and the results would be unpredictable.

So, you say to set the value of R_{equiv} equal to zero prior to the loop. But, this will result in the numerator of the product-over-sum equation being zero, which makes the value of R_{equiv} zero in each loop iteration. The easiest solution is to set R_{equiv} to the value of the first resistor during the first loop iteration. Then, the value of R_{equiv} is recalculated with each subsequent loop iteration. Of course, if there is only one resistor in the circuit (*Number* = 1), the loop is executed only once with the value of R_{equiv} being set to this single resistor value.

Notice also that a counter (*Count*) must be initialized to 0 prior to the loop. The value of *Count* must then be incremented with each loop iteration to prevent an infinite loop. The looping continues until the value of *Count* equals the number of resistors in the circuit (*Number*). When this happens, the loop statements are not executed again and the equivalent resistance is displayed.

Following the algorithm, you can easily code a C++ program, like this:

Coding the Program

```
//ACTION 6-2A (ACT06-02.CPP)
#include <iostream.h>   //FOR cin AND cout

void main()
{
//DEFINE VARIABLES
    int Count = 0;          //LOOP COUNTER
    int Number = 0;         //NUMBER OF RESISTORS IN CIRCUIT
    float R_equiv = 0.0;    //RESISTANCE OF CIRCUIT IN OHMS
    float R = 0.0;          //INDIVIDUAL RESISTANCE VALUES IN OHMS

//WRITE PROGRAM DESCRIPTION MESSAGE AND GET NUMBER
//OF PARALLEL RESISTORS
    cout << "This program will calculate the equivalent resistance\n"
            "of any number of parallel resistors." << endl << endl;
    cout << "Enter the number of resistors in the parallel circuit: ";
    cin >> Number;

//CALCULATE EQUIVALENT RESISTANCE USING WHILE
    while (Count < Number)
    {
        ++Count;
        cout << "Enter the value for resistor #" << Count << endl;
        cin >> R;
        if (Count == 1)
            R_equiv = R;
        else
            R_equiv = (R_equiv * R) / (R_equiv + R);
    } //END WHILE
```

```
    cout.setf(ios::fixed);
    cout.precision(2);
    cout << "The equivalent resistance for the parallel circuit is:  "
         << R_equiv << " ohms" << endl;
} //END main()
```

Here is what you would see on the display when this program is executed:

This program will calculate the equivalent resistance
of any number of parallel resistors.

Enter the number of resistors in the parallel circuit:
3.↵
Enter the value for resistor #1
10.↵
Enter the value for resistor #2
12.↵
Enter the value for resistor #3
15.↵
The equivalent resistance for the parallel circuit is: 4.00 ohms

Next, suppose you want to use the **do/while** control structure to perform the same task. Remember the major difference is that the **do/while** loop statements are always executed at least once.

Planning the Solution

BEGIN
    Write a program-description message.
    Write a user prompt to enter the number of resistors in the circuit.
    Read (*Number*).
    Set *Count* = 0.
    Do
        Set *Count* = *Count* + 1.
        If Number == 0 Then
          Break
        Write prompt to enter resistor #(*Count*).
        Read (*R*).
        If *Count* == 1 Then
          Set R_{equiv} = R.

Else

$\quad$ Calculate $R_{equiv} = (R_{equiv} \times R) / (R_{equiv} + R)$.

While (*Count < Number*).

Write (R_{equiv}).

END.

$\quad$ Here you can see that the only difference between this algorithm and the previous **while** algorithm is the addition of an **if** statement that will cause the loop to break if the user enters a value of zero for the number of resistors in the circuit. Remember that a **do/while** loop is always executed at least once. Therefore, the loop must be broken and no calculation performed if there are no resistors in the circuit. This is an ideal application for the use of a **break** statement within a **do/while** loop. We did not need to use this option with the **while** loop. (Why?) Here's the resulting program.

Coding the Program

```
//ACTION 6-2B

#include <iostream.h>    //FOR cin AND cout
void main()
{
//DEFINE VARIABLES
   int Count = 0;           //LOOP COUNTER
   int Number = 0;          //NUMBER OF RESISTORS IN CIRCUIT
   float R_equiv = 0.0;     //RESISTANCE OF CIRCUIT IN OHMS
   float R = 0.0;           //INDIVIDUAL RESISTANCE VALUES IN OHMS

//WRITE PROGRAM DESCRIPTION MESSAGE AND GET NUMBER
//OF PARALLEL RESISTORS
   cout << "This program will calculate the equivalent resistance\n"
           "of any number of parallel resistors. " << endl << endl;
   cout << "Enter the number of resistors in the parallel circuit: ";
   cin >> Number;
//CALCULATE EQUIVALENT RESISTANCE USING DO/WHILE
   do
   {
        if (Number == 0)        //BREAK IF NUMBER IS ZERO
           break;
        ++Count;
        cout << "Enter the value for resistor #" << Count << endl;
        cin >> R;
```

```
        if (Count == 1)
            R_equiv = R;
        else
            R_equiv = (R_equiv * R) / (R_equiv + R);
}//END DO/WHILE
while (Count < Number);
cout.setf(ios::fixed);
cout.precision(2);
cout << "The equivalent resistance for the parallel circuit is:  "
        << R_equiv << " ohms" << endl;
} //END main()
```

The output of this program is the same as that of the **while** loop program.

Finally, let's rewrite the algorithm and code a program to employ the **for** iteration control structure. Remember that with the **for** structure, the loop is executed a fixed number of times as the loop counter ranges from its initial to final value. So, why not set the initial counter value to 1 and make a test against the number of resistors in the parallel circuit? Here's the idea in the form of an algorithm:

Planning the Solution

BEGIN
    Write a program-description message.
    Write a user prompt to enter the number of resistors in the circuit.
    Read (*Number*).
    For *Count* = 1 to *Number*
        Write prompt to enter resistor #(*Count*).
        Read (*R*).
        If *Count* == 1 then
            Set R_{equiv} = R.
        Else
            Calculate R_{equiv} = (R_{equiv} × R) / (R_{equiv} + R).
    Write (R_{equiv}).
END.

Here, the loop executes as *Count* ranges from 1 to *Number*. The counter is incremented and tested as part of the **for** control structure. An **if/else** is used as before to initialize the value of R_{equiv} to the first resistor value during the first loop iteration. Here's the program:

Coding the Program

```
//ACTION 6-2C

#include <iostream.h>    //FOR cin AND cout

void main()
{
//DEFINE VARIABLES
   int Number = 0;          //NUMBER OF RESISTORS IN CIRCUIT
   float R_equiv = 0.0;     //RESISTANCE OF CIRCUIT IN OHMS
   float R = 0.0;           //INDIVIDUAL RESISTANCE VALUES IN OHMS

//WRITE PROGRAM DESCRIPTION MESSAGE AND GET NUMBER
//OF PARALLEL RESISTORS
   cout << "This program will calculate the equivalent resistance\n"
           "of any number of parallel resistors." << endl << endl;
   cout << "Enter the number of resistors in the parallel circuit:  ";
   cin >> Number;

//CALCULATE EQUIVALENT RESISTANCE USING FOR
   for (int Count = 1; Count <= Number; ++Count)
   {
        cout << "Enter the value for resistor #" << Count << endl;
        cin >> R;
        if (Count == 1)
           R_equiv = R;
        else
           R_equiv = (R_equiv * R) / (R_equiv + R);
   } //END FOR
   cout.setf(ios::fixed);
   cout.precision(2);
   cout << "The equivalent resistance for the parallel circuit is:  "
        << R_equiv << " ohms" << endl;
} //END main()
```

Notice how the algorithm statement *For Count = 1 to Number* is coded in C++ as for (int Count = 1; Count <= Number; ++Count). The value of *Count* is first initialized to 1. Then, to allow *Count* to range from 1 to *Number*, the test must be *Count <= Number*. This allows the final iteration to occur when the value of *Count* equals the value of *Number* and forces the loop to break when the value of *Count* exceeds the value of *Number*. Of course, the value of *Count* is incremented as part of the **for** statement. Do we need a **break** statement here to terminate the program if the user enters a 0 for *Number*? The answer is no. (Why?) The output of this program is the same as that for the previous two programs.

DEBUGGING TIP

When desk-checking a loop, always check the *loop boundaries*. The loop boundaries occur at the initial and final value of the loop control variable. Checking these values will help prevent *off-by-one* errors, where the loop executes one time more or one time less than it is supposed to.

CHAPTER SUMMARY

In this chapter, you learned about the three iteration control structures employed by C++: **while**, **do/while**, and **for**. The **while** is a pretest looping structure, the **do/while** a posttest looping structure, and the **for** a fixed repetition looping structure. As a result, the following general guidelines should be considered when deciding which looping structure to use in a given situation:

- Use **while** whenever there is a possibility that the loop statements will not need to be executed.
- Use **do/while** when the loop statements must be executed at least once.
- Use **for** when it can be determined exactly how many times the loop statements must be executed. Thus, if the number of loop iterations is predetermined by the value of a variable or constant, use a **for** loop.

The **break** and **continue** statements can be used to interrupt loop iterations. Execution of the **break** statement within a loop forces the entire loop structure to terminate immediately and pass control to the next statement following the loop structure. Execution of the **continue** statement within a loop terminates only the current loop iteration.

QUESTIONS AND PROBLEMS

Questions

1. Name the three iteration control structures employed by C++.

2. Which iteration control structure(s) will always execute the loop at least once?

3. Which iteration control structure(s) evaluates the test expression before the loop is executed?

4. Which iteration control structure(s) should be employed when it can be determined in advance how many loop repetitions there should be?

5. What will the following loop do?
   ```
   while (3)
     cout << "Hello" << endl;
   ```

6. Explain the difference between the execution of **break** and **continue** within a loop.

In questions 7–17, determine the output generated by the respective program segment. Assume that the appropriate header files have been included.

7.
```
int A = 1;
while (17 % A != 5)
{
  cout << A << " " << 17 % A << endl;
  ++A;
}//END WHILE
```

8.
```
int B = 2;
do
{
  cout << B << " " << B / 5 << endl;
  B *= 2;
}//END DO/WHILE
while (B != 20);
```

9.
```
int B = 2;
do
{
  cout << B << " " << B / 5 << endl;
  B *= 2;
}//END DO/WHILE
while (B != 32);
```

10.
```
int Number = 1;
int Product = 1;
do
{
  ++Number;
  Product *= Number;
}//END DO/WHILE
while (Number < 5);
cout << "The product is:  " << Product << endl;
```

11.
```
int Count = -3;
while (Count < 3)
{
  if (!Count)
    continue;
  cout << Count << '\t';
  ++Count;
}//END WHILE
```

12.
```
int Count = -3;
while (Count < 3)
{
  ++Count;
  if (!Count)
    continue;
  cout << Count << '\t';
}//END WHILE
```

13.
```
int Count = -3;
while (Count < 3)
{
  ++Count;
  if (!Count)
    break;
  cout << Count << '\t';
}//END WHILE
```

14.
```
cout << "Angle\tSin\tCos" << endl;
cout << "-----\t---\t---" << endl;
const float PI = 3.14159;
cout.setf(ios::fixed);
cout.precision(3);
for (int Angle = 0; Angle < 91; Angle += 5)
  cout << Angle << '\t' << sin(Angle * PI/180)
       << '\t' << cos(Angle * PI/180) << endl;
```

15.
```
for (int Row = 1; Row < 6; ++Row)
{
  for (int Col = 1; Col < 11; ++Col)
    cout << Row << ',' << Col << '\t';
  cout << endl;
}//END FOR
```

16.
```
int Count = 0;
const int MAXCOUNT = 5;
while (Count < MAXCOUNT)
{
  for (int I = 1; I < MAXCOUNT + 1; ++I)
    cout << I;
  cout << endl;
  ++Count;
}//END WHILE
```

17.
```
int const MAXCOUNT = 5;
int Times = 3;
do
{
  int Count = 0;
  while (Count < MAXCOUNT)
  {
    for (int J = 1; J < Count + 1; ++J)
      cout << J;
    ++Count;
    cout << endl;
  }//END WHILE
  cout << endl;
  --Times;
}//END DO/WHILE
while (Times != 0);
```

18. When will the following loop terminate?

```
enum Boolean {FALSE,TRUE};  //DECLARE BOOLEAN DATA CLASS
Boolean Flag = TRUE;        //DEFINE BOOLEAN VARIABLE

int Number = 0;             //INPUT VARIABLE
int Sum = 0;                //SUM VARIABLE
char Query = 'N';           //CONTINUE QUERY

while (Flag == TRUE)
{
    cout << "Enter an integer number:" << endl;
```

```
                        cin >> Number;
                        cout << "Want to continue (y/n)?" << endl;
                        cin >> Query;
                        if ((Query == 'n') || (Query == 'N'))
                        {
                            Flag = FALSE;
                            cout << "Loop terminated" << endl;
                        }//END IF
                        else
                        {
                            Sum = Sum + Number;
                            cout << "The sum is now " << Sum << endl;
                        }//END ELSE
                    }//END WHILE
```

Problems

Least Difficult

1. Write a program that will compute the average of any number of test scores using a **while** loop.

2. Revise the program in problem 1 to employ a **do/while** loop.

3. Revise the program in problem 1 to employ a **for** loop.

4. Write a C++ program that will find the equivalent resistance of any number of resistors in series. Employ the **while** control structure.

5. Revise the program in problem 4 to employ the **do/while** control structure.

6. Revise the program in problem 4 to employ the **for** control structure.

7. Using the formula $C = 5/9(F - 32)$, generate a Celsius conversion table for all even temperatures from 32 degrees to 212 degrees Fahrenheit.

More Difficult

8. Write a menu-driven program that will calculate the equivalent resistance of any number of resistors in a series or a parallel circuit. Provide for loop control of the menu-driven program.

9. Write a program that will calculate the mean ($\bar{x}$) and standard deviation (σ) of a series of numbers. The mean of a series of numbers is the same as the average of the numbers. The standard deviation of a series of numbers is found using the following formula:

$$\sigma = \sqrt{\frac{(x_1 - \bar{x})^2 + (x_2 - \bar{x})^2 + \cdots + (x_n - \bar{x})^2}{n}}$$

10. Some programming languages, like BASIC, allow you to use a STEP command within a **for** statement, like this:

FOR Counter = <initial value> TO <final value> STEP N DO

The STEP command allows the loop counter to increment by some value (N), other than the value 1, with each loop iteration.

Write a **for** loop in C++ that will emulate this STEP operation. Provide for user entry of any desired step value. To demonstrate its operation, use your step loop to display every fifth integer, from 1 to 100.

11. To make the digital timer program given in this chapter work properly, you must insert a time delay within the seconds loop so that the seconds counter is incremented precisely once every second. To do this, you can insert a **for** loop that simply decrements a large counter, like this:

for(long int Timer = 4000000; Timer > 0; – –Timer);

This loop will not do anything but waste time. However, the amount of time delay is dependent on the initial counter value and the clock speed of your system CPU. Insert such a delay loop into the timer program given in this chapter, and, by trial and error, determine a counter value that will provide a one-second delay for your system. Compile, execute, and observe the program output.

12. Using the ideas you saw in the digital timer program in this chapter, write a C++ program to display the output of a 4-bit binary counter. A 4-bit binary counter simply counts in binary from 0000 to 1111. The first count value is 0000, the second is 0001, the third is 0010, and so on, until it reaches the final count value of 1111. Insert a delay in the program so that the counter increments once every 2 seconds. Change the delay value and observe the effect on the count frequency. (*Hint:* You will need four nested loops, one for each bit within the count value.)

Most Difficult

13. Write a program that will find the equivalent resistance of a series–parallel circuit of any arbitrary configuration. A series–parallel circuit is one in which there are both series and parallel resistor connections. (*Hint:* When combining resistors in such a circuit, you must start with the last resistor, at

the end of the circuit, and work toward the first resistor, at the beginning of the circuit.)

14. Write a program that employs a **while** loop to read a file called "scores" that contains an unknown number of test scores. Display the scores along with their average.

7

FUNCTIONS IN-DEPTH

INTRODUCTION
7-1 FUNCTIONS THAT RETURN A SINGLE
  VALUE: NON-VOID FUNCTIONS
  The Function Header
  The Statement Section
  Calling Non-Void Functions
  Actual Arguments versus Formal
    Parameters
7-2 VOID FUNCTIONS
  Value versus Reference Parameters
  Locating Functions Within Your Program
7-3 FUNCTION PROTOTYPES
  Default Parameters
  Function Overloading

PROBLEM SOLVING IN ACTION:
  STRUCTURED PROGRAMMING
7-4 SCOPING-OUT VARIABLES AND
  CONSTANTS ⇒ BLOCK STRUCTURE
  The Scope of Variables
  The Scope of Constants
  Static Variables
7-5 RECURSION
PROBLEM SOLVING IN ACTION:
  STRUCTURED PROGRAMMING
CHAPTER SUMMARY
QUESTIONS AND PROBLEMS
  Questions
  Problems

INTRODUCTION

In Chapter 1, you were introduced to structured design using stepwise refinement and structured programming using C++ functions. In the last few chapters, we have developed top-down structured program designs, but have employed a flat implementation when coding these designs. As a result, we have been coding C++ programs that consist of one main section defined by function *main()*. It is now time to learn how to code structured designs using a structured C++ program that employs functions. As you know, functions are the basis for structured programming in the C++ language. In addition, functions provide the only method of communicating with objects in object-oriented programming. So this chapter is crucial to your learning of both structured programming and object-oriented programming in the C++ language.

You have already used built-in, or predefined, functions in your programs. All of these functions are part of the various header files included with C++. Now it is time to develop your own functions and employ them to create modular, well-structured C++ programs as well as your own classes and objects later on when you study object-oriented programming. Functions that you create for your own use in a program are called **user-defined** functions. In this sense, the "user" is you, the programmer.

> A **user-defined function** is a block of statements, or a subprogram, that is written to perform a specific task required by you, the programmer.

A function is given a name and **called**, or **invoked**, using its name each time the task is to be performed within the program. The program that calls, or invokes, a function is often referred to as the **calling program**.

Functions eliminate the need for duplicate statements within a program. Given a task to be performed more than once, the statements are written just once for the function. Then, the function is called each time the task must be performed. In addition, the use of functions enhances the program listing clarity and readability. And most important, the use of functions within a structured language such as C++ allows you to solve very large, complex problems using a top-down program-design approach as well as to construct classes and objects in object-oriented programming. In C++, the function can be made to serve two roles. A function can be made to return a single value to the calling program. This type of function is referred to as a *non-void* function in C++. Functions can also be written to perform specific tasks or return multiple values to the calling program. These functions are called *void* functions in C++.

7-1 FUNCTIONS THAT RETURN A SINGLE VALUE: NON-VOID FUNCTIONS

You have already had some experience with functions that return a single value in C++. Recall the standard functions that you learned about in Chapter 4, such as *sqrt()*, *sin()*, and *cos()*, just to mention a few. You found that C++ included several predefined mathematical, string, and I/O functions. However, suppose you want to perform some operation that is not a predefined function in C++, such as cube. Because C++ does not include any standard function for the cube operation, you could code the operation as a statement in your program, like this:

cube = x $*$ x $*$ x;

Then, you insert this statement into your program each time the value of *x* must be cubed. However, wouldn't it be a lot easier simply to insert the command *cube(x)* each time *x* is to be cubed, where C++ knows what to do just as it knows how to execute *sqrt(x)*? You can do this by defining your own *cube()* function. Such a function is called a ***user-defined function***, for obvious reasons.

A user-defined function is a subprogram that, when invoked, performs some task or returns a single value that replaces the function name wherever the name is used in the calling program. Thus, if *cube()* is a user-defined function that will cube a value, say, *x*, the statement cout << cube(x); will invoke the function and cause the cube of *x* to be displayed. Now you need to learn how to create such user-defined functions.

Here is the format that you must use when defining your own functions:

> ### *USER-DEFINED FUNCTION FORMAT*
>
> **//FUNCTION HEADER**
>   <return data class> <function name> (<parameter list>)
>
> { //BEGIN FUNCTION STATEMENT BLOCK
>
> **//LOCAL VARS AND CONSTS**
>   <local constant and variable objects should go here>
>
> **//FUNCTION STATEMENTS or BODY**
>   function statement #1;
>   function statement #2;
>   •
>   •
>   •

```
        function statement #n;
        return <return value>;
} //END FUNCTION STATEMENT BLOCK
```

The function definition format consists of three main sections: a ***function header*** line, any ***local variable*** or ***constant objects*** required by the function, and a ***statement*** section.

The Function Header

The ***function header*** provides the data ***interface*** for the function.

> A ***function interface***, or ***header***, is a statement that forms a common boundary between the function and its calling program.

This idea is illustrated by Figure 7-1. Notice that the header dictates what data the function will *accept* from the calling program and what data the function will *return* to the calling program. When developing function headers, your perspective needs to be relative to the function. You must ask yourself two things:

1. What data must the function accept from the calling program in order to perform its designated task?

2. What data, if any, must the function return to the calling program in order to fulfill its designated task?

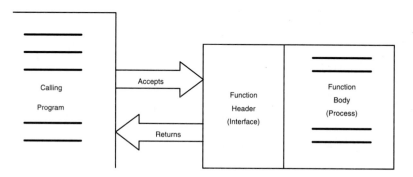

Figure 7-1 The function header forms the interface between the calling program and the function.

In general, the function header consists of the following three parts:

- The data class of the value to be returned by the function, if any.
- The name of the function.
- A parameter listing.

The Return Data Class

The first thing that appears in the function header is the data class of the return value. Recall that a function can be made to return a single value that replaces the function name wherever the name appears in a calling program. The value that replaces the function name in the calling program is referred to as the **return value**. When a function is used for this purpose, the data class of the return value must be specified in the function heading. For example, suppose that our *cube()* function returns the cube of an integer. Because the cube of an integer is an integer, the function will return an integer value. As a result, the return value data class must be **int** and specified in the function header, like this:

int cube(<parameter listing>)

On the other hand, if our *cube()* function were to cube a floating-point value, the return class would have to be **float**, and the header would look like this:

float cube(<parameter listing>)

When a function does not return any value to the calling program, you must use the keyword **void** as the return class, like this:

void SampleFunction(<parameter listing>)

Functions that do not return a value to the calling program are used to perform specific tasks, such as I/O. More about these types of functions later.

The Function Name

The function name can be any legal identifier in C++. However, the function name *should not* begin with an underscore symbol because some debuggers always place an underscore symbol in front of the function name if an error is found in the function. The function name should be descriptive of the operation that the function performs, just as *cube* describes the cubing of a value. When you invoke the function within your calling program, you will use this name.

Two things to remember:

1. The function name can never be used *inside of the function*. In other words, the following statement inside the *cube( )* function will generate an error:

    cube = x * x * x;

    There is one exception to this rule called **recursion**, which will be discussed later.

2. The function identifier can never be used on the left side of the assignment symbol *outside of the function*. Therefore, the following statement will cause an error in the calling program:

    cube = x * x * x;

The Parameter Listing

The function parameter listing includes variables, called **parameters**, that will be *passed* from the calling program and evaluated by the function. Think of a parameter as a function variable, waiting to receive a value from the calling program when the function is invoked. To determine the function parameters, ask yourself: What data must the function *accept* to perform its designated task? Suppose that our *cube( )* function will cube integer values. Then, the function must accept an integer value from the calling program and return an integer value to the calling program. Thus, our *function interface* can be described as follows:

Function *cube( )*:   Cubes an integer.
Accepts: An integer value.
Returns: An integer value.

Let's designate *x* as the integer object that the function will accept. In C++, a given parameter must be specified in the function header by indicating its data class followed by its identifier. As a result, the appropriate parameter listing for the *cube( )* function would be *(int x)*. Putting everything together, the complete header would be

                          int cube(int x)
        Return class ──┘ | └── Function parameter
                          Function name

If the *cube()* function were to cube floating-point values, the appropriate header would be

float cube(float x)
Return class ——┘ | └—— Function parameter
Function name

Example 7-1

Suppose you want to write a user-defined function to calculate the voltage in a dc circuit using Ohm's law. Write an appropriate function heading.

Solution

Let's call the function *Voltage*, because this is what the function must return to the calling program each time the function is called.

To develop the function header, we will treat the function like a black box and ask ourselves the following two questions: (1) What data must the function *accept* from the calling program in order to perform the application task? (2) What must it *return* to the calling program? The answers to these questions will dictate the function header, or interface. To answer the first question, think about what the function must evaluate. In order to calculate voltage using Ohm's law, the function must evaluate two things: current and resistance. So let's use the words *Current* and *Resistance* as our parameters. Of what data class should the parameters be? The obvious choice is floating-point, because you want to allow the function to evaluate decimal values of current and resistance. Thus, the function must accept a floating-point value of *Current* and a floating-point value of *Resistance*.

Next, you must decide what data the function must *return* to the calling program. Because the function is evaluating floating-point values, it makes mathematical sense that the returned value should also be a floating-point value.

Now, the function interface can be described as follows:

Function *Voltage()*: Calculates voltage using Ohm's law.
Accepts: A floating-point value for *Current* and a floating-point
                    value for *Resistance*.
Returns: A floating-point value for *Voltage*.

Once you have decided what the function accepts and returns, the function header is easily constructed in C++ syntax as follows:

float Voltage (float Current, float Resistance)

The Statement Section

The statement section of the function includes those operations that the function must perform to return a value to the calling program. Look at the general format for a user-defined function again. As you can see, the entire statement section is framed with curly braces. After the opening curly brace, you should begin the statement section by declaring any constant objects and defining variable objects that will be used within the function. Any constant or variable objects listed here are called *local*, because they are defined only for local use within the function itself. Local constants and variables have no meaning outside of the function in which they are defined. *You do not duplicate any of your function parameters here.* You list only additional constants or variables that the function might require during its execution. A common example of a local variable is a loop counter that is employed as part of a **while**, **do/while**, or **for** loop within the function. Actually, you can declare local constants and define local variables anyplace within the function as long as they are listed prior to their use. However, good style dictates that they be declared/defined at the beginning of the statement section of the function.

CAUTION

Do not confuse local variables with function parameters. A local variable is defined after the opening brace of a function for use within that function. A function parameter is defined in the function header as a place holder for argument values passed to the function when the function is called. It will also be used within the function to supply data from the calling program to the function.

The executable statements of the function follow any local declarations/definitions. The last statement in a non-void function is the **return** statement. The **return** statement is used when a single value must be returned to the calling program. So, if our *cube()* function must return the cube of *x*, an appropriate return statement would be

return x * x * x;

Combining the function header and statement section for the cube function will give us the complete function as follows:

```
int cube(int x)
{
   return x * x * x;
}//END Cube()
```

Obviously, this is a relatively simple function that doesn't require any local definitions or executable statements other than the **return** statement.

Example 7-2

Complete the *Voltage()* function whose header was developed in Example 7-1.

Solution

Ohm's law requires the function to multiply *Current* by *Resistance* to get *Voltage*. Thus, the only statement required in the function is a **return** statement that will return the product of *Current* and *Resistance*. By putting it all together, the complete function becomes

```
float Voltage(float Current, float Resistance)
{
   return Current * Resistance;
}//END Voltage()
```

DEBUGGING TIP

A common source of error in coding a non-void function is to make an assignment to the function name within the function, as follows:

```
float Voltage(float Current, float Resistance)
{
   return Voltage = Current * Resistance;
}//END Voltage()
```

This will always cause a compiler error, because you are attempting to return the function name. You must return a value, which, in this case, is the product of *Current* and *Resistance*.

Example 7-3

Write a function to return the sum of all integers from 1 to some maximum integer value, called *Max*. The function must obtain the value of *Max* from the calling program.

Solution

Let's call this function *Sum()*. Now, the function must *accept* an integer value, called *Max*, from the calling program. Because the function is to sum all the integers from 1 to *Max*, it must return an integer value. Thus, our function interface can be described as follows:

Function *Sum()*:   Sums all integers from 1 to *Max*.
Accepts: An integer value, *Max*.
Returns: An integer value.

Using this information, the function header becomes

int Sum(int Max)

The next step is to determine if there are any local variables required by the function statements. You can use a **for** loop to calculate the sum of integers from 1 to *Max*. However, the **for** statement requires a counter variable. This is a classic application for a local variable. Let's call this local counter variable *Count*. Next, you also need a temporary variable within the **for** loop to keep a running subtotal of the sum each time the loop executes. Let's call this local variable *SubTotal*. Using these ideas, the complete function is

```
int Sum(int Max)
{
  int SubTotal = 0;    //TEMP SUBTOTAL VARIABLE

  for (int Count = 1; Count <= Max; ++Count)
     SubTotal = SubTotal + Count;
  return SubTotal;
}//END Sum()
```

Why can't you use *Sum* instead of *SubTotal* within the function **for** loop? This would cause an error during compilation. The reason? *Sum* is the function name and cannot appear within the body of the function except when used as part of a recursive operation (to be discussed later).

Calling Non-Void Functions

You call, or invoke, a non-void function just about anywhere in your program just as you call many of the standard functions in C++. For example, you can call a function by using an assignment operator or a *cout* statement, like this:

```
y = cube(2);
```

or

```
cout << cube(2);
```

In both cases, the value 2 is passed to the function to be cubed. Thus, in our *cube()* function, the parameter *x* takes on the value 2. The function will return the cube of 2, which is 8. With the assignment statement, the variable *y* will be assigned the value 8, and the *cout* statement causes the value 8 to be displayed on the monitor.

Here are two other ways that our *cube()* function can be called:

```
int A = 2;
y = cube(A);
```

 or

```
cout << cube(A);
```

In these cases, the function is cubing the variable *A*, where *A* has been previously assigned the value 2. Thus, the value of *A*, or 2, is passed to the function. In our *cube()* function, the parameter *x* takes on the value of *A*.

Functions can also be called as part of arithmetic expressions or relational statements. For instance, our *cube()* function can be called as part of an arithmetic expression, like this:

```
int A = 2;
y = 1 + cube(A) * 2;
```

What will be assigned to *y* ? Well, C++ evaluates the *cube()* function first to get 8, then performs the multiplication operation to get 16, and finally adds 1 to 16 to get 17.

You also can use functions as part of relational operations, like this:

```
if (cube(A) >= 27)
```

When will the relationship be true? When *A* is greater than or equal to 3, right? When *A* is greater than or equal to 3, *cube(A)* is greater than or equal to 27. Just remember that when a function is designed to return a single value to the calling program, the *value returned replaces the function name wherever the name is used in the calling program.*

PROGRAMMING NOTE

You will normally call non-void functions within your program using an assignment statement, a *cout* object, or as part of an arithmetic operation. Remember to think of the function call as a *value*. That is, a value replaces the function call where it appears in the program. Ask yourself: "Does a *value* make sense here?" For example, the following statements all make sense, because a value can easily be substituted for the function call:

```
Result = cube(A);
cout << cube(A);
Solution = 2 * cube(A) + 5;
```

On the other hand, the following statement would not make sense and would cause a compile error, because the compiler sees just a single value coded as an executable statement.

```
cube(A);
```

Actual Arguments versus Formal Parameters

Some terminology is appropriate at this time. In the foregoing *cube()* example, the variable *A* used in the calling program is called an ***actual argument***. On the other hand, the corresponding variable *x* used in the function header is called a ***formal parameter***.

> ***Actual arguments*** are values/variables used within the function call, and ***formal parameters*** are variables used within the function header that receive the actual argument values.

Thus, we say that the formal parameter in our *cube()* function, *x*, takes on the value of the actual argument, *A*, used in the function call. Here are some things that you will want to remember about actual arguments and formal parameters:

- Actual argument variables must be defined in the calling program. This will be function *main()*, unless functions are calling other functions.
- The data class of the corresponding actual arguments and formal parameters should be the same.

- Formal parameters are place holders for the actual argument values during the execution of the function. Formal parameters are always listed in the parameter section of the function heading.
- The number of actual arguments used during the function call must be the same as the number of formal parameters listed in the function heading, except when default parameters are used. Default parameters will be discussed shortly.
- The correspondence between actual arguments and formal parameters is established on a one-to-one basis according to the respective listing orders.
- Although the actual argument and formal parameter variables often have different variable names, they can be the same. When this is the case, the respective variable objects must still be defined in the calling program and must also appear in the parameter listing of the function.

DEBUGGING TIP

Always remember to check that the number and data classes of the actual arguments in a function call match the number and data classses of the formal parameters in the function header on a one-to-one basis, according to their respective listing orders. Each argument in the function call *must* correspond to one and only one parameter in the function header, and the respective ordering *must* be the same. You will always get a compiler error if the number of actual arguments does not match the number of formal parameters, unless default parameters are employed. However, you will often not get a compiler error if their data classes do not match or the respective ordering is different. The result here will be garbage, and its source might be very difficult to locate.

 Quick Check

1. What is the role of a function in a C++ program?
2. The three main sections of a function are the _____, _____, and _____ sections.

3. What is the purpose of the function header in a C++ program?

4. List the three parts of a function header.

5. A function variable, waiting to receive a value from the calling program, is called a _____.

6. What is the purpose of a **return** statement in a function?

7. Explain the difference between an actual argument in a calling program and a formal parameter in a function header.

7-2 VOID FUNCTIONS

Functions that do not return a single value to the calling program are often written to return multiple values or perform some specific task. These are called *void* functions.

A *void function* is a function that returns multiple values or performs some specific task, rather than returning a single value to the calling program.

When a function is not returning a single value to the calling program, you must use the keyword **void** as the return data class. In addition, these functions may or may not require parameters. When no parameters are required, you simply leave the parameter listing blank to indicate to the compiler that the function does not need to receive any values from the calling program. Functions that do not return a value or do not require any parameters are the simplest type of functions in C++. For example, suppose that you want to write a function that will display the following header on the monitor each time it is called:

$$\text{NAME} \quad \text{STREET} \quad \text{ADDRESS} \quad \text{STATE} \quad \text{CITY} \quad \text{ZIP}$$
$$\underline{\quad\quad} \quad \underline{\quad\quad} \quad \underline{\quad\quad\quad} \quad \underline{\quad\quad} \quad \underline{\quad\quad} \quad \underline{\quad}$$

Let's call this function *DisplayHeader()*. To develop the function header, ask yourself what the function must *accept* to perform its designated task and what it must *return*. In this case, the function is simply displaying constant header information and does not need to accept any data or return any data. Thus, our function interface can be described as follows:

Function *DisplayHeader( )*:	Displays fixed header information.
Accepts:	Nothing.
Returns:	Nothing.

Using this information, the header becomes

void DisplayHeader()

Look at the function header and you will see the keyword **void** used as the function return class. The keyword **void** used here indicates to the compiler that there is no return value. Furthermore, notice that there are no parameters required by this function, because the parameter listing is left blank. In other words, the function does not return a value and does not require any arguments to evaluate. It simply performs a given task, in this case displaying a header. To display the header, all you need is a *cout* statement in the body of the function. Putting everything together, the function becomes

```
void DisplayHeader()
{
 cout << "\tNAME\tSTREET ADDRESS\tCITY\tSTATE\tZIP"
        "\n\t____\t_____\t____\t____\t___" << endl;
}//END DisplayHeader()
```

Finally, you do not see a **return** statement at the end of the function, because no single value is being returned by the function.

How would you call this function in your program? Simple; just use the function name as a statement within the calling program each time the header must be displayed, like this:

DisplayHeader();

No actual arguments are listed in the function call, because no arguments need to be evaluated by the function.

PROGRAMMING NOTE

When calling a void function, simply list the function name and required arguments as a single statement within your program. *Do not* call a void function with an assignment operator or *cout* object as you do non-void functions. The following calls on *DisplayHeader( )* would, at best, cause a compiler error,

```
Header = DisplayHeader();      //ERROR
cout << DisplayHeader();       //ERROR
```

The correct call is simply

```
DisplayHeader();
```

Value versus Reference Parameters

The preceding *DisplayHeader()* function did not require any formal parameter listing, because it did not need to receive any arguments from the calling program to evaluate. When formal parameters are required for evaluation by the function, they must be listed in the function header in one of two ways: as **value parameters** or as **reference parameters**.

Value Parameters

You have been using value parameters up to this point in this chapter. Value parameters allow for *one-way communication* of data from the calling program to the function. This concept is illustrated in Figure 7-2a.

> A **value parameter** provides for one-way communication of data from the calling program to the function.

Observe that the actual argument values in the calling program are passed (by value) to the formal parameters in the function. Another way to think of it is that the formal parameter receives a *copy* of the actual argument value. When the function operates on a value parameter, it is operating on a copy, rather than the original value in the calling program. Thus, the actual argument value in the calling program is protected from being accidentally changed by the function. The important thing to remember when using value parameters is that any manipulation of the formal parameters within the function does not affect the actual argument values used for the function call. For instance, consider the following function:

```
void PassByValue(int x,int y)
{
```

//INCREMENT AND DECREMENT FORMAL PARAMETERS
```
  ++x;
  --y;
```

//DISPLAY FORMAL PARAMETER VALUES
```
  cout << "x = " << x << endl;
  cout << "y = " << y << endl;
}//END PassByValue()
```

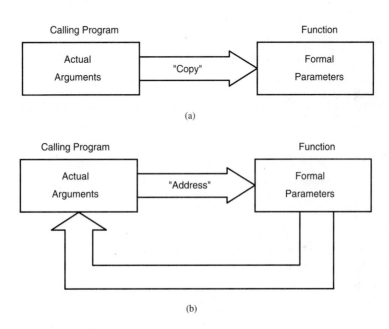

Figure 7-2 Passing parameters (a) by value and (b) by reference.

Here, the parameters x and y are value parameters. Notice that, within the function, the value of x is incremented and the value of y is decremented. Then, the resulting values are displayed using a *cout* statement. Now, suppose the above function is called by the following program:

```
void main()
{
//DEFINE ACTUAL ARGUMENT VARIABLES
  int A = 0;
  int B = 0;
```

```
//CALL FUNCTION
  PassByValue(A,B);

//DISPLAY ACTUAL ARGUMENT VALUES
  cout << "A = " << A << endl;
  cout << "B = " << B << endl;
}//END main()
```

First, notice how the function is called. It is simply a statement in the calling program. The function name is listed, followed by the required actual arguments within parentheses. The actual arguments are *A* and *B*, because they are listed in the function call. When the function call is executed, the value of *A* is passed to the value parameter *x*, and the value of *B* is passed to the value parameter *y*. Another way to say this is that *x* receives a copy of *A* and *y* receives a copy of *B*. Notice that before the function call, the calling program initializes both *A* and *B* to the value 0. As a result, both *x* and *y* receive the value 0 from the calling program. The function then increments the value of *x*, decrements the value of *y*, and displays the new values of *x* and *y*. However, the operations on *x* and *y* have no effect on the actual arguments (*A* and *B*) in the calling program. The values of *A* and *B* remain 0. Notice that after the function call, the calling program displays the values of *A* and *B*. What would you see on the display by executing the program? Well, the *PassByValue()* function displays *x* and *y*, then *main()* displays *A* and *B*. Therefore, the resulting display is

```
x = 1
y = −1
A = 0
B = 0
```

Reference Parameters

Reference parameters, sometimes called ***variable parameters***, differ from value parameters in that they provide two-way communication between the calling program and the function, as illustrated in Figure 7-2b.

> A ***reference parameter*** provides two-way communication of data between the calling program and function.

Observe the two-way communication path: The actual argument values are passed to the formal parameters in the function, and then the formal parameter values are passed back to the actual arguments. This allows the function to change the actual argument values in the calling program. Recall that a *value parameter* is simply a copy of the actual argument value; therefore, any operations on the parameter within the function have no effect on its original argument value. On the other hand, a *reference parameter* represents the *address* in memory of the actual argument value. As a result, any changes made to the reference parameter within the function will change what's stored at that address. This obviously changes the original value of the actual argument in the calling program.

To create a reference parameter, you simply insert an ampersand, &, prior to the appropriate parameter identifiers in the function heading. Let's change our preceding example to use reference parameters, as follows:

```
void PassByReference(int &x,int &y)
{
//INCREMENT AND DECREMENT FORMAL PARAMETERS
  ++x;
  --y;

//DISPLAY FORMAL PARAMETER VALUES
  cout << "x = " << x << endl;
  cout << "y = " << y << endl;
}//END PassByReference()
```

The major change here is to insert an ampersand prior to *x* and *y* in the function heading. Of course, the function name has also been changed to reflect the new application. What would you see on the display as a result of executing the following program?

```
void main()
{
//DEFINE ACTUAL ARGUMENT VARIABLES
  int A = 0;
  int B = 0;

//CALL FUNCTION
  PassByReference(A,B);

//DISPLAY ACTUAL ARGUMENT VALUES
  cout << "A = " << A << endl;
  cout << "B = " << B << endl;
} //END main()
```

Because *x* and *y* are now reference parameters and not value parameters, any operations that affect *x* and *y* within the function will also affect the values of the actual arguments, *A* and *B*, used in the function call. Here are the values displayed by the program:

```
x = 1
y = -1
A = 1
B = -1
```

As you can see, the new values of *x* and *y* are passed back to *A* and *B*, respectively. We use that term "passed back" to describe the action. However, remember that nothing is actually being passed back, because the function is simply operating on the addresses of the actual arguments, *A* and *B*.

Example 7-4

What will be displayed as a result of the following program?

```
void main()
{
//DEFINE ACTUAL ARGUMENT VARIABLES
  int A = 0;
  int B = 0;

//CALL FUNCTION
  DisplayParameters(A,B);

//DISPLAY ACTUAL ARGUMENT VALUES
  cout << "A = " << A << endl;
  cout << "B = " << B << endl;
} //END main()


//*****************************************************************
//
//THIS FUNCTION DEMONSTRATES THE USE OF VALUE VERSUS
//REFERENCE PARAMETERS
//
//*****************************************************************
void DisplayParameters(int &x, int y)
{
//INCREMENT AND DECREMENT FORMAL PARAMETERS
  ++x;
  --y;
```

```
//DISPLAY FORMAL PARAMETER VALUES
  cout << "x = " << x << endl;
  cout << "y = " << y << endl;
} //END DisplayParameters()
```

Solution

Here you see an entire program that incorporates a function. The function is located immediately following the closing brace of function *main()*. The function is then called within the statement section of *main()* by simply listing its name followed by a listing of the required actual arguments. Notice that the actual arguments (*A* and *B*) are defined as integer objects in *main()*. Now look at the function heading. The formal parameters are *x* and *y*. Both are integers; however, *x* is a reference parameter, whereas *y* is a value parameter. Observe the use of the ampersand prior to *x*. This defines *x* as a reference parameter. However, a comma follows *x*, ending this definition. Then, *y* is defined separately as a value parameter (no ampersand). As a result, the value of *x* is passed back to *main()*, but the value of *y* is not. Here's what you would see on the display:

```
x = 1
y = -1
A = 1
B = 0
```

Example 7-5

Write a function called *Exchange()* that will accept two integer objects from the calling program and return the objects with their values exchanged.

Solution

This is an ideal application for reference parameters because, to exchange the object values, the exchange process within the function must have an effect on the original object values in the calling program. So, the function must accept two integer objects and return the same two objects with the values exchanged. Here's a description of the function interface:

Function *Exchange()*:	Exchanges the values of two integer objects.
Accepts:	Two integer objects.
Returns:	The same two integer objects.

Because the function must return the same two integer variables that it accepts, both will be reference parameters. Let's label the parameters *Object1* and *Object2*. The function header then becomes

```
void Exchange(int &Object1, int &Object2)
```

Notice the use of the ampersand to indicate that the parameters are reference parameters. Because *Object1* and *Object2* are reference parameters, the values of the actual argument objects used in the function call will be exchanged. Now, to exchange the two object values within the function, you must create a temporary local variable object so that one of the values is not lost. Using this idea, the complete function is

```
void Exchange(int &Object1, int &Object2)
{
  //DEFINE TEMPORARY LOCAL VARIABLE
  int Temp;

  //EXCHANGE OBJECT VALUES
  Temp = Object1;
  Object1 = Object2;
  Object2 = Temp;
} //END Exchange()
```

To call this function in a program, you simply list the function name and provide two variable objects to be exchanged, like this:

```
Exchange(A,B);
```

Of course, *A* and *B* must be defined and initialized with values within the calling program, somewhere prior to this function call.

CAUTION

Although functions that employ reference parameters might have a **void** return class, they are, in fact, returning values to the calling program via the reference parameters. Do not get the idea of the function return class confused with the idea of returning values via reference parameters. They are two different things.

Locating Functions Within Your Program

As you can see from Example 7-4, user-defined functions are located just after the closing brace of function *main()*. There is no limit on the number of user-defined functions that can be used in a program. To call a function that returns a single value, you must insert the function name where you want the value to be returned. To call a void function, you simply list its name as a statement within the calling program. Of course, in both cases, any actual arguments required by the function must be listed within parentheses after the function name when it is called. In addition, the number of actual arguments used in the function call must be the same as the number of formal parameters defined in the respective function header, unless default parameters are used.

The placement of functions in a C++ program is summarized in Figure 7-3. Notice the block structure of the overall program. Function *main()* forms the overall outer program block, and the user-defined functions form the inner blocks that are nested within function *main()* via the function calls. This is why C++ is called a **block-structured language**. From now on, when we develop C++ programs, we will attempt to divide the overall programming problem into a group of simpler subproblems whose combined solution solves the original problem. How will these subproblems be coded? You've got it—as functions! This is the essence of structured programming and top-down software design.

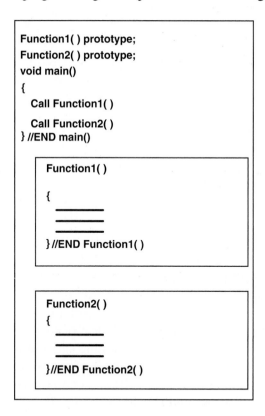

Figure 7-3 Functions are usually placed after *main()* in a C++ program.

Quick Check

1. What must be used as the return data class when a function does not return a single value to the calling program?

2. What two things must be considered when developing a function header?

3. One-way communication of data from the calling program to a function is provided via _____ parameters.

4. Two-way communication of data between the calling program and a function is provided via _____ parameters.

5. To specify a reference parameter in a function header, you must use the _____ symbol prior to the parameter identifier.

6. Where is the body of a function normally located in a C++ program?

7-3 FUNCTION PROTOTYPES

You undoubtedly noticed the presence of a ***function prototype*** in Figure 7-3. A ***function prototype***, sometimes referred to as a ***function declaration***, is a *model* of the *interface* to the function that can be used by the compiler to check calls to the function for the proper number of arguments and the correct data classes of the arguments.

> A ***function prototype*** is a model of the interface to the function.

Prototyping forces the compiler to perform additional data class checking of your function calls, thus aiding in the detection of programming errors associated with function calls. For example, if a function expects to receive an integer value and the programmer tries to pass it a character string, the compiler can detect the error because C++ requires that the function prototype be specified prior to the function call. Because prototyping forces the compiler to check for errors during compile time, it does not affect the size or speed of the run-time program. Although it takes the compiler slightly longer to perform this error-checking task, any errors detected via prototyping can save hours of debugging time had prototyping not been employed. For these reasons, function prototypes are required by the C++ language. You should be aware, however, that function prototyping is optional in the C language. As a result, the C++ language is considered more strongly typed than the C language.

In the foregoing definition of a prototype, you see it provides a model of the interface to the function. Well, the function interface is the function header; therefore, the function prototype is simply a copy of the function header used by the compiler to verify the calls to the function. Thus, the prototype dictates what classes of data the function will accept from the calling program and what classes of data the function will return to the calling program.

You see from Figure 7-3 that the function prototypes are located just prior to function *main()*. The function prototype can be nothing more than a copy of the function header followed by a semicolon, like this:

```
void Student(int Number, float Average, char Grade);
```

Here, the prototype tells the compiler that the function *Student()* will not be returning a value to the calling program. In addition, *Student()* expects to receive three parameters when it is called. The first parameter will be interpreted as an integer, the second as a floating-point value, and the third as a character. If the function is called with more than or fewer than the number of parameters listed in the prototype, the compiler will generate an error, unless defalt parameters are specified. If the function is called with parameters that belong to different data classes than those listed in the prototype, the parameters will be treated as if they were the respective data classes listed. Here is a program that uses the *Student()* function whose prototype was shown above:

```
#include <iostream.h>   //FOR cin AND cout

//FUNCTION PROTOTYPE
   void Student(int Number, float Average, char Grade);

void main()
{
   Student(5, 85.6, 'B');
} //END main()

//*********************************************************
//THIS FUNCTION WILL DISPLAY A STUDENT'S AVERAGE AND
//GRADE
//*********************************************************
void Student(int Number, float Average, char Grade)
{
```

```
    cout.setf(ios::fixed);
    cout.precision(1);
    cout << "There are " << Number << " tests, resulting "
         << "in an average of " << Average << " and a grade of "
         << Grade << '.' << endl;
} //END Student()
```

The output generated by this program is

There are 5 tests, resulting in an average of 85.6 and a grade of B.

As you can see, the actual arguments in the function call were passed to *Student()* and used to construct the *cout* statement. If more or fewer parameters had been used in the function call, a compiler error would have been the result. But what would happen if the argument data classes were not the same as those listed in the prototype? Consider this function call:

Student('B', 'A', 67);

This call would not produce a compiler error, because the number of parameters is correct. However, the compiler would interpret the first parameter as an integer, the second as a floating-point value, and the third as a character value. As a result, the output generated by the function call would be

There are 66 tests, resulting in an average of 65.0 and a grade of C.

Do you see what happened? The function used the integer equivalent of the character 'B' for the first parameter, the floating-point equivalent of the character 'A' for the second parameter, and the character equivalent of the integer 67 for the third parameter. Of course, these equivalencies are derived from the ASCII character code. So, the lesson here is to make sure that the argument data classes match the formal parameter data classes, or you may get unpredictable results.

Look at the *Student()* function prototype again, and you will see that it is just a copy of the function header. Because of this, prototypes are easily coded into your program by using the block copy feature of your editor. Once you code a function, simply mark the function header and copy it to the prototype area just prior to function *main()*. Don't forget to add a semicolon at the end of the prototype, because the copied function header will not have one.

You may also list your function prototypes without any parameter identifiers, like this:

void Student(int, float, char);

After all, the compiler is not interested in the parameter names, it is only interested in the number of parameters and their data classes. One final point: If you forget to include a prototype for a function you will get the familiar "prototype expected" error when you compile your program. You will also get this error if you forget to include a header file for a standard function in your program because prototypes for the standard functions in C++ are included in the respective function header files.

DEBUGGING TIP

Remember that a semicolon must terminate a function prototype. You will get a "declaration syntax error" error message during compilation if it is missing. However, there must *not* be a semicolon at the end of a function header. You will get a "declaration terminated incorrectly" error message during compilation if it is present.

Default Parameters

When a parameter has a default value, the parameter assumes its default value when no argument is supplied for that parameter in the function call.

A *default parameter* is a function parameter that is assigned a default value in either the function prototype or the function header, but not both.

Consider the following program:

```
//PREPROCESSOR DIRECTIVES
#include <iostream.h>   //FOR cin AND cout

//FUNCTION PROTOTYPE
int Volume(int Length, int Width = 5, int Height = 2);

void main()
{
//DEFINE FUNCTION ARGUMENT VARIABLES
  int  L = 10;                  //LENGTH
  int W = 15;                   //WIDTH
  int H = 12;                   //HEIGHT
//FUNCTION CALLS
```

```
        cout << "The volume for this function call is:  " << Volume(L,W,H)
            << endl << endl;
        cout << "The volume for this function call is:  " << Volume(L,W)
            << end << endl;
        cout << "The volume for this function call is:  " << Volume(L)
            << endl << endl;
        cout << "The volume for this function call is:  " << Volume(3,3,3)
            << endl << endl;
    } //END main()


//FUNCTION DEFINITION
int Volume(int Length, int Width, int Height)
{
    cout << "The formal parameters for this function call are: " << Length <<  ", "
        << Width << ", " << Height << endl;
    return  Length * Width * Height;
}//END Volume()
```

Here you see a prototype for function *Volume( )* where the *Width* and *Height* parameters are assigned default values of 5 and 2, respectively. Looking at the function definition, you see that the function simply writes its formal parameter values and returns the product of these values. Now, look at the function calls in the body of *main( )*. Notice how the function is called several times, each time with a different set of actual arguments. Here is what you would see on your monitor after executing this program:

```
The formal parameters for this function call are:  10, 15, 12
The volume for this function is:  1800

The formal parameters for this function call are:  10, 15, 2
The volume for this function call is:  300

The formal parameters for this function call are:  10, 5, 2
The volume for this function call is:  100

The formal parameters for this function call are:  3, 3, 3
The volume for this function call is:  27
```

The first time the function is called, all three arguments are supplied by the way of the three variables *L*, *W*, and *H*, which are initialized to 10, 15, and 12, respectively, in *main( )*. The second time the function is called, only *L* and *W* are supplied as function arguments. Because the *Height* argument is not supplied, the compiler inserts the default *Height* value of 2 for this argument. Thus, the returned volume is 10 * 15 * 2, or 300. In the third call, only the value of *L* is supplied as a function argument, and the compiler inserts the default values of 5 and 2 for the *Width* and *Height* arguments, respectively. This results in a volume value of 10 * 5 * 2, or 100. Finally, in the last function call, all three arguments are hard-coded into the call, and the resulting volume is 3 * 3 * 3, or 27.

Here are some things that you will want to remember when using default parameters:

- Default parameter values are supplied by the compiler in a function call when an argument is not provided in the call for a given parameter.
- Default values can be provided in either the function prototype or function header, but not both.
- Once you assign a default value to a parameter in either a function prototype or header, all the remaining parameters must have default values. So, if a default value is specified for parameter *n*, then default parameters must also be specified for parameters *n* + 1, *n* + 2, and so on.
- The default values for a given parameter must be the correct data class for that parameter.

Function Overloading

The idea of function overloading is important to programming in C++. When a function is overloaded, it is designed to perform differently when it is supplied with a different number of arguments or argument data classes. In other words, the same function exhibits different *behavior* with a different number of arguments or argument data classes. Thus, a given function might *behave* one way when supplied one argument and an entirely different way when supplied two arguments. For example, consider the following program:

```
#include <iostream.h>   //FOR cin AND cout

//FUNCTION PROTOTYPES
int Area(int);
int Area(int, int);
float Area(float);

void main()
{
//DEFINE FUNCTION ARGUMENT VARIABLES
  int Side = 3;
```

```
    int Length = 4;
    int Width = 5;
    float Radius = 6.25;

//FUNCTION CALLS
    cout << "The area of the square is:  " << Area(Side) << endl;
    cout << "The area of the rectangle is: " << Area(Length,Width) << endl;
    cout << "The are of the circle is: " << Area(Radius) << endl;
} //END main()

//THIS FUNCTION FINDS THE AREA OF A SQUARE
int Area(int S)
{
   return S * S;
} //END Area()

//THIS FUNCTION FINDS THE AREA OF A RECTANGLE
int Area(int L, int W)
{
   return L * W;
} //END Area()

//THIS FUNCTION FINDS THE AREA OF A CIRCLE
float Area(float R)
{
   return 3.14159 * R * R;
} //END Area()
```

Look at the function prototyping section. The first thing you see is three different prototypes for *Area()*. In the first prototype, *Area()* requires a single integer argument and returns an integer value. In the second prototype, *Area()* requires two integer arguments and returns an integer value. In the third prototype, *Area()* requires a single floating-point argument and returns a floating-point value. Looking at the function definitions at the bottom of the program, you find that the single function *Area()* is defined three different times to do three different things. The way *Area()* will *behave* is determined by the number and classes of the arguments supplied when it is called. If a single integer argument is provided when *Area()* is called, it will return the area of a square. If two integer arguments are supplied in the call, *Area()* will return the area of a rectangle, which is not square. However, if a single floating-point argument is supplied in the call, *Area()* will return the area of a circle. Here is the result of the program execution:

The area of the square is: 9

The area of the rectangle is: 20

The area of the circle is: 122.718

Obviously, you could say that *Area()* is *overloaded* with work, because it is performing three different tasks, depending on the number and data classes of the arguments used in its call. Overloading is used where the tasks are very similar, differing only in the number of arguments required by the function or the data classes of the arguments. Without overloading, you would have to invent different names for each similar task instead of just one, thus requiring you and your program users to remember all of them.

Function overloading is related to the concept of ***polymorphism***, which is one of the cornerstones of object-oriented programming, as you will find out later. I am introducing it here so that you understand the concept. You will see how it is applied when you learn about OOP in a later chapter. By the way, function overloading is not possible in the C language.

 Quick Check

1. What is the primary purpose of a function prototype?

2. Where is a function prototype normally located in a C++ program?

3. True or false: Parameters listed in a function prototype can be listed only by data class, without any corresponding identifiers.

4. True or false: Default parameters can appear on either the function prototype or function header, but not both.

5. True or false: Once a default parameter is specified in a function prototype, the remaining parameters in the parameter listing must be default parameters.

6. When overloading a function, what determines how the function will behave?

PROBLEM SOLVING IN ACTION: STRUCTURED PROGRAMMING

Problem

In previous chapters, we developed a loop-controlled, menu-driven Ohm's law program. However, although we developed a structured design, we have employed a flat implementation when coding the design. It is now time to do it right and employ structured programming via functions to implement the structured design. Here is the problem definition that we developed earlier:

Defining the Problem

Output: A program menu that prompts the user to select a voltage, current, or resistance calculation option.
Invalid entry messages as required.
A voltage, current, or resistance value, depending on the program option that the user selects.

Input: A user response to the menu (V, I, R, or Q).
If V is selected: User enters values for current and resistance.
If I is selected: User enters values for voltage and resistance.
If R is selected: User enters values for voltage and current.
If Q is selected: Terminate the program.

Processing: Calculate the selected option.
Case V: *Voltage = Current × Resistance.*
Case I: *Current = Voltage / Resistance.*
Case R: *Resistance = Voltage / Current.*
Case Q: Terminate the program.
Repeat the menu until the user chooses to terminate the program.

Planning the Solution

The structure chart that we developed earlier is shown again in Figure 7-4. Here is the set of algorithms we developed earlier:

Initial Algorithm

     main()
     BEGIN
        Do
           Call *DisplayMenu()* function.

Call *OhmsLaw()* function.
While *Choice* ≠ 'q' AND *Choice* ≠ 'Q'
END.

First Level of Refinement

DisplayMenu()
BEGIN
　Display a program menu that prompts the user to choose a voltage (V),
　current (I), resistance (R), or quit (Q) option.
　Read (*Choice*).
END.

OhmsLaw()
BEGIN
　Case V:　Call function *CalculateVoltage()*.
　Case I:　Call function *CalculateCurrent()*.
　Case R:　Call function *CalculateResistance()*.
　Case Q:　Terminate program.
　Default:　Write an invalid entry message and ask the user to select again.
END.

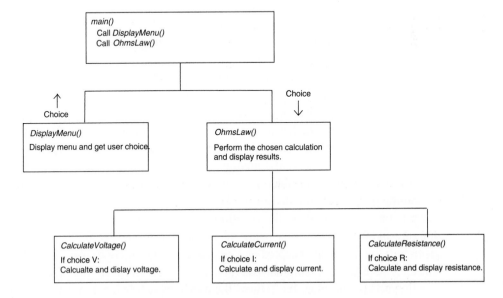

Figure 7-4　A structure diagram for the Ohm's law problem.

Coding the Program

Now, to implement the design, we need to construct the functions. The main task here is to develop the function interfaces. To do this, we must develop a problem definition for *each* function. The problem definition developed earlier addresses output, input, and processing for the overall program, *main()*. This is still needed to define the problem for the program as a whole. However, to construct the function interfaces, we must address problem definition from the perspective of the function. In other words, we must consider the output, input, and processing of each individual function. The *input* to the function is what the function must *accept* in order to perform its designated task, the *output* from the function is what the function *returns*, and the processing is the task the function will perform.

We will start with the *DisplayMenu()* function. You must ask yourself two questions: 1) "What does the function need to *accept* (input) to perform its designated task?" and 2) "What does the function need to *return* (output) to the calling program?" The task of the *DisplayMenu()* function is to display the menu and return the user's choice to its calling function, *main()*. Thus, this function does not need to accept anything from *main()* to perform its task, but needs to return a single value to *main()*, which is the user's menu choice. This is shown in the structure diagram by the variable *Choice* coming out of *DisplayMenu()*. Notice that nothing is going into this function. Here is the problem definition from the perspective of this function:

Function *DisplayMenu()*:   Display menu and get user entry.
Accepts: Nothing.
Returns: Menu choice obtained from user.

The function definition describes the function interface. The first decision you need to make is whether to use a void function or a non-void function. Use a non-void function if the function produces a single value that is returned to the calling program. Use a void function if the function does not accept or return anything or accepts a variable(s), changes it, and returns the altered variable(s) to the calling program. In other words, if the structure diagram indicates that a single value is being produced by the function, use a non-void function. If the structure diagram indicates nothing is being accepted or returned by the function, or if a given variable is being accepted and returned by the function, use a void function. These guidelines are summarized in Table 7-1. Because our *DisplayMenu()* function accepts nothing, but returns the user's menu choice, it must be a non-void function. So, the return class must be **char**, because the user's choice will be a character from the menu.

TABLE 7-1 FUNCTION RETURN CLASS

Returns	Return Data Class
A single value	Non-Void
Nothing	Void
Multiple values	Void

Next, we must decide the function parameters. Table 7-2 provides the guidelines for determining whether a given parameter must be a value or a reference parameter.

TABLE 7-2 FUNCTION PARAMETERS

Accepts/Returns	Parameter
Nothing accepted	None
Accepts without returning (one-way)	Value
Accepts and returns (two-way)	Reference

No parameters are required for *DisplayMenu()*, because it does not accept anything. Thus, the function interface is simply

```
char DisplayMenu()
```

Now, we simply place the *DisplayMenu()* code developed earlier inside the function. Here is the complete function:

```
char DisplayMenu()
{
//DEFINE LOCAL CHOICE VARIABLE
  char Choice = 'Q';
```

```
//GENERATE MENU AND GET USER'S CHOICE
  cout << "\n\n\t\t\tEnter V to find voltage" << endl << endl
       << "\t\t\tEnter I to find current" << endl << endl
       << "\t\t\tEnter R to find resistance" << endl << endl
       << "\t\t\tEnter Q to quit" << endl << endl
       << "\tPlease enter your choice:  ";
  cin >> Choice;

//RETURN CHOICE
  return Choice;
} //END DisplayMenu()
```

Notice that our *Choice* variable is now defined as a local variable inside the function. In addition, a **return** statement is placed at the end of the function to return *Choice* to its calling function, *main( )*.

Next, let's develop the *OhmsLaw( )* function. We begin by developing the function interface. From the structure diagram, it is easy to see the following:

Function *OhmsLaw( )*:	Perform chosen calculation and display results.
Accepts:	Menu entry, *Choice*, obtained from *main( )*.
Returns:	Nothing.

From the interface description, it is easy to see that we must use a void function, because nothing is returned by the function. Even though the function is displaying the results, it *is not* returning any values to its calling function, *main( )*. However, this function needs to accept the menu choice from *main( )*. This means that we need a function parameter. Now the question is: "Is the parameter a value parameter or a reference parameter?" Well, if the parameter is one-way, into the function, it must be a value parameter. If the parameter is two-way, in and out of the function, it must be a reference parameter. Because this parameter is accepted, but not returned, it must be a value parameter, right? The required parameter is a character, so the function interface becomes

```
void OhmsLaw(char Choice)
```

Now, inserting our switch statement code into the body of the function, the complete function becomes:

```
void OhmsLaw(char Choice)
{
```

```
//SET OUTPUT PRECISION
cout.setf(ios::fixed);
cout.precision(2);

switch (Choice)
{
  case 'v':
  case 'V' :  cout << "\n\nThe voltage value is:  " << CalculateVoltage()
                   << " volts." << endl;
              break;

  case 'i':
  case 'I' :  cout << "\n\nThe current value is:  " << CalculateCurrent()
                   << " milliamperes."  << endl;
              break;

  case 'r':
  case 'R' :  cout << "\n\nThe resistance value is:  " << CalculateResistance()
                   << " kilohms."  << endl;
              break;

  case 'q':  //TERMINATE PROGRAM
  case 'Q':  cout << "Program terminated" << endl;
             break;

             //DISPLAY INVALID ENTRY MESSAGE
  default :  cout << "\n\nThis is an invalid entry." << endl;

  }//END SWITCH
}//END OhmsLaw()
```

Notice that the function employs our earlier **switch** statement, which acts on the user choice, *Choice*, received as a parameter from the calling function, *main()*. Next, you see that each Ohm's law case calls another function as part of a *cout* statement to calculate the required voltage, current, or resistance, depending on the value of *Choice*. Each Ohm's law function will return a single value of voltage, current, or resistance, depending on which **case** is executed. Does this give you a hint as to what type of functions these will be (void or non-void)? Finally, notice that there is no **return** statement in our *OhmsLaw()* function, because it is a void function.

Here are the interface descriptions for each of the Ohm's law functions:

Function *CalculateVoltage()*:   Get current and resistance from user and use
                                   Ohm's law to calculate voltage.
Accepts: Nothing.
Returns: Voltage.

Function *CalculateCurrent()*:   Get voltage and resistance from user and use
                                   Ohm's law to calculate current.
Accepts: Nothing.
Returns: Current.

Function *CalculateResistance()*: Get voltage and current from user and use
                                   Ohm's law to calculate resistance.
Accepts: Nothing.
Returns: Resistance.

Each of these functions will have the same interface, except, of course, for the function name. Each function will be a non-void function, because a single value is being produced and returned by the function. No parameters are required, because none of the functions need to accept any data from the calling function, *OhmsLaw()*. You are probably thinking each function needs the two unknown quantities in the Ohm's law equation in order to make the required calculation. However, these quantities will be obtained from the user within each of the functions and not from the *OhmsLaw()* calling function. Here are the resulting function interfaces:

```
float CalculateVoltage()
float CalculateCurrent()
float CalculateResistance()
```

Now, here is each complete function:

```
float CalculateVoltage()
{
//DEFINE LOCAL VARIABLES
  float Current = 0.0;          //CURRENT IN MILLIAMPERES
  float Resistance = 0.0;       //RESISTANCE IN KILOHMS

//GET CURRENT AND RESISTANCE
  cout << "\nEnter the current value in milliamperes\tI = ";
  cin >> Current;
  cout << "\nEnter the resistance value in kilohms\tR = ";
  cin >> Resistance;
```

```
//TEST FOR RESISTANCE < 0 AND CALCULATE VOLTAGE
  if (Resistance < 0)
  {
        cout << "\n\nThis is an invalid entry. Please"
                " select again." << endl;
        return 0.0;
  }//END IF
  else
        return Current * Resistance;
}//END CalculateVoltage;

float CalculateCurrent()
{
//DEFINE LOCAL VARIABLES
  float Voltage = 0.0;          //VOLTAGE IN VOLTS
  float Resistance = 0.0;       //RESISTANCE IN KILOHMS

//GET VOLTAGE AND RESISTANCE
  cout << "\nEnter the voltage value in volts\tV = ";
  cin >> Voltage;
  cout << "\nEnter the resistance value in kilohms\tR = ";
  cin >> Resistance;

//TEST FOR RESISTANCE <= ZERO AND CALCULATE CURRENT
  if (Resistance <= 0)
  {
    cout << "\n\nThis is an invalid entry. Please"
              " select again." << endl;
    return 0.0;
  }//END IF
  else
    return Voltage / Resistance;
}//END CalculateCurrent()

float CalculateResistance()
{
//DEFINE LOCAL VARIABLES
  float Voltage = 0.0;          //VOLTAGE IN VOLTS
  float Current = 0.0;          //CURRENT IN MILLIAMPERES

//GET VOLTAGE AND CURRENT
  cout << "\nEnter the voltage value in volts\tV = ";
  cin >> Voltage;
```

```
   cout << "\nEnter the current value in milliamperes\tI = ";
   cin >> Current;

//TEST FOR CURRENT == 0 AND CALCULATE RESISTANCE
   if (Current == 0)
   {
      cout << "\n\nThis is an invalid entry. Please"
              " select again." << endl;
      return 0.0;
   }//END IF
   else
      return Voltage / Current;
}//END CalculateResistance()
```

Notice that each of the functions obtains the data required for the calculation from the user. The input data are tested. If invalid, an appropriate message is generated; otherwise, the function returns the required value. Notice that there are two **return** statements in each function. Because we have defined the functions as non-void, they *must* return a value, regardless of any terminating conditions. This is why there is a *return 0.0* statement after the invalid entry message in each function. I have chosen to return the value 0.0 in this situation, because we must return a floating-point value.

DEBUGGING TIP

A non-void function *must always* return a value, or a compiler error will result. So, regardless of the path of execution a non-void function takes, it must lead to a **return** statement.

We are now ready to combine everything into a complete program. Here it is:

```
#include <iostream.h>   //FOR cin AND cout

//FUNCTION PROTOTYPES
char DisplayMenu();              //DISPLAYS OHMS LAW MENU
void OhmsLaw(char Choice);       //GETS MENU CHOICE AND
                                 //CALLS REQUIRED OHMS LAW FUNCTION
float CalculateVoltage();        //CALCULATES VOLTAGE
float CalculateCurrent();        //CALCULATES CURRENT
float CalculateResistance();     //CALCULATES RESISTANCE
```

```
void main()
{

//DEFINE FUNCTION ARGUMENT VARIABLE
  char Choice = 'Q';              //USER MENU CHOICE


//DISPLAY PROGRAM DESCRIPTION MESSAGE
  cout << "This program will calculate dc voltage, current, or\n"
          "resistance given the other two values. " << endl << endl;

do
{
  Choice = DisplayMenu();        //CALL DisplayMenu()
  OhmsLaw(Choice);               //CALL OhmsLaw()
} //END DO/WHILE
while ((Choice != 'q') && (Choice != 'Q'));
} //END main()

//FUNCTION TO DISPLAY THE MENU AND RETURN USER CHOICE
char DisplayMenu()
{
//DEFINE LOCAL VARIABLE
  char Choice = 'Q';

//GENERATE MENU AND GET USER'S CHOICE
  cout << "\n\n\t\t\tEnter V to find voltage" << endl << endl
       << "\t\t\tEnter I to find current" << endl << endl
       << "\t\t\tEnter R to find resistance" << endl << endl
       << "\t\t\tEnter Q to quit" << endl << endl
       << "\tPlease enter your choice:  ";
  cin >> Choice;

//RETURN CHOICE
  return Choice;
} //END DisplayMenu()

//FUNCTION TO CALL REQUIRED OHMS LAW FUNCTION
void OhmsLaw(char Choice)
{
//SET OUTPUT PRECISION
  cout.setf(ios::fixed);
  cout.precision(2);
```

```
        switch (Choice)
        {
          case 'v':
          case 'V' :   cout << "\n\nThe voltage value is:  " << CalculateVoltage()
                            << " volts." << endl;
                       break;

          case 'i':
          case 'I' :   cout << "\n\nThe current value is:  " << CalculateCurrent()
                            << " milliamperes."  << endl;
                       break;

          case 'r':
          case 'R' :   cout << "\n\nThe resistance value is:  " << CalculateResistance()
                            << " kilohms."  << endl;
                       break;

          case 'q':    //TERMINATE PROGRAM
          case 'Q':    cout << "Program terminated" << endl;
                       break;

                       //DISPLAY INVALID ENTRY MESSAGE
          default :    cout << "\n\nThis is an invalid entry." << endl;
        }//END SWITCH
}//END OhmsLaw()

//FUNCTION TO CALCULATE VOLTAGE
float CalculateVoltage()
{
//DEFINE LOCAL VARIABLES
  float Current = 0.0;            //CURRENT IN MILLIAMPERES
  float Resistance = 0.0;         //RESISTANCE IN KILOHMS

//GET CURRENT AND RESISTANCE
  cout << "\nEnter the current value in milliamperes\tI = ";
  cin >> Current;
  cout << "\nEnter the resistance value in kilohms\tR = ";
  cin >> Resistance;

//TEST FOR RESISTANCE < 0 AND CALCULATE VOLTAGE
  if (Resistance < 0)
  {
     cout << "\n\nThis is an invalid entry. Please"
              " select again." << endl;
```

```
      return 0.0;
   }//END IF
   else
      return Current * Resistance;
}//END CalculateVoltage;

//FUNCTION TO CALCULATE CURRENT
float CalculateCurrent()
{
//DEFINE LOCAL VARIABLES
   float Voltage = 0.0;        //VOLTAGE IN VOLTS
   float Resistance = 0.0;     //RESISTANCE IN KILOHMS

//GET VOLTAGE AND RESISTANCE
   cout << "\nEnter the voltage value in volts\tV = ";
   cin >> Voltage;
   cout << "\nEnter the resistance value in kilohms\tR = ";
   cin >> Resistance;

//TEST FOR RESISTANCE <= ZERO AND CALCULATE CURRENT
   if (Resistance <= 0)
   {
      cout << "\n\nThis is an invalid entry. Please"
              " select again." << endl;
      return 0.0;
   }//END IF
   else
      return Voltage / Resistance;
}//END CalculateCurrent()

//FUNCTION TO CALCULATE RESISTANCE
float CalculateResistance()
{
//DEFINE LOCAL VARIABLES
   float Voltage = 0.0;     //VOLTAGE IN VOLTS
   float Current = 0.0;     //CURRENT IN MILLIAMPERES

//GET VOLTAGE AND CURRENT
   cout << "\nEnter the voltage value in volts\tV = ";
   cin >> Voltage;
   cout << "\nEnter the current value in milliamperes\tI = ";
   cin >> Current;
```

```
//TEST FOR CURRENT == 0 AND CALCULATE RESISTANCE
  if (Current == 0)
  {
    cout << "\n\nThis is an invalid entry. Please"
            " select again." << endl;
    return 0.0;
  }//END IF
  else
    return Voltage / Current;
}//END CalculateResistance()
```

One of the first things you see at the top of the program are the function prototypes. These are simply copied from the function headers with a semicolon added to the end of each. Good style dictates that each prototype should be commented according to the purpose of the function. Remember that C++ requires a prototype for each function so that it can check the correctness of the function calls. Next, you should be impressed by the simplicity of function *main()*. All that is being done here is writing a program description message and calling our two main functions within a program control loop. Most of the real work of the program is being done within the functions. That's structured programming! The rest of the program contains each of the functions that we discussed earlier.

DOCUMENTATION NOTE

It's a good idea to include all your program documentation within the program listing. Then, anyone looking at the listing can readily see the program design through the problem definitions and algorithms, without having to go through the code. I suggest that my students place the appropriate problem definition and algorithm for each function in comments, just prior to the function in the program code. This means that the original problem definition and initial algorithm should be placed in comments just prior to *main()*. Then, each function interface description and algorithm should be placed in comments just prior to the respective function code. This way, there are no doubts about what the various parts of the program are doing.

7-4 SCOPING-OUT VARIABLES AND CONSTANTS ⇒ BLOCK STRUCTURE

In the last two sections, you observed the use of local variables.

> A *local variable* is a variable that is defined within a specific block of code, such as a function.

A local variable is created for use only within a function block and has no meaning outside of the respective function. Don't get local variables confused with the function parameters listed in the function heading. Local function variables are defined after the opening brace of a function, and parameters are defined in the function heading.

To make variables global in C++, you must define them outside of function *main()*. This makes them global to function *main()*, as well as to any functions called by *main()*. Of course, this would be all the functions defined in a given program. This is why global variables are sometimes called *file variables* in C++.

> A *global variable* is a variable that can be used by all functions of a given program, including *main()*.

To illustrate the use of local and global variables, look at the block structure in Figure 7-5. Here, the global variable is *X0* and the local variable is *X1*. The function can perform operations on both *X0* and *X1*. However, *main()* can operate only with *X0*, because *X1* is not defined outside of the *Function1()* block. Any attempt to use *X1* outside of *Function1()* will result in an error. In addition, any value assigned to *X1* during the *Function1()* execution is destroyed and cannot be retrieved for subsequent executions of the function.

Now look at Figure 7-6. This time, there are two functions, both of which define *X1* as a local variable. Again, the global variable is *X0* and can be used within *main()*, as well as within any other functions defined in the program. The variable *X1* can be used only within the two functions. However, any operations on *X1* within *Function1()* do not affect the value of *X1* in *Function2()*, and vice versa. In other words, the *X1* in *Function1()* is considered a separate variable from the *X1* in *Function2()*. It's as if they are two completely different variables! This provides a very important feature of structured programming, called *modularity*.

```
int X0;                   // GLOBAL VARIABLE
Function1( ) prototype;

main( )
{
    ___
    ___
    ___
}//END main()


    Function1( )
    {
    int X1;            // LOCAL VARIABLE
    ___
    ___
    }//END Function1()
```

Figure 7-5   *X0* is global to entire program, and *X1* is local to *Function1()*.

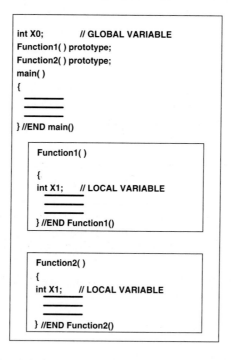

Figure 7-6   *X0* is global to the entire program, and *X1* is local to both *Function1()* and *Function2()*, but treated as two unique variables.

To realize the importance of modularity, suppose that you are a member of a programming team that must develop the software to solve a very complex industrial problem. The easiest way to solve any complex problem is to divide the problem into simpler, more manageable subproblems. Then, solve the subproblems and combine their solutions in order to solve the overall complex problem. This is called **top-down design**. Using the top-down design approach, your team leader divides the complex programming problem into simpler subproblems and then asks each member of the team to write a function to solve a given subproblem. How does this relate to the use of local variables? Well, you can write your function using any local variables you wish, without worrying that another team member might use the same local variables. Even if two team members use the same local variable identifiers, the functions will still execute independently when they are combined in the main program. This allows a top-down team approach to software design, something that is not available in nonstructured languages like BASIC. The functions in a structured language act as modular building blocks to form the overall program. This is why a structured language, like C++, is often referred to as a modular, block-structured language.

The Scope of Variables

A global variable defined prior to *main( )* has **file scope**, because it is accessible to any block in the same file. On the other hand, a local variable defined in a function is said to have **block scope**, because it is available only within the function block in which it is defined.

The **scope** of a variable refers to the largest block in which a given variable is accessible.

A term often associated with scope is **visibility**. You could say that the visibility of a global variable is the entire program file, and the visibility of a local variable is the block in which it is defined. Look at the following code to get the idea.

```
//FUNCTION PROTOTYPES
void Function1();
void Function2();

int X0;          //GLOBAL TO ENTIRE PROGRAM

void main()
{
```

```
  int X1;          //LOCAL TO main();
}//END main()

int X2;            //GLOBAL TO Function1() AND Function2()

void Function1()
{
  int X3;          //LOCAL TO Function1()
}//END Function1()

void Function2()
{
  int X0;          //LOCAL TO Function2()
}//END Function2()
```

Here, *X0* has file scope, because it is visible, or global, to all blocks in the program. However, *X1* has block scope, because it is defined local to *main()* and therefore is visible only in *main()* and cannot be accessed by *Function1()* or *Function2()*. Next, *X2* is defined after *main()*, but prior to any functions. Thus, the scope of *X2* extends to any functions defined after *X2*, making it visible to *Function1()* and *Function2()*, but not to *main()*. How about *X3*? Here, *X3* is defined inside of *Function1()* and, therefore, is local to this function and cannot be used by any other function, including *main()*. Finally, notice that the variable *X0* is also defined in *Function2()* as a local variable. Is there a problem here, because *X0* is also global to the entire program? No! The local variable *X0* in *Function2()* is independent of the global variable *X0* defined prior to *main()*. Because *X0* is defined locally in *Function2()*, any operations on *X0* within this function will not affect the global variable *X0*. It's as if they are two separate variables.

In summary, we could make the following statements concerning the scope of the variables in the foregoing program.

- *X0* is visible to the entire program. However, the *X0* in *Function2()* is different from the global *X0*.
- *X1* is visible to *main()*, but not visible to *Function1()* or *Function2()*.
- *X2* has a scope that extends to *Function1()* and *Function2()*, but not *main()*.
- *X3* has a block scope of *Function1()*.

All of the functions except *Function2()* have access to the global variable *X0*. As a result, the value of *X0* can be altered by any of these functions. The altering of a global variable by a function is referred to as a ***side effect***. In most cases, *side effects are undesirable*. It is not good practice to alter global variables within a function, because it defeats the modularity characteristic of a structured language. Therefore, *always define your variable objects as locally as possible* within a given function block. One exception to this rule is when several functions need to share a common variable or data structure.

The Scope of Constants

Constants, like variables, can also be termed global or local. In other words, you can declare constants globally prior to *main()*, or locally within a function. The scope of a constant works just like that of a variable. Its scope is the largest block in which it is available. However, the general rule for declaring constants is just the opposite of defining variables—you should *declare constant objects as globally as possible*. In other words, all constants should be declared prior to *main()* if possible.

Declaring constants globally allows all functions access to a given constant. No side effects are possible, because a constant cannot be changed by the program. Moreover, constants are not always constant. Remember the *Postage* and *SalesTax* constants we used in Chapter 2? These constants are subject to change over a period of time. When they must be changed, you only need to make a change in one place in the program if they are declared globally. However, if they are declared locally, a change must be made in each function in which they are declared.

Static Variables

Earlier, I stated that any value assigned to a local variable within a function block is destroyed and cannot be retrieved for subsequent executions of the function. This is true unless you use the keyword **static** in front of the variable definition. By making a local variable static, its value is retained from one call to the next of the function in which it is defined. A static variable acts like a local variable in that it is not accessible outside of the function block in which it is defined. However, a static variable has the *lifetime* of a global variable in that it remains defined throughout the execution of the program. Here's a program that should illustrate this idea:

```
#include <iostream.h>   //FOR cin AND cout

//FUNCTION PROTOTYPE
void StaticExample(int);
```

```
void main()
{
//CALL FUNCTION THREE TIMES
  StaticExample(1);
  StaticExample(2);
  StaticExample(3);
}//END main()

//THIS FUNCTION ILLUSTRATES THE USE OF A STATIC VARIABLE
void StaticExample(int Call)
{
  static int Count = 0;
  if (Call == 1)
    Count = 1;
  cout << "The value of Count in call #" << Call << " is:  " << Count << endl;
  ++Count;
}//END StaticExample()
```

From the function prototype, you see that *StaticExample()* expects to receive an integer and doesn't return any value to the calling program. Looking at the function implementation, you find that a variable called *Count* is defined as a local *static* variable within the function. The value of this variable is displayed on the monitor each time the function is called. After *Count* is displayed, its value is incremented in the last statement of the function. On the first call, *Count* will be initialized to the value 1 by the **if** statement within the function. On all subsequent calls, the value of *Count* is not initialized. Thus, its value has to be the value it had when leaving the previous function call. Notice that in function *main()*, *StaticExample()* is called three times. Here is what you would see on the display:

```
The value of Count in call #1 is:  1
The value of Count in call #2 is:  2
The value of Count in call #3 is:  3
```

In order for this output to occur, the value of the static variable *Count* had to be retained from one function call to the next. What happens if you remove the keyword **static** from in front of the variable object definition? Here are the results that I obtained on my monitor:

```
The value of Count in call #1 is:  1
The value of Count in call #2 is:  1046
The value of Count in call #3 is:  1046
```

As you can see, *Count* was initialized to the value 1 in the first call. However, its value was not retained for subsequent calls. In fact, you cannot predict its value on subsequent calls, because it might be any arbitrary memory value. So, the lesson to be learned here is that if you want a local variable to retain its value from one call of a function to the next, define the variable as a static variable using the keyword **static** in front of the local variable definition.

Quick Check

1. Where must a constant that has file scope be placed in a C++ program?

2. A local variable has _____ scope.

3. The altering of a global variable by a function is referred to as a _____.

4. How can you retain the value of a local function variable from one call of the function to the next?

7-5 RECURSION

The C++ language supports a very powerful process called ***recursion***.

> ***Recursion*** is a process whereby an operation calls itself until a primitive state is reached.

A recursive function is a function that calls itself. That's right, with the power of recursion, a given function can actually contain a statement that calls, or invokes, the same function, thereby calling itself.

To get the idea of recursion, consider a typical compound interest problem. Suppose you deposit $1000 in the bank at a 12 percent annual interest rate, but it is compounded monthly. What this means is that the interest is calculated and added to the principle on a monthly basis. Thus, each time the interest is calculated, you get interest on the previous month's interest. Let's analyze the problem a bit closer.

Your initial deposit is $1000. Now, the annual interest rate is 12 percent, which translates to a 1 percent monthly rate. Because interest is compounded monthly, the balance at the end of the first month will be

$$\text{Month 1 balance} = \$1000 + (0.01 \times \$1000) = \$1010$$

As you can see, the interest for month 1 is $0.01 \times \$1,000$, or $10.00. This interest amount is then added to the principle ($1,000) to get a new balance of $1010. Using a little algebra, the same calculation can be made like this:

$$\text{Month 1 balance} = 1.01 \times \$1000 = \$1010$$

Now, how would you calculate the interest for the second month? You would use the balance at the end of the first month as the principle for the second month calculation, right? So, the calculation for month 2 would be

$$\text{Month 2 balance} = 1.01 \times \$1010 = \$1020.10$$

For month 3, the calculation would be

$$\text{Month 3 balance} = 1.01 \times \$1020.10 = \$1030.30$$

Do you see a pattern? Notice that to calculate the balance for any given month, you must use the balance from the previous month. In general, the calculation for any month becomes

$$\textit{Balance} = 1.01 \times \textit{Previous Balance}$$

Let's let B_i represent the balance of any given month and B_{i-1} the previous month's balance. Using this notation, the balance for any month, B_i is

$$B_i = 1.01 \times B_{i-1}$$

Let's use this relationship to calculate what your balance would be after four months. Here's how you must perform the calculation:
First, the balance for month 4 is

$$B_4 = 1.01 \times B_3$$

However, to find B_4 you must find B_3 like this:

$$B_3 = 1.01 \times B_2$$

Then B_2 must be found like this:

$$B_2 = 1.01 \times B_1$$

Finally, B_1 must be found like this:

$$B_1 = 1.01 \times B_0$$

Now, you know that B_0 is the original deposit of $1000. This is really the only thing known, aside from the interest rate. Therefore, working backwards, you get

$$B_1 = 1.01 \times \$1000 = \$1010$$

$$B_2 = 1.01 \times \$1010 = \$1020.10$$

$$B_3 = 1.01 \times \$1020.10 = \$1030.30$$

$$B_4 = 1.01 \times \$1030.30 = \$1040.60$$

This is a classic example of recursion, because in order to solve the problem, you must solve the previous problem condition using the same process, and so on, until you encounter a known condition (in our case, the initial $1000 deposit). This known condition, or state, is called a ***primitive state***. Thus, a recursive operation is an operation that calls itself until a primitive state is reached. Likewise, a recursive function is one that calls, or invokes, itself until a primitive state is reached.

Now, suppose we wish to express the preceding compound interest calculation as a recursive function. The mathematical function would be

$$B_0 = 1000 \text{ and } B_i = 1.01 \times B_{i-1} \text{ (for } i > 0)$$

This mathematical function can be expressed in pseudocode form, like this:

```
If i == 0 Then
    Bᵢ = 1000
Else
    Bᵢ = 1.01 × Bᵢ₋₁
```

Next, let's assume the we use a variable called *Deposit* to represent the initial deposit and a variable called *Rate* to represent the annual interest rate.

Then, our balance could be calculated using recursion, as follows:

$$\text{If } i == 0 \text{ Then}$$
$$B_i = Deposit$$
$$\text{Else}$$
$$B_i = (1 + Rate / 12 / 100) \times B_{i-1}$$

If a programming language supports recursive operations, a software function can be coded directly from the above algorithm. Because C++ employs the power of recursion, the C++ function is

```
float Balance(int i)
{
  if (i==0)
    return Deposit;
  else
    return (1 + Rate / 12 / 100) * Balance(i – 1);
} //END Balance()
```

That's all there is to it! This function will calculate the balance at the end of any month *i* passed to the function. Notice how the function calls itself in the **else** clause. Here's how it works. When the computer encounters the recursive call in the **else** clause, it must temporarily delay the calculation to evaluate the recursive function call just as we did as part of the compounded interest calculation. When it encounters the **else** clause a second time, the function calls itself again, and keeps calling itself each time the **else** clause is executed until the primitive state is reached. When this happens, the **if** clause is executed (because *i* is zero), and the recursive calling ceases.

Now, let's insert this function into a program to calculate compounded interest, as follows:

```
#include <iostream.h>   //FOR cin AND cout

//FUNCTION PROTOTYPES AND GLOBAL VARIABLES
float Balance(int);         //RETURN NEW BALANCE
float Deposit = 0.0;        //INITIAL DEPOSIT
float Rate = 0.0;           //ANNUAL INTEREST RATE

void main()
{
```

```
//DEFINE FUNCTION ARGUMENT VARIABLE
  int Months = 0;          //NUMBER OF MONTHS AFTER INITIAL
                           //DEPOSIT TO DETERMINE BALANCE

//GET   DEPOSIT, NUMBER OF MONTHS, AND INTEREST RATE
  cout << "Enter the initial balance:  $";
  cin >> Deposit;
  cout << "Enter the number of months to compound:  ";
  cin >> Months;
  cout << "Enter the annual interest rate:  ";
  cin >> Rate;

//SET FIXED OUTPUT AND PRECISION
  cout.setf(ios::fixed);
  cout.precision(2);

//DISPLAY RESULTS, MAKING RECURSIVE FUNCTION CALL
  cout << "\n\nWith an initial deposit of $" << Deposit
       << " and an interest rate of " << Rate
       << "% \nthe balance at the end of " << Months
       << " months would be $" << Balance(Months) << endl ;
} //END main()


//****************************************************************
//
//THIS RECURSIVE FUNCTION WILL CALCULATE A BANK BALANCE
//BASED ON A MONTHLY COMPOUNDED INTEREST RATE
//
//****************************************************************
float Balance(int i)
{
  if (i==0)
    return Deposit;
  else
    return (1 + Rate / 12 / 100) * Balance(i – 1);
} //END Balance()
```

This program prompts the user to enter the deposit, number of months to compound, and the current annual interest rate. The *Deposit* and *Rate* variables are defined globally for example purposes so that we can concentrate on the recursive function. The number of months to compound is passed to the function as a value parameter. Actually, the deposit and rate variables could be defined locally to *main()* and passed to the function as value parameters. This will be left as an exercise at the end of the chapter. Once the user enters the required values, the recursive calls are made, and the program will write the ending balance. Here is a sample of the program output:

Enter the initial deposit: **$1000.**↵
Enter the number of months to compound: **4.**↵
Enter the annual interest rate: **12.**↵

With an initial deposit of $1000 and an interest rate of 12%
the balance at the end of 4 months would be $1040.60

During any recursive call, all information required to complete the calculation after the recursive call is saved by the computer in a memory area called a **stack**. As the recursive calls continue, information is saved on the memory stack until the primitive state is reached. Then the computer works backward from the primitive state, retrieving the stack information to determine the final result. The process that the computer goes through is identical to what we did when working the compound interest problem and is illustrated in Figure 7-7. The values shown in the figure assume a $1000.00 initial deposit and an interest rate of 12% per year, compounded monthly. Notice that the last thing placed into the stack is the first thing retrieved from the stack when recursion begins to "unwind." This principle is known as *last-in-first-out*, or **LIFO**. All stacks operate using the LIFO principle.

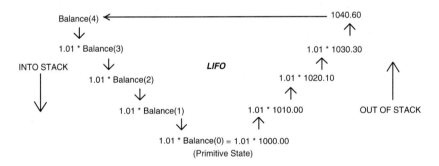

Figure 7-7 As recursion winds up, calculation information is placed into a memory stack until a primitive state is reached. Recursion then unwinds by retrieving the calculation information out of the stack and using substitution to generate the final result.

CAUTION

A word of caution: A recursive function must always reach a primitive state. If it does not, the function will keep calling itself forever, resulting in a memory overflow run-time error. Why?

Example 7-6

Write a recursive C++ function to find the sum of all integers from 1 to some number, N.

Solution

Think about this operation for a minute. Isn't it a classic recursive operation? To find the sum of integers 1 to, say, 5, couldn't you add 5 to the sum of integers from 1 to 4? Then, to find the sum of integers from 1 to 4, you add 4 to the sum of integers from 1 to 3, and so on, right? Expressed in symbols,

$Sum\ 5 = 5\ +\ Sum\ 4$
$Sum\ 4 = 4\ +\ Sum\ 3$
$Sum\ 3 = 3\ +\ Sum\ 2$
$Sum\ 2 = 2\ +\ Sum\ 1$
$Sum\ 1 = 1$

Notice that *Sum* 1 is the primitive state, because its value is known. Now, translating this process to a recursive function, you get

$$Sum\ 1 = 1 \ \ \text{and} \ \ Sum\ N = N + Sum\ (N - 1) \ \ (\text{for } N > 1)$$

This function can be expressed in pseudocode, like this:

If $N == 1$ Then
   $Sum = 1$
Else
   $Sum = N + Sum\ (N - 1)$

The C++ function is then coded directly from the algorithm as

```
//***************************************************
//
//THIS RECURSIVE FUNCTION WILL CALCULATE SUM OF
//INTEGERS 1 THRU N
//
//***************************************************
```

```
int Sum(int N)
{
  if (N == 1)
    return 1;
  else
    return N + Sum(N – 1);
} //END Sum()
```

Although recursion is a very powerful feature of any language, you should be aware that it is not always the most efficient method of solving a problem. Whenever we talk about computer efficiency, we must consider two things: *execution speed* and *memory usage*. When using recursion, the computer must keep track of each recursive call so that it can work backward to obtain a solution. This requires large amounts of both memory and time. As a result, a recursive solution to a problem may not always be the most efficient solution. *All* recursive problems can also be solved nonrecursively using iteration. For instance, consider the sum of integers from 1 to *N* done recursively in Example 7-6. This problem can be solved using an iterative function, like this:

```
//****************************************************
//
//THIS ITERATIVE FUNCTION WILL CALCULATE SUM OF
//INTEGERS 1 THRU N
//
//****************************************************
int Sum(int N)
{
  int SubTotal = 0;          //SUM SUBTOTAL
  for (int Count = 1; Count <= N; ++Count)
    SubTotal = SubTotal + Count;
  return SubTotal;
} //END Sum()
```

So, why use recursion? Probably the main reason is that many recursive solutions are much simpler than iterative solutions. In addition, there are some problems in data structures, such as linked lists and binary trees, where recursion isn't a mere convenience, it is essential to keep the code manageable. Here are two guidelines that should help you decide when to use recursion:

1. Consider a recursive solution only when a *simple* iterative solution is not possible.

2. Use a recursive solution only when the execution and memory efficiency of the solution is within acceptable limits, considering the system limitations.

By the way, notice how the two variables, *Count* and *Temp*, are used as local variables in the preceding function. This is an ideal application for nonstatic local variables, because they need to be used only within this function block and do not need to be saved from one function call to the next.

Quick Check

1. True or false: There is no way that a C++ function can call itself.

2. Explain why we can describe recursion as a "winding" and "unwinding" process.

3. What terminates a recursive function call?

4. A factorial operation (*N*!) finds the product of all integers from 0 to some positive integer *N*. Thus, 5! = 5 * 4 * 3 * 2 * 1. Write the pseudocode required to find *N*!, where *N* is any integer. (*Note:* By definition, 0! = 1.)

5. True or false: An advantage of recursion is that it does not require a lot of memory to execute.

6. True or false: All recursive problems can also be solved using iteration.

PROBLEM SOLVING IN ACTION: STRUCTURED PROGRAMMING

In Chapter 1, we employed stepwise refinement to design a solution for a bank account application. We coded the solution using a flat implementation because, at that time, you did not know how to implement a structured design using C++ functions. Let's revisit this application with our newly gained knowledge of functions.

Here's the problem statement again:

Problem

Your local bank has contracted you to design a structured program that will process savings account data. Develop a set of related algorithms using the top-down structured program design method that could be coded using a structured programming language.

Here is how we defined the overall problem in terms of output, input, and processing:

Defining the Problem

Output: The program must generate a report showing the account transactions and balance for a given savings account in a given month.

Input: We will assume that the user will enter the monthly transaction information.

Processing: The program must process deposits, withdrawals, and calculate interest to determine the monthly balance.

This will serve as our problem definition for the initial algorithm, *main()*.

Planning the Solution

Next, using structured design and stepwise refinement we constructed the structure diagram in Figure 7-8 along with the following set of related algorithms.

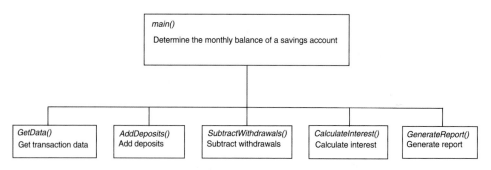

Figure 7-8   A structure diagram for the banking problem.

Initial Algorithm

    main()
    BEGIN
        Call the function to get the transaction data.
        Call the function to add the account deposits.
        Call the function to subtract the account withdrawals.
        Call the function to calculate the account interest.
        Call the function to generate the account report.
    END.

First Level of Refinement

    GetData()
    BEGIN
        Write a prompt to enter the current account balance.
        Read(*Balance*).
        Write a prompt to enter the monthly deposits.
        Read(*Deposits*).
        Write a prompt to enter the monthly withdrawals.
        Read(*Withdrawals*).
    END.

    AddDeposits()
    BEGIN
        Calculate *Balance = Balance + Deposits*.
    END.

    SubtractWithdrawals()
    BEGIN
        Calculate *Balance = Balance − Withdrawals*.
    END.

    AddInterest()
    BEGIN
        Calculate *Balance = Balance + (Balance * Interest)*.
    END.

> *GenerateReport()*
> BEGIN
>   Write(*Balance*).
>   Write(*Deposits*).
>   Write(*Withdrawals*).
> END.

With our new-found knowledge of functions, we can modify the structure diagram, as shown in Figure 7-9. Notice what has been added. First, the box at the top is labeled *main()* and simply calls the individual functions in the order that they are needed to solve the problem. Second, data objects being passed to/from the functions are shown on the lines connecting *main()* to the functions. Objects the function accepts are shown to the left of the connecting line, and objects the function returns are shown to the right of the line, as follows:

- If a given data object goes one way into the function, it is a value parameter.
- If a given data object goes one way out of the function, it is a return value.
- If a given data object goes two ways in and out of the function, it is a reference parameter.

To construct the expanded structure diagram, you must consider a problem definition for each function by describing the function interface in terms of what it accepts and returns. Let's begin with the *GetData()* function.

Function *GetData()*:	Get current account balance, deposits, and withdrawals from the user.
Accepts: and	A variable object placeholder for balance, deposits, withdrawals.
Returns:	Balance, deposits, and withdrawals.

The *GetData()* function must obtain user entries and return them to the calling program, *main()*. As a result, the function must accept a variable object placeholder for each user entry. The function will obtain a value from the user to fill each variable placeholder and then return that variable to *main()*. This interface description is represented on the structure diagram in Figure 7-9 by showing the variables *Balance*, *Deposits*, and *Withdrawals* going both into and out of the *GetData()* function module. This means that all three must be reference parameters, resulting in a function interface of

void GetData(float &Balance, float &Deposits, float &Withdrawals)

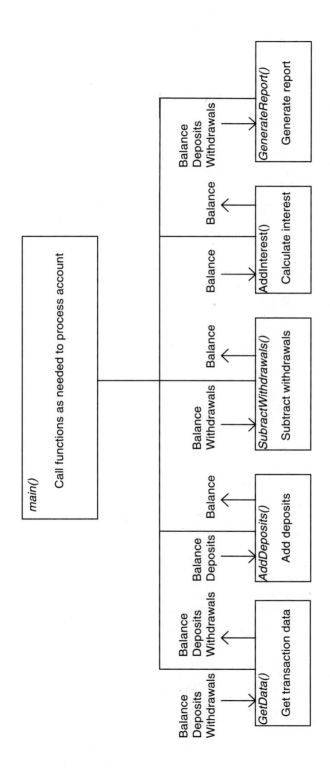

Figure 7-9 An expanded structure diagram shows data items flowing to/from the bank account functions.

The *AddDeposits( )* function interface can be described as follows:

Function *GetData( )*:	Add deposits to the current balance.
Accepts:	The current account balance and deposits.
Returns:	A new account balance.

This function requires that the function receive the current account balance and deposits in order to calculate and return the new account balance. As a result, *Balance* and *Deposits* are accepted by the function, *Balance* is then changed by adding *Deposits*, and *Balance* is returned to *main( )*, as shown in the structure diagram. Notice that *Balance* is going two ways, into the function and out of the function, whereas *Deposits* is going only one way into, the function. This means that *Balance* must be a reference parameter, and *Deposits* must be a value parameter. Therefore, the resulting function interface must be

void AddDeposits(float &Balance, float Deposits)

The *SubtractWithdrawals( )* function must receive the current account balance and withdrawals, subtract the withdrawals, and return the new account balance. With this information, its interface can be described as follows:

Function *SubtractWithdrawals( )*:	Subtract withdrawals from the current balance.
Accepts:	The current account balance and withdrawals.
Returns:	A new account balance.

The structure diagram illustrates this information by showing *Balance* going two ways into the function and out of the function, whereas *Withdrawals* is going only one way, into the function. Thus, *Balance* must be a reference parameter, and *Withdrawals* must be a value parameter. The resulting function interface is

void SubtractWithdrawals (float &Balance, float Withdrawals)

Next, the *AddInterest( )* function must receive the account balance, calculate the monthly interest, and return the balance. This function can be described as follows:

Function *AddInterest( )*:	Add monthly interest to account balance.
Accepts:	The current account balance.
Returns:	A new account balance.

Here, the account balance is accepted by the function, changed by adding the monthly interest, and returned to *main()* by the function. Transcribing this information to the structure diagram, you find that *Balance* goes into and out of the *AddInterest()* function module. The resulting interface is

void AddInterest(float &Balance)

Finally, the *GenerateReport()* function must receive the account balance, deposits, and withdrawals in order to generate the required account report. This function can, therefore, be described as follows:

Function *GenerateReport()*: Generate account report.
Accepts: The current account balance, deposits, and withdrawals.
Returns: Nothing.

In order to generate the account report, the function must receive the account balance, deposits, and withdrawals from *main()*. However, these values are not being modified and returned; they are being displayed only as part of the report by the function. Thus, the structure diagram indicates *Balance*, *Deposits*, and *Withdrawals* going only one way, into the function module. This means that they all must be value parameters, right? The resulting function interface is

void GenerateReport(float Balance, float Deposits, float Withdrawals)

Make sure that you see how the interface description for each function is illustrated on the structure diagram and how the structure diagram is translated directly into the foregoing C++ interface code. If a given data object only comes out of the function, it is a return value. Observe that there are no variables that only come out of any of the functions. As a result, all of the functions have return classes of **void**. If a given object only goes into the function, it is a value parameter. If a given object goes both into and out of a function, it is a reference parameter and must be preceded by an ampersand symbol in the prototype.

Finally, using the function interfaces, algorithms, and combining everything, we get the following code:

Coding the Program

```
//ACTION 7-2 (ACT07-02.CPP)
//THIS IS A STRUCTURED PROGRAM THAT WILL PROCESS
//SAVINGS ACCOUNT DATA INTO A MONTHLY STATEMENT
```

```
#include <iostream.h>   //FOR cin AND cout

//DEFINE GLOBAL INTEREST CONSTANT
const float INTEREST = 0.01;   //CURRENT MONTHLY INTEREST RATE

//FUNCTION PROTOTYPES
void GetData(float &Balance, float &Deposits, float &Withdrawals);
void AddDeposits(float &Balance, float Deposits);
void SubtractWithdrawals (float &Balance, float Withdrawals);
void AddInterest(float &Balance);
void GenerateReport(float Balance, float Deposits, float Withdrawals);

void main()
{
//DEFINE FUNCTION ARGUMENT VARIABLES
  float Balance = 0.0;          //ACCOUNT BALANCE
  float Deposits = 0.0;         //MONTHLY DEPOSITS
  float Withdrawals = 0.0;      //MONTHLY WITHDRAWALS

//DISPLAY PROGRAM DESCRIPTION MESSAGE
   cout << "This program will generate a banking account report based"
           "on information entered by the user" << endl << endl;

  //CALL FUNCTIONS
  GetData(Balance,Deposits,Withdrawals);
  AddDeposits(Balance,Deposits);
  SubtractWithdrawals(Balance,Withdrawals);
  AddInterest(Balance);
  GenerateReport(Balance,Deposits,Withdrawals);
} //END main()

//THIS FUNCTION GETS THE MONTHLY ACCOUNT
//INFORMATION FROM THE USER
void GetData (float &Balance, float &Deposits, float &Withdrawals)
{
  cout << "Enter the account balance:  $";
  cin  >> Balance;
  cout << "Enter the deposits this month:  $";
  cin >> Deposits;
  cout << "Enter the withdrawals this month:  $";
  cin >> Withdrawals;
} //END GetData()

//THIS FUNCTION ADDS THE MONTHLY DEPOSITS
//TO THE ACCOUNT BALANCE
void AddDeposits(float &Balance, float Deposits)
```

```
{
  Balance = Balance + Deposits;
} //END AddDeposits()

//THIS FUNCTION SUBTRACTS THE MONTHLY WITHDRAWALS
//FROM THE ACCOUNT BALANCE
void SubtractWithdrawals (float &Balance, float Withdrawals)
{
  Balance = Balance – Withdrawals;
} //END SubtractWithdrawals()

//THIS FUNCTION ADDS MONTHLY INTEREST
//TO THE ACCOUNT BALANCE
void AddInterest(float &Balance)
{
  Balance = Balance + (Balance * INTEREST);
} //END AddInterest()

//THIS FUNCTION DISPLAYS THE MONTHLY ACCOUNT REPORT
void GenerateReport(float Balance, float Deposits, float Withdrawals)
{
  cout << "The account balance is currently:  $" << Balance << endl;
  cout << "Deposits were:  $" << Deposits << endl;
  cout << "Withdrawals were:  $" << Withdrawals << endl;
} //END GenerateReport()
```

That's it! You should now have the knowledge to understand all facets of this problem, from the structured design to the structured C++ program.

CHAPTER SUMMARY

In this chapter, you learned how to write and use functions in C++. All user-defined functions to be used in *main()* are defined after the closing brace of *main()*. The function is defined by writing a function header, which includes the function return class, the function name, and a parameter listing. The body, or statement section, of the function then follows the function header. Unlike the C language, the C++ language requires that each function have a prototype. The function prototypes must be listed prior to *main()* and must include the return data class of the function, the function name, and a listing of the parameter data classes. Prototypes are used by the compiler to check for the proper number of arguments when the function is called. Functions in C++ can be made to return a single value to the calling program or perform some specific task. When a function is designed to return a single value to the calling program, the value returned replaces the function name wherever the name is used in the calling program. Thus, the function name can appear as part of an assignment operator, a *cout* statement, an arithmetic operator, or a test statement. When a function is designed to perform a specific task, the function is called by using the function name (followed by a list of actual arguments) as a statement in the program.

Actual arguments are data passed to the function when the function is called. Formal parameters are defined within the function header and take on the value(s) of the actual arguments when the function is called. Furthermore, parameters can be passed between the calling program and function by value or reference. When passing parameters by value, the actual arguments in the calling program are not affected by operations on the formal parameters within the function. When passing parameters by reference, the actual arguments in the calling program will reflect any changes to the formal parameters within the function. Thus, passing parameters by value is one-way communication of data from the calling program to the function. Passing parameters by reference is two-way communication of data from the calling program to the function and back to the calling program. In C++, reference parameters are defined using an ampersand (&) prior to the parameter name in the function heading.

In addition to parameters, functions can operate with local variables that are defined within the function body. Such local variables are visible only for use within the function in which they are defined. Local variables are destroyed once the function execution is terminated, unless they are defined as static local variables. A static variable retains its value from one call of a function to the next. Global, or file, constants and variables are available for use by any functions in a given program and must be defined prior to *main()*. The scope of a constant or variable refers to the largest block in which it is visible. A side effect occurs when a function changes the value of a global variable. Variables always should be defined as locally as possible, whereas constants should be declared as globally as possible.

A recursive function is a function that calls itself until a primitive state is reached. There must always be a primitive state to terminate a recursive function call. Otherwise, a run-time error will occur. Recursive operations are performed as part of an **if/else** statement. The primitive state forms the **if** clause, and the recursive call is part of the **else** clause of the statement. All recursive operations also can be performed using iteration. Because recursion eats up time and memory as compared to iteration, you should consider recursion only when a simple iterative solution is not possible and when the execution and memory efficiency of the solution are within acceptable limits.

QUESTIONS AND PROBLEMS

Questions

1. What three things must be specified in a function header?

2. Explain the difference between an actual argument and a formal parameter.

3. Which of the following are invalid function headings? Explain why they are invalid.
   a. float Average (Num1, Num2)
   b. int Largest (X,Y : int)
   c. float Smallest (float a,b)
   d. string Result (char Character)

4. Write the appropriate headings for the following functions:
   a. Inverse of x: $1/x$
   b. *Tan (x)*
   c. Convert a decimal test score value to a letter grade.
   d. Convert degrees Fahrenheit to degrees Celsius.
   e. Compute the factorial of any integer N ($N!$)
   f. Compute the average of three integer test scores.

5. True or false: When a function does not have a return data class, you must indicate this with the keyword **null**.

6. Explain the difference between a value parameter and a reference parameter.

7. When passing a parameter to a function by reference,
   a. The actual argument takes on the formal parameter value.
   b. The formal parameter takes on the actual argument value.
   c. The actual argument reflects any changes to the formal parameter after the function execution.
   d. a and b
   e. b and c
   f. a and c

8. When using an assignment operator to call a function, the function must include a _____ statement.

9. Which of the following are invalid function prototypes? Explain why they are invalid.
   a. void PrintHeader();
   b. int Error(float Num1, char Num2);
   c. void GetData (&int Amount, char Date);
   d. float Average (int Number, float Total)
   e. char Sample (int, char, float);

10. True or false: A variable object defined in *main( )* has visibility in all functions called by *main( )*.

11. Which of the following are value parameters and which are reference parameters?

   a. char Prob_a (char &A, char &B, float X, int Y);

   b. int Prob_b (int Num1, int Num2, int Num3, float &Avg);

   c. float Prob_c (int, float, char &);

12. Write the appropriate headers for the following functions:

   a. A function called *Sample( )* that must return a floating-point value and receive an integer, a floating-point value, and a character (in that order) when it is called.

   b. A function called *Skip( )* that will cause the printer to skip a given number of lines where the number of lines to skip is obtained from the calling program.

   c. A function called *Swap( )* that will swap the values of two integer variables obtained from the calling program and return the swapped values to the calling program.

   d. A function called *Hypot( )* that will return the hypotenuse of a right triangle, given the values of the two sides from the calling program.

13. Write prototypes for the functions in question 12.

14. Write C++ statements that will call the four functions in question 12.

15. Given the following function,

```
void Swap(int &X, int &Y)
{
  int Temp;
  Temp = X;
  X = Y;
  Y = Temp;
} //END Swap()
```

determine the output for each of the following segments of code that call function *Swap( )*.

   a.
```
A = 2;
B = 10;
cout << "A = " << A << "  B = " << B << endl;
Swap(A,B);
cout << "A = " << A << "  B = " << B << endl;
```

   b.
```
A = 20;
B = -5;
cout << "A = " << A << "  B = " << B << endl;
if (A < B)
   Swap(A,B);
else
```

```
        Swap(B,A);
        cout << "A = " << A << "  B = " << B << endl;
 c. Num1 = 1;
    Num2 = 5;
    for (int Count = 5; Count; --Count)
    {
        Swap(Num1,Num2);
        cout << "Num1 = " << Num1 << "  Num2 = " << Num2 << endl;
        ++Num1;
        --Num2;
    } //END FOR
```

16. Explain the difference between a local and global variable.

17. What is meant by the scope of a variable?

18. What is a side effect?

19. True or false: Variable objects should be defined as locally as possible and constant objects as globally as possible.

20. A local variable has _____ scope.

21. Suppose that a local integer object called *SubTotal* must retain its value from one call of a function to the next. Write a definition for this object.

22. Suppose that a function must have access to a variable defined in *main()*. How must this be accomplished?

23. Explain recursion.

24. When should you consider a recursive solution to a problem?

Problems

Least Difficult

Write functions to perform the following tasks:

1. Convert a temperature in degrees Fahrenheit to degrees Celsius.

2. Find x^y, where x is a real value and y is an integer value.

3. Calculate $Tan(\theta)$, for some angle θ in degrees.

4. Find the inverse $(1/x)$ of any real value x.

5. Find the maximum of two integer values.

6. Find the minimum of two integer values.

7. Find $N!$ using iteration.

8. Find $N!$ using recursion.

9. Place the functions that you developed in problems 7 and 8 in a menu-driven program that will allow the user to select either an iterative or recursive solution to *N*!. Execute each option for the same value of *N*, and determine the amount of time it takes to execute each option with the given value of *N*. Repeat this process for increasing values of *N*. What conclusions can you draw about iterative versus recursive solutions?

10. Examine a range of values, and return the Boolean value true if a value is within the range and false if the value is outside of the range.

11. Find your bank balance at the end of any given month for some initial deposit value and interest rate. Define the number of months, deposit, and interest rate variables in *main()* and pass them to your function.

12. Display your name, class, instructor, and hour. *Note*: To display your name and instructor, the function must accept a character array. To make the function accept an array, you simply provide an array definition in your function header. For example, suppose that you define an array in *main()* to hold your name, as follows:

    char Name[MAX];

    To receive this array from *main()*, you simply repeat the array definition in your function header, like this:

    Display(char Name[MAX], ...

    Of course, the function return class and parameters for the instructor's name and class hour must be added to the header.

13. Cause the printer to skip a given number of lines, where the number of lines to be skipped is passed to the function.

14. Swap, or exchange, any two floating-point values.

15. Compare some new floating-point value to a maximum value obtained from the calling program. Replace the maximum value with the new value if the new value is greater than the maximum value. Use the function that you developed in problem 14 for the exchange operation.

More Difficult

In problems 16–20, write three independent functions for each problem, as follows:

*   *One function to read the required input values.*

*   *A second function to perform the required calculations using the input values from the first function.*

*   *A third function to display the results of the second function.*

16. Revise the payroll program you developed for Ma and Pa in problem 12 of Chapter 4 to employ functions. Recall that the payroll program will calculate Herb's net pay given the following information:

> Employee's name
> Number of weekly hours worked
> Hourly rate of pay
> FICA (7.15%)
> Federal withholding (16%)
> State withholding (4.75%)

Ma or Pa will be required to enter only the first three items when running the program. The program must generate a report using the following format:

```
Employee Name: XXXXXXXXXXXXXXXXXXXXX

Rate of Pay:                        $XXXXX
Hours Worked:                        XXXXX
Gross Pay:                          $XXXXX
Deductions:
    FICA                            $XXXXX
    Federal withholding             $XXXXX
    State withholding               $XXXXX
                                   -----------
    Total Deductions                $XXXXX
Net Pay:                            $XXXXX
```

Note: To get the employee's name, the function must accept and return a character array. To make the function accept and return an array, you simply provide an array definition in your function header. For example, suppose that you define an array in *main()* to hold your name, as follows:

char Name[MAX];

To accept this array from *main()* and return it to *main()*, you simply repeat the array definition in your function header, like this:

Display(char Name[MAX], ...

Of course, the function return class and additional parameters required for this function must be added to the header.

17. Find the height at which the ladder in Figure 7-10 makes contact with the wall, given the length of the ladder and the distance the base of the ladder is from the wall.

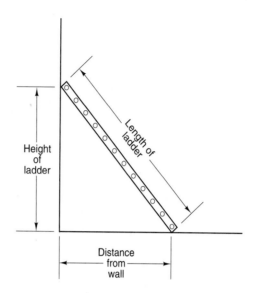

Figure 7-10   A ladder for problem 17.

Most Difficult

18. A Fibonacci sequence of numbers is defined as follows:

$$F_0 = 0$$
$$F_1 = 1$$
$$F_n = F_{n-1} + F_{n-2}, \text{ for } n > 1$$

This says that the first two numbers in the sequence are 0 and 1. Then, each additional Fibonacci number is the sum of the two previous numbers in the sequence. Thus, the first 10 Fibonacci numbers are

$$0, 1, 1, 2, 3, 5, 8, 13, 21, 34$$

Here, we say that the first number occupies position 0 in the sequence, the second number position 1 in the sequence, and so on. Thus, the last position in a 10-number sequence is position 9.

   Develop a program that employs a recursive function to generate a Fibonacci sequence of all numbers up to some position *n* entered by the user.

19. Develop a program that employs an iterative function to generate a Fibonacci sequence of all numbers up to some position *n* entered by the user.

20. Measure the amount of time it takes each of the programs in problems 18 and 19 to generate a Fibonacci sequence of 50 elements. What do you conclude about the efficiency of recursion versus iteration? Why does the recursive program take so long?

ARRAYS

INTRODUCTION
8-1 THE STRUCTURE OF AN ARRAY
   The Array Elements
   The Array Indices
8-2 DEFINING ONE-DIMENSIONAL
   ARRAYS IN C++
8-3 ACCESSING ARRAYS
   Inserting Elements into One-Dimensional
    Arrays
   Extracting Elements from One-Dimensional
    Arrays
8-4 PASSING ARRAYS AND ARRAY
   ELEMENTS TO FUNCTIONS

PROBLEM SOLVING IN ACTION:
   SEARCHING AN ARRAY USING
   ITERATION (SEQUENTIAL SEARCH)
PROBLEM SOLVING IN ACTION: SORTING
   AN ARRAY USING ITERATION
   (INSERTION SORT)
PROBLEM SOLVING IN ACTION:
   SEARCHING AN ARRAY USING
   RECURSION (BINARY SEARCH)
8-5 INITIALIZING ARRAYS
     Default Initialization of Global and
      Static Arrays
CHAPTER SUMMARY
QUESTIONS AND PROBLEMS
   Questions
   Problems

INTRODUCTION

This chapter will introduce you to a very important topic in any programming language: *arrays*. The importance of arrays cannot be overemphasized, because they lend themselves to so many applications.

> An *array* is an indexed data structure that is used to store data elements of the same data class.

Arrays simply provide an organized means for locating and storing data, just as the post office boxes in your local post office lobby provide an organized means of locating and storing mail. This is why an array is referred to as a *data structure*. The array data structure can be used to store just about any class of data, including integers, floats, characters, arrays, pointers, and records (structs). In addition, arrays are so versatile that they can be used to implement other data structures, such as stacks, queues, linked lists, and binary trees. In fact, in some languages, like FORTRAN, the array is the only data structure available to the programmer, because most other structures can be implemented using arrays.

8-1 THE STRUCTURE OF AN ARRAY

An array is a data structure. In other words, an array consists of data elements that are organized, or structured, in a particular way. This array data structure provides a convenient means of storing large amounts of data in primary, or user, memory. There are both one-dimensional and multidimensional arrays. In this chapter, you will learn about one-dimensional arrays. Then, in a later chapter, you will literally expand this knowledge into multidimensional arrays.

To get the idea of an array, look at the illustration in Figure 8-1. Here you see a single row of post office boxes as you might find in any common post office lobby. As you know, each box has a post office (P.O.) box number. In Figure 8-1, our P.O. box numbers begin with 0 and go up to some finite number N. How do you locate a given box? By using its P.O. box number, right? However, the P.O. box number has nothing to do with what's inside the box. It is simply used to locate a given box. Of course, the contents of a given box is the mail delivered to that box. The reason the postal service uses the P.O. box method is that it provides a convenient, well-organized method of storing and accessing the mail for its postal customers. An array does the same thing in a computer program; it provides a convenient, well-organized method of storing and accessing data for you, the programmer. By the way, how many post office boxes are there in Figure 8-1? Because the first box number is 0 and the last is *N*, there must be *N* + 1 boxes.

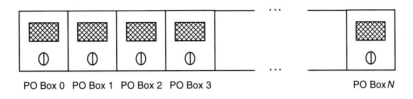

PO Box 0 PO Box 1 PO Box 2 PO Box 3   PO Box *N*

Figure 8-1 A one-dimensional array is like a row of post office boxes.

You can think of a one-dimensional array, like the one shown in Figure 8-2, as a row of post office boxes. The one-dimensional array consists of a single row of storage locations, each labeled with a number called an **index**. Each index location is used to store a given class of data. The data stored at a given index location is referred to as an array **element**. Thus, a one-dimensional array is a sequential list of storage locations that contain individual data elements that are located, or accessed, via indices.

Element 0	Element 1	Element 2	Element 3		Element *N*
[0]	[1]	[2]	[3]		[*N*]

INDICES

Figure 8-2 A one-dimensional array, or list, is a sequential list of storage locations that contain data elements that are located via indices.

The two major components of any array are the elements stored in the array and the indices that locate the stored elements. Don't get these two array components confused! Although array elements and indices are related, they are completely separate quantities, just as the contents of a post office box is something different from its P.O. box number. With this in mind, let's explore array elements and indices a bit further.

The Array Elements

The elements of an array are the data stored in the array. These elements can be any class of data that you have seen so far. Thus, a given array can store integer elements, floating-point elements, character, and Boolean elements. In addition to these standard data-class elements, an array can also be used to store enumerated data elements. In fact, the elements in an array even can be other arrays. However, there is one major restriction that applies to the array elements: *The elements in a given array all must be of the same data class.*

As you will see shortly, you must define arrays in a C++ program. Part of the definition is to specify the class of the elements that the array will store. Once a given array is defined for a certain data class, only elements of that class should be stored in that array.

The Array Indices

The array indices locate the array elements. In C++, the compiler automatically assigns integer indices to the array element list beginning with index 0. So, the first element of the array in Figure 8-2 is located at index 0, and the last element is located at index *N*. The indices begin with 0 and go to *N*, so there must be *N* + 1 elements in the array. Also, because this is a one-dimensional array, or *list*, we say that it has a ***dimension*** of 1 × (*N* + 1), meaning that there is one row of *N* + 1 elements. The dimension of an array indicates the size of the array, just as the dimension of a piece of lumber indicates its size.

 Quick Check

1. The two major components of an array are the _____ and _____.

2. True or false: The elements within a given array can be any combination of data classes.

8-2 DEFINING ONE-DIMENSIONAL ARRAYS IN C++

All arrays in C++ must be defined. In order to define an array, you must specify three things:

1. The data class of the array elements.
2. The name of the array.
3. The size of the array.

Here's the general format:

ONE-DIMENSIONAL ARRAY FORMAT

<element data class> <array name> [<number of array elements>];

The first thing you see in the definition is the data class of the array elements. The array data class is followed by the array identifier, or name, which is followed by the number of elements that the array will store enclosed within square brackets, [ ]. A semicolon terminates the definition. For instance, the following defines an array of 10 characters whose name is *Characters*.

char Characters [10];

Example 8-1

Write definitions for the following arrays:

a. An array called *Integers* that will store 10 integers.
b. An array called *Reals* that will store five floating-point values.
c. An array called *Characters* that will store 11 characters.
d. An array called *Class* that will store the grades of 25 students. Assume the grades A, B, C, D, and F are defined in an enumerated data class called *Grades*.
    What index locates the last element in each of the above arrays?

Solution

a. int Integers[10];
b. float Reals[5];
c. char Characters[11];

d. enum Grades {F, D, C, B, A};
    Grades Class[25];
    The index that locates the last element in each of the above arrays is one less than the defined size of the array.

In each of the preceding definitions, the element data class is listed first, followed by the array identifier, followed by the size of the array enclosed in square brackets. Each definition should be fairly obvious, except perhaps the *Class* array definition. In this definition, the data class of the array is the enumerated data class called *Grades*, which must be declared prior to the array definition. So, we would say that the *Class* array can store elements whose data class is *Grades*. Thus, the elements that can be stored in the *Class* array are limited to the enumerated data class elements of F, D, C, B, and A. Take note that these are not considered characters by the compiler, but rather elements of an enumerated data class called *Grades*.

Quick Check

1. Define an array called *TestScores* that will store up to 15 test scores.

2. What is the dimension of the array in question 1?

3. What is the index of the first element of the array in question 1?

4. What is the index of the last element of the array in question 1?

5. Define an array called *ThisSemester* that will store elements of an enumerated class called *Courses*, which includes the courses that you are taking this semester.

6. Suppose that the index of the last element in an array is [25]. How many elements will the array store?

8-3 ACCESSING ARRAYS

Accessing the array means to insert elements into the array for storage or to get stored elements from the array.

Inserting Elements into One-Dimensional Arrays

There are basically three major ways to insert elements into an array: by using a *direct assignment* statement, by *reading*, or by using *loops*.

Direct Assignment

Here's the general format for inserting an element into an array using a direct assignment:

DIRECT ASSIGNMENT FORMAT (INSERTING ARRAY ELEMENTS)

<array name> [array index] = element value;

Using the following array definitions,

```
char Characters[6];
int Integers[3];
```

direct assignments might go something like this:

```
Characters[0] = 'H';
Characters[5] = '\0';
Integers[0] = 16;
Integers[2] = -22;
```

In each of these instances, an element is placed in the first and last storage positions of the respective array. The character 'H' is placed in the first position of the *Characters* array, and the null terminator is placed in the last position of this array. Recall that the first position of an array is always [0], and the last array position is always one less than the array size. The integer 16 is placed in the first position of the *Integers* array, and the integer −22 placed in the last position of this array.

Observe that the respective array name is listed, followed by the array index within brackets. An assignment operator (=) is then used, followed by the element to be inserted. The data class of the element being inserted should be the same as the data class defined for the array elements; otherwise, you could get unpredictable results when working with the array elements.

DEBUGGING TIP

Remember that C++ array indices are integer values. This means that any specified index is converted to its integer equivalent. For instance, you can specify an index as a character, like this: *Array*['A']; however, C++ sees this as *Array*[65], because the integer equivalent of the character 'A' is 65 from the ASCII code. Likewise, you can specify an index using a floating-point value, like this: *Array*[1.414]; however, C++ sees this as *Array*[1], because the integer portion of 1.414 is 1. Enumerated data elements can also be used as indices, because the compiler equates enumerated elements to integers, according to the listing order of the enumerated data class declaration. To avoid confusion and potential problems, I suggest that you always use integer values for your indices, unless the application specifically dictates otherwise.

Reading Elements into the Array

You can also use any of the C/C++ input functions or objects to insert array elements from a keyboard entry, like this:

```
cin >> Characters[1];
cin >> Integers[0];
```

Here, the user must type the respective array element value on the keyboard and press the **ENTER** key to execute each statement. A character should be entered for the first *cin* statement and an integer for the second *cin* statement. (Why?) The character entered from the keyboard will be stored in the second position (index [1]) of the *Characters* array, whereas the integer entered from the keyboard will be stored in the first position (index [0]) of the *Integers* array.

Inserting Array Elements Using Loops

The obvious disadvantage to using direct assignments to insert array elements is that a separate assignment statement is required to fill each array position. You can automate the insertion process by using a loop structure. Although any of the three loop structures (**while, do/while, for**) can be employed, the **for** structure is the most common. Here's the general format for using a **for** loop:

> ### INSERTING INTO A ONE-DIMENSIONAL ARRAY USING A **for** LOOP
>
> ```
> for (int Index = 0; Index < Array Size;  ++Index)
>         <assign or read to Array[Index]>
> ```

Consider the following program:

```
//FILLING AN ARRAY USING A FOR LOOP
#include <iostream.h>   //FOR cin AND cout

//DECLARE ARRAY SIZE
const int MAX = 10;

void main()
{
  int Sample[MAX];        //DEFINE INTEGER ARRAY

  cout << "Enter a list of " << MAX << " elements and press"
          "the ENTER key after each entry." << endl;
  for (int i = 0; i < MAX; ++i)
    cin >> Sample[i];
} //END main()
```

First, you see a global constant called *MAX* declared. Notice where *MAX* is used in the program. It is the array-size value and the final counter value in the **for** loop. Using a constant like this allows you to change the size of the array easily. Here, the array size is 10 elements. To change the size of the array, you only need to make a change one place in the program under the constant declaration.

Next, look at the array definition. The array *Sample* is defined locally as an array of integer elements. The user is told to "Enter a list of *MAX* (where *MAX* is 10) values and press the **ENTER** key after each entry." Once this prompt is displayed, the program enters a **for** loop. The loop counter variable is *i*, which ranges from 0 to *MAX*. When the loop counter reaches the value of *MAX*, the loop is broken, because the loop test is *i* < *MAX*. It is important to use the "less than" (<) test here rather than the "less than or equal to" (<=) test; otherwise, the loop will execute one too many times. (Why?) The loop counter is employed as the index value for the array. With each loop iteration, a single *cin* statement is executed to insert an element into the array at the respective position specified by the loop counter, *i*.

Let's analyze the *cin* statement. First, the identifier *Sample* is listed with the loop counter variable *i* as the array index in brackets. What does *i* do with each loop iteration? It increments from 0 to *MAX*, right? As a result, the first loop iteration reads a value into *Sample*[0], the second iteration reads a value into *Sample*[1], and so on, until the last loop iteration reads a value into the last array position *Sample*[*MAX* – 1]. When the loop counter increments to the value of *MAX* at the end of the last loop iteration, the loop is broken and no more elements are inserted into the array. That's all there is to it! The array is filled!

You can also use loops for assigning values to array elements. For instance, using the foregoing definitions, consider this loop:

```
for (int i = 0; i < MAX; ++i)
   Sample[i] = 2 * i;
```

This time, the array elements are assigned twice the loop counter value with each loop iteration. What values are actually inserted into the array? How about the 10 even integers from 0 through 18?

Extracting Elements from One-Dimensional Arrays

First, let me caution you that the word *extract* is not a good term here. Why? Because, in general, the word *extract* means to remove something. When we extract an element from an array, we don't actually remove it! We simply *copy* its value. The element remains stored in the array until it is replaced by another value using an insertion operation. As with insertion, you can extract array elements using one of three general methods: *direct assignment*, *writing*, or *looping*.

Direct Assignment

Extracting array elements using assignment statements is just the reverse of inserting elements using an assignment statement. Here's the general format:

> ### DIRECT ASSIGNMENT FORMAT (EXTRACTING ARRAY ELEMENTS)
>
> <variable object identifier> = <array name> [array index];

As an example, suppose we make the following definitions:

```
const int MAX = 10;
int Sample[MAX];
int x;
```

As you can see, the array *Sample*[] consists of 10 integer elements. Now, assuming the array has been filled, what do you think the following statements do?

```
x = Sample[0];
x = Sample[MAX – 1];
x = Sample[3] * Sample[5];
x = 2 * Sample[2] – 3 * Sample[7];
```

The first statement assigns the element stored in the first array position to the variable *x*. The second statement assigns the element stored in the last array position to the variable *x*. The third statement assigns the product of the elements located at indices [3] and [5] to *x*. Finally, the fourth statement assigns two times the element at index [2] minus three times the element at index [7] to *x*. The last two statements illustrate how arithmetic operations can be performed using array elements.

In all of the foregoing cases, the array element values are not affected by the assignment operations. The major requirement is that *x* should be defined as the same data class as the array elements so that you don't get unexpected results.

As a final example, consider these assignment statements:

```
Sample[0] = Sample[MAX – 1];
Sample[1] = Sample[2] + Sample[3];
```

Can you determine what will happen here? In the first statement, the first array element is replaced by the last array element. Is the last array element affected? No, because it appears on the right side of the assignment operator. In the second case, the second array element at index [1] is replaced by the sum of the third and fourth array elements at indices [2] and [3]. Again, the third and fourth array elements are not affected by this operation, because they appear on the right side of the assignment operator.

Writing Array Elements

cout objects can be used to display array elements. Let's use the same array to demonstrate how to write array elements. Here's the array definition again:

```
const int MAX = 10;
int Sample[MAX];
```

Now what do you suppose the following statements will do?

```
cout << Sample[0] << endl;
cout << Sample[MAX – 1] << endl;
cout << Sample[1] / Sample[2] << endl;
cout << sqrt(Sample[6]) << endl;
```

The first statement will display the element contained at index [0] of the array. The second statement will display the last element of the array, located at index [$MAX - 1$]. The third statement will divide the element located at index [1] by the element located at index [2] and display the integer quotient. Finally, the fourth statement will display the square root of the element located at index [6]. None of the array element values is affected by these operations.

Extracting Array Elements Using Loops

As with inserting elements into an array, extracting array elements using loops requires less coding, especially when extracting multiple elements. Again, any of the loop structures can be used for this purpose, but **for** loops are the most common.

Consider the following program:

```
//DISPLAYING AN ARRAY USING A FOR LOOP

#include <iostream.h>   //FOR cin AND cout

//DECLARE ARRAY SIZE
const int MAX = 10;

void main()
{
  int Sample[MAX];       //DEFINE INTEGER ARRAY

  for (int i = 0; i < MAX; ++i)
    Sample[i] = i * i;
  for (i = 0; i < MAX; ++i)
    cout << Sample[i] << '\t';
} //END main()
```

Here again, the array is defined locally as an array of *MAX* (10) integer values. The array name is *Sample*. Notice that the loop counter variable *i* is used as the array index in both **for** loops. The first loop will fill the array locations with the square of the loop counter. Then, the second loop will display each of the array elements located from index [0] to index [*MAX* − 1]. A *cout* statement is used to display the array elements horizontally across the face of the display. Notice also that each time an element is displayed, a tab is written after the element to separate it from the next sequential element. Here is what you would see on the display:

0   1   4   9   16   25   36   49   64   81

DEBUGGING TIP

Be careful not to specify an array index that is out of range. Such an index would be one that is less than zero or greater than the maximum index value. For example, suppose that you define an array like this:

```
const int MAX = 10;
char Array[MAX];
```

A common mistake using this definition would be to attempt to access the element *Array[MAX]*. However, remember that array indices in C++ begin with 0; therefore, *MAX* specifies one position beyond the maximum index value of the array. The maximum index value in this array is *MAX* − 1. In a loop situation, the following loop statement would create the same problem:

```
for (int i = 0; i <= MAX, ++i)
    cout << A[i];
```

Again, the last loop iteration specifies an array index of *MAX*, which is out of the index range. To prevent this error, the test must be *i* < *MAX* or *i* <= *MAX* − 1.

When an array index is out of range, you *will not* get a compiler error. At best, you will get garbage. At worst, you might destroy something in memory that is required by your program or operating system, resulting in a program or system crash. Errors such as this are very difficult to locate. So, be safe and make sure that your indices are always within their specified range.

Quick Check

1. Write a **for** loop that will fill the following array from user entries:

    char Characters[15];

2. Write a **for** loop that will display the contents of the array in question 1.

8-4 PASSING ARRAYS AND ARRAY ELEMENTS TO FUNCTIONS

You can pass an entire array to a function or pass single array elements to a function. The important thing to remember is that to pass the entire array, you must pass the address of the array. In C and C++, *the array name is the address of the first element (index [0]) of the array*. Let's begin by looking at the required function header. Here is typical prototype for passing a one-dimensional array to a function:

void Weird (char Array[MAX]);

Looking at the prototype, you see that the function does not return a value. There is one character parameter called *Array[MAX]*. The single set of square brackets after the parameter identifier indicates that the parameter is a one-dimensional array with a size of *MAX*. When passing arrays to a function, the function must know how large an array to accept. Now, the array identifier references the address of the array, so the array is passed *by reference* to the function. Thus, any operations on the array within the function will affect the original array contents in the calling program. Also, because the parameter is the address of the array, no ampersand symbol, &, is required to pass the array by reference. In fact, the use of an ampersand prior to the array parameter will cause a compile error.

Next, to call this function and pass the array, you simply use the following statement:

Weird(Name);

Of course, this call assumes that *Name* is the array name in the calling program. (Remember that the actual argument identifier and the formal parameter identifier *can be* different.) The call to *Name* references the address of the array, so the array address is passed to the function rather than a copy of the array. Thus, any operations on the array within the function will affect the original array elements. Here's a complete program:

```
//PASSING AN ARRAY TO A FUNCTION

#include <iostream.h>   //FOR cin AND cout

//DECLARE ARRAY SIZE
const int MAX = 3;

 //FUNCTION PROTOTYPE
void Weird(char Array[MAX]);

void main()
{
  //DEFINE CHARACTER ARRAY
  char Name[MAX];

  //FILL Name ARRAY WITH CHARACTERS
  Name[0] = 'I';
  Name[1] = 'B';
  Name[2] = 'M';

  //DISPAY Name ARRAY
  cout << "The contents of Name[] before Weird() is:  " << endl;
  for(int i = 0;i < MAX;++i)
    cout << Name[i];

  //CALL FUNCTION Weird()
  Weird(Name);

  //DISPLAY Name ARRAY
  cout << "\n\nThe contents of Name[] after Weird() is:  " << endl;
  for(i = 0;i < MAX;++i)
    cout << Name[i];
} //END main()
```

```
//THIS FUNCTION DECREMENTS EACH OF THE ARRAY ELEMENTS
void Weird(char Array[MAX])
{
  for (int i = 0; i < MAX; ++i)
    --Array[i];
} //END Weird()
```

The array *Name*[] is defined as an array of characters and filled using direct assignment with the characters 'I', 'B', 'M' in *main( )*. The characters stored in the array are displayed on the monitor using a **for** loop. Then, the function *Weird( )* is called using the array name, *Name*, as its argument. This passes the address of the array to function *Weird( )*, where each of the elements in the array is decremented. What do you suppose the user will see on the monitor after executing the program? Well, this is why things are "weird."

The contents of Name[] before Weird() is:
IBM

The contents of Name[] after Weird() is:
HAL

The point here is that the decrement operation within the function affected the original array elements. Thus, the word *IBM* was converted to the word *HAL*. Is there anything weird here? Recall that HAL was the artificially intelligent computer in the book and movie *2001: A Space Odyssey*. Is there a message here or is this just a coincidence? You will have to ask the author, Arthur Clarke, to find out.

One final point: You cannot pass the entire array by value to a function. If you do not want operations within the function to affect the array elements, you should pass the array to the function, make a temporary local copy of the array within the function, and then operate on this temporary array.

On the other hand, you can pass individual array elements by value to a function. Look at the following function prototype:

void PassByValue(int ArrayElement);

The header says that the function does not return any value and expects to receive an integer value from the calling program. Suppose the function were called as follows:

PassByValue(Scores[0]);

Notice that the actual argument in the function call is *Scores*[0]. This will cause a copy of the element stored at index [0] in the *Scores*[] array to be passed to the function by value. As a result, any operations on this element within the function will not affect the element value in the original *Scores*[] array. If you want the element to reflect any operations within the function, you must pass it by reference using the ampersand symbol in the function prototype, like this:

```
void PassByReference(int &ArrayElement);
```

Now, any call to the function will pass the address of the element to the function, thereby passing the element by reference. The following program illustrates how array elements can be passed by value or reference.

```
//PASSING ARRAY ELEMENTS BY VALUE AND REFERENCE

#include <iostream.h>   //FOR cin AND cout

//DECLARE ARRAY SIZE
const int MAX = 3;

//FUNCTION PROTOTYPES
void PassByValue(int ArrayElement);
void PassByReference(int &ArrayElement);

void main()
{
  int Scores[MAX];
  Scores[0] = 10;
  Scores[1] = 20;
  Scores[2] = 30;
  cout << "Element at Scores[0] before PassByValue is:  "
       << Scores[0] << endl;
  PassByValue(Scores[0]);
  cout << "Element at Scores[0] after PassByValue is:  "
       << Scores[0] << endl;

  cout << "Element at Scores[0] before PassByReference is:  "
       << Scores[0] << endl;
  PassByReference(Scores[0]);
  cout << "Element at Scores[0] after PassByReference is:  "
       << Scores[0] << endl;
} //END main()
```

```
void PassByValue(int ArrayElement)
{
  ++ArrayElement;
} //END PassByValue()

void PassByReference(int &ArrayElement)
{
  ++ArrayElement;
} //END PassByReference()
```

The output produced by the program reflects the effect of the two functions on the array element.

Element at Scores[0] before PassByValue is: 10
Element at Scores[0] after PassByValue is: 10
Element at Scores[0] before PassByReference is: 10
Element at Scores[0] after PassByReference is: 11

Study the last two programs to make sure that you understand how entire arrays and individual array elements are passed to functions.

Example 8-2

Write a program that uses an array to store a maximum of 25 test scores and calculate their average. Use one function to fill the array with the scores, a second function to calculate the average, and a third function to display all the scores along with the calculated average.

Solution

We will begin in true structuring style and develop the interfaces for the required functions. Let's call the three functions *GetScores()*, *Average()*, and *DisplayResults()*. Now, the *GetScores()* function must obtain the test scores from the user and place them in an array. Thus, the function must accept the array structure and return the array containing the test scores. This leads to the following function interface description:

Function *GetScores()*:   Obtains test scores from user and places them in an array.

Accepts: A placehoder for the number of test scores and the test scores array structure of size *MAX*.

Returns: The number of test scores and the test scores array filled with scores entered by the user.

The function interface requires that it must accept and return the array structure. Let's assume that the test scores will be decimal values and, therefore, require a floating-point array. By using these ideas, the function prototype becomes

```
void GetScores (int &Number, float Scores[MAX]);
```

From here, writing the function is easy. We will employ a *cin* statement within a **for** loop in the function body to fill the array with the test scores. Here's the entire function:

```
void GetScores (int & Number, float Scores[MAX])
{
  cout << "How many scores do you want to average?" << endl;
  cin >> Number;
  cout << "Enter each score, and press ENTER after each entry." << endl;
  for (int i = 0; i < Number; ++i)
  {
    cout << "Enter score #" << i + 1 << ":  ";
    cin >> Scores[i];
  } //END FOR
} //END GetScores()
```

Within the function body you see that the user is prompted to enter the number of test scores and each individual score. The scores are entered and placed in the array via a *cin* statement within a **for** loop. Notice that the value the user enters for *Number* is employed to terminate the **for** loop. Also notice that *Number* is a reference parameter. As a result, it will be returned to the calling program for use by other functions.

Next, a function called *Average()* must be written to average the test scores in the array. This function must accept the array to obtain the test scores and return a single floating-point value that is the average of the scores. So, the function interface description is as follows:

Function *Average()*:   Computes the average of the test scores.

Accepts: The number of test scores to average and the test score array of of size *MAX*.

Returns: A single value that is the average of the test scores.

This time, the array must be passed to the function and the function must return a single value. Therefore, the function prototype becomes

```
float Average(int Number, float Scores[MAX]);
```

The body of the function simply adds up all the test scores in the array and divides by their number. Here is the complete function:

```
float Average(int Number, float Scores[MAX])
{
  float Total = 0.0;
  for (int i = 0; i < Number; ++i)
    Total += Scores[i];
  return Total/Number;
} //END Average()
```

There are two local function variables defined: *Total* and *i*. *Total* will act as a temporary variable to accumulate the sum of the scores, and variable *i* is the loop counter variable. The variable *Total* is first initialized to 0. Then the loop is used to obtain the array elements, one at a time, and to add them to *Total*. Observe that the loop counter (*i*) acts as the array index within the loop. Thus, the array elements, from index [0] to [*Number* – 1], are sequentially extracted with each loop iteration and added to *Total*. The last test score is located at index [*Number* – 1]. Once the loop calculates the sum total of all the test scores, a **return** statement is used to return the calculated average.

Finally, the *DisplayResults()* function must display the individual test scores obtained from the user along with their average. To do this, we must pass the array to the function to obtain the test scores. Here's the function description:

Function *DisplayResults()*:   Displays the individual test scores and their average.

Accepts: The number of scores to display and the test scores array of size *MAX*.

Returns: Nothing.

To display the average, we will simply call the *Average()* function within this function as part of a *cout* statement. The entire function then becomes

```
void DisplayResults(int Number, float Scores[MAX])
{
  cout << endl << endl;
  cout << "Test Scores" << endl;
  cout << "-----------" << endl;
  cout.setf(ios::fixed);
  cout.precision(2);
  for (int i = 0; i < Number; ++i)
    cout << Scores[i] << endl;
  cout << "\nThe average of the above scores is:  "
       << Average(Scores) << endl;
} //END DisplayResults()
```

Again, a **for** loop is employed to display the individual test scores. Notice how the *Average()* function is called in the final *cout* statement to calculate the test average.

Now, putting everything together, we get the following program:

```
//***************************************************************************
//
//THIS PROGRAM WILL CALCULATE A TEST AVERAGE
//FROM SCORES ENTERED BY THE USER INTO AN ARRAY
//
//***************************************************************************

#include <iostream.h>        //FOR cin AND cout

//GLOBAL CONSTANT
const int MAX = 25;          //MAXIMUM NUMBER OF SCORES

//FUNCTION PROTOTYPES
void GetScores (int &Number, float Scores[MAX] );
float Average(int Number, float Scores[MAX]);
void DisplayResults(int Number, float Scores[MAX]);

void main()
{
 //DEFINE NUMBER OF SCORES VARIABLE AND TEST SCORES ARRAY
  int Number = 0;            //ACTUAL NUMBER OF SCORES
  float Scores[MAX];         //ARRAY DEFINITION

 //CALL FUNCTION TO GET SCORES AND DISPLAY RESULTS
  GetScores(Number, Scores);        //CALL FUNCTION GetScores()
  DisplayResults(Number, Scores);   //CALL FUNCTION DisplayResults()
} //END main()

//***************************************************************************
//
//THIS FUNCTION WILL GET THE SCORES FROM THE USER
//AND PLACE THEM INTO THE SCORES ARRAY
//
//***************************************************************************
void GetScores (int &Number, float Scores[MAX])
{
  cout << "How many scores do you want to average?" << endl;
  cin >> Number;
  cout << "Enter each score, and press ENTER after each entry." << endl;
```

```
    for (int i = 0; i < Number; ++i)
    {
      cout << "Enter score #" << i + 1 << ":  ";
      cin >> Scores[i];
    } //END FOR
  } //END GetScores()


//****************************************************************************
//
//THIS FUNCTION WILL CALCULATE THE AVERAGE OF THE
//SCORES IN THE ARRAY
//
//****************************************************************************
float Average(int Number, float Scores[MAX])
{
  float Total = 0.0;
  for (int i = 0; i < Number; ++i)
    Total += Scores[i];
  return Total/Number;
} //END Average()


//****************************************************************************
//
//THIS FUNCTION DISPLAYS THE ARRAY SCORES AND THE
//FINAL SCORE AVERAGE
//
//****************************************************************************
void DisplayResults(int Number, float Scores[MAX])
{
  cout << endl << endl;
  cout << "Test Scores" << endl;
  cout << "-----------" << endl;
  cout.setf(ios::fixed);
  cout.precision(2);
  for (int i = 0; i < Number; ++i)
    cout << Scores[i] << endl;
  cout << "\nThe average of the above scores is:  "
       << Average(Number, Scores) << endl;
} //END DisplayResults()
```

As you can see, a global constant (*MAX*) is first declared. This will be the maximum number of elements in the array. After the global constant is defined, the three function prototypes are listed. Now, look at the statement section of *main()*. Are you surprised at its simplicity? Function *main()* is relatively short, because all the work is done in the other functions. This is the "beauty" of structured programming! All *main()* does is call the two other functions in the order that they are needed. You see that at the beginning of *main()*, a variable called *Number* is defined to hold the actual number of test scores entered by the user. This value will be passed to and from the functions as needed. Then, the array, called *Scores[]*, is defined as an array of *MAX*, or 25, floating-point elements. The array name is *Scores,* so this identifier must be used when accessing the array. After the array is defined, the *GetScores()* function is called, followed by the *DisplayResults()* function. Observe that, in both cases, both *Number* and the array, *Scores*, are passed to the function by listing their names as the function arguments. The function *GetScores()* is first called to obtain the scores from the user and to insert them into the array. Next, the function *DisplayResults()* is called. Again, the number of scores, *Number*, and the test scores array, *Scores*, are passed to the function by listing their respective names as arguments in the function call. This function displays the test scores from the array and calls the *Average()* function to calculate the test average.

You now have all the ingredients you need to write programs using the versatile one dimensional arrays. Next, you will learn how to search and array for a given element value as well as sort the elements in an array. What follows are some classic searching and sorting algorithms that are important for you to learn, regardless of the programming language that you are using. Of course, we will implement these classic algorithms using the C++ language.

 Quick Check

1. True or false: An array name is the address of index [1] of the array.

2. Write a prototype for a function called *Sample()* that must alter the following array:

    char Characters[15];

    Assume that the function does not return any values except the altered array.

4. Write a prototype for a function called *Test()* that will alter a single array element in the array defined in question 2.

5. Write a statement that will call the function prototyped in question 3 to alter the element stored at index [5] of the array defined in question 2.

PROBLEM SOLVING IN ACTION: SEARCHING AN ARRAY USING ITERATION (SEQUENTIAL SEARCH)

Many applications require a program to search for a given element in an array. Two common algorithms used to perform this task are ***sequential***, or ***serial***, ***search*** and ***binary search***. Sequential search is commonly used for unsorted arrays, and binary search is used on arrays that are already sorted. In this problem, you will learn about sequential search; then in a later problem, you will learn about binary search.

Problem

Develop a function that can be called to sequentially search an array of integers for a given element value and return the index of the element if it is found in the array.

Defining the Problem

Because we are dealing with a function, the problem definition will focus on the function interface. As a result, we must consider what the function will accept and what the function will return. Let's call the function *SeqSearch()*. Now, from the problem statement, you find that the function must search an array of integers for a given element value. Thus, the function needs two things to do its job: (1) the array to be searched, and (2) the element for which to search. These will be our function parameters. Do these need to be value or reference parameters? Well, the function will not be changing the array or the element being searched for, right? Therefore, the parameters will be value parameters.

Next, we need to determine what the function is to return to the calling program. From the problem statement, you see that the function needs to return the index of the element being searched for if it is found in the array. All array indices in C++ are integers, so the function will return an integer value. But, what if the element being searched for is not found in the array? We need to return some integer value that will indicate this situation. Because array indices in C++ range from 0 to some finite positive integer, let's return the integer –1 if the element is not found in the array. Thus, we will use –1 to indicate the "not-found" condition, because no array index in C++ can have this value. Here is the function interface description:

Function *SeqSearch()*:   Searches an integer array for a given element value.

Accepts: An array of integers and the element for which to search.

Returns: The array index of the element if found, or the value –1
                                               if the element is not found.

The preceding function interface description provides all the information required to write the function interface. Here it is:

int SeqSearch(int A[MAX], int Element)

The interface dictates that the function will accept two things: (1) an array of *MAX* integer elements, and (2) an integer value, called *Element*, that will be the value for which to search.

The next task is to develop the sequential search algorithm.

Planning the Solution

Sequential search does exactly what it says: It *sequentially* searches the array, from one element to the next, starting at the first array position and stopping when either the element is found or it reaches the end of the array. Thus, the algorithm must test the element stored in the first array position, then the second array position, then the third, and so on until the element is found or it runs out of array elements. This is obviously a repetitive task of testing an array element, then moving to the next element and testing again, and so on. Consider the following algorithm that employs a **while** loop to perform the repetitive testing operation:

SeqSearch() **Algorithm**

SeqSearch()
BEGIN
   Set *Found* = false.
   Set *Index* = first array index.
   While (*Element* is not *Found*) AND (*Index* <= last array index) Do
     If (*A[Index]* == *Element*) Then
       Set *Found* = true.
     Else
       Increment *Index.*
   If (*Found* == true) Then
     Return *Index.*
   Else
     Return –1.
END.

The idea here is to employ a Boolean variable, called *Found*, to indicate if the element was found during the search. The variable *Found* is initialized to false, and a variable called *Index* is initialized to the index of the first element in the array. Notice the **while** loop test. Because of the use of the **AND** operator, the loop will continue as long as the element is not found *and* the value of *Index* is less than or equal to the last index value of the array. Another way to say this is that the loop will repeat until the element is found *or* the value of *Index* exceeds the last index value of the array. Think about it!

Inside the loop, the value stored at location [*Index*] is compared to the value of *Element*, received by the function. If the two are equal, the Boolean variable *Found* is set to true. Otherwise, the value of *Index* is incremented to move to the next array position.

When the loop terminates, either the element was found or not found. If the element was found, the value of *Found* will be true, and the value of *Index* will be the array position, or index, at which the element was found. Thus, if *Found* is true, the value of *Index* is returned to the calling program. If the element was not found, the value of *Found* will still be false from its initialized state, and the value −1 is returned to the calling program. That's all there is to it!

Coding the Program

Here is the C++ code that reflects the foregoing algorithm:

```
//ACTION 8-1 (ACT08-01.CPP)
int SeqSearch(int A[MAX], int Element)
{
  enum Boolean {FALSE, TRUE};      //DEFINE FALSE = 0 AND TRUE = 1
  Boolean Found = FALSE;           //INITIALIZE Found TO FALSE
  int i = 0;                       //ARRAY INDEX VARIABLE

//SEARCH ARRAY UNTIL FOUND OR REACH END OF ARRAY
  while ((!Found) && (i < MAX))
  {
   if (A[i] == Element)            //TEST ARRAY ELEMENT
     Found = TRUE;                 //IF EQUAL, SET Found TO TRUE
   else                            //ELSE INCREMENT ARRAY INDEX
     ++i;
  } //END WHILE

//IF ELEMENT FOUND, RETURN ELEMENT POSITION IN ARRAY
//ELSE RETURN −1.
```

```
    if (Found)
      return i;
    else
      return -1;
} //END SeqSearch()
```

There should be no surprises in this code. At the top of the function, you see the header that is identical to the function interface developed earlier. Then you see an enumerated data class created to define FALSE and TRUE. Recall that the default values for enumerated data elements are the integers, beginning with 0. Thus, FALSE is defined to be the value 0, and TRUE is defined to be the value 1. This allows us to use the identifiers FALSE and TRUE within our program to represent the integer values 0 and 1, respectively. In addition, Boolean tests can be made against these values, because C++ interprets a 0 as a logical FALSE and a 1 as a logical TRUE.

The variable *Found* is defined as an object of our enumerated Boolean data class and set to FALSE. We will use the variable *i* as our array index variable. This variable is defined as an integer and set to the first array index, 0. Remember that arrays in C++ always begin with index 0. The **while** loop employs the **AND** (&&) operator to test the values of *Found* and *i*. The loop will repeat as long as the element is not found (!*Found*) and the value of *i* is less than the size of the array, *MAX*. Remember that when the size of the array is *MAX*, the last array index is *MAX* − 1. So, when *i* exceeds the maximum array index, *MAX* − 1, the loop breaks. When the loop is broken, the value of *Found* is tested. If *Found* is TRUE, the value of *i* is returned; if *Found* is FALSE, the value −1 is returned to indicate that the element was not found in the array.

PROBLEM SOLVING IN ACTION: SORTING AN ARRAY USING ITERATION (INSERTION SORT)

To sort an array means to place the array elements in either ascending or descending order from the beginning to the end of the array. There are many common algorithms used for sorting. There is *insertion sort*, *bubble sort*, *selection sort*, *quick sort*, *merge sort*, and *heap sort*, just to mention a few. In a data structures course, you will most likely learn about and analyze all of these sorting algorithms. In this problem, we will develop the *insertion sort* algorithm and code it as a function in C++.

Problem

Develop a function that can be called to sort an array of characters in ascending order using the ***insertion sort*** algorithm.

Defining the Problem

Again, we will code the algorithm as a C++ function, so the problem definition will focus on the function interface, leading us to the function prototype. Let's call our function *InsertSort()*. Think about what *InsertSort()* needs to do its job. Well, it must receive an unsorted array of characters and return the same array as a sorted array, right? Does it need anything else? No, additional data are not required by the function, because the only thing being operated upon is the array itself.

What about return values? Does the function need to return a single value or a set of values? The function does not return any single value, but must return the sorted array. Therefore, the return type of the function must be **void**, and the array must be a reference parameter, right? Remember that when arrays are passed to C++ functions, they are always treated as reference parameters because the array name represents an address in memory. So, here's our *InsertSort()* function interface description:

Function *InsertSort()*:   Sorts an array of characters in ascending order.

Accepts: An unsorted array of characters.

Returns: A sorted array of characters.

From the preceding description, the function interface is easily coded as

```
void InsertSort(char Array[MAX])
```

The interface says that *InsertSort()* will receive a character array of size *MAX*. The return type is **void**, because no single value is returned. However, because the entire array is being passed to the function, any sorting operations on the array within the function will be reflected in the calling program. Now for the insertion sort algorithm.

Planning the Solution

Before we set up the algorithm, let's see how insertion sort works. Look at Figure 8-3. We will assume that we are going to sort a five-character array in ascending order. Before getting into the details, look at the figure from top to bottom and from left to right. The unsorted array is shown at the top of the figure, and the sorted array is shown at the bottom of the figure. Notice that shading is employed in the figure to show the sorting process from top to bottom. As we proceed from the unsorted array at the top, the shading increases, showing the portion of the array that is sorted, until the entire array is shaded at the bottom of the figure.

The top-to-bottom sequence shows that we will make four passes through the array to achieve the sorted array shown at the bottom of the figure. With each pass, an element is placed into its sorted position *relative to the elements that occur before it* in the array. The first pass begins with the first element, 'E', sorted as indicated by the shading. The single character 'E' is considered to be sorted by itself, because it does not have any elements preceding it. Thus, the task in this first pass is to sort the second element, 'D', relative to the character 'E' that precedes it.

The second pass begins with the characters 'D' and 'E' sorted, as indicated by the shading. The task in this pass is to sort the third character, 'C', relative to these two characters. In the third pass, the elements 'C', 'D', and 'E' are sorted, and the task is to sort the character 'B' relative to these characters. Remember, in each pass, the task is to sort the first character of the unsorted portion of the array relative to the characters that precede it in the sorted portion of the array. The process continues until all the characters are sorted, as shown at the bottom of the figure. With each pass, you are essentially repeating what was done in the previous pass. As a result, you can identify a repetitive process, from pass to pass, from the top to the bottom of the figure. This repetition will result in a loop structure in our algorithm.

Now, the question is: What happens during each pass to eventually sort the entire array? Well, during each pass, the first element in the unsorted (unshaded) portion of the array is examined by comparing it to the sorted sequence of elements that precede it. If this element is less than the element preceding it, the two elements are exchanged. Once the element is exchanged with its predecessor, it is compared with its new predecessor element. Again, if it is less than its predecessor, the two elements are exchanged.

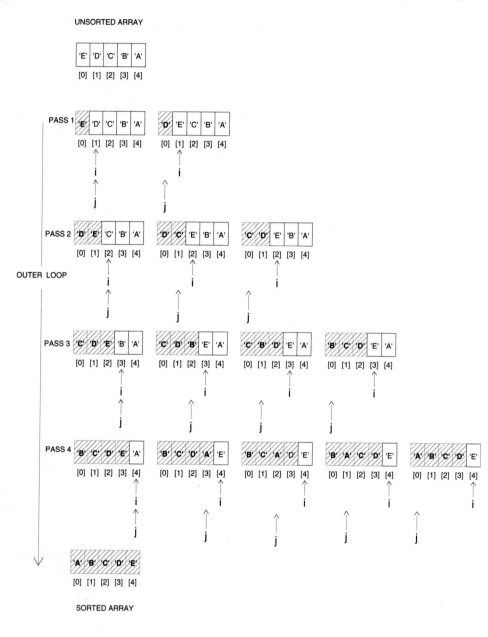

Figure 8-3   Insertion sort is a nested repetition process.

This process is repeated until one of two things happens: (1) the element is greater than or equal to its predecessor, or (2) the element is in the first position of the array (index [0]). In other words, the left-to-right compare/exchange process shown in Figure 8-3 ceases when the element under examination has been "inserted" into its proper position in the sorted portion of the array. This compare/exchange process represents repetition from left to right in the figure and will result in another loop structure in our algorithm. So, we can identify two repetitive processes in the figure: one from top to bottom and one from left to right. How are the two repetitive processes related? Well, it seems that for each top-to-bottom pass through the array, the compare/exchange process is executed from left to right. Thus, the left-to-right process must be nested within the top-to-bottom process. This will be reflected in our algorithm by two loop structures: one controlling the left-to-right compare/exchange process that must be nested inside a second loop controlling the top-to-bottom process. Look at the figure again to make sure that you see this nested repetition. Now that you have an idea of how insertion sort works, here is the formal algorithm:

InsertSort( ) **Algorithm**

InsertSort( )
BEGIN
  Set i = second array index.
  While (i <= last array index) Do
    Set $j = i$.
    While ((j > first array index) AND ($A[j] < A[j-1]$)) Do
      Exchange $A[j]$ and $A[j-1]$.
      Decrement j.
    Increment i.
END.

The variables i and j in the algorithm correspond to the i and j shown in Figure 8-3. The variable i controls the outer loop, and j controls the inner loop. Notice that i begins at the second array index. Why not the first array index? Because the first element in the array is always sorted relative to any preceding elements, right? So, the first pass begins with the second array element. The first statement in the outer loop sets j equal to i. Thus, both i and j locate the first element in the unsorted portion of the array at the beginning of each pass. Now, the inner loop will exchange the element located by j, which is $A[j]$, with its predecessor element, which is $A[j-1]$, as long as j is greater than the first array index *and* element A[*j*] is less than element A[*j*– 1]. Once the exchange is made, *j* is decremented. This forces *j* to follow the element being inserted into the sorted portion of the array. The exchanges continue until either there are no elements preceding element A[*j*] that are less than element A[*j*] or the element is inserted into the first element position.

Once the inner loop is broken, element A[*j*] is inserted into its correct position relative to the elements that precede it. Then, another pass is made by incrementing the outer loop control variable *i*, setting *j* to *i*, and executing the inner loop again. This nested looping process continues until *i* is incremented past the last array position.

Study the preceding algorithm and compare it to Figure 8-3 until you are sure that you understand *InsertSort()*. Now for the C++ code.

Coding the Program

We have already developed the *InsertSort()* function interface. The algorithm is easily coded as a function in C++, like this:

```
//ACTION 8-2  (ACT08-02.CPP)
//EXCHANGE FUNCTION
void Exchange(char &x, char &y)
{
  char Temp;                    //CREATE TEMPORARY VARIABLE
  Temp = x;                     //SET Temp TO x
  x = y;                        //SET x TO y
  y = Temp;                     //SET y TO Temp
} //END Exchange()

//INSERTION SORT FUNCTION
void InsertSort(char A[MAX])
{
  int i;                        //OUTER LOOP CONTROL VARIABLE
  int j;                        //INNER LOOP CONTROL VARIABLE
  i = 1;                        //SET i TO SECOND ARRAY INDEX
  while (i < MAX)               //MAKE MAX – 1 PASSES THRU ARRAY
  {
    j = i;                      //j LOCATES FIRST ELEMENT
                                //OF UNSORTED ARRAY
    while ((j > 0) && (A[j] < A[j – 1])) //COMPARE/EXCHANGE A[j] AND A[j – 1]
    {
      Exchange(A[j], A[j – 1]);
```

```
        --j;                        //MAKE j FOLLOW INSERT ELEMENT
      } //END INNER WHILE
        ++i;                        //MAKE i LOCATE FIRST ELEMENT OF
                                    //UNSORTED PORTION

    } //END OUTER WHILE
  } //END InsertSort()
```

Here you see two functions coded in C++. Recall that the *InsertSort()* algorithm requires an exchange operation. A function called *Exchange()* has been coded to accomplish this task. Notice that this function has two reference parameters that are characters. Thus, the function receives two characters that are exchanged by using a temporary local variable (*Temp*) within the function. The exchanged characters are sent back to the calling program via the reference parameters. Of course, the calling program will be our *InsertSort()* function.

The *InsertSort()* code should be straightforward from the algorithm that we just analyzed. Study the code and compare it to the algorithm. You will find that they are identical from a logical and structural point of view. You might notice how the *Exchange()* function is called within *InsertSort()*. The array elements $A[j]$ and $A[j - 1]$ are passed to the function. These elements are simply characters, right? So, the function receives two characters and exchanges them. The respective characters in the array reflect the exchange operations, because *Exchange()* employs reference parameters.

PROBLEM SOLVING IN ACTION: SEARCHING AN ARRAY USING RECURSION (BINARY SEARCH)

In this problem, we will develop another popular searching algorithm, called **binary search**. The binary search algorithm that we will develop will employ recursion, although it can also be done using iteration. One of the major differences between binary search and sequential search is that binary search requires that the array be sorted prior to the search, whereas sequential search does not have this requirement. If, however, you have a sorted array to begin with, binary search is much faster than sequential search, especially for large arrays. For example, if you were to apply sequential search to an array of 1000 integers, the sequential search algorithm will make an *average* of 500 comparisons to find the desired element. Even worse, if the desired element is in the last array position, sequential search will make 1000 comparisons to find the element. On the other hand, a binary search would require a maximum of 10 comparisons to find the element, even if it is in the last array position! Of course, you must pay a price for this increased efficiency. The price you must pay is that of a more complex algorithm. So, when searching a sorted array, the advantage of sequential search is simplicity, whereas the advantage of binary search is efficiency.

Problem

Develop a C++ function that can be called to search a sorted array of integers for a given element value and return the index of the element if it is found in the array. Employ a recursive binary search to accomplish this task.

We will be developing a C++ function, so our problem definition will again focus on the function interface. However, before we can consider the function interface, we must see how a recursive binary search works, because the search algorithm will dictate our function parameters. So, let's first deal with the algorithm and then develop the function interface.

Planning the Solution

Binary search represents a natural recursive operation. Remember that the idea behind recursion is to divide and conquer. You keep dividing a problem into simpler subproblems of exactly the same type until a primitive condition occurs. This is not the same as top-down software design, which divides problems into simpler subproblems. The difference with recursion is that the subproblems are exactly the same type of problem as the original problem. For example, suppose that you are searching for a name in a telephone book. Imagine starting at the beginning of the telephone book and looking at every name until you found the right one. This is exactly what sequential search does. Wouldn't it be much faster, on the average, to open up the book in the middle? Then, determine which half of the book contains the name that you are looking for, divide this section of the book in half, and so on, until you obtain the page on which the desired name appears. Here is an algorithm that describes the telephone book search just described

A Recursive Telephone Book Search Algorithm

TeleSearch()
BEGIN
    If (the telephone book only contains one page) Then
        Look for the name on the page.
    Else
        Open the book to the middle.
        If (the name is in the first half) Then

> *TeleSearch*(first half of the book for the name).
>
> Else
>> *TeleSearch*(second half of the book for the name).

END.

Do you see how this search is recursive? You keep performing the same basic operations until you come to the page that contains the name for which you are looking. In other words, the *TeleSearch()* function keeps calling itself in the nested **if/else** statement until the correct page is found. The reason that this is called a *binary* search process is that you must divide the book by 2 (*bi*) each time the algorithm calls itself.

Now, let's see how this process can be applied to searching an array of integers. We will call our recursive binary search function *BinSearch()* and will develop our algorithm in several steps. Here is the first-level algorithm.

BinSearch() **Algorithm: First Level**

BinSearch()
BEGIN
   If (the array has only one element) Then
      Determine if this element is the element being searched for.
   Else
      Find the midpoint of the array.
      If (the element is in the first half) Then
         *BinSearch(*first half*)*.
      Else
         *BinSearch(*second half*)*.
END.

Notice how this algorithm is almost identical to the *TeleSearch()* algorithm. Here, the divide-and-conquer searching process continues until the array is reduced to one element that is tested against the element for which we are searching. Do you see how the search keeps calling itself until the primitive condition occurs? Although this algorithm provides the general binary search idea, we need to get more specific in order to code the algorithm. To do this, we must ask ourselves what data *BinSearch()* needs to accomplish its task. Well, like sequential search, it needs an array to search and the element for which to search, right? However, sequential search dealt with one array of a given size, whereas binary search needs to deal with arrays of different sizes as it keeps dividing the original array in half. Not only are these arrays of different sizes, but the first and last indices of each half are different. As a result, we must provide *BinSearch()* with the boundaries of the array that it is dealing with at any given time. This can be done by passing the first and last indices of the given array to the function. Let's call these indices *First* and *Last*.

We are now ready to write the function-interface description:

Function *BinSearch()*:   Searches a sorted array of integers for a given value.

Accepts: An array of integers, an element for which to search, the
                                          first index of the array being searched, and the last index
                                          of the array being searched.

Returns: The array index of the element, if found, or the value
                                          −1 if the element is not found.

This description gives us enough information to write the C++ function interface, as follows:

int BinSearch(int A[], int Element, int First, int Last)

Here, *BinSearch()* will return an integer value that represents the index of the element being searched for. Again, you will see that the value −1 will be returned if the element is not found in the array. The function receives the integer array being searched (*A[]*), the element being searched for (*Element*), the first index of the array being searched (*First*), and the last index of the array being searched (*Last*). Notice that no size is provided for the array being searched because the function will recursively search arrays of different sizes.

The next problem is to determine what the value of *First* and *Last* will be for any given array during the search. Well, remember that we must divide any given array in half to produce two new arrays each time a recursive call to *BinSearch()* is made. Given any array where the first index is *First* and the last index is *Last*, we can determine the middle index, like this:

$$Mid = (First + Last) / 2$$

By using this calculation, the first half of the array begins at *First* and ends at *Mid* − 1, and the second half of the array begins at *Mid* + 1 and ends at *Last*. This idea is illustrated in Figure 8-4.

But, notice that neither half of the array contains the middle element. By using this technique, the two halves do not make a whole, right? So, before the split is made, suppose that we test the middle element to see if it is the element that we are looking for. The following test will do the job.

If $(A[Mid] == Element)$ Then
Return Mid.

If this test is true prior to the split, we have found the element that we are looking for, and we can cease the recursive calls. Otherwise, the element stored in $A[Mid]$ is not the element that we are looking for, and this array position can be ignored during the rest of the search. If this is the case, we will split the array and continue the recursive process. However, we have just added a second primitive condition to our recursive algorithm. Here are the two primitive conditions that we now have:

1. The array being searched has only one element.
2. $A[Mid] == Element$.

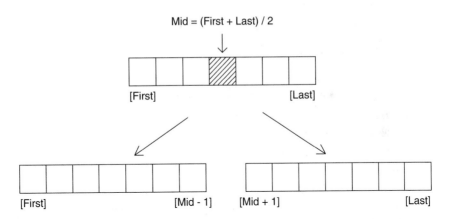

Figure 8-4 Recursive binary search requires that an array be divided in half with each recursive call.

Either of these primitive conditions will cause the recursive calls to cease. Now, let's consider the first primitive condition more closely. How do we know if the array being searched has only one element? Well, as the recursive calls continue without finding the element, the array will eventually be reduced to a single element. If this is the element that we are looking for, the test *If A[Mid] == Element* will be true, and the recursive calls will stop. If this is not the element that we are looking for, the value of *First* will become greater than the value of *Last* on the next split. Why? Because if you think about the splitting action of the algorithm, you will realize that each recursive call causes *First* to increase and *Last* to decrease. Thus, if the element is not in the array, the value of *First* will eventually become larger than the value of *Last*. So we can use this idea to test for the element not being in the array, as well as use it for a primitive condition. Thus, we will replace the original primitive condition with the following statement:

If (*First* > *Last*) Then
Return –1

If this condition occurs, the value –1 is returned, indicating that the element was not found, and the recursive calls cease.

Now, let's apply this knowledge to a second-level algorithm. Here it is:

BinSearch() **Algorithm: Second Level**

```
BinSearch(A, Element, First, Last)
BEGIN
   If (First > Last) Then
     Return –1.
   Else
     Set Mid = (First + Last) / 2.
     If (A[Mid] == Element) Then
       Return Mid.
     Else
       If (the element is in the first half) Then
               BinSearch(A, Element, First, Mid – 1).
       Else
               BinSearch(A, Element, Mid + 1, Last).
END.
```

It is much clearer now that our algorithm is performing recursion, because you see the function calling itself in either one of two places, depending on which half of the split array the element is likely to be found. Also, observe where the two primitive cases are tested. If, at the beginning of any recursive call, *First* > *Last*, the element is not in the array, and the recursive calls cease. In addition, if, after calculating *Mid*, we find the element at *A[Mid]*, the recursive calls cease. In both cases, the function has finished executing, and a value is returned to the calling program. The last thing our algorithm needs is a way to determine if the element being searched for is likely to be in the first half or the second half of the split array. Here is where the requirement for a sorted array comes in. If the array is sorted, the element will likely be in the first half of the array when *Element < A[Mid]*; otherwise, the element is likely to be in the second half of the array. Notice that we are using the term "likely." We cannot guarantee that the element is in either half, because it might not be in the array at all! All we can do is to direct the search to that half where the element is likely to be, depending on the sorted ordering of elements. So, we can now complete our algorithm using this idea. Here is the final algorithm:

BinSearch( ) **Algorithm**

BinSearch(A, Element, First, Last)
BEGIN
If (*First > Last*) Then
    Return –1.
Else
    Set *Mid = (First + Last) / 2.*
    If (*A[Mid] == Element)* Then
      Return *Mid.*
    Else
     If (*Element < A[Mid]*) Then
        BinSearch(A, Element, First, Mid – 1).
     Else
        BinSearch(A, Element, Mid + 1, Last).
END.

Notice how ***elegant*** the algorithm is. By elegant, I mean that the rather complicated binary search process is reduced to just a few statements. You *know* there is a lot going on here, but recursion allows us to express all of this processing in just a few statements. As you can see, recursive algorithms often provide simple solutions to problems of great complexity, where an equivalent iterative solution might be rather complex. This is not always the case, because some recursive solutions are impractical relative to speed and memory efficiency. Remember the rule of thumb when considering recursion: Consider a recursive solution to a problem only when a simple iterative solution is not possible. You should be aware that binary search has a relatively simple iterative solution. You will code this solution for one of the problems at the end of the chapter.

Coding the Program

The required C++ function now can be easily coded from the final algorithm. Here it is:

```
//ACTION 8-3  (ACT08-03.CPP)
int BinSearch(int A[ ], int Element, int First, int Last)
{
  int Mid;                           //ARRAY MIDPOINT
  if (First > Last)                  //IF ELEMENT NOT IN ARRAY
    return –1;                       //RETURN –1, ELSE CONTINUE SEARCH
  else
  {
    Mid = (First + Last) / 2;        //FIND MIDPOINT OF ARRAY
    if (Element == A[Mid])           //IF ELEMENT IS IN A[MID]
      return Mid;                    //RETURN MID
    else                             //ELSE SEARCH APPROPRIATE HALF
      if (Element < A[Mid])
          return BinSearch(A, Element, First, Mid – 1);
      else
          return BinSearch(A, Element, Mid + 1, Last);
  } //END OUTER ELSE
} //END BinSearch()
```

You should not have any trouble understanding this code, because it reflects the function interface and algorithm just developed. The only difference here is that the recursive calls on *BinSearch()* must be part of a **return** statement. Remember that C++ requires all execution paths of a non-void function to lead to a **return** statement.

8-5 INITIALIZING ARRAYS

Before leaving this chapter, you need to know how to initialize arrays at the time they are defined. Arrays, like variables, can be initialized when they are created. The initializing values can be supplied for any array, wherever the array is defined in the program. Let's consider some example array definitions to illustrate how arrays can be initialized.

int Integers[3] = {10,20,30};

In this definition, an integer array of three elements has been defined. The three integer elements have been initialized to the values 10, 20, and 30, respectively. Notice the syntax. The array definition is followed by an assignment operator, which is followed by the initialization values enclosed within curly braces. Here is what you would see if you inspected the array using a debugger:

DEBUGGER RESULTS

Inspecting *Integers*

[0]   10
[1]   20
[2]   30

As you can see, the first initialization value, 10, is placed at index 0 of the array, the value 20 is placed at index 1, and the value 30 is placed at the last index position, which is 2. Now, what do you suppose happens if you were to provide fewer initialization values than there are positions in the array? Well, suppose you define the array like this:

int Integers[3] = {10,20};

Here is what you would find when inspecting the array using a debugger:

DEBUGGER RESULTS

Inspecting *Integers*

[0]   10
[1]   20
[2]   00

As you can see, the compiler has initialized the last position of the array with zero. Zero is the default initialization value for integer arrays when not enough values are supplied to fill the array.

The next obvious question is: What happens if you supply too many initialization values? For instance, suppose you define the array like this:

int Integers[3] = {10,20,30,40};

In this case, you will get a compiler error stating, "too many initializers." One way to solve this problem is to increase the size of the array. Another, more preferred, way is to define the array without any specified size, as follows:

int Integers[] = {10,20,30,40};

With this definition, the compiler will set aside enough storage to hold all the initialization values. Here is what you would see if you inspected this array definition using a debugger:

DEBUGGER RESULTS

Inspecting *Integers*

[0]   10
[1]   20
[2]   30
[3]   40

Next, let's consider character arrays. Suppose that you define a character array of size 5, like this:

char Characters[5] = {'H','E','L','L','O'};

Again you see that the initialization values are enclosed in curly braces after an assignment operator. Here is what a debugger would reveal:

DEBUGGER RESULTS

Inspecting *Characters*

[0]   'H'
[1]   'E'
[2]   'L'
[3]   'L'
[4]   'O'

You see here that the five initialization characters are placed in the array starting at index zero and ending at the last index position, 4. What happens if you supply fewer initialization characters than are required to fill the array? Well, suppose that you define the array this way:

char Characters[5] = {'H','E'};

The contents of the array would now be as follows:

DEBUGGER RESULTS

Inspecting *Characters*

```
[0]    'H'
[1]    'E'
[2]    '\0'
[3]    '\0'
[4]    '\0'
```

This time, the compiler has inserted a null terminator character as the default character to fill the array. On the other hand, if you supply too many characters, the compiler will generate a "too many initializers" error message. Again, the safe way to handle this problem is to let the compiler determine the array size to fit the number of initialization values.

Finally, let's consider how to initialize character arrays with string values. Remember, a string is nothing more than an array of characters, terminated with a null terminator. Here is how a character array can be initialized with a string value:

char Characters[6] = "HELLO";

Notice that the syntax is different. The initialization string must be enclosed in double quotation marks rather than curly braces. Another thing you see is that the size of the array is one larger than the number of characters in the string. The reason for this becomes obvious when you inspect the array using a debugger. Here is what you would see:

DEBUGGER RESULTS

Inspecting *Characters*

    [0]   'H'
    [1]   'E'
    [2]   'L'
    [3]   'L'
    [4]   'O'
    [5]   '\0'

Recall that a string must be terminated with a null terminator. Making the size of the array one larger than the number of string characters allows room for the compiler to insert the null terminator. If you don't leave room for the null terminator, it will be truncated (dropped) from the array, and you *will not* get an error message. Again, the best way to avoid this problem is to let the compiler determine the size of the array, like this:

char Characters[] = "HELLO";

With this definition, the compiler will create enough array positions to hold all the string characters with the null terminator inserted as the last character in the array.

Default Initialization of Global and Static Arrays

Arrays can be defined and initialized anywhere in your C++ program. The scope of an array works just like the scope of a variable or constant. An array defined prior to *main()* is visible in the entire source file in which it is defined. An array defined within a block has block scope and, therefore, is visible only within the block in which it is defined.

If you define an array globally or as a **static** array and don't provide any initialization values, the compiler will initialize the array with the respective default value (zeros for integer and floating-point arrays, and null terminators for character arrays). Here's an example:

int Integers[5];
void main()
{
static char Characters[5];
} //END main()

The integer array has been defined globally, and the character array has been defined as a local static array within *main()*. Inspecting these arrays with a debugger would reveal the following:

DEBUGGER RESULTS

Inspecting *Integers*	Inspecting *Characters*
[0] 0	[0] '\0'
[1] 0	[1] '\0'
[2] 0	[2] '\0'
[3] 0	[3] '\0'
[4] 0	[4] '\0'

The debugger shows that the global integer array has been initialized with zeros, whereas the static character array has been initialized with null terminator characters. If you define an array of local block scope that is not static and do not initialize it, no default initialization values will be supplied by the compiler. The array will contain garbage! Thus, if we were to remove the keyword **static** from the above *Characters* array definition, the debugger would reveal arbitrary memory values in the array.

Here is a summary of the foregoing discussion:

- Integer, floating-point, and character arrays are initialized by using an assignment operator after the array definition, followed by a listing of the individual initializing values within curly braces.
- Too few initializing values will result in default values (zeros for integer and floating-point arrays, and null terminators for character arrays) being inserted in the extra array positions.
- Too many initializing values will result in a compiler error.
- Character arrays can be initialized with a string by enclosing the string within double quotes.
- The size of a string array must be one greater than the number of characters within the string to leave room for the null terminator character.
- If no size is specified in the array definition, the compiler will create just enough storage to hold the initialization values.

- Global arrays and static arrays are always initialized with the respective default values when no initialization values are supplied in the array definition.
- Local arrays that are not static will not be initialized with any specific values, unless they are supplied in the array definition.

Quick Check

1. Define an array and initialize it with the integer values –3 through +3.

2. What is the dimension of the array that you defined in question 1?

3. Show the contents of the following array:

    char Language[5] = {'C','+','+'};

4. Show the contents of the following array:

    char Language[] = "C++";

5. Suppose that you define a character array globally without any initializing values. What does the compiler store in the array?

CHAPTER SUMMARY

An array is an important data structure used to locate and store elements of a given data class. The two components of any array are the elements that are stored in the array and the indices that locate the stored elements. Array elements can be any given data class, and array indices are always integers ranging from [0] to [*MAX* – 1], where *MAX* is the size of the array.

There are both one-dimensional arrays and multidimensional arrays. A one-dimensional array, or list, is a single row of elements. It has dimensions of $1 \times n$, where *n* is the number of elements in the list. In C++, the maximum index in any dimension is the size of the dimension (*n*) minus 1.

Arrays are defined in C++ by specifying the element data class, the array name, and the size of the array. To access the array elements, you must use direct assignment statements, read/write statements, or loops. The **for** loop structure is the most common way of accessing multiple array elements.

Searching and sorting are common operations performed on arrays. ***Sequential search*** is an iterative search that looks for a given value in an array by sequentially comparing the value to the array elements, beginning with the first array element, until the value is found in the array or until the end of the array is reached. ***Binary search*** can be iterative or recursive. Binary search keeps dividing the array in half, directing itself to the half where the value is likely to be found. Binary search requires that the array be sorted, whereas sequential search does not have this requirement. On the other hand, binary search is much faster than sequential search, especially on large sorted arrays.

Many real-world applications require that information be sorted. There are several common sorting algorithms, including ***insertion sort***, ***bubble sort***, ***selection sort***, and ***quick sort***. All of these algorithms operate on arrays. The insertion sort algorithm is an iterative process that inserts a given element in the array in its correct place relative to the elements that precede it in the array. You will be acquainted with bubble sort and selection sort in the chapter problems.

QUESTIONS AND PROBLEMS

Questions

1. What three things must be specified in order to define an array?

Use the following array definition to answer questions 2–7.
char Characters[15];

2. What is the index of the first array element?

3. What is the index of the last array element?

4. Write a statement that will place the character 'Z' in the third cell of the array.

5. Write a statement that will display the last array element.

6. Write the code necessary to fill the array from keyboard entries. Make sure to prompt the user before each character entry.

7. Write a loop that will display all the array elements vertically on the screen.

8. Show the contents of the following array:
int Integers[5] = {1,2,3};

9. Show the contents of the following array:

   char Characters[5] = {'C','+','+'};

10. What is wrong with the following array definition?

    char OOP[3] = "C++";

    How would you correct the problem in this definition?

11. Write a statement to define a floating-point array that will be initialized with all zeros and is local to *main()*.

12. What is wrong with the following array definition?

    int Numbers[4] = {0,1,2,3,4};

13. Given the following array definition,

    int Values[10];

    write a statement to place the product of the first and second array elements in the last element position.

Use the following array definition to answer questions 14–18:

    const int MAX = 4;
    char String[MAX] = "C++";

14. Write the prototype for a function called *StringLength()* that will receive the entire array and return the length of the string.

15. Write a prototype for a function called *StringElement()* that will receive a single element of the string so that any operation on that element within the function will not affect the element value within the array.

16. Write a statement to call the function in question 15 and pass the first element of the array to the function.

17. Write a prototype for a function called *ChangeElement()* that will receive a single element of the string so that any change to that element within the function will change the element value in the array.

18. Write a statement to call the function in question 17 and pass the last element of the array to the function.

19. In general, what element position will be returned by the sequential and binary search functions developed in this chapter if there are multiple occurrences of the element in the array?

20. Why is binary search faster, on the average, than sequential search?

21. When would sequential search be faster than binary search?

22. Revise the *InsertSort()* algorithm to sort the array in descending order.

Problems

Least Difficult

1. Write a program to fill an array with all the odd integers from 1 to 99. Write one function to fill the array and another function to display the array, showing the odd integers across the screen separated by commas.

2. Write a function to read the user's name from a keyboard entry and place it in a character array. Write another function to display the user's name stored in the array. Test your functions via an application program.

3. Write a program to read a list of 25 character elements from a keyboard entry and display them in reverse order. Use one function to fill the list with the entered elements and another function to display the list.

4. Write a program that uses six character arrays to store the user's name, street address, city, state, zip code, and telephone number. Provide one function to fill the arrays and another to display the array contents using proper addressing format.

More Difficult

5. Write a program to test the *SeqSearch()* function developed in this chapter. Use the *srand()* and *rand()* functions available in *stdlib.h* to fill an array with random integer values prior to applying *SeqSearch()*. A call to *srand(1)* must be made first to initialize the random number generator. Then, a call to *rand()* will return an integer value between 0 and RAND_MAX, where RAND_MAX is defined by your compiler. For example, the following code will generate 10 random integers between 0 and 99:

    ```
    srand(1);
    for (int I = 0; I < 10 ; ++I)
        cout << rand() % 100 << endl;
    ```

    The *srand()* function is called first with an argument value of 1 to initialize the random number generator so that the same 10 numbers are not generated each time the loop is executed. The % 100 operation *scales* the value returned by *rand()* to produce a range of values between 0 and 99.

6. Write a program to test the *BinSearch()* function developed in this chapter. Use the standard *srand()* and *rand()* functions available in *stdlib.h* to fill an array with random integer values as described in problem 5. Then, apply *InsertSort()* to sort the array prior to using *BinSearch()*. Note: If you use the *InsertSort()* code developed in this chapter, you must change the code to sort an integer array rather than a character array.

Most Difficult

7. Here is the iterative solution for binary search in pseudocode form:

    BinarySearch()
    BEGIN
        Set Found = false.
        While (!Found AND First <= Last) Do
            Set Mid = (First + Last) / 2.
            If (Element == A[Mid]) Then
                Set Found = true.
            Else
                If (Element < A[Mid]) Then
                    Set Last = Mid – 1.
                Else
                    Set First = Mid + 1.
        If (Found) Then
            Return Mid.
        Else
            Return –1.
    END.

    Code this algorithm as a C++ function to search for a given element in an integer array. Write an application program to test the function. Remember to sort the array using a sorting function prior to calling the binary search function.

8. Another common iterative sorting algorithm is ***bubble sort***. Here's the algorithm:

    BubbleSort()
    BEGIN
        Set Passes = 1.
        Set Exchange = true.
        While (Passes < Number of Array Elements) AND (Exchange == true)
            Set Exchange = false.
            For Index = (First Array Index) To (Last Array Index – Passes)
                If A[Index] > A[Index + 1]
                    Swap(A[index], A[Index + 1]).
                    Set Exchange = true.
            Set Passes = Passes + 1.
    END.

    The bubble sort algorithm makes several passes through the array, comparing adjacent values during each pass. The adjacent values are exchanged if the first value is larger than the second value. The process terminates when $N - 1$ passes have been made (where N is the number of elements in the array) or when no more exchanges are possible.

Your job is to code the previous algorithm as a C++ function called *BubbleSort()*. In addition, you will have to code a *Swap()* function that can be called by the *BubbleSort()* function to exchange two array elements as shown in the algorithm. Write your functions to sort a character array. Incorporate them into a program that will test the sorting procedure. Why is bubble sort less efficient that insertion sort?

9. Another common iterative sorting algorithm is **selection sort.** The algorithm goes like this:

SelectSort()
BEGIN
    For Index1 = (First Array Index) To (Last Array Index) Do
        Set Position = Index1.
        Set Smallest = A[Position].
        For Index2 = (Index1 + 1) To (Last Array Index) Do
            If A[Index2] < Smallest
                Set Position = Index2.
                Set Smallest = A[Position].
        Set A[Position] = A[Index1].
        Set A[Index1] = Smallest.
END.

As with bubble sort, selection sort makes several passes through the array. The first pass examines the entire array and places the smallest element in the first array position. The second pass examines the array beginning at the second element. The smallest element in this array segment is found and placed in the second array position. The third pass examines the array beginning at the third element, finds the smallest element in this array segment, and places it in the third element position. The process continues until there are no more array segments left.

Your job is to code the previous algorithm as a C++ function called *SelectionSort()*. Write your function to sort a character array. Then use it in a program that will test the sorting procedure.

Why is selection sort less efficient than insertion sort?

10. Write a program that will take an *unsorted* integer array and find the location of the maximum value in the array. (*Hint:* Copy the array into another array and sort this second array to determine its maximum value. Then search the original array for this value.)

CLASSES AND OBJECTS IN-DEPTH

INTRODUCTION
9-1 STRUCTURES
    Declaring Structures
    Defining Structure Objects
    Initializing Structures When They Are
      Defined
    Storing Information into Structures
    Retrieving Information from Structures
    Nested Structures
9-2 CLASSES AND OBJECTS
    The Idea of Classes and Objects
    Classes
    Encapsulation
    Information Hiding
    Objects
9-3 MEMBER FUNCTIONS

Constructors
Scoping Inside of Functions
Access Functions
Messages
Putting Everything Together in a Complete
    Program
9-4 MULTIFILE PROGRAM
    CONSTRUCTION
PROBLEM SOLVING IN ACTION:
    BUILDING A MULTIFILE C++
    PROGRAM
CHAPTER SUMMARY
QUESTIONS AND PROBLEMS
    Questions
    Problems

INTRODUCTION

This chapter will introduce you to the important topic of object-oriented programming (OOP) and is intended to prepare you for further study of the topic. This means that you will need to study OOP further to become a competent object-oriented programmer.

Recall that C++ was first created to add object-oriented programming ability to the C language. With object-oriented programming, you construct complex programs from simpler program entities called *objects*, which are real instances, or specimens, of abstract *classes*. Object-oriented programs are organized as a collection of objects that cooperate with each other. Thus, object-oriented programming employs objects, rather than algorithms, as the fundamental building blocks for program development.

Object-oriented programming facilitates the extension and reuse of general-purpose classes in other applications with minimal modification to the original code. Although this can be accomplished with ordinary functions in algorithmic programming, OOP provides an important feature called *inheritance*, which is a mechanism for deriving new classes from existing ones. As a result, classes are related to each other to create a hierarchy of classes through inheritance. This inheritance feature also allows new applications to "inherit" code from existing applications, thereby making the programming chore much more productive.

In summary, the goals of OOP are to improve programmer productivity by managing software complexity via the use of classes and their associated objects that provide for reusable code via the class inheritance feature.

Up to this point you have been learning how to construct programs using a structured top-down approach. Although the overall design of any software is a top-down process, writing object-oriented programs requires a different approach. You create object-oriented programs from the inside out by expanding on classes. For example, you might approach a banking problem by creating a bank account class that defines the basic data that all accounts must contain (account number, balance, etc.) as well as the fundamental operations that are performed on bank accounts (deposit, withdrawal, etc.). This basic bank account class can then be expanded into classes that define specific types of bank accounts, such as checking accounts, super-now accounts, savings accounts, and so on.

There are four concepts central to OOP: *encapsulation with information hiding*, *inheritance*, *polymorphism*, and *dynamic binding*. In this chapter, you will be exposed to the idea of encapsulation and information hiding. The next chapter is devoted entirely to inheritance. The concepts of polymorphism and dynamic binding are beyond the scope of this text and, as a result, will only be covered lightly in the next chapter.

Object-oriented programming has its own unique terminology. Be sure to grasp the terminology as you progress through the chapter. A glossary of OOP terms is provided at the end of this text for quick reference.

When Bjarne Stroustrup created classes for the C++ language, he expanded on the existing C language *structure*. Therefore, it is only appropriate that we discuss C++ structures as a lead-in to C++ classes.

9-1 STRUCTURES

Like an array, a structure is a data structure, meaning that it provides a well-organized, convenient means of storing data. In many programming languages, such as BASIC and FORTRAN, the only data structure available is the array. Recall that when you define an array, you must specify the number of elements it contains (its size) and the data class of its elements. The idea that all the elements must be the same data class is a serious limitation of an array. For instance, suppose an academic application requires a data structure for storing student information. Such information might include the student's name, student number, GPA, year enrolled, and whether or not the student has graduated. This information is composed of a variety of unique data classes. As a result, an array would not be a suitable data structure for this application. Fortunately, C++ provides the structure data class that permits information of different data classes to be conveniently stored, accessed, and manipulated. You should be aware that structures are also called *records* in some other programming languages, such as Pascal.

In this section, you will learn how to define and access C++ structures. In addition, you will learn how to create very powerful complex data structures by building structures of structures, called *nested structures*.

> A *structure* is a collection of *members*.

A *structure* is a collection of members. A *structure member* is simply an item of meaningful data. For example, the string of characters that form your name can be classified as a member, the collection of numbers that form your student number can be a member, and the collection of numbers and the decimal point that form your GPA can form a member. Thus, a student structure might consist of a collection of student-related members, as shown in Figure 9-1. Notice that each member within the structure is a unique data class, whereas the collection of all the members (the structure) represents different data classes.

A structure can contain any number of members, with each member having a unique name, called the ***member name***. Thus, the member names in the student structure are *Name*, *StudentNumber*, *GPA*, *YearEnrolled*, and *Graduated*. Now that you have an idea of the format of a simple structure, you are ready to learn how to declare structures in C++.

Student Structure

Member Name	Member Data Class
Name	A character string
StudentNumber	An integer value
GPA	A floating-point value
YearEnrolled	An integer value
Graduated	A Boolean value

Figure 9-1 A student structure consists of a collection of related student members.

Declaring Structures

Like enumerated data, a structure is a user-defined data structure that must be declared before it can be used. Here's the declaration format:

STRUCTURE DECLARATION FORMAT

struct <structure name>
{
   <member 1 data class> <member 1 name>;
   <member 2 data class> <member 2 name>;
               .
               .
               .
   <member n data class> <member n name>;
}; //END STRUCT

As you can see, the structure declaration in C++ literally shows that the structure is a collection of individual members, each identified by its data class and member name. After the keyword **struct**, you must first list the structure identifier, or name. The name can be any valid identifier, but should be descriptive of the structure meaning. The structure name is followed by a left curly brace, {, which is followed by a list of the individual members that make up the structure. The structure declaration is concluded with a right curly brace, }.

The individual members are declared using an indentation scheme below the keyword **struct**. Here are some things you will want to remember about the member declarations:

- Each member within the structure must have a unique name. However, a given member name may be used again in another structure declaration.
- A data class must be specified for each member. All the data classes discussed so far are legal. Thus, a member can be an integer, float, character, Boolean, or enumerated data class. Of course, if a member is an enumerated data class, the enumerated data class must be declared prior to the structure declaration.

Defining Structure Objects

Like the enumerated data class, a structure is accessed using one or more objects that must be defined after the structure declaration. Here we go again with the two words *declaration* and *definition*. Remember the technical difference? A declaration simply specifies the name and format of the data structure, but does not reserve storage. On the other hand, a definition reserves storage. Thus, each object definition for a given structure creates an area in memory where data will be stored according to the declared structure format. Structure objects can be defined in two ways: (1) by listing them immediately after the closing brace of the structure declaration or (2) by listing the structure name followed by the corresponding objects anyplace in the program prior to their use. Clearly, the object name must be different from the structure name. Now, let's declare some structures and define their associated objects.

Example 9-1

Declare the following structures:

a. A *Student* structure, consisting of the student's name, student number, year enrolled, GPA, and whether or not the student has graduated. Define an object called *Fred* to access the *Student* structure.

b. An *Automobile* structure, consisting of the automobile year, color (blue, black, yellow, red, or green), and price. Make provision to use this same structure for a *Ford, Chevy,* or *Dodge*.

c. A *Weather* structure, consisting of the date, temperature, barometric pressure, and conditions. Assume that there are three reportable conditions: clear, cloudy, and rain. Make provision to use this structure for storing morning, afternoon, evening, and night weather information.

Solution

a.
```
struct Student
  {
   char Name[30];         //STUDENT NAME
   int StudentNumber;     //STUDENT NUMBER
   int YearEnrolled;      //YEAR STUDENT ENROLLED
   float GPA;             //STUDENT GPA
   int Graduated;         //TRUE IF GRAD, FALSE IF NOT GRAD
  } Fred;                 //STRUCTURE OBJECT
```

This structure declaration is straightforward. The structure name is *Student*, which contains five members: *Name*, *StudentNumber*, *YearEnrolled*, *GPA*, and *Graduated*. Observe that the *StudentNumber* and *YearEnrolled* are both objects of the integer data class, but declared on separate lines. They could be listed on the same line, but many software engineers prefer to use separate line declarations for clarity and program readability. The *Name* member is declared as a character array member so that we can easily store a character string in this member. Why is the *Graduated* member an integer member?

Finally, notice that the structure object is *Fred,* which is different from the structure name *Student*, and is defined just after the closing brace of the structure declaration.

b.
```
enum Colors {Blue, Black, Yellow, Red, Green};
struct Automobile
  {
   int Year;              //AUTO YEAR
   Colors Color;          //AUTO COLOR
   float Price;           //AUTO PRICE
  } Ford, Chevy, Dodge;   //STRUCTURE OBJECTS
```

You see two different twists in this structure declaration. First, the enumerated data class *Colors* is used as the data class of the *Color* member. Thus, the automobile color can be Blue, Black, Yellow, Red, or Green. Of course, the enumerated data class *Colors* must be declared prior to the structure declaration.

Second, you see that the structure has three objects: *Ford*, *Chevy*, and *Dodge*. This creates three separate structures of the same format in memory, one for each structure object.

c.
```
enum Conditions {Clear, Cloudy, Rain};
struct Weather
  {
```

```
char Date[10];              //DATE OF WEATHER OBSERVATION
float Temperature;          //TEMPERATURE
float Pressure;             //BAROMETRIC PRESSURE
Conditions Condition;       //GENERAL WEATHER CONDITIONS
} Morning, Afternoon, Evening, Night;  //STRUCTURE OBJECTS
```

Here again, an enumerated data class is employed for the weather *Condition* member. In addition, four structure objects are defined so that a separate weather structure can be stored for morning, afternoon, evening, and night.

Example 9-2

In Example 9-1, the structure objects were defined immediately after the respective structure declarations. Assuming that this was not done, define the same objects for these structures that could be inserted anyplace in the program prior to their use to access the respective structure.

Solution:

a. Student Fred;

b. Automobile Ford;
   Automobile Chevy;
   Automobile Dodge;

c. Weather Morning;
   Weather Afternoon;
   Weather Evening;
   Weather Night;

In each of the preceding cases, the respective structure name is listed, followed by the object that will be used to access the structure. Thus, a structure object can be created immediately after the structure declaration or anyplace in the program code prior to its use.

DEBUGGING TIP

A common mistake when declaring structures is to omit the semicolon after the closing brace of the structure declaration. Such an omission will result in the compiler generating a number of different error messages, depending on what follows the declaration. In fact, this bug can be very difficult to find, because the error messages generated will most likely have nothing to do with the real problem.

Initializing Structures When They Are Defined

Structure objects can be initialized when they are defined just like any other variable object. This means that they can be initialized if they are defined as part of the structure declaration or anywhere where they are defined after the structure declaration. To initialize a structure object, you must use an assignment operator, =, after the variable identifier and place the initializing values within curly braces. Here's the general format:

INITIALIZING STRUCTURE OBJECTS

```
<structure name> <structure object name> = {member 1 value,
                                            member 2 value,
                                                    •
                                                    •
                                                    •
                                            member n value};
```

As an example, let's consider the *Student* structure that was declared in Example 9-1. Here's the declaration again:

```
struct Student
 {
   char Name[30];        //STUDENT NAME
   int StudentNumber;    //STUDENT NUMBER
   int YearEnrolled;     //YEAR STUDENT ENROLLED
   float GPA;            //STUDENT GPA
   int Graduated;        //TRUE IF GRAD, FALSE IF NOT GRAD
 }; //END Student
```

Applying this format, we can initialize the object *Fred* as follows:

```
Student Fred = {"Fred Smith",
               12345,
               1990,
               3.15,
               0};
```

Here, you will find a value for each of the members declared in the *Student* structure. As you can see, an assignment operator is used with the individual initializing values separated by commas and enclosed within curly braces following the assignment operator. The order of the initializing values must be the same as that of their respective members in the structure declaration. The initializing values could have been listed on the same line as the object, but good style dictates that each initializing value appear on a separate line just like its respective member declaration. This allows anyone looking at the code to immediately associate an initializing value with a member name in the structure.

Example 9-3

In Example 9-1, we declared a *Weather* structure. Then, in Example 9-2, we defined four objects for this structure. Repeat the structure declaration and object definitions; however, this time initialize the *Afternoon* object to the following values:

Date:	12/28/96
Temperature:	41
Pressure:	30.15
Condition:	Cloudy

Solution

Here is the *Weather* structure declaration from Example 9-1:

```
enum Conditions {Clear, Cloudy, Rain};
struct Weather
{
  char Date[10];          //DATE OF WEATHER OBSERVATION
  float Temperature;      //TEMPERATURE
  float Pressure;         //BAROMETRIC PRESSURE
  Conditions Condition;   //GENERAL WEATHER CONDITIONS
}; //END Weather
```

To define the four objects, you must list the structure name followed by the object names. To initialize any of the objects you must use an assignment operator followed by the initializing values enclosed within curly braces. Using this idea, the *Weather* objects are defined as follows.

```
Weather Morning;
Weather Evening;
Weather Night;
Weather Afternoon = {"12/28/96",
                     41,
                     30.15,
                     Cloudy
                    };
```

You see that the *Afternoon* object is initialized, and the others are not. If any of the other objects must be initialized, you use the same format. The object *Afternoon* was placed last in the object listing for clarity. Actually, this object, along with its initializing values, could be placed anywhere in the object listing as long as the correct syntax is applied.

Storing Information into Structures

When accessing a structure, you will either store information into the structure or retrieve information from the structure. Of course, you are actually accessing the members that make up the structure when storing or retrieving structure data. You can access the structure members in one of two ways: (1) by using the dot operator, •, or (2) by using the pointer operator, →. I will discuss the dot operator in this chapter, leaving the pointer operator discussion for a later chapter. You get information into a structure through initialization, direct assignment, or reading from the keyboard. The initialization process has already been discussed, so let's see how direct assignment and reading from the keyboard work.

Direct Assignment

When assigning information to a structure, you must assign the information directly to the respective member within the structure. How can you access a given member? Well, think about the structure declaration and object definition. How do you access the structure itself? By using the structure object, right? Next, how do you suppose you would access a given member within the structure? Of course, by using its member name! So, the **path** to a given member within the structure is via the structure object and the respective member name. Consider the *Student* structure in Example 9-1. Suppose you wish to store a name in the *Name* member. Ask yourself: "Self, what *path* must I take to get to the name member?" Well, you must use the structure object, *Fred*, to get you to the structure and the member name, *Name*, to get you to the required member within the structure. You must provide the path to a given member using the dot operator.

Using the Dot Operator to Access Structure Data

Here's the C++ syntax required when using the dot operator:

> ### *ASSIGNING DATA TO STRUCTURES USING THE DOT OPERATOR*
>
> `<structure object name>•<member name> = data;`

Notice that the structure object name is listed first, followed by the dot operator, •, followed by the required member name, an assignment operator, =, and the data to be stored. Here are just a few examples of how you might store information into the structure objects defined in Example 9-1.

```
strcpy(Fred.Name, "Fred Smith");
Fred.StudentNumber = 0001;
Fred.YearEnrolled = 1990;
Fred.GPA = 4.0;
Fred.Graduated = 1;
```

As you can see, the "dot'" notation provides a path directly to the member in which the information is to be stored. One final point: The data being stored in a given member should be the same data class that has been declared for that member.

Reading Information into a Structure

Now suppose you want the user to enter the information into the structure via the system keyboard. When this is desired, you simply employ an input statement, while accessing the members using the dot operator. As an example, suppose the user must enter information into the *Student* structure declared in Example 9-1. If *Fred* is defined as a structure object, you use the dot operator, like this:

```
cout << "Enter the student name:  ";
gets (Fred.Name);
cout << "Enter the student number:  ";
cin >> Fred.StudentNumber;
cout << "Enter the year the student enrolled:  ";
cin >> Fred.YearEnrolled;
cout << "Enter the student GPA:  ";
cin >> Fred.GPA;
cout << "Has the student graduated? (Y/N):  ";
cin >> Answer;
if (Answer == 'y' || Answer == 'Y')
   Fred.Graduated = 1;
else
   Fred.Graduated = 0;
```

As you can see, the appropriate user prompts have been inserted via *cout* statements. The respective data are then read from the keyboard using a *gets()* function or *cin* statement. Notice that a *gets()* function is employed to obtain the string data. In addition, an **if/else** statement is used to make the correct Boolean assignment on the *Graduated* member.

Retrieving Information from Structures

You retrieve structure information using the assignment operator or a *cout* statement. Again, the dot operator is employed to access the members. Here's the general format:

RETRIEVING STRUCTURE INFORMATION USING ASSIGNMENT

<variable object name> = <structure object name>•<member name>;

RETRIEVING STRUCTURE INFORMATION USING cout

cout << <structure object name>•<member name>;

Here are some examples using the *Student* structure defined in Example 9-1:

```
Number = Fred.StudentNumber;
Grad = Fred.Graduated;
cout << Fred.Name << endl;
cout << Fred.GPA << endl;
```

The first two statements show how the assignment operator is used to copy the structure information to another variable object within the program using the dot operator. Remember, however, that the object *Fred* must be defined as a structure object to use the dot operator. Clearly, the variable receiving the assignment must be defined as the same data class as the respective member information. Consequently, *Number* and *Grad* must be defined as integers for this application.

The second two statements show how *cout* is employed to retrieve structure information.

Example 9-4

Your instructor needs a student structure consisting of the following items:
* Student name

- Student number
- Major
- Semester test scores
- Semester test average
- Equivalent letter grade of the test average

a. Declare an appropriate structure.
b. Write a function that will allow the instructor to fill the structure from the keyboard.
c. Write a function that will display the contents of the structure.

Solution

a. The structure is a student structure for a given class. Consequently, let's give the structure an appropriate name, such as *Student*. Then, we can use the class name, such as *CS1*, as the structure object to access the grades of a given class.

   Next, there are six members that need to be declared as part of the structure. Let's call them *Name*, *StudentNumber*, *Major*, *TestScores*, *TestAverage*, and *TestGrade*. The *Name*, *StudentNumber*, and *Major* members will be declared as character array members because they will store string values.

   Several individual test scores must be stored, so we will declare the *TestScores* member as an array of floating-point elements.

   Next, we will declare the *TestAverage* member an integer member, because we will use a rounded-off average of the test scores.

   Finally, the *Grade* member must be a character member to represent a letter grade. Here's a structure declaration that will work:

```
struct Student
{
    char Name[30];              //STUDENT NAME
    char StudentNumber[15];     //STUDENT NUMBER
    char Major[20];             //STUDENT MAJOR
    float TestScores[15];       //STUDENT TEST SCORES
    float TestAverage;          //AVERAGE OF TEST SCORES
    char TestGrade;             //STUDENT GRADE
}; //END Student

Student CS1;                    //STRUCTURE OBJECT
```

   Notice in particular that the *TestScores* member is declared as an array of fifteen floating-point elements. The value 15 was used to allow for a maximum of fifteen test scores. The structure object is called *CS1*.

b. Here's a function that will fill the structure:

```
//THIS FUNCTION WILL FILL THE STUDENT STRUCTURE WITH
//VALUES ENTERED FROM THE KEYBOARD
```

```
void FillStructure(int &Number, Student &S)
{
 int TestTotal = 0;
 cout << "Enter the student name:  ";
 gets(S.Name);
 cout << "Enter the student number:  ";
 gets(S.StudentNumber);
 cout << "Enter the student major:  ";
 gets(S.Major);
 cout << "How many test scores are there?:  ";
 cin >> Number;
 for (int i = 0; i < Number; ++i)
 {
   cout << "Enter test score " << i + 1 << ":  ";
   cin >> S.TestScores[i];
   TestTotal += S.TestScores[i];
 } //END FOR
 S.TestAverage = TestTotal/Number;
 if (S.TestAverage < 60)
    S.TestGrade = 'F';
 if (S.TestAverage >= 60 && S.TestAverage < 70)
    S.TestGrade = 'D';
 if (S.TestAverage >= 70 && S.TestAverage < 80)
    S.TestGrade = 'C';
 if (S.TestAverage >= 80 && S.TestAverage < 90)
    S.TestGrade = 'B';
 if (S.TestAverage >= 90 && S.TestAverage <= 100)
    S.TestGrade = 'A';
} //END FillStructure()
```

First, observe the function header. The function name is *FillStructure*. There are two reference parameters, *Number* and *S*, as designated by the ampersand symbol, *&*. It is important to note that *S* is a reference parameter that has a data class of *Student*, which is the structure we declared in part a. This allows the *Student* structure to be passed by reference to the function. The structure object in the calling program will be the structure object, *CS1*; the structure object within the function is the reference parameter *S*. Consequently, any operations on the *S* structure within this function will affect the *CS1* structure passed to the function when it is called.

Next you see that a local function variable called *TestTotal* is defined. You will observe its use shortly.

Now look at how the structure is being filled. The structure parameter, *S*, must be referenced here, because it will take on the values of the structure object, *CS1*, in the calling program. Notice that in all cases, the structure dot operator, •, is employed to fill the respective members. The first member to be filled is the *Name* member. This is accomplished by prompting the user and reading the member name, *Name,* using the *gets()* function. After the student name is read, the user is prompted to enter the student number and major. This information is read into the structure and stored using the member names *StudentNumber* and *Major*, respectively.

Next, the user is prompted for the number of test scores that will be entered into the structure. A reference parameter, *Number,* receives this value. This value is needed to control the number of times that the subsequent **for** loop will be executed.

A **for** loop is used to fill the *TestScores* array. A local variable, *i,* is incremented from 0 to the number (*Number*) of test scores. With each loop iteration, the user is prompted for the respective score value, and the corresponding entry is read into the *TestScores* array. In addition to filling the array member, the **for** loop calculates a running total (*TestTotal*) of the test scores as they are entered.

The next member to be filled is the *TestAverage* member. Observe that this member is filled using an assignment statement. The total sum of the test scores (*TestTotal*) is divided by the number of scores (*Number*) and assigned to the *TestAverage* member.

Finally, the *TestGrade* member is filled using a series of **if** statements. As you can see, the **if** statements translate the numerical average to a letter grade. A given **if** simply assigns the appropriate letter grade to the *TestGrade* member. You might be wondering why a **switch** statement was not used here in place of the five **if** statements. Well, remember, the selector in a **switch** statement *cannot* be a floating-point value. In this application, the selector would be the variable *TestAverage*, which is a floating-point object. Here is a sample of what the user will see when this function is executed:

```
Enter the student name:  Bjarne Stroustrup↵
Enter the student number:  1↵
Enter the student major:  Computer Science↵
How many test scores are there?  3↵
Enter test score 1:  98.7↵
Enter test score 2:  97↵
Enter test score 3:  95.2↵
```

c. A function to display the student structure follows:

```
//THIS FUNCTION WILL FILL DISPLAY THE STUDENT STRUCTURE
void DisplayStructure(int Number, Student S)
{
  cout << "\nStudent Name:  " << S.Name
       << "\n\n\tStudent Number: " << S.StudentNumber
       << "\n\tMajor:  " << S.Major
       << "\n\tTest Scores:  ";
```

```
for (int i = 0; i < Number; ++i)
   cout << S.TestScores[i] << ", ";
cout << "\tTest Average:  " << S.TestAverage
     << "\n\tTest Grade:  " << S.TestGrade << endl;
} //END DisplayStructure()
```

This function employs two value parameters, *Number* and *S*. The parameter *Number* will receive the number of test scores entered by the user to control the subsequent **for** loop execution. The structure parameter, *S*, will receive the structure from the calling program and becomes the structure object within the function. (Why are value parameters used here instead of reference parameters?) The student's name, number, and major are displayed first along with appropriate headings. Then the individual test scores are displayed using a **for** loop.

After the individual test scores are displayed, the *TestAverage* and *TestGrade* members are displayed, respectively. Here is the display generated by the *DisplayStructure()* function with the values obtained by the *FillStructure()* function:

```
Student Name:  Bjarne Stroustrup

        Student Number:  1
        Major:  Computer Science
        Test Scores:  98.7, 97, 95.2,
        Test Average:  96
        Test Grade:  A
```

Finally, you might be wondering what the entire program looks like. Here it is:

```
#include <iostream.h>      //FOR cin AND cout
#include <stdio.h>         //FOR gets()

struct Student
{
   char Name[30];            //STUDENT NAME
   char StudentNumber[15];   //STUDENT NUMBER
   char Major[20];           //STUDENT MAJOR
   float TestScores[15];     //STUDENT TEST SCORES
   float TestAverage;        //AVERAGE OF TEST SCORES
   char TestGrade;           //STUDENT GRADE
}; //END Student
```

```
//FUNCTION PROTOTYPES
void FillStructure(int &Number, Student &S);   //FILL STRUCTURE
void DisplayStructure(int Number, Student S); //DISPLAY STRUCTURE


void main()
{
  Student CS1;                       //DEFINE STRUCTURE OBJECT
  int Number = 0;                    //DEFINE NUMBER OF TESTS
  FillStructure(Number, CS1);        //FILL THE STRUCTURE
  DisplayStructure(Number,CS1);      //DISPLAY THE STRUCTURE
} //END main()

//THIS FUNCTION WILL FILL THE STUDENT STRUCTURE WITH
//VALUES ENTERED FROM THE KEYBOARD
void FillStructure(int Number, Student &S)
{
  int TestTotal = 0;
  cout << "Enter the student name:  ";
  gets(S.Name);
  cout << "Enter the student number:  ";
  gets(S.StudentNumber);
  cout << "Enter the student major:  ";
  gets(S.Major);
  cout << "How many test scores are there?:  ";
  cin >> Number;
  for (int i = 0; i < Number; ++i)
  {
    cout << "Enter test score " << i + 1 << ":  ";
    cin >> S.TestScores[i];
    TestTotal += S.TestScores[i];
  } //END FOR
  S.TestAverage = TestTotal/Number;
  if (S.TestAverage < 60)
     S.TestGrade = 'F';
  if (S.TestAverage >= 60 && S.TestAverage < 70)
     S.TestGrade = 'D';
  if (S.TestAverage >= 70 && S.TestAverage < 80)
     S.TestGrade = 'C';
  if (S.TestAverage >= 80 && S.TestAverage < 90)
     S.TestGrade = 'B';
  if (S.TestAverage >= 90 && S.TestAverage <= 100)
     S.TestGrade = 'A';
} //END FillStructure()

//THIS FUNCTION WILL DISPLAY THE STUDENT STRUCTURE
void DisplayStructure(int Number, Student S)
```

```
    {
      cout << "\nStudent Name:  " << S.Name
           << "\n\n\tStudent Number: " << S.StudentNumber
           << "\n\tMajor:  " << S.Major
           << "\n\tTest Scores:  ";
      for (int i = 0; i < Number; ++i)
        cout  << S.TestScores[i] << ", ";
      cout << "\n\tTest Average:  " << S.TestAverage
           << "\n\tTest Grade:  " << S.TestGrade << endl;
    } //END DisplayStructure()
```

It is important to note that the structure is declared prior to *main()* so that the function prototypes can employ this structure as a data class. The actual structure object, *CS1*, is defined at the beginning of *main()* and passed to the functions when they are called. That's all there is to it!

Nested Structures

Now that you know how to work with single structures, it is time to literally build on this knowledge and create structures of structures. That's right, we can create a structure that contains other structures, called ***nested structures***.

A ***nested structure*** is a structure within a structure. In other words, a nested structure is a member of another structure.

In the last section, we worked with a student structure that contained the student's name, number, major, and test results. From an organizational perspective, it might make more sense to create a separate structure to hold the test results and include, or nest, this structure inside of the student structure. This way those test members that relate closely to each other are stored in a separate structure. Thus, our new nested student structure will contain the following members:

- A student name member
- A student number member
- A major member
- A nested structure member that contains test results

Here are the required C++ declarations:

```
struct Tests
{
  float TestScores[15];        //STUDENT TEST SCORES
  float TestAverage;           //AVERAGE OF TEST SCORES
  char TestGrade;              //STUDENT GRADE
}; //END Tests

struct Student
{
    char Name[30];             //STUDENT NAME
    char StudentNumber[15];    //STUDENT NUMBER
    char Major[20];            //STUDENT MAJOR
    Tests Test;                //NESTED TEST STRUCTURE
}; //END Student
```

Next, we will define an object for the *Student* structure as follows:

```
Student CS1;
```

As you can see, the nested *Tests* structure is declared first and then included as a member within the main *Student* structure. The declaration for a nested structure uses the same format as that of any structure declaration. In the main *Student* structure, the nested *Tests* structure becomes the data class for the *Test* member. Thus, each member within the nested structure actually forms a submember of the main structure member. You can actually have multiple levels of nesting. In other words, you can have a structure within a structure within a structure, and so on.

Now you are probably wondering how you can gain access to the nested structure members. For instance, how can you get to the *TestScores* member within the nested *Tests* structure? Well, the structure object, *CS1*, will get you into the main *Student* structure; then the nested member *Test* will get you into the nested structure, *Tests*; and finally the member name, *TestScores*, will get you into the required member. Thus, assignment statements such as

```
CS1.Test.TestScores[0] = 95;
CS1.Test.TestScores[1] = 87;
CS1.Test.TestScores[2] = 93;
```

would allow you to place three test scores into the *TestScores* member. Here, both the structure object, *CS1*, and the nested structure member name, *Test*, must be referenced within the statement followed by the desired submember name. Listing the structure object followed by the nested structure member name "opens up" any submembers within the nested structure. In this case, we have opened up the

TestScores[] submember. Notice that the dot operator is used to access the member in the main *Student* structure, and the dot operator is employed again to access the submember in the nested *Tests* structure. Now, using this idea, let's construct a function to fill this new student structure. Here it is:

```
//THIS FUNCTION WILL FILL THE STUDENT STRUCTURE WITH
//VALUES ENTERED FROM THE KEYBOARD
void FillStructure(Student &S)
{
  int TestTotal = 0;
  cout << "Enter the student name:  ";
  gets(S.Name);
  cout << "Enter the student number:  ";
  gets(S.StudentNumber);
  cout << "Enter the student major:  ";
  gets(S.Major);
  cout << "How many test scores are there?  ";
  cin >> TestNumber;
  for (int i = 0; i < TestNumber; ++i)
  {
    cout << "Enter test score " << i + 1 << ":  ";
    cin >> S.Test.TestScores[i];
    TestTotal += S.Test.TestScores[i];
  } //END FOR
  S.Test.TestAverage = TestTotal/TestNumber;
  if (S.Test.TestAverage < 60)
    S.Test.TestGrade = 'F';
  if (S.Test.TestAverage >= 60 && S.Test.TestAverage < 70)
    S.Test.TestGrade = 'D';
  if (S.Test.TestAverage >= 70 && S.Test.TestAverage < 80)
    S.Test.TestGrade = 'C';
  if (S.Test.TestAverage >= 80 && S.Test.TestAverage < 90)
    S.Test.TestGrade = 'B';
  if (S.Test.TestAverage >= 90 && S.Test.TestAverage <= 100)
    S.Test.TestGrade = 'A';
} //END FillStructure()
```

Look at the function header and you will see that the function employs a reference parameter for the main structure, *Student.* Even though the *Student* structure contains a nested structure, all we need to pass to the function is an object of the main structure. (Why is a reference parameter required here?) Within the function, you will find that the nested structure members are accessed using the parameter, *S,* to the main structure member, followed by a dot to the nested structure member, followed by another dot to the submember as described above. Once the nested structures are "opened up'" using their respective names, the submembers are filled directly using the respective submember names. Study the preceding function! You should now have all the prerequisite knowledge to understand its operation.

How about a function to display the contents of the foregoing structure? Here's one that will do the job:

```
//THIS FUNCTION WILL DISPLAY THE STUDENT STRUCTURE
void DisplayStructure(Student S)
{
  cout << "\nStudent Name:  " << S.Name
       << "\n\n\tStudent Number: " << S.StudentNumber
       << "\n\tMajor:  " << S.Major
       << "\n\tTest Scores:  ";
  for (int i = 0; i < TestNumber; ++i)
    cout  << S.Test.TestScores[i] << ", ";
  cout << "\n\tTest Average:  " << S.Test.TestAverage
       << "\n\tTest Grade:  " << S.Test.TestGrade << endl;
} //END DisplayStructure()
```

Now, let's place these two functions in a program that will allow the user to fill and display the structure. Here's the program:

```
#include <iostream.h>   //FOR cin AND cout
#include <stdio.h>        //FOR gets()

//TESTS STRUCTURE DECLARATION
struct Tests
{
  float TestScores[15];        //STUDENT TEST SCORES
  float TestAverage;           //AVERAGE OF TEST SCORES
  char TestGrade;              //STUDENT GRADE
}; //END Tests

struct Student
{
   char Name[30];              //STUDENT NAME
   char StudentNumber[15];     //STUDENT NUMBER
   char Major[20];             //STUDENT MAJOR
   Tests Test;                 //NESTED TEST STRUCTURE
}; //END Student
```

```
//FUNCTION PROTOTYPES
void FillStructure(Student &S);      //FILL STRUCTURE VIA USER ENTRIES
void DisplayStructure(Student S);    //DISPLAY STRUCTURE MEMBERS

//GLOBAL VARIABLE
int TestNumber = 0;

void main()
{
  Student CS1;                       //DEFINE STRUCTURE OBJECT
  FillStructure(CS1);                //FILL STRUCTURE
  DisplayStructure(CS1);             //DISPLAY STRUCTURE
} //END main()

//THIS FUNCTION WILL FILL THE STUDENT STRUCTURE WITH
//VALUES ENTERED FROM THE KEYBOARD
void FillStructure(Student &S)
{
  int TestTotal = 0;
  cout << "Enter the student name:  ";
  gets(S.Name);
  cout << "Enter the student number:  ";
  gets(S.StudentNumber);
  cout << "Enter the student major:  ";
  gets(S.Major);
  cout << "How many test scores are there?  ";
  cin >> TestNumber;
  for (int i = 0; i < TestNumber; ++i)
  {
    cout << "Enter test score " << i + 1 << ":  ";
    cin >> S.Test.TestScores[i];
    TestTotal += S.Test.TestScores[i];
  } //END FOR
  S.Test.TestAverage = TestTotal/TestNumber;
  if (S.Test.TestAverage < 60)
     S.Test.TestGrade = 'F';
  if (S.Test.TestAverage >= 60 && S.Test.TestAverage < 70)
     S.Test.TestGrade = 'D';
  if (S.Test.TestAverage >= 70 && S.Test.TestAverage < 80)
     S.Test.TestGrade = 'C';
  if (S.Test.TestAverage >= 80 && S.Test.TestAverage < 90)
     S.Test.TestGrade = 'B';
  if (S.Test.TestAverage >= 90 && S.Test.TestAverage <= 100)
     S.Test.TestGrade = 'A';
} //END FillStructure()
```

```
//THIS FUNCTION WILL DISPLAY THE STUDENT STRUCTURE
void DisplayStructure(Student S)
{
  cout << "\nStudent Name:  " << S.Name
       << "\n\n\tStudent Number: " << S.StudentNumber
       << "\n\tMajor:  " << S.Major
       << "\n\tTest Scores:  ";
  for (int i = 0; i < TestNumber; ++i)
    cout  << S.Test.TestScores[i] << ", ";
  cout << "\n\tTest Average:  " << S.Test.TestAverage
       << "\n\tTest Grade:  " << S.Test.TestGrade << endl;
} //END DisplayStructure()
```

You should now have all the knowledge you need to completely understand this program.

 Quick Check

1. True or false: All the members of a given structure must have the same data class.

2. Declare a structure called *Account* that has four floating-point members named *Deposits*, *Withdrawals*, *InterestRate*, and *Balance*.

3. Define an unitialized object called *Checkbook* for the structure you declared in question 2.

4. Define an object called *Passbook* for the structure you declared in question 2, and initialize it to the following values:

    > Deposits of $1500.00
    > Withdrawals of $500
    > Interest Rate of 10%
    > Balance of $2345.49

Use the following structure declaration to answer questions 5–13:

```
struct Account
{
  float Deposits;        //ACCOUNT DEPOSITS
  float Withdrawals;     //ACCOUNT WITHDRAWALS
  float InterestRate;    //ANNUAL INTEREST RATE IN PERCENT FORM
```

```
    float Balance;              //ACCOUNT BALANCE
}; //END Account
Account Checkbook;          //DEFINE CHECKBOOK OBJECT
Account Passbook;           //DEFINE PASSBOOK OBJECT
```

5. The structure objects are _____.

6. Write a statement to assign a value of $250.00 to the *Deposits* member of the *Checkbook* structure.

7. Write a statement to assign a value of 12% to the *InterestRate* member of the *Passbook* structure.

8. Write a statement to allow the user to input a value for the *Withdrawals* member of the *Checkbook* structure.

9. Write a statement to allow the user to input a value for the *Deposits* member of the *Passbook* structure.

10. Write a statement to display the account balance in the *Checkbook* structure.

11. Write a statement to display the account balance in the *Passbook* structure.

12. Write a header for a function called *Input()* that would obtain user entries for the *Checkbook* structure.

13. Write a header for a function called *Output()* that would display the contents of the *Passbook* structure.

Use the following structure declarations to answer questions 14–19:

```
struct Address
{
    char Street[25];        //EMPLOYEE STREET ADDRESS
    char City[25];          //EMPLOYEE CITY
    char State[2];          //EMPLOYEE ZIP CODE
    char Zip[10];
}; //END Address
struct Employee
{
    char Name[25];          //EMPLOYEE NAME
    int ID;                 //EMPLOYEE ID
    Address Addr;           //NESTED EMPLOYEE ADDRESS STRUCTURE
    float Salary;           //EMPLOYEE SALARY
}; //END Employee
Employee  JD;               //DEFINE EMPLOYEE OBJECT
```

14. How are the structures nested?

15. Write a statement to assign "John Doe" for the employee name.

16. Write the statements to allow the user to enter the employee's state of residence.

17. Write the statements to allow the user to enter the employee's salary.

18. Write a header for a function called *DisplayEmployee( )* that will display the data stored in the *Employee* structure.

19. Write the statements required for the function in question 18 to display the employee data.

9-2 CLASSES AND OBJECTS

A thorough understanding of classes and objects is essential to developing object-oriented code. You have been working with the standard C++ data classes since Chapter 2. Using these classes you have created constant and variable objects to manipulate within your programs. So, you should now have a good feeling for the class/object concept. It is now time to learn how to create your own classes and objects that provide all the ADT characteristics of the standard classes. Before we get into the details, let's reinforce your class/object knowledge with a real-world example of how they might be used in a commercial program.

The Idea of Classes and Objects

For now, you can think of a class as a model, or pattern, for its objects. If you have used a word processor, you are aware that most word processing programs include templates for business letters, personal letters, interoffice memos, press releases, etc. (*Note*: Be aware that OOP uses the term *template* in a different sense than it is used here in word processing.) The idea is to first open one of the built-in general-purpose template files when you want to generate, let's say, an interoffice memo. An example of such a template from Microsoft's Word for Windows® is provided in Figure 9-2.

As you can see, the template provides the accepted interoffice memo formatting, the memo type style, and any fixed information, such as headings and the date. Using this template, you fill in all the object information required for the memo, including the text of the memo as shown in Figure 9-3.

InterOffice Memo

To:	Recipient
From:	Sender
Date:	June 13, 1996
Subject:	The Subject of the Memo

CC:

Figure 9-2   A *class* can be thought of as a model, or pattern, like this memo template from Microsoft's Word for Windows®.

InterOffice Memo

To:	All C++ Students
From:	Prof. Andrew C. Staugaard, Jr.
Date:	June 13, 1996
Subject:	Classes and Objects

This memo represents an object of the class shown in Figure 9-2. The class provides a general framework from which objects are created. It is important that you understand this concept.

CC:

Your Instructor

Figure 9-3   An *object* is a particular instance, or specimen, of a class, as this memo is an instance of the memo template of Figure 9-2.

In other words, you provide the details that might make one memo different from another. You can think of a class as the memo template and the actual memo that you generate as an object of that template. Different memos made from the same memo template would represent unique objects of the same class. The class template provides the framework for each of its object memos. All the object memos would have the same general format and type style defined by the class template, but would have different text information defined by a given object memo. You could load in another template file, let's say for a business letter, that would represent a different class. Then using this template, you could construct different object business letters from the business letter template.

The word *class* in OOP is used to impart the notion of classification. Objects defined for a class share the fundamental framework of the class. Thus, the class is common to the set of objects defined for it. In the preceding example, the interoffice memo template defines the characteristics that are common to all interoffice memos created by Word for Windows®. In fact, many current word processing programs, like Word for Windows®, employ classes and objects for this purpose. A given class provides the foundation for creating specific objects, each of which share the general characteristics and *behavior* of the class.

As you can see from this example, classes and objects are closely related. In fact, it is difficult to discuss one without the other. The important difference is that a class is only an ***abstraction***, or pattern, whereas an object is a real entity. The interoffice memo class is only an abstraction for the real memo object that can be physically created, printed, and mailed. As another example, think of a class of fish. The fish class describes the general characteristics and behavior of all fish. However, the notion of a fish only provides an abstraction of the real thing. To deal with the real thing, you must consider specific fish objects such as a bass, trout, marlin, and so on. A fish, in general, behaves as you would expect a fish to behave, but a particular kind of fish has its own unique behavior.

Classes

In order to completely understand the nature of a class, we must consider two levels of definition: the ***abstract*** level and the ***implementation*** level.

The Abstract Level

The abstract level of a class provides the *essence* of the class. Here's how we define a class at the abstract level.

> At the abstract level, a ***class*** can be described as an *interface* that defines the behavior of its objects.

A class can be described as an interface, because its main purpose is to describe the operations, or functions, that can be performed by its objects. In this way, it defines the behavior common to all of its objects. By behavior, we mean how an object of a given class acts and reacts when it is accessed.

The abstract view of a class as an interface provides its *outside* view while hiding its internal structure and behavioral details. Thus, an object of a given class can be viewed as a black box, as shown in Figure 9-4.

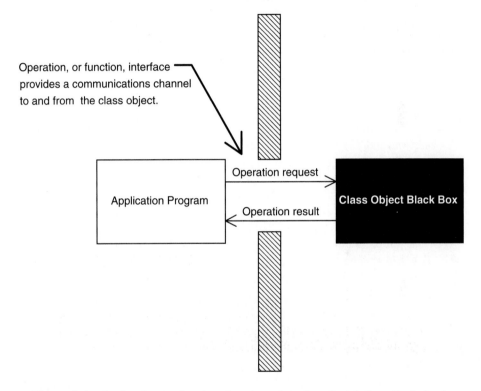

Figure 9-4   At the abstract level, a class is an interface that defines the behavior of its objects.

As you can see, the operation, or function, interface provides a communications channel to and from the class object. The application program generates an operation request to the object, and the object responds with the desired result. The interface dictates *what* must be supplied to the object and *how* the object will respond. As a result, a class, through its operation interfaces, defines how its objects will behave. At the client application level, you treat the class object as a black box because you do not care about what goes on inside the object. All you care about is how to work with the object. These concepts should not be new to you because you have been using the standard integer, floating-point, and character classes all along.

The Implementation Level

The class implementation provides its *inside* view, showing the secrets of its data organization and function implementation. As a result, the class implementation reveals the secrets of its behavior, because it is primarily concerned with the operations that define the abstract level, or interface.

> At the implementation level, a ***class*** is a syntactical unit that describes a set of data and related operations that are common to its objects.

The implementation of a class consists of two major sections: (1) a public section and (2) a private section. Any item declared in a class is called a class ***member***. Consequently, to implement a class we create public members and private members.

The Public Section

The public section of the class can consist of both ***member data*** and ***member functions***. The member data and functions are "public" because they can be accessed anywhere within the scope of a given class. In other words, member data can be changed and member functions can be called from outside the class, as long as the class is visible at the time of access. As you might suspect, it is the public member functions that form the interface to the class objects.

There is nothing special about public member functions, except that they are used to operate on the private members of the class. The important thing to remember is that *no functions outside of a given class can access the private members of the class*, unless they are special ***friend functions*** defined for a given class. Friend functions are beyond the scope of this text, so we will assume that *only* the member functions defined for a given class can access the private members of that class. You should be aware that member functions are sometimes called ***methods*** in object-oriented programming.

The Private Section

The private section of a class can consist of both ***member data*** and ***member functions***. The private member data can be variable objects of any data class in

C++, including **int**, **char**, **float**, **bool**, **enum**, as well as arrays and pointers. In addition, private members can be functions. We say that these members are "private" because they are *accessible only by the public member functions defined for the class*. This means that the private member data can be changed only by the public member functions in the class or that private member functions can be called only by the public member functions.

The Class Declaration

The implementation level of a class can be clearly seen by its declaration format, as follows:

CLASS DECLARATION FORMAT

class <class name>
{
public:
<return class> <function 1 name> (<function 1 parameter listing>);
<return class> <function 2 name> (<function 2 parameter listing>);
        •
        •
        •
<return class> <function n name> (<function n parameter listing>);
<data class> <variable object name 1>;
<data class> <variable object name 2>;
        •
        •
        •
<data class> <variable object name n>;

private:
<data class> <variable object name 1>;
<data class> <variable object name 2>;
        •
        •
        •
<data class> <variable object name n>;
<return class> <function 1 name> (<function 1 parameter listing>);
<return class> <function 2 name> (<function 2 parameter listing>);
        •
        •
        •
<return class> <function n name> (<function n parameter listing>);
}; //END CLASS

The declaration begins with the keyword **class**, followed by the class name. The entire class declaration is enclosed in a set of curly braces. Normally, the public section of the class is declared first using the keyword **public** followed by a colon and a listing of the public members. The private section of the class is declared second using the keyword **private** followed by a colon and a listing of the private members of the class. You might see the public and private sections reversed in some texts; however, I will always declare the public section first, to emphasize the fact that the public member functions are the important aspect of the class, because they define the class behavior and its interface.

To declare a function as a member of a class, you list the function prototype. The entire member function definition, often called an *implementation*, is provided after the class declaration.

Encapsulation

Encapsulation is simply the idea of packaging things together in a well-defined programming unit. A structure is encapsulated because it is a collection of data members that are combined into a well-defined structure unit. The class in C++ obviously provides for encapsulation by packaging both data and function members into a single class unit. In fact, a C++ class is an extension of a structure that encapsulates both data and function members.

> *Encapsulation* means to package data and/or operations into a single well-defined programming unit.

Information Hiding

The idea of encapsulation can be enhanced with *information hiding*.

> *Information hiding* means that there is a binding relationship between the information, or data, and its related operations so that operations outside of an encapsulated unit cannot affect the information inside the unit.

With information hiding, there is a *binding* relationship between the information and the operations that are performed on that information. The class provides for information hiding in C++. The public section provides the interface that is accessible outside the class, and the private section provides the information that is accessible only from within the class itself. Only the member functions declared for the class can operate on the private class members. Thus, the private section of a class provides the information hiding. Without encapsulation and information hiding, there is no such binding relationship. In programming languages that do not support information hiding, you define data structures and the code that operates on those data structures separately. Then, you place both in a single source code file while attempting to treat the data and code as separate modules within the file. After all, isn't this the idea behind structured programming that has worked for you until now? Although such an approach seems reasonable, it can create problems. Because there is no defined, or explicit, binding relationship between the data and the code, another programmer could write functions to access and inadvertently change the data.

For instance, suppose that you are writing a program for a bank that calculates bank account interest. To write such a program, you would define an account balance variable, among others, and write functions to change the balance based on deposits, withdrawals, interest rate, and so on. These functions would be written according to the policies dictated by the bank—and the government, for that matter. Would you want another programmer to be able to write functions that would affect the account balances differently than yours? Even worse, would you want the transactions of one account to affect the balance of another account? Of course not!

With information hiding, you can truly separate the account data and the functions operating on those data into two separate sections, a private section and a public section, but bind them tightly together in an encapsulated class unit. Only those member functions in the public section can operate on the private account data. This means that outside functions written by another programmer cannot corrupt the data. Thus, only the operations that you have defined for a given type of account can be applied to that type of account and no others. In addition, these same operations applied to one account cannot affect another account of the same type. The class dictates the data format and legal operations for all accounts of a given type. Then, individual accounts of the same type are created as objects of the account class. Let's illustrate this idea with an example.

Encapsulation Without Information Hiding

Here is how a banking program might be coded using C, without the information hiding ability of C++.

```cpp
#include <iostream.h>   //FOR cin AND cout

//DECLARE Account STRUCTURE
struct Account
{
   float Balance;               //ACCOUNT BALANCE
   float InterestRate;          //ANNUAL INTEREST RATE IN PERCENT
}; //END Account

//FUNCTION PROTOTYPES
void Initialize(Account Acct, float Bal, float Rate);//INITIALIZE DATA
void AddInterest(Account Acct);              //ADD MONTHLY INTEREST
void Deposit(Account Acct, float Amount);    //ADD DEPOSIT
void Withdraw(Account Acct, float Amount);   //SUBTRACT WITHDRAWAL
float CurrentBalance(Account Acct);          //RETURN BALANCE

void main()
{
//DEFINE STRUCTURE OBJECTS
   Account Acct1;
   Account Acct2;

//INITIALIZE STRUCTURE DATA AND ADD INTEREST
   Initialize(Acct1, 1000, 10);
   CurrentBalance(Acct1);

//ATTEMPT TO CORRUPT ACCOUNT DATA
   Acct1.Balance = 1000000;          //THIS OPERATION IS LEGAL
                                     //USING A STRUCT
   Acct2.Balance = Acct1.Balance;    //THIS OPERATION IS LEGAL
                                     //USING A STRUCT

//OUTPUT ACCOUNT BALANCES
   cout << "Your Account 1 balance is: $" << CurrentBalance(Acct1) << endl;
   cout << "Your Account 2 balance is: $" << CurrentBalance(Acct2) << endl;;
} //END main()

//INITIALIZE STRUCTURE DATA
void Initialize(Account Acct, float Bal, float Rate)
{
   Acct.Balance = Bal;
   Acct.InterestRate = Rate;
} END Initialize()
```

```
//CALCULATE MONTHLY BALANCE
void AddInterest(Account Acct)
{
  Acct.Balance += Acct.Balance * Acct.InterestRate/12/100;
} //END AddInterest()

//ADD DEPOSIT
void Deposit(Account Acct, float Amount)
{
  Acct.Balance += Amount;
} //END Deposit()
//SUBTRACT DEPOSIT
void Withdraw(Account Acct, float Amount)
{
  Acct.Balance -= Amount;
} //END Withdraw()


//RETURN MONTHLY BALANCE
float CurrentBalance(Account Acct)
{
  return Acct.Balance;
} //END CurrentBalance()
```

This program starts off by declaring a bank account structure called *Account.* The structure defines the account variables and is encapsulated, because the account variables are packaged within a single structure (struct). Five functions, called *Initialize(), AddInterest(), Deposit(), Withdraw(),* and *CurrentBalance(),* are prototyped and defined to initialize the structure objects, add monthly interest to the balance, make a deposit, make a withdrawal, and return the account balance, respectively. Two structure objects, called *Acct1* and *Acct2*, are defined at the beginning of *main()*. Notice that function *Initialize()* is called to initialize the *Acct1* structure. The account balance is set to $1000 and the interest rate is set to 10%. A call to function *AddInterest()* is then made to calculate a new monthly balance. Next, a successful attempt is made to alter the balance in both accounts, resulting in the following balances:

Your Account 1 balance is: $1000000
Your Account 2 balance is: $1000000

Wow! Both accounts have been corrupted, most likely illegally, by the insertion of two lines of code. Not only has the *Acct1* balance been corrupted, but the corrupted *Acct1* balance has been transferred to *Acct2*. This can happen only if the data and related functions are not tightly bound, as is the case with this structure and its related functions. This points out a definite weakness in the traditional algorithmic approach to programming.

Encapsulation with Information Hiding

Now, let's see how to protect the bank account data using a class. Look closely at the following program:

```
#include <iostream.h>   //FOR cin AND cout

//DECLARE Account CLASS
class Account
{
public:
  void Initialize(float Bal, float Rate);     //INITIALIZE PRIVATE DATA
  void AddInterest();                          //ADD MONTHLY INTEREST
  void Deposit(float Amount);                  //ADD DEPOSIT
  void Withdraw(float Amount);                 //SUBTRACT WITHDRAWAL
  float CurrentBalance();                      //RETURN BALANCE

private:
  float Balance;                               //ACCOUNT BALANCE
  float InterestRate;                          //ANNUAL INTEREST IN PERCENT
}; //END Account

void main()
{
//DEFINE ACCOUNT OBJECTS
  Account  Acct1;
  Account  Acct2;

//INITIALIZE OBJECT DATA AND ADD INTEREST
  Acct1.Initialize(1000, 10);
  Acct1.AddInterest();

//ATTEMPT TO CORRUPT ACCOUNT DATA
//Acct1.Balance = 1000000;            //THIS OPERATION IS ILLEGAL
                                      //USING A CLASS
//Acct2.Balance = Acct1.Balance;      //THIS OPERATION IS ILLEGAL
                                      //USING A CLASS
```

```
//OUTPUT ACCOUNT BALANCES
  cout << "Your Account 1 balance is:  $" << Acct1.CurrentBalance() << endl;
  cout << "Your Account 2 balance is:  $" << Acct2.CurrentBalance() << endl;
} //END main()

//INITIALIZE ACCOUNT OBJECT DATA
void Account :: Initialize(float Bal, float Rate)
{
  Balance = Bal;
  InterestRate = Rate;
} //END Initialize()

//CALCULATE MONTHLY BALANCE
void Account :: AddInterest()
{
  Balance += Balance * InterestRate/12/100;
} //END AddInterest()

//ADD DEPOSIT
void Account :: Deposit(float Amount)
{
  Balance += Amount;
} //END Deposit()

//SUBTRACT DEPOSIT
void Account :: Withdraw(float Amount)
{
  Balance -= Amount;
} //END Withdraw

//RETURN MONTHLY BALANCE
float Account :: CurrentBalance()
{
  return Balance;
} //END CurrentBalance()
```

This program does basically the same thing as the previous program. Don't worry about the coding details for now, as they will be covered shortly. This time the bank account is declared as a class. The class consists of the same account variables as the earlier struct; however, they are now private members of the class and can be accessed only by the public member functions of the class. There are five public member functions: *Initialize(), AddInterest(), Deposit(), Withdraw(),* and *CurrentBalance().* These functions accomplish the same tasks as the functions defined in the previous program. At the beginning of *main()*, you see two objects, *Acct1* and *Acct2*, defined for the *Account* class. The *Acct1* object data are then initialized by a call to the *Initialize()* function, and a new monthly balance is calculated for this account by calling the *AddInterest()* function. Next, an attempt is made to corrupt the balances of both the *Acct1* and *Acct2* objects. However, in this program, the attempt is unsuccessful, as verified by the following account balance values:

Your Account 1 balance is: $1008.75
Your Account 2 balance is: $0

Notice that the *Acct1* balance reflects the interest calculation and would not be corrupted by the illegal assignment to $1,000,000. Likewise, the *Acct2* balance remains $0, indicating that it would not be corrupted by the assignment of the *Acct1* balance. In fact, these two assignment statements have been commented out of the program because they are illegal operations and will cause a compile error. This means that the compiler will enforce information hiding when using a class.

The effect of this program is to bind the data and the code operating on that data so tightly that the data cannot be corrupted by any outside code. This is encapsulation with information hiding! The private section of a class hides the data from any operations that are not defined for the class. It is difficult to provide information hiding in some programming languages, like C, because the overhead is too great. On the other hand, a class in C++ inherently enforces information hiding.

There is a cost, however. You must use a function call to access private data. This reduces the efficiency of the code slightly. On the other hand, using the compiler to enforce the rules that relate data to code can pay off in a big way when it comes time to debug a large program. In addition, object-oriented code is much easier to maintain because the classes and their objects closely match the application. Finally, once object-oriented code is developed for a given application program, it can be easily reused in another program that has a similar application. Consider a windows program. All windowing programs employ the same window classes. To create a new windows application program, you simply "inherit" the general window classes and customize them to the new application.

The ideas of encapsulation and information hiding are not new. Only languages like Ada, Modula II, and C++, which easily and efficiently provide for encapsulation and information hiding, are new. These concepts have been around as long as computers. Common examples of information hiding include those data and routines that are part of BIOS to control your PC keyboard, monitor, and file access. Also, the file-handling routines built into most compilers employ information hiding. Imagine what would happen if you could inadvertently corrupt these data and routines (system crash, lost unrecoverable files, etc.). You can use these built-in routines just by knowing how to operate them, but you cannot get at the inner workings of the routines. Likewise, you can operate your CD player via its controls without worrying about the inner workings of the player. Imagine what might happen if a nontechnical user could get to the inner workings of your CD player. This is why it is so important to think of a class in the abstract sense of an interface.

You should be aware that some texts equate encapsulation with information hiding. However, remember that encapsulation does not necessarily relate to information hiding. Each language permits various parts of a programming entity to be accessible to the outside world. Those parts that are not visible to the outside world represent the information hiding aspect of encapsulation. C structures, for example, are encapsulated and permit all member data to be visible and manipulated by outside operations and, therefore, do not provide any information hiding. C++ classes are encapsulated, but, in addition, provide information hiding through the private declaration section of the class.

Now, let's take a closer look at the foregoing *Account* class declaration. Here is the declaration again, without the rest of the program:

```
class Account
{
public:
    void Initialize(float Bal, float Rate);    //INITIALIZE PRIVATE DATA
    void AddInterest();                         //ADD MONTHLY INTEREST
    void Deposit(float Amount);                 //ADD DEPOSIT
    void Withdraw(float Amount);                //SUBTRACT WITHDRAWAL
    float CurrentBalance();                     //RETURN BALANCE

private:
    float Balance;                              //ACCOUNT BALANCE
    float InterestRate;                         //MONTHLY INTEREST RATE
}; //END Account
```

The declaration begins by describing the class interface via its public function prototypes. The public section begins with the keyword **public**. This class contains five public member functions. All the functions operate on the private data members. The *Initialize()* function initializes the private members to beginning values received from the calling program, but does not return any data to the calling program. The *AddInterest()* function calculates a new balance from the current private member values. The *Deposit()* function adds an amount received from the calling program to the account balance. The *Withdraw()* function subtracts an amount received from the calling program from the account balance. Finally, the *CurrentBalance()* function returns the value of the account balance to the calling program. You see that only the function prototypes are listed in the class declaration. The entire function definition, or ***implementation***, is separate from the class declaration.

After the public section, you find a listing of the private members that make up the private section of the declaration. There are two private floating-point members, *Balance* and *InterestRate,* which are listed after the keyword **private** in the class declaration.

Example 9-5

Write class declarations for the following:

a. A rectangle class that consists of the rectangle length and width with functions to initialize the private members, calculate the perimeter of the rectangle, and calculate the area of the rectangle.
b. A circle class that consists of the circle radius with functions to initialize the private member, calculate the circumference of the circle, and calculate the area of the circle.

Solution

a. The rectangle class requires three public functions: *Initialize()*, *Perimeter()*, and *Area()* and two private members, *Length* and *Width*. Here's the declaration:

```
class Rectangle
{
public:
    void Initialize(float L, float W);    //INITIALIZE PRIVATE DATA
    float Perimeter();                    //RETURN PERIMETER
    float Area();                         //RETURN AREA

private:
    float Length;                         //RECTANGLE LENGTH
    float Width;                          //RECTANGLE WIDTH
}; //END Rectangle
```

The *Initialize()* function receives length and width values from the calling program. This function does not require any return class, because it is operating directly on the private members of the class. The *Perimeter()* and *Area()* do not receive any data from the calling program, but both will return floating-point values to the calling program. Because the private data and public functions are so tightly bound within the class, you *do not pass the private data to or from the public functions as you would in structured programming.*

b. The circle class requires three public member functions: one to initialize the radius, one to calculate the circumference, and one to calculate the area. The only private member required is the circle radius. Here's the declaration:

```
class circle
{
public:
    void Initialize(float R);          //INITIALIZE PRIVATE DATA
    float Circumference();             //RETURN CIRCUMFERENCE
    float Area();                      //RETURN AREA

private:
    float Radius;                      //CIRCLE RADIUS
}; //END Circle
```

The *Initialize()* function receives an initializing radius value from the calling program and doesn't return any values, because it is operating directly on the private data member. The *Circumference()* and *Area()* functions do not receive any parameters from the calling program, but return the circumference and area of the circle, respectively. The single private member is the circle radius, which is declared as a floating-point value.

STYLE TIP

When naming function members to be used in C++ classes, you should use a verb when the purpose of the function is to perform some designated task and a noun when the function returns a value. For instance, in the foregoing example, the function that performs the initialization task of the private class members was named *Initialize()*, and the function that returned the area of the rectangle and circle was name *Area()*.

Objects

You should now have a pretty good handle on what an object is. Here is a technical definition for your reference.

An *object* is an instance, or specimen, of a given class. An object of a given class has the structure and behavior defined by the class that is common to all objects of the same class.

An object is a real thing that can be manipulated in a program. An object must be defined for a given class to use the class, just as a variable object must be defined for an integer to use the **int** data class. You have been using classes and objects all along when, for example, you think of an integer variable as an object of the **int** class. An object defined for a class has the structure and behavior dictated by the class, which are common to all objects defined for the class. You see from the foregoing definition that an object is an "instance" of a class. The word *instance* means an example or specimen of something. In this case, you could say that an object is an example or specimen of a class. If you have a class of dogs, then a Brittany Spaniel is an example or specimen of a dog. The same idea applies between objects and classes.

Defining Objects

You define an object for a class just as you define an object for a structure. When the object is defined, memory is allocated to store the class for which the object is defined. Many different objects can be defined for a given class with each object made up of the data described by the class and responding to functions defined by the class. However, the private member data are hidden from one object to the next, even when multiple objects are defined for the same class. Objects are usually nouns. This means that they are persons, places, or things, like a *Square* object for a *Rectangle* class, a *Checkbook* object for a *Bank Account* class, a *FileWindow* object for a *Window* class, and so on. You create objects just as you create variables for standard classes. Here is the required object definition format:

FORMAT FOR DEFINING CLASS OBJECTS

<class name> <object name>;

When defining objects, you simply list the object name after the class name. You will normally define objects separate from the class declaration because the object definition will appear in the application program, whereas the class declaration will appear in a header file. More about this later.

Example 9-6

Create a *Square* object for a class called *Rectangle* and a *Checkbook* object for a class called *BankAccount*.

Solution

The *Square* object definition is

Rectangle Square;

The *Checkbook* object definition is

BankAccount Checkbook;

 Quick Check

1. What do we mean when we say that a class defines the behavior of its objects?

2. True or false: Encapsulation ensures information hiding.

3. True or false: Private class members can be accessed only via public member functions.

4. Combining data with the functions that are dedicated to manipulating the data so that outside operations cannot affect the data is known as _____.

5. True or false: A struct is an encapsulated unit.

6. Information hiding is provided by the _____ section of a class.

7. The behavioral secrets of a class are revealed at the _____ level.

8. Define an object called *PickUp* for a class called *Truck*.

9. Define an object called *StationWagon* for a class called *Automobile*.

9-3 MEMBER FUNCTIONS

The member functions in a class provide the interface to the class objects. Recall that to include a function as part of a class declaration, you simply list the function prototype in the public section of the class. The body of the function, or *implementation*, is given separately from the class declaration.

> A function *implementation* is the definition of the function that includes the function header and the body of the function.

In object-oriented programming, a function implementation is the same as a function definition. Here is the general format required to implement a function:

FORMAT FOR A FUNCTION IMPLEMENTATION

```
<return class> <class name> :: <function name> (<parameter listing>)
{

//BODY OF FUNCTION GOES HERE

}//END FUNCTION
```

As an example, remember that earlier we declared a class called *Account* that included a function called *Initialize()*. The *Initialize()* function was used to set the private members of the class to initial values. Here is the class declaration again:

```
class Account
{
public:
  void Initialize(float Bal, float Rate);   //INITIALIZE PRIVATE DATA
  void AddInterest();                        //ADD MONTHLY INTEREST
  void Deposit(float Amount);                //ADD DEPOSIT
  void Withdraw(float Amount);               //SUBTRACT WITHDRAWAL
  float CurrentBalance();                    //RETURN BALANCE

private:
  float Balance;                             //ACCOUNT BALANCE
  float InterestRate;                        //MONTHLY INTEREST RATE
}; //END Account
```

The important thing to remember is that the class declaration shows only the function prototypes that define the class interface. The details of how a given function works are provided in the function implementation. Here is the implementation for the *Initialize()* function:

```
void Account :: Initialize(float Bal, float Rate)
{
  Balance = Bal;
  InterestRate = Rate;
} //END Initialize()
```

Look closely at the function header and you will see a double colon, **::**, separating the class name and the function name. The double colon is called the **scoping operator**. To implement a function as part of a class, you *must* include the scoping operator in the function header to tell the compiler that the function is part of a class. In other words, the foregoing function header tells the compiler that "the *Initialize()* function has scope within the *Account* class." Once the function header is properly coded using the scoping operator, the body of the function is coded within curly braces just like any other function body.

Example 9-7

Write function implementations for the following *Rectangle* class:

```
class Rectangle
{
public:
  void Initialize(float L, float W);      //INITIALIZE PRIVATE DATA
  float Perimeter();                      //RETURN PERIMETER
  float Area();                           //RETURN AREA

private:
  float Length;                           //RECTANGLE LENGTH
  float Width;                            //RECTANGLE WIDTH
}; //END Rectangle
```

Solution

The *Initialize()* function is used to set the private class members to initial values received from the calling program. As a result, the function implementation is

```
void Rectangle :: Initialize(float L, float W)
{
  Length = L;
  Width = W;
} //END Initialize()
```

The *Perimeter()* function needs to calculate and return the perimeter of the rectangle. Here is the appropriate implementation:

```
float Rectangle :: Perimeter()
{
  return 2 *(Length + Width);
} //END Perimeter()
```

The *Area()* function must calculate and return the area of the rectangle, resulting in an implementation of

```
float Rectangle :: Area()
{
  return Length * Width;
} //END Area()
```

In all of the above member function implementations, you see the scoping operator employed to tell the compiler the class scope of the function. In addition, notice that each function operates on or with the private members of the class.

PROGRAMMING NOTE

Remember, when function members of a class operate directly on private data members of the class, you *do not* pass the member data to and from the functions as you would with traditional structured programming. The reason is that the function and data members are so tightly bound within the class that passing of class data is not necessary.

Constructors

A **constructor** is a special class function that is used to initialize an object automatically when the object is defined.

Although a constructor is a function used to initialize an object, it is often used to allocate dynamic memory, open files, and generally get an object ready for processing. In several previous examples, you have seen the *Initialize()* function used to set the private class members to initial values. However, to set the values of a given object using this function, you would have to call the *Initialize()* function someplace in the program code. The advantage of using a constructor is that the constructor function is called automatically when an object is defined.

Here are the rules governing the creation and use of constructors:

- The name of the constructor is the same as the name of the class.
- The constructor cannot have a return class, not even **void**.
- The constructor can have default parameters.
- A class cannot have more than one constructor; however, the constructor can be overloaded.
- Overloaded constructors with default parameters can cause ambiguity problems for the compiler.
- Constructors should not be developed for tasks other than to initialize an object for processing.

To illustrate how to set up a constructor, consider the following *Rectangle* class declaration:

```
class Rectangle
{
public:
  Rectangle(float L, float W);     //CONSTRUCTOR
  float Perimeter();               //RETURN PERIMETER
  float Area();                    //RETURN AREA

private:
  float Length;                    //RECTANGLE LENGTH
  float Width;                     //RECTANGLE WIDTH
}; //END Rectangle
```

This is the declaration for the *Rectangle* class that you saw earlier, with one big difference: It includes a constructor. Here, the constructor is *Rectangle()*, which takes the place of the *Initialize()* function that you observed earlier. Aside from the comment, you can recognize the constructor because it has the same name as the class and does not have any return class, not even **void**. The format of the *Rectangle()* constructor header is illustrated in Figure 9-5.

Once the constructor is declared in the class declaration, it must be defined, or implemented. Here is how the *Rectangle()* constructor might be implemented:

```
Rectangle :: Rectangle(float L, float W)
{
  Length = L;
  Width = W;
} //END Rectangle()
```

The implementation shows that the two private class members, *Length* and *Width*, are being initialized to the values received by the constructor parameters, *L* and *W*, respectively, just like our former *Initialize()* function.

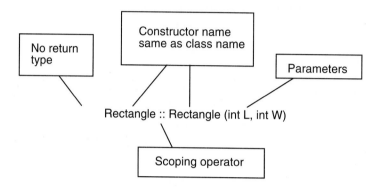

Figure 9-5 The format of a constructor header.

Now, the next question is: How is the constructor called? Well, the reason for using a constructor over a regular function to initialize an object is that the constructor is called automatically when an object is defined. So, let's define two objects for the *Rectangle* class and therefore automatically call the constructor.

```
Rectangle  SmallBox(2,3);
Rectangle  LargeBox(10,20);
```

Here, *SmallBox* and *LargeBox* are defined as objects of the *Rectangle* class. Notice that two argument values are passed to each object. The *SmallBox* object receives the argument values (2,3) and the *LargeBox* receives the argument values (10,20). What do you suppose happens with these arguments? You're right, the argument values are passed to the constructor, which is automatically called to set the *Length* and *Width* of the *SmallBox* object to 2 and 3, respectively. Likewise, the *Length* and *Width* of the *LargeBox* object are initialized to the values 10 and 20, respectively. So, the idea is to list the constructor arguments in parentheses after the object name when the object is defined. This passes the arguments to the constructor, which is automatically called to perform its initializing task.

Default Parameters for Constructors

Like any other function, a constructor can have default parameters. Recall that a default parameter is used when no arguments are supplied for that parameter. The default parameter values *must be supplied in the function prototype*. This means that the default parameter values must be present in the class declaration. Here is our *Rectangle* class again with default parameters inserted into the constructor prototype:

```
class Rectangle
{
public:
  Rectangle(float L = 0, float W = 0);    //CONSTRUCTOR
  float Perimeter();                      //RETURN PERIMETER
  float Area();                           //RETURN AREA

private:
  float Length;                           //RECTANGLE LENGTH
  float Width;                            //RECTANGLE WIDTH
}; //END Rectangle
```

Now, when we define our objects, like this,

```
Rectangle  SmallBox;
Rectangle  LargeBox(4,5);
```

the *SmallBox* object will have its *Length* and *Width* initialized to the default parameter values (0,0), and the *LargeBox* object will have its *Length* set to 4 and its *Width* set to 5. Notice that no argument values are present in the *SmallBox* object definition. When this is the case, the compiler will substitute the default values for any missing parameters.

Overloaded Constructors

Any function, even a constructor, can be overloaded. Recall from Chapter 7 that an overloaded function is one that performs different tasks depending on the number and/or class of arguments that it receives. Let's overload our *Rectangle()* constructor as follows:

```
class Rectangle
{
public:
  Rectangle(float S);            //CONSTRUCTOR FOR
                                 //A SQUARE  RECTANGLE

  Rectangle(float L, float W);   //CONSTRUCTOR FOR
                                 //A NONSQUARE RECTANGLE
```

```
float Perimeter();                    //RETURN PERIMETER
float Area();                         //RETURN AREA

private:
  float Length;                       //RECTANGLE LENGTH
  float Width;                        //RECTANGLE WIDTH
}; //END Rectangle
```

You are probably thinking that there are two constructors in the foregoing declaration. No, there is a single constructor called *Rectangle()*, which is overloaded. You can tell that the *Rectangle()* constructor is overloaded, because it has two different sets of parameters.

Now, let's look at the constructor implementations. Here they are:

```
//IMPLEMENTATION OF SQUARE CONSTRUCTOR
Rectangle :: Rectangle(float S)
{
  Length = Width = S;
} //END Rectangle()

//IMPLEMENTATION OF NONSQUARE CONSTRUCTOR
Rectangle :: Rectangle(float L, float W)
{
  Length = L;
  Width = W;
} //END Rectangle()
```

There are two implementations of this constructor, because it is overloaded. The first implementation is for a square and the second for a nonsquare rectangle. The square implementation sets the *Length* and *Width* members of the rectangle equal to the same value, *S,* that is received when the constructor is called. The nonsquare implementation sets the *Length* and *Width* to two different values, *L* and *W,* when the constructor is called. What determines which implementation is used? Well, if the constructor is called with a single argument, the square implementation is executed. If the constructor is called with two arguments, the nonsquare implementation is executed. How is the constructor called? Of course, by defining objects for the class. Here is a sample object definition:

```
Rectangle  Square(1);
Rectangle  Box(2,3);
```

Here, two objects, *Square* and *Box*, are defined. In addition, a single argument of (1) is passed to the *Square* object, and a double argument of (2,3) is passed to the *Box* object. What do you suppose happens? When the *Square* object is defined, the first constructor implementation is executed, setting the *Length* and *Width* of the *Square* object to the same value, 1. When the *Box* object is defined, the second constructor implementation is executed, setting the *Length* to 2 and the *Width* to 3.

CAUTION

When overloading a constructor and using default values, you can easily create *ambiguity* as to which constructor implementation should be executed. Such ambiguity *always* results in a compiler error.

Be careful to prevent ambiguity when using default values with overloaded constructors. For example, suppose we would have declared the *Rectangle* class as follows:

```
class Rectangle //THIS CLASS DECLARATION CREATES AMBIGUITY
{
public:
  Rectangle(float Side = 0);              //CONSTRUCTOR FOR
                                          //A SQUARE
  Rectangle(float L = 0, float W = 0);    //CONSTRUCTOR FOR
                                          //A NONSQUARE
  float Perimeter()                       //RETURN PERIMETER;
  float Area();                           //RETURN AREA

private:
  float Length;                           //RECTANGLE LENGTH
  float Width;                            //RECTANGLE WIDTH
}; //END Rectangle
```

Then we define our objects like this:

```
Rectangle  Square;
Rectangle  Box;
```

When this code is compiled, the compiler will generate an "ambiguity" error message. Why? Because the compiler doesn't know which constructor implementation to execute. Does it execute the implementation containing one parameter or the implementation containing two parameters? For this reason, it is wise not to use default parameters with an overloaded constructor. Obviously, there can never be an ambiguity problem with nonoverloaded constructors, because there is only one implementation for the constructor.

Scoping Inside of Functions

There can be a problem using a constructor, or any class function for that matter, when the private member names are the same as the function parameter names. For instance, suppose that we declare a simple *Circle* class that contains a private member called *Radius*. You then decide to use the *Radius* name as a parameter for the constructor. Here is the appropriate class declaration:

```
class Circle
{
public:
  Circle(float Radius = 0);        //CONSTRUCTOR
private:
  float Radius;                    //CIRCLE RADIUS
}; //END Circle
```

There is nothing wrong with this declaration. The problem arises in the constructor implementation. Consider the following implementation:

```
//CONSTRUCTOR IMPLEMENTATION
Circle :: Circle(float Radius)
{
Radius = Radius;
} //END Circle()
```

The implementation will compile; however, it will initialize *Radius* to garbage! Look at the statement within the implementation and you will see ambiguity in the use of the *Radius* name. It appears that *Radius* is being assigned to itself. How does the compiler know what *Radius* to use? Is *Radius* the variable defined as the private class member, or is *Radius* the value received by the constructor, or both? We must tell the compiler that the *Radius* on the left side of the assignment operator is the private class member and the *Radius* on the right side of the assignment operator is the value received by the constructor. There are two ways to solve this problem: (1) by using the scoping operator, or (2) by using the **this** pointer.

The Scoping Operator Revisited

You were introduced to the double colon scoping operator, ::, when you learned how to code the header of a member function implementation. The scoping operator simply defines the scope of something. In the case of a function header, it is used to tell the compiler that the function belongs to a certain class and therefore has class scope. The scoping operator can also be used inside of a function to define the scope of a variable. Using the scoping operator, we can fix the previous ambiguity problem by coding the *Circle()* constructor implementation as follows:

```
//CONSTRUCTOR IMPLEMENTATION
Circle :: Circle(float Radius)
{
Circle :: Radius = Radius;
} //END Circle()
```

The addition of the scoping operator in the constructor statement tells the compiler that the *Radius* on the left side of the assignment operator belongs to the *Circle* class. Therefore, the *Radius* on the right side of the assignment operator must be the function parameter. Now there is no ambiguity between the two *Radius* names.

The "this" Pointer

All the member functions of a class carry with them an invisible pointer, called **this**, that points to the object that called the function. (Pointers will be discussed in detail later.) Although the pointer is invisible, it can be used to prevent ambiguity problems like the one in the foregoing *Circle()* constructor. Here is how the **this** pointer can be employed in the constructor implementation to solve an ambiguity problem:

```
//CONSTRUCTOR IMPLEMENTATION
Circle :: Circle(float Radius)
{
this –> Radius = Radius;
} //END Circle()
```

The compiler knows that **this** points to the object that called the constructor, and it knows what class the object belongs to. As a result, this –> Radius references the private member *Radius* of the *Circle* class. Now there is no ambiguity between the two *Radius* names.

PROGRAMMING TIP

A simple solution to the use of duplicate names in a program is to make sure that you employ different names to avoid any ambiguity. For instance, the radius of a circle could be named *Radius*, *Rad*, or *R*, depending on where it is used in the program. Thus, the *Circle()* constructor could be coded like this:

```
//CONSTRUCTOR IMPLEMENTATION
Circle :: Circle(float Rad)
{
Radius = Rad;
} //END Circle()
```

This represents much better overall programming style and is less confusing to anyone looking at the code.

Example 9-8

Declare a *Point* class that defines an (x,y) coordinate for a cursor position on the monitor. Provide a constructor to initialize the coordinate when an object is defined for *Point*. The default coordinate should be (0,0). Include a function, called *Plot*, as part of the class that will display the string "C++" at the (x,y) coordinate location. Finally, code a statement required to define an object, *P*, of the *Point* class, and initialize this object to point to the middle of the monitor screen. Also, write a statement to call the *Plot* function.

Solution

First, the class declaration:

```
//Point CLASS DECLARATION
class Point
{
public:
  Point(int x = 0, int y =0);      //CONSTRUCTOR
  void Plot ();                    //PLOT POINT(X,Y)

private:
  int x;                           //X-COORDINATE
  int y;                           //Y-COORDINATE
}; //END Point
```

This declaration should be straightforward. The *Point* class consists of two private integer members, *x* and *y*, that will form the coordinate. A constructor function is included to initialize the *x* and *y* values and provide a default coordinate of (0,0). The *Plot* function will use the *x* and *y* member values to position the cursor at an (*x,y*) coordinate on the screen and display the string "C++". To see how the functions work, we need to develop their implementations. Here they are:

```
//CONSTRUCTOR IMPLEMENTATION
Point :: Point(int x, int y)
{
  this -> x = x;
  this -> y = y;
} //END Point()
```

```
//PLOT IMPLEMENTATION
void Point :: Plot()
{
 for(int i = 0; i < y; ++i)        //MOVE CURSOR DOWN y LINES
   cout << endl;
 for ( i = 0; i < x; ++i)          //MOVE CURSOR OVER x LINES
   cout << ' ';
 cout << "C++" << endl;           //DISPLAY "C++"
} //END Plot()
```

The constructor implementation applies the **this** pointer to prevent ambiguity between the *x,y* class members and the *x,y* constructor parameters. The *Plot* implementation uses the *x,y* class members within **for** loops to position the cursor at the (*x,y*) position on the monitor. Once the cursor is positioned, the final *cout* statement displays the string "C++" at the cursor position.

A statement to define an object, *P*, of the *Point* class and initialize *P* to point to the middle of the screen is

```
Point  P(40,12);
```

This statement defines *P* and calls the constructor to initialize the (*x,y*) coordinate to (40,12), which is the approximate middle of the screen. The following statement will call the *Plot* function to move the cursor to the (*x,y*) coordinate position and display the string.

```
P.Plot();
```

To call a nonconstructor function, you simply list the object, a dot, and then the function name with any required arguments. Of course, the *Plot* function doesn't require any arguments, because it operates directly on the private members of the object.

Access Functions

Remember that the only way to access the private members of an object are with a member function. Even if we simply want to examine the private members of an object, we need to use a public function that is declared within the same object class. Such a function needs to return only the private member(s) to the calling program. Access functions are used for this purpose.

An ***access function*** is a function that returns only the values of the private members of an object.

Let's revisit one of our *Rectangle* class declarations, adding access functions to it, as follows:

```
class Rectangle
{
public:
    Rectangle(float L, float W);        //CONSTRUCTOR
    float Perimeter();                  //RETURN PERIMETER
    float Area();                       //RETURN AREA
    float CurrentLength();              //ACCESS LENGTH
    float CurrentWidth();               //ACCESS WIDTH

private:
    float Length;                       //RECTANGLE LENGTH
    float Width;                        //RECTANGLE WIDTH
}; //END Rectangle
```

Two new member functions called *CurrentLength()* and *CurrentWidth()* have been added here to return the *Length* and *Width* private member values, respectively. The only purpose of an access function is to return the value of a private member, so the implementation requires only a **return** statement, as follows:

```
//IMPLEMENTATION OF LENGTH ACCESS FUNCTION
float Rectangle :: CurrentLength()
{
  return Length;
} //END CurrentLength()

//IMPLEMENTATION OF WIDTH ACCESS FUNCTION
float Rectangle :: CurrentWidth()
```

```
{
  return Width;
} //END CurrentWidth()
```

When either of these implementations is executed, the respective private member value is returned to the calling program. So, if we define *Box* to be an object of *Rectangle*, you can call either access member using dot notation to examine the private members. For instance, to display the member values of *Box*, the access functions could be called as part of *cout* statements, like this:

```
cout << "The length of the box is:  " << Box.CurrentLength() << endl;
cout << "The width of the box is:  " << Box.CurrentWidth() << endl;
```

Messages

A ***message*** is a call to a member function.

The term ***message*** is used for a call to a member function with the idea that when we are calling a member function, we are sending a message to the object. The object responds to the calling program by sending back return values. This idea is illustrated in Figure 9-6. As you will see shortly, objects communicate with each other using messages.

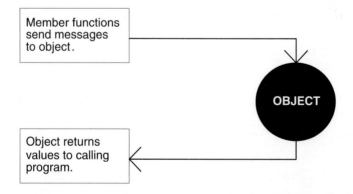

Figure 9-6 Messages are the means of communicating with an object.

To generate a message to an object, you must call one of its member functions. You call a member function by using the dot operator. The required format is

SENDING A MESSAGE USING THE DOT OPERATOR

<object name>•<function name> (argument listing);

You see that the syntax is very much like that required to access a structure. Here is our *Rectangle* class again with all the features that we have added up to this point:

```
class Rectangle
{
public:
  Rectangle(float L = 0, float W = 0);    //CONSTRUCTOR
  float Perimeter();                      //RETURN PERIMETER
  float Area();                           //RETURN AREA
  float CurrentLength();                  //ACCESS LENGTH
  float CurrentWidth();                   //ACCESS WIDTH

private:
  float Length;                           //RECTANGLE LENGTH
  float Width;                            //RECTANGLE WIDTH
}; //END Rectangle()
```

Let's define three *Rectangle* objects called *Box1*, *Box2*, and *Box3*. Here are the required definitions:

```
Rectangle Box1(2,3);           //Box1 OBJECT DEF
Rectangle Box2(3,4);           //Box2 OBJECT DEF
Rectangle Box3;                //Box3 OBJECT DEF
```

Next, let's send messages to all the functions of the three boxes using *cout* statements. We will use a separate *cout* statement for each message so that you can easily observe the required syntax. Here are the messages:

```
cout << "The length of Box1 is:  " << Box1.CurrentLength() << endl;
cout << "The width of Box1 is:  " << Box1.CurrentWidth()<< endl;
cout << "The perimeter of Box1 is:  " << Box1.Perimeter()<< endl;
cout << "The area of Box1 is:  " << Box1.Area()<< endl << endl;

cout << "The length of Box2 is:  " << Box2.CurrentLength()<< endl;
cout << "The width of Box2 is:  " << Box2.CurrentWidth()<< endl;
cout << "The perimeter of Box2 is:  " << Box2.Perimeter()<< endl;
cout << "The area of Box2 is:  " << Box2.Area() << endl << endl;
```

```
cout << "The length of Box3 is:  " << Box3.CurrentLength()<< endl;
cout << "The width of Box3 is:  " << Box3.CurrentWidth()<< endl;
cout << "The perimeter of Box3 is:  " << Box3.Perimeter()<< endl;
cout << "The area of Box3 is:  " << Box3.Area()<< endl << endl;
```

Observe that each group of four *cout* statements deals with a different box object. Each group sends messages to its respective object via the dot operator. That's all there is to it!

Putting Everything Together in a Complete Program

We now have all the ingredients to build a complete program. Here it is:

```
#include <iostream.h>    //FOR cin AND cout

//Rectangle CLASS DECLARATION
class Rectangle
{
public:
    Rectangle(float L = 0, float W = 0);      //CONSTRUCTOR
    float Perimeter();                        //RETURN PERIMETER
    float Area();                             //RETURN AREA
    float CurrentLength();                    //ACCESS LENGTH
    float CurrentWidth();                     //ACCESS WIDTH

private:
    float Length;                             //RECTANGLE LENGTH
    float Width;                              //RECTANGLE WIDTH
}; //END Rectangle

void main()
{
//DEFINE OBJECTS
    Rectangle Box1(2,3);                      //Box1 OBJECT DEF
    Rectangle Box2(3,4);                      //Box2 OBJECT DEF
    Rectangle Box3;                           //Box3 OBJECT DEF

//DISPLAY LENGTH, WIDTH, PERIMETER, AND AREA OF BOX OBJECTS
    cout << "The length of Box1 is:  " << Box1.CurrentLength() << endl;
    cout << "The width of Box1 is:  " << Box1.CurrentWidth()<< endl;
    cout << "The perimeter of Box1 is:  " << Box1.Perimeter()<< endl;
    cout << "The area of Box1 is:  " << Box1.Area()<< endl << endl;
```

```
    cout << "The length of Box2 is:  " << Box2.CurrentLength()<< endl;
    cout << "The width of Box2 is:  " << Box2.CurrentWidth()<< endl;
    cout << "The perimeter of Box2 is:  " << Box2.Perimeter()<< endl;
    cout << "The area of Box2 is:  " << Box2.Area() << endl << endl;

    cout << "The length of Box3 is:  " << Box3.CurrentLength()<< endl;
    cout << "The width of Box3 is:  " << Box3.CurrentWidth()<< endl;
    cout << "The perimeter of Box3 is:  " << Box3.Perimeter()<< endl;
    cout << "The area of Box3 is:  " << Box3.Area()<< endl << endl;
} //END main()

//CONSTRUCTOR IMPLEMENTATION
Rectangle :: Rectangle(float L, float W)
{
  Length = L;
  Width =  W;
} //END Rectangle()

//IMPLEMENTATION OF Perimeter() FUNCTION
float Rectangle :: Perimeter()
{
  return 2 * (Length + Width);
} //END Perimeter()

//IMPLEMENTATION OF Area() FUNCTION
float Rectangle :: Area()
{
  return Length * Width;
} //END Area()

//IMPLEMENTATION OF CurrentLength() FUNCTION
float Rectangle :: CurrentLength()
{
  return Length;
} //END CurrentLength()

//IMPLEMENTATION OF CurrentWidth() FUNCTION
float Rectangle :: CurrentWidth()
{
  return Width;
} //END CurrentWidth()
```

You see that our program includes the *Rectangle* class declaration, which includes five public function members and two private members. The functions consist of a constructor with default values, two access functions, and two functions that return the perimeter and area of the rectangle. Three objects are defined for the *Rectangle* class, and then messages are sent to the objects by calling all their respective functions. Here is the output from the program:

```
The length of Box1 is:  2
The width of Box1 is:  3
The perimeter of Box1 is:  10
The area of Box1 is:  6

The length of Box2 is:  3
The width of Box2 is:  4
The perimeter of Box2 is:  14
The area of Box2 is:  12

The length of Box3 is:  0
The width of Box3 is:  0
The perimeter of Box3 is:  0
The area of Box3 is:  0
```

This program summarizes most of what has been covered in the last two sections. Before going on, study the program to make sure that you understand everything in it. Many important OOP concepts are demonstrated here.

 Quick Check

1. The operator employed in a function header that designates the function as being a member of a given class is the _____ operator.

2. The complete definition of a member function, which includes the function header and body, is called the function _____.

3. Write a header for a member function called *Wheels()* that will return the number of wheels from a class called *Truck*.

4. A member function that is used specifically to initialize class data is called a _____.

5. How do you know which member function in a class is the constructor function?

6. True or false: The return class of a constructor function is optional.

7. How do you call a class constructor?

8. All member functions of a class carry with them a built-in pointer to the object that called the function, which is called _____.

9. How do you call a nonconstructor member function of a class?

10. A member function that returns only the values of the private class members is called a _____ function.

11. Why is the term "message" used for a call to a member function?

9-4 MULTIFILE PROGRAM CONSTRUCTION

Up to this point, we have been working with relatively simple C++ programs for learning purposes. Commercial programs, on the other hand, can get very complex, involving several thousand lines of code. Remember what to do when tackling a complex problem? You're right, divide it into simpler subproblems, the old "divide-and-conquer" strategy. The same is true when building a large program. Rather than placing everything into a single source file and compiling/linking this file into an executable file, we place different parts of the program in separate files, edit them separately, compile them separately, and then link them all together to create the executable file. This is the way the pros do it!

From the beginning, you have included header files in your C++ programs. These header files primarily provide interfaces to the standard functions and objects used in your program. The C and C++ languages were developed around the idea of using many separate files for a programming project and linking them together to create the executable file. There are several reasons for this approach. First, it allows you to create smaller, more manageable files. This facilitates a team approach to software development. Each team member writes, debugs, and compiles his/her own part of the project code independent of the other team members. When all the individual files are completed, they are linked to create a common executable program.

Second, programs made of separately compiled files are easier to maintain. When changes need to be made to the program, only those files affected by the change need to be modified and recompiled. In many cases, the unaffected files do not need to be recompiled.

Third, you can hide any important proprietary parts of the program code from the user by only providing the user with the binary object code for those parts. What really makes one C++ program different from another are the member function implementations. So, suppose that you provide the class declarations to the user as a *.cpp* source file and the function implementations as a *.obj* object file. The class declaration provides a listing of all the data members as well as the function prototypes. The function prototypes provide the required interface to an object of that class. This is all the user needs to know to use the class. He or she does not need to know how the functions are implemented. The function implementations can be compiled into a binary object file and supplied to the user. The user can then include the class declaration file in his/her applications program and link it along with the function implementation object file to create the final executable file. This encourages programmers to write object-oriented code that can be reused in other programs and shared with other programmers without compromising confidentiality. This idea is illustrated in Figure 9-7.

You should be aware of the rules for what must be recompiled and linked if things change in the class declaration header file or the function implementation file. If the ".*h*" class declaration header file is modified, then *every* ".*cpp*" source file that includes the header file must be recompiled. On the other hand, if the ".*cpp*" function implementation file is modified, then only this file must be recompiled. In either case, the entire application project must be relinked.

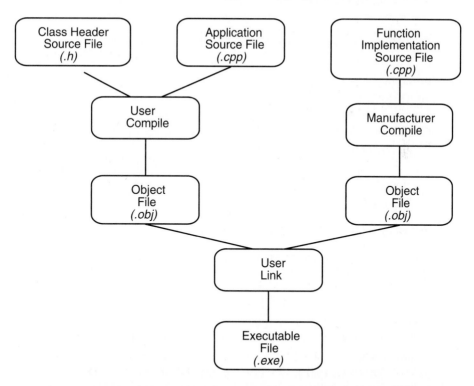

Figure 9-7 Object interfaces can be made public by supplying users with the class header files as source code, while hiding the function implementations in object files.

PROBLEM SOLVING IN ACTION: BUILDING A MULTIFILE C++ PROGRAM

C++ compilers and commercial programs are constructed using the multifile concept. The software manufacturers provide you with all the standard header files that include the function prototypes as source code, but do not supply you with the source code for the function implementations. Thus, you cannot alter and possibly corrupt the standard function implementations.

Most C++ compilers allow you to build your own multifile programs. In this problem, you will see how a typical C++ compiler allows you to build multifile programs through the use of its *project manager*. When using the project manager, you specify all the files required to build an application program. This information is kept in a *project file*.

A *project file* identifies the files that need to be compiled and linked to create a given executable program.

You can add or delete files to and from your project, view/edit individual files in the project, and set options for a file in the project. When working with program files in the project, the project manager automatically updates the information kept in the project file and identifies those files that need to be re-compiled and linked to produce an executable program. If a given program file is altered, only that file is recompiled by the project manager. This saves program development time.

As an example, let's build a project out of the *Rectangle* program that we developed at the end of the last section. We will place the *Rectangle* class declaration in a separate file called *rectangl.h*, like this:

//rectangl.h HEADER FILE

//Rectangle CLASS DECLARATION
class Rectangle
{
public:
    Rectangle(float L = 0, float W = 0);   //CONSTRUCTOR
    float Perimeter();   //RETURN PERIMETER
    float Area();   //RETURN AREA
    float CurrentLength();   //ACCESS LENGTH
    float CurrentWidth();   //ACCESS WIDTH

```
private:
  float Length;                          //RECTANGLE LENGTH
  float Width;                           //RECTANGLE WIDTH
}; //END Rectangle
```

Next, we will place all the function implementations in a separate file called *rectangl.cpp*, like this:

```
//rectangl.cpp IMPLEMENTATION FILE

#include "rectangl.h"      //FOR Rectangle CLASS

//CONSTRUCTOR IMPLEMENTATION
Rectangle :: Rectangle(float L, float W)
{
  Length = L;
  Width =  W;
} //END Rectangle()

//IMPLEMENTATION OF Perimeter() FUNCTION
float Rectangle :: Perimeter()
{
  return 2 * (Length + Width);
} //END Perimeter()

//IMPLEMENTATION OF Area() FUNCTION
float Rectangle :: Area()
{
  return Length *  Width;
} //END Area()

//IMPLEMENTATION OF CurrentLength() FUNCTION
float Rectangle :: CurrentLength()
{
  return Length;
} //END CurrentLength()

//IMPLEMENTATION OF CurrentWidth() FUNCTION
float Rectangle :: CurrentWidth()
{
  return Width;
} //END CurrentWidth()
```

The first executable statement that you see in this file is a preprocessor directive that includes the *rectangl.h* class declaration header file. This directive is required so that the *rectangl.cpp* file can be compiled to produce a *rectangl.obj* file. The file will not compile unless the class header file in included, because without it, the compiler doesn't know the class declaration from which the functions are derived. Notice that double quotes are employed around the header file name so that the compiler will look for the file in the system working directory. This is where a source file that you have developed will most likely be located.

Finally, you will write a separate application file. Let's call this file *myprog.cpp*. Here it is:

```
//myprog.cpp APPLICATION FILE

#include "rectangl.h"     //FOR Rectangle CLASS
#include <iostream.h>   //FOR cin AND cout
void main()
{
//DEFINE OBJECTS
  Rectangle Box1(2,3);                    //Box1 OBJECT DEF
  Rectangle Box2(3,4);                    //Box2 OBJECT DEF
  Rectangle Box3;                         //Box3 OBJECT DEF

//DISPLAY LENGTH, WIDTH, PERIMETER, AND AREA OF BOX OBJECTS
  cout << "The length of Box1 is:  " << Box1.CurrentLength() << endl;
  cout << "The width of Box1 is:  " << Box1.CurrentWidth()<< endl;
  cout << "The perimeter of Box1 is:  " << Box1.Perimeter()<< endl;
  cout << "The area of Box1 is:  " << Box1.Area()<< endl << endl;

  cout << "The length of Box2 is:  " << Box2.CurrentLength()<< endl;
  cout << "The width of Box2 is:  " << Box2.CurrentWidth()<< endl;
  cout << "The perimeter of Box2 is:  " << Box2.Perimeter()<< endl;
  cout << "The area of Box2 is:  " << Box2.Area() << endl << endl;

  cout << "The length of Box3 is:  " << Box3.CurrentLength()<< endl;
  cout << "The width of Box3 is:  " << Box3.CurrentWidth()<< endl;
  cout << "The perimeter of Box3 is:  " << Box3.Perimeter()<< endl;
  cout << "The area of Box3 is:  " << Box3.Area()<< endl << endl;
} //END main()
```

Here is where the objects are defined for the program. In addition, function *main()* appears here along with any other functions that are part of the application program. This file must also include the *rectangl.h* header file, because it won't compile unless the compiler knows the class declaration for which the objects are being defined.

Now we have three separate files: *rectangl.h*, *rectangl.cpp*, and *myprog.cpp*. At this point, you could compile the *rectangl.cpp* function implementation file to produce a *rectangl.obj* object file. Then, compile the *myprog.cpp* application file and link it with the *rectangl.obj* object file to produce an executable program called *myprog.exe*. This would require separate compiling and linking steps. However, there is an easier way using, a project manager. Once a project file is open, you can add and delete files to and from the project. For this project, you will add the *myprog.cpp* application file and the *rectangl.cpp* implementation file. You **do not** add the *rectangl.h* header file to the project because it is included as part of the other two files. Figure 9-8 depicts the composition of our project file.

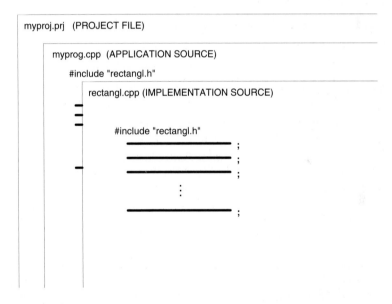

Figure 9-8   A project file includes all the program files needed to create an executable application file.

Once the project is built, you simply compile the project file. When the project file is compiled, it will automatically perform the compiling and linking steps required to produce an executable file called *myproj.exe*. In addition, if there are any errors in any of the files that make up the project, the project manager will open the file in error for editing. Once the error is corrected, you can attempt to compile the project again from that point. Furthermore, at any time, you can edit and compile any of the component files independently of the project file.

After building a project, you can open the project at any time. When a given project is opened, the compiler will load the files that are part of that project so that they can be viewed and altered if necessary. In addition, you can obtain a listing of any included header files for a project. From here, you can also view and edit any of the included files. When a project is recompiled, the project manager only compiles those files that have been changed, resulting in reduced compile time.

At this point, it might be a good idea to build, compile, and execute your own project for the *Rectangle* program, using your compiler's project manager.

 Quick Check

1. State three reasons for using the multifile approach for developing software.
2. What file(s) in a C++ software project provide the interfaces to the class objects?
3. Why might a software manufacturer not supply you with the member function implementation source code?
4. A file that identifies the files that need to be compiled and linked to create an executable program is the _____ file.
5. When building a C++ project, which files must be listed in the project manager?
6. Why don't you list header files in the project manager?

CHAPTER SUMMARY

A structure is a collection of member data. Unlike an array, the elements that make up a structure, the members, can be different data classes. Structures are declared in C++ using the keyword **struct**. In addition, a structure object must be defined to access the structure information. Storage for a structure is not allocated until an object is defined for that structure.

Structure data are accessed by using the dot operator. To gain access to a member using dot notation, the structure object is listed first, followed by a dot, followed by the member name.

Nested structures are structures within structures. Thus, a nested structure is actually a member of another structure. A given nested structure is declared using the standard structure declaration format. The nested structure must be declared first, followed by the main structure. The main structure then includes the nested structure as the data class of a member within its declaration. When accessing nested structures, the nested structure member name must be listed in the dot notation path.

Object-oriented programs are developed from the inside out by expanding on simple classes. The fundamental components of any object-oriented program are the class and its objects. At the abstract level, a class can be described as an interface, because it defines the behavior common to all of its objects. At the implementation level, a class is a construct that describes a set of data and related operations that are common to its objects. The abstract level provides an outside view of a class, whereas the implementation level provides the inside view of the class, disclosing its behavioral secrets. At the implementation level, a class is comprised of public and private members. The private class members are hidden from the outside, because they can only be accessed using the public member functions. This provides for information hiding within the class.

Encapsulation is the idea of packaging things together in a well-defined programming unit. A structure, or struct, is encapsulated, because it consists of a collection of data members. A class in C++ is also encapsulated, because it consists of a collection of data members and related functions. However, a C struct does not provide information hiding, whereas a C++ class does provide information hiding through its private declarations.

An object is an instance, or specimen, of a class. Thus, an object of a given class has the structure and behavior defined by the class. The functions defined for a given class are called member functions. There are various types of member functions, including constructor functions and access functions. The member functions provide a means of communication with the object via messages. Messages are sent to an object by calling the member functions that perform a given task on the hidden object data. The object responds via the values returned by the member functions.

Object-oriented programs are normally constructed using a multifile approach. Class declarations are placed in separate header files. All the member function implementations for a given class are placed in a separate file that includes the class header file. Finally, the application program is placed in a separate file that includes all the class header files. The individual files are edited and compiled separately, then linked together to form an executable file. This facilitates a team approach to software development and makes such programs easier to maintain. Moreover, the user can be supplied the source code of the class header files and the object code of the function implementation files. This encourages reuse of the object-oriented code while protecting the implementation of that code from corruption by the user. Most C++ compilers include a project manager that facilitates the multifile approach to building programs.

QUESTIONS AND PROBLEMS

Questions

1. What is a structure?

2. How do the contents of a structure differ from that of an array?

3. Why is an object definition required to access a structure?

4. What operator is employed for accessing structure members?

5. True or false: Structures cannot be part of other structures.

6. True or false: Structure members can be initialized when the structure object is defined.

7. True or false: A given structure can contain members of any legal data class.

Use the following structure declarations to answers questions 8–11 and problems 1–3:

```
//PITCHING STATS STRUCTURE DECLARATION
struct Pitching
{
  int Wins;              //NUMBER OF WINS
  int Losses;            //NUMBER OF LOSSES
  float ERA;             //EARNED RUN AVERAGE
}; //END Pitching

//HITTING STATS STRUCTURE DECLARATION
struct Batting
{
  int AtBat;             //NUMBER AT BATS
  int HomeRuns;          //NUMBER HOME RUNS
  int RBIs;              //NUMBER RUNS BATTED IN
  float Average;         //BATTING AVERAGE
}; //END Batting
```

```
//NL BASEBALL PITCHER STRUCTURE DECLARATION
struct BaseballPitcher
  {
    char Name[30];      //PITCHER NAME
    char Team[30];      //PITCHER TEAM
    int Year;           //YEAR OF STATS
    Pitching Pitch;     //NESTED PITCHING STATS STRUCTURE
    Batting Bat;        //NESTED BATTING STATS STRUCTURE
  }; //END BaseballPitcher
BaseballPitcher  Pitcher;      //DEFINE STRUCTURE OBJECT
```

8. Explain the structure nesting.

9. Write statements to assign the structure members with the following data:

Name:	John Smoltz
Team:	Atlanta Braves
Year:	1989
Wins:	12
Losses:	11
ERA:	2.94
At Bats:	20
Home Runs:	0
RBIs:	11
Average:	.190

10. Write statements to display the structure data assigned in question 9.

11. Suppose that you define an object to the preceding *BaseballPitcher* structure as follows:

    BaseballPitcher Pitcher;

    Write a prototype for a function that would fill the structure members from keyboard entries.

12. Define the following OOP terms:

    Class at the abstract level
    Class at the implementation level
    Encapsulation
    Information Hiding
    Object
    Instance
    Member
    Function Implementation
    Constructor

Access Function
Overloaded Constructor
Message

13. What are the two major sections that make up a class declaration?

14. What is the scope of a private class member?

15. What is the scope of a public class member?

16. The concept of combining data with a set of operations that are dedicated to manipulating the data so tightly that outside operations cannot affect the data is called _____.

17. A computer window can be considered an object of a window class. What data and operations might be part of this object?

18. Where are function prototypes normally placed in a class declaration?

19. True or false: The abstract definition for a class provides the inside view of the class.

20. What is meant by the term "behavior" relative to a class object?

21. True or false: A class is an interface.

22. A member function that simply displays the values of class data members is called a _____ function.

23. What is the purpose of a constructor?

24. Suppose that a member function called *Initialize()* is part of a class called *Student*. The prototype for the *Initialize()* function is

```
void Initialize();
```

a. Write a header line for the function implementation.

b. Write a statement to call the *Initialize()* function for the object *IsaacNewton* of the *Student* class.

Use the following class declaration to answer questions 25–32:

```
class Student
{
public:
  Student(char Nam[] = "None",     //CONSTRUCTOR
          char Maj[] = "None",
          int Num = 0,
          float GPA = 0);
  void Initialize();               //INITIALIZE FROM USER ENTRIES
  void StudentData();              //ACCESS STUDENT DATA
```

```
private:
  char Name[25];                    //STUDENT NAME
  char Major[20];                   //STUDENT MAJOR
  int StudentNumber;                //STUDENT NUMBER
  float GPA;                        //STUDENT GPA
}; //END Student
```

25. What is the name of the constructor function?

26. Write a statement to define John Doe as a student object that will be initialized to the default values in the constructor.

27. Jane Doe (student #456) is a Computer Science major with a GPA of 3.58. Write a statement to define Jane Doe as a student object that will be initialized to the proper data values.

28. Write an implementation for the *Student()* function.

29. Write an implementation for the *Initialize()* function that will allow the user to enter the data values from the keyboard.

30. Write a statement that will allow the user to initialize the Jane Doe object from the keyboard.

31. Write an implementation for the *StudentData()* function, assuming that this function will display the student data.

32. Write a statement that will display the data in the John Doe student object.

33. True or false: A constructor may have parameters.

34. Suppose that you have a class called *Circle()*. What will be the corresponding constructor name?

35. When are constructors normally used in a C++ object-oriented program?

36. Given the following function implementation

```
Dogs :: Dogs(int Legs)
{
  Legs = Legs;
} //END Dogs()
```

    a. What special type of function is this?

    b. What problem would the compiler encounter when attempting to compile this implementation?

    c. Rewrite the implementation using the scoping operator to correct any problems.

    d. Rewrite the implementation using the **this** pointer to correct any problems.

37. What operator is used to send a message to an object?

38. Explain why you should use a multifile approach when developing C++ programs.

39. Suppose that you want to develop a commercial object-oriented program whereby you provide the user with the function interfaces while hiding their implementations. Explain how such a program would be organized and supplied to the user.

40. Explain the rules for recompiling and relinking when things are modified in a class header file or a function implementation file for a given application.

Problems

Least Difficult

1. Write a function to fill the structure members of the foregoing *BaseballPitcher* structure from the keyboard.

2. Write a function to display the structure members of the foregoing *BaseballPitcher* structure.

3. Write a program that incorporates the functions you developed in problems 1 and 2 to fill and display a baseball pitcher's stats.

4. Declare a *Name* structure consisting of a person's last name, first name, and middle initial.

5. Define an object for the structure in problem 4 and write the code to initialize it with your name.

6. Declare an *Address* structure consisting of a street number, street name, city, state, and zip code.

7. Define an object for the structure in problem 6 and write the code to initialize it with your address.

8. Declare a *Person* structure consisting of the *Name* and *Address* structures declared in problems 4 and 6.

9. Write a function to fill the structure in problem 8 from keyboard entries

10. Write a function to display the contents of the structure declared in problem 8.

11. Write a program that incorporates the functions developed in problems 9 and 10 to fill and display a person's name and address.

More Difficult

12. Modify the program given in Section 9-1 to include a nested structure for laboratory grades similar to the one given for test grades. Compile and execute your program to verify its operation.

13. Declare a class called *Employee* as part of a header file called *employe.h*. The class is to have data members to store the employee's name, hourly rate, and hours worked. The class is to have member functions to perform the following tasks:

    - A constructor function to initialize the hourly rate to a minimum wage of $4.25 per hour and the hours worked to 0.
    - A function to get the employee's name from the user.
    - A function to get the hourly rate of pay from the user.
    - A function to get the hours worked from the user.
    - Three separate access functions to display each of the data members.
    - A function to return weekly pay, including overtime pay, where overtime is paid at a rate of time-and-a-half for any hours worked over 40.

14. Write the implementations for the functions in problem 13 and place them in a file called *employe.cpp*.

15. Write an application program that defines an object for the class declared in problem 13 and tests the functions in problem 14. Place this program in a file called *pay.cpp*.

16. Build a project from the files created in problems 13 to 15. Compile, debug, and run the project file.

Use the multifile approach when writing your programs to solve the following problems.

17. Create an invoice object that contains all the information necessary to process one line of an invoice. Assume that the invoice must include the following data and functions:

    Data:
    Quantity Ordered
    Quantity Shipped
    Part Number
    Part Description
    Unit Price
    Extended Price
    Sales Tax Rate
    Sales Tax Amount
    Shipping
    Total

Functions:

- A function to initialize all the data items to 0, except the Sales Tax Rate, which should be initialized to 5%.
- A function to allow the user to initialize all the data items from the keyboard.
- A function to calculate the Extended Price of the item.
- A function to calculate the Sales Tax Amount of the item.
- A function to calculate the Total Amount of the invoice.
- A function to display the invoice data with header information in a businesslike format.

Most Difficult

18. A stack ADT is ideal to implement using a class, because it must include the stack data elements as well as the functions that operate on those elements in a tightly bound manner. As a result, object-oriented programming is perfect for implementing stacks. Here is a declaration for a *Stack* class:

```
class Stack
{
public:
    Stack();                    //CONSTRUCTOR INITIALIZES TOP TO -1
    void ClearStack();          //CLEAR STACK BY SETTING TOP TO -1
    int EmptyStack();           //CHECKS FOR EMPTY STACK
    int FullStack();            //CHECKS FOR FULL STACK
    void Push(char Char);       //PLACE ELEMENT ON TOP
    char Pop();                 //REMOVE ELEMENT FROM TOP

private:
    char Data[MAX];             //CHARACTER ARRAY TO HOLD THE STACK
    int Top;                    //Top LOCATES TOP ELEMENT OF STACK
}; //END Stack
```

This stack can hold MAX character elements as seen by the character array declaration within the class. An integer member called *Top* is declared to access the top element of the stack. Thus, *Top* provides the array index of the top element in the stack. The stack is empty when *Top* is −1 and the stack is full when *Top* is MAX − 1. Write the stack function implementations according to the following criteria:

- *Stack()* is a constructor function that initializes *Top* to −1.
- *ClearStack()* sets *Top* to −1.
- *EmptyStack()* tests to see if *Top* = −1.
- *FullStack()* tests to see if *Top* = MAX − 1 .

- *Push()* checks to see if the stack is full by calling the *FullStack()* function. Then it must increment *Top* and place *Element* in the array at the index pointed to by *Top*.

- *Pop()* checks to see if the stack is empty by calling the *EmptyStack()* function. If the stack is not empty, it returns the character element located at the array index pointed to by *Top* and decrements *Top*.

Write an application program to completely test your stack class.

19. Write a 12-hour clock program that declares a *Clock* class to store hours, minutes, seconds, A.M., and P.M. Provide functions to perform the following tasks:

- Set hours, minutes, seconds to 00:00:00 by default.

- Initialize hours, minutes, seconds, A.M., and P.M. from user entries.

- Allow the clock to tick by advancing the seconds by one and at the same time correcting the hours and minutes for a 12-hour clock value of A.M. or P.M.

- Display the time in hours:minutes:seconds A.M./P.M. format.

Write an application program that allows the user to set the clock and tick the clock at 1-second intervals while displaying the time.

CLASS INHERITANCE

INTRODUCTION
10-1 WHY USE INHERITANCE?
10-2 DECLARING AND USING DERIVED
        CLASSES
    Single versus Multiple Inheritance
    Using *#ifndef*: An Implementation Detail
10-3 POLYMORPHISM AND DYNAMIC
        BINDING

    Polymorphism
    Dynamic versus Static Binding
CHAPTER SUMMARY
QUESTIONS AND PROBLEMS
    Questions
    Problems

INTRODUCTION

One of the most important properties of object-oriented programming is *inheritance*. In fact, some believe that a program that doesn't employ inheritance is not an object-oriented program.

> *Inheritance* is that property of object-oriented programming that allows one class, called a *derived class*, to share the structure and behavior of another class, called a *base class*.

The natural world is full of inheritance. All living things inherit the characteristics, or traits, of their ancestors. Although you are different in many ways from your parents, you are also the same in many ways because of the genetic traits that you have inherited from them. In object-oriented programming, inheritance allows newly created classes to inherit members from existing classes. These new *derived*, or *child*, classes will include their own members and members inherited from the *base*, or *parent*, class. So, you can view a collection of classes with common inherited members as a *family* of classes, just like the family that you belong to. Classes are related to each other through inheritance. Such inheritance creates a class hierarchy.

In this chapter, I will first explain why inheritance is important and then illustrate its use via a practical example. Finally, we will discuss the two more important aspects of OOP: *polymorphism* and *dynamic binding*.

10-1 WHY USE INHERITANCE?

One reason to use inheritance is that it allows you to reuse the code from a previous programming project without starting from scratch to reinvent the code. Many times the code developed for one program can be reused in another program. Although the new program might be slightly different from the old, inheritance allows you to build on what was done previously. Why reinvent the wheel?

Another reason for using inheritance is that it allows you to build a *hierarchy* among classes. The classes that include those things that are most commonly inherited are at the top of the hierarchy, just as your ancestors are at the top of your genetic family hierarchy. Take a banking situation, for example. A general bank account class is used to define variables, such as an account number and account balance, and member functions, such as deposit, that are common to all bank accounts. Then, classes that define a checking account, super-now account, and savings account can all be derived from the bank account **base** class. This way, they will inherit the account number and balance members as well as the deposit function of the general bank account class. Although the derived classes may have their own unique members, they all include the bank account base class as part of their structure. Thus, a general bank account class would be at the top of a banking class hierarchy. This idea is illustrated by the hierarchy diagram in Figure 10-1.

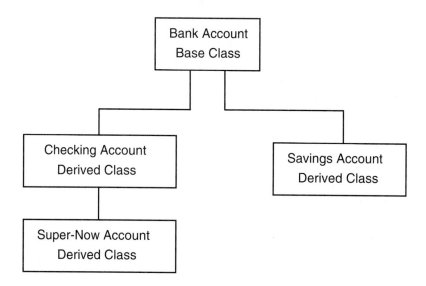

Figure 10-1   The *Checking* and *Savings* classes are derived from the *Bank Account* base class, which has data and function members common to both of these derived classes. The *Super-Now* class is derived from the *Checking* class and will inherit data and function members from both the *Checking* and *Bank Account* classes.

In fact, the left side of the hierarchy diagram in Figure 10-1 shows two levels of inheritance. The *Bank Account* class is inherited by both the *Checking* class and the *Savings* class. In addition, the *Checking* class is inherited by the *Super-Now* class. Notice that the *Super-Now* class inherits the *Bank Account* class indirectly through the *Checking* class. A family of classes related like this is referred to as a ***class hierarchy***.

PROGRAMMING TIP

The important link between a derived class and its base class is the IS-A link. The IS-A relationship must exist if inheritance is used properly. For instance, a checking account IS-A bank account. A super-now account IS-A checking account. However, a savings account IS **NOT** A checking account; it IS-A banking account. Thus, a savings account should *not* be derived from a checking account, but a more general bank account class. Always consider the IS-A link when creating inheritance. If there is no IS-A relationship, inheritance should not be used.

 Quick Check

1. A parent class is called a _____ class in C++.

2. A child class is called a _____ class in C++.

3. A collection of classes with common inherited members is called a _____.

4. List at least two reasons for using inheritance.

5. True or false: The proper use of inheritance would allow a line class to be derived from a point class.

6. True or false: The proper use of inheritance would allow a pixel class to be derived from a point class.

7. True or false: The proper use of inheritance would allow a pickup truck class to be derived from a truck class.

10-2 DECLARING AND USING DERIVED CLASSES

A derived class is declared using the following format:

FORMAT FOR DECLARING DERIVED CLASSES

class <derived class>:**public** <base class>
{
  <Derived Class Member Functions>

  <Derived Class Member Data>
}; //END CLASS

Let's illustrate inheritance via the classes of bank accounts shown in Figure 10-1. Look at the figure again. You see that the *Checking* and *Savings* classes are derived from the *Bank Account* base class, and the *Super-Now* class is derived from the *Checking* class. Here is how we will set up the various account classes:

Bank Account Class

The *Bank Account* class is at the top of the hierarchy diagram and, therefore, will be the base class for the entire family. It will contain member data and functions that are common to all types of bank accounts. The structure of this class will be as follows:

Function Members
- A function to make deposits.
- A function to access the account number.
- A function to access the account balance.

Data Members
- An account number.
- An account balance.

Checking Account Class

The *Checking* account class will inherit the *Bank Account* class members. In addition, it will contain the following members:

Function Members
- A constructor function to initialize the *Checking* account data members.
- A function that will cash a check by receiving a check amount and debit the account balance accordingly.

Data Members
- A minimum balance value that will dictate when a per-check charge is to be made.
- A value that will be charged on each check cashed when the account balance is less than the minimum required balance.

Super-Now Checking Account Class

A super-now acount is simply an interest-bearing checking account. As a result, this class will inherit the *Checking* account class members and, therefore, will also inherit the *Bank Account* class members. In addition, the *Super-Now* account class will contain the following members:

Function Members
- A constructor function to initialize the *Super-Now* checking account data members.
- A function that will credit interest to the account if the balance is above the required minimum.

Data Members
- An annual interest rate value that is credited to the account balance on a monthly basis, if the account balance remains above a minimum required level.

Savings Account Class

The savings account class is derived from the original *Bank Account* base class. In addition to the *Bank Account* class members, the *Savings* account class will contain the following:

Function Members
- A constructor function to initialize the *Savings* account data members.
- A function that will credit interest to the account.
- A function that will debit the account for a withdrawal.

Data Members
  • An annual interest rate value that is credited to the account balance on a monthly basis.

Now, we begin our program construction by declaring our *Bank Account* base class, as follows:

//BANK ACCOUNT HEADER FILE (account.h)

#ifndef ACCOUNT_H
#define ACCOUNT_H

//BANK ACCOUNT BASE CLASS DECLARATION
class BankAccount
{
public:
  void Deposit(float Dep);   //ADD DEPOSIT
  int AccountNum();   //RETURN ACCOUNT NUMBER
  float CurrentBalance();   //RETURN ACCOUNT BALANCE

protected:
  int AccountNumber;   //ACCOUNT NUMBER
  float Balance;   //ACCOUNT BALANCE
}; //END BankAccount
#endif

First, you see that the class declaration is provided in a header file called *account.h*. Next, you see three preprocessor directives: *#ifndef* and *#define* at the beginning of the file and *#endif* at the end of the file. These directives are required because this header file will be included in several additional files. The specific purpose of these directives will be discussed shortly. Looking at the *BankAccount* class declaration, you see that it contains three function members and two data members. The three public functions are *Deposit()*, *AccountNum()*, and *CurrentBalance()*. The *Deposit()* function will be used to make a deposit to the account. The *AccountNum()* and *CurrentBalance()* functions are access functions that are used to retrieve the account number and balance, respectively. You might be wondering why there is no constructor function to initialize the data members of the class. Well, when inheritance is used properly, there are no objects created for the base class. When no objects are created for a class, the class is called an **abstract class**. An abstract class never needs a constructor, because there will be no objects created for it. Only the derived classes will have objects, and the constructors will be placed in each of the derived classes. These constructors will be used to initialize the data members inherited from the base class. You will see how this works shortly.

The data members of the *BankAccount* base class are *AccountNumber* and *Balance*. Notice that they are declared as ***protected members*** using the keyword **protected**.

A ***protected member*** of a class is a member that is accessible to both the base class and any derived classes of the base class in which it is declared. Thus, a protected member of a base class is accessible to any class within the class family, but not accessible to things outside the class family.

You could say that a protected member of a base class has accessibility that is somewhere between that of a private member and a public member. If a member is a private member of a base class, it is *not* accessible to a derived class. However, a protected member of a base class is accessible to any derived classes. On the other hand, a protected member is "protected" from being accessed outside of the class family, thereby preserving information hiding within the family. Next, we develop an implementation file, called *account.cpp*, for the base class, as follows:

```
//ACCOUNT IMPLEMENTATION FILE (account.cpp)

#include "account.h"      //FOR BankAccount CLASS

//IMPLEMENTATION FOR Deposit() FUNCTION
void BankAccount :: Deposit(float Amount)
{
  Balance += Amount;
} //END BankAccount()

//IMPLEMENTATION FOR AccountNum() FUNCTION
int BankAccount :: AccountNum()
{
  return  AccountNumber;
} //END Deposit()

//IMPLEMENTATION FOR CurrentBalance() FUNCTION
float BankAccount :: CurrentBalance()
{
  return  Balance;
} //END CurrentBalance()
```

The function implementations shown in this file should be self-explanatory.

Now, let's declare our first derived class. This class, called *Checking,* will be derived from the *BankAccount* class, as follows:

```
//CHECKING ACCOUNT HEADER FILE (checking.h)

#ifndef CHECKING_H
#define CHECKING_H

#include "account.h"      //FOR BankAccount CLASS

//CHECKING ACCOUNT DERIVED CLASS DECLARATION
class Checking:public BankAccount
{
public:
  Checking(int AcctNum = 0000,
           float Bal = 0,                //CONSTRUCTOR
           float Min = 1000,
           float Chg = .5);
  void CashCheck(float Amt);             //CASH A CHECK

protected:
  float Minimum;                         //MINIMUM BALANCE TO
                                         //AVOID CHECK CHARGE

  float Charge;                          //PER-CHECK CHARGE
}; //END Checking
#endif
```

Again, the *Checking* class declaration is coded as a header file. The header file name is *checking.h.* Looking at the class declaration, you see that the *Checking* class is derived from the *BankAccount* class. This is indicated by the colon between the derived class (*Checking*) and the base class (*BankAccount*) in the class declaration. The base class header file (*account.h*) must be included in this file to make the declaration. Furthermore, notice the use of the keyword **public** prior to the base class name. This designation makes the *BankAccount* class a public base class to the derived *Checking* class.

> A **public base class** allows all public members of the base class to be public in the derived class.

When a base class is designated as **public** in the derived class declaration, the inherited members of the public base class maintain their access level in the derived class. Thus, the inherited protected members remain protected, and the inherited public members remain public in the derived class. In our example, the public members of the *BankAccount* class are the *Deposit()*, *AccountNum()*, and *CurrentBalance()* functions. The use of the keyword **public** prior to the base class name, *BankAccount*, in the derived *Checking* class declaration makes all of these functions public to the *Checking* class just as if they were declared as part of the public section of the *Checking* class. Without the use of the keyword **public,** the public functions of the *BankAccount* class would *not* be accessible to any program using an object of the *Checking* class. In other words, without the base class being public, an application program could not call any of the base class functions via a derived class object.

For example, suppose an application program defines an object called *JohnDoe* for the *Checking* derived class, like this:

Checking JohnDoe;

If the *BankAccount* base class is not made public, then a message to its *CurrentBalance()* function via the *JohnDoe* object would cause a compiler error. Thus, the statement

JohnDoe.CurrentBalance();

would not compile, because *CurrentBalance()* is not public for *Checking*.

Now, back to the *Checking* class declaration. Two member functions are declared for the *Checking* class: *Checking()* and *CashCheck()*. The *Checking()* function is a constructor that is used to initialize all four data members of the class. (Why does this class have four data members, when only two are shown in the foregoing declaration?) Notice that each data member has a default value. The *CashCheck()* function is used to debit the account balance by cashing a check.

You see that the *Checking* class has two protected members, *Minimum* and *Charge*. The *Minimum* data member will be used to store a minimum balance value, whereby no per-check charge is made if the account balance is above the stored minimum value. The *Charge* data member will be used to store a per-check charge for writing checks if the account balance is less than *Minimum*. Notice that both *Minimum* and *Charge* are designated as protected members, because they will be inherited by the *Super-Now* class (see Figure 10-1).

Of course, because *Checking* is derived from *BankAccount*, the protected *BankAccount* class members, *AccountNumber* and *Balance*, are inherited by the *Checking* class. Thus, *Checking* actually has four data members, *AccountNumber* and *Balance*, which are inherited from *BankAccount*, as well as *Minimum* and *Charge*, which are declared in *Checking*.

PROGRAMMING TIP

You will avoid confusion about when to use the keywords **protected** and **public** relative to inheritance if you remember the following points:

- Use the keyword **protected** in a base class declaration if you want to allow access to private members of the base class by the derived class. The protected members will be accessible within the class family, but not outside of the family.
- Use the keyword **public** when declaring a derived class if you want the public members of the base class to be public for the derived class.

The **protected** and **public** options are provided in C++ to provide flexibility during inheritance. With the proper use of these options, you can specify precisely which base class members are to be inherited by the derived classes. If you do not want the private members of a base class inherited, do not protect the private class members of the base class. If you do not want the public members of the base class inherited, do not use the keyword **public** in the derived class declaration.

Next, we need to construct an implementation file for the *Checking* class. Let's call the file *checking.cpp*. Here it is:

```
//CHECKING IMPLEMENTATION FILE (checking.cpp)
#include "checking.h"    //FOR Checking CLASS
#include <iostream.h>

//IMPLEMENTATION FOR Checking() CONSTRUCTOR
Checking :: Checking (int AcctNum, float Bal, float Min, float Chg)
{
  AccountNumber = AcctNum;
  Balance = Bal;
  Minimum = Min;
  Charge = Chg;
} //END Checking()

//IMPLEMENTATION FOR CashCheck() FUNCTION
void Checking :: CashCheck (float Amt)
{
  if (Amt > Balance)                         //TEST FOR OVERDRAW
    cout << "Cannot cash check, account overdrawn. << endl ";
```

```
    else                            //CASH CHECK
        if (Balance < Minimum)      //DEBIT BALANCE WITH
            Balance -= Amt + Charge;  //CHECK AMOUNT AND CHARGE
        else                        //DEBIT BALANCE WITH
            Balance -= Amt;         //CHECK AMOUNT
} //END CashCheck()
```

As you can see, the *Checking()* constructor function sets the values of *AccountNumber*, *Balance*, *Minimum*, and *Charge* from values received by the function when an object is defined for the class. Recall that a class constructor is automatically called when an object is defined for the class. Of course, if values are not provided in the object definition, the data members are initialized to their respective default values. The *CashCheck()* function receives an amount (*Amt*) from the calling object and generates an error message if this amount exceeds the account balance. Otherwise, the check is cashed, and the account balance is debited accordingly. Notice that a check-cashing charge is applied if the amount of the check is less than the required minimum balance.

Looking back at Figure 10-1, you see that a *SuperNow* class is derived from the *Checking* class. A super-now account is one where you get interest on your checking account if you maintain a minimum balance. In addition, no per-check charge is made if the balance stays above the minimum. This is a perfect place to declare a derived class of the *Checking* class, because the *SuperNow* class can inherit the *Minimum* and *Charge* data members as well as the *CashCheck()* function of the *Checking* class. So, let's develop a header file for the *SuperNow* class and call it *supernow.h*. Here's one that will work:

```
//SUPER-NOW ACCOUNT HEADER FILE (supernow.h)
#include "checking.h"    //FOR Checking CLASS

//SUPER-NOW ACCOUNT DERIVED CLASS DECLARATION
class  SuperNow:public Checking
{
public:
  SuperNow(int AcctNum = 0,
           float Bal = 0,              //CONSTRUCTOR
           float Min = 5000,
           float Chg = .5,
           float Rate = 12);
  void AddInterest();                  //ADD INTEREST TO BALANCE
protected:
  float InterestRate;                  //ANNUAL INTEREST RATE
}; //END SuperNow
```

First, you see that the *checking.h* header file is included, because the *SuperNow* class is derived from this class. The *SuperNow* class declaration uses the keyword **public** so that the public functions of *Checking* are inherited by *SuperNow*. There are two additional functions declared for this class: the *SuperNow()* constructor function, which initializes the data members of the class; and the *AddInterest()* function, which will credit the account balance with interest at a rate specified by the *InterestRate* data member.

The only data member unique to this class is *InterestRate*, which specifies the annual interest rate to be applied to the account. However, through inheritance, there are four additional data members. What are they? Well, *AccountNumber* and *Balance* are inherited from the *BankAccount* class via the *Checking* class, and *Minimum* and *Charge* are inherited directly from the *Checking* class. Here is the implementation file for the class:

```
//SUPER-NOW IMPLEMENTATION FILE (supernow.cpp)

#include "supernow.h"    //FOR SuperNow CLASS

//IMPLEMENTATION FOR SUPER-NOW CONSTRUCTOR
SuperNow :: SuperNow (int AcctNum,
                      float Bal,
                      float Min,
                      float Chg,
                      float Rate)
{
  AccountNumber = AcctNum;
  Balance = Bal;
  Minimum = Min;
  Charge = Chg;
  InterestRate = Rate;
} //END SuperNow()

//IMPLEMENTATION FOR AddInterest() FUNCTION
void SuperNow :: AddInterest()
{
  float Interest;
  if (Balance >= Minimum)
  {
    Interest = Balance * (InterestRate/12/100);
    Balance += Interest;
  } //END IF
} //END AddInterest()
```

The file is called *supernow.cpp*. As you can see, the *SuperNow()* constructor function initializes all class data members. The *AddInterest()* function adds monthly interest to the account if the account balance is greater than or equal to the minimum required balance.

The last class that we need to declare is the *Savings* account class. Here's the declaration:

```
//SAVINGS ACCOUNT HEADER FILE (savings.h)
#include "account.h"     //FOR BankAccount CLASS

//SAVINGS ACCOUNT DERIVED CLASS DECLARATION
class Savings: public BankAccount
{
public:
  Savings( int AcctNum = 0,
             float Bal = 0,                //CONSTRUCTOR
             float Rate = 12.0);
  void AddInterest();                     //ADD INTEREST TO BALANCE
  void Withdraw(float Amt);               //SUBTRACT WITHDRAWAL

protected:
  float InterestRate;                     //ANNUAL INTEREST RATE
}; //END Savings
```

There are three additional functions defined for the *Savings* class. The *Savings()* constructor function is used to initialize the class data members. The *AddInterest()* function is used to credit the account balance with monthly interest earnings. The *Withdraw()* function is used to debit the account balance when a savings withdrawal is made. Moreover, because the *Savings* class is derived from the *BankAccount* class, it inherits the *Deposit()* function.

The *Savings* class also inherits the *AccountNumber* and *Balance* data members from the *BankAccount* class. In addition, an *InterestRate* data member is defined for this class. The *InterestRate* data member will store an annual savings account interest rate value.

Here is the associated implementation file:

```
//SAVINGS IMPLEMENTATION FILE (savings.cpp)
#include "savings.h"     //FOR Savings CLASS

//IMPLEMENTATION FOR Savings() CONSTRUCTOR
Savings :: Savings(int AcctNum, float Bal, float Rate)
{
  AccountNumber = AcctNum;
```

```
  Balance = Bal;
  InterestRate = Rate;
} //END Savings()

//IMPLEMENTATION FOR Withdraw() FUNCTION
void Savings :: Withdraw(float Amt)
{
  Balance -= Amt;
} //END Withdraw()

//IMPLEMENTATION FOR AddInterest() METHOD
void Savings :: AddInterest()
{
  float Interest;
  Interest = Balance * (InterestRate/12/100);
  Balance += Interest;
} //END AddInterest()
```

The function implementations should be self-explanatory by now. Notice, however, that this *AddInterest()* function differs from the *AddInterest()* function in the *SuperNow* class. The *Savings* class *AddInterest()* function does not depend on a minimum balance, whereas the *SuperNow* class *AddInterest()* function does.

We can use the **Venn diagram** shown in Figure 10-2 to summarize the bank account class family hierarchy. Notice how the class inheritance patterns can be seen by the intersections between the classes.

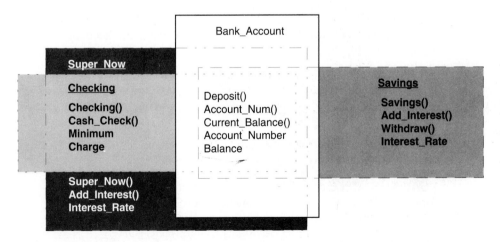

Figure 10-2   A Venn diagram of the bank account class family hierarchy.

Finally, we need an application file to exercise our class family. Here is one that will demonstrate most of the family features:

```
//BANKING APPLICATION FILE (banking.cpp)

#include "account.h"      //FOR BankAccount CLASS
#include "checking.h"     //FOR Checking CLASS
#include "supernow.h"     //FOR SuperNow CLASS
#include "savings.h"      //FOR Savings CLASS
#include <iostream.h>     //FOR cin AND cout

void main()
{
//DEFINE BANKING ACCOUNT OBJECTS
   Checking BjarneStroustrup1(0001);
   SuperNow JohnMcCarthy1(0002);
   Savings GraceHopper1(0003);
   Checking GraceHopper2(0004);

//MONTHLY CHECKING ACCOUNT TRANSACTIONS
   BjarneStroustrup1.Deposit(1500);
   BjarneStroustrup1.CashCheck (500.00);
   BjarneStroustrup1.CashCheck (500.00);
   BjarneStroustrup1.CashCheck (700.75);
   BjarneStroustrup1.CashCheck (200.00);
   GraceHopper2.Deposit(2500);
   GraceHopper2.CashCheck(25.75);
   GraceHopper2.CashCheck(75.25);

//MONTHLY SUPER-NOW ACCOUNT TRANSACTIONS
   JohnMcCarthy1.Deposit(2000.00);
   JohnMcCarthy1.CashCheck(200.00);

//MONTHLY SAVINGS ACCOUNT TRANSACTIONS
   GraceHopper1.Deposit(2000.00);
   GraceHopper1.Withdraw(350);

//MONTHLY REPORT OF ACCOUNT BALANCES
   cout.setf(ios::fixed | ios::showpoint);
   cout.precision(2);
   JohnMcCarthy1.AddInterest();
   GraceHopper1.AddInterest();
   cout << "\t\t\tAccount Balances" << endl << endl;
```

```
    cout << "Account Number:  "
         << BjarneStroustrup1.AccountNum()
         << "\tBjarne Stroustrup:  $"
         << BjarneStroustrup1.CurrentBalance() << endl;

    cout << "Account Number:  "
         << JohnMcCarthy1.AccountNum()
         << "\tJohn McCarthy:  $"
         << JohnMcCarthy1.CurrentBalance() << endl;

    cout << "Account Number:  "
         << GraceHopper1.AccountNum()
         << "\tGraceHopper:  $"
         << GraceHopper1.CurrentBalance() << endl;

    cout << "Account Number:  "
         << GraceHopper2.AccountNum()
         << "\tGraceHopper:  $"
         << GraceHopper2.CurrentBalance() << endl;
} //END main()
```

The application file is called *banking.cpp* and begins by including all of the class header files. The class header files must be included because the respective class objects are defined in this application file. Looking at function *main()* within the file, you see that several objects are defined for the various banking account classes. The object name corresponds to the customer name. A suffix is added to the customer name so that the same customer can have more than one bank account. For instance, you see that *GraceHopper1* is a checking account object, and *GraceHopper2* is a savings account object. Notice also that a unique account number is specified when each object is defined. As a result, the customer account number in the base class is initialized with this value. All other data members will take on their respective default values, because only the account number value is specified during the object definition.

Next, monthly transactions are listed for each type of account. Can you determine what should happen in each transaction? Finally, a monthly balance report of each account is generated on the display monitor. What will be the balance for each account at the end of the month, using the indicated transactions in the order that they appear?

A project file is needed to efficiently develop such a program in C++. For this program, the project file would reference all the *.cpp* implementation files and the *.cpp* application file.

Single versus Multiple Inheritance

Up to this point, we have been dealing with single inheritance. Actually, there are two types of inheritance possible: ***single inheritance*** and ***multiple inheritance***. Single inheritance occurs when the inherited class members can be traced back to a single parent class. The type of inheritance depicted in Figure 10-1 is single inheritance. Multiple inheritance occurs when the inherited class members can be traced back to more than one parent class. As an example of multiple inheritance, consider the *iostream.h* header file that you have been including in your programs to use the *cout* and *cin* objects. The *iostream.h* header file declares the *iostream* class. This class is derived from two parent classes: *istream* and *ostream*. The *istream* class provides the members necessary for formatted input, and the *ostream* class provides the members necessary for formatted output.

As a result of multiple inheritance, the *iostream* class inherits both the required input and output members. In addition, the *istream* and *ostream* classes are derived from a single class called *ios*. The *ios* base class provides file operations common to both input and output and maintains internal flags used by *istream* and *ostream*. Single inheritance allows both *istream* and *ostream* to inherit these common members. The diagram in Figure 10-3 illustrates the *ios* family hierarchy. Here, we have single inheritance from *ios* to *istream/ostream* and multiple inheritance from *istream/ostream* to *iostream*.

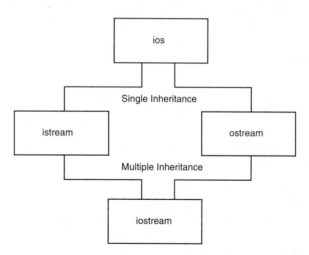

Figure 10-3 Single inheritance exists between the *ios* class and the *istream/ostream* classes. Multiple inheritance occurs between the *istream/ostream* classes and the *iostream* class.

Using *#ifndef* : An Implementation Detail

To close this section, I need to discuss the *#ifndef* preprocessor directive as promised earlier. You observed the use of this directive along with the *#define* and *#endif* directives in the *BankAccount* and *Checking* class declarations. These classes are base classes, so they need to be included as header files in more than one file. For example, *account.h* is included in *checking.h*, *savings.h*, and *banking.h* files. Because *account.h* provides the declaration for the *BankAccount* class, the compiler sees multiple declarations for this class via the multiple include directives. It's as if you defined a variable several times in a single source file. Such an oversight causes a "multiple declaration for…" compiler error. The *BankAccount* class must be included in multiple files for inheritance purposes, so you must tell the compiler that you are only declaring it once. This is the purpose of the *#ifndef* directive. So, always use the following format when declaring base classes in C++:

DECLARING BASE CLASSES IN C++

#ifndef <HEADER FILE NAME> _H
#define <HEADER FILE NAME> _H

< BASE CLASS DECLARATION>

#endif

Consult your compiler reference manual if you need more information on the *#ifndef* directive.

 Quick Check

1. True or false: When declaring a derived class, the derived class is listed first followed by a colon and the base class.

2. True or false: A public base class allows its public members to be used by any of its derived classes.

3. True or false: A protected base class member is protected from any use by the derived classes of that base class.

4. When base class header files are included in multiple implementation and application files, you must use the _____ directive to avoid "multiple declaration" compile errors.

5. What would be wrong with deriving the *Savings* class from the *Super_Now* class in the program discussed in this section?

6. What type of inheritance occurs when all the inherited members in a family can be traced back to more than one parent class?

10-3 POLYMORPHISM AND DYNAMIC BINDING

In the Chapter 9 introduction, it was stated that there were four concepts central to OOP: encapsulation with data hiding, inheritance, polymorphism, and dynamic binding. We have thoroughly explored the first two. For completeness, we will now briefly discuss the latter two concepts of polymorphism and dynamic binding.

Polymorphism

The term "polymorphic" is Greek meaning "of many forms." Polymorphism can be associated with functions or objects, as shown in the following definitions:

A *polymorphic* function is one that has the same name for different classes of the same family, but has different implementations for the various classes.

A *polymorphic* object is one that has the same name as objects of other classes in a class hierarchy so that each object, although related through a common base class, may have different behavior.

As you can see, polymorphism allows functions of the same name and objects of the same name to behave differently within a class family. You have just seen an example of a polymorphic function in our bank account class family. Can you identify which function it is from the class header files? You're right if you thought the *AddInterest()* function. Notice that this function is defined in both the *SuperNow* and *Savings* classes. The function interface is identical in both classes; however, the implementation is different in each class. In effect, we are hiding alternative operations behind the common *AddInterest()* interface. This means that the two objects defined for these classes will respond to the common operation, *AddInterest()*, in different ways. Languages that do not support polymorphism, such as Pascal and C, require large switch/case statements to implement this effect.

Polymorphism allows objects to be more independent, even though they are members of the same class family. Moreover, new classes can be added to the family without changing existing ones. This allows systems to evolve over time, meeting the needs of a changing application. Consider a word processing program where the system is required to print many different types of documents. Recall from Chapter 9 that many such programs employ classes to define the structure and behavior of a given type of document. Each document class will have a *Print()* function to print a specific document in its correct format. Such a function would be a polymorphic function, because it would have a common interface, but behave differently for different document objects.

Polymorphism is accomplished using overloaded functions or *virtual functions*. Overloaded functions were discussed earlier in Chapters 7 and 9. However, virtual functions are something new. The difference between the two has to do with the different techniques that are used by C++ to call the function. Overloaded functions are called using *static binding*, and virtual functions are called using *dynamic binding*.

Dynamic versus Static Binding

Binding relates to the actual time when the code for a given function is attached, or bound, to the function.

> *Dynamic*, or *late*, *binding* occurs when a polymorphic function is defined for several classes in a family but the actual code for the function is not attached, or bound, until execution time. A polymorphic function that is dynamically bound is called a *virtual* function.

Dynamic binding is implemented in C++ through *virtual functions*. With dynamic binding, the selection of code to be executed when a virtual function is called is delayed until execution time. This means that when a virtual function is called, the executable code determines at run time which version of the function to call. Remember, virtual functions are polymorphic and, therefore, have different implementations for different classes in the family.

Static binding occurs when a polymorphic function is defined for several classes in a family and the actual code for the function is attached, or bound, at compile time. Overloaded functions are statically bound.

Static binding, on the other hand, occurs when the function code is "bound" at compile time. This means that when a nonvirtual function is called, the compiler determines at compile time which version of the function to call. Overloaded functions are statically bound, whereas virtual functions are dynamically bound. With overloaded functions, the compiler can determine which function to call based on the number of and data classes of the function parameters. However, virtual functions have the same interface within a given class family. Therefore, pointers must be used during run time to determine which function to call. Any ideas on how this is accomplished? (*Hint:* Remember that each function can be traced to its correct class via its calling object's unique ***this*** pointer.) Fortunately, you don't have to worry about how the binding is accomplished, because this is taken care of automatically by the compiler.

You should be aware that virtual functions are most often declared in a base class in C++ using the keyword **virtual**. When a function is declared as a virtual function in a base class, the compiler knows that the base class definition might be overridden in a derived class. The base class definition is overridden by defining a different implementation for the same function in a derived class. If the base class definition is not overridden in a given derived class, then the base class definition is available to the derived class.

 Quick Check

1. True or false: A virtual function is polymorphic.

2. True or false: All polymorphic functions are virtual functions.

3. True or false: The virtual function interface is identical for each version of the function in a given class family.

4. Overloaded functions are _____ bound.

5. Virtual functions are _____ bound.

6. The implementation code for a dynamically bound function is determined at _____.

CHAPTER SUMMARY

Inheritance is an important property of object-oriented programming that allows one class, called a derived class, to share the structure and behavior of another class, called a base class. The derived class should always be related to its base class via the IS-A relationship. There is both single inheritance and multiple inheritance. Single inheritance occurs when the inherited class members can be traced to a single base class. Multiple inheritance occurs when the inherited class members can be traced back to more than one base class. You control the amount of data member inheritance by designating the members as private, protected, or public in the base class declaration. You control the amount of function inheritance by designating the base class as public or nonpublic (by default) in the derived class declaration.

Polymorphism has to do with functions and objects that have the same name, but different behavior within a class family. Polymorphism allows functions and objects to be more independent and class families to be more flexible. Overloaded functions and virtual functions are polymorphic. Overloaded functions are statically bound to their code during compile time, whereas virtual functions are dynamically bound to their code during run time.

QUESTIONS AND PROBLEMS

Questions

1. Define the following terms:
    Base Class
    Derived Class
    Inheritance
    Single Inheritance
    Multiple Inheritance
    IS-A
    Polymorphism
    Dynamic Binding
    Static Binding

2. Suggest several real-world applications for the use of inheritance.

3. What relationship must be considered between a potential derived class and its base class when developing inheritance?

4. Given a base class called *Point*, write the class declaration header line for a derived class called *Pixel*. Assume that the functions in *Point* are to be public in *Pixel*.

5. Explain how a protected class member differs from a private class member and a public class member.

6. When should you use the keyword **public** in a derived class declaration?

7. When should you use the #*ifndef* directive in a class header file?

8. Why is a virtual function polymorphic?

9. Explain the difference between static binding and dynamic binding.

Problems

Least Difficult

1. Determine the output generated by the application program (*banking.cpp*) given in this chapter.

2. Code the class header and implementation files for the banking program given in this chapter. Then, write your own application program to exercise the class family in different ways. See if you can predict the results of your banking transactions.

More Difficult

3. Add a *CreditCard* class to the *BankAccount* class family developed in this chapter. The *CreditCard* class should inherit the *BankAccount* class directly. Provide functions to debit monthly charges and interest from the account balance. Write an application program to exercise a *CreditCard* object and report the balance due.

4. Declare a *ResistorCircuit* base class that contains the following members:

Function Members

- A function that will allow the user to enter the resistor values and the number of resistors in the circuit.

- A function that will display the resistor values along with the equivalent resistance of the circuit.

Data Members

- The resistor values stored in an array.
- The number of resistors in the circuit.
- The equivalent resistance of the circuit.

5. Declare two derived classes called *SeriesCircuit* and *ParallelCircuit* that inherit the *ResistorCircuit* class declared in problem 4. Provide the following functions in these derived classes:

SeriesCircuit( ):

A function to calculate the equivalent resistance of a series circuit.

ParallelCircuit( ):

A function to calculate the equivalent resistance of a parallel circuit.

6. Write an application program that defines a series resistance object and a parallel resistance object from the classes declared in problems 4 and 5. Include statements in the program that will exercise the object functions to calculate circuit resistance of the respective objects.

11

POINTERS

INTRODUCTION
11-1 THE IDEA OF POINTERS
11-2 DEFINING POINTERS AND
      INITIALIZING POINTER DATA
  Static Pointers
  Dynamic Pointers
11-3 ACCESSING POINTER DATA AND
      POINTER ARITHMETIC
  Pointer Arithmetic
11-4 ARRAYS OF POINTERS ⇒
      INDIRECTION
11-5 USING POINTERS AS FUNCTION
      ARGUMENTS AND PARAMETERS
11-6 POINTERS TO FUNCTIONS

11-7 STRUCTURE AND OBJECT POINTERS
  Defining Structure Pointers
  Using the Pointer Operator to Access
    Structure Data
  Reading Information into a Structure
  Retrieving Information from Structures
  Defining Object Pointers
  Using the Pointer Operator to Send
    Messages to Objects
  Destructors
CHAPTER SUMMARY
QUESTIONS AND PROBLEMS
  Questions
  Problems

INTRODUCTION

Pointers are fundamental to programming in either the C or C++ language. A pointer represents a physical address in memory.

A ***pointer*** represents a physical memory address.

Although you may not have realized it, you have been working with pointers already. For instance, recall that an array name actually represents the memory address of the first element of an array. Furthermore, by preceding a variable identifier with an ampersand, &, you are representing the memory address of the variable. Therefore, an array name and a variable preceded with an ampersand are actually pointers. However, these pointers are ***constant pointers***, because the address to which they point can never be changed by the program. On the other hand, a ***variable pointer*** is a pointer whereby the address to which it points can be changed by the program. In this chapter, you will learn how to use variable pointers in preparation for their use in the chapters that follow. Pointers provide a powerful and efficient means of accessing data, especially when the data are part of a data structure, such as an array. This is an important topic, so stay with me.

11-1 THE IDEA OF POINTERS

Let's begin by comparing a pointer to a variable. Assume for a moment that *Value1* and *Value2* are defined as integer variables and initialized to the values of 10 and 20, respectively. Also, assume that *p1* and *p2* are defined as pointers. The boxes in Figure 11-1 illustrate these assumptions.

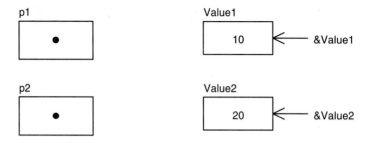

Figure 11-1   *p1* and *p2* are pointers, and *Value1* and *Value2* are integer variables.

In Figure 11-1, you see the boxes labeled *Value1* and *Value2* storing the integers 10 and 20, respectively. Now, you already know that *&Value1* and *&Value2* represent the memory *addresses* of the variables. Thus, *&Value1* locates the box containing the integer 10, and *&Value2* locates the box containing the 20. The boxes labeled *p1* and *p2* contain a dot, •, indicating that they do not point to anything at this time.

Because *p1* and *p2* are pointer variables, we can reassign them at any time to point to data in memory. For instance, we can assign the address of *Value1* to *p1* and the address of *Value2* to *p2*, like this:

```
p1 = &Value1;
p2 = &Value2;
```

There is no problem with these assignments because *p1*, *p2*, *&Value1*, and *&Value2* all represent memory addresses. What you get is illustrated by Figure 11-2(a).

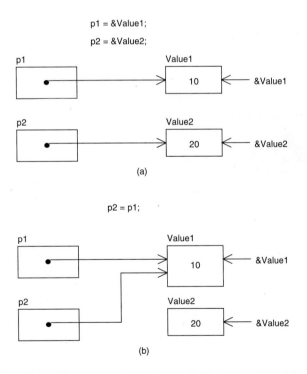

Figure 11-2 The effect of (a) assigning the address of a variable to a pointer, and (b) assigning a pointer to a pointer.

After these assignments, *p1* and *&Value1* both locate the value 10 in memory, and *p2* and *&Value2* locate the value 20 in memory. Likewise, both *p1* and *p2* are pointers, so we can assign *p1* to *p2*, like this:

p2 = p1;

The result of this assignment is illustrated in Figure 11-2(b). Notice now that *p1*, *p2*, and *&Value1* all locate the value 10. In fact, we can alter *p1* and *p2* to point to any address in memory, because they are variable pointers. However, we cannot alter *&Value1* or *&Value2*, because they are constant pointers, which cannot be altered.

It is important to note that in Figure 11-2(b), there is only one *Value1*; however, we have three pointers locating this value. Thus, if we change the value of *Value1*, there is still only one variable to be changed, not three. For instance, suppose we make the following assignment:

Value1 = 30;

After this assignment, *p1*, *p2*, and *&Value1* will all locate the new value, 30, in memory.

Quick Check

1. Suppose that *pchar* is a pointer to a character and *Character* is a character variable. Write a statement to make *pchar* point to the character stored in *Character*.

2. Write a statement that will make an integer pointer called *p1int* point to the same integer to which an integer pointer called *p2int* is pointing.

3. True or false: If *Character* is defined as a character variable, then *&Character* can be altered at any time.

4. True or false: If *pchar* is defined as a character pointer, then *pchar* can be altered at any time.

11-2 DEFINING POINTERS AND INITIALIZING POINTER DATA

To define a pointer, you must tell the compiler the class of data to which the pointer is pointing, just as you do when defining a variable. Here's the general format:

> ### *POINTER DEFINITION FORMAT*
>
> <data class being pointed to> *<pointer identifier>;

Here are some sample pointer definitions:

```
int  *IntegerPointer;
char *CharacterPointer;
float *FloatPointer;
```

The first definition says that *IntegerPointer* is a pointer to an integer value, the second says that *CharacterPointer* points to a character, and finally *FloatPointer* points to a floating-point value. Note the use of the asterisk, or star, in all the definitions. The star must immediately precede the pointer identifier. This is what tells the compiler that you are defining a pointer variable rather than a common variable. From now on, I will refer to a pointer variable as simply a pointer.

The *star*, *, in front of a pointer variable denotes "the contents of." In other words, *p1* is read as "the contents of the memory location where *p1* is pointing." In the preceding pointer definitions, the * indicates the data class to which the pointer is pointing. Thus, the definintion int *IntegerPointer says that the contents of memory to which *IntegerPointer* is pointing is an integer.

There are two ways to initialize a pointer to point to a value.

1. Allocating memory **statically** by defining a variable and then making the pointer point to the variable value.

2. Allocating memory **dynamically** and initializing the pointer to point to a value.

Static Pointers

Let's define a pointer to an integer and an integer variable as follows:

```
int *p1;
int Value;
```

Using these definitions, we can then make the following *static* assignments:

```
p1 = &Value;
*p1 = 25;
```

Figure 11-3 illustrates the results of the preceding operations. Pointer *p1* is defined as a pointer to an integer. Variable *Value* is defined as an integer variable. The first assignment makes *p1* point to the variable *Value*. The second assignment stores the value 25 in memory where *p1* is pointing. Notice the use of the star symbol, *, again. A star in front of a pointer variable means "the contents of." Therefore, the second assignment reads "Store the value 25 in the contents of memory to where *p1* is pointing." Of course, this is the same memory location as *&Value*. We can say that **p1* is an **alias** for the variable *Value*, because the integer value stored in *Value* can also be accessed via **p1*.

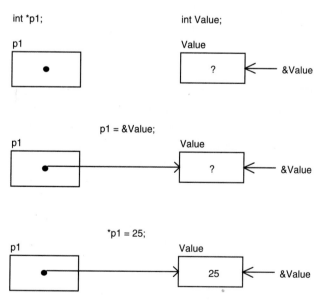

Figure 11-3   Initializing a static pointer.

There is no ambiguity in the use of the star to define a pointer and to initialize a pointer to point to a value. Both reference "the contents of." When defining a pointer, the ∗ indicates that "the contents of" memory pointed to by the pointer will be a given a data class. When initializing a pointer to point to a value, the ∗ indicates "the contents of" memory pointed to by the pointer will be a given value.

We say that this type of initialization is *static* because the allocation of memory used to store the value is fixed and cannot go away. Once the variable is defined, the compiler sets aside enough memory to store a value of the given data class. This memory remains reserved for this variable and cannot be used for anything else until the function in which the pointer is defined is terminated. In other words, you cannot *deallocate* the memory set aside for a variable. The pointer to that variable can be changed, but the amount of memory set aside for the variable remains.

DEBUGGING TIP

It is very easy to make incorrect assignments when working with pointers. For example, using the foregoing pointer definitions, the following three assignments will create an error:

```
*p1 = &Value;
p1 = Value;
p1 = 25;
```

In all cases, an attempt is made to "mix apples and oranges." In the first case, an attempt is made to assign an address (*&Value*) to a value, because *∗p1* is a value. In the second case, an attempt is made to assign a value (*Value*) to an address, because *p1* is an address. Likewise, in the third case, an attempt is made to assign a value to an address. The correct assignments would be

```
*p1 = Value;
p1 = &Value;
*p1 = 25;
```

Dynamic Pointers

The second way to initialize a pointer to point to a value is by allocating memory *dynamically*. By allocating memory dynamically, we mean to set aside memory when it is needed to store a value of a given data class. Then, once the value is no longer needed, we can deallocate the memory and make it available for other use by the system. Again we will define *p1* as an integer pointer, as follows:

int *p1;

Now, we can initialize *p1* dynamically to point to a value, like this:

p1 = new int;
*p1 = 25;

       Figure 11-4 illustrates the results of these operations.

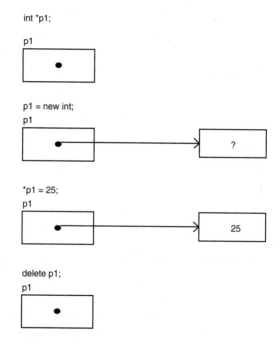

Figure 11-4   Initializing a dynamic pointer.

       This time, we did not need to first initialize *p1* to the address of a static variable. Rather, the **new** operator creates enough memory to hold an integer value pointed to by *p1*. Then, we stored the value 25 in that memory area. Once memory is allocated dynamically like this, we can deallocate the same memory area by using the **delete** operator, as follows:

delete p1;

This operation will free up the memory pointed to by *p1* for other use by the program and/or system. It is important to note that the **delete** operator *does not* delete the pointer; it simply releases the memory area to which the pointer points. Therefore, after the preceding statement is executed, *p1* still exists as a pointer that does not point to anything, but can be again initialized to point to another integer by using the **new** operator.

The **new** operator is used to dynamically allocate memory for pointer data, and the **delete** operator is used to deallocate memory pointed to by a pointer.

Example 11-1

Determine the output generated by the following program:

```
#include <iostream.h>    //FOR cout

void main()
{
//DEFINE TWO POINTERS AND A VARIABLE
    int *p1;
    int *p2;
    int Index;

//INITIALIZE POINTER DATA STATICALLY
    p1 = &Index;
    Index = 10;

//INITIALIZE POINTER DATA DYNAMICALLY
    p2 = new int;
    *p2 = 20;

//DISPLAY POINTER DATA
    cout << "The contents of memory pointed to by p1 is: " << *p1 << endl;
    cout << "The contents of memory pointed to by p2 is: " << *p2 << endl;

//DEALLOCATE MEMORY POINTED TO BY p2
    delete p2;
} //END main()
```

Solution

The output generated by the program is

```
The contents of memory pointed to by p1 is 10
The contents of memory pointed to by p2 is 20
```

Notice that the program initializes the *p1* pointer data statically and the *p2* pointer data dynamically. Both produce the same results; however, the memory pointed to by *p1* is set aside until the program terminates, whereas the memory pointed to by *p2* is deallocated immediately after the *cout* statement. Notice also how the pointer data are accessed in the *cout* statement. The ∗ is employed to indicate that "the contents of" memory pointed to by the pointer is to be displayed. What do you suppose would happen if the ∗ were omitted? Well, because a pointer is a memory address, you would see the actual memory address, in hex, assigned to the pointer. This leads us to our next topic.

 Quick Check

1. Define a static character pointer called *pchar* and a character variable called *Character*.

2. Write a statement to make *pchar* point to the variable *Character* defined in question 1.

3. Write a statement to initialize *pchar* defined in question 1 to the character 'A'.

4. True or false: The assignment *pchar* = 'Z' is legal, as long as *pchar* is defined as a character pointer.

5. When a pointer is initialized dynamically, the _____ operator must be used in the pointer definition.

6. Write the statements to initialize a dynamic character pointer called *pchar* to the value 'B'.

7. Write a statement that will deallocate the memory allocated in question 6.

8. True or false: When you deallocate pointer memory using the **delete** operator, the respective pointer is deleted.

11-3 ACCESSING POINTER DATA AND POINTER ARITHMETIC

You have already seen how to access the data pointed to by a pointer through the use of the star, ∗, operator. Remember, ∗*p* means "the contents of memory pointed to by *p."* Let's see how we can expand on this knowledge by using a pointer to a string. Consider the following pointer definition:

char *sptr = "HAL";

The foregoing definition creates a character pointer called *sptr*. In addition, the pointer data are initialized to the string "HAL". If you were to view the data stored to where *sptr* is pointing via a debugger, you would observe the following:

DEBUGGER RESULTS

Inspecting *sptr*

[0]   'H'
[1]   'A'
[2]   'L'
[3]   '\0'

As you can see, *sptr* locates the entire string in memory just as an array name locates an array in memory. In fact, you see that the compiler has placed the string in an array located by the variable pointer *sptr*. Now, what do you suppose you would see on the display after the following *cout* statements were executed?

cout << *sptr << endl;
cout << sptr[0] << endl;

Even though the pointer data are initialized to a string, *sptr* is still only a character pointer. Therefore, the first *cout* statement will display the single character 'H'. Likewise, the compiler has placed the string into an array pointed to by *sptr*, so the second statement will also produce the single character stored at index [0] in the array, which is the single character 'H'.

Next, what do you suppose will be displayed by the following?

cout << sptr << endl;

With this definition, *sptr* is simply a pointer to an array of characters. In other words, the compiler will treat it just like an array name when used like this. As a result, the foregoing statement will display the entire string "HAL". Remember, although *sptr* is treated just like an array name in this operation, it is different! When *sptr* is defined as a pointer to a character array, it is a variable pointer and therefore could be altered to point to another location in memory. On the other hand, if *sptr* were an array name, it would be a constant pointer and could not be altered to point to a different location.

Next, consider the following two statements:

```
cout << *(sptr + 1) << endl;
cout << (sptr + 1)[0] << endl;
```

The first statement is read "Display the contents of *sptr* + 1." Because *sptr* locates the first character in the array, (*sptr* + 1) must locate the second array character, right? Therefore, the contents of (*sptr* + 1) must be the character 'A'. This statement doesn't change the pointer location; it simply *offsets* the pointer for the purpose of the *cout* operation. The second statement will produce the same character 'A'. This statement would be read as "Display the character stored at index [0] of location (*sptr* + 1)." This time, the pointer is being treated just like an array name; however it might be a bit confusing, because the character 'A' is located at index [1] in the array. This is true relative to *sptr*, but relative to (*sptr* + 1), index [0] locates the second character in the array, which is the character 'A'. What character do you suppose is stored at (*sptr* + 1)[1] ? You're right if you thought the character 'L'. How about position (*sptr* + 2)[0] ? Again, you would be accessing the character 'L'. Think about it! These concepts are illustrated in Figure 11-5.

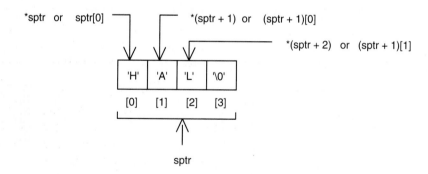

Figure 11-5   Accessing string pointer data.

Pointer Arithmetic

Unlike an array name, which is a constant pointer and cannot be altered, a pointer is a variable pointer, which can be altered. As a result, you can perform certain arithmetic operations on pointers.

Keep in mind that a pointer is an address. As a result, only those arithmetic operations that "make sense" are legal. You can add or subtract an integer constant to or from a pointer. Adding or subtracting an integer, say, *x*, to or from a pointer will produce a new pointer, which is *x* elements away from the original pointer.

Adding or subtracting a floating-point constant to or from a pointer would not make sense, considering that an address must result from the operation. Likewise, it wouldn't make sense to multiply or divide a pointer by a constant, considering that a pointer is an address.

Here is what you *should not* do:

- You should not add two pointers.
- You should not multiply two pointers.
- You should not divide two pointers.

 CAUTION

Performing arithmetic operations on pointers may be hazardous to your system! Pointers can be altered to point anywhere in the system memory, so you could accidentally make a pointer operate in an area of memory being used by the operating system for other system chores. The result of such an accident is usually a system crash, which can only be corrected by rebooting the system.

One thing you *can* do is subtract two pointers when both pointers are pointing to the same array. When you subtract two pointers that point to the same array, you get a constant value, which is the number of array positions, or elements, between the two pointers. So, if *p1* is a pointer that points to index [0] in an array, and *p2* is a pointer that points to index [5] in the same array, then *p2 – p1* will yield the value 5.

Legal arithmetic operations on pointers are ***scaled***. This means that when you perform pointer arithmetic, the compiler scales the result relative to the data class being pointed to, rather than bytes of memory. For instance, you know that an integer requires 2 bytes of storage, therefore requiring two memory addresses to store an integer value. So, if *iptr* is a pointer to an integer, then adding 1 to *iptr* yields a pointer that will point 2 bytes, or addresses, away from where *iptr* was originally pointing. Likewise, if *iptr1* points to index [1] in an integer array, and *iptr2* points to index [2] of the same integer array, then *iptr2 – iptr1* will yield the constant value 1, even though the two addresses being pointed to are 2 bytes from each other.

Example 11-2

Determine the output generated by the following program:

```
#include <iostream.h>    //FOR cout

void main()
{
//DEFINE THREE CHARACTER POINTERS AND
//INITIALIZE ONE TO A STRING
  char *sptr1;
  char *sptr2;
  char *sptr= "HAL";

//DISPLAY POINTER DATA
  cout << "*sptr --> " << *sptr << endl;
  cout << "sptr[0] --> "<< sptr[0] << endl;
  cout << "*(sptr + 1) --> " << *(sptr + 1) << endl;
  cout << "(sptr + 1)[0] --> " << (sptr + 1)[0] << endl;
  cout << "*(sptr + 2) --> " << *(sptr + 2) << endl;

//ADD ONE TO sptr AND OUTPUT STRING
  ++sptr;
  cout << "sptr --> " << sptr << endl;

//SUBTRACT ONE FROM sptr AND OUTPUT STRING
  --sptr;
  cout << "sptr --> " << sptr << endl;

//WEIRD
  for (int i = 0; i < 3; ++i)
    *(sptr + i) = *(sptr + i) + 1;
  cout << "sptr --> " <<  sptr << endl;

//INITIALIZE sptr1, sptr2 AND OUTPUT DIFFERENCE
  sptr1 = sptr;
  sptr2 = sptr + 2;

//OUTPUT sptr2 – sptr1
  cout << "sptr2 – spt1 = " << sptr2 – sptr1 << endl;
} //END main()
```

Solution

Here is what you would see on the display:

```
*sptr -->  H
```

```
sptr[0] --> H
*(sptr + 1) --> A
(sptr + 1)[0] --> A
*(sptr + 2) --> L
sptr --> AL
sptr --> HAL
sptr --> IBM
sptr2 - sptr1 = 2
```

The first five single character outputs demonstrate the operations discussed earlier. See if you can verify the output characters knowing that *sptr* is initialized to the string "HAL". The sixth output, "AL", results from adding 1 to *sptr* and then displaying the string located by *sptr*. Adding 1 to *sptr* yields a new pointer that points to the second character in the string. The seventh output, "HAL", is produced by subtracting 1 from *sptr* to make it point to its original location at the beginning of the string. The eighth output, "IBM", results from a **for** loop that adds 1 to each character in the string pointed to by *sptr*. The body of the **for** loop is the single statement *$*(sptr + i) = *(sptr + i) + 1$*. Think about what this statement does. When i is 0, the statement becomes *$*(sptr) = *(sptr) + 1$*. Doesn't this add one to the value pointed to by *sptr* and assign this sum back to the contents of *sptr*? Well, *$*sptr$* is the character 'H'. If you add one to this character value, you get the character 'I'. As a result, the first loop iteration replaces the character 'H' in *$*stpr$* with the character 'I'. Likewise, the second iteration replaces 'A' with 'B' and the third iteration replaces 'L' with 'M'. After the loop terminates, the string pointed to by *sptr* is "IBM", which can be verified by observing the output generated by the respective *cout* statement.

Finally, the last output is produced by initializing *sptr1* to point to the beginning of the string and *sptr2* to point to the end of the string. The output is the value 2, which is the number of elements between *sptr1* and *sptr2*.

 Quick Check

1. Define a string pointer called *pstring* and initialize it to the string "C++".

2. Write a statement to display the entire string in question 1.

3. Write a statement to display just the first character of the string in question 1.

4. Write a statement to display just the last character of the string in question 1.

5. Write a statement to display the last two characters of the string in question 1.

6. Suppose that *p1* is a pointer that points to index [5] of an array of double floating-point values, and *p2* is a pointer that points to index [15] of the same array. Then *p2 – p1* will yield the value _____.

11-4 ARRAYS OF POINTERS ⇒ INDIRECTION

We can easily define an array that stores pointers, thus creating an *array of pointers*. Here is how it's done:

```
char *PtrArray[2];
PtrArray[0] = "Dog";
PtrArray[1] = "Cat";
```

The first line of code defines an array of pointers to character data. The star in front of the array name is used to specify an array of pointers. The array size is 2, so this array holds two pointers, or addresses. This definition represents two levels of ***indirection***, because an array name is always a pointer and this pointer points to the pointers contained in the array.

> ***Indirection*** has to do with the levels of addressing it takes to access data.

The two lines of code following the array definition are used to initialize the array. The pointer at position [0] of this array is initialized to point to the string "Dog", and the pointer (address) contained at position [1] of the array is initialized to point to the string "Cat". Notice that the "pointer" is initialized to point to a given string.

Although the array is easily defined and initialized, interpreting the indirection gets a bit tricky. Study Figure 11-6 to get an idea of how the array data are accessed using pointers. First, you see that each position in the array is a pointer that locates an entire string. Thus, *PtrArray*[0] locates the string "Dog" and *PtrArray*[1]   locates the string "Cat". You also see that **PtrArray* and **(PtrArray + 1)* locate the same two strings, "Dog" and "Cat", respectively, because the *contents of PtrArray* is the address of the first string and the *contents of (PtrArray + 1)* is the address of the second string. What do you suppose is pointed to by **PtrArray + 1*? This statement offsets the contents of the first pointer by 1, resulting in a string pointer that points one character away from the original pointer. Thus, **PtrArray + 1* points to the string "og". Next, because

PtrArray locates the entire string "Dog", what do you suppose is located by *(PtrArray*[0])? You're right if you thought the first character, 'D', of the first string, "Dog". Likewise, *(PtrArray*[0] + 1) locates the second character, 'o', of this same string. How would you access the character 'C' in the second string? How about *(PtrArray*[1])? Extending this idea, *(PtrArray*[1] + 2) will locate the character 't' of the second string.

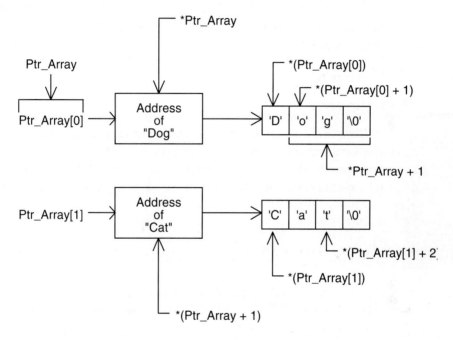

Figure 11-6 An array of pointers pointing to strings.

Let's look at a practical application for an array of pointers.

Example 11-3

Write a program to define an array of pointers, called *Names*, to strings. Initialize the array pointers to point to the strings "Andy", "Brenda", "Neil", "Lori", and "Doug", and display the strings using the array of pointers.

Solution

First, we must define an array of pointers and initialize the pointers to point to the given strings. This can be accomplished in one line, as follows:

```
char *Names[] = {"Andy", "Brenda", "Neil", "Lori", "Doug", NULL};
```

This defines an array of pointers called *Names*. The pointers point to character strings. There is no array size specified, so the number of pointers in the array depends on the number of initializing string values. The pointers are initialized to point to the five string values given in the problem statement. In addition, the last pointer in the array is initialized to point to **NULL**. The word **NULL** is predefined in the standard C++ library header files, such as *iostream.h* and *stdio.h*. Any pointer can be tested for equality or inequality to **NULL**. As a result, it can be used to terminate a loop that will display the string values. Here's such a loop:

```
int i = 0;
while (*(Names + i) != NULL)
{
   cout  << *(Names + i) << endl;
   ++i;
} //END WHILE
```

The **while** statement displays the strings pointed to by *(Names + i)*. Thus, the first loop iteration will display the string pointed to by *(Names + 0)*, which is the string "Andy". The second iteration will display the string pointed to by *(Names + 1)*, which is the string "Brenda", and so on. The loop terminates when *(Names + i)* points to **NULL**. In our example, this happens when *i* equals the value 5, because *(Names + 5)* was initialized as a pointer to **NULL**. Notice that the loop test is *(*(Names + i) != NULL)*. Here is the complete program:

```
//*********************************************************************************
//
//THIS PROGRAM WILL DEFINE AN ARRAY OF POINTERS TO POINT
//TO STRINGS AND THEN DISPLAY THE STRINGS USING POINTERS
//
//*********************************************************************************

#include <iostream.h>    //FOR cout

//DEFINE AND INITIALIZE ARRAY OF POINTERS TO STRINGS
char *Names[] = {"Andy", "Brenda", "Neil", "Lori", "Doug", NULL};

void main()
{
  int i = 0;

//DISPLAY NAMES IN ARRAY UNTIL NULL POINTER IS ENCOUNTERED
  while (*(Names + I) != NULL)
  {
   cout << *(Names + i) << endl;
   ++i;
  } //END WHILE
} //END main()
```

The output produced by the program is

Andy
Brenda
Neil
Lori
Doug

Quick Check

1. Define an array of pointers called *Courses* to point to the strings "Calc", "Assembler", and "C++".

2. What is located at *Courses* using the array in question 1?

3. What is located at *Courses*[2] using the array in question 1?

4. What is located at *Courses* + 2 using the array in question 1?

5. What is located at *(*Courses*[1] + 3)?

6. The concept of using several levels of addressing to access data is known as
    _____.

11-5 USING POINTERS AS FUNCTION ARGUMENTS AND PARAMETERS

When you use a pointer as an argument in a function call, you are passing the address that the pointer references to the function. Recall that when you pass an address to a function, you are passing by reference rather than by value. When passing by reference, any operations on the parameter variables within the function will alter the corresponding actual argument variables listed in the function call. Up to this point, you had only two ways to pass variables to a function by reference: (1) by using the ampersand symbol, &, prior to the parameter in the function header, or (2) by passing an array using an array name. Well, think about what you are doing in both cases. You are passing an *address* to the function, right? Because a pointer is an address, we can also pass by reference using a pointer variable. Consider the following program:

```
#include <iostream.h>        //FOR cout

//FUNCTION PROTOTYPE
void Swap(int *, int *);

void main()
{
  int Value1 = 10;
  int Value2 = 20;
  int *Pointer2 = &Value2;
  cout << "The values before the function call are " << Value1
      << " " << Value2 << endl;
  Swap(&Value1,Pointer2);
  cout << "The values after the function call are " << Value1
      << " " << Value2 << endl;
} //END main()

//FUNCTION WILL EXCHANGE THE TWO PARAMETER VALUES
void Swap(int *p1, int *p2)
{
  int Temp;
  Temp = *p1;
  *p1 = *p2;
  *p2 = Temp;
} //END Swap()
```

At the beginning of this program, a function called *Swap()* is prototyped to accept two integer pointers. Notice the syntax in the prototype. The int * specification means that the function expects to receive an integer pointer. Looking at the function definition at the end of the program, you see that the function simply exchanges the two integer values that it receives from the calling program. In function *main()*, you find that two integer variables are defined and initialized to the values of 10 and 20, respectively. Then, a pointer variable called *Pointer2* is defined to point to the value of *Value2*. In the function call, the address of *Value1* is passed using the ampersand symbol, &, as we did earlier in the text. In addition, the address of *Value2* is also passed as the second argument via pointer *Pointer2*. Therefore, both variables are passed by reference to the function. The function expects to "see" two addresses, because its prototype dictates that it will accept two pointers. The variables are passed by reference, so their values will be swapped by the function. Here is the output generated by the program:

The values before the function call are 10 20
The values after the function call are 20 10

  Look at the actual arguments and the prototype parameters again. You probably don't have any question about the second argument versus the second parameter, because both are pointers. But, what about the first argument versus the first parameter? Is there a problem here, because an & symbol is used for the argument and a * symbol is used for the corresponding parameter? No! Both are addresses of integers; therefore, there is no mismatch between the class of data being passed to the function and the class of data being received by the function.

  Next, let's see how strings can be passed to functions using pointers. Look at the following program:

```
#include <iostream.h>   //FOR cout

//FUNCTION PROTOTYPE
void DisplayString(char *);

void main()
{

//DEFINE AND INITIALIZE A POINTER TO A STRING
char *String = "Hello World";

//CALL FUNCTION TO DISPLAY STRING
  DisplayString(String);
} //END main()

//****************************************************************************
//
//THIS FUNCTION DISPLAYS THE STRING POINTED TO BY *String
//
//****************************************************************************
void DisplayString(char *String)
{
  cout << "The string value is:  " << String << endl;
} //END DisplayString()
```

  First, you see a pointer defined to point to a string of characters and initialized to the string value "Hello World". Nothing is new here. Next, you see the function prototype. The prototype shows a void function that will accept a character pointer. Looking at the function implementation, you see that the function simply displays the string value whose address is pointed to by *String*.

The function call in *main( )* passes the pointer to the function by listing the pointer identifier as the function argument. The pointer already represents an address, so you must never use the ampersand symbol, &, prior to a pointer name in a function call. So, in summary, the address of the string is passed to the function, where it is used to display the string value. That's all there is to it!

The foregoing program represents one level of indirection using a pointer that points to a character string. Next, let's consider two levels of indirection by defining an array of pointers to strings and see how such a structure is passed to and operated upon by a function. We will use the same array of pointers employed in Example 11-3. Here is the definition/initialization again:

char *Names[] = {"Andy", "Brenda", "Neil", "Lori", "Doug", NULL};

Remember, *Names* is a pointer to an array of pointers, thereby creating two levels of indirection. Now, we will develop a prototype for a function that will display the string values pointed to by the array pointers. Consider this:

void DisplayNames(char **);

Notice that the function parameter is *char **. The reason that two stars are required is that it requires two levels of indirection to get to the fundamental character elements. Using this prototype, we will write a function to display the string values, as follows:

```
void DisplayNames(char **Names)
{
  cout << "The names in the array are:" << endl;
  while (*Names != NULL)
  {
    cout << *Names << endl;
    ++Names;
  } //END DisplayNames()
```

First, you see that the function header reflects the prototype. Next, you see that a **while** loop is employed to display the string values. The last pointer in the array is initialized to **NULL**, so we can test for the null condition in the **while** statement as we did in Example 11-3. The *cout* statement within the loop displays the strings pointed to by the pointers in the *Names* array. Observe how the two levels of indirection are working here. To access the individual characters, you must use **Names*; to access the entire string at a given pointer address, you use

∗Names. Thus, *∗∗Names* points to the character 'A', and *∗Names* points to the string "Andy".

The real power of pointers is demonstrated where the loop is incrementing from one string to the next to provide the sequential string display. To do this, you simply increment from one string pointer to the next by incrementing the array pointer *Names* using a *++Names* statement. That's all there is to it!

Finally, the function call is

```
DisplayNames(Names);
```

Again, you see that you only need to list the pointer array name as the argument in the function call. Putting everything together, you get the following program:

```
//***********************************************************************************
//
//THIS PROGRAM WILL DEFINE AN ARRAY OF POINTERS TO
//POINT TO STRINGS  AND THEN DISPLAY THE STRINGS BY PASSING
//THE POINTER ARRAY TO A FUNCTION
//
//***********************************************************************************
#include <iostream.h>   //FOR cout

//FUNCTION PROTOTYPE
void DisplayNames(char ∗∗);

void main()
{
//DEFINE AND INITIALIZE ARRAY OF POINTERS TO STRINGS
char ∗Names[] = {"Andy", "Brenda", "Neil", "Lori", "Doug", NULL};

//CALL FUNCTION TO DISPLAY NAMES
  DisplayNames(Names);
} //END main()

//*********************************************************************
//
//THIS FUNCTION DISPLAYS THE STRINGS POINTED TO
//BY THE ARRAY
//
//*********************************************************************
void DisplayNames(char ∗∗Names)
{
  cout << "The names in the array are:" << endl;
```

```
  while (*Names != NULL)
  {
    cout << *Names << endl;
    ++Names;
  } //END WHILE
} //END DisplayNames()
```

 Quick Check

1. True or false: When a pointer is used in a function call, any operations on the pointer data in the function will affect the pointer data in the calling program.

2. True or false: A pointer argument in a function call must have a corresponding pointer parameter in the function prototype.

3. Write a prototype for a function called *MyFunc()* that will receive a pointer to a string.

4. Write a prototype for a function called *MyFunc()* that will receive an array of pointers to strings.

5. Assuming that *MyNames* is defined as an array of pointers to strings, write a statement that will call the function in question 4.

11-6 POINTERS TO FUNCTIONS

In this section, we will use pointers to point to functions. The idea is similar to using pointers to point to arrays. Recall that an array name is actually a constant pointer that locates the array in memory. Likewise, a function name is actually a constant pointer that locates the function code in memory. In both cases, these pointers are fixed and cannot be made to point to different arrays or functions, respectively. However, a pointer variable does not have this limitation. An array pointer variable can be altered to point to different arrays of the same type. Likewise, we can create a function pointer variable that can be altered to point to different functions of the same type. Consider the following:

```
#include <iostream.h>   //FOR cout

//FUNCTION PROTOTYPES
void DisplayHeader(char *);
```

```
void DisplayName(char *);
void DisplayAddress(char *);
void (*FunctionPtr)(char *);

void main()
{
  char *Garbage = "  ";
  char *Name = "Jane Doe";
  char *Address = "C++ City, USA";
  FunctionPtr = DisplayHeader;
  FunctionPtr(Garbage);
  FunctionPtr = DisplayName;
  FunctionPtr(Name);
  FunctionPtr = DisplayAddress;
  FunctionPtr(Address);
} //END main()

void DisplayHeader(char *Garbage)
{
  cout << "\tNAME\t\tADDRESS\n"
       << "\t----\t\t-------" << endl;
} //END DisplayHeader()

void DisplayName(char *Nam)
{
  cout << '\t' << Nam;
} //END DisplayName()

void DisplayAddress(char *Addr)
{
  cout << '\t' << Addr << endl;
} //END DisplayAddress()
```

When analyzing a program, always look at the prototypes first. Here we see four void functions that each accept a character pointer. The first three function prototypes should be self-explanatory by now. However, notice that the last function prototype employs a * symbol prior to the function name. In addition, the * and function name are enclosed within parentheses. This is a prototype for a variable function pointer. Because *FunctionPtr()* is a variable function pointer, it can be made to point to any function of the same type. By the same type, we mean a function that accepts and returns the same classes of data. Notice that all the function prototypes indicate that they are the same function type. At the beginning of *main()*, you see three character pointers defined and initialized to string values. Next, you see that the *DisplayHeader()* function is assigned to the *FunctionPtr()* function. This makes *FunctionPtr()* point to the *DisplayHeader()* function. Thus, we can use *FunctionPtr()* to display the header information instead of *DisplayHeader()*, because they both locate the same code. Notice that *Garbage* is passed to the function as an actual argument in the function call. Actually, *DisplayHeader()* does not need to accept any data, because it simply displays fixed header information contained in the function definition. However, to permit the assignment of *DisplayHeader()* to *FunctionPtr()*, they must have the same parameter data classes. So, garbage string data are passed, but not utilized.

Next, you see that the *DisplayName()* function is assigned to our variable function pointer. *FunctionPtr()* is then called using the *Name* argument to display the name string just as if you had called *DisplayName()*. Finally, *DisplayAddress()* is assigned to *FunctionPtr()* and called using *Address* as an argument. As a result, the address string is displayed. Here is what you would see on your monitor after executing the program:

<u>Name</u>   <u>Address</u>
Jane Doe C++ City, USA

Figure 11-7 illustrates how the function pointer in the preceding program can be made to point to different functions using an assignment statement.

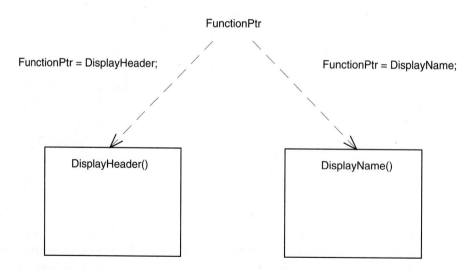

Figure 11-7   A function pointer can be made to point to different functions.

Quick Check

1. True of false: A function name is a constant pointer.

2. Write a prototype for a variable function pointer called *MyFuncPtr* that can be used to point to functions that receive a single integer value and return a single integer value.

3. Given the following function prototypes,

   int Square(int);
   int Cube(int);

   write a statement to make the function pointer defined in question 2 point to the *Square()* function;

   Write a statement to make the function pointer defined in question 2 point to the *Cube()* function.

4. True or false: When a function pointer is created, the parameter data classes and return type must match those of any function to which it must point.

11-7 STRUCTURE AND OBJECT POINTERS

In earlier chapters, you learned how to define static structure and class objects. By static, we mean not dynamic. In other words, static objects do not allocate memory dynamically. You can, however, define structure and object pointers just as you can simple variable pointers. Then, to access structure and object members, you employ the pointer operator, –>, –>, instead of the dot operator. So, let's first see how to use structure pointers. Then, we will move on to object pointers.

Defining Structure Pointers

Recall that you can allocate pointer memory statically by defining a variable, then making a pointer point to that variable, or dynamically by using the **new** operator. We can allocate memory statically and dynamically for structures in the same way. To allocate memory statically, you define a structure object in the normal manner and then define a pointer to point to the structure object using the following format:

FORMAT FOR DEFINING STATIC STRUCTURE POINTERS

<structure name> <object name>;
<structure name> *<pointer name>;
<pointer name = &<object name>;

As an example, suppose that we have declared a structure called *Student*. Then, we can define a pointer to this structure as follows:

```
Student CS1;        //DEFINE STATIC STRUCT OBJECT, CS1
Student *Janet;     //DEFINE STRUCT POINTER, Janet
Janet = &CS1;       //MAKE Janet POINT TO CS1 STRUCT
```

Here, we define a static object, *CS1*, and a pointer, *Janet*, for the *Student* structure. Then, we make the pointer point to the structure object by assigning the address of the structure object to the pointer. This creates a pointer, *Janet*, to the *CS1* structure.

To allocate structure memory dynamically, you first define a pointer for the structure and then allocate memory for that pointer using the **new** operator. Here's the format:

FORMAT FOR DEFINING DYNAMIC STRUCTURE POINTERS

<structure name> *<pointer name>;
<pointer name = **new** <structure name>;

Let's create a dynamic pointer to the *Student* structure. Here's how:

```
//DEFINE DYNAMIC POINTER
Student *Andy;          //DEFINE STRUCT POINTER, Andy
Andy = new Student;     //ALLOCATE DYNAMIC MEMORY FOR Andy
```

Now we have allocated memory dynamically for our *Student* structure using the **new** operator. A pointer, called *Andy*, is first defined for the *Student* structure;

then, memory is allocated dynamically for *Andy* using the **new** operator. Of course, when the structure is no longer needed in the program, you must deallocate this memory using the **delete** operator, like this:

delete Andy;

Using the Pointer Operator to Access Structure Data

–>, The pointer operator, –>, is specifically designed for accessing structure data using pointers. To use this operator, you must first define a pointer, either statically or dynamically, to point to the structure. Then, simply use the pointer operator to point to a given member. Earlier we defined two structure pointers named *Janet* and *Andy*. To get to the individual members within either of these structures, you must use the pointer operator, –>. Here is the general format for the pointer operator:

> ### ASSIGNING DATA TO STRUCTURES USING THE POINTER OPERATOR
>
> <structure pointer> –> <member name> = data;

Notice also that the pointer operator is coded by using a dash, –, followed by a right-angle bracket, >. No space is allowed between the two symbols. By using this format, the members within the *Janet* and *Andy* structures can be assigned data, as follows:

```
strcpy(Janet –> Name,  "Janet Smith");
Janet –> StudentNumber = 0001;
Janet –> YearEnrolled = 1993;
Janet –> GPA = 4.0;
Janet –> Graduated = 0;

strcpy(Andy –> Name, "Andy Jones");
Andy –> StudentNumber = 0002;
Andy –> YearEnrolled = 1992;
Andy –> GPA = 3.5;
Andy –> Graduated = 0;
```

DEBUGGING TIP

Remember, you must employ dot notation, •, to access structure members when using nonpointer structure objects. On the other hand, you must use the pointer operator, –>, when accessing structure members using pointers to the structure. The pointer operator is coded using a dash, –, followed by a right-angle bracket, >, with no spacing.

Reading Information into a Structure

Now suppose you want the user to enter the information into the structure via the system keyboard. When this is desired, you simply employ an input statement, while accessing the members using the pointer operator. As an example, suppose the user must enter information into the *Janet* structure declared earlier. Here's how such an operation would be coded:

```
cout << "Enter the student name:  ";
gets (Janet –> Name);
cout << "Enter the student number:  ";
cin >> Janet –> StudentNumber;
cout << "Enter the year the student enrolled:  ";
cin >> Janet –> YearEnrolled;
cout << "Enter the student GPA:  ";
cin >> Janet –> GPA;
cout << "Has the student graduated? (Y/N):  ";
char Answer;
cin >> Answer;
if (Answer == 'y' || Answer == 'Y')
  Janet –> Graduated = 1;
else
  Janet –> Graduated = 0;
```

Retrieving Information from Structures

You retrieve structure information using the assignment operator or a *cout* statement. Again, the pointer operator is employed to access the members when using pointers. Here's the general format:

> ### RETRIEVING STRUCTURE INFORMATION USING ASSIGNMENT
>
> <variable name> = <structure pointer> –> <member name>;
>
> ### RETRIEVING STRUCTURE INFORMATION USING *cout*
>
> cout << <structure pointer> –> <member name>;

Here are some examples using the *Student* structure declared earlier and the dynamic pointer, *Andy*, defined for this structure:

```
Number = Andy –> StudentNumber;
Grad = Andy –> Graduated;
cout << Andy –> Name << endl;
cout << Andy –> GPA << endl;
```

The first two statements show how the assignment operator is used to copy the structure information to another variable within the program. Clearly, the variable receiving the assignment must be defined as the same data class as the respective member information. Consequently, *Number* and *Grad* must be defined as integers for this application.

The second two statements show how *cout* is employed to retrieve structure information. Again, the pointer operator is used to get to the required structure member.

Example 11– 4

Your instructor needs a student structure consisting of the following items:

- Student name
- Student number
- Major
- Semester test scores
- Semester test average
- Equivalent letter grade of the test average

a. Declare an appropriate structure and define a dynamic pointer called *BjarneStroustrup* for this structure.

b. Write a function that will allow the instructor to fill the structure from the keyboard.

c. Write a function that will display the contents of the structure.

Solution

a. Here's a structure declaration and dynamic pointer definition that will do the job:

```
struct Student
 {
   char Name[30];
   char StudentNumber[15];
   char Major[20];
   float TestScores[15];
   float TestAverage;
   char TestGrade;
 }; //END Student

Student *BjarneStroustrup;
BjarneStroustrup = new Student;
```

   Notice in particular that the *TestScores* member is declared as an array of 15 floating-point elements. The value 15 was used to allow for a maximum of fifteen test scores. The structure pointer is a dynamic pointer variable called *BjarneStroustrup*.

b. Here's a function that will fill the structure:

```
void FillStructure(int &Number, Student *S)
 {
  int TestTotal = 0;
  cout << "Enter the student name:  ";
  gets(S –> Name);
  cout << "Enter the student number:  ";
  gets(S –> StudentNumber);
  cout << "Enter the student major:  ";
  gets(S –> Major);
  cout << "How many test scores are there?  ";
  cin >> Number;
  for (int i = 0; i < Number; ++i)
  {
    cout << "Enter test score " << i + 1 << ":  ";
    cin >> S –> TestScores[i];
    TestTotal += S –> TestScores[i];
  } //END FOR
  S –> TestAverage = TestTotal/Number;
  if (S –> TestAverage < 60)
    S –> TestGrade = 'F';
```

```
      if (S -> TestAverage >= 60 && S -> TestAverage < 70)
         S -> TestGrade = 'D';
      if (S -> TestAverage >= 70 && S -> TestAverage < 80)
         S -> TestGrade = 'C';
      if (S -> TestAverage >= 80 && S -> TestAverage < 90)
         S -> TestGrade = 'B';
      if (S -> TestAverage >= 90 && S -> TestAverage <= 100)
         S -> TestGrade = 'A';
   } //END FillStructure()
```

First, observe the function header. The function name is *FillStructure()*. There are two reference parameters, *Number* and *S*. It is important to note that *S* is a pointer variable whose data class is *Student*, which is the structure we declared in part a. This allows a pointer to the *Student* structure to be passed by reference to the function. The structure variable in the calling program will be the structure pointer variable, *BjarneStroustrup*, and the structure variable within the function is the structure pointer variable *S*. Consequently, any operations on the structure within this function employ the pointer variable, *S*.

Now look at how the structure is being filled. The structure pointer, *S*, must be referenced here, because it will take on the values of the structure pointer, *BjarneStroustrup*, in the calling program. Notice that in all cases, the structure pointer operator, $->$, is employed to fill the respective members. Here is a sample of what the user will see when this function is executed:

```
Enter the student name:  Bjarne Stroustrup↵
Enter the student number:  1↵
Enter the student major:  Computer Science↵
How many test scores are there?  3↵
Enter test score 1:  98.7↵
Enter test score 2:  97↵
Enter test score 3:  95.2↵
```

c. A function to display the student structure follows:

```
void DisplayStructure(int Number, Student *S)
{
cout << "\nStudent Name:  " << S -> Name
     << "\n\n\tStudent Number:  " << S -> StudentNumber
     << "\n\tMajor:  " << S -> Major
     << "\n\tTest Scores:  ";
  for (int i = 0; i < Number; ++i)
     cout  << S -> TestScores[i] << ", ";
  cout << "\n\tTest Average:  " << S -> TestAverage
       << "\n\tTest Grade:  " << S -> TestGrade << endl;
  } //END DisplayStructure()
```

Again, the function employs a pointer parameter, $*S$, that will receive the structure pointer from the calling program. This becomes the structure pointer variable within the function. Here is the display generated by the *DisplayStructure()* function with the values obtained by the *FillStructure()* function:

Student Name: Bjarne Stroustrup

      Student Number: 1
      Major: Computer Science
      Test Scores: 98.7, 97, 95.2,
      Test Average: 96
      Test Grade: A

Finally, you might be wondering what the entire program looks like. Here it is:

```
#include <iostream.h>      //FOR cin AND cout
#include <stdio.h>         //FOR gets()

//STUDENT STRUCTURE DECLARATION
struct Student
  {
    char Name[30];
    char StudentNumber[15];
    char Major[25];
    float TestScores[25];
    float TestAverage;
    char TestGrade;
  }; //END Student

//FUNCTION PROTOTYPES
void FillStructure(int &Number, Student *S);
void DisplayStructure(int Number, Student *S);


void main()
{
  int Number = 0;
                                                    //NUMBER OF TEST SCORES
    Student *BjarneStroustrup;                      /DEFINE POINTER
    BjarneStroustrup = new Student;                 //ALLOCATE MEMORY

    FillStructure(Number, BjarneStroustrup);        //CALL FILL FUNCTION
    DisplayStructure(Number, BjarneStroustrup); //CALL DISPLAY FUNCTION

    delete BjarneStroustrup;                        //DEALLOCATE MEMORY
} //END main()
```

```cpp
//THIS FUNCTION WILL FILL THE STUDENT STRUCTURE WITH
//VALUES ENTERED FROM THE KEYBOARD
void FillStructure(int &Number, Student *S)
{
 int TestTotal = 0;
 cout << "Enter the student name:  ";
 gets(S -> Name);
 cout << "Enter the student number:  ";
 gets(S -> StudentNumber);
 cout << "Enter the student major:  ";
 gets(S -> Major);
 cout << "How many test scores are there?:  ";
 cin >> Number;
 for (int i = 0; i < Number; ++i)
 {
   cout << "Enter test score " << i + 1 << ":  ";
   cin >> S -> TestScores[i];
   TestTotal += S -> TestScores[i];
 } //END FOR
 S -> TestAverage = TestTotal/Number;
 if (S -> TestAverage < 60)
   S -> TestGrade = 'F';
 if (S -> TestAverage >= 60 && S -> TestAverage < 70)
   S -> TestGrade = 'D';
 if (S -> TestAverage >= 70 && S -> TestAverage < 80)
   S -> TestGrade = 'C';
 if (S -> TestAverage >= 80 && S -> TestAverage < 90)
   S -> TestGrade = 'B';
 if (S -> TestAverage >= 90 && S -> TestAverage <= 100)
   S -> TestGrade = 'A';
} //END FillStructure()

//THIS FUNCTION WILL FILL DISPLAY THE STUDENT STRUCTURE
void DisplayStructure(int Number, Student *S)
{
 cout << "\nStudent Name:  " << S -> Name
      << "\n\n\tStudent Number: " << S -> StudentNumber
      << "\n\tMajor:  " << S -> Major
      << "\n\tTest Scores:  ";
 for (int i = 0; i < Number; ++i)
   cout  << S -> TestScores[i] << ", ";
 cout << "\n\tTest Average:  " << S -> TestAverage
      << "\n\tTest Grade:  " << S -> TestGrade << endl;
} //END DisplayStructure()
```

It is important to note that the structure is declared prior to *main()* so that the function prototypes can employ this structure as a data class. Observe that the function prototypes list a pointer to the structure name, *Student*, as the parameter in each case. Thus, each function expects to receive a pointer to the *Student* structure. The actual structure pointer variable, *BjarneStroustrup*, is defined at the beginning of *main()* and passed to the functions when they are called. Lastly, the **delete** operator is employed at the end of *main()* to deallocate the structure memory.

Defining Class Object Pointers

Pointers for class objects are defined very much like structure pointers. Object pointers can be set up as static or dynamic pointers using the following formats:

FORMAT FOR DEFINING STATIC OBJECT POINTERS

```
<class name>  <object name>;
<class name>  *<pointer name>;
<pointer name = &<object name>;
```

FORMAT FOR DEFINING DYNAMIC OBJECT POINTERS

```
<class name>  *<pointer name>;
<pointer name> = new <class name>;
```

If you are defining a pointer to a static object, you must define the object first and then define a pointer and make it point to the address of the object. When defining dynamic objects, the object name must be a pointer, and the keyword **new** must be employed to create the dynamic object. Notice that the class name must appear again after the keyword **new**. Of course, if you create a dynamic object, you should delete it using the keyword **delete** when you are finished with it.

For example, suppose that we have declared a class called *Rectangle*. Then object pointers can be defined as follows:

```
//DEFINE A STATIC OBJECT POINTER
  Rectangle Box(1,2);              //DEFINE STATIC OBJECT, Box
  Rectangle *Box1;                 //DEFINE OBJECT POINTER, Box1
  Box1 = &Box;                     //MAKE Box1 POINT TO Box
```

```
//DEFINE DYNAMIC OBJECT POINTER
   Rectangle *Box2;                    //DEFINE Box2 OBJECT POINTER
   Box2 = new Rectangle(2,3);          //ALLOCATE Box2 MEMORY
```

In the first case, a static object called *Box* is defined for the *Rectangle* class; then a pointer called *Box1* is defined for the same class. Finally, the address of the *Box* object is assigned to the object pointer so that the pointer points to the object. In the second case, an object pointer called *Box2* is created for the *Rectangle* class; then an object is allocated dynamically using the **new** operator. Notice that the *Box* object has the argument *(1,2)*. This obviously means that constructor is called when the object is defined. Here, the constructor will initialize the rectangle length to 1 and width to 2. There is nothing new here. The arguments *(1,2)* are passed to the object when it is defined. The object pointer, *Box1*, is made to point to this object and, therefore, will reference a rectangle object with a length of 1 and width of 2. Now, look at the dynamic object definition for *Box2*. Something *is* new here. The constructor arguments of *(2,3)* are placed *after the class specification*. This is where you must pass constructor arguments to dynamic objects.

PROGRAMMING NOTE

When initializing data with a dynamic object constructor, the initializing arguments must be placed after the class specification in the **new** statement.

Using the Pointer Operator to Send Messages to Objects

–>When a pointer is defined for an object, you must use the pointer operator, –>, to send messages to the object. Here's the idea:

SENDING A MESSAGE USING THE POINTER OPERATOR

<object name> –> <function name> (argument listing);

You see that the syntax is very much like that required to access a structure. The pointer operator must be used when the object name is a pointer; otherwise, you use the dot operator. Here is a *Rectangle* class similar to the one we declared in Chapter 9:

```
class Rectangle
{
public:
  Rectangle(float L = 0, float W = 0);      //CONSTRUCTOR
  float Perimeter();                        //RETURN PERIMETER
  float Area();                             //RETURN AREA
  float CurrentLength();                    //ACCESS LENGTH
  float CurrentWidth();                     //ACCESS WIDTH

private:
  float *Length;                            //RECTANGLE LENGTH
  float *Width;                             //RECTANGLE WIDTH
}; //END Rectangle
```

Notice that the private members, *Length* and *Width*, have been defined as pointers. More about this later. Now, let's repeat our earlier definitions for two *Rectangle* objects called *Box1* and *Box2*. Recall that we defined *Box1* to be a pointer to a static object and *Box2* to be a dynamic object pointer. Here are the definitions:

```
//DEFINE A STATIC OBJECT POINTER
  Rectangle Box(1,2);                //DEFINE STATIC OBJECT, Box
  Rectangle *Box1;                   //DEFINE OBJECT POINTER, Box1
  Box1 = &Box;                       //MAKE Box1 POINT TO Box

//DEFINE DYNAMIC OBJECT POINTER
  Rectangle *Box2;                   //DEFINE Box2 OBJECT POINTER
  Box2 = new Rectangle(2,3);         //ALLOCATE Box2 MEMORY
```

Finally, let's send messages to all the functions of the two boxes using *cout* statements. We will use a separate *cout* statement for each message so that you can easily observe the required syntax. Here are the messages:

```
cout << "The length of Box1 is:  " << Box1 -> CurrentLength() << endl;
cout << "The width of Box1 is:  " << Box1 -> CurrentWidth() << endl;
cout << "The perimeter of Box1 is:  " << Box1 -> Perimeter() << endl;
cout << "The area of Box1 is:  " << Box1 -> Area() << endl <<endl;

cout << "The length of Box2 is:  " << Box2 -> CurrentLength() << endl;
cout << "The width of Box2 is:  " << Box2 -> CurrentWidth() << endl;
cout << "The perimeter of Box2 is:  " << Box2 -> Perimeter() << endl;
cout << "The area of Box2 is:  " << Box2 -> Area() << endl;
```

Observe that each group of four *cout* statements deals with a different box object. Both groups send messages to their respective boxes using the pointer operator. Here is what you would see on the display as a result of the above code:

```
The length of Box1 is:  1
The width of Box1 is:  2
The perimeter of Box1 is:  6
The area of Box1 is:  2

The length of Box2 is:  2
The width of Box2 is:  3
The perimeter of Box2 is:  10
The area of Box2 is:  6
```

Destructors

The last thing we need to cover, relative to pointers, is the use of a ***destructor*** function within an object. The primary use for a destructor is to deallocate memory allocated dynamically by a constructor.

> A ***destructor*** is the counterpart of a constructor and is used to "clean up" an object after it is no longer needed.

Like a constructor, a destructor is called automatically. However, rather than being called when the object is defined, a destructor is called *when program execution leaves the block of code in which the object is defined.* Here are some rules governing the use of destructors:

- The name of the destructor is the same as the name of the class.
- The destructor cannot have a return type, not even **void**.
- The destructor cannot have any parameters.
- A class cannot have more than one destructor.
- The destructor cannot be overloaded.

Here is another declaration for our *Rectangle* class that includes a destructor:

```
class Rectangle
{
public:
    Rectangle(float L=0, float W=0);        //CONSTRUCTOR
```

```
    float Perimeter();                    //RETURN PERIMETER
    float Area();                         //RETURN AREA
    float CurrentLength();                //ACCESS LENGTH
    float CurrentWidth();                 //ACCESS WIDTH
    ~Rectangle();                         //DESTRUCTOR
private:
  float *Length;                          //RECTANGLE LENGTH
  float *Width;                           //RECTANGLE WIDTH
}; //END Rectangle
```

First, look at the private member declarations, and you will see that they are defined as pointer variables. This has been done to facilitate the use of a destructor, because we will use the constructor to allocate memory dynamically for these members. Next, you see that the constructor prototype has not changed from the one you observed earlier. The constructor receives two floating-point values that will be used to initialize the private members of the class. Now look at the destructor prototype. Like the constructor, the destructor has the same name as the class, but its name is preceded with a tilde symbol, ~. In addition, there is no return type, and there are no parameters. Destructors cannot have a return type, and generally no parameters are needed.

Now, here are implementations for both the constructor and destructor:

```
//IMPLEMENTATION OF CONSTRUCTOR
Rectangle :: Rectangle(float L, float W)
{
  Length = new float;
  *Length = L;
  Width = new float;
  *Width = W;
} //END Rectangle()

//IMPLEMENTATION OF DESTRUCTOR
Rectangle :: ~Rectangle()
{
  delete Length;
  delete Width;
} //END ~Rectangle()
```

In the constructor implementation, you find that the private class members, *Length* and *Width*, are being allocated dynamically using the **new** operator. Once allocated, each is set with an initializing value received by the constructor. In the destructor implementation, you see that the memory allocated to *Length* and

Width is deallocated using the **delete** operator. Notice the destructor header line. The format for the header of this typical destructor is illustrated in Figure 11-8.

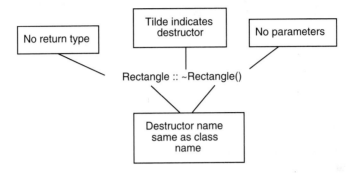

Figure 11-8   Header format for a destructor.

So, when an object is defined for the *Rectangle* class, the constructor is called automatically, which allocates memory for the private members of the object and initializes them to the values of *L* and *W* received by the constructor. Then, the destructor is called automatically when program execution leaves the block of code in which the object is defined. The destructor deallocates the memory that was allocated by the constructor.

Let's put everything together in a complete program for our rectangle class. First the header file that declares the class:

```
//Rectangle CLASS DECLARATION  (rectangl.h)
class Rectangle
{
public:
    Rectangle(float L = 0, float W = 0);    //CONSTRUCTOR
    float Perimeter();                       //RETURN PERIMETER
    float Area();                            //RETURN AREA
    float CurrentLength();                   //ACCESS LENGTH
    float CurrentWidth();                    //ACCESS WIDTH
    ~Rectangle();                            //DESTRUCTOR

private:
    float *Length;                           //RECTANGLE LENGTH
    float *Width;                            //RECTANGLE WIDTH
};  //END Rectangle
```

Next, the implementation file:

```
#include "rectangl.h"      //FOR Rectangle CLASS

//CONSTRUCTOR IMPLEMENTATION
Rectangle :: Rectangle(float L, float W)
{
  Length = new float;
  *Length = L;
  Width = new float;
  *Width = W;
} //END Rectangle

//IMPLEMENTATION OF DESTRUCTOR
Rectangle :: ~Rectangle()
{
  delete Length;
  delete Width;
} //END ~Rectangle()

//IMPLEMENTATION OF Perimeter() FUNCTION
float Rectangle :: Perimeter()
{
  return 2 * (*Length + *Width);
} //END Perimeter()

//IMPLEMENTATION OF Area() FUNCTION
float Rectangle :: Area()
{
  return *Length *  *Width;
} //END Area()

//IMPLEMENTATION OF CurrentLength() FUNCTION
float Rectangle :: CurrentLength()
{
  return *Length;
} //END CurrentLength()

//IMPLEMENTATION OF CurrentWidth() FUNCTION
float Rectangle :: CurrentWidth()
{
  return *Width;
} //END CurrentWidth()
```

And finally the application code:

```
#include "rectangl.h"      //FOR Rectangle CLASS
#include <iostream.h>   //FOR cin AND cout

void main()
{
//DEFINE OBJECTS
  Rectangle Box(1,2);              //DEFINE  Box STATIC OBJECT
  Rectangle *Box1;                 //DEFINE Box1 OBJECT POINTER
  Box1 = &Box;                     //MAKE Box1 POINT TO Box
  Rectangle *Box2;                 //DEFINE AN OBJECT POINTER
  Box2 = new Rectangle(2,3);       //ALLOCATE Box2  MEMORY

//DISPLAY LENGTH, WIDTH, PERIMETER, AND AREA OF BOX OBJECTS
  cout.setf(ios::fixed);
  cout.precision(2);
  cout << "The length of Box1 is:  " << Box1 ->  CurrentLength() << endl;
  cout << "The width of Box1 is:  " << Box1 ->  CurrentWidth() << endl;
  cout << "The perimeter of Box1 is:  " << Box1 ->  Perimeter() << endl;
  cout << "The area of Box1 is:  " << Box1 ->  Area() << endl;

  cout << "\nThe length of Box2 is:  " << Box2 ->  CurrentLength() << endl;
  cout << "The width of Box2 is:  " << Box2 ->  CurrentWidth() << endl;
  cout << "The perimeter of Box2 is:  " << Box2 ->  Perimeter() << endl;
  cout << "The area of Box2 is:  " << Box2 ->  Area() << endl;
}//END main()
```

Now we have a multifile C++ program that employs object pointers both statically and dynamically. Take a close look at how pointers are being utilized here. First, the private class members are integer pointers that are being dynamically allocated by the constructor and then deallocated by the destructor. Next, *Box1* is being defined as a pointer to a static object, and *Box2* is defined as a pointer to a dynamic object. When this program is compiled, linked, and executed, you will obtain the following results:

```
The length of Box1 is:  1.00
The width of Box1 is:  2.00
The perimeter of Box1 is:  6.00
The area of Box1 is:  2.00

The length of Box2 is:  2.00
The width of Box2 is:  3.00
The perimeter of Box2 is:  10.00
The area of Box2 is:  6.00
```

Quick Check

Use the following structure declaration to answer questions 1–9:

```
struct Account
{
  float Deposits;          //ACCOUNT DEPOSITS
  float Withdrawals;       //ACCOUNT WITHDRAWALS
  float InterestRate;      //ANNUAL INTEREST RATE IN PERCENT
  float Balance;           //ACCOUNT BALANCE
}; //END Account
Account *Passbook;
Account *Checkbook;
Passbook = new Account;
Checkbook = new Account;
```

1. The structure pointer variables are _____ .

2. Write a statement to assign a value of $250.00 to the *Deposits* member of the *Checkbook* structure.

3. Write a statement to assign a value of 12% to the *InterestRate* member of the *Passbook* structure.

4. Write a statement to allow the user to input a value for the *Withdrawals* member of the *Checkbook* structure.

5. Write a statement to allow the user to input a value for the *Deposits* member of the *Passbook* structure.

6. Write a statement to display the account balance in the *Checkbook* structure.

7. Write a statement to display the account balance in the *Passbook* structure.

8. Write the header for a function called *Input()* that would obtain user entries for the *Checkbook* structure.

9. Write a header for a function called *Output()* that would display the contents of the *Passbook* structure.

10. Write a definition for a dynamic object called *PickUp* for a class called *Truck*. Assume that the *Truck* class has a constructor that initializes the number of wheels for the truck. A pick-up truck has four wheels.

11. Write a statement that will send a message to an access function called *Wheels* that will return the number of wheels on the truck.

12. Write a statement to deallocate the *PickUp* object memory.

13. When should a destructor be used as part of a class declaration?

CHAPTER SUMMARY

A pointer represents a physical memory address. Pointers can be used to point to anything in memory, including other pointers. You can initialize a pointer by allocating memory statically or dynamically. To initialize a pointer statically, you must define a variable first and then make the pointer point to the address of the variable. To initialize a pointer dynamically, you must use the **new** operator. Dynamic memory allocation is most efficient, because memory can be allocated and deallocated as needed in the program.

You can add and subtract integer values to or from a pointer. The result will be a pointer that is displaced from the original pointer value by the number added or subtracted. The displacement is relative to the size of the data pointed to by the pointer. We therefore say that pointer arithmetic is scaled. If you subtract two pointers pointing to the same array, you get the number of elements between the two pointer locations, regardless of the data-class size. You cannot add, multiply, or divide pointers.

Variable pointers can be altered to point to any data of the same class. A constant pointer, like an array or function name, cannot be changed to point to anywhere other than where it has been originally defined to point.

Pointers can be used as function arguments and parameters. Because a pointer is an address, a pointer parameter is a reference parameter. Therefore, any operations on the pointer parameter within the function affect the pointer data in the calling program.

Like array names, function names are actually constant pointers. A function name points to the function code in memory. You can create variable function pointers that can be made to point to any other function of the same type. This means that the interface, or prototype, of the variable function pointer must match the interface, or prototype, of any function to which it will point.

Pointers can be created to point to static or dynamic structures and objects. When accessing structure and object members via a pointer, you must use the –> pointer operator in lieu of the dot operator. An object destructor is the counterpart of an object constructor and is commonly used to deallocate dynamic memory created by a constructor. An object destructor is executed automatically when the program leaves the block of code in which the object is defined.

QUESTIONS AND PROBLEMS

Questions

1. What is a pointer?

2. Explain the difference between static memory allocation and dynamic memory allocation.

3. Define a static pointer to point to the character 'Z'.

4. Define a dynamic pointer to point to the character 'Z'.

5. Write a statement that will deallocate the memory pointed to by the pointer in question 4.

6. If *p* is defined as a pointer, what is the meaning of *p?

7. Define a pointer to point to the string "This text is great!"

8. What would you see when you view the data pointed to by the pointer in question 7 using your C++ debugger?

9. Given the following pointer definition,

   char *String = "Computer Science";

   what output will be generated by the following statements?
   a. cout << String << endl;
   b. cout << *String << endl;
   c. cout << String[0] << endl;
   d. cout << *(String + 1) << endl;
   e. cout << (String + 1)[1] << endl;
   f. cout << *String + 5 << endl;

10. List the arithmetic operations that can and cannot be performed with pointers.

11. Suppose *p1* is pointing to index [2] in a given array and *p2* is pointing to index [7] of the same array. What is the result of subtracting *p1* from *p2*?

12. Define an array of pointers called *Courses* that point to the following strings:
   "Assembler"
   "C++"
   "Data Structures"
   "Data Communications"

13. Write a function that contains a loop that will display each of the strings in question 12 using pointers.

14. Explain why using pointer parameters in a function facilitates passing data by reference.

15. Three functions meet the following interface criteria:

    Accepts: A character, a float, and an integer pointer.

    Returns: An integer.

    Write the prototype for a variable function pointer called *FunctionPtr()* that can be made to point to any of the three functions.

Use the following structure declarations to answer questions 16–19 and problems 8–10:

```
//PITCHING STATS STRUCTURE DECLARATION
struct Pitching
{
  int Wins;          //NUMBER OF WINS
  int Losses;        //NUMBER OF LOSSES
  float ERA;         //EARNED RUN AVERAGE
}; //END Pitching

//HITTING STATS STRUCTURE DECLARATION
struct Batting
{
  int AtBat;         //NUMBER AT BATS
  int HomeRuns;      //NUMBER HOME RUNS
  int RBIs;          //NUMBER RUNS BATTED IN
  float Average;     //BATTING AVERAGE
}; //END Batting

//NL BASEBALL PITCHER STRUCTURE DECLARATION
struct BaseballPitcher
{
  char Name[30];     //PITCHER NAME
  char Team[30];     //PITCHER TEAM
  int Year;          //YEAR OF STATS
  Pitching Pitch;    //NESTED PITCHING STATS STRUCTURE
  Batting Bat;       //NESTED BATTING STATS STRUCTURE
}; //END BaseballPitcher
```

16. Define a dynamic pointer called *Pitcher* for this structure declaration.

17. Write statements to assign the structure members with the following data:

Name:	John Smoltz
Team:	Atlanta Braves
Year:	1989

Wins:	12
Losses:	11
ERA:	2.94
At Bats:	20
Home Runs:	0
RBIs:	11
Average:	.190

18. Write statements to display the structure data assigned in question 17.

19. Write a prototype for a function that would fill the structure members from keyboard entries.

20. True or false: A destructor may or may not have parameters.

21. Suppose that you have a constructor called *Circle()*. What will be the corresponding destructor name?

22. When are destructors normally used in a C++ object-oriented program?

Problems

Least Difficult

1. Write a program that will fill a character array with a string of up to 25 characters using pointers, and display the string in reverse order using pointers.

2. Write a program that will determine whether a word is a palindrome. Place a word entered by the program user into an array and use pointers to compare the character elements for the palindrome determination. (*Note:* A palindrome is a word that is spelled the same way both forward and backward. Example: "MOM.")

More Difficult

3. Suppose that you have the following strings in an array:
   "BOB"
   "ANDY"
   "JANET"
   "BRENDA"
   "LARRY"
   "ZANE"
   "ANDREW"
   "DAVID"
   "RON"

Write a program using pointers to initialize an array with the foregoing names in the order given. Employ a function in the program to sort the names within the array using the following sort algorithm:

For i = 0 to Array Size
    For j = i + 1 to Array Size
        If Array[i] > Array[j]
            Swap Array[i] and Array[j]

Employ another function that employs pointers to display the array names to verify the sorting operation.

Most Difficult

4. In Section 11-5, we created an array of pointers to strings. Because each pointer locates a separate string, the individual strings can be of different lengths. If you view the strings as a two-dimensional array of characters (see Chapter 14), the right side of the array has a ragged edge, because the strings have different lengths. For this reason, such an array is called a ***ragged edge array***. Write a program that uses an array of pointers to point to a ragged edge array of characters that contains the names of some students in your class. Write functions to enter the names into the array and display the names.

5. A ***stack*** is a sequential data structure whereby the last element placed into the stack is the first element to be removed from the stack. This idea is referred to as *last-in, first-out* (*LIFO*). The last element placed into the stack is located by a pointer called *Top*. Suppose that you use an array to implement a stack and a pointer called *Top*. As you add elements to the stack, *Top* increments through the array; as you remove elements from the stack, *Top* decrements through the array. Adding elements to a stack is called a ***Push*** operation, and removing elements from a stack is called a ***Pop*** operation.

    Write two functions, called *Push()* and *Pop()*, that employ a pointer called *Top* to push and pop character elements to and from a stack contained in an array. Remember, the only legal way to access the stack is through the single pointer *Top*. Place your functions in a program that will allow you to test the functions. Here are the function descriptions to help you get started:

Function *Push()*:	Places an element onto the stack.
Accepts:	An element to be pushed and a pointer called *Top*, which locates the position in the array where the element is to be placed.
Returns:	Nothing.

Function *Pop()*:   Removes an element from the stack.

Accepts: A pointer called *Top*, which locates the position
                                     in the array from where the element is to be
                                     obtained.

Returns: The popped element.

6. When pushing and popping elements to and from a stack that is being held in
    an array, you must have a way of determining when the stack is empty or full.
    You know the stack is empty when the *Top* pointer points to array position
    NULL. You know the stack is full when *Top* points to the maximum array
    index. Write two functions called *EmptyStack()* and *FullStack()* that will
    return a nonzero (true) value if the stack is empty or full, respectively, and a
    zero (false) value if the stack is not empty or full, respectively.

7. You can use stacks to test a word to see if it's a palindrome. Here's the idea:
    Enter the word to be tested into two separate stacks. Pop the elements from
    one of the two stacks and place them in a third stack. Pop the two remaining
    stacks and compare the popped elements character by character as they are
    popped. Continue popping until two elements do not match or until the stacks
    are empty. As soon as you find two elements that are not the same, you don't
    have a palindrome. On the other hand, if no mismatches have been detected
    after all the elements are popped, you have a palindrome. Why does this
    work?
        Write a program that uses this idea to test a word to see if it is a
    palindrome. Employ the functions that you developed in problems 5 and 6.

8. Write a header file called *p11-08.h* for the foregoing *BaseballPitcher*
    structure.

9. Write an implementation file called *p11-09.cpp* that incorporates functions to
    fill and display the *BaseballPitcher* structure in problem 8 using a structure
    pointer.

10. Write an application file called *p11-10.cpp* to test the header and
    implementation files developed in problems 8 and 9.

Use the following class declaration to do problems 11 and 12:

```
class Employee
{
public:
  Employee(float Rate = 0.0, float Hours = 0.0);          //CONSTRUCTOR
  void GetData();                 //GETS EMPLOYEE DATA FROM USER
  void CalculatePay();            //CALCULATES WEEKLY PAY, WITH OVERTIME
  void DisplayData();             //DISPLAYS PAYROLL DATA
  ~Employee();                    //DESTRUCTOR
```

```
private:
  char Name[25];      //EMPLOYEE NAME
  float *Rate;        //HOURLY RATE OF PAY
  float *Hours;       //WEEKLY HOURS WORKED
  float *Pay;         //GROSS WEEKLY PAY
}; //END Employee
```

11. Code the foregoing class declaration as a header file, and develop an implementation file for the member functions of the *Employee* class.

12. Develop an application file to test the code you developed in problem 11.

13. Create a dynamic invoice object that contains all the information necessary to process one line of an invoice. Assume that the invoice must include the following data and functions:

> *Data*:
> > Quantity Ordered
> > Quantity Shipped
> > Part Number
> > Part Description
> > Unit Price
> > Extended Price
> > Sales Tax Rate
> > Sales Tax Amount
> > Shipping
> > Total
>
> *Functions*:
> > - A function to initialize all the data items to 0, except the Sales Tax Rate, which should be initialized to 5%.
> > - A function to allow the user to initialize all the data items from the keyboard.
> > - A function to calculate the Extended Price of the item.
> > - A function to calculate the Sales Tax Amount of the item.
> > - A function to calculate the Total Amount of the invoice.
> > - A function to display the invoice data with header information in a businesslike format.

Use dynamic pointers to implement the object data.

ADTs

12

INTRODUCTION
12-1 THE CONCEPT OF DATA
        ABSTRACTION REVISITED
12-2 ADT STACK
    Implementing the Stack ADT
12-3 ADT QUEUE
    Implementing the Queue ADT

12-4 ADT LIST
    Linked Lists
    Implementing the Linked List ADT
CHAPTER SUMMARY
QUESTIONS AND PROBLEMS
        Questions
        Problems

INTRODUCTION

Abstract data types, or ADTs, provide for data abstraction. You were introduced to data abstraction in Chapter 2. Recall that the idea behind data abstraction is to combine data with a set of operations that are defined for that data in one neat encapsulated package called an ADT. The ADT can then be used by knowing what the operations do, without needing to know the details of how the computer system implements the data or its operations. You have been using data abstraction since Chapter 2 when you first learned about the standard C++ classes. In each case, you learned about the structure of the data within the class, the operations that could be performed by a given object of a class, and how to use those operations. You were not concerned about how the computer stores the data or how the operations were implemented. You could concentrate on their use rather than their implementation.

Data abstraction is an important software development and programming tool. When developing software with ADTs, you can concentrate on the ADT data and related operations, without worrying about the inner implementation details of the ADT. Data abstraction provides for generality, modularity, and protection when developing software. The C++ class is the ideal construct for implementing ADTs.

I will begin this chapter with a general review and discussion of ADTs. In the first section, I will discuss all the facets of an ADT so that you completely understand all of its implications. Then, the remaining three sections will use object-oriented programming to build three classic ADTs: the stack, the queue, and the linked list.

12-1 THE CONCEPT OF DATA ABSTRACTION REVISITED

Let's begin with a simple definition for an ADT and then look at some important characteristics of an ADT.

> An *abstract data type (ADT)* is a collection of data and related operations.

- *Abstraction*

   The term *abstract* means that the data and related operations are being viewed without considering any of the details of *how* the data or operations are implemented in the computer system. You have been working with abstract data types thoughout this book, without knowing it. For instance, consider the *float* data class used in C++. Have you been concerned about how floating-point values are stored in memory? Have you been concerned about how the C++ compiler implements floating-point operations? Of course not! All that you are concerned about is the general structure of a floating-point value, what operations are available to be used with floating-point values, and how to use these floating-point operations. The implementation details are left to the C++ compiler designer.

This whole idea of abstraction facilitates the design of modular software and the development of algorithms for software design, because abstraction allows us to hide implementation details, thereby facilitating more general thinking.

- *An ADT includes both data and related operations.*

Think of an ADT as a black box that contains *private* data and *public* operations. Sound familiar? You know what the box does and how to use it through its *public* operations, or interface. However, you are not concerned about what goes on inside the box. The ADT black box concept facilitates modular software design.

The Data: An ADT defines the data to be operated upon as well as the operations that can be performed on the data. An ADT is not the same thing as a data structure. A data structure provides a way of structuring, or organizing, data within a programming language. You will be concerned about data structures when you implement an ADT, because you will have to decide how to organize and store the ADT data. However, on the surface, you are not concerned with these implementation details in order to access and manipulate the ADT data. The data in an ADT must be private, which means that it is hidden from any operations that are not defined for the ADT.

The Operations: The ADT includes operations, or functions, that manipulate the ADT data. These operations are public, which means that they are used by outside software to access and manipulate the private ADT data. Again, all you are concerned about at the abstract level is what these operations do and how to use them. As a result, the interface to the operations within the ADT must be complete enough to describe totally the effect that they have on the data. However, you are not concerned about how they do what they do.

- *An ADT provides a means to encapsulate details whereby the data are completely hidden from their surroundings.*

Recall that *encapsulation* with *information hiding* allows you to combine data with the operations that are dedicated to manipulating the data so tightly that outside operations cannot affect the data. This allows the application program to be oblivious to how the ADT data are stored. In addition, information hiding provides for data protection. Only those operations that are defined for the ADT can operate on the ADT data. As a result, the data cannot be corrupted intentionally or unintentionally by using "unauthorized" operations.

- *ADT operations provide loose coupling to the outside world via a function interface.*

The operations defined for an ADT provide the interface between the outside world and the ADT. In other words, the only way to gain access to the ADT is through the ADT operation, or function, interfaces. Again, the ADT is like a black box that is connected to its surroundings via its function interfaces. The function interfaces provide the communications channel between an application program and the ADT. This idea is illustrated in Figure 12-1. This figure should look familiar to you, because it is basically the same figure used to illustrate a class in Chapter 9. As you might now suspect, the class in C++ provides an ideal implementation of an ADT.

By using ADTs during software development, we gain *modularity*, *generality*, and *protection*. We gain modularity, because ADTs can be thought of as black box building blocks during software development. We gain generality, because algorithms can be developed that depend only on the function interface to the ADT without considering the implementation details of the ADT. In addition, once an ADT is developed, it is available for general use in many applications without rewriting the ADT code. We gain protection through information hiding. Private data stored within an ADT cannot be corrupted intentionally or unintentionally.

The preceding definition of an ADT completely describes the C++ class that we developed in an earlier chapter. Recall that a class includes both data (private members) and related operations (public functions) that are encapsulated. In addition, the private member data are completely hidden from anything outside the class. Finally, the class is coupled to its outside world via the class function interfaces (prototypes). That is, to access the class data from the outside, you must invoke the public member functions of the class. This is why C++ is ideal for coding ADTs.

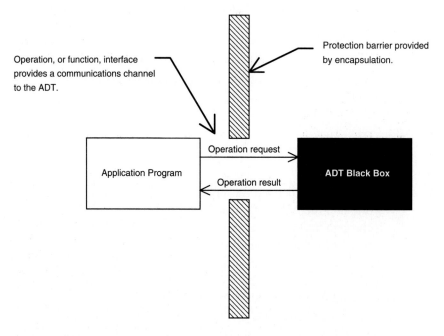

Figure 12-1 The ADT is like a black box that is connected to its surroundings via its function interfaces.

The remainder of this chapter is devoted to building some classic ADTs. As you study these ADTs, keep in mind the general ideas of data abstraction presented in this section.

 **Quick Check**

1. What term is used to indicate that data and its related operations are being viewed without considering any of the details of how the data or operations are implemented in the computer system?

2. Give an example of an ADT with which you have been working in the C++ language.

3. The ADT black box concept facilitates _____ software design.

4. True or false: A data structure and an abstract data type are the same thing.

5. Data protection in an ADT is provided by _____.

6. The interface to an ADT is through its _____.

7. Why do you gain modularity through the use of ADTs?

8. Why do you gain generality through the use of ADTs?

12-2 ADT STACK

You have been introduced to the stack ADT via some of the programming problems in previous chapters. Now it is time to take a closer look at this important ADT. Stacks are common in a wide variety of applications in computer science. For example, you observed the use of a stack when you studied recursion in Chapter 7. With recursion, a stack is employed to save information as the recursive function calls are made. Once the primitive state is reached, the stack information is retrieved to determine the final recursive function value.

In general, a stack is used to reverse the order of data placed in it. Now, let's see how a stack works, beginning with a formal definition for a stack:

> A *stack* is a collection of data elements and related operations whereby all the insertions and deletions of elements to and from the stack are made at one end of the stack called the *top*. A stack operates on the *last-in*, *first-out*, or *LIFO*, principle.

To get the idea of a stack, think of a stack of trays in a spring-loaded bin, such as that which you might find in a cafeteria line. Such a stack is illustrated in Figure 12-2. When you remove a tray from the stack, you remove it from the *top* of the stack. If you were to add a tray onto the stack, you would place it on the *top* of the stack. All insertions and deletions of trays to and from the stack are made at the *top* of the stack. In other words, the last tray placed onto the stack will be the first tray removed from the stack. This characteristic is commonly referred to as *last-in*, *first-out*, or simply *LIFO*. Examples of the LIFO principle are hard to find in everyday life. For instance, suppose that you enter a grocery store check-out line. If the line is operating on the LIFO principle, the last person in the line would be the first one to be checked out. It might be quite some time until you were able to pay for your groceries, especially if other people keep entering the line. Think about how unfair such a line would be! To be fair, a grocery store line must operate on a *first-in*, *first-out*, or *FIFO*, principle. This principle is associated with *queues* and will be discussed in the next section. Although the LIFO principle is not very common in everyday life, it is very common in many problems that arise in computer science.

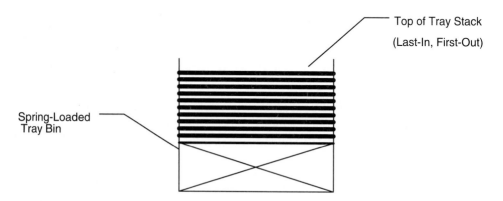

Figure 12-2   A stack obeys the last-in, first-out (LIFO) principle, like this stack of cafeteria trays.

Now, let's consider the cafeteria tray stack again. What operations do you suppose could be performed on such a stack? Well, first of all, you can move an empty tray bin into position in preparation for adding trays to the bin. Then, you can begin adding trays to the bin to form a stack of trays. When a single tray is added to the stack, it can only be added at the *top* position and no other position. Adding an element to a stack is referred to as a *push* operation. You can remove a tray from the *top* of the stack, and, normally, you can't remove a tray from any position other than the top of the stack. Removing an element from a stack is called a *pop* operation. You could also inspect the *top* tray, but no others. You could see if the stack of trays were empty, but if not empty, you would not know how many trays were in the stack. Given the situation, you are forced to access the trays from the *top* of the stack. The stack of trays provide a very good analogy to stacks in computer science, because the operations that can be performed on a stack of trays form the basis for the stack ADT in computer science. Here is a summary of legal stack operations:

- CreateStack() $\Rightarrow$ Creates an empty stack.
- Push() $\Rightarrow$ Places an element on the top of a stack.
- Pop() $\Rightarrow$ Removes an element from the top of a stack.
- TopElement() $\Rightarrow$ Inspects the top element of the stack, leaving the stack unchanged.
- EmptyStack() $\Rightarrow$ Determines if the stack is empty.

Now we are ready to define our stack ADT. Remember, to define an ADT, we must include both a definition for the ADT data as well as any operations that will be needed to manipulate the data. Consider the following ADT definition:

ADT Stack

Operations, or Interface:

CreateStack()
Creates an empty stack.

Push()
Adds a new element to the top of a stack.

Pop()
Removes the top element of a stack.

TopElement()
Copies the top element of the stack, leaving the stack unchanged.

EmptyStack()
Determines if the stack is empty.

Data:

A collection of data elements that can be accessed at only one location, called the *top* of the stack.

Implementing the Stack ADT

The ADT definition given before provides all the information needed to work with a stack. The operations are clearly defined in order to access and manipulate the stack data. Now it is time to consider the implementation details in order to create stacks in C++. Remember, however, that the following implementation details are not part of the ADT definition. We can always change how we implement the stack ADT, but the stack ADT definition will remain constant.

It is perfectly natural to use a one-dimensional array to hold a stack. We must use an existing structure to implement our stack, because there is no inherent built-in stack class available in C++, or most other high-level languages for that matter.

Creating a Stack Using an Array

We will create an array of some arbitrary length and create an integer variable called *Top* to keep track of the top element on the stack. Remember, we only need to keep track of the top element of the stack, because, by definition, access to the stack elements must be through the top of the stack. To initialize the stack, we will set *Top* to the value −1, as shown in Figure 12-3.

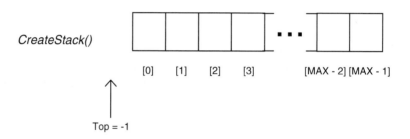

Figure 12-3   Setting *Top* to the value −1 will create an empty stack.

First, look at the array. It is defined with indices ranging from [0] to [*MAX* − 1] and, therefore, can hold *MAX* elements. The array will be used to hold a stack so that the first stack element will be placed at position [0] in the array, the second stack element at position [1], and so on. We will create an integer variable called *Top* that will "point" to the array index that locates the top element in the stack. In Figure 12-3, the value of *Top* is set to −1 to indicate that the stack is empty. The value −1 is used to indicate an empty stack condition, because there is no −1 index in the array. So, using this idea, all we have to do to create a new empty stack is to define an array and set *Top* to the value −1. How do you know if the stack ever becomes empty when processing the stack data? Of course, the stack is empty if the value of *Top* is −1. The algorithm required to create a stack using our array implementation is straightforward. Here it is:

CreateStack( ) **Algorithm**

BEGIN
    Set *Top* = −1.
END.

Now we are ready to start pushing elements onto the stack.

Pushing Elements onto a Stack

The first element pushed onto an empty stack will be placed in position [0] of the array. However, before the first element can be placed into the array, the value of *Top* must be incremented to point to position [0]. Let's suppose that we have created a character array to form a stack of characters. Then we execute the following operation:

Push('A')

The push operation causes the value of *Top* to be incremented from −1 to 0, and then the character 'A' is placed at position [*Top*], or [0], of the array. Next, suppose we execute another push operation, like this:

Push('B')

This push operation causes *Top* to be incremented from 0 to 1, and then the character 'B' is placed on the top of the stack, which is now array position [1]. Lastly, let's execute a third push operation, like this:

Push('C')

Now we are pushing the character 'C' onto the stack. Again, the value of *Top* is incremented, and this character is placed into array position [*Top*], or [2]. This sequence of three push operations is illustrated in Figure 12-4.

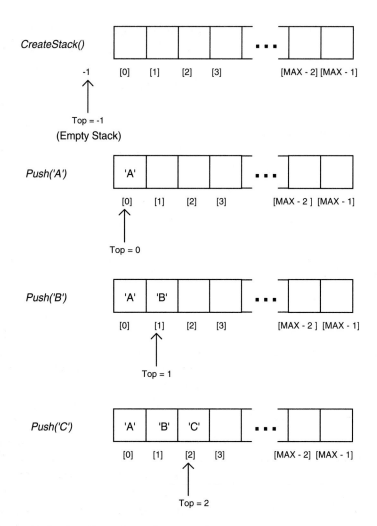

Figure 12-4 The effect of creating a stack and pushing three character elements onto the stack.

It is important to note that the value of *Top* must be incremented *prior* to placing the element on the stack. Thus, we say that the *Push()* operation preincrements the stack pointer, *Top*. Here is an algorithm for *Push()*:

Push() **Algorithm**

BEGIN
    If the stack is not full

                     Increment *Top*.

                     Place element at array position [*Top*].

           Else

                     Display full stack message.

       END.

Notice that a test is made to determine if the stack is full, because you cannot push an element onto a full stack. When would our stack be full? Well, the stack is full when the array is full, right? The maximum array position is *MAX* − 1, so the stack will be full when *Top* has the value *MAX* − 1.

Popping Elements from a Stack

Now we are ready to illustrate several popping operations. Given the stack in Figure 12-4, suppose that we execute a single pop operation, like this:

Pop()

What happens to the stack? Well, *Top* is pointing to the *last* element placed on the stack (the character 'C') so all we need to do is to remove the element at array position [*Top*], or [2]. However, once the element is removed, the value of *Top* must be decremented to locate the new top of the stack. Thus, in Figure 12-4, the character 'C' at position [2] is removed, and the value of *Top* is decremented from 2 to 1 to locate array position [1], which is the new top of the stack.

Next, suppose we execute a second pop operation. This operation removes the character 'B', and *Top* is decremented to array position [0]. Finally, if we execute a third pop operation, the character 'A' is removed from the stack, and *Top* is decremented to the value −1, indicating an empty stack. This sequence of events is shown in Figure 12-5. Remember that the *Pop()* operation decrements *Top* after the element is removed from the stack. Thus, we say that the *Pop()* operation postdecrements the stack pointer. Here is an algorithm for *Pop()*:

Pop() Algorithm

       BEGIN

           If the stack is not empty

                     Remove element at array position [*Top*].

                     Decrement *Top*.

           Else

                     Display empty stack message.

       END.

Notice that a test must be made to determine if the stack is empty, because you cannot pop an element from an empty stack. How do you know when the stack is empty? Of course, when *Top* has the value −1.

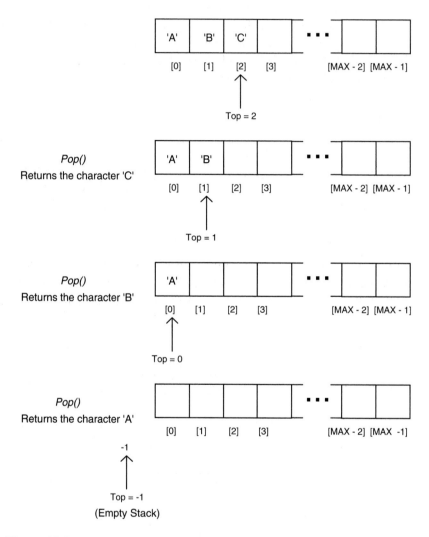

Figure 12-5 The effect of popping three character elements from the stack in Figure 12-4.

One final point: Although the stack is empty after the three popping operations in Figure 12-5, the array still contains the 'A', 'B', and 'C' character elements. These elements could be accessed by reading the array. However, remember that, by definition, an ADT restricts the data access to only those operations defined for the ADT. Therefore, the only possible way to access the array is through the stack operations, *Push()* and *Pop()*, defined for the stack ADT. Any direct array access would violate the idea of an ADT. This is why object-oriented programming is ideal for implementing ADTs. With object-oriented programming, we can make the array a **private** data member of a class, thereby restricting its access to only those operations defined for the ADT. As a result, the ADT data are completely hidden from the outside world.

Inspecting the Top Element of a Stack

The last operation of our stack ADT that we need to illustrate is the *TopElement()* operation. Recall that this operation makes a copy of the top element on the stack, leaving the stack unchanged. So, let's assume that we start with the stack in Figure 12-4 and execute a *TopElement()* operation, like this:

TopElement()

Like the *Pop()* operation, the *TopElement()* operation reads the element at array position [*Top*]. However, unlike the *Pop()* operation, *TopElement()* does not decrement the stack pointer, *Top*. This operation is illustrated in Figure 12-6.

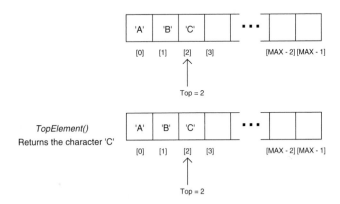

Figure 12-6   The effect of the *TopElement()* operation.

The algorithm for *TopElement()* is straightforward. Here it is:

TopElement( ) **Algorithm**

BEGIN
    If the stack is not empty
        Copy element at array position [*Top*].
    Else
        Display empty message.
END.

Coding the Stack ADT

We are now ready to code our stack ADT. We will code the ADT as a class to enforce encapsulation and information hiding. Here is the stack ADT class coded as a C++ header file called *stack.h*:

//STACK CLASS DECLARATION (stack.h)

```
#ifndef STACK_H
#define STACK_H

const int MAX = 5;                    //MAXIMUM STACK SIZE
enum {EMPTY = -1, FULL = MAX - 1};    //DEFINE EMPTY = -1
                                      //AND FULL = MAX - 1
enum {FALSE, TRUE};                   //DEFINE FALSE = 0 AND
                                      //TRUE = 1

class Stack
{
public:
  Stack();                    //CONSTRUCTOR FOR CreateStack()
  int EmptyStack();           //CHECKS FOR EMPTY STACK
  int FullStack();            //CHECKS FOR FULL STACK
  void Push(char Char);       //PLACE ELEMENT ON TOP
  char Pop();                 //REMOVE ELEMENT FROM TOP
  char TopElement();          //INSPECT TOP ELEMENT

private:
  char S[MAX];        //CHARACTER ARRAY TO HOLD THE STACK
  int Top;            //Top LOCATES TOP ELEMENT OF STACK
}; //END Stack
#endif
```

First, you see a constant, called *MAX,* defined. This constant will dictate the maximum size of the array, or stack. Next, you see several enumerated data elements defined. We set *EMPTY* to the value −1 to designate an empty stack. Then, we set *FULL* to the value *MAX* − 1 to designate a full stack. You know why *EMPTY* is set to −1. But why is *FULL* set to *MAX* − 1? Well, theoretically, the size of a stack is limited only by the amount of memory available in the system to hold the stack. However, because we are using an array to hold the stack, the maximum stack size is limited by the size of the array. The size of this array implementation is *MAX,* which means that the last array index is [*MAX* − 1]. Therefore, when the top of the stack is located at array index [*MAX* − 1], the stack is full.

The last two enumerated data elements defined in the header file are *FALSE* and *TRUE.* The element *FALSE* is set to 0, and the element *TRUE* is set to 1. These elements take on the values 0 and 1, respectively, by default, according to the way that C++ assigns default values to enumerated data. They will be used as return values when testing the stack for an empty or a full condition.

The stack ADT is defined as a class called *Stack.* The public members of the class include the operations defined for the stack ADT. First, you see the *Stack()* constructor. This constructor will take the place of the *CreateStack()* operation. Remember how a constructor works? When an object is defined for a class, the constructor is automatically called to initialize the private members of the class. Here, the constructor function will be coded to set the value of *Top* to *EMPTY,* or −1. Isn't this what the *CreateStack()* operation must do? We could not use the name *CreateStack(),* because a constructor must have the same name as the class.

Next, you see the *EmptyStack()* function listed. This function will return the integer 1 (*TRUE*) if the stack is empty, or 0 (*FALSE*) if the stack is not empty. The next function defined is *FullStack().* This function will be used to determine if the stack is full. The function will return the integer 1 (*TRUE*) if the stack is full or 0 (*FALSE*) if the stack is not full. (What constitutes a full stack?) You have noticed that in our formal ADT definition, we did not have a *FullStack()* operation, and, in theory, no such operation is needed for the stack ADT. However, *FullStack()* is required in this implementation, because we are using a finite array to hold the stack.

The last three functions defined for the class are *Push(), Pop(),* and *TopElement().* You already know the purpose of these functions. However, take a close look at each function prototype. The *Push()* function accepts a character, *Char,* to be pushed onto the stack. It does not return any value, because it will simply place *Char* into the array at the top position. The *Pop()* function does not have any formal parameters, because it will read the element at the top position of the stack array. The return type of *Pop()* is a character, because it will return the popped element to the calling program. Likewise, the *TopElement()* function does not require any formal parameters, because it simply reads the top element of the stack. The return type is character, because it will return a copy of the top element to the calling program.

The private members of the class are the character array, *S[ ]*, and the integer variable, *Top*. The size of the array is *MAX*, which means that the stack can hold *MAX* elements. However, remember that the last array index is [*MAX* − 1]. It goes without saying that array *S[ ]* will hold a stack of characters whose top element is located by *Top*.

PROGRAMMING NOTE

The C++ class fully encapsulates the stack ADT. As a result, only those operations defined in the class can operate on the stack data. Even though the stack is being implemented with an array, the stack array is private and, therefore, cannot be corrupted by any operations outside of the class. When using the stack, you are forced to use only those operations defined by the stack ADT. This is why encapsulation and information hiding are so important when creating ADTs. As you can see, the class in C++ inherently provides the encapsulation and data hiding required by ADTs.

Now we need to look at the implementation file for the *Stack* class functions.

```
//STACK IMPLEMENTATION FILE (stackop.cpp)

#include "stack.h"        //FOR stack CLASS
#include <iostream.h>   //FOR cin AND cout

//IMPLEMENTATION OF Stack() CONSTRUCTOR
Stack :: Stack()
{
  Top = EMPTY;          //SET TOP TO -1
} //END Stack()

//IMPLEMENTATION OF EmptyStack()
int Stack :: EmptyStack()
{
  if (Top == EMPTY)     //IF STACK EMPTY RETURN TRUE
    return TRUE;         //ELSE RETURN FALSE
```

```
  else
    return FALSE;
} //END EmptyStack()

//IMPLEMENTATION OF FullStack()
int Stack :: FullStack()
{
  if (Top == FULL)          //IF STACK FULL RETURN TRUE
    return TRUE;            //ELSE RETURN RETURN FALSE
  else
    return FALSE;
} //END FullStack()

//IMPLEMENTATION OF Push()
void Stack :: Push(char Char)
{
  if (!FullStack())         //IF STACK NOT FULL, INCREMENT TOP
  {                         //AND ADD ELEMENT TO STACK
    ++Top;
    S[Top] = Char;
  }
  else
    cout << "The stack is full!" << endl;
} //END Push()

//IMPLEMENTATION OF Pop()
char Stack :: Pop()
{
  char Character;
  if (!EmptyStack())        //IF STACK NOT EMPTY, RETURN ELEMENT
  {                         //AND DECREMENT TOP
    Character = S[Top];
    - -Top;
    return Character;
  } //END IF
  else
  {
    cout << "The stack is empty!" << endl;
    return '#';             //RETURN '#' TO INDICATE STACK EMPTY
  } //END ELSE
} //END Pop()

//IMPLEMENTATION OF TopElement()
char Stack :: TopElement()
```

```
{
  if (!EmptyStack())        //IF STACK NOT EMPTY, RETURN ELEMENT
     return S[Top];
  else                      //ELSE RETURN '#' FOR EMPTY STACK
  {
     cout << "The stack is empty! " << endl;
     return '#';
  } //END ELSE
} //END TopElement()
```

The file is named *stackop.cpp*. You see that the stack header file, *stack.h*, is included in this file. The first implementation is for the constructor function, *Stack()*. This function simply creates a new stack by setting *Top* to *EMPTY*, or −1. Next, the *EmptyStack()* function returns *TRUE* if the stack is empty or *FALSE* if the stack is not empty. What constitutes an empty stack? Of course, when the value of *Top* is −1. This is the test that is made in the **if/else** statement. Notice how the enumerated data elements defined in the stack header file are used here. Remember that *EMPTY* is defined as −1, *TRUE* is defined as 1, and *FALSE* is defined as 0.

The structure of the *FullStack()* implementation is similar to *EmptyStack()*. However, *FullStack()* checks to see if the value of *Top* is equal to *FULL*. Recall that *FULL* is defined in the header file as *MAX* − 1. This value is the maximum array index value. When *Top* reaches *MAX* − 1, the array is full, thereby making the stack full.

The implementation of the *Push()* function employs an **if/else** statement to check for a full stack condition. You cannot push an element onto a full stack. The condition is checked by calling the *FullStack()* function. If the stack is not full, the value of *Top* is incremented, and the character, *Char*, received by the function is stored in the stack array at position *S[Top]*. If the stack is full, an appropriate message is displayed.

The *Pop()* function employs an **if/else** statement to check for an empty stack condition. You cannot pop an element from an empty stack. Here, the *EmptyStack()* function is called as part of the **if/else** statement. If the stack is not empty, the element at array position *S[Top]* is obtained and assigned to the local variable *Character*. (Why is a local variable required here?) The value of *Top* is then decremented, and the character, *Character*, is returned to the calling program.

Finally, the *TopElement()* function is similar to the *Pop()* function in that it checks for an empty stack condition and, if the stack is not empty, returns the character at array position *S[Top]*. Notice, however, that the value of *Top* is not altered, thereby leaving the stack unchanged.

Now all we need is an application program to test our stack ADT. Here is one that will do the job:

//APPLICATION FILE TO TEST THE STACK ADT (stackapp.cpp)

```
#include "stack.h"        //FOR stack CLASS
#include <iostream.h>     //FOR cin AND cout

void main()
{
  char Character;         //CHARACTER TO BE STACKED
  int Number = 0;         //NUMBER OF CHARACTERS TO BE STACKED
  int Count = 0;          //LOOP COUNTER

  Stack Stk;              //DEFINE STACK OBJECT

//GET NUMBER OF ELEMENTS TO STACK
  cout << "You cannot enter more than " << MAX
       << " elements.  \nHow many elements do you have to enter? " << endl;
  cin >> Number;

//PUSH ELEMENTS ONTO STACK
  while (Count < Number)
  {
    ++Count;
    cout << "\nEnter a character element:  ";
    cin >> Character;
    Stk.Push(Character);
  } //END WHILE

//INSPECT TOP ELEMENT OF THE STACK
  cout << "\nThe top element of the stack is:  "
       << Stk.TopElement() << endl;

//POP AND WRITE STACK ELEMENTS
  cout << "\nThe contents of the stack are:  ";
  while (!Stk.EmptyStack())
    cout << Stk.Pop();

//ATTEMPT TO POP AN EMPTY STACK
  Stk.Pop();
} //END main()
```

The program begins by including the stack ADT header file, *stack.h*. There are several local variables declared at the beginning of *main()*. These variables will be used to process the stack information, as you will see shortly. An object called *Stk* is defined for our *Stack* class. The user is first prompted for the number of characters to be entered onto the stack. A **while** loop is used to push the entered characters onto the stack one character at a time. Notice that the **while** loop will execute as long as the number of characters entered is less than the number dictated by the user. The user is prompted within the loop to enter one character at a time. After the character is read from the user, it is pushed onto the stack by calling the *Push()* function.

The next segment of code inspects and displays the top character on the stack with a call to the *TopElement()* function.

The final segment of code pops the entire stack and displays the stack elements one character at a time. A **while** loop is used to pop and display the stack elements. The loop is controlled by making a call to the *EmptyStack()* function. As a result, the loop will execute until the stack is empty.

Finally, notice that a single call to *Pop()* is made after the stack is emptied. This call is made to test the *Pop()* function relative to an empty stack. Here is a sample run of the program:

```
You cannot enter more than 5 elements.
How many elements do you have to enter?
3↵

Enter a character element:  A↵

Enter a character element:  B↵

Enter a character element:  C↵

The top element of the stack is:  C

The contents of the stack are:  CBA

The stack is empty!
```

Observe what has happened. The user entered three characters in the order 'A', 'B', 'C'. The program shows that the last character entered, 'C', is on the top of the stack. Then, the contents of the stack are popped and displayed. Notice that the output order is reversed from the input order because of the LIFO principle. Finally, the attempt to pop an empty stack resulted in the appropriate message to the user, thus verifying the integrity of the *Pop()* function.

Quick Check

1. Suppose that the user filled a stack using the application test program in this section. What would happen if a call was made to the *Push()* function after the stack was full?

2. Because we are using an array implementation for a stack, why can't you randomly access the stack elements using array operations, rather than accessing them through *Top*?

3. With our array implementation of a stack, a *Push()* operation requires that the stack pointer be _____.

4. True or false: With our array implementation of a stack, the stack is full when the value of *Top* becomes equal to *MAX*, where *MAX* is the maximum number of elements that the array can hold.

5. With our array implementation of a stack, the stack is empty when the value of *Top* is _____.

6. What is the functional difference between the *Pop()* function and the *TopElement()* function?

7. There is no *FullStack()* operation defined for the stack ADT. Why did we have to include a *FullStack()* function in our implementation?

12-3 ADT QUEUE

A *queue* is another important ADT in computer science. There are more examples of queues in the real world than stacks, because queues have the *first-in, first-out*, or *FIFO*, property. For instance, the grocery store line mentioned in the last section is a queue. Aircraft in a holding pattern waiting to land at a busy airport represent a *queuing* operation. As aircraft approach the airport traffic area, they are placed in a holding pattern so that the first one in the pattern is the first one to land. We say that the aircraft are being *queued* into the pattern. A computer scientist would never say that the aircraft are being *stacked* in the pattern, right? Can you think of other real-world examples of queuing operations?

Recall that the LIFO property of stacks reverses the order of the stack elements from input to the stack to output from the stack. Queues, on the other hand, exhibit the FIFO property which preserves the order of the elements from input to output. Now for a formal definition of a queue.

A *queue* is a collection of data elements in which all insertions of elements into the queue are made at one end of the queue, called the *rear* of the queue; and all deletions of elements from the queue are made at the other end of the queue, called the *front* of the queue. A queue operates on the *first-in*, *first-out*, or *FIFO* principle.

From this definition, you see that queue access occurs at one of two ends of the queue. If an element is added to the queue, it is added to the rear of the queue just as in a grocery store checkout line. On the other hand, if an element is removed from the queue, it is removed from the front of the queue, as with the grocery store line. Of course, you can't remove an element from an empty queue.

We are now ready to define our queue ADT as follows:

ADT Queue

Operations, or Interface:

CreateQ
  Creates an empty queue.

Insert()
  Adds an element to the rear of a queue.

Remove()
  Removes an element from the front of a queue.

FrontElement()
  Copies the front element of a queue, leaving the queue unchanged.

EmptyQ()
  Determines if the queue is empty.

Data:

A collection of data elements with the property that elements can only be added at one end, called the ***rear*** of the queue, and elements can only be removed from the other end, called the *front* of the queue.

Implementing the Queue ADT

Like a stack, the queue ADT is not predefined in C++ or most other programming languages. Therefore, we must implement it using something that is predefined in the language. Again we will use the versatile array to implement the queue. However, we need to make use a special array called a ***circular***, or ***wraparound***, array. Look at the array in Figure 12-7 to see how we can create a queue using a circular array.

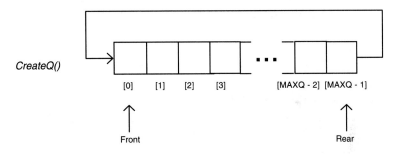

Figure 12-7 Setting *Front* to 0 and *Rear* to *MAXQ* − 1 will create a queue using a circular array implementation.

Creating a Queue Using a Circular Array

You see an array whose size is *MAXQ* and highest index is *MAXQ* − 1. To make the array hold a queue, we need to initialize two integer variables that locate the front and rear of the queue. Here, *Front* is initialized to 0 so that it locates position [0] of the array, and *Rear* is initialized to *MAXQ* − 1 so that it locates the last array position. Thus, an appropriate algorithm for *CreateQ()* is

CreateQ() **Algorithm**

BEGIN
   Set *Front* = 0.
   Set *Rear* = *MAXQ* − 1.
END.

Now, here's the idea behind a circular array. When we are using an external integer variable, such as *Front* or *Rear*, to locate elements in the array, we will advance the variable through the index range of the array, in our case from 0 to *MAXQ* − 1. When the variable needs to be advanced past the last array index, *MAXQ* − 1, we will force it to the first array index, 0. Thus, the variable will be advanced as follows:

0, 1, 2, 3, … , (*MAXQ* − 1), 0,1,2, 3, … , (*MAXQ* − 1), 0, 1, 2, 3, …

This way, the advancing process can continue in a circle indefinitely. All we need to accomplish this task is an **if/else** statement, like this:

If *Rear* == *MAXQ* − 1
   Set *Rear* = 0.
Else
   Set *Rear* = *Rear* + 1.

Here you see that the **else** statement increments *Rear*, unless the value of *Rear* is *MAXQ* − 1. If this is the case, *Rear* is set to 0. Of course, we will do the same thing with *Front* to make it wrap around.

Now we are ready to begin inserting and removing elements to and from the queue. Remember, we will insert elements at the rear of the queue and remove elements from the front of the queue.

Inserting Elements into a Queue

To insert an element into the queue, we must first advance *Rear* and then place the element at array position [*Rear*]. Thus, suppose we start with the array shown in Figure 12-7 and execute the following three insertion operations:

Insert('A')
Insert('B')
Insert('C')

The sequence of events created by these three operations is illustrated in Figure 12-8.

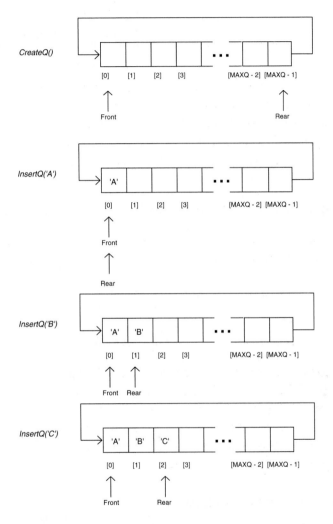

Figure 12-8 The effect of creating a queue and inserting three character elements into the queue.

We begin with the queue being initialized using *CreateQ()*. Remember that *CreateQ()* initializes *Front* with the value 0 and *Rear* with the value *MAX* − 1. When the first character, 'A', is inserted into the queue, the value of *Rear* must be advanced prior to the character being placed in the array. However, because *Rear* locates the last array index, *MAXQ* − 1, the value of *Rear* is forced to 0 using the wraparound idea. Once *Rear* is advanced to 0, the character 'A' is placed at array position [*Rear*], or [0]. Notice that both *Front* and *Rear* locate the character 'A'. This is *always* the case when there is only one element in the queue.

The second character to be inserted is the character 'B'. Again, *Rear* is advanced to locate the next array position. This time, however, the value of *Rear* is **not** *MAXQ* − 1. Therefore, 1 is added to *Rear* so that it locates the next sequential array position, [1]. The character 'B' is then placed at array position [*Rear*], or [1].

The third insert operation places that character 'C' at array position [2]. Notice that *Front* has not been affected by the insert operations and locates the first character inserted into the queue.

Here is an algorithm that reflects the *Insert()* operation:

Insert() **Algorithm**

BEGIN
    If the queue is not full
        If *Rear* == *MAXQ* − 1
            Set *Rear* = 0.
        Else
            Set *Rear* = *Rear* + 1.
        Place element at array position [*Rear*].
    Else
        Display full queue message.
END.

The first thing that must be done is to check for a full queue. How do you know when the queue is full? Or, for that matter, how do you know when the queue is empty? Well, because we are using an array implementation, the queue is full when the array is full, and the queue is empty when the array is empty, right? But, how can we use *Front* and/or *Rear* to determine when the array is full or empty? Your first thought might be that the queue is full when an element is placed in the last array position, thereby making *Rear* take on the value *MAX* − 1. But, from Figure 12-7, you see that this condition also reflects an empty queue condition. In fact, because of the circular nature of the array, there is no way to determine a full or empty queue condition using the values of *Front* and *Rear* unless we alter the nature of our implementation. Think about it!

The simplest way to determine an empty or full queue condition is to count the number of elements being inserted and removed from the queue. When an element is inserted into the queue, we will increment an element counter. When an element is removed from the queue, we will decrement the element counter. In this way, the queue is empty when the counter value is 0 and full when the counter value reaches the size of the array, *MAXQ*. To do this, we must add an additional processing step to our *Insert()* algorithm that will increment the element counter. Here is a modified *Insert()* algorithm that will permit us to determine a full queue condition:

Modified *Insert()* Algorithm

```
BEGIN
    If the queue is not full
            Increment element counter.
            If Rear == MAXQ − 1
                    Set Rear = 0.
            Else
                    Set Rear = Rear + 1.
            Place element at array position [Rear].
    Else
            Display full queue message.
END.
```

You should be aware that there is another way to implement a queue using a circular array that doesn't require an element counter to determine the empty/full conditions. However, this implementation requires that you sacrifice one array position by not allowing any queue elements to be placed in this position. This implementation will be left as a programming exercise at the end of the chapter.

Now, back to the algorithm. If the queue is not full, the element counter is incremented, and the **if/else** wraparound statement is executed to advance *Rear*. Once *Rear* is advanced, the element is placed in array position [*Rear*]. Note that *Rear* must be advanced prior to placing the element in the array. Of course, if the queue is full, no action is taken on the queue, and an appropriate message is displayed.

Removing Elements from a Queue

Let's remove the three elements that were inserted in Figure 12-8 by executing the following *Remove()* operations:

Remove( )
Remove( )
Remove( )

This sequence of events is illustrated in Figure 12-9.

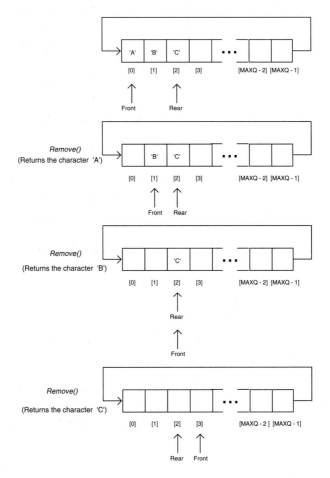

Figure 12-9   The effect of removing three character elements from the queue in Figure 12-8.

Elements are removed from the front of the queue. As a result, the first element to be removed from the queue is the character 'A' at array position [*Front*], or [0]. Once the element is removed, *Front* is advanced to the next circular array position. Now the character 'B' is at the front of the queue. The second *Remove()* operation removes this character and advances *Front* to position [2]. Now the only remaining element in the queue is the character 'C'. Notice that both *Front* and *Rear* locate this character, because it is the only element in the queue. A third *Remove()* operation removes the character 'C', leaving an empty queue. How can it be that the queue is empty, because *Front* and *Rear* are not in their initialized positions? Moreover, *Front* has moved ahead of *Rear*. Is this a problem? No! Remember how we have defined an empty and a full queue? It does not matter where *Front* and *Rear* are located in determining the empty or full queue conditions. All that matters is the value of the element counter. If the element counter is 0, the queue is empty. If the element counter is *MAXQ*, the queue is full.

Here is an algorithm for the *Remove()* operation:

Remove() **Algorithm**

```
BEGIN
    If the queue is not empty
            Decrement element counter.
            Remove the element at array position [Front].
            If Front == MAXQ − 1
                    Set Front = 0.
            Else
                    Set Front = Front + 1.
    Else
            Display empty queue message.
END.
```

The algorithm begins by checking for the empty queue condition. If the queue is not empty, the element counter is decremented, and *Front* is advanced via the **if/else** wraparound statement. If the queue is empty, an appropriate message is displayed.

Inspecting the Front Element of a Queue

The next thing we need to do is to develop the *FrontElement()* operation. Suppose we execute the following statement on the queue created back in Figure 12-8:

FrontElement()

The results of this operation are shown in Figure 12-10. Here you find that neither *Front* nor *Rear* is affected by the *FrontElement()* operation. The operation simply returns the front character of the queue. The following algorithm will support this operation:

FrontElement() **Algorithm**

> BEGIN
>> If the queue is not empty
>>> Copy the element at array position [*Front*].
>> Else
>>> Display an empty queue message.
> END.

If the queue is not empty, the algorithm simply copies the element at the front position of the queue. Comparing this to the *Remove()* algorithm, you find that there is no operation on the element counter or the *Front* position locator.

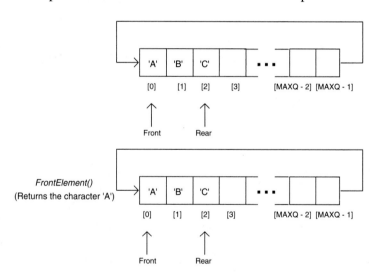

Figure 12-10   The effect of inspecting the queue created in Figure 12-8.

Coding the Queue ADT

We are now ready to code the queue ADT. To assure encapsulation and information hiding, we will code the ADT as a class. Here's the class declaration:

```
//QUEUE CLASS DECLARATION (queue.h)

#ifndef QUEUE_H
#define QUEUE_H
const int MAXQ = 5;                 //MAXIMUM QUEUE SIZE
enum {EMPTY = 0, FULL = MAXQ};      //DEFINE EMPTY = 0 AND
                                    //FULL = MAXQ

enum {FALSE, TRUE};                 //DEFINE FALSE = 0 AND
                                    //TRUE = 1

class Queue
{
public:
  Queue();                          //CONSTRUCTOR TO IMPLEMENT CreateQ()
  int EmptyQ();                     //CHECKS TO SEE IF QUEUE IS EMPTY
  int FullQ();                      //CHECKS TO SEE IF QUEUE IS FULL
  void Insert(char Char);           //ADD ELEMENT TO REAR
  char Remove();                    //REMOVE ELEMENT FROM FRONT
  char FrontElement();              //INSPECT FRONT ELEMENT

private:
  char Q[MAXQ];                     //CHARACTER ARRAY TO HOLD THE QUEUE
  int Front;                        //Front LOCATES FRONT ELEMENT OF QUEUE
  int Rear;                         //Rear LOCATES REAR ELEMENT OF QUEUE
  int ElementCount;                 //ELEMENT COUNTER
}; //END Queue
#endif
```

The foregoing file is coded as an include file called *queue.h.* At the beginning of the file, you find the same type of constant and enumerated data definitions as we coded in the stack ADT. Notice, however, that *EMPTY* is defined with a value of 0, and *FULL* is defined with a value of *MAXQ.* These definitions will be used when testing the element counter for the empty and full conditions, respectively.

The public functions that are listed in the class are those defined for the queue ADT, with the exception of the *FullQ()* operation. Why do we need a *FullQ()* operation for our implementation? The same reason that we needed a *FullStack()* operation for our stack implementation. We are dealing with a finite array data structure. Note also that the *CreateQ()* operation is implemented by the class constructor.

The private section begins by defining a character array called *Q[]* as a private member. As a result, this queue will store character elements. The size of the array is *MAXQ*, where *MAXQ* has been declared as the constant 5 for example purposes. There are three private integer variables: *Front, Rear*, and

ElementCount. You now should be aware of their use in this implementation. Again, it is important to stress the hiding of these private class members. No operations outside of the class can affect the contents of *Q[ ]* or the values of *Front*, *Rear*, or *ElementCount*. As a result, any queue object created for this class cannot be corrupted by intentional or unintentional operations outside of the queue class.

Next we need an implementation file to define the class functions. The file is called *queueop.cpp* and is provided as follows:

```
//QUEUE IMPLEMENTATION FILE (queueop.cpp)
#include "queue.h"      //FOR queue CLASS
#include <iostream.h>   //FOR cin AND cout

//IMPLEMENTATION OF Queue() CONSTRUCTOR
Queue :: Queue()
{
  Front = 0;                     //SET FRONT TO FIRST ARRAY POSITION
  Rear = MAXQ – 1;               //AND REAR TO LAST ARRAY POSITION
  ElementCount = EMPTY;          //SET Q ELEMENT COUNTER TO 0
} //END Queue()

//IMPLEMENTATION OF EmptyQ()
Queue :: EmptyQ()
{
  if (ElementCount == EMPTY) //IF Q  EMPTY, RETURN TRUE
    return TRUE;             //ELSE RETURN FALSE
  else
    return FALSE;
} //END EmptyQ()

//IMPLEMENTATION OF FullQ()
Queue :: FullQ()
{
  if (ElementCount == FULL)    //IF Q FULL, RETURN TRUE
    return TRUE;               //ELSE RETURN FALSE
  else
    return FALSE;
} //END FullQ()

//IMPLEMENTATION OF Insert()
void Queue :: Insert(char Char)
{
  if (!FullQ())                //IF Q NOT FULL
  {                            //ADD ONE TO ELEMENT COUNT
```

```
    ++ ElementCount;
    if (Rear == MAXQ − 1)        //INCREMENT REAR USING WRAPAROUND
      Rear = 0;
    else
      ++Rear;
    Q[Rear] = Char;              //INSERT CHARACTER INTO Q
  } //END IF
  else
    cout << "The queue is full!" << endl;
} //END Insert()

//IMPLEMENTATION OF Remove()
char Queue :: Remove()
{
  char Character;
  if (!EmptyQ())                //IF Q NOT EMPTY
  {
    −−ElementCount;             //DECREMENT ELEMENT COUNT
    Character = (Q[Front]);     //SAVE FRONT ELEMENT
    if (Front == MAXQ − 1)      //INCREMENT FRONT USING WRAPAROUND
      Front = 0;
    else
      ++Front;
    return Character;           //RETURN SAVED FRONT ELEMENT
  }
  else
  {
    cout << "The queue is empty" << endl;
    return '#';                 //RETURN '#' TO INDICATE QUEUE EMPTY
  } //END ELSE
} //END Remove()

//IMPLEMENTATION OF FrontElement()
char Queue :: FrontElement()
{
  if (!EmptyQ())                //IF Q NOT EMPTY
    return Q[Front];            //RETURN FRONT ELEMENT
  else                          //ELSE RETURN '#' FOR EMPTY Q
  {
    cout << "The queue is empty!" << endl;
    return '#';
  } //END ELSE
} //END FrontElement()
```

In this file, all of the queue algorithms discussed earlier have been coded. Compare each coded function to its algorithm so that you understand what's going on. There were no algorithms developed for the *EmptyQ()* and *FullQ()* operations, because they are so straightforward. Observe that the code for the *EmptyQ()* and *FullQ()* functions simply tests the element counter for an *EMPTY* or *FULL* condition. Recall that *EMPTY* is defined as 0 and *FULL* is defined as *MAXQ*.

The following application file, called *queueapp.cpp*, has been created to test our queue ADT:

```
//APPLICATION FILE TO TEST THE QUEUE ADT (queueapp.cpp)
#include "queue.h"      //FOR queue CLASS
#include <iostream.h>   //FOR cin AND cout

void main()
{
   char Character;        //CHARACTER TO BE QUEUED
   int Number = 0;        //NUMBER OF CHARACTERS TO BE QUEUED
   int Count = 0;         //LOOP COUNTER
   Queue Q;               //DEFINE QUEUE OBJECT

//GET NUMBER OF ELEMENTS TO QUEUE
   cout << "You cannot enter more than " << MAXQ
        << " elements. \nHow many elements do you have to enter? " << endl;
   cin >> Number;

//INSERT ELEMENTS INTO QUEUE
   while (Count < Number)
   {
     ++Count;
     cout << "\nEnter a character element: ";
     cin >> Character;
     Q.Insert(Character);
   } //END WHILE

//INSPECT FRONT ELEMENT WITHOUT CHANGING QUEUE
   cout << "\nThe front element of the queue is: "
        << Q.FrontElement();

//REMOVE AND WRITE QUEUE ELEMENTS
   cout << "\nThe contents of the queue are: ";
   while (!Q.EmptyQ())
     cout << Q.Remove();
```

```
//ATTEMPT TO REMOVE FROM EMPTY QUEUE
  Q.Remove();
} //END main()
```

The test program defines *Q* as an object of class *Queue*. Elements are then inserted into *Q* one at time from user entries via a **while** loop. Notice that the loop executes as long as the number of elements entered does not exceed the number of elements the user specified for entry. Once the user elements are inserted into the queue, the front element is inspected by a call to the *FrontElement()* function. The next segment of code removes and displays the queue elements. If the queue is not empty, a **while** loop is entered to remove and display all of the queue elements one at a time. The termination of the loop is controlled by a call to *EmptyQ()*. As a result, the loop statements will execute, removing and displaying one element with each iteration, until the queue is empty. Finally, a single call is made to *RemoveQ()* in an attempt to remove an element from an empty queue. This call was made to test the *RemoveQ()* function. Here are the results of executing the test program:

You cannot enter more than 5 elements.
How many elements do you have to enter?
3↵

Enter a character element: **A**↵

Enter a character element: **B**↵

Enter a character element: **C**↵

The front element of the queue is: A

The contents of the queue are: ABC

The queue is empty!

In this test run, the user has entered the characters 'A', 'B', and 'C'. The front character, 'A', is copied and displayed to verify the *FrontElement()* function. Then all of the characters of the queue are removed and displayed. Notice that the characters are displayed in the same order in which they were entered, thereby verifying the FIFO principle. The last line on the display verifies that the *Remove()* function checks for the empty queue condition.

Quick Check

1. Suppose that the user filled a queue using the application test program in this section. What would happen if a call were made to the *Insert()* function after the queue was full?

2. True or false: With our array implementation of a queue, an *Insert()* operation requires that *Front* be advanced prior to placing the element in the array.

3. Write the pseudocode required to advance *Front* for the circular array implementation of a queue.

4. True or false: With the circular array implementation of a queue, *Front* can never have a higher value than *Rear*.

5. Using the circular array implementation of a queue, how can you tell when there is only one element in the queue?

6. Theoretically, the size of a queue is unlimited. Why did we have to include a *FullQ()* function in our implementation?

7. Explain how to determine when the queue is empty and when the queue is full using our array implementation.

12-4 ADT LIST

You have already been dealing with lists, even though we have not made a formal definition of a list, but now is the time to do so.

> A *list* is a *sequence* of data elements whose basic operations are insertion and deletion of elements to and from the list.

The arrays, stacks, and queues that you have studied so far are lists. Each of these lists represents a *sequence* of data elements. The term *sequence* implies ordering. This means that the list has a first element, a second element, and so on. In an array, the elements are ordered from the first array position to the last array position. In a stack, the elements are ordered from the top of the stack (last element in) to the bottom of the stack (first element in). In a queue, the elements are ordered from the front of the queue to the rear of the queue. Stacks and queues, however, are special kinds of lists, because the insert and delete operations are defined to be at the end(s) of the list. An array has no such restriction, because you can access the list randomly, inserting and deleting elements from any position in the list. Thus, stacks and queues must be sequentially accessed, whereas arrays can be randomly accessed.

In each of the lists you have studied so far, the sequencing of the elements is *implicit*. This means that the element sequence is inherent to the structure definition. The sequencing of elements in an array is given implicitly, because the first element is stored in position [0], the second element in position [1], and so on. Thus, given any element in the array, you can always locate its successor element. Given the element at array position [5], you know that its successor is at array position [6]. In a stack, the sequencing of elements is given implicitly from top to bottom. Given the element located at *Top*, you know that the next element is located at *Top* − 1. In a queue, the sequencing is from front to rear. Given an element located at *Front*, you know that its successor is located at *Front* + 1. In all of these lists, once you locate the first element, you can locate the second, and so on, via the natural ordering of the structure. However, there is one kind of list where the sequencing of elements must be provided *explicitly*. This means that given any element in the list, the location of its successor must be clearly specified, because its location is not inherent within the natural sequencing of the list elements. Such a list is called a *linked list*.

Linked Lists

First, consider the following formal definition of a linked list:

> A *linked list* is a sequential collection of data elements such that, given any element in the list, the location of its successor element is specified by an *explicit* link, rather than by its natural position in the collection.

Now, here's the idea: A linked list consists of a sequence of *nodes*. A node contains two things: an *element* and a *locator*, or *link*. The element is the information that is stored in the node, and the locator is the link that locates the *next* node in the list. This idea is illustrated in Figure 12-11.

NODE

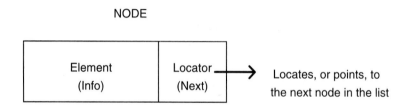

Figure 12-11   A single node in a linked list.

The element part of the node may contain a simple integer, character, or string as well as an entire structure that contains many other data elements. For instance, the element part of a node could be a *struct* that contains your name, address, and telephone number. We will call this the *Info* part of the node. The locator part of the node is the explicit locator, or link, to the next sequential node in the list. We will call this the *Next* part of the node. We say that *Next* locates, or points to, the next node in the list. Now, look at the sample linked list in Figure 12-12.

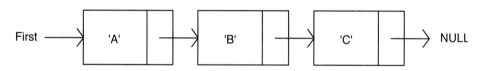

Figure 12-12   A linked list containing three nodes.

The linked list in Figure 12-12 contains three nodes storing character information. The first node is located by a locator called *First*. We must always have a means of locating the first node in the list and will usually designate this as *First*. Notice that *First* locates, or points to, the first node in the list. The first node locates, or points to, the second node, and so on. The last node points to *NULL*, because there are no more nodes in the list. We will use the term *NULL* to designate the end of the list. It is easy to see that the list is sequentially ordered from the first to the last node and the ordering is given explicitly via the *Next* part of each node.

Now we need to develop some notation that will be used to discuss linked lists. We will implement our linked list using pointers and, therefore, refer to a node locator as a pointer. Here are some notation and terminology that will be employed when discussing linked lists:

Node(P) refers to the entire node pointed to by *P*.
Info(P) refers to the information part of the node pointed to by *P*.
Next(P) refers to the next, or pointer, part of the node pointed to by *P*.
The *predecessor node* to *Node(P)* is the node just before *Node(P)*.
The *successor node* to *Node(P)* is the node just after *Node(P)*.

This linked list notation and terminology is illustrated in Figure 12-13.

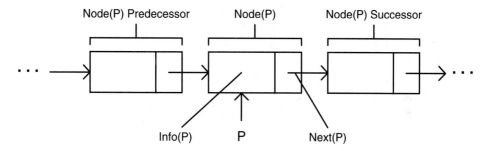

Figure 12-13 Notation and terminology used with linked lists.

Of special interest is *Next(P)*. *Next(P)* is always a pointer and points to *Node(P)'s* successor node, unless *Node(P)* is the last node in the list. If this is the case, *Next(P)* has the value *NULL*.

To get familiar with this notation, consider the following algorithm:

```
        BEGIN
          Set P = First.
          While P ≠ NULL
            Write Info(P).
            Set P = Next(P).
        END.
```

Can you determine what the algorithm does? Well, notice that *P* is made to point to the first node in the list by setting *P* to *First*. Then, the **while** loop will execute as long as *P* is not equal to *NULL*. Each time the loop is executed, the information in the node pointed to by *P* (*Info(P)*) is written and *P* is advanced to point to the next sequential node in the list. In other words, the list is *traversed* from the first node to the last. At each node, the information stored in the node is written. Now that you have a general feel for a linked list, it is time to define our linked list ADT, as follows:

ADT Linked List

Operations, or Interface:

CreateList( )
  Creates an empty list.

InsertNode( )
  Adds a data element to the beginning of the list.

DeleteNode( )
  Removes a specified data element from the list.

TraverseList( )
  Traverses the list, processing the list information as required.

EmptyList( )
  Determines if the list is empty.

Data:

  A sequential collection of data elements.

Implementing the Linked List ADT

The natural way to implement a linked list is by using pointers. As you can see from the ADT definition, we have defined five linked list operations. We now need to show how pointers can be used to implement these operations. For each of the operations, we will develop an algorithm using the linked list notation given earlier. Then, we will code the algorithms in C++.

Creating an Empty Linked List

The first thing that must be done before building a linked list is to create an empty list. An empty list will be a list with no nodes in it, right? So, to create a list without any nodes, all we need to do is set *First* to *NULL*, as in Figure 12-14.

$$\text{First} \longrightarrow \text{NULL}$$

Figure 12-14   An empty list is created by making *First* point to *NULL*.

Remember that (1) we will be using pointers to implement our linked list, (2) *First* will be the pointer that locates the first node in the list, and (3) *NULL* will define the end of the list. So, if we make *First* point to *NULL*, we have an empty list. Here's the simple algorithm:

CreateList( ) **Algorithm**

BEGIN
 Set *First = NULL*.
END.

Inserting Data into a Linked List

Next, we need to develop an algorithm to insert a data element into the linked list. Because the linked list data elements are contained in nodes, this operation requires that a node be added to the list. Looking at the ADT definition, you see that we will always add a node at the beginning of the list. To accomplish this task, we need to do four things:

1. Create a new node.
2. Fill the node with the data to be stored.
3. Make the new node point to the first node in the list.
4. Make *First* point to the new node.

For example, suppose that we have a linked list of the two characters 'A' and 'B', in that order. Then, we execute the following operation to insert the character 'C' into the list:

Insert('C')

The sequence of events that must be performed to insert a new node containing the character 'C' at the beginning of the list are shown in Figure 12-15.

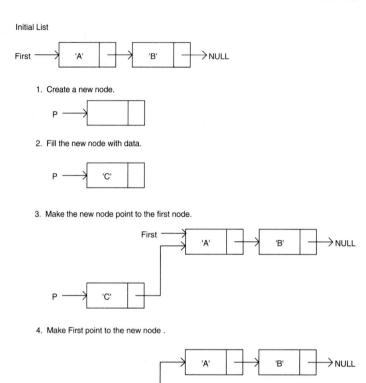

Figure 12-15   Inserting a node at the beginning of a linked list.

To create the new node, we simply make a temporary pointer, *P*, point to an empty node. As you will find out shortly, a node will be coded as a struct that contains a data, or *Info*, member and a pointer, or *Next*, member. The new node struct will literally be created from nothing using dynamic memory allocation and the **new** operator. So, to create a new node and make *P* point to this node, we will use the following statement in our algorithm:

$$\text{Set } P = \text{new } Node.$$

Next, the information field of the new node is filled with the data element, in this case the character 'C'. To accomplish this task, we will place the following statement in the algorithm:

$$\text{Set } Info(P) = \text{'C'}.$$

This statement says to "place the character 'C' in the information part of the node pointed to by *P*."

Once the data are in the new node, we must add the node to the list. The node is to be added at the beginning of the list, so we make the new node point to the first node in the list. Notice from Figure 12-15 that, prior to this step, *First* is pointing to where the new node needs to point. As a result, all we need to do is to assign *First* to the pointer, or *Next*, part of the new node. The following pseudocode statement will accomplish this task:

Set *Next(P)* = *First*.

The above statement says to "Assign *First* to the pointer part of the node pointed to by *P*." Performing this assignment places the new node at the beginning of the list. However, *First* is now pointing to the second node in the list and needs to be moved to point to our new node. Our new node is currently being pointed to by *P*. Thus, to make *First* point to the new node, all we have to do is to set *First* to *P*, like this:

Set *First* = *P*.

That's all there is to it. Here's the complete algorithm:

InsertNode( ) **Algorithm**

```
BEGIN
  Set P = new Node.
  Set Info(P) = Data Element.
  Set Next(P) = First.
  Set First = P.
END.
```

Make sure that you understand how the four statements in the above algorithm accomplish the four tasks shown in Figure 12-15, especially in light of the notation that is being used. You might have noticed that, because our *InsertNode( )* algorithm places the new node at the beginning of the list, the character 'C' is placed out of its natural order, relative to the other nodes in the list. An **ordered linked list** is a linked list whereby all the data elements are in some natural order from the first node to the last node in the list. To create an ordered linked list, our *InsertNode( )* algorithm must be changed to search the list for the correct insertion point prior to adding the node to the list. This will be left as an exercise at the end of the chapter.

Deleting Data from a Linked List

Deleting data from a linked list requires that we delete the node containing the data from the linked list. Deleting a node from a linked list is the most difficult operation to be performed. As a result, we will develop several algorithm levels, working up to one that can be coded in C++.

Looking at the ADT definition for *DeleteNode()*, you see that we must delete a specified data element from the list. This means that, given an element to delete, we must search for the element in the list. Then, once the element is found, adjust the list pointers to eliminate the node that contains the element to be deleted. So, our first-level algorithm becomes

DeleteNode( ) **Algorithm (First Level)**

> BEGIN
>> Search the list for the element to be deleted.
>> Adjust the list pointers to eliminate the node that
>> contains the element to be deleted.
> END.

Searching a Linked List

We will employ a simple sequential search to find the node to be deleted. This means that, beginning with the first node, we must test the element stored in the information part of the node against the specified element to delete and advance to the next node, repeat the testing procedure, and so on, until we get to the end of the list. Here is an algorithm that will do the job:

Linked List Search Algorithm

> BEGIN
> If the list is empty
>> Write an appropriate message.
> Else
>> Set $P = First$.
>> Set $PredP = NULL$.
>> Set $Found$ = false.
>> While (NOT *Found*) AND ($P \neq NULL$)
>>> If *Info(P)* == *Element*

> Set *Found* = true.
> > Else
> > > Set *PredP* = *P*.
> > > Set *P* = *Next(P)*.
>
> END.

The first thing that must be done is to test for an empty list, because you cannot delete a node from a list that is empty. If the list is empty, an appropriate message is written to the user; otherwise, the search process is started.

There are two key pointer variables employed for the search. We will use the pointer *P* as a pointer to traverse the list, beginning at *First* and ending when *P* becomes *NULL*. In addition to *P*, we will employ another pointer called *PredP* that follows *P* through the list as the search progresses. As a result, the pointer *PredP* will always point to the node just prior to the node to which *P* is pointing. Recall that this is the predecessor node to *Node(P)*. This idea is illustrated in Figure 12-16.

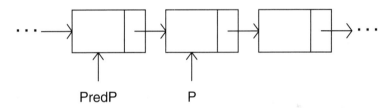

Figure 12-16 During the list search procedure, *P* will point to the node being tested, and *PredP* will point to the predecessor node to *Node(P)*.

A **while** loop is employed to control the search. Notice that the loop tests for two conditions: (NOT *Found*) and (*P* ≠ *NULL*). The **AND** operator requires that both tests be true for the search to proceed. As a result, the search will stop when either the element is found or when *P* becomes *NULL*. Within the loop, we use an **if/else** statement to test the information contained in *Node(P)*. If *Info(P)* is equal to the element being searched for, the Boolean variable is set to true, and the loop will break. Otherwise, both pointers are advanced to the next respective node in the list. Do you see how the statement *Set Pred(P)* = *P* makes *PredP* point to *Node(P)* and the statement *Set P* = *Next(P)* makes *P* point to *Node(P)*'s successor node?

So, when the search loop is broken, *P* is pointing to the node to be deleted, and *PredP* is pointing to this node's predecessor. But, what if the element being searched for was not in the list? In this case, *P* will move all the way through the list and stop when it becomes *NULL*. Also, what if the node to be deleted is the first node in the list? Well, in this case, *P* and *PredP* will not be advanced at all and will have their original values of *First* and *NULL*, respectively.

Deleting a Node in a Linked List

Next, let's develop the pseudocode required to actually delete a node from the list. This task follows the foregoing search algorithm, so we will use the values of *Found*, *P*, and *PredP* to delete the required node. Here's the delete algorithm:

Delete Algorithm

```
BEGIN
  If (Found)
    If (PredP == NULL)
      Set First = Next(P).
    Else
      Set Next(PredP) = Next(P).
  Else
      Write a message that the element was not
      found in the list.
END.
```

Here, the first thing to do is to check to see if the element being searched for was found during the search. If *Found* is true coming out of the search algorithm, the element was found, and the node must be deleted. Otherwise, the element was not found and an appropriate message must be written to the user. If the element was found, a nested **if/else** statement is employed to delete the respective node. If the node to be deleted is the first node in the list, we simply make *First* point to the second node in the list by setting *First* to *Next(P)*. This deletes the first node in the list. How do you know if the node to be deleted is the first node in the list? Of course, *PredP* has the value *NULL* after exiting the search algorithm. If *PredP* does not have the value *NULL,* the node to be deleted is not the first node in the list. In this case, the nested **else** makes the pointer from *Node(P)*'s predecessor jump around *Node(P)* and point to *Node(P)*'s successor. This is accomplished by setting *Next(PredP)* to *Next(P)*. The diagram in Figure 12-17 illustrates this operation:

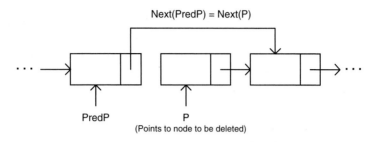

Figure 12-17 Setting *Next(PredP)* to *Next(P)* deletes *Node(P)* from the list.

Now putting the search algorithm together with the delete node algorithm, we get an algorithm for our ADT *DeleteNode()* operation that can be coded in C++. Here is the final algorithm:

DeleteNode() **Algorithm**

```
BEGIN
  If the list is empty
     Write an appropriate message.
  Else
     Set P = First.
     Set PredP = NULL.
     Set Found = false.
     While (NOT Found) AND (P ≠ NULL)
        If Info(P) == Element
           Set Found = true.
        Else
           Set PredP = P.
           Set P = Next(P).
     If (Found)
        If (PredP == NULL)
           Set First = Next(P).
        Else
           Set Next(PredP) = Next(P).
     Else
        Write a message that the element was not found
        in the list.
  END.
```

Traversing a Linked List

You have already observed a traversal algorithm. Here is one that is customized to fit our ADT definition for *TraverseList( )*:

TraverseList( ) **Algorithm**

```
BEGIN
   If the list is not empty
      Set P = First.
      While P ≠ NULL
         Write Info(P).
         Set P = Next(P).
   Else
         Write a message to indicate an empty list.
END.
```

The algorithm begins by checking for an empty list. If the list is not empty, a temporary list pointer, *P*, is initialized to the beginning of the list. A **while** loop is then executed to process the information stored in the nodes. In this case, we are simply writing the node information, *Info(P)*. Once the node information is written, *P* is advanced to point to the next node in the list. The loop continues writing the node information and advancing *P* through the list until the value of *P* becomes *NULL*. Of course, an appropriate message is written to the user if the list is empty.

Checking for an Empty List

To complete our ADT implementation, we must develop an algorithm for the *EmptyList( )* operation. Recall that this operation simply checks to see if the list is empty. How do you know when the list is empty? Right, when *First* has the value *NULL*. As a result, the algorithm is

EmptyList( ) **Algorithm**

```
BEGIN
   If First == NULL
      Return true.
```

```
        Else
            Return false.
        END.
```

As you can see, *EmptyList()* returns the Boolean value true if the value of *First* is *NULL*; otherwise, it returns the value false. We can now call upon this operation in the other operations when we need to test for an empty list.

Coding the Linked List ADT

We are now ready to code the linked list ADT. How do you suppose that we will code it in C++? You guessed it, using a class to assure complete encapsulation with information hiding. First, the class declaration:

```
//LINKED LIST CLASS DECLARATION FILE (list.h)
#ifndef LIST_H
#define LIST_H

#include <iostream.h>            //REQUIRED TO DEFINE NULL POINTER

enum {FALSE,TRUE};              //DEFINE FALSE = 0 AND TRUE = 1

//NODE STRUCTURE DECLARATION
struct Node
{
  char Info;                    //INFORMATION PART OF NODE
  Node *Next;                   //POINTER TO NEXT NODE
}; //END Node

class List
{
public:
  List();                       //CONSTRUCTOR TO
                                //IMPLEMENT  CreateList()
  ~List();                      //DESTRUCTOR TO
                                //DEALLOCATE LIST MEMORY
  void InsertNode(char Char);   //FUNCTION TO INSERT A NODE
  void DeleteNode(char Char);   //FUNCTION TO DELETE A
                                //SPECIFIED NODE
  void TraverseList();          //FUNCTION TO TRAVERSE LIST
  int  EmptyList();             //FUNCTION TO TEST FOR
                                //EMPTY  LIST
```

```
private:
  Node *First;          //DEFINE First AS A POINTER TO NODE STRUCT
}; //END List
#endif
```

The class declaration is placed in a header file called *list.h*. Before the *List* class is declared, a struct called *Node* is declared. Remember that a linked list node has two parts: an information part and a pointer part. As a result, the *Node* struct has two parts. The information part is defined as a character field called *Info*. This means that our linked list will hold character data. The pointer part of the node is defined as a pointer field called *Next*. Notice that the data pointed to by *Next* is the *Node* struct itself. This means that the *Next* pointer will point to a struct that has the same definition as the *Node* struct in which *Next* is defined. Isn't this what we want to do? The *Next* pointer in a node needs to point to another node of the same structure, right?

Following the *Node* struct declaration, we declare a class called *List*. The class must consist of the linked list node structure and the functions required to operate on that structure. All we have to do to define the entire linked list is define a pointer to the first node in the list. From here, each node locates its successor node via its *Next* pointer. So the single private member of the class is a pointer, called *First*, which will locate the first node in the list. Notice that *First* is a pointer to our *Node* struct.

The first function declared in the class is the class constructor, called *List()*. This constructor function implements the *CreateList()* operation and will be coded to set *First* to *NULL*.

The second function declared is the class destructor, called *~List()*. This is an ideal application for a destructor! We will be generating new nodes by dynamically allocating memory. When we delete a node, we will deallocate the memory required for that node. So, why not deallocate the memory allocated to the entire list by using a destructor when we are done processing the list? In other words, our *~List()* destructor will delete the entire list by deallocating all memory allocated to the list when we are done processing the list. This function is not part of our ADT definition and is only included because of the use of dynamic memory allocation.

Next you see the remaining four operations required for the *Linked List* ADT. You are now aware of the purpose of these four operations. The task at hand is to code the respective algorithms developed for these operations as part of an implementation file. The function implementation file is called *listop.cpp*. Here it is:

```
//LINKED LIST IMPLEMENTATION FILE (listop.cpp)

#include "list.h"          //FOR list CLASS
#include <iostream.h>   //FOR cin AND cout

//IMPLEMENTATION OF CONSTRUCTOR List()
List :: List()
{
  First = NULL;
} //END List()

//IMPLEMENTATION OF DESTRUCTOR, ~List()
List :: ~List()
{
  Node *P;              //DEFINE P AS A POINTER TO
                        //THE NODE STRUCT
  Node *Temp;           //DEFINE Temp AS POINTER TO
                        //THE NODE STRUCT
  P = First;            //SET P = FIRST
  while (P!= NULL)      //TRAVERSE LIST UNTIL P = NULL
  {
    Temp = P -> Next;   //MAKE Temp POINT TO NEXT NODE IN LIST
    delete P;           //DEALLOCATE NODE(P)
    P = Temp;           //MAKE P POINT TO NEXT NODE
  } //END WHILE
} //END ~List()
//IMPLEMENTATION OF InsertNode()
void List :: InsertNode(char Char)
{
  Node *P;                   //DEFINE P AS A POINTER TO
                             //THE NODE STRUCT
  P = new Node;              //ALLOCATE MEMORY FOR NODE(P)
  P -> Info = Char;          //PLACE CHAR IN INFO(P)
  P -> Next = First;         //INSERT NODE(P) AT BEGINNING
  First = P;                 //MOVE First TO NODE(P)
} //END InsertNode()

//IMPLEMENTATION OF DeleteNode()
void List :: DeleteNode(char Char)
{
  int Found = FALSE;   //INITIALIZE Found TO FALSE
  Node *P;             //DEFINE P AS A POINTER TO NODE STRUCT
  Node *PredP;         //DEFINE PredP AS A POINTER TO NODE STRUCT
```

```
    P = First;                //START P AT FIRST NODE
    PredP = NULL;             //START PredP AT NULL

//IF LIST EMPTY, WRITE EMPTY MESSAGE. ELSE
//SEARCH FOR ELEMENT TO BE DELETED
  if (EmptyList())
      cout << "\nYou cannot delete a node from an empty list!" << endl;
  else
  {
      while (!Found && P != NULL)          //TRAVERSE LIST UNTIL FOUND
                                           //OR P == NULL
      {
          if (P -> Info == Char)           //TEST INFO(P)
             Found = TRUE;
          else                             //ADVANCE POINTERS
          {
             PredP = P;                    //CATCH PredP UP TO P
             P = P-> Next;                 //ADVANCE P
          } //END ADVANCE ELSE
      } //END SEARCH LOOP

//DELETE NODE IF FOUND. ELSE WRITE NOT FOUND MESSAGE
      if (Found)
      {
          //DOES NODE(P) HAVE A PREDECESSOR?
          //IF NOT, DELETE FIRST NODE. ELSE DELETE NODE(P)
          if (PredP == NULL)
          {
             First = P -> Next;            //MOVE FIRST TO SECOND NODE
             delete P;                     //DEALLOCATE NODE(P)
          } //END DELETE FIRST NODE
          else
          {
             PredP -> Next = P -> Next;    //MAKE NEXT(PredP) JUMP
                                           //AROUND NODE(P)
             delete P;                     //DEALLOCATE NODE(P)
          } //END DELETE NODE(P)
      } //END IF FOUND
      else                                 //WRITE NOT FOUND MESSAGE
          cout << "\nThe character '" << Char << "' is not in the list!" << endl;
  } //END SEARCH ELSE
} //END DeleteNode()
```

```
//IMPLEMENTATION OF TraverseList()
void List :: TraverseList()
{
  Node *P;              //DEFINE P AS A POINTER TO  NODE STRUCT
  P = First;            //START P AT FIRST NODE

  //IF LIST IS NOT EMPTY, TRAVERSE LIST
  //AND WRITE INFO(P). ELSE WRITE LIST EMPTY MESSAGE
  if (!EmptyList())
  {
    while (P != NULL)            //TRAVERSE LIST UNTIL P = NULL
    {
      cout << P -> Info << " -> ";   //WRITE INFO(P)
      P = P -> Next;             //ADVANCE P
    } //END WHILE
    cout << "NULL " << endl;     //WRITE "NULL"
  } //END IF NOT EMPTY
  else                           //WRITE EMPTY LIST MESSAGE
    cout << "\nThe list is empty!" << endl;
} //END TraverseList()

//IMPLEMENTATION OF EmptyList()
int List :: EmptyList()
{
  if (First == NULL)
    return TRUE;
  else
    return FALSE;
} //END EmptyList()
```

Now remember, we are implementing our linked list ADT using dynamic pointers. The first implementation that you see in the foregoing code is for the constructor, *List()*. This function simply initializes a new list by setting *First* to *NULL*. Next, the destructor function, *~List()* begins by defining temporary pointers, *P* and *Temp*, to the *Node* struct. The pointer *P* is initialized to point to the first node in the list by setting it to *First*. A **while** loop is then executed until the value of *P* becomes *NULL*. Within the loop, *Temp* is set to the next node in the list, and the **delete** operator is executed to deallocate the memory being used by *Node(P)*. Once the node memory is deallocated, *P* is advanced to the next node in the list by setting *P* to *Temp*. (Why do we need *Temp*?)

The remaining function implementations simply reflect their respective algorithms. However, take special note of how dynamic pointers are employed to code the algorithm. For example, notice how the *InsertNode()* function allocates memory for a new node by executing the **new** operator. The statement P = new Node; allocates memory dynamically for a *Node* struct and then makes *P* point to that struct. In the *DeleteNode()* function, the statement delete P; deallocates the memory occupied by the *Node* struct to which *P* is pointing. The pseudocode operations used in our algorithms are implemented in C++ using pointers, as summarized in Table 12-1.

TABLE 12-1 LINKED LIST PSEUDOCODE
VERSUS C++ POINTER CODE

Pseudocode	C++ Pointer Code
Info(P)	P –> Info
Node(P)	*P
Next(P)	P –> Next

Make a sincere effort to understand how each of the algorithms developed in this section is coded using dynamic pointers in the foregoing implementation file. You now possess all the knowledge required to understand this code.

Last but not least, we need an application file to test our linked list ADT. Here is the one that I used:

```
//APPLICATION FILE TO TEST LIST ADT (listapp.cpp)

#include "list.h"        //FOR list CLASS
#include <iostream.h>   //FOR cin AND cout

void main()
{
  char Character;       //CHARACTER TO BE INSERTED INTO LIST
  int Number = 0;       //NUMBER OF CHARACTERS TO BE INSERTED
  int Count = 0;        //LOOP COUNTER

  List L;               //DEFINE LIST OBJECT

//INSERT SPECIFIED NUMBER OF ELEMENTS INTO LIST
  cout << "How many nodes do you want to insert? " << endl;
  cin >> Number;
```

```
  while (Count < Number)
  {
    ++Count;
    cout << "\nEnter a character element:  ";
    cin >> Character;
    L.InsertNode(Character);
  } //END WHILE

//TRAVERSE AND WRITE LIST ELEMENTS
  cout << "\nThe contents of the list are:  ";
  L.TraverseList();

//DELETE A SPECIFIED CHARACTER  FROM THE LIST
  cout << "\nWhich character element do you want to delete? ";
  cin >> Character;
  L.DeleteNode(Character);

//TRAVERSE AND WRITE LIST ELEMENTS
  cout << "\nThe contents of the list are:  ";
  L.TraverseList();
} //END main()
```

The application file name is *listapp.cpp*. The code begins by including the *list.h* header file as well as other standard header files that are required. An object, *L*, is defined for the *List* class. The user is then prompted to enter any number of list elements. Is the user restricted to some maximum number of elements as with our stack and queue implementations? No! This is the advantage of using a dynamic pointer implementation. As long as memory is available, we can add as many elements to the list as we want. (Why were we limited with our stack and queue implementations?)

Once a list is constructed, the list is traversed by calling *TraverseList( )* to display the list elements. Then the user is prompted to delete a specified character from the list. The character is deleted, and the list is traversed and displayed again. Here's a sample run:

How many nodes do you want to insert?
3↵

Enter a character element: **A**↵

Enter a character element: **B**↵

Enter a character element: **C**↵

The contents of the list are: C –> B –> A –> NULL

Which character element do you want to delete? **B.⏎**

The contents of the list are: C –> A –> NULL

Quick Check

1. True or false: In a linked list, the sequencing of the nodes is implicit.

2. The two parts of a linked list node are the _____ and _____.

3. If *Node(P)* is the last node in the list, the value of *Next(P)* is _____.

4. True of false: In a pointer implementation of a linked list, we know that the list is empty when the value of *First* is zero.

5. What happens if you reverse the order of steps 3 and 4 in the insertion process illustrated in Figure 12-15?

6. Will the list search algorithm given in this section detect multiple occurrences of the same element in a linked list?

7. What happens if the statements *Set Pred(P) = P* and *Set P = Next(P)* are reversed in the linked list search algorithm?

8. Write an algorithm using the pseudocode notation developed in this section for the list destructor function, *~List( )*.

CHAPTER SUMMARY

The definition of an ADT includes the following key concepts:

*   *An ADT provides for data abstraction.*
*   *An ADT includes both data and related operations.*
*   *An ADT provides a means to encapsulate and hide information details whereby the ADT data is completely hidden from its surroundings.*
*   *ADT operations provide coupling to the outside world via a function interface.*

Data abstraction is an important software development and programming tool. When developing software with ADTs, you can concentrate on the ADT data and related operations, without worrying about the inner implementation details of the ADT. Data abstraction provides for generality, modularity, and protection when developing software.

Three classic ADTs are stack, queue, and linked list. The stack ADT provides for a collection of data elements whereby elements are always added and removed from one end of the stack, called the *Top* of the stack. As a result, stacks operate on the last-in, first-out (LIFO) principle, which reverses the ordering of data elements from input to the stack to output from the stack. The queue ADT provides for a collection of data elements whereby elements are always added to the rear of the queue and removed from the front of the queue. Thus, queues operate on the first-in, first-out (FIFO) principle, which preserves the ordering of data elements from input to the queue to output from the queue. The linked list ADT provides for a list of data elements whereby elements are always added to the beginning of the list (with the exception of an ordered linked list) and removed from a specified position in the list. Linked lists consist of nodes that contain an information part and a pointer part. The pointer part of any node locates the next sequential node in the list. Arrays, stacks, and queues provide for implicit sequencing of data, whereas linked lists provide for explicit sequencing of data.

Object-oriented programming is ideal for implementing ADTs because of its data hiding ability. When an ADT is coded as a class, only those operations that are defined for the ADT can be used to access and manipulate the ADT data.

QUESTIONS AND PROBLEMS

Questions

1. Why is data abstraction an important software development tool?

2. What three things are gained by using ADTs during software development?

3. Suppose that we implement a queue using a noncircular array. The queue is initialized so that $Front = Rear = 0$. Then, as we add elements to the queue, we increment *Rear* and insert the element into the array at position [*Rear*]. When we remove elements from the queue, we remove the element at position [*Front*] and increment *Front*. What problem is encountered with this implementation? Can the problem be corrected? If so, how? What do you suppose the disadvantage is to this implementation versus the one given in this chapter.

4. How do you know that there is only a single element in a queue using the implementation discussed in this chapter?

5. Suggest a way of implementing a queue using a noncircular array. (*Hint:* Always keep *Front* at position [0] in the array.) What is the disadvantage of this implementation compared to the circular array implementation?

6. Would a compiler use a stack or a queue to keep track of return addresses for nested function calls?

7. Use the stack ADT to write the pseudocode required to remove the element just below the top element of a stack.

8. How must the class header files for the stack, queue, and linked list ADTs given in this chapter be changed to store integers?

9. How must the class header files for the stack, queue, and linked list ADTs given in this chapter be changed to store floating-point numbers?

10. How must the class header files for the stack, queue, and linked list ADTs given in this chapter be changed to store structures (structs)?

11. Use the queue ADT to write the pseudocode required to move the element at the rear of the queue to the front of the queue.

12. Suppose that *P* is pointing to some given node in a linked list. What is pointed to by the expression *Next(Next(P))*?

13. Suppose that *P* is pointing to some given node in a linked list. What information is accessed by the expression *Info(Next(P))*?

14. Verify, through desk-checking, that the linked list *DeleteNode()* algorithm developed in this chapter works for the last node in the list.

Problems

Least Difficult

1. Change the stack ADT implementation given in this text to store integers. Write an application program to test your integer stack.

2. Change the queue ADT implementation given in this text to store floating-point numbers. Write an application program to test your floating-point queue.

3. Code the linked list ADT given in this chapter, and write an application program to test the following features:
    *   Deleting the first node in the list.
    *   Deleting the last node in the list.
    *   Deleting a node from an empty list.

4. A palindrome is a word that has the same spelling both forward and backward. Three examples are the words MOM, DAD, and ANNA. Write a program that uses a stack and a queue to determine if a word entered by the user is a palindrome.

5. Write a program that uses only stacks to determine if a word entered by the user is a palindrome. (*Hint:* You will need three stacks. Why?)

More Difficult

6. A problem with the array implementation of a stack is that the array is finite, thus requiring a *FullStack()* operation. A dynamic pointer implementation of a linked list does not have this limitation. Implement the stack ADT using a dynamic linked list. (*Hint:* Make the top of the stack point to the first node in the list. In fact, replace *First* with *Top*. Then always insert and delete at this first node when you push and pop data, respectively.)

7. You can implement a queue in a circular array without using an element counter to determine the empty/full conditions. To do this, you must sacrifice an array position so that no element is ever stored in this position. In this implementation, *Front* will locate the empty array position, and the empty position will always precede the actual front element in the queue. This idea is shown in Figure 12-18.

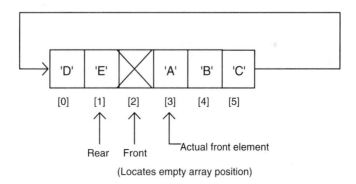

Figure 12-18   An alternative way to implement a queue using a circular array.

With this implementation, the queue is empty when *Front = Rear*, and the queue is full when *Rear + 1 = Front*. To insert an element into the rear of the queue, you must preincrement *Rear*. To remove an element from the front of the queue, you must preincrement *Front*. The queue can be initialized to an empty condition by setting *Front = Rear = MAXQ − 1*.

Write a program using object-oriented code for this implementation. Be sure to write a test program to see if the implementation works.

Does it really matter relative to data abstraction which implementation is used for the queue: this one or the one given in the chapter? Both implementations do the same thing relative to the ADT definition, right?

8. A problem with the array implementation of a queue is that the array is finite, thus requiring a *FullQ()* operation. A dynamic linked list does not have this limitation. Implement the queue ADT using a dynamic linked list. (*Hint:* Make *Front* point to the first node in the list and *Rear* point to the last node in the list.)

9. Change the linked list ADT given in this text to store structs consisting of a name, address, and telephone number. Write an application program to test your linked list.

Most Difficult

10. An ordered linked list is one in which the information in the list is ascending or descending from the first node to the last node in the list. To develop an ordered linked list ADT, the *InsertNode()* operation needs to search for the proper insertion point of the information being added to the list prior to inserting the node into the list.

    Develop an ordered linked list ADT to store character data in ascending order, from the beginning to the end of the list. (*Hint:* You will need to employ two pointers as we did in the *DeleteNode()* operation.) Write an application program to test your ordered linked list.

11. Modify the ADT developed in problem 10 to store a list of address structs, where each struct contains a name (last, first), address, and telephone number. The list should be in ascending order according to the last name. Write an application program to test your address list.

FILE I/O:
A CASE FOR INHERITANCE

INTRODUCTION

13-1 FUNDAMENTAL CONCEPTS AND
    IDEAS
    Classes Provide the Basis for C++ Files
    Creating File Streams in C++: The File
        Stream Definition

13-2 ACCESSING FILE INFORMATION

    The File Window
    File Operations

CHAPTER SUMMARY

QUESTIONS AND PROBLEMS
    Questions
    Problems

INTRODUCTION

All the data classes and structures you have learned about so far have provided a means of organizing and storing data in primary memory. However, recall that primary memory is relatively small and, more importantly, volatile. In other words, when the system is turned off or power is lost for any reason, all information stored in primary memory goes to "bit heaven." The obvious solution to this problem is to store any long-term data in secondary memory, because secondary memory is nonvolatile.

In Chapter 3, you learned how to read and write disk files. In this chapter, you will expand on this knowledge and learn how to create and manipulate your own disk files in C++. A file provides a means of storing information in a convenient and organized manner in secondary memory, such as magnetic disk. There are two basic types of files in C++: character, or text, files and binary files. Text files are used to store ASCII or EBCDIC data, such as that produced by a text editor. Binary files are used to store executable code, such as that of a compiled program. In this chapter, we will discuss input and output of text files.

13-1 FUNDAMENTAL CONCEPTS AND IDEAS

> A *file* is a data structure that consists of a sequence of components.

A file is a *sequence* of components. This means that the data elements, called **components**, are arranged within the file sequentially, or serially, from the first component to the last component. As a result, when accessing files, the file components must be accessed in a sequential manner from one component to the next. A common analogy for a file is an audio cassette tape. Think of the songs on the tape as the file components. How are they stored on the tape? You're right, sequentially from the first song to the last. How must you access a given song? Right again, by sequencing forward or backward through the tape until the desired song is found. Thus, like a cassette tape, a file is a sequential, or serial, storage medium. This makes file access relatively slow as compared to other random-access storage mediums.

You might be tempted to think of a file as a one-dimensional array, but there are some important differences. First, files provide a means for you to store information within a program run as you do with arrays. But, unlike arrays, files also allow you to store information between program runs. Second, many compilers require you to access the file components in sequence, starting with the first file component. You cannot jump into the middle of a file as you can an array to access a given component. However, C++ does provide a means of semirandom direct access using the *seek* operations. More about this later. Third, files are not declared with a specific dimension as are arrays. Once you declare a file, its size is theoretically unlimited. Of course, the file size is actually limited by the amount of storage space available in secondary memory, such as a disk.

In Chapter 3, you learned that all C++ file I/O is based on the concept of file streams.

A *file stream* provides a channel for data to flow between your program and the outside world.

In particular, a file stream provides a channel for the flow of data from some source to some destination. Think about what happens when you are typing characters on the keyboard when prompted by a program. You can think of the characters as flowing, or streaming, from the keyboard into the program. Likewise, when your program generates a character display, you can easily visualize the characters streaming from the program to the display.

Classes Provide the Basis for C++ Files

All program I/O is supported by files that operate on predefined classes in C++. The familiar *cin* and *cout* objects that you have been using in your programs for keyboard input and display output are objects of the *iostream* file class. The *cin* and *cout* objects invoke predefined file streams. Thus, we say that standard input is read from the *cin stream* and standard output is written to the *cout stream*. When you include the *iostream.h* header file in your program, the *cin* and *cout* file streams are defined automatically. Of course, the only files that you can access conveniently with *cin* and *cout* are the keyboard and display files that are "attached" to these file streams.

For accessing disk files, you must use one of three classes: *ifstream, ofstream,* or *fstream*. The *ifstream* class is used to perform input, or read, operations from disk files; the *ofstream* class is used to perform output, or write, operations to disk files; and the *fstream* class can be used to perform both read and write operations on disk files. All three of these classes are declared in the *fstream.h* header file.

Class inheritance provides the basis for C++ file streams. A hierarchy diagram of the C++ file class family is provided in Figure 13-1. Above the dashed line in Figure 13-1, you find the classes declared in *iostream.h*, and below the line, you see the classes declared in *fstream.h*. Notice all the *fstream* classes are derived from the *iostream* classes. As a result, by including the *fstream.h* header file in your program, you have access to the predefined file streams (*cin, cout*) as well as file streams that you will define for disk I/O. File streams that you will define for disk I/O are referred to as **named** file streams.

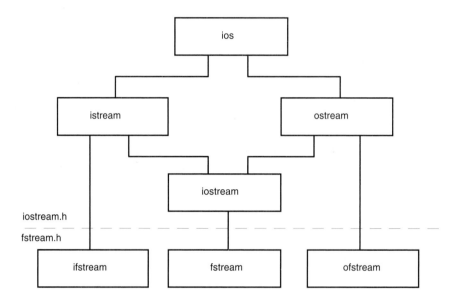

Figure 13-1   The file class hierarchy in C++.

Creating File Streams in C++: The File Stream Definition

Let's review how to create your own file streams in C++. To create a named file stream, you must do two things:

1. Define a file stream object for one of the *fstream.h* file classes.
2. Attach the file stream object to a particular disk file to **open** the file.

When you create a named file, the first thing you must do is define an object for one of the named file classes. File stream objects that are used exclusively for input are defined as objects of the *ifstream* class. Thus, the statement

ifstream Input;

defines *Input* as an input file stream object. You use the *ofstream* class to define file stream objects that are used exclusively for output. Thus, the statement

ofstream Output;

defines *Output* as an output file stream object. Finally, you must use the *fstream* class when defining objects that will be used for both file input and output. The statement

fstream InputOutput;

defines *InputOutput* as both an input and output file stream object.

Next, you must attach the file stream object to a physical file. When a file stream object is attached to a physical disk file, the disk file is opened for access. This requires the use of the *open()* function, which is inherited by all the file stream classes. Here is the format required to call this function:

FORMAT TO OPEN A DISK FILE

<file stream object>•**open** (<disk file name>, <file open mode>,
<file protection mode>);

The first thing that must be specified is the file stream object. The object name is followed by a dot, which is followed by the *open()* function and its required arguments. From your knowledge of OOP, you know that this statement simply calls the *open()* function defined in the respective file stream class.

The *open()* function can have up to three arguments: a disk file name, an open-mode designator, and a protection-mode designator. The disk file name must adhere to the requirements of the operating system. For DOS systems, the file name cannot exceed eight characters. A three-character extension, separated from the file name by a dot, is optional. Thus, DOS file names, such as *sample*, *sample.dat*, and *sample12.dat*, are all legal file names. The physical disk file name can be specified directly within double quotes (i.e., "*sample.dat*") or indirectly as a character array variable.

The open-mode designator argument defines what type of file access is to be performed. The eight predefined mode designators available in C++ are listed in Table 13-1.

TABLE 13-1 OPEN-MODE DESIGNATORS DEFINED IN C++

Mode	Definition
ios :: in	Open file for reading
ios :: out	Open file for writing
ios :: ate	Seek to end-of-file upon opening
ios :: app	Open for appending to end-of-file
ios :: nocreate	Open fails if file does not exist
ios :: noreplace	Open fails if file exists
ios :: trunc	Open file and discard existing contents
ios :: binary	Binary file: CRLF pairs not translated

The third argument possible in the *open()* function call is the protection-mode designator. The four protection modes defined for C++ files are listed in Table 13-2. You will normally not be concerned with the file-protection mode and therefore do not need to list one as an argument in the *open()* function.

TABLE 13-2 FILE-PROTECTION MODES DEFINED IN C++

Mode	Access Protection
S_IREAD	Read only
S_IWRITE	Write only
S_IREAD	S_IWRITE	Read and write

Suppose that we want to open a file stream called *InputOutput*. The file stream is defined for the *fstream* class and is to be attached to a disk file called *test.dat*. In addition, the program will both read and write the file. The appropriate open statement would be

InputOutput.open("test.dat", ios :: in | ios :: out);

As you can see, the file stream object calls the *open()* function using the dot operator. The physical disk file to be opened is placed within double quotes as the first argument in the function call. The first argument could also be a string (character array) variable that holds the disk file name. The second argument provides the file-mode designators. Here, two designators are ORed together using the ¦ bitwise OR operator to tell the compiler that the file can be both read from (*ios :: in*) or written to (*ios :: out*). No protection mode is listed for this file.

The read/write mode(s) must always be specified when a file stream object is opened for the *fstream* class, because by definition, this class is used for both input and output (reading/writing) file access. Read/write modes do not need to be specified when opening files defined for the *ifstream* or *ofstream* classes, because such files are input and output files, respectively, by default. For instance, if *Output* is defined as a file stream object of the *ofstream* class, the open statement simply would be

```
Output.open("test.dat");
```

On the other hand, if *Input* is defined as a file stream object of the *istream* class, the open statement would be

```
Input.open("test.dat");
```

The first four mode designators in Table 13-1 are the most commonly used. However, you should take special note of the last designator, *ios :: binary*. By default, all files in C++ are character, or text, files. To designate a file as a noncharacter file, you designate it as mode *ios :: binary*. Again we are going to deal only with text files in this chapter.

Example 13-1

Write statements to create the following disk files:

a. A file stream called *Read* that will read from a disk file called *sample.doc*.
b. A file stream called *Write* that will write to a disk file called *sample.doc*.
c. A file stream called *ReadWrite* that will read and write a disk file called *sample.doc*.
d. A file stream called *Append* that will append a file whose name is stored in a character array called *FileName[]*.

Solution

a. ifstream Read;
   Read.open("sample.doc");
b. ofstream Write;
   Write.open("sample.doc");
c. fstream ReadWrite;
   readWrite.open("sample.doc", ios :: in ¦ ios :: out);

Again, notice that the *ios :: in* and *ios :: out* file modes are ORed together to create a read/write file when the *fstream* class is specified.

d. ofstream Append;
   Append.open(FileName, ios :: app);

Here, the *ios :: app* mode is specified, because the file is to be appended. To append a file means to add components to the end of the file.

Quick Check

1. True or false: A file is a random-access data structure.

2. What two basic types of files are possible in C++?

3. A channel where data can flow between your C++ program and the outside world is called a _____.

4. Standard output in C++ is written to the _____ file stream.

5. What class is used in C++ to perform input, or read, operations from disk files?

6. True or false: The *iostream* class provides an example of multiple inheritance.

7. Write a statement to define *MyFile* as an output file stream object.

8. Write a statement to define *YourFile* as an input/output file stream object.

9. Write a statement that will open the file stream in question 7 for a text file called *ASCII.dat*.

10. To add information to the end of a file, you must use the _____ file mode.

13-2 ACCESSING FILE INFORMATION

Before getting into specific file access routines, let's take a minute to discuss the more important overall concept of file access.

The File Window

Files can be thought of as a means for a program to communicate with the "outside world." Information can be read into the program by placing it in a file and having the program read that file. In the same way, the program can write information to the outside world by writing to a file. As you know, C++ treats the user keyboard as an input file and the display monitor as an output file. Now, the question is: "How does your program communicate with the file?" The answer is: "Through something called a *file window*, sometimes called a *file pointer*." In other words, your program "sees" the outside file components through something called a file window. This concept is illustrated by Figure 13-2.

FILE OF CHARACTERS

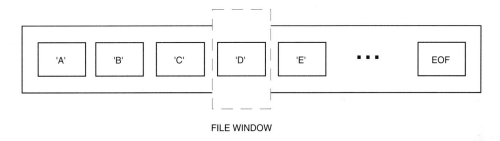

FILE WINDOW

Figure 13-2   File components are accessed through a file window.

In Figure 13-2, the file consists of a sequence of character components. To access a given character, the window must be positioned over that character so that it can be "seen." Once the window is positioned over the desired character, information can be read from, or written to, that character component position within the file.

When you open a file, a window is automatically created to access the file components. This window is technically referred to as a *file stream buffer*. Consequently, the file stream buffer, or window, is the link between the program and the file components.

File Operations

Now that you know how a file is created and structured, you need to learn about some general operations that will allow you to work with files. The following discussion will center on C++. I should caution you, however, that file operations in C differ somewhat from file operations in C++, because file operations in C++ are structured around classes. As a result, there are operations available in C++ that are not available in C, and a program written in C++ might not compile in C.

It is probably best to look at a comprehensive example in order to learn how to access C++ files. Let's begin by developing our own class that will be used specifically for file access. We will include member functions in the class that allow us to perform the following common file-access routines:

- Initialize a private data member with a disk file name entered by the user.
- Write, or create, a new file.
- Read and display an existing file.
- Append an existing file.
- Change an existing file.

Here is the class declaration:

```
//files.h  FOR FILES CLASS

#ifndef FILES_H
#define FILES_H

#include <fstream.h>      //FOR FILE STREAM BASE CLASS

class Files : public fstream
{
public:
  void GetName();         //GETS DISK FILE NAME FROM USER
  void WriteFile();       //WRITES DATA TO USER DISK FILE
  void ReadFile();        //READS USER DISK FILE
  void AppendFile();      //APPENDS USER DISK FILE
  void ChangeFile();      //CHANGES USER DISK FILE DATA

private:
  char FileName[13];      //USER DISK FILE NAME
}; //END Files
#endif
```

First, you see that the *fstream.h* header file is included prior to the class declaration. The *fstream.h* header file is included because it contains the *fstream* class declaration. The *fstream* class forms the base class for our *Files* class, as you can see from the class declaration. As a result, our *Files* class will inherit all the members of the predefined *fstream* class.

The declaration provides for a single private data member called *FileName*. This *FileName* character array will be used to store the name of the disk file being attached to our file stream objects. Notice that the array can store up to 13 character elements to provide for an 8-character file name, a dot, a 3-character extension, and a null terminator. This file name supports DOS files. If you are using a different operating system, you will need to name your files according to the respective operating system file naming rules. Four public functions are part of the class to provide the file-access routines previously listed. Our *Files* class declaration will be stored in a header file called *files.h*.

Next, we need to develop an implementation file for each of the member functions. Let's take them in order, beginning with the *GetName()* function.

Getting A Disk File Name from the User

The *GetName()* function simply gets a physical disk file name from the user and initializes the *FileName* member of our *Files* class to the string entered by the user. Here's the implementation:

```
//getname.cpp IMPLEMENTATION FILE FOR GetName() FUNCTION

#include "files.h"          //FOR files CLASS

void Files :: GetName()
{
//GET THE FILE NAME FROM USER TO
//INITIALIZE FILE NAME DATA MEMBER
   cout << "What file name do you want to use?\n"
        << "Note:  Not more that 8 characters with"
        << " a 3 character extension." << endl;
   cin >> FileName;
} //END GetName()
```

The opening comment indicates that the *GetName()* implementation is stored in a file called *getname.cpp*. The *files.h* file must be included in this file, because *files.h* contains our *Files* class declaration, of which *GetName()* is a member. The body of the implementation is straightforward, and you should not have any trouble understanding it at this point.

Writing, or Creating, a New File

Next, we need to develop an implementation for the *WriteFile()* function. This function must accomplish the task of creating a new file if it doesn't already exist, or completely rewriting an existing file with new components. Here are the general file operations required to accomplish this task:

• Define an output file stream object.

- Open the file stream in the output mode and attach it to a disk file name.
- Get the new file components from the user and write them to the file.
- Close the file stream.

We will place the *WriteFile()* implementation in the following *write.cpp* file:

```
//write.cpp  IMPLEMENTATION FILE FOR WriteFile()

#include "files.h"              //FOR files CLASS
#include <stdlib.h>             //FOR exit()
#include <string.h>             //FOR strcmp()

void Files :: WriteFile()
{
//LOCAL CONSTANTS AND VARIABLES
const int SIZE = 81;           //MAX LINE SIZE
char Line[SIZE];               //LINE BUFFER

//DEFINE OUTPUT FILE OBJECT
ofstream Output;

//OPEN FILE
Output.open(FileName);
if (!Output)
{
  cerr << "This file cannot be opened.";
  exit(1);
}//END IF

//GET FILE COMPONENTS AND WRITE TO FILE
cout << "Enter a file component or DONE when finished:" << endl;
cin >> Line;
while (strcmp(Line,"DONE"))
{
  Output << Line << endl;
  cout << "Enter a file component or DONE when finished:" << endl;
  cin >> Line;
}//END WHILE

//CLOSE FILE
Output.close();

}//END WriteFile()
```

First, notice that each of the major operations that need to be performed in this implementation is commented so that it can be easily identified in the code. The code begins by including the header files that are needed in this implementation. Of course, our class header file (*files.h*) must be included, because *WriteFile()* is a member function of our *Files* class. Before anything can be done with a file, a file stream object must be defined and opened. The object is called *Output* and is defined for the *ofstream* class, which is inherited via our *Files* class. The *ofstream* class is used here because *WriteFile()* only writes information to the file. Next, the *Output* stream object is opened by calling the *open()* function. (How does the *Output* object have access to this function?) The only argument needed in the *open()* function is the physical disk file name that will be attached to the *Output* stream object. Recall that our *GetName()* function obtains the disk file name from the user and initializes the *FileName* member of the class to the user entry. The *open()* function has access to this value because, by inheritance, *open()* is a member of our *Files* class. Observe that *FileName* is provided as the argument for the *open()* function.

After the file stream is opened, an **if** statement is inserted to determine if the file stream can be opened. If, for any reason, the file stream cannot be opened, the file stream object will return a value of zero. If a value of zero is returned, an error message is displayed via a *cerr* object, and the program is aborted via an *exit()* function. The *cerr* object does basically the same thing as *cout*. However, the *cerr* object is usually employed for file operations rather than *cout*, because some programs might attach *cout* to a file other than the standard display monitor file. The *exit()* function causes the program to abort and return to the operating system. In addition, *exit()* closes any files that were previously opened by the program.

The next section of code gets the file components from the user and writes them to the file. By default, the file is a character file. Here, we are obtaining character strings from the user via the *cin* object and storing them in a local character array called *Line*. The maximum size of *Line* is 81 characters to allow for a maximum string of 80 characters and a null terminator. Recall that the width of a typical monitor screen is 80 characters. Once a string is obtained from the user, it is written to our *Output* file stream object using the familiar << insertion operator. We say that the << operator "inserts" the string into the file stream. In our case, the string contained in *Line* is inserted into the *Output* file stream. In addition to the string contained in *Line*, an *endl* is inserted into the stream to produce a carriage return/line feed (CRLF) as a delimiter to separate the strings within the file. Notice that the user read and file write operations are both part of a **while** loop that iterates once for each component the user has to enter. The loop breaks when the user enters the string "DONE". Here is what the file looks like on disk, assuming the strings "Andy", "Janet", and "Ron" were written to the file. Notice that *endl* produced two characters on the disk, a carriage return (CR) character and a line feed (LF) character. The file is terminated by an end-of-file (EOF) marker character.

```
A n d y CR LF J a n e t CR LF R o n CR LF EOF
```

The last thing to do is to close the file stream. This is accomplished by a call to the *close()* function. The *close()* function is the counterpart to the *open()* function. Unlike the *open()* function, the *close()* function does not require any arguments. ***Open file streams must always be closed before exiting the program***. In fact, it is a good idea to close a file stream as soon as you are done accessing it so that you don't forget. For this reason, we will always close any open file streams immediately when we are done accessing them within a file-handling routine.

Reading and Displaying an Existing File

The next implementation we need to deal with is the *ReadFile()* implementation. The operations that must be performed here are as follows:

- Define an input file stream object.
- Open the file stream in input mode and attach it to a disk file name.
- Read the file components and display them to the user.
- Close the file stream.

We will store this implementation in a separate file called *read.cpp*, as follows:

```
//read.cpp IMPLEMENTATION FILE FOR ReadFile()

#include "files.h"        //FOR Files CLASS
#include <stdlib.h>       //FOR exit()

void Files :: ReadFile()
{
//LOCAL CONSTANTS AND VARIABLES
const int SIZE = 81;             //MAX LINE SIZE
```

```
char Line[SIZE];                    //LINE BUFFER

//DEFINE INPUT FILE OBJECT
ifstream Input;

//OPEN FILE
Input.open(FileName);
if (!Input)
{
  cerr << "This file cannot be opened." << endl;
  exit(1);
}//END IF

//READ FIRST FILE COMPONENT
cout << "The current file contents are:" << endl;
Input >> Line;

//TEST FOR EOF, DISPLAY, AND READ NEXT COMPONENT
while (!Input.eof())
{
  cout << Line << endl;
  Input >> Line;
}//END WHILE

//CLOSE FILE
Input.close();

}//END ReadFile()
```

You see that our *files.h* file is again included in this file, because the *ReadFile()* function is part of our *Files* class. The file stream object is called *Input* and is defined for the *ifstream* class. The *ifstream* class is used, because all we will do is read a file. Next, the file stream is opened and attached to the disk file name stored in *FileName*. Again, an error message is generated, and the program aborted if, for some reason, the file stream cannot be opened.

The first character string is read via an *Input >> Line* statement prior to the loop test. The familiar >> extraction operator extracts a string from the *Input* file stream and places it in a local character array called *Line*. Once the first string is read, a **while** loop is encountered to read the remaining strings. Notice the loop test. *eof()*, There is a standard function available in the *ios* class called *eof()*. (How does our implementation inherit this function?) The *eof()* function returns a 1 (true) when the file window is at the end-of-file position; otherwise, a value of 0 (false) is returned. The end-of-file (EOF) position is defined as the position just after the last component in the file. Our *Input* object calls the *eof()* function in the loop test via the statement *!Input.eof()*. The test will be true and the loop statements will execute as long as the window is not at the EOF position. Within the loop, the first statement displays the string just read via a *cout* statement. The loop then reads the next string. The loop continues to iterate until the EOF marker is detected. Finally, after all the file components are read and displayed, the loop terminates and the file stream is closed.

It is important to analyze the window positioning during the file read operations. Given a file containing the strings "Andy", "Janet", and "Ron", the first *Input >> Line* statement extracts the characters 'A', 'n', 'd', 'y' from the *Input* file stream and terminates when the CR character is encountered. This results in the file window being positioned at the first CR character, as follows:

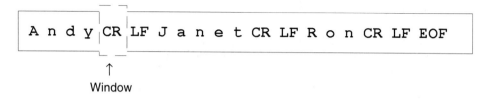

The next *Input >> Line* statement skips the CR and LF characters and extracts the characters 'J', 'a', 'n', 'e', 't' from the *Input* file stream, leaving the window positioned at the next CR character, as follows:

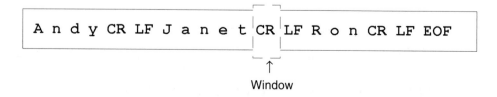

The loop continues to read the remaining characters in the file in this fashion until the end-of-file marker is encountered.

Appending an Existing File

Appending a file means to add information to the end of the file. The operations required to perform this task are as follows:

- Define an output file stream object.
- Open the file stream in append mode, and attach it to a disk file name.

- Get the additional file components from the user, and write them to the file.
- Close the file stream.

This implementation will be stored in a separate file called *append.cpp*. The code required to append an existing file is almost the same as that for creating a new file. The only difference is the open-mode argument specified in the *open()* function. Here's the required implementation code:

```
//append.cpp  IMPLEMENTATION FILE FOR AppendFile()

#include "files.h"        //FOR Files CLASS
#include <stdlib.h>       //FOR exit()
#include <string.h>       //FOR strcmp()

void Files :: AppendFile()
{
//LOCAL CONSTANTS AND VARIABLES
 const int SIZE = 81;        //MAX LINE SIZE
 char Line[SIZE];            //LINE BUFFER

//DEFINE APPEND FILE OBJECT
 ofstream Append;

//OPEN FILE
Append.open(FileName, ios :: app);
if (!Append)
{
  cerr << "\nThis file cannot be opened.";
  exit(1);
}//END IF

//GET FILE FILE COMPONENTS AND APPEND TO FILE
cout << "Enter new file component or DONE when finished:" << endl;
cin >> Line;
while (strcmp(Line,"DONE"))
{
  Append << Line << endl;
  cout << "Enter new file component or DONE when finished:" << endl;
  cin >> Line;
}//END WHILE

//CLOSE FILE
Append.close();
}//END AppendFile()
```

Comparing this code to the *WriteFile( )* code, you will find that the only difference is in the name of the object (*Append* versus *Output*) and the open-mode argument (*ios :: app* versus *ios :: out*). Does this tell you anything about how the open mode positions the file window? Well, the *ios :: out* mode positions the window at the beginning of the file, and, in addition, erases any information in an existing file. As a result, any write operations to the file create entirely new information in the file. On the other hand, the *ios :: app* mode positions the window at the end of the file and does not erase existing information. Therefore, any write operations to the file add information to the end of the file.

Changing an Existing File

The last function we need to discuss is the *ChangeFile( )* function. This function requires the following file operations:

- Define an input/output file stream object.
- Open the file stream in both input and output mode, and attach it to a disk file name.
- Get the component to be changed from the user, and search the file for the component.
- Seek the position of the component to be changed.
- Erase the old component information from the file.
- Seek the end-of-file position.
- Write the new component information to the end of the file.
- Close the file stream.

The idea here is to get the component to be changed from the user and then search the file for that component. Once found, we will erase the old component information from the file and ask the user to provide the new component information. The new component information then will be written to the end of the file. Let's get into the code. By the way, this implementation will be stored in a file called *change.cpp*. Here it is:

//change.cpp IMPLEMENTATION FILE FOR ChangeFile()

```
#include "files.h"      //FOR Files CLASS
#include "string.h"     //FOR strcmp()
#include "stdlib.h"     //FOR exit()
```

```
//DECLARE LINE SIZE BUFFER AND BOOLEAN DATA CLASS
const int SIZE = 81;      //MAX LINE SIZE
enum Boolean {FALSE, TRUE};

void Files :: ChangeFile()
{
//LOCAL CONSTANTS AND VARIABLES
char  OldLine[SIZE];      //LINE TO CHANGE
char NewLine[SIZE];       //NEW LINE
char Entry[SIZE];         //USER ENTRY FOR LINE TO CHANGE
int WindowPos  = -2;      //CURRENT WINDOW POSITION
Boolean  Flag = FALSE; //FLAG TO INDICATE FILE COMPONENT FOUND

//DEFINE INPUT/OUTPUT FILE OBJECT
fstream Change;

//OPEN FILE OBJECT
Change.open(FileName, ios :: in | ios :: out);
if (!Change)
{
   cerr << "\nThis file cannot be opened.";
   exit(1);
}//END IF

//GET COMPONENT TO CHANGE FROM USER
cout << "\nWhich line do you wish to change?" << endl;
cin >> Entry;

//READ A FILE COMPONENT
Change >> OldLine;

//TEST FOR EOF, PROCESS, AND READ NEXT COMPONENT
while (!Change.eof())
{
        //COMPARE FILE COMPONENT TO USER ENTRY
        if (!strcmp(OldLine,Entry))
        {
                //SET FLAG TO TRUE IF FOUND
                Flag = TRUE;
                //SEEK BEGINNING OF FOUND COMPONENT
                Change.seekg(WindowPos + 2,ios :: beg);
                //REPLACE COMPONENT WITH *'s
                for (int i = 1; i <= strlen(OldLine); ++i)
                        Change << '*';
                //ADD CRLF
                Change << endl;
```

```
        //GET NEW COMPONENT FROM USER
        cout << "Line found, what do you wish to change it to?" << endl;
        cin >> NewLine;
        //SEEK END OF FILE POSITION
        Change.seekg(0,ios :: end);
        //ADD NEW COMPONENT TO END OF FILE
        Change << NewLine << endl;
        break;
    }//END IF

    //SAVE CURRENT WINDOW POSITION
    WindowPos = Change.tellg();

    //READ A FILE COMPONENT
    Change >> OldLine;
}//END WHILE
//WRITE MESSAGE TO USER IF COMPONENT NOT FOUND
if (!Flag)
   cout << "Line not found." << endl;
//CLOSE FILE
Change.close();
}//END ChangeFile()
```

The code begins by including several header files that are required for this implementation file. Several local items are defined at the beginning of the *ChangeFile()* implementation. You will discover their use shortly. A file stream object called *Change* is defined for the *fstream* class. The *fstream* class is required here because we will use this object to both read and write the file. The file stream is then opened and attached to the disk file name stored in *FileName*. In addition, notice that the file stream is opened for mode *ios :: in* and mode *ios :: out*. Recall that you must specify the input/output modes when using the *fstream* class, because no default mode is assumed.

After the file stream is opened, the user is prompted to enter the component information to be changed. The user entry is placed in a local character array called *Entry*. Next, the first file string is read via a *Change >> Oldline* statement. The >> extraction operator extracts this first string from the *Change* input file stream and places it in the *Oldline* character array. A **while** loop is then executed to search for the user entry (*Entry*). Notice that the **while** loop will execute until one of two conditions occurs: (1) when the end-of-file (EOF) marker is encountered, or (2) when the component being searched for is found. The loop test checks for the EOF marker. The **if** statement within the loop is used to compare the user entry to the file string just read. If the two strings are equal, the file string is replaced with *'s, and a new component obtained from the user is written at the end of the file. The loop is then broken via a **break** statement.

If the two strings are unequal, the statements within the **if** are bypassed, and a variable called *WindowPos* is set to the current window position. This is accomplished when the *Change* object invokes a function of the *istream* class called *tellg()*. (How does this program inherit *tellg()*?) The *tellg()* function returns the current position of the file window. (You should be aware that there is a comparable function, called *tellp()*,defined for the *ostream* class. We are using *tellg()* rather than *tellp()* to be consistent with an input operation.) The value returned by *tellg()* represents the number of bytes the window is located from the beginning of the file. This value is assigned in the program to a variable called *WidowPos* that will be used later. After the current window position is saved in *WindowPos*, another string is read and tested. Thus, the loop continues to iterate until the end-of-file marker is encountered or the string being searched for is found.

Now, let's take a closer look at what goes on inside the **if** statement. First, a Boolean flag is set to indicate that the string being search for was found. Next, the file window is repositioned to the beginning of the string just found when the *Change* file object invokes an inherited function called *seekg()*. The *seekg()* function positions the file window a given number of bytes from a specified point in the file. Here is the statement that we are using to call *seekg()*:

Change.seekg(WindowPos + 2, ios :: beg);

This statement places the file window at the beginning of the found component, *OldLine*. The first argument, *WindowPos + 2*, contains the number of bytes that the *Oldline* component is located from the beginning of the file. Why are we specifying *WindowPos + 2*? Well, let's assume that our file contains the strings "Andy", "Janet", "Ron" and we are searching for the string "Janet". Here is the window status after the first read operation:

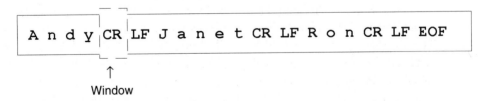

This window position is saved in *WindowPos* prior to reading the next string. Next, the string we are looking for ("Janet") is read, and the window is now positioned as follows:

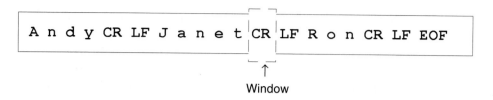

Window

Prior to this read operation, the window was at the previous CR character position, which is saved in *WindowPos*. Now, the idea is to erase this string by replacing it with *'s. However, in order to write over the string "Janet", the file window must be repositioned at the 'J' character, like this:

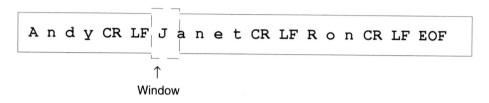

Window

Now, to get to this character, the window must be moved a distance of *WindowPos + 2* bytes from the beginning of the file. Recall that, before the last read operation, the file window was at the CR character just after "Andy". However, after "Janet" is read, the window moves to the CR character just after "Janet". Therefore, if the component being searched for is found, the window must be repositioned to the beginning of this component so that it can be erased from the file. To position the window on the 'J' in "Janet", the window must be moved a distance of *WindowPos + 2* from the beginning of the file. This is why we stored the previous window position in *WindowPos* just prior to reading the last component. The + 2 accounts for the CR and LF delimiting characters separating the two strings.

The second argument in the function call, *ios :: beg*, tells the compiler to move the window relative to the beginning of the file. So, the first argument in *seekg()* specifies the number of bytes to move the window, and the second argument specifies the starting point. In our case, we must move the window *WindowPos + 2* bytes from the beginning of the file. There are three possible starting points for the second argument of *seekg()*: the beginning of the file (*ios :: beg*), the current position of the file window (*ios :: cur*), and the end of the file (*ios :: end*). Thus, we can move the file window so many bytes from the beginning of the file, the current position of the file window, or the end of the file. The *seekg()* function recognizes the three possible arguments of *ios :: beg*, *ios :: cur*, or *ios :: end*.

Now that the searched-for component has been found, it is effectively erased by replacing it with asterisks. This is accomplished using a **for** loop that iterates a number of times equal to the length of the found component, *OldLine*. Notice the call to the *strlen()* function in the loop test. The *strlen()* function calculates the length of the *Oldline* component. The resulting length determines when the loop will terminate. With each loop iteration, an asterisk (*) is written to the file so that the *OldLine* component is overwritten with *'s.

The task now is to get the new component information from the user and append it to the end of the file. The user is prompted for the new component information, which is obtained by *cin* and stored in the character array called *Newline*. To append the new information to the file, the file window must be moved to the end-of-file position. This is accomplished with a call to the *seekp()* function. The *seekp()*function is analogous to the *seekg()* function used earlier. However, *seekp()* is inherited via *ostream*, and *seekg()* is inherited via *istream*. Thus, the *seekp()* function should be used in conjunction with file write operations and *seekg()* used with file read operations. Actually, either could be used here, because both are inherited by this program. We are using *seekp()* to be consistent with its purpose, because we are about to perform a file write operation. Here is the statement we are using to call *seekp()*:

Change.seekp(0, ios :: end);

Notice the two arguments. The first argument, 0, tells the compiler to move the file window 0 bytes from the second argument specification. Thus, the window will be positioned 0 bytes from the *end* of the file. Table 13-3 summarizes the *tell* and *seek* functions available for window manipulation.

TABLE 13-3 FILE WINDOW FUNCTIONS IN C++

Function	Class	Purpose
tellg()	istream	Returns window position of the input file stream.
tellp()	ostream	Returns window position of the output file stream.
seekg()	istream	Positions window of the input file stream.
seelp()	ostream	Positions window of the output file stream.

After the window is positioned at the end of the file, the *NewLine* component is written to the file via the statement

Change << NewLine << endl;

Once the new component is appended to the file, a **break** statement is executed to break the **while** loop.

The next segment of code checks *Flag* to determine if the component searched for was found during the previous search loop. If the component was not found in the file, an appropriate message is displayed to the user.

The Application Program

Now all we need is an application program to test our *Files* class. Here is one, called *fileapp.cpp*, that will exercise all of the file operations that we have just developed:

```
//fileapp.cpp  APPLICATION FILE FOR FILE I/O

#include "files.h"        //FOR Files CLASS
#include <iostream.h>  //FOR cin AND cout
#include <ctype.h>       //FOR toupper()
void main()
{
//DECLARE MyFile OBJECT AND LOCAL VARIABLES
  Files MyFile;
  char Choice;

//GET FILE NAME FROM USER
  MyFile.GetName();

//GENERATE FILE-ACCESS MENU
  do
  {
   cout  << "\n\n\t\tWrite and create a new file (W)"
            "\n\n\t\tRead and display file (R)"
            "\n\n\t\tAppend file (A)"
            "\n\n\t\tChange file (C)"
            "\n\n\t\tQuit(Q)"
            "\n\n\n\t\t\tENTER CHOICE ---> " << endl;
   cin >> Choice;
   Choice = toupper(Choice);
   switch (Choice)
   {
    case 'W':  MyFile.WriteFile();
              break;
    case 'R':  MyFile.ReadFile();
              break;
```

```
         case 'A':  MyFile.AppendFile();
                        break;
         case 'C':  MyFile.ReadFile();
                        MyFile.ChangeFile();
                        break;
         default :  cout << "Invalid choice." << endl;
      } //END SWITCH
    } //END DO/WHILE
    while (Choice != 'Q');
} //END main()
```

Again, you see our *files.h* header file included so that we can define an object for our *Files* class. Function *main()* begins by defining an object called *MyFile* of the *Files* class. This object is then used to call our *GetName()* function to obtain a disk file name from the user. A menu is then generated on the screen that allows the user to exercise any of the file operations that are part of the *Files* class. Of course, these are the operations that we just developed. Once the user selects a given menu option, the respective class function is called via the *MyFile* object. Notice in particular that both the *ReadFile()* and *ChangeFile()* functions are called for the "Change file (C)" menu option to allow the user to examine the existing contents of the file via the *ReadFile()* function prior to entering a component to be changed.

 Quick Check

1. True of false: File operations in C++ are the same as those in C.

2. List the major operations that are required to create a new file.

3. List the major operations that are required to read an existing file.

4. What is the difference, relative to the position of the file window, between using the *ios :: out* versus the *ios :: app* file modes when opening a file?

5. How does the *change.cpp* program in this section inherit the *tellg()* function?

6. What does the *tellg()* function return to the calling program?

7. True or false: The *tellg()* function should be used with input files, whereas the *tellp()* function should be used with output files.

8. What function must be used to position the file window for an output file?

9. What three predefined starting points are available to the *seekg()* and *seekp()* functions?

10. The distance to move the file window from the specified starting point when using *seekg()* or *seekp()* must be expressed in _____ units.

CHAPTER SUMMARY

A file is a data structure that consists of a sequence of components. Files provide a means for your program to communicate with the outside world. Any I/O operations performed by your program, even keyboard input and display output, are handled via files. Files in C++ can be either ASCII character files, called text files, or binary files. The default type of file is the character file. If a file is to be a binary file, the binary file mode must be specified when the file stream is opened.

All file I/O in C++ is in the form of file streams that employ predefined classes. The *ifstream* class is used to create input file stream objects, the *ofstream* class is used to create output file stream objects, and the *fstream* class is used to create file stream objects that will be used for both input and output. All three of these file stream classes are declared in the *fstream.h* header file. File streams that you create are called named file streams. To create a named file stream, you must define a file stream object for one of the *fstream.h* file classes and attach the stream object to a particular disk file using the *open()* function. The *open()* function can have up to three arguments: a physical disk file name, a file-mode designator, and a protection mode designator. See Tables 13-1 and 13-2 for a list of the predefined file-mode and protection mode designators.

Once a file stream is opened, it is ready for processing. The individual components within a file are accessed via a file stream window. The window must be positioned over the component to be accessed. When a file is opened, the window, sometimes called a file stream buffer, is automatically created to access the file components. Typical tasks that are performed on disk files include writing new files, reading existing files, appending existing files, and changing the information in existing files. The C++ language has various predefined functions to facilitate the coding of these tasks, some of which are given in Table 13-3. After a file stream is processed, it must always be closed using the *close()* function.

QUESTIONS AND PROBLEMS

Questions

1. Describe the structure of a file.

2. What is a file stream?

3. What is a file stream window and how is it used during file processing?

4. What three predefined classes provide the basis for C++ files?

5. What header file provides the predefined file class declarations in C++?

6. What two operations must be performed to create a named file stream in C++?

7. The *open()* function can have up to three arguments. What are they? What is the purpose of each argument?

8. True or false: The *ios :: out* file stream mode does not need to be designated for an object defined for the *ofstream* class.

9. When must the *ios :: app* mode be specified when opening a file stream?

10. What mode must be specified to open a binary file stream?

11. Write statements to create the following disk file streams:

    a. A character file stream called *FileIn* that will read a disk file called *mydata.txt*.

    b. A binary file stream called *BinaryIn* that will read a disk file called *mydata.bin*.

    c. A binary file stream called *BinaryI_O* that will both read and write a disk file called *mydata.bin*.

    d. A character file stream called *AddTo* that will append a file whose name is stored in a character array called *Name*.

12. True or false: When a file stream is opened for the *ofstream* class and no append mode is specified, the file stream window is placed at the beginning of the file, and all components in an existing file are overwritten by any subsequent write operations to the file.

13. List the major operations that must be performed in order to change the contents of an existing file.

14. Write a statement that will store the current position of the *MyFile* file stream window in a variable called *Position*. Assume that *MyFile* is defined for the *ofstream* class.

15. Write a statement that will move the file stream window in question 14 to a position that is *Position* bytes from the current position of the window.

16. Write a statement that will position the *MyFile* file stream window to the beginning of the file. Assume that *MyFile* is defined for the *ifstream* class.

17. Write a statement that will position the *MyFile* file stream window to the end of the file. Assume that *Myfile* is defined for the *ofstream* class.

18. Write a statement that will write a string called *String* to an output file stream object called *MyFile*.

19. Write a statement that will read a string component at the current window position of an input file stream called *MyFile* and place it in a character array called *String*.

20. Write a loop structure that will search for a string called *String* in a file stream called *MyFile* and set *Flag* to true if the string is found.

Problems

Least Difficult

Perform the following tasks for problems 1–5:

- Add the specified function to the *Files* class developed in this chapter.
- Write an implementation file for the specified function.
- Add the specified function to the application program menu in *fileio.cpp* in order to test the function.

1. A function called *Copy()* that will copy an existing file to a new file.

2. A function called *Erase()* that will erase an existing file.

3. A function called *Compare()* that will compare the contents of two files and report to the user if they are the same or different.

More Difficult

4. A function called *CleanUp()* that will clean up a file by removing the asterisks inserted by the *Change()* function developed in this chapter. The cleaned-up file should have no blank lines or fill characters.

5. A function that will read a file and then rewrite it to a new file with every line preceded by a sequential line number. The line number must be left justified on the screen when the file is displayed.

Most Difficult

6. Using the techniques discussed in this chapter, write and test a program that will handle a parts inventory file of the following information:

   - Part Name
   - Part Number
   - Part Price
   - Quantity on Hand

   Develop functions that will allow a user to create the parts inventory file, read and display the file, append the file, and change information in the file. (*Hint*: Define the parts inventory information as private members of your inventory files class.)

MULTIDIMENSIONAL ARRAYS

INTRODUCTION
14-1 TWO-DIMENSIONAL ARRAYS
  Defining Two-Dimensional Arrays in C++
  Accessing Two-Dimensional Array
    Elements
14-2 ARRAYS OF MORE THAN TWO
    DIMENSIONS

PROBLEM SOLVING IN ACTION:
  SIMULTANEOUS EQUATION
  SOLUTION
    Determinants
    Cramer's Rule
CHAPTER SUMMARY
QUESTIONS AND PROBLEMS
    Questions
    Problems

INTRODUCTION

A multidimensional array is simply an extension of a one-dimensional array. Rather than storing a single list of elements, you can think of a multidimensional array as storing multiple lists of elements. For instance, a two-dimensional array stores lists in a two-dimensional table format of rows and columns, where each row is a list. The rows provide the vertical dimension of the array, and the columns provide the horizontal array dimension. A three-dimensional array stores lists in a three-dimensional format of rows, columns, and planes, where each plane is a two-dimensional array. The rows provide the vertical dimension, the columns provide the horizontal dimension, and the planes provide the depth dimension of the array.

In this chapter, you will learn about two- and three-dimensional arrays: Arrays larger than this are seldom needed in programming. The chapter will conclude with a comprehensive problem-solving exercise employing two-dimensional arrays to solve sets of simultaneous equations using Cramer's rule.

14-1 TWO-DIMENSIONAL ARRAYS

The most common multidimensional array is the ***two-dimensional*** array shown in Figure 14-1. Here, you see that a two-dimensional array contains multiple rows. It's as if several one-dimensional arrays are combined to form a single rectangular structure of data. As a result, you can think of this rectangular data structure as a ***table*** of elements.

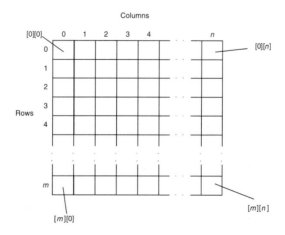

Figure 14-1 The structure of a two-dimensional array.

Observe that the two-dimensional array in Figure 14-1 is composed of elements that are located by rows and columns. The rows are labeled on the vertical axis and range from 0 to m. The columns are labeled on the horizontal axis and range from 0 to n. How many rows and columns are there? Each dimension starts with index [0], so there must be $m + 1$ rows and $n + 1$ columns, right? As a result, we say that this two-dimensional array has a dimension, or size, of $m + 1$ rows by $n + 1$ columns, written as $(m + 1) \times (n + 1)$.

How many elements are in the array? You're right: $(m + 1)$ times $(n + 1)$ elements! How do you suppose a given element is located? You're right again: by specifying its row and column index values. For instance, the element in the upper left-hand corner is located at the intersection of row 0 and column 0, or index [0][0]. Likewise, the element in the lower right-hand corner is located where row m meets column n, or index [m][n]. We say that two-dimensional arrays in C/C++ are ***row major ordered***. This means that the row index is listed first, followed by the column index.

Defining Two-Dimensional Arrays in C++

You define a two-dimensional array in C++ almost the same as you define a one-dimensional array. Here's the general format:

TWO-DIMENSIONAL ARRAY FORMAT

<element data class> <array name> [<number of rows>][<number of columns>];

The only difference between this definition and that required for a one-dimensional array is found within the size specification. You must specify both the row and column sizes, as shown.

Example 14-1

Given the following two-dimensional array definitions, sketch a diagram of the array structures showing the respective row/column indices.

a. float Table[5][7];
b. const int ROWS = 5;
    const int COLS = 7;
    float Table[ROWS][COLS];

c. const int CURRENT = 26;
   const int RESISTANCE = 1001;
   int Voltage[CURRENT][RESISTANCE];

d. const int WEEKS = 6;
   const int DAYS = 7;
   int May[WEEKS][DAYS];

e. const int ROW = 57;
   const int SEAT = 10;
   int SeatOccupied[ROW][SEAT];

Solution

a. See Figure 14-2(a). This is a rectangular array, or table, whose rows range from 0 to 4 and columns range from 0 to 6. Remember that, because array indices start with [0], the last index in a given array dimension is one less than its size. The array name is *Table*, and it will store floating-point values.

b. See Figure 14-2(a) again. This array is identical to the first array. The only difference here is in the way the array is defined. Notice that the row and column indices are defined as [*ROWS*][*COLS*], where *ROWS* and *COLS* are defined as constants.

c. See Figure 14-2(b). Here, the rows are called *CURRENT* and range from 0 to 25. The array columns are labeled *RESISTANCE* and range from 0 to 1000. The array name is *Voltage*, and it will store integer elements. Obviously, the array will store the *Voltage* values corresponding to *CURRENT* values from 0 to 25 and *RESISTANCE* values from 0 to 1000, using Ohm's law.

d. See Figure 14-2(c). This array is constructed to store the dates for the month of *May*, just like a calendar. Look at a common calendar if you have one handy. Isn't a given month simply a table of integers whose values are located by a given week and a given day within that week? As you can see from Figure 14-2(c), the array structure duplicates a monthly calendar. The rows are labeled 0 through 5, representing the six possible weeks in any given month. The columns of the array are labeled 0 through 6, representing the seven days of the week.

e. See Figure 14-2(d). This last array also has a practical application. Can you determine what it is from the definition? Notice that it is an array of integer elements. The rows range from 0 to 56, and the columns range from 0 to 9, as shown. The array name is *SeatOccupied*. Suppose that you use this array to store integer values of 0 and 1, where 0 represents the Boolean value of false and 1 represents the Boolean value of true. Then, this array could be used in a reservation program for a theater or airline flight to indicate whether or not a given seat is occupied or not occupied.

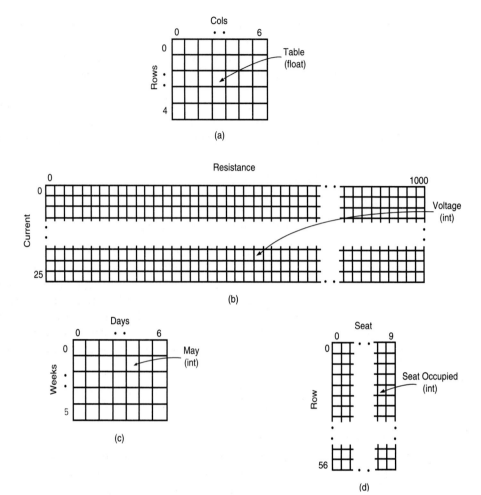

Figure 14-2   Four two-dimensional arrays for Example 14-1.

Example 14-2

How many elements will each of the arrays in Example 14-1 store, and what class of elements will they store?

Solution

a. The array in Figure 14-2(a) will store 5 × 7, or 35 elements. The elements will be floating-point values.

b. The array in Figure 14-2(b) has 26 rows, from 0 to 25, and 1001 columns, from 0 to 1000. Thus, the array will store 26 × 1001 = 26,026 integer elements.

c. The array in Figure 14-2(c) has 6 rows and 7 columns and, therefore, will store $6 \times 7 = 42$ integer elements.

d. The array in Figure 14-2(d) has 57 rows and 10 columns and will store $57 \times 10 = 570$ integer elements that will be treated as Boolean values.

The foregoing figures can be verified by using the *sizeof()* function. The *sizeof()* function returns the *number of bytes* required to store an expression or a data class. So, coding the following statements will display the number of elements in each array:

```
cout << sizeof(Table)/sizeof(float) << endl;
     << sizeof(Voltage)/sizeof(int) << endl;
     << sizeof(May)/sizeof(int) << endl;
     << sizeof(SeatOccupied)/sizeof(int) << endl;
```

Here, the *sizeof()* function is called twice to calculate the number of elements in each array. Notice that the size of the array in bytes is divided by the size of the data class of the array in bytes. The quotient, therefore, should be the number of elements that the array can store, right? You should be aware that the preceding code is totally portable between systems that might represent data types using a different number of bytes. This calculation will always determine the *number of elements* in the respective array, regardless of how many bytes are employed to store a given data class.

Accessing Two-Dimensional Array Elements

You access two-dimensional array elements in very much the same way as one-dimensional array elements. The difference is that to locate the elements in a two-dimensional array, you must specify a row index and a column index.

You can access the array elements using direct assignment, reading/writing, or looping.

Direct Assignment of Two-Dimensional Array Elements

The general format for direct assignment of element values is as follows:

> ### *TWO-DIMENSIONAL ARRAY DIRECT ASSIGNMENT FORMAT*
> ### *(inserting elements)*
>
> <array name> [row index][column index] = element value;

TWO-DIMENSIONAL ARRAY DIRECT ASSIGNMENT FORMAT (*extracting elements*)

<variable identifier> = <array name> [row index][column index];

First, you see the format for inserting elements into a two-dimensional array, followed by the format for obtaining elements from the array. Notice that in both instances you must specify a row and column index to access the desired element position. The row index is specified first, followed by the column index. By using the arrays defined in Example 14-1, possible direct assignments for insertion might be

```
Table[2][3] = 0.5;
Voltage[2][10] = 20;
May[1][3] = 8;
SeatOccupied[5][0] = 1;
```

In the first case, the floating-point value 0.5 is placed in row [2], column [3] of the *Table* array. In the second case, a value of 20 is inserted into row [2], column [10] of the *Voltage* array. Notice that this voltage value corresponds to a current value of 2 and a resistance value of 10 when using Ohm's law. In the third case, a value of 8 is placed in row [1], column [3] of the *May* array. Finally, the last case assigns the integer value 1 to row [5], column [0] of the *SeatOccupied* array. If interpreted as a Boolean value, this would indicate that the seat is occupied.

By using the same arrays, direct assignment statements to extract elements might be

```
Sales = Table[0][0];
Volts = Voltage[5][100];
Today = May[2][4];
Tomorrow = May[2][5];
SeatTaken = SeatOccupied[3][3];
```

In each of these statements, the element value stored at the row/column position within the respective array is assigned to a variable identifier. Of course, the variable identifier should be defined as the same data class as the array element being assigned to it.

Remember that extraction operations have no effect on the array elements. In other words, the elements are not actually removed from the array; their values are simply "copied" to the assignment variable.

Reading and Writing Two-Dimensional Array Elements

cin statements can be used to insert two-dimensional array elements, and *cout* statements can be used to extract array elements, like this:

```
cin >> Table[1][1];
cout << Table[1][1];
cin >> Voltage[5][20];
cout << Voltage[5][20];
cin >> May[1][3];
cout << May[1][3];
if (SeatOccupied[3][1])
  cout << "TRUE" << endl;
else
  cout << "FALSE" << endl;
```

Again, you can see that both a row and a column index must be specified. The *cin* statements will insert elements obtained from a keyboard entry. The *cout* statements will then extract the array element just inserted and simply "echo" the user entry back to the display. Notice that the last *cout* statement is contained within an **if/else** statement to determine if the element is a Boolean true or false value. This statement will produce a TRUE or FALSE on the display, depending on the contents of location [3][1] of the *SeatOccupied* array.

Using Loops to Access Two-Dimensional Arrays

As you know, loops provide a more efficient way to access arrays, especially when working with large multidimensional arrays. The thing to remember with multidimensional arrays is that *a separate loop is required for each dimension of the array*. In addition, the loops must be nested. Thus, a two-dimensional array requires two nested loops.

Look at the calendar pictured in Figure 14-3. As you have seen, this calendar can be stored in memory using a two-dimensional array. How do you suppose you might go about filling the calendar with the dates required for a given month? A logical approach would be to fill in all of the dates of week 0, from *Sun* to *Sat*, then go to week 1 and fill in its dates, then fill in the week 2 dates, and so on.

Think about what the array indices must do to perform this filling operation. The week index would start at [0], and then the days index would begin at [0] and increment through the days of the week to [6]. This will fill the first week. To fill the second week, the week index must be incremented to 1, with the days index starting at [0] and incrementing to [6] all over again. To fill the third week, the week index is incremented to 2, and the days index incremented from [0] to [6] again. In other words, you are filling in the dates week by week, one week at a time. Each time the week index is incremented, the days index starts at [0] and increments to [6], before the week index is incremented to the next week.

May

	Sun	Sat	Mon	Tue	Wed	Thu	Fri
	[0]	[1]	[2]	[3]	[4]	[5]	[6]
Week [0]							1
Week [1]	2	3	4	5	6	7	8
Week [2]	9	10	11	12	13	14	15
Week [3]	16	17	18	19	20	21	22
Week [4]	23	24	25	26	27	28	29
Week [5]	30	31					

Figure 14-3   May calendar.

Does this suggest two loops, one to increment the week index and a second to increment the days index? Moreover, doesn't this process suggest that the days loop must be nested within the week loop, because the days must run through its entire range for each week?

Here's the general loop structure for accessing elements in a two-dimensional array.

LOOPING FORMAT FOR ACCESSING TWO-DIMENSIONAL ARRAY ELEMENTS

```
for (int Row Index = 0; Row Index < Row Size; ++Row Index)
    for (int Col Index = 0; Col Index < Col Size; ++Col Index)
        <Process Array[Row Index][Col Index]>
```

You see that the column index loop is nested within the row index loop. Thus, the column loop runs through all of its iterations for each iteration of the row loop. The actual insertion takes place within the column loop. Let's look at an example to get the idea.

Example 14-3

Write a function using loops to fill a calendar array for the month of *May*. Write another function to display the *May* calendar.

Solution

We will begin by defining the month array as before.

```
const int WEEKS = 6;
const int DAYS = 7;
int May[WEEKS][DAYS];
enum DaysOfWeek {Sun,Mon,Tue,Wed,Thur,Fri,Sat};
```

In addition, you see that an enumerated data class called *DaysOfWeek* has been defined. This enumerated data class will be used to access the days of the week within the array, as you will see shortly.

Next, we must write a function to fill the array with the dates for May. But first, we must consider the function interface. The function must receive the array, get the dates from the user, and return the filled array to the calling program. Thus, the function-interface description becomes as follows:

Function *FillMonth()*:   Obtains dates of the month from the user and fills a two-dimensional integer array.

Accepts: A two-dimensional integer array of size *WEEKS × DAYS*.

Returns: A two-dimensional integer array of size *WEEKS × DAYS*.

Now, here's a function that will do the job:

```
//THIS FUNCTION WILL FILL A 2-DIM ARRAY FOR A
//CALENDAR MONTH
void FillMonth(int Month[WEEKS][DAYS])
{
 cout << "What month do you want to fill and display?  "
 cin >> ThisMonth;
 cout << "Enter the dates of the month, beginning Sunday of the first\n"
         "week in the month.  If there is no date for a given day\n"
         "enter a 0.  Press the ENTER key after each entry." << endl;
 for (int Week = 0; Week < WEEKS; ++Week)
  for (int Day = Sun; Day < Sat + 1; ++Day)
  {
    cout << "\nEnter the date for Week " << Week
        << " day " << Day << ":  ";
    cin >> Month[Week][Day];
  } //END DAY LOOP
} //END FillMonth()
```

The first few lines of the function provide a few simple directions to the user and obtain the month to be filled and displayed. The array-filling operation takes place within the two **for** loops. Notice that the *Week* loop is the outer loop, and the *Day* loop is the inner loop. Here's how it works: The *Week* counter begins with 0, and the *Day* counter begins with *Sun*. As a result, the first date is inserted into *Month*[0][*Sun*], corresponding to Sunday of week 0 in the month. Notice that the array name is *Month*. How can this be, because we defined *May* as the array name? Well, the array *May* will be the actual argument used in the function call. However, *Month* is the formal parameter listed in the function header. Thus, the function will receive the *May* array from the calling program, fill it, and return it to the calling program. The reason I used a different array name (*Month*) in the function is to make it more general. For example, additional arrays, such as *June*, *July*, *August*, and the like, could be defined to create arrays for these months. Again, these would act as actual arguments when calling the function. The respective month arrays (*June*, *July*, *August*, etc.) could then be filled separately using separate calls to this same function. In each case, the function parameter *Month* would take on the actual array argument used in the function call. Now, back to the loops. After an element is read into *Month* [0][*Sun*], the inner **for** loop increments the *Day* counter to *Mon*, and an element is read into *Month* [0][*Mon*]. Notice that the *Week* counter remains the same. What is the next array position to be filled? You're right: *Month* [0][*Tue*]. In summary, the inner *Day* loop will increment from *Sun* to *Sat* for each iteration of the outer *Week* loop. Thus, the first iteration of the outer *Week* loop will fill

> *Month* [0][*Sun*]
> *Month* [0][*Mon*]
> *Month* [0][*Tue*]
> *Month* [0][*Wed*]
> *Month* [0][*Thur*]
> *Month* [0][*Fri*]
> *Month* [0][*Sat*]

The second iteration of the outer *Row* loop will fill the second week, like this:

> *Month* [1][*Sun*]
> *Month* [1][*Mon*]
> *Month* [1][*Tue*]
> *Month* [1][*Wed*]
> *Month* [1][*Thur*]
> *Month* [1][*Fri*]
> *Month* [1][*Sat*]

This filling process will continue for weeks 2, 3, 4, and 5. The looping is terminated when a value is read into the last array position, *Month* [5][*Sat*].

Now, let's look at a similar function to display our *May* calendar once it has been filled. Again, consider the following function interface description:

Function *DisplayMonth( )*:   Displays the two-dimensional-calendar month array.

Accepts: A two-dimensional array of size *WEEKS* × *DAYS*.

Returns: Nothing.

Here is the completed function:

```
//THIS FUNCTION WILL DISPLAY THE CALENDAR MONTH ARRAY
void DisplayMonth(int Month[WEEKS][DAYS])
{
 cout << "\n\n\t\tCALENDAR FOR THE MONTH OF " << ThisMonth
      << "\n\n\tSun\tMon\tTue\tWed\tThur\tFri\tSat\" << endl;
 for (int Week = 0; Week < WEEKS; ++Week)
 {
  cout << endl;
  for (int Day = Sun; Day < Sat + 1; ++Day)
   cout << '\t' << Month[Week][Day];
 } //END WEEK LOOP
} //END DisplayMonth()
```

Again, *Month* is the formal parameter defined in the function header. The first part of the function statement section simply writes the header information required for the calendar. Then, the nested **for** loops are executed to display the array contents. The basic loop structures are the same as those we discussed for the filling operation: The *Day* counter is incremented from *Sun* through *Sat* for every iteration of the *Week* loop. Thus, the array contents are displayed in a row-by-row, or week-by-week, fashion. Notice that a *cout* statement is used to display the element values. The *cout* statement is the only statement within the inner **for** loop.

Now, putting everything together, here is the entire program:

```
//********************************************************
//
//THIS PROGRAM WILL FILL AND DISPLAY
//A 2-DIM ARRAY FOR A CALENDAR MONTH
//
//********************************************************
#include <iostream.h>        //FOR cin AND cout

//GLOBAL CONSTANTS AND ENUMERATED DATA
const int WEEKS = 6;
const int DAYS = 7;
```

```
char ThisMonth[10];
enum DaysOfWeek {Sun,Mon,Tue,Wed,Thur,Fri,Sat};

//FUNCTION PROTOTYPES
void FillMonth(int May[WEEKS][DAYS]);
void DisplayMonth(int May[WEEKS][DAYS]);

void main()
{
//ARRAY DEFINITION
   int May[WEEKS][DAYS];
//FUNCTION CALLS
   FillMonth(May);
   DisplayMonth(May);
} //END main()

//THIS FUNCTION WILL FILL A 2-DIM ARRAY FOR A
//CALENDAR MONTH
void FillMonth(int Month[WEEKS][DAYS])
{
  cout << "What month do you want to fill and display?" << endl;
  cin >> ThisMonth;
  cout << "Enter the dates of the month, beginning Sunday of the first\n"
          "week in the month.  If there is no date for a given day\n"
          "enter a 0.  Press the ENTER key after each entry." << endl;
  for (int Week = 0; Week < WEEKS; ++Week)
   for (int Day = Sun; Day < Sat + 1; ++Day)
   {
     cout << "\nEnter the date for Week " << Week
         << " day " << Day << ":  ";
     cin >> Month[Week][Day];
    } //END DAY LOOP
} //END FillMonth()


//THIS FUNCTION WILL DISPLAY THE CALENDAR MONTH ARRAY
void DisplayMonth(int Month[WEEKS][DAYS])
{
  cout << "\n\n\t\tCALENDAR FOR THE MONTH OF "  << ThisMonth
      << "\n\n\tSun\tMon\tTue\tWed\tThur\tFri\tSat" << endl << endl;
  for (int Week = 0; Week < WEEKS; ++Week)
  {
    cout << endl;
    for (int Day = Sun; Day < Sat + 1; ++Day)
     cout << '\t' << Month[Week][Day];
   } //END WEEK LOOP
} //END DisplayMonth()
```

First, you see that *WEEKS*, *DAYS*, *ThisMonth*, and *DaysOfWeek* have been declared globally so that all functions have access to them. Notice that the statement section of *main()* is short. Function *main()* simply defines the array and calls the two other functions. In each function call, the actual array argument, *May*, is employed. As stated earlier, other monthly arrays could also be defined to create additional monthly calendars. In fact, all 12 months could be defined to create a yearly calendar. To fill or display a given month, you simply use that array name in the respective function call.

Assuming that the user executes this program and keys in the proper dates for May, the program will generate the following calendar display:

CALENDAR FOR THE MONTH OF MAY

Sun	Mon	Tue	Wed	Thur	Fri	Sat
0	0	0	0	0	0	1
2	3	4	5	6	7	8
9	10	11	12	13	14	15
16	17	18	19	20	21	22
23	24	25	26	27	28	29
30	31	0	0	0	0	0

Of course, this calendar could also be printed by defining a print object and using it to write the array.

Example 14-4

Write a program that uses an array to store the names of all the students in your C++ class. Use one function to insert the student names into the array and a second function to display the contents of the array once it is filled. Assume that there are no more than 25 characters in any student name and the maximum class size is 20 students.

Solution

First, an array must be defined to hold the student names in your C++ class. The student names are strings, so we must define a two-dimensional array of characters so that each name string will occupy a row in the array. Consider the following:

```
const int MAX_STUDENTS = 20;
const int MAX_CHARACTERS = 26;
char CPP[MAX_STUDENTS][MAX_CHARACTERS];
```

Here, the array name is *CPP*, and it is defined as a character array with 20 rows and 26 columns. This will allow for 20 name strings with a maximum of 25 characters per string. (An extra column must be provided for the null terminator character.)

Next, we will work on the function that gets the student names from the user. We will call this function *GetStudents()*. Here is the function interface description:

Function *GetStudents()*:   Obtains student names from the user and fills a two-
                              dimensional character array.

Accepts: A placeholder for the number of students and
                              a two-dimensional character array of size
                              $MAX\_STUDENTS \times MAX\_CHARACTERS$.

Returns: The number of students and a two-dimensional
                              character array of size
                              $MAX\_STUDENTS \times MAX\_CHARACTERS$.

This interface requires that the two-dimensional *CPP* array be passed to the function and then returned filled with the student names. Of course, passing an array to a function is easy, regardless of its size, because you simply use the array name as the actual function argument. Here is the complete function:

```
//*****************************************************************************
//
//THIS FUNCTION GETS THE STUDENT NAMES FROM THE
//USER AND ENTERS THEM INTO THE ARRAY
//
//*****************************************************************************
void GetStudents(int &N, char Students[MAX_STUDENTS][MAX_CHARACTERS])
{
 cout << "Enter number of students:  ";
 cin >> N;
 for (int Row = 0; Row < N; ++Row)
 {
  cout << "\nEnter student number " << Row + 1 << ":  ";
  cin >> ws;
  cin.getline(&Students[Row][0],MAX_STUDENTS);
 } //END FOR
} //END GetStudents()
```

Again, you see a different name employed for the array in the function header. This makes the function more generic, because you might want to use this same function to fill other arrays from other classes. The function begins by prompting the user to enter the number of students in the class and then reading this number and assigning it to a reference parameter called *N*. The value entered will provide a maximum value for the row counter in the **for** loop. Next, you see a single **for** loop. Is there a problem here, because we are filling a two-dimensional array? No, this single loop is all that is required, because we are filling the array with strings, not individual characters. Notice that the loop counter increments only the row index. The column index is fixed at [0]. This will place the first string in the array beginning at [0][0], the second string at [1][0], the third string at [2][0], and so on. The standard *getline()* function is used to read the strings. Recall that, when *cin >>* will terminate when a whitespace character is encountered, thereby interpreting first and last names as two separate strings. Look at the argument used in the *getline()* function call. An ampersand symbol is used to tell *getline()* to place the string beginning at the *address* associated with *Students[Row][0]*. When reading strings into a two-dimensional array, we must tell the compiler to insert the string beginning at a specified address. So, the first string is inserted into the array beginning at the memory address associated with index [0][0], the second string begins at the memory address associated with index [1][0], and so on.

Next, we will write a function called *DisplayStudents()* to display the array of student names. Here is the interface description for this function:

Function *DisplayStudents()*:	Displays the strings of a two-dimensional array.
Accepts:	The number of students and a two-dimensional character array of size *MAX_STUDENTS × MAX_CHARACTERS*.
Returns:	Nothing.

The parameter listing for this function will be identical to the previous function, because it accepts the same array structure. Here is the entire function:

```
//***************************************************************************
//
//THIS FUNCTION DISPLAYS THE CONTENTS OF THE ARRAY
//
//***************************************************************************
void DisplayStudents(int N, char Students[MAX_STUDENTS][MAX_CHARACTERS])
{
  cout << "The students entered in the array are:" << endl;
  for (int Row = 0; Row < N; ++Row)
    cout << "\nArray position [" << Row << "] [0]  " << &Students[Row][0];
} //END DisplayStudents()
```

Again, you see a single **for** loop employed, because we need to reference only the beginning address of each string. The ampersand symbol is required in front of the array name in the *cout* statement to specify the string address. Without the ampersand, you would only see the first character of each string. (Why?)

PROGRAMMING TIP

Multiple strings are stored in two-dimensional arrays row by row. When accessing strings that are stored in a two-dimensional array, you must specify the beginning address of the string. This is done by using the ampersand symbol, &, prior to the array name and specifying the respective string row and fixing the column at zero, like this: *&StringArray[Row][0]*.

In addition to displaying the student names, the *cout* statement is formatted to display the array position of each name string. Here is a sample of what you would see on the monitor:

```
Array position [0][0]  Brenda Snider
Array position [1][0]  Anna Simon
Array position [2][0]  Doug Hahn
Array position [3][0]  Steve Weston
```

Finally, the entire program follows:

```
//****************************************************************************
//
//THIS PROGRAM WILL FILL A 2-DIM CHARACTER ARRAY WITH
//STRINGS ENTERED BY THE USER  AND THEN DISPLAY THE
//FILLED ARRAY
//
//****************************************************************************

#include <iostream.h>          //FOR cin AND cout

//GLOBAL CONSTANTS
const int MAX_STUDENTS = 20;
const int MAX_CHARACTERS = 26;

//FUNCTION PROTOTYPES
void GetStudents(int &N, char Students[MAX_STUDENTS][MAX_CHARACTERS]);
void DisplayStudents(int N, char Students[MAX_STUDENTS][MAX_CHARACTERS]);

void main()
{
  int Number = 0;                       //ACTUAL NUMBER OF STUDENTS
  char CPP[MAX_STUDENTS][MAX_CHARACTERS];   //DEFINE ARRAY
  GetStudents(Number,CPP);              //CALL FUNCTION TO FILL ARRAY
  DisplayStudents(Number,CPP);          //CALL FUNCTION TO DISPLAY ARRAY
} //END main()
```

```
//***************************************************************************
//
//THIS FUNCTION GETS THE STUDENT NAMES FROM THE
//USER AND ENTERS THEM INTO THE ARRAY
//
//***************************************************************************
void GetStudents(int &N, char Students[MAX_STUDENTS][MAX_CHARACTERS])
{
  cout << "Enter number of students:  ";
  cin >> N;
  for (int Row = 0; Row < N; ++Row)
  {
   cout << "\nEnter student number " << Row + 1 << ":  ";
   cin >> ws;
   cin.getline(&Students[Row][0],MAX_STUDENTS);
  } //END FOR
} //END GetStudents()

//***************************************************************************
//
//THIS FUNCTION DISPLAYS THE CONTENTS OF THE ARRAY
//
//***************************************************************************
void DisplayStudents(int N, char Students[MAX_STUDENTS][MAX_CHARACTERS])
{
  cout << "The students entered in the array are:" << endl;
  for (int Row = 0; Row < N; ++Row)
    cout << "\nArray position [" << Row << "] [0]  " << &Students[Row][0];
} //END DisplayStudents()
```

 Quick Check

1. Given the following two-dimensional array definition,

    float Sample[10][15];

    what is the maximum row index? What is the maximum column index?

2. What will the following statement display when applied to the array defined in question 1?

    cout << sizeof(Sample)/sizeof(float) << endl;

3. Write a statement that will read a value from the keyboard and place it in the first row and last column of the array defined in question 1.

4. Write a statement that will display the value stored in the second row and third column of the array defined in question 1.

5. Write the code, using **for** loops, that will display the elements of the array defined in question 1 in row/column format.

6. Write a prototype for a function called *Display()* that will display the contents of the array defined in question 1.

7. Write a statement to call the function in question 6.

8. A two-dimensional array in C++ is _____ major order.

14-2 ARRAYS OF MORE THAN TWO DIMENSIONS

Arrays of more than two dimensions are required for some applications. In this text, we will only consider three-dimensional arrays, because few common applications require larger arrays. The easiest way to picture a three-dimensional array is to imagine a cube such as that shown in Figure 14-4. Think of a three-dimensional array as several two-dimensional arrays combined to form a third dimension, depth. The cube is made up of rows (vertical dimension), columns (horizontal dimension), and planes (depth dimension). Thus, a given element within the cube array is located by specifying its plane, row, and column. See if you can verify for yourself the element positions indicated in Figure 14-4.

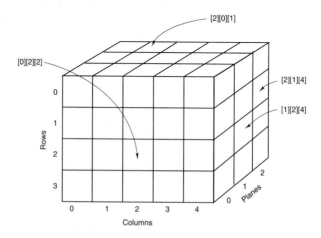

Figure 14-4 A $3 \times 4 \times 5$ three-dimensional array.

Now, let's look at a practical example of a three-dimensional array so you can see how one is defined and accessed in C++. Think of this excellent textbook as a three-dimensional array where each page of the book is a two-dimensional array made up of rows and columns. The combined pages then form the planes within a three-dimensional array that make up the book. Let's suppose there are 45 lines on each page that form the rows for the array and 80 characters per line that form the columns of the array. If there are 750 pages in the book, there are 750 planes in the array. Thus, this book array is a $45 \times 80 \times 750$ array. What are the array elements, and how many are there? Well, the array elements must be characters, because characters form the words within a page. In addition, there must be $45 \times 80 \times 750 = 2,700,000$ of them, including blanks, because this is the size of the book in terms of rows, columns, and pages.

How might our book array be defined in C++? How about this:

```
const int PAGES = 750;
const int LINES = 45;
const int COLUMNS = 80;
char TextBook[PAGES][LINES][COLUMNS];
```

You should be able to understand this definition from your work with one- and two-dimensional arrays. There are three dimensions [*PAGES*], [*LINES*], and [*COLUMNS*] that define the size of the *TextBook* array. A three-dimensional array in C/C++ is **plane major ordered**. This is why the plane size is specified first, followed by the row size, followed by the column size. The array data class is *char*, because the elements are characters. Of course, additional arrays could be used to create arrays for other books of the same general dimensions, right? Well, theoretically yes, but just one of these book arrays would be too large for most PC systems. In most systems, the definition would result in a "array size too big" error when the program is compiled.

Next, how do you suppose you might access the book information? The easiest way is to use nested loops. How should the loops be nested? Because the array is plane major ordered, the page loop must be the outermost loop, and the column loop the innermost loop. This leaves the row loop to be inserted between the page and column loops. Translating this to our book array, you get

```
for (int Page = 0; Page < PAGES; ++Page)
       for (int Line = 0; Line < LINES; ++Line)
              for (int Column = 0; Column < COLUMNS; ++Column)
                     <process TextBook[Page][Line][Column]>
```

By using this nesting approach, the *Column* loop is executed 80 times for each iteration of the *Line* loop, which is executed 45 times for each iteration of the *Page* loop. Of course, the *Page* loop is executed 750 times. This **for** structure would process elements one line at a time for a given page. Notice the use of the variables *Page*, *Line*, and *Column* as the loop counters. These variables must be different from the constants (*PAGES, LINES, COLUMNS*) used to define the array, because they are local to the **for** loops.

CAUTION

When you define an array, C++ actually sets aside enough primary memory to store the array. This memory is reserved exclusively for the defined array and cannot be used for other programming or system chores. In other words, a large array "eats up" a lot of memory. For instance, the foregoing book array contains 2,700,000 character elements. Each character requires 1 byte of memory to store, so C++ will allocate about 2637K bytes of user memory for the book array. This is much more than is available in some PC systems and would create an "array size too big" error during compilation. So be careful that your arrays don't get too big for your system to store. There are other, more memory-efficient, ways to store large amounts of data—a dynamic linked list.

Example 14-5

Given the foregoing *TextBook* array definition:

a. Write a program segment that could be used to fill the book.
b. Write a program segment that could be used to print the entire book.
c. Write a program segment that could be used to print page 2 of the book.

Solution:

a. Using the three foregoing nested loops, you could fill the book, like this:

```
for (int Page = 0; Page < PAGES; ++Page)
        for (int Line = 0; Line < LINES; ++Line)
                for (int Column = 0; Column < COLUMNS; ++Column)
                        cin.get(TextBook[Page][Line][Column]);
```

The innermost loop employs a *get()* function to read one character at a time and place it in the indexed position. The *cin* extraction operator (>>) will not work here, because >> ignores whitespace, which would obviously be part of the text material.

b. A *print* object is employed in the innermost loop to print the book:

```
for (int Page = 0; Page < PAGES; ++Page)
  for (int Line = 0; Line < LINES; ++Line)
  {
    print << endl;
    for (int Column = 0; Column < COLUMNS; ++Column)
      print << TextBook[Page][Line][Column];
  } //END MIDDLE FOR
```

Notice the single *print* statement used in the middle loop to provide a CRLF after a given line has been printed. Of course, the *print* object must be defined as discussed in Chapter 3 for these statements to compile.

c. You need only two loops to print a given page number, as follows:

```
for (int Line = 0; Line < LINES; ++Line)
{
  print << endl;
  for (int Column = 0; Column < COLUMNS; ++Column)
      print << TextBook[1][Line][Column];
} //END FOR
```

Observe that the *Page* index is fixed at [1] within the *cout* statement in order to print page 2 of the book. (Remember that the first page of the book is actually at page index [0].) How could this segment be modified to print any page desired by the user? Think about it! This will be left as an exercise at the end of the chapter.

 Quick Check

1. What problem might be encountered when defining large multidimensional arrays?

2. A three-dimensional array in C++ is _____ major ordered.

3. Define a three-dimensional array of integers that has 10 planes, 15 rows, and 3 columns.

4. How many bytes of storage are occupied by the array that you defined in question 3?

5. Write the code necessary to display the contents of the array that you defined in question 3, one plane at a time.

PROBLEM SOLVING IN ACTION: SIMULTANEOUS EQUATION SOLUTION

Problem

Recall from your algebra class that a set of simultaneous equations exists when you have two or more equations with two or more common unknowns. For instance, consider the following:

$$7x - 5y = 20$$
$$-5x + 8y = -10$$

Here you have two equations and two unknowns. To solve the equations, you must find both x and y. This is impossible using just one of the equations alone, but does not present a problem when both equations are solved "simultaneously," or together. One thing you might remember from algebra class is that in order to solve simultaneous equations, there must be at least as many equations as there are unknowns. This is why you cannot solve for two unknowns using a single equation. However, two unknowns can be solved using two or more equations.

Determinants

A common way to solve simultaneous equations is by using determinants. You might recall from algebra that a ***determinant*** is simply a *square array*. By a square array, we mean an array that has the same number of rows and columns. Here is a simple 2×2, called an ***order*** 2, determinant:

$$\begin{vmatrix} A_1 & B_1 \\ A_2 & B_2 \end{vmatrix}$$

The elements are A_1, B_1, A_2, and B_2. (*Note:* These elements will be numeric values when we actually use determinants to solve simultaneous equations.) Notice the vertical "bars" on the left and right sides of the array. These bars are used to indicate that the array is a determinant. This determinant is called an order 2 determinant, because it has two rows and two columns. There are also order 3, order 4, order 5, and so on, determinants. In each case, the determinant is a square array. Here is an order 3 determinant:

$$\begin{vmatrix} A_1 & B_1 & C_1 \\ A_2 & B_2 & C_2 \\ A_3 & B_3 & C_3 \end{vmatrix}$$

Expansion of a Determinant

A determinant is said to be expanded when you replace the array with a single value. An order 2 determinant expansion is the simplest. To get the idea, look at the following:

$$\begin{vmatrix} A_1 & B_1 \\ A_2 & B_2 \end{vmatrix} = A_1 B_2 - A_2 B_1$$

Imagine the two diagonals in the determinant. There is one diagonal running from top-left to bottom-right. We will call this the *down diagonal*, which forms the product $A_1 B_2$. The second diagonal runs from bottom-left to top-right. We will call this the *up diagonal*, which forms the product $A_2 B_1$. In the expansion on the right side of the equals sign, you see that the up-diagonal product is subtracted from the down-diagonal product.

Example 14-6

Expand the following determinants:

a. $\begin{vmatrix} 20 & -5 \\ -10 & 8 \end{vmatrix}$

b. $\begin{vmatrix} 7 & 20 \\ -5 & -10 \end{vmatrix}$

c. $\begin{vmatrix} 7 & 5 \\ -5 & 8 \end{vmatrix}$

Solution

a. $\begin{vmatrix} 20 & -5 \\ -10 & 8 \end{vmatrix} = (20)(8) - (-10)(-5) = 160 - 50 = 110$

b. $\begin{vmatrix} 7 & 20 \\ -5 & -10 \end{vmatrix} = (7)(-10) - (-5)(20) = -70 - (-100) = -70 + 100 = 30$

c. $\begin{vmatrix} 7 & 5 \\ -5 & 8 \end{vmatrix} = (7)(8) - (-5)(5) = 56 - (-25) = 56 + 25 = 81$

Expansion of an order 3 determinant is a bit more challenging. Here is a general order 3 determinant again:

$$\begin{vmatrix} A_1 & B_1 & C_1 \\ A_2 & B_2 & C_2 \\ A_3 & B_3 & C_3 \end{vmatrix}$$

To manually expand this determinant, you must rewrite the first two columns to the right of the determinant, and then use the diagonal method, as follows:

$$\begin{array}{ccccc} A_1 & B_1 & C_1 & A_1 & B_1 \\ A_2 & B_2 & C_2 & A_2 & B_2 \\ A_3 & B_3 & C_3 & A_3 & B_3 \end{array} = A_1B_2C_3 + B_1C_2A_3 + C_1A_2B_3 - A_3B_2C_1 - B_3C_2A_1 - C_3A_2B_1$$

Here, you create three down diagonals that form the products $A_1B_2C_3$, $B_1C_2A_3$, and $C_1A_2B_3$, and three up diagonals that form the products $A_3B_2C_1$, $B_3C_2A_1$, and $C_3A_2B_1$. The three up-diagonal products are subtracted from the sum of the three down-diagonal products. This is called the "method of diagonals" for expanding order 3 determinants. I should caution you, however, that the method of diagonals does not work for determinants larger than order 3. To expand determinants larger than order 3, you must use the method of *cofactors*. The cofactor method is a recursive process and will be left as an exercise at the end of the chapter.

Example 14-7

Expand the following order 3 determinant:

$$\begin{vmatrix} 6 & -2 & -4 \\ 15 & -2 & -5 \\ -4 & -5 & 12 \end{vmatrix}$$

Solution

Rewriting the first two columns to the right of the determinant, you get

$$\begin{array}{ccccc} 6 & -2 & -4 & 6 & -2 \\ 15 & -2 & -5 & 15 & -2 \\ -4 & -5 & 12 & -4 & -5 \end{array}$$

Now, multiplying the diagonal elements and adding/subtracting the diagonal products, you get

$$+ (6)(-2)(12) + (-2)(-5)(-4) + (-4)(15)(-5)$$
$$- (-4)(-2)(-4) - (-5)(-5)(6) - (12)(15)(-2)$$

Finally, performing the required arithmetic gives you

$$+ (-144) + (-40) + (300)$$
$$- (-32) - (150) - (-360)$$

$$= -144 - 40 + 300 + 32 - 150 + 360$$

$$= 358$$

As you can see from the preceding example, expanding an order 3 determinant can get a bit tricky! You have to pay particular attention to the signs. One simple sign error during your arithmetic will result in an incorrect expansion. Wouldn't it be nice if a computer program could be written to perform the expansion? This is an ideal application for a C++ function, because the expansion operation returns a single value.

An Order 2 Determinant Expansion Function

Let's write a C++ function to expand an order 2 determinant. We will assume that the elements in the determinant are stored in a 2×2 array. This array must be passed to the function, and then the function must evaluate the array and return a single expansion value. Here is the function interface description:

Function *Expand()*:   Expands an order 2 determinant.

Accepts: A 2×2 array.

Returns: The expansion value.

By using this interface description, the function prototype becomes

float Expand(float Determinant[2][2]);

The function name is *Expand()*. The formal parameter is *Determinant*[2][2], because this is the size of the array that will be expanded. The data class of the returned expansion value is *float*. Now, the *Determinant* array has row indices, which range from [0] to [1], and column indices, which range from [0] to [1]. Here is the array showing the row/column index layout:

$$\begin{array}{cc} [0][0] & [0][1] \\ [1][0] & [1][1] \end{array}$$

Remember that these are only the array indices and not the elements stored in the array. Recall that to expand the determinant, the up diagonal must be subtracted from the down diagonal. Thus, the product of indices [1] [0] and [0] [1] must be subtracted from the product of [0] [0] and [1] [1]. Using this idea in our function, we get a single **return** statement, as follows:

```
return   Determinant[0][0] ∗ Determinant[1][1]
          – Determinant[1][0] ∗ Determinant[0][1];
```

That's all there is to it! Here is the complete function:

```
//THIS FUNCTION WILL EXPAND A 2 x 2 DETERMINANT
float Expand(float Determinant[2][2])
{
   return  Determinant[0][0] ∗ Determinant[1][1]
          – Determinant[1][0] ∗ Determinant[0][1];
} //END Expand()
```

Writing a function to expand an order 3 determinant will be left as an exercise at the end of the chapter.

Cramer's Rule

Cramer's rule allows you to solve simultaneous equations using determinants. Let's begin with two equations and two unknowns.

An equation is said to be in ***standard form*** when all the variables are on the left-hand side of the equals sign and the constant term is on the right-hand side of the equals sign. Here is a general equation containing two variables in standard form:

$$Ax + By = C$$

This equation has two variables, x and y. The x-coefficient is A and the y-coefficient is B. The constant term is C.

Here is a set of two general simultaneous equations in standard form:

$$A_1x + B_1y = C_1$$
$$A_2x + B_2y = C_2$$

The common variables between the two equations are x and y. Subscripts 1 and 2 denote the coefficients and constants of equations 1 and 2, respectively. Cramer's rule allows you to solve for x and y using determinants, like this:

$$x = \frac{\begin{vmatrix} C_1 & B_1 \\ C_2 & B_2 \end{vmatrix}}{\begin{vmatrix} A_1 & B_1 \\ A_2 & B_2 \end{vmatrix}} \qquad y = \frac{\begin{vmatrix} A_1 & C_1 \\ A_2 & C_2 \end{vmatrix}}{\begin{vmatrix} A_1 & B_1 \\ A_2 & B_2 \end{vmatrix}}$$

As you can see, the determinants are formed using the coefficients and constants from the two equations. Do you see a pattern? First, look at the denominator determinants. They are identical and are formed using the x- and y-coefficients directly from the two equations. However, the numerator determinants are different. When solving for x, the numerator determinant is formed by replacing the x-coefficients with the constant terms. When solving for y, the numerator determinant is formed by replacing the y-coefficients with the constant terms. Here's an example:

Example 14-8

Solve the following set of simultaneous equations using Cramer's rule:

$$x + 2y = 3$$
$$3x + 4y = 5$$

Solution

Forming the required determinants, you get

$$x = \frac{\begin{vmatrix} 3 & 2 \\ 5 & 4 \end{vmatrix}}{\begin{vmatrix} 1 & 2 \\ 3 & 4 \end{vmatrix}} \qquad y = \frac{\begin{vmatrix} 1 & 3 \\ 3 & 5 \end{vmatrix}}{\begin{vmatrix} 1 & 2 \\ 3 & 4 \end{vmatrix}}$$

Expanding the determinants and dividing gives you x and y:

$$x = \frac{(3)(4) - (5)(2)}{(1)(4) - (3)(2)} = \frac{2}{-2} = -1 \qquad y = \frac{(1)(5) - (3)(3)}{(1)(4) - (3)(2)} = \frac{-4}{-2} = 2$$

Implementing Cramer's Rule in C++

Think about the "functions" you just went through using Cramer's rule to solve the previous set of simultaneous equations. There are three major tasks to be performed:

- Task 1: Obtain the equation coefficients and constants.

- Task 2: Form the determinants, both numerator and denominator.
- Task 3: Expand the determinants.

We have already developed a function to perform the third task. We must now develop C++ functions to accomplish the first two tasks.

To perform Task 1, we must write a function that will obtain the coefficients and constants of the equations to be solved. There are two equations and three items (two coefficients and a constant) that must be obtained from each equation. Does this suggest any particular data structure? Of course, a 2×3 array! So, let's write a function to fill a 2×3 array from coefficient and constant terms of the two equations that will be entered by the user. Here it is:

```
//THIS FUNCTION WILL FILL AN ARRAY WITH THE
//EQUATION COEFFICIENTS
void Fill(float Equations[2][3])
{
  for(int Row = 0; Row < 2; ++Row)
  {
    cout  << "Enter the variable coefficients and constant for equation "
          << Row + 1 << "\nNote the equation must be in standard form."
          << endl << endl;
    for(int Col = 0; Col < 3; ++Col)
      {
          if (Col == 2)
            cout << "Enter the constant term:  ";
          else
            cout << "Enter the coefficient for variable " << Col + 1 << ":  ";
          cin >> Equations[Row][Col];
      } //END COLUMN LOOP
  } //END ROW LOOP
} //END Fill()
```

Such a function should be nothing new to you, because it simply employs nested **for** loops to fill an array. The function name is *Fill()*. It fills an array called *Equations* that must be defined as a 2×3 array in the calling program. The array will be passed to the function by reference using the array name in the function call. Once the function fills the array, it is passed back to the calling program.

Given the following two general equations in standard form,

$$A_1 x + B_1 y = C_1$$
$$A_2 x + B_2 y = C_2$$

The *Fill()* function will fill the 2×3 array, like this:

$$A_1 \quad B_1 \quad C_1$$
$$A_2 \quad B_2 \quad C_2$$

As you can see, the first equation coefficients and constant term are inserted into the first row of the array. The second row of the array stores the coefficients and constant term of the second equation. Of course, the function assumes that the user will enter the coefficients and constants in their proper order.

To accomplish Task 2, we will develop a function to form the determinants from the equation coefficients and constants. How can we obtain the coefficients and constants? You're right: from the 2×3 array that was just filled! Now, how many unique determinants does Cramer's rule require to solve two equations and two unknowns? Three: a numerator determinant for the x unknown, a numerator determinant for the y unknown, and a denominator determinant that is the same for both the x and y unknowns. All of the determinants must be order 2, right?

So, our function must obtain the single 2×3 array that was filled with coefficients and constants in the *Fill()* function and generate three 2×2 arrays that will form the two numerator and one denominator determinant required by Cramer's rule. Here's the function:

```
//THIS FUNCTION WILL FORM THE DETERMINANTS
void FormDet(float Equations[2][3], float x[2][2],  float y[2][2], float D[2][2])
{
  for(int Row = 0; Row < 2; ++Row)
   for(int Col = 0; Col < 2; ++Col)
    {
       x[Row][Col] = Equations[Row][Col];
       y[Row][Col] = Equations[Row][Col];
       D[Row][Col] = Equations[Row][Col];
    } //END COLUMN LOOP
  x[0][0] = Equations[0][2];
  x[1][0] = Equations[1][2];
  y[0][1] = Equations[0][2];
  y[1][1] = Equations[1][2];
} //END FormDet()
```

First, look at the function header. The name of the function is *FormDet()*. This function requires four parameters: *Equations*[2][3], *x*[2][2], *y*[2][2], and *D*[2][2]. *Equations*[2][3] is the 2×3 array containing the coefficients and constants from the *Fill()* function. The *x*[2][2] parameter represents the numerator determinant for the *x* unknown. The *y*[2][2] parameter represents the numerator determinant for the *y* unknown. The *D*[2][2] parameter represents the denominator determinant for both the *x* and *y* unknowns.

Next, look at the statement section of the function. The first two columns of the equation array are copied into each of the determinant arrays using **for** loops. Then, the constant terms are inserted into the *x* and *y* determinant arrays at the required positions using direct assignment. The formation pattern results from Cramer's rule. Notice that in all instances, the determinants are formed using the elements from the 2 × 3 *Equations* array of coefficients and constants generated by the *Fill()* function.

Now we have all the ingredients for a C++ program that will solve two equations and two unknowns using Cramer's rule. Combining our *Fill()* function, our *FormDet()* function, and our *Expand()* function into a single program, we get the following:

```
//*****************************************************************************
//
//THIS PROGRAM WILL SOLVE TWO EQUATIONS AND TWO
//UNKNOWNS USING CRAMER'S RULE (ACT14-01.CPP)
//
//*****************************************************************************

#include <iostream.h>   //FOR cin AND cout

//FUNCTION PROTOTYPES
void Fill(float Equations[2][3]);
void FormDet(float Equations[2][3], float x[2][2], float y[2][2], float D[2][2]);
float Expand(float Determinant[2][2]);

void main()
{
//ARRAY DEFINITIONS
  float Equations[2][3];
  float x[2][2];
  float y[2][2];
  float D[2][2];

//CALL FUNCTIONS TO FILL EQUATION ARRAY
//AND FORM DETERMINANTS
  Fill(Equations);
  FormDet(Equations, x, y, D);
```

```
//IF DENOMINATOR = 0, WRITE ERROR MESSAGE.
//ELSE CALCULATE x AND y
  if(!Expand(D))
    cout << "\nDenominator = 0.  Equations are unsolvable." << endl;
  else
    cout << "\nThe value of the first variable is: "
         << Expand(x)/Expand(D)
         << "\n\nThe value of the second variable is: "
         << Expand(y)/Expand(D) << endl;
} //END main()

//********************************************************************************
//
//THIS FUNCTION WILL FILL AN ARRAY WITH THE EQUATION
//COEFFICIENTS
//
//********************************************************************************
void Fill(float Equations[2][3])
{
  for(int Row = 0; Row < 2; ++Row)
  {
    cout << "\nEnter the variable coefficients and constant for equation "
         << Row + 1 << "\nNote the equation must be in standard form."
         << endl << endl;
    for(int Col = 0; Col < 3; ++Col)
      {
        if (Col == 2)
          cout << "Enter the constant term:  ";
        else
          cout << "Enter the coefficient for variable " << Col + 1 << ":  ";
        cin >> Equations[Row][Col];
      } //END COLUMN LOOP
  } //END ROW LOOP
} //END Fill()

//****************************************************************
//
//THIS FUNCTION WILL FORM THE DETERMINANTS
//
//****************************************************************
void FormDet(float Equations[2][3], float x[2][2], float y[2][2], float D[2][2])
{
```

```
    for(int Row = 0; Row < 2; ++Row)
      for(int Col = 0; Col < 2; ++Col)
        {
           x[Row][Col] = Equations[Row][Col];
           y[Row][Col] = Equations[Row][Col];
           D[Row][Col] = Equations[Row][Col];
        } //END COLUMN LOOP
     x[0][0] = Equations[0][2];
     x[1][0] = Equations[1][2];
     y[0][1] = Equations[0][2];
     y[1][1] = Equations[1][2];
} //END FormDet()


//***************************************************************************
//
//THIS FUNCTION WILL EXPAND A 2 x 2 DETERMINANT
//
//***************************************************************************
float Expand(float Determinant[2][2])
{
   return  Determinant[0][0] * Determinant[1][1]
            - Determinant[1][0] * Determinant[0][1];
} //END Expand()
```

Observe that all the arrays are defined local to *main()*. *Equations* is a 2×3 array that will store the coefficients and constants of the two equations. This is followed by definitions for the three 2×2 determinant arrays. The prototypes for our three functions are given prior to *main()*, and the functions themselves are listed after *main()*.

Now, look at the statement section of the *main()*. The *Fill()* function is called first to obtain the coefficient and constant terms of the two equations. The actual argument used for the function call is the name of the equations array, *Equations*. Next, the *FormDet()* function is called to form the required determinants. The actual arguments used in this function call are *Equations*, *x*, *y*, and *D*. The *Equations* argument is required to pass the 2×3 array to the function. The *x*, *y*, and *D* arguments are required to pass the three determinant arrays to the function and back.

Finally, look at how the *Expand()* function is invoked. It is first invoked as part of an **if/else** statement to see if the denominator determinant value is zero. If it is, the equations cannot be solved using Cramer's rule because division by zero is undefined. If the denominator determinant is not zero, the *Expand()* function is invoked twice to calculate the first unknown (x) within a *cout* statement like this: *Expand(x) / Expand(D)*. This expands the x determinant, expands the common denominator determinant, and divides the two to obtain the value of the first unknown (x). The function is called twice again to find the second unknown (y).

Given the following two equations

$$x + 2y = 3$$
$$3x + 4y = 5$$

here is what you would see when the program is executed:

Enter the variable coefficients and constant for equation 1
Note the equation must be in standard form.

Enter the coefficient for variable 1: **1**↵
Enter the coefficient for variable 2: **2**↵
Enter the constant term: **3**↵

Enter the variable coefficients and constant for equation 2
Note the equation must be in standard form.

Enter the coefficient for variable 1: **3**↵
Enter the coefficient for variable 2: **4**↵
Enter the constant term: **5**↵

The value for the first variable is: −1

The value for the second variable is: 2

Do you think that you could develop a similar program to solve a set of three simultaneous equations? You now have all the required knowledge! Guess what you will be doing in the programming exercises at the end of the chapter.

CHAPTER SUMMARY

A two-dimensional array, or table, is a combination of two or more element rows, or lists. It has dimension $m \times n$, where m is the number of rows in the array, and n is the number of array columns. A three-dimensional array is the combination of two or more two-dimensional arrays. It is comprised of rows, columns, and planes. Thus, a three-dimensional array has dimension $p \times m \times n$, where p is the number of planes in the array, m is the number of array rows, and n is the number of columns. In C++, two-dimensional arrays are row major ordered, and three-dimensional arrays are plane major ordered.

A separate **for** loop is required to access each array dimension. In addition, the loops must be nested when accessing multidimensional arrays. Thus, to access a three-dimensional array, the column loop is nested in the row loop, which is nested in the plane loop.

There are many technical applications for arrays. A common use of an array is to store determinants that are used to solve systems of simultaneous equations using Cramer's rule.

QUESTIONS AND PROBLEMS

Questions

Use the following array definitions to answer questions 1–11:

float SemesterScores[10];

const int MULTIPLIER = 12;
const int MULTIPLICAND = 20;
int Product[MULTIPLIER][MULTIPLICAND];

bool Cube[3][7][4];

enum Colors {Brown, Black, Red, Orange, Yellow, Green, Blue, Violet,
            Gray, White};

float ColorCode[10][10][10];

1. Sketch a diagram showing each array structure and its indices.

2. List the identifiers that must be used to access each array.

3. What are the dimensions of each array?

4. How many elements will each array store?

5. List ail of the possible element values for the *Cube* array.

6. Write a C++ statement that will display the element in the fourth row and second column of the *Product* array.

7. Write a C++ statement that will assign any legal element to the second row and last column of the *Product* array.

8. Write a C++ statement that will display the element values in the third row, second column, and third plane of the *Cube* and *ColorCode* arrays. Assume

that the enumerated data class elements will be used as indices to access the *ColorCode* array.

9. Write C++ statements that will insert values into the *ColorCode* array using the following color code combinations and associated values:

a. Brown, Black, Red = 1000
b. Brown, Black, Green = 1000000
c. Yellow, Violet, Red = 4700
d. Red, Red, Red = 2200

10. Write the C++ code required to fill each array from keyboard entries.

11. Write the C++ code required to display each array, and include appropriate table headings.

Problems

Least Difficult

1. Write a program to read 15 integer elements from the keyboard and store them in a 3×5 array. Once the elements have been read, display them as a 5×3 array. (*Hint:* Reverse the rows and columns.)

2. Write a function that will display any given page of the book array used in Example 14-5. Assume that the user will enter the page number to be displayed.

3. Write a program that will store the state table for a 4-bit decade counter (BCD). Write functions to fill and display the state table. Here is what its state table looks like:

State	Count
0	0000
1	0001
2	0010
3	0011
4	0100
5	0101
6	0110
7	0111
8	1000
9	1111

4. Write a program that employs two functions to fill and print a calendar for the current month.

More Difficult

Employ the program developed in the chapter case study to solve problems 5–7.
Modify the program to meet the given application.

5. The circuit diagram in Figure 14-5 shows two unknown currents, I_1 and I_2.
    An engineer writes two equations that describe the circuit, as follows:

$$300 I_1 + 500(I_1 - I_2) - 20 = 0$$
$$200 I_2 + 500(I_2 - I_1) + 10 = 0$$

    Put these equations in standard form, and solve for the two currents using the
    software developed in the chapter case study.

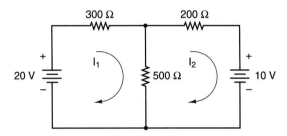

Figure 14-5   A two-loop circuit for problem 5.

6. Look at the lever in Figure 14-6. If you know one of the weights and all the
    distances of the weights from the fulcrum, you can calculate the other two
    weights using two simultaneous equations. The two equations have the
    following general form,

$$w_1 d_1 + w_2 d_2 = w_3 d_3$$

    where

    w_1, w_2, and w_3 are the three weights.

    d_1, d_2, and d_3 are the distances the three weights are located from the
    fulcrum, respectively.

    Using this general equation format, you get two equations by knowing two
    balance points. Suppose weight w_3 is 5 pounds, and you obtain a balance
    condition for the following distance values:

    Balance point 1:

$$d_1 = 3 \text{ in.}$$
$$d_2 = 6 \text{ in.}$$
$$d_3 = 36 \text{ in.}$$

Balance point 2:

$$d_1 = 5 \text{ in.}$$
$$d_2 = 4 \text{ in.}$$
$$d_3 = 30 \text{ in.}$$

Find the two unknown weights, w_1 and w_2.

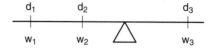

Figure 14-6   A lever/fulcrum arrangement for problem 6.

7.   The following equations describe the tension, in pounds, of two cables supporting an object. Find the amount of tension on each cable (T_1 and T_2).

$$0.5T_2 + 0.93T_1 - 120 = 0$$
$$0.42T_1 - 0.54T_2 = 0$$

Most Difficult

8.   Write a function to fill a 3×4 array with the coefficients and constant terms from three simultaneous equations expressed in standard form. Assume that the user will enter the array elements in the required order.

9.   Write a function to display the equation array in problem 8.

10.   Using Cramer's rule, write a function to form 3×3 determinants from the 3×4 equation array you filled in problem 8.

11.   Write a function to expand an order 3 determinant.

12.   Employ the functions you developed in problems 8 through 11 to write a program that will solve a set of three simultaneous equations.

13.   Use the program in problem 12 to solve the three currents (I_1, I_2, I_3) in the Wheatstone bridge circuit shown in Figure 14-7. Here are the equations that an engineer writes to describe the circuit:

$$2000(I_1 - I_2) + 4000(I_1 - I_3) - 10 = 0$$
$$2000(I_2 - I_1) + 8000I_2 + 5000(I_2 - I_3) = 0$$
$$5000(I_3 - I_2) + 3000I_3 + 4000(I_3 - I_1) = 0$$

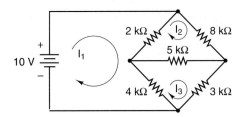

Figure 14-7   The three-loop Wheatstone Bridge circuit for problem 13.

14. Suppose the perimeter of a triangle is 14 inches. The shortest side is half as long as the longest side and 2 inches more than the difference of the two longer sides. Find the length of each side using the program you developed in problem 12.

15. Assume the following table represents the monthly rental price of six resort cabins over a 5-year period.

YEAR

		FIRST	SECOND	THIRD	FOURTH	FIFTH
	1	200	210	225	300	235
	2	250	275	300	350	400
CABIN	3	300	325	375	400	450
	4	215	225	250	250	275
	5	355	380	400	404	415
	6	375	400	425	440	500

Write a program that employs functions to perform the following tasks:
- Fill a two-dimensional array with the table.
- Compute the total rental income for each cabin by year, and store the yearly totals in a second array.
- Compute the percentage increase/decrease in price between adjacent years for each cabin, and store the percentages in a third array.
- Generate a report showing all three arrays in table form with appropriate row/column headings.

16. The method of *cofactors* used to find a value of a determinant is a recursive process. Write a function that will find the value of an order n determinant, where the order of the determinant, n, is entered by the user. Incorporate this function into a program that will find the solution to n equations of n

unknowns. (You might need to consult a good linear algebra textbook for information on using the method of cofactors to solve a determinant.)

17. Write a program that employs pointers to find the maximum and minimum elements in a two-dimensional integer array. Initialize the array from the keyboard using user entries.

APPENDIX A

QUICK-CHECK SOLUTIONS

CHAPTER 1

SECTION 1-1

1. English-like statements that require less precision than a formal programming language are called *pseudocode* statements.

2. Some questions that must be answered when defining a computer programming problem are as follows:
    *   What outputs are needed?
    *   What inputs are needed?
    *   What processing is needed to produce the output from the input?

3. To test and debug a program you can desk-check, compile, debug it using a debugger, and run it.

4. Commenting is important within a program because it explains what the program does and makes the program easier to read and maintain.

SECTION 1-2

1. It is important to use an algorithm in the planning of a program to define what steps are needed to produce the desired final result. An algorithm keeps you from "spinning your wheels."

2. The three major categories of algorithmic language operations are sequence, decision, and iteration.

3. Three decision operations are **if/then**, **if/else** and **switch/case**.

4. Three iteration operations are **while**, **do/while**, and **for**.

SECTION 1-3

1. Abstraction allows you to "see the forest for the trees," because it permits you to initially concentrate on the problem at hand, without agonizing over the implementation details of a computer language.

2. Stepwise refinement begins with the initial abstract algorithm and step by step divides it into one or more related algorithms that provide more and more implementation detail.

3. A codeable level of an algorithm is reached when all the statements have been reduced to the pseudocode operations listed in Table 2-1.

CHAPTER 2

SECTION 2-1

1. C++ is referred to as a midlevel language because it provides low-level access to system hardware and software while having the advantages of a high-level language.

2. The steps that must be performed to translate a C++ source code program to an executable program are as follows:
   - Write the source code.
   - Compile the source code into object code.
   - Link the object code to other required routines to form the executable program.

3. An object file (*.obj*) is produced by the compile step.

4. An executable file (*.exe*) is produced by the linking step.

5. The purpose of the linking step is to integrate the program with any additional routines that are required for proper program execution.

6. The major difference between the C language and the C++ language is that C++ allows for object-oriented programming whereas C does not.

SECTION 2-2

1.   A *class* describes the data attributes and behavior of its objects.

2.   Data classes that are predefined within a programming language are called *standard* data classes.

3.   A set of data elements by you, the programmer, to meet a given application is called an *enumerated* data class.

4.   The three major data class categories in a structured programming language are the *scalar*, *structured*, and *pointer* data categories.

5.   Behavior, as related to ADTs, descibes how the ADT will act and react to a given operation.

6.   Another name for a struct is a *record*.

SECTION 2-3

1.   The range of values that can be provided via the standard *int* data class is −32768 to +32767.

2.   An overflow error occurs when, as a result of a calculation, a value exceeds its predefined range.

3.   The two ways that floating-point values can be represented in a C++ program are using either *decimal* or *exponential* format.

4.   The following values will be returned when these functions are executed:

     toascii('B') = 66
     toascii('?') = 63

5.   The extended character set defined for the IBM PC must use the **unsigned char** data class.

6.   A character string is stored in a data structure called an *array*.

7.   Twenty-nine bytes of storage are required to store the string "The United States of America". Remember that you must include room for the null terminator character.

8.   The ANSI C++ standard specifies a Boolean class called **bool** which includes the elements **true** and **false**.

SECTION 2-4

1.   The two reasons for declaring/defining constants and variables in a C++ program are as follows:

- The compiler must know the value of a constant before it is used and must reserve memory locations to store variables.
- The compiler must know the data class of constants and variables to determine their data attributes and behavior.

2. The following will declare a constant called *PERIOD* that will insert a period wherever it is referenced in a program.

   const char PERIOD = '.' ;

3. The following will declare a constant called *BOOK* that will insert the string "Structuring Techniques" wherever it appears in a program.

   const char BOOK[ ] = "Structured and Object-Oriented Techniques";

4. Given a string variable that must store a string of up to 25 characters, an array size of 26 must be defined to store the string variable.

5. The following will define a string variable called *Course* that will be initialized to a string value of "Data Structures".

   char Course[ ] = "Data Structures" ;

SECTION 2-5

1. Enumerated data classes allow the programmer to define a problem more clearly and make the program more readable than standard data classes.

2. The following will define an enumerated data class called *Automobiles*, which consists of 10 popular automobile brands.

   enum Automobiles {Ford, BMW, Geo, Chrysler, Volvo, Nissan, Mazda,
                       Porsche, Cadillac, Toyota};

3. The compiler assigns the numeric value of 0 (zero) to the first element in an enumerated data class.

SECTION 2-6

1. Any C++ program consists of two sections called the *preprocessor* and *main function* sections.

2. The following is an *#include* directive to include a standard header file called *stdlib.h* into a program, assuming that the header file is located in the system default directory.

   #include <stdlib.h>

3. A subprogram that returns a single value, a set of values, or performs some specific task in C++ is called a *function*.

4. Global constants must be declared before the main function identifier, *main()*, so that they are accessible to the entire program.

5. Variable objects can be defined anywhere in the program as long as they are defined prior to their use. However, good style dictates that they be defined at the beginning of the function block in which they are used.

6. True: Constants should be declared as globally as possible, whereas variables should be declared as locally as possible.

7. D. Comments are inserted into a C++ program using double forward slashes, like this: //COMMENT.

8. At a minimum, the program should include the following comments:

The beginning of the program should be commented with the programmer's name, date the program was written, date the program was last revised, and the name of the person doing the revision. In other words, a brief ongoing maintenance log should be commented at the beginning of the program.

The beginning of the program should be commented to explain the purpose of the program, which includes the problem definition. This provides an overall perspective by which anyone, including you, the programmer, can begin debugging or maintaining the program.

Preprocessor directives should be commented as to their purpose.

Constants and variables should be commented as to their purpose.

Major sections of the program should be commented to explain the overall purpose of the respective section.

Individual program lines should be commented when the purpose of the code is not obvious relative to the application.

All major subprograms (functions in C++) should be commented just like the main program function.

The end of each program block (right curly brace) should be commented to indicate what the brace is ending.

SECTION 2-7

1. A methodology that requires software to be designed using a top/down modular approach is called *structured design*.

2. In C++, individual program modules are implemented using *functions*.

3. C. In C++, user-defined function code is placed after *main()*.

Chapter 3

SECTION 3-1

1. The file that must be included to use *cout* is the *iostream.h* header file.

2. The operator that must be employed to insert information into the *cout* stream is the << stream insertion operator.

3. The following is a *cout* statement to display my name as a fixed string of information.

   cout << "Andy" << endl;

4. The following is a *cout* statement to display my name when it is stored in a string variable called *Name*.

   cout << Name << endl;

5. The escape sequence that must be used to generate a CRLF is '\n'.

6. The file that must be included to use the *setw()* field-width manipulator is the *iomanip.h* header file.

7. The following *cout* statement that will display the value of a floating-point variable called *Number* left-justified within a field width of 10 columns and a precision of 2 decimal places.

   cout.setf(ios::fixed ¦ ios:: left);

   cout.precision(2);

   cout << setw(10) << Number;

8. The difference between using a '\n' versus an *endl* within a *cout* statement is that the '\n' escape sequence only generates a CRLF, whereas the *endl* manipulator generates a CRLF and flushes the output stream buffer.

SECTION 3-2

1. The operator that must be employed to extract data from the *cin* input stream is the >> extraction operator.

2. The following statements will prompt the user to enter a value for an integer variable called *Number* using *cin* to read the user entry.

   cout << "Please enter an integer :" << endl;
   cin >> Number;

3. Blanks, tabs, new lines (CRLFs), and carriage returns are all considered whitespace.

4. The following statement will read a single whitespace character and store it in a variable called *Whitespace*.

   cin.get(Whitespace);

5. The following statement will display the single whitespace character read in question 4.

   cout.put(Whitespace);

6. True: When reading character data, *cin* will read only one character at a time.

7. When using the >> operator to read string data, the *cin* statement will terminate when whitespace is encountered.

8. The *getline()* function can be used as *cin.getline()* to include whitespace when reading string data.

9. The *gets()* or *fgets()* function should be used in lieu of *cin* when reading string data after reading numeric or character data.

10. The following employs the *gets()* function to read a string of up to 25 characters and stores it in a variable called *Name*:

    char Name[26];
    gets(Name);

11. The function *gets()* converts the CRLF character to a null terminator.

12. The function *fgets()* reads and stores the CRLF character and then adds a null terminator.

SECTION 3-3

1. The *fstream.h* header file must be included to read/write disk files.

2. The class used to define input file objects is the *ifstream* class.

3. The class used to define output file objects is the *ofstream* class.

4. The three tasks that must always be executed to process any disk file are (1) define a file object, (2) open a file and attach it to the object, and (3) close the file.

5. ifstream MyInput;
   ofstream MyOutput;

6. MyInput.open("data");
   MyOutput.open("results");

7. //READ FIRST INTEGER
      MyInput >> Integer;

   //READ AND PROCESS FILE DATA USING A LOOP
   while (!MyInput.eof())

```
{ //BEGIN LOOP
  TimesTen = 10 * Integer;              //MULTIPLY INTEGER BY 10
  MyInput >> Integer;                   //READ AN INTEGER FROM INPUT FILE
  MyOutput << TimesTen << endl;         //WRITE PRODUCT TO OUTPUT FILE
} //END LOOP
```

8.   `#include <fstream.h>  //FOR FILE I/O`

```
void main()
{
//DEFINE VARIALBES
  int Integer;                          //INTEGER VARIABLE FOR INPUT DATA
  int TimesTen;                         //INTEGER VARIABLE FOR TIMES 10 PRODUCT

//DEFINE FILE OBJECTS AND OPEN FILES
  ifstream MyInput;          //DEFINE INPUT OBJECT
  ofstream MyOutput;         //DEFINE OUTPUT OBJECT

  MyInput.open("data");      //OPEN INPUT FILE
  MyOutput.open("results");  //OPEN OUTPUT FILE

//READ FIRST INTEGER
  MyInput >> Integer;

//READ AND PROCESS FILE DATA USING A LOOP
while (!MyInput.eof())
{ //BEGIN LOOP
  TimesTen = 10 * Integer;              //MULTIPLY INTEGER BY 10
  MyInput >> Integer;                   //READ AN INTEGER FROM INPUT FILE
  MyOutput << TimesTen << endl;         //WRITE PRODUCT TO OUTPUT FILE
} //END LOOP

  MyInput.close();           //CLOSE INPUT FILE
  MyOutput.close();          //CLOSE OUTPUT FILE
} //END main()
```

CHAPTER 4

SECTION 4-1

1.   The order in which C++ performs arithmetic operations is as follows:

( ) * / % + −

Any operations inside of parentheses are performed first, then (from left-to-right) multiplication, division, and modulus, and then (from left-to-right) addition and subtraction.

2.   The statement $--x$; is equivalent to the statement $x = x - 1$;

3.   The statement, "The division operator will produce an integer result when either of the operands is an integer," is false because this happens only when both the numerator and denominator operands are integers.

4.   True: The modulus operator is only defined for integers.

5.   The difference between using the preincrement operator versus the postincrement operator on a variable is that a preincrement operator increments the variable before any expression involving the variable is evaluated and a postincrement operator increments the variable after any expression involving the variable is evaluated. It is important to be careful as to which one you use, especially when the variable is used as part of a compound expression, because undesirable results can be produced if the wrong incrementing operator is used.

6.   The result of $10 / 100$ is 0, becasue both operands are integers, and the $/$ operator generates an integer result when both operands are integers.

SECTION 4-2

1.   The statement $x += 5$; is equivalent to the statement $x = x + 5$;.

2.   The statement $x /= y$; is equivalent to the statement $x = x/y$;.

SECTION 4-3

1.   Operators that allow two values to be compared are called *relational* operators.

2.   In C++, a logical false is equated to the value 0 (*zero*).

3.   The difference between the $=$ operator and the $==$ operator in C++ is that the $=$ operator assigns the statement on the right to the variable on the left and the $==$ operator compares two quantities to determine if they are equal.

4.   The value Boolean value true (1) is generated as a result of the operation $4 > 5 - 2$, because 4 is greater than $(5 - 2)$, or 3.

5.   The Boolean value false (0) is generated as a result of the operation $(5 != 5)$ **AND** $(3 == 3)$, because $(5 != 5)$ is false, making the entire **AND** statement false.

SECTION 4-4

1. In order to use a standard function in your program, you must include its *header*, or *include*, *file*.

2. The answer to this question depends on the compiler that you are using. To get an on-line description of a standard function using the TURBO C++ compiler while working in the edit mode, press **CTRL + F1**, and select the function from the on-line help index. An alternative way is to place the cursor on the desired function name in the edit mode, and press **CTRL + F1**.

3. The *strcpy()* function must be employed to assign string data to a string variable in a C++ program.

4. The statement strcpy(Compiler,"C++"); will assign the string "C++" to a string variable called *Compiler*.

5. The *strcmp()* function should be used instead of Boolean relational operators when comparing string values because Boolean relational operators do not give correct logical results when comparing strings.

CHAPTER 5

SECTION 5-1

1. True: A test expression that evaluates to any nonzero value is considered true.

2. True: When a test expression in an **if** statement evaluates to zero, the related **if** statements are bypassed.

3. The correct **if** statement reads as follows:

    ```
    if (x == y)
        cout << "There is a problem here" << endl;
    ```

    The test expression needs to be a comparison, not an assignment.

4. The && (**AND**) operator must be employed to test if all conditions are true.

5. The !&& (**NOT AND**) operators must be employed to test if one of several conditions is false.

6. The ¦¦ (**OR**) operator must be employed to test if one of several conditions is true.

7. The *cout* statement will be executed when x is zero, because $!x = !0 = 1 = $ true.

SECTION 5-2

1. True: When the test expression in an **if/else** operation evaluates to zero, the **else** statements are executed.

2. The following pseudocode needs an **else** statement because, without an **else** statement, both statements, "It's payday" and "It's not payday", would be written when the **if** test is true.

    If *Day* == *Friday*
        Write("It's pay day").
    Write("It's not pay day").

3. True: Framing with curly braces can be eliminated when an **if** or **else** statement section only has a single statement.

SECTION 5-3

1. Indentation is important when operations are nested for code readability and to be able to see at a glance which statements belong to which **if** or **else** statements.

2. True: The innermost nested **else** always goes with the closest **if**.

Consider the following pseudocode for questions 3–5:
    If *Value* < 50
      If *Value* > –50
          Write ("Red").
      else
          Write ("White").
    else
      Write ("Blue").

3. "Red" will be written when the value is greater than –50 and less than 50.

4. "White" will be written when the value is less than or equal to –50.

5. "Blue" will be written when the value is greater than or equal to 50.

6. The equivalent **if-else-if-else** logic is
    If *Value* >= 50
        Write ("Blue")
    else
        If *Value* <= –50
            Write ("White")
        else
            Write ("Red")

SECTION 5-4

1. The selection of a particular case in a **switch** statement is controlled by a *matching* process.

2. If you have *n* cases in a **switch** statement and there are no **break** statements in any of the cases, all of the cases will be executed sequentially when a match is made on the first case.

3. The statement "There are never any times when a case should not contain a **break** statement" is false, because there may be times when several subsequent cases need to be executed as the result of a match to a given case.

4. A statement that can be inserted at the end of a **switch** statement to protect against invalid entries is the **default** statement.

5. A common application for **switch** statements is for *menu-driven programs*.

CHAPTER 6

SECTION 6-1

1. True: A **while** loop breaks when the test expression evaluates to zero.

2. False: The **while** loop is a pretest loop not a posttest loop.

3. The **while** loop statements need to be framed, because without the framing, the value of *x* is never changed and you will have an infinite loop.

4. The correct the code for question 3 is as follows:
```
x = 10;
while (x > 0)
{
    cout << "This is a while loop" << endl;
    --x;
} //END WHILE
```

5. The loop will never execute, because the loop test is false. Notice that *x* is initialized to 1 and is never < = 0.

6. This is an infinite loop. Notice that *x* is initialized to 1 and is incremented with each loop iteration. Thus, the **while** test of x > = 0 is always true.

SECTION 6-2

1. True: A **do/while** loop breaks when the test expression evaluates to zero.

2. True: A **do/while** loop is a posttest loop.

3. The value of *x* is never changed within the loop, thereby creating an infinite loop.

4. The correct code for question 3 is as follows:

```
x = 10;
do
{
    cout << "This is a do/while loop" << endl;
    --x;
} //END DO/WHILE
while (x > 0);
```

5. The loop will execute once, because a **do/while** loop is a posttest loop.

6. Without the limitations of the computer, the loop will execute infinitely, because *x* starts out greater than 0 and is incremented inside of the loop. But, considering the physical limitations of the computer, it will execute 32,768 times before wrapping around to −32,768 and causing the test to be false.

SECTION 6-3

1. The three things that can appear in the first line of a **for** loop structure are as follows:
    *   The loop counter initialization.
    *   The loop test expression.
    *   The increment/decrement of the counter.

2. True: The loop counter in a **for** loop is altered after the loop statements are executed in a given iteration.

3. True: A **for** loop can always be replaced by a **while** loop, because they are basically the same looping structure, just coded differently.

4. The loop will execute zero times, because the test condition *x* is 0 (false) on the first test.

5. The loop will execute 11 times.

6. The **for** loop statements must be framed when there is more than one statement to be executed within the loop.

7. If you have two nested loops, with the inner loop executing 5 times and the outer loop executing 10 times, there will be 50 total iterations. The inner loop will execute 5 times for every outer loop iteration (5×10).

8. In a down-to loop, the loop counter is always *decremented*.

SECTION 6-4

1. The statement that will cause only the current iteration of a loop to be aborted is the **continue** statement.

2. The **break** and **continue** statements are normally used as part of an **if** statement within a loop structure.

3. The loop will execute twice. When x is incremented to 1 at the end of the first iteration, the **if(x)** statement will be true (nonzero) in the second iteration, causing the **break** statement to execute to abort the loop structure.

CHAPTER 7

SECTION 7-1

1   The role of a function in a C++ program is to eliminate the need for duplicate statements. The use of functions allows you to solve large complex problems by dividing the problem into smaller, more easily manageable subproblems (top/down approach).

2   The three main sections of a function are the *function header*, *local variables* or *constants*, and *statement* sections.

3. The function header in a C++ program is the data interface for the function. It forms a common boundary between the function and its calling program.

4. The three parts of a function header are as follows:
    *   The data class of the value to be returned by the function, if any.
    *   The name of the function.
    *   A parameter listing.

5. A function variable waiting to receive a value from the calling program is called a *parameter.*

6. A **return** statement in a function is used when a single value must be returned to the calling program.

7. The difference between an actual argument in a calling program and a formal parameter in a function header is that the actual argument contains the value passed to the formal parameter in the function header. In other words, the formal parameter receives the value from the actual argument in the calling program.

SECTION 7-2

1. **void** must be used as the return data class when a function does not return a single value to the calling program

2. The two things that must be considered when developing a function header are as follows:
   - What the function must accept to perform its task.
   - What the function must return.

3. One-way communication of data from the calling program to a function is provided via *value* parameters.

4. Two-way communication of data between the calling program and a function is provided via *reference* parameters.

5. To specify a reference parameter in a function header, you must use the & *(ampersand)* symbol prior to the parameter identifier.

6. The body of a function is normally located after the closing brace of *main()*.

SECTION 7-3

1. The primary purpose of a function prototype is to allow the compiler to check for any mismatches between the actual arguments in a function call and the formal parameters that the function expects to receive.

2. A function prototype is normally located after the preprocessor directives and before function *main()* in a C++ program.

3. True: Parameters listed in a function prototype can be listed only by data class, without any corresponding identifiers.

4. True: Default parameters can appear on either the function prototype or function header, but not both.

5. True: Once a default parameter is specified in a function prototype, the remaining parameters in the parameter listing must be default parameters.

6. When overloading a function, the return data class as well as the number and data classes of the function parameters will determine how the function will perform.

SECTION 7-4

1. A constant that has file scope must be placed *outside* and *prior to* function *main()* in a C++ program.

2. A local variable has *block* scope.

3. The altering of a global variable by a function is referred to as a *side effect*.

4. To retain the value of a local function variable from one call of the function to the next, the keyword **static** must be used in front of the variable declaration.

SECTION 7-5

1. The statement "There is no way that a C++ function can call itself" is false because C++ supports recursion, which allows a function to call itself.

2. We can describe recursion as a "winding" and "unwinding" process, because recursion "winds" values onto a stack, and when the primitive state is reached, it "unwinds" the values to calculate the final result.

3. When the primitive state is reached, a recursive function call is terminated.

4. The pseudocode required to find *N!*, where *N* is any integer is

   If N == 0 Then
       Factorial = 1.
   Else
       Factorial = N * Factorial (N − 1).

5. The statement "An advantage of recursion is that it does not require a lot of memory to execute" is false because recursion uses large amounts of memory to keep track of each recursive call.

6. True: All recursive problems can also be solved using iteration.

CHAPTER 8

SECTION 8-1

1. The two major components of an array are the *index* and *element.*

2. The statement "The elements within a given array can be any combination of data classes" is false because the elements within a given array must all be of the same data class.

SECTION 8-2

1. float TestScores[15];

2. The dimension of the array in question 1 is 1×15.

3. The index of the first element of the array in question 1 is [0].

4. The index of the last element of the array in question 1 is [14].

5. enum Courses{CS1, Calc, Physics, English, Speech};
    Courses ThisSemester[5];

6. If the index of the last element in an array is [25], the array will store 26 elements, since the first element index is [0].

SECTION 8-3

1. The **for** loop required to fill the array char Characters[15]; is

    for (int Index = 0; Index < 15; ++ Index)
        cin >> Characters [Index];

2. The **for** loop that will display the contents of the above array is

    for (int Index = 0; Index < 15; ++ Index)
        cout << Characters [Index] << '\t';

SECTION 8-4

1. The statement "An array name is in the address of index [1] of the array" is false because the array name locates index [0] of the array.

2. A prototype for a function called *Sample()* that must alter the array is

    char Characters[15]; is
    void Sample (char Characters [15]);

3. A prototype for a function called *Test()* that will alter a single array element in the array in question 2 is

    void Test (char &Element);

4. A statement that will call the above function to alter the element stored at index [5] of the array in question 2 is

    Test (Characters [5]);

SECTION 8-5

1. An array definition initialized with the integer values −3 through +3 is

    int Numbers[7] = { −3,−2,−1,0,1,2,3 };
    or
    int Numbers[] = { −3,−2,−1,0,1,2,3 };

2. The dimension of the above array is 1 × 7.

3. The contents of the array char Language[5] = {'C','+','+'}; are

    ['C'] ['+'] ['+'] ['\0'] ['\0']

4. The contents of the array char Language[] = "C++"; are

['C'] ['+'] ['+'] ['\0']

5. A null terminator character ('\0') is placed in each array position of a globally defined character array without any initializing values.

CHAPTER 9

SECTION 9-1

1. The statement "All the members of a given structure must have the same data class" is false because a structure can have members of different data classes.

2. A declaration for structure called *Account* that has four floating-point members named *Deposits*, *Withdrawals*, *InterestRate*, and *Balance* is

```
struct Account
{
    float Deposits;          //ACCOUNT DEPOSITS
    float Withdrawals;       //ACCOUNT WITHDRAWALS
    float InterestRate;      //ANNUAL INTEREST RATE IN PERCENT FORM
    float Balance;           //ACCOUNT BALANCE
}; //END Account
```

3. A definition for an uninitialized variable called *Checkbook* for the structure declared in question 2 is

```
Account Checkbook;
```

4. The following is a definition for a variable called *Passbook* for the structure declared in question 2 and initialized to the stated values

```
Account Passbook = {1500.00,
                    500.00,
                    12,
                    2345.49};
```

The following structure declarations are used to answer questions 5–13:

```
struct Account
{
    float Deposits;          //ACCOUNT DEPOSITS
    float Withdrawals;       //ACCOUNT WITHDRAWALS
    float InterestRate;      //ANNUAL INTEREST RATE IN DECIMAL FORM
    float Balance;           //ACCOUNT BALANCE
}; //END Account
Account Checkbook;           //DEFINE CHECKBOOK OBJECT
Account Passbook;            //DEFINE PASSBOOK OBJECT
```

5. The structure variables are *Checkbook* and *Passbook*.

6. A statement to assign a value of $250.00 to the *Deposits* member of the *Checkbook* structure is

    Checkbook.Deposits = 250.00;

7. A statement to assign a value of 12% to the *InterestRate* member of the *Passbook* structure is

    Passbook.InterestRate = 12; //ANNUAL PERCENT FORM

8. A statement to allow the user to input a value for the *Withdrawals* member of the *Checkbook* structure is

    cout << "Enter amount of withdrawals:" << endl;
    cin >> Checkbook.Withdrawals;

9. A statement to allow the user to input a value for the *Deposits* member of the *Passbook* structure is

    cout << "Enter amount of deposits:" << endl;
    cin >> Passbook.Deposits;

10. A statement to display the account balance in the *Checkbook* structure is

    cout << "The Account Balance is:" << Checkbook.Balance << endl;

11. A statement to display the account balance in the *Passbook* structure is

    cout << "The Account Balance is: " << Passbook.Balance << endl;

12. The header for a function called *Input()* that would obtain user entries for the *Checkbook* structure is

    void Input (Account &Checkbook)

13. A header for a function called *Output()* that would display the contents of the *Passbook* structure is

    void Output (Account Passbook)

The following structure declarations are used to answer questions 14–19:

```
struct Address
{
    char Street[25];        //EMPLOYEE STREET ADDRESS
    char City[25];          //EMPLOYEE CITY
    char State[2];          //EMPLOYEE STATE
    char Zip[10];           //EMPLOYEE ZIP CODE
}; //END Address

struct Employee
{
    char Name[25];          //EMPLOYEE NAME
```

```
    int ID;                  //EMPLOYEE ID
    Address Addr;            //NESTED EMPLOYEE ADDRESS STRUCTURE
    float Salary;            //EMPLOYEE SALARY
}; //END Employee
Employee  JD;    //DEFINE EMPLOYEE OBJECT
```

14. The *Address* structure is nested inside of the *Employee* structure.

15. A statement to assign "John Doe" for the employee name is

    ```
    strcpy(JD.Name,"John Doe");
    ```

16. Statements to allow the user to enter the employee's state of residence are

    ```
    cout  <<  "Enter the employee's state of residence:" << endl;
    gets (JD.Addr.State);
    ```

17. Statements to allow the user to enter the employee's salary are

    ```
    cout  <<  "Enter the employee's salary:" << endl;
    cin  >>  JD.Salary;
    ```

18. A header for a function called *DisplayEmployee()* that will display the data stored in the *Employee* structure is

    ```
    void DisplayEmployee (Employee Employ)
    ```

19. Statements required for the function in question 18 to display the employee information are

    ```
    void DisplayEmployee (Employee Employ)
    {
      cout << "Employee Name:  " << Employ.Name
           << "\nEmployee ID:  "  << Employ.ID
           << "\nEmployee Address:  " << "\n\t\t" << Employ.Addr.Street
           << "\n\t\t" << Employ.Addr.City << ", " << Employ.Addr.State
           << ' ' << Employ.Addr.Zip
           << "\nEmployee Salary:  " << Employ.Salary << endl;
    } //END DisplayEmployee;
    ```

SECTION 9-2

1. By a class defining the behavior of its objects, we mean that the class defines how its objects act and react when they are accessed.

2. False: Data hiding is not ensured by encapsulation, because encapsulation dictates only that the data and/or functions are packaged together in a well-defined unit.

3. True: Private class members can be accessed only via public member functions.

4. Combining data with the functions that are dedicated to manipulating the data so that outside operations cannot affect the data is known as *information*, or *data*, *hiding*.

5. True: A struct is an encapsulated unit.

6. Information hiding is provided by the *private* section of a class.

7. The behavioral secrets of a class are revealed at the *implementation* level.

8. A definition of an object called *PickUp* for a class called *Truck* is

    Truck PickUp;

9. A definition of an object called *StationWagon* for a class called *Automobile* is

    Automobile StationWagon;

SECTION 9-3

1. The operator employed in a function header that designates the function as being a member of a given class is the *scoping*, ::, operator.

2. The complete definition of a member function that includes the function header and body is called the function *implementation*.

3. A header for a member function called *Wheels()* that will return the number of wheels from a class called *Truck* is

    int Truck :: Wheels(void);

4. A member function that is used specifically to initialize class data is called a *constructor*.

5. You can tell which member function in a class is the constructor, because the constructor has the same name as the class and has no return class.

6. The statement "The return class of a constructor function is optional" is false because a constructor cannot have a return class.

7. A class constructor is called automatically when an object is defined for that class.

8. All member functions of a class carry with them a built-in pointer to the object that called the function, which is called *this*.

9. You can call a nonconstructor member function of a class by listing the object name, a dot, and the function name with any required arguments.

10. A member function that returns only the values of the private class members is called an *access* function.

11. The term "message" is used for a call to a member function because when an object function is called, we are sending information to the object, and the object sends back information.

SECTION 9-4

1. Three reasons for using the multifile approach for developing software are as follows:
   - It allows the creation of smaller, more manageable files.
   - Programs are easier to maintain.
   - The programmer can hide important program code from the user.
2. Header files in a C++ software project provide interfaces to the class objects.
3. A software manufacturer might not supply you with the member function implementation source code to keep the user from altering and possibly corrupting the function implementations, or to hide the function implementations for proprietary reasons.
4. A file that identifies the files that need to be compiled and linked to create an executable program is the *project* file.
5. When building a C++ project, the *.cpp* files, such as the application and implementation files, must be listed in the project manager.
6. You don't list header files in the project manager because the header files are already included in the *.cpp* files as *#include* preprocessor directives.

CHAPTER 10

SECTION 10-1

1. A parent class is called a *base* class in C++.
2. A child class is called a *derived* class in C++.
3. A collection of classes with common inherited members is called a *family of classes*.
4. Two reasons for using inheritance are
   - Inheritance allows you to reuse code without having to start from scratch.
   - Inheritance allows you to build a hierarchy among classes.
5. False: The proper use of inheritance would not allow a line class to be derived from a point class, because a line IS NOT A point.
6. True: The proper use of inheritance would allow a pixel class to be derived from a point class, because a pixel IS-A point.
7. True: The proper use of inheritance would allow a pickup truck class to be derived from a truck class, because a pickup truck IS-A truck.

SECTION 10-2

1. True: When declaring a derived class, the derived class is listed first followed by a colon and the base class.

2. True: A public base class allows its public members to be used by any of its derived classes.

3. The statement "A protected base class member is protected from any use by the derived classes of that base class" is false because the derived classes of a base class have access to the base's protected members.

4. When base class header files are included in multiple implementation and application files, you must use the *#ifndef* directive to avoid "multiple declaration" compile errors.

5. The main reason that *Savings* should not be derived from *SuperNow* is that a savings account is *not* a checking account. Such an inheritance would not be natural.

6. *Multiple inheritance* occurs when all the inherited members in a family can be traced back to more than one parent class.

SECTION 10-3

1. True: A virtual function is always a polymorphic function.

2. False: All polymorphic functions are not virtual, because an overloaded function is polymorphic, but not virtual.

3. True: The virtual function interface is identical for each version of the function in a given class family.

4. Overloaded functions are *statically* bound.

5. Virtual functions are *dynamically* bound.

6. The implementation code for a dynamically bound function is determined at run time.

CHAPTER 11

SECTION 11-1

1. Suppose that *pchar* is a pointer to a character and *Character* is a character variable. A statement to make *pchar* point to the character stored in *Character* is

    pchar = &Character;

2. A statement that will make an integer pointer called *p1int* point to the same integer to which an integer pointer called *p2int* is pointing is

    p1int = p2int;

3. The statement "If *Character* is defined as a character variable, then *&Character* can be altered at any time" is false because *&Character* represents a constant pointer and cannot be changed by the program.

4. True: If *pchar* is defined as a character pointer, then *pchar* can be altered at any time.

SECTION 11-2

1. A definition for a static character pointer called *pchar* and a character variable called *Character* is

    char *pchar;
    char Character;

2. A statement to make *pchar* point to the variable *Character* defined in question 1 is

    pchar = &Character;

3. A statement to initialize *pchar* defined in question 1 to the character 'A' is

    *pchar = 'A';

4. The statement "The assignment *pchar* = 'Z' is legal, as long as *pchar* is defined as a character pointer" is false because *pchar* must be assigned to another pointer, not a character. The correct assignment would be

    *pchar = 'Z';

5. When a pointer is initialized dynamically, the **new** operator must be used in the pointer definition.

6. The statements required to initialize a dynamic character pointer called *pchar* to the value 'B' are

    pchar = new char;
    *pchar = 'B';

7. A statement that will deallocate the memory allocated in question 6 is

    delete pchar;

8. The statement, "When you deallocate pointer memory using the **delete** operator, the respective pointer is deleted" is false because the pointer remains, and only the memory space that was used by the pointer is deallocated.

SECTION 11-3

1. A statement that defines a string pointer called *pstring* and initializes it to the string "C++" is

    char *pstring = "C++";

2. A statement to display the entire string in question 1 is

    cout << pstring << endl;

3. A statement to display just the first character of the string in question 1 is

    cout << *pstring << endl;

    or

    cout << pstring[0] << endl;

4. A statement to display just the last character of the string in question 1 is

    cout << pstring[2] << endl;

    or

    cout << *(pstring + 2) << endl;

5. A statement to display the last two characters of the string in question 1 is

    cout << *(pstring + 1) << *(pstring + 2) << endl;

    or

    cout << pstring[1] << pstring[2] << endl;

6. Suppose that *p1* is a pointer that points to index [5] of an array of double floating-point values and *p2* is a pointer that points to index [15] of the same array. Then, *p2 − p1* will yield the value 10.

SECTION 11-4

1. A definition for an array of pointers called *Courses* to point to the strings "Calc", "Assembler", and "C++" is

    char *Courses[] = {"Calc", "Assembler", "C++", NULL};

2. "Calc" is located at *Courses using the array in question 1.

3. The string "C++" is located at *Courses*[2] using the array in question 1.

4. "lc" is located at *Courses + 2 using the array in question 1.

5. The single character 'e' is located at *(*Courses*[1] + 3).

6. The concept of using several levels of addressing to access data is known as *indirection*, or *indirect addressing*.

SECTION 11-5

1. True: When a pointer is used in a function call, any operations on the pointer data within the function will affect the pointer data in the calling program.

2. True: A pointer argument in a function call must have a corresponding pointer parameter in the function prototype.

3. A prototype for a function called *MyFunc()* that will receive a pointer to a string is

   void MyFunc(char *);

4. A prototype for a function called *MyFunc()* that will receive an array of pointers to strings is

   void MyFunc(char **);

5. Assuming that *MyNames* is defined as an array of pointers to strings, a statement that will call the function in question 4 is

   MyFunc(MyNames);

SECTION 11-6

1. True: A function name is a constant pointer.

2. A prototype for a variable function pointer called *MyFuncPtr* that can be used to point to functions that receive a single integer value and return a single integer value is

   int (* MyFuncPtr) (int);

3. Given the following function prototypes,

   int Square(int);
   int Cube(int);

   a statement to make the function pointer defined in question 2 point to the *Square()* function is

   MyFuncPtr = Square;

   a statement to make the function pointer defined in question 2 point to the *Cube()* function is

   MyFuncPtr = Cube;

4. True: When a function pointer is created, the parameter data classes and return data class must match those of any function to which it must point.

SECTION 11-7

The following structure declaration is used to answer questions 1–9:

```
struct Account
{
    float Deposits;        //ACCOUNT DEPOSITS
    float Withdrawals;     //ACCOUNT WITHDRAWALS
    float InterestRate;    //ANNUAL INTEREST RATE IN PERCENT FORM
    float Balance;         //ACCOUNT BALANCE
}; //END Account
Account *Passbook;
Account *Checkbook;
Passbook = new Account;
Checkbook = new Account;
```

1. The structure pointer variables are called *Checkbook* and *Passbook*.

2. A statement to assign a value of $250.00 to the *Deposits* member of the *Checkbook* structure is

    ```
    Checkbook –> Deposits = 250.00;
    ```

3. A statement to assign a value of 12% to the *InterestRate* member of the *Passbook* structure is

    ```
    Passbook –> InterestRate = 12;        //PERCENT FORM
    ```

4. A statement to allow the user to input a value for the *Withdrawals* member of the *Checkbook* structure is

    ```
    cout << "Enter amount of withdrawals: ";
    cin >> Checkbook –> Withdrawals;
    ```

5. A statement to allow the user to input a value for the *Deposits* member of the *Passbook* structure is

    ```
    cout << "Enter amount of deposits: ";
    cin >> Passbook –> Deposits;
    ```

6. A statement to display the account balance in the *Checkbook* structure is

    ```
    cout << "The Account Balance is: " << Checkbook –> Balance << endl;
    ```

7. A statement to display the account balance in the *Passbook* structure is

    ```
    cout << "The Account Balance is: " << Passbook –> Balance << endl;
    ```

8. The header for a function called *Input()* that would obtain user entries for the *Checkbook* structure is

    ```
    void Input (Account *Checkbook)
    ```

9. A header for a function called *Output()* that would display the contents of the *Passbook* structure is

void Output (Account *Passbook)

10. The definition for a dynamic object called *PickUp* for a class called *Truck* with four wheels is

Truck *PickUp;
PickUp = new Truck(4);

11. A statement that will send a message to an access function called *Wheels* that will return the number of wheels on the truck is

PickUp –> Wheels();

12. A statement to deallocate the *PickUp* object memory is
delete PickUp;

13. A destructor should be used in a class declaration when private members of the class have been defined dynamically. The destructor function is used to deallocate the dynamic member memory.

CHAPTER 12

SECTION 12-1

1. The term *abstract* is used to indicate that data and its related operations are being viewed without considering any of the details of how the data or operations are implemented in the computer system.

2. *Float*, *int*, or any of the other data classes are examples of ADTs that we have been working with in the C++ language.

3. The ADT black box concept facilitates *modular* software design.

4. The statement "A data structure and an abstract data class are the same thing" is false, because a data structure provides a way of structuring or organizing data and an ADT defines the data to be operated on as well as the operations that can be performed on the data.

5. Data protection in an ADT is provided by *encapsulation and information hiding*.

6. The interface to an ADT is through its *function interface*.

7. You gain modularity through the use of ADTs, because ADTs are building blocks for use in software development.

8. You gain generality through the use of ADTs, because algorithms can be developed that depend only on the ADT function interface without concern for the implementation details of the ADT.

SECTION 12-2

1. If the user filled a stack using the application test program in this section and a call was made to the *Push()* function after the stack was full, *FullStack()* would return a value of true and the message "The stack is full!" would be displayed on the screen.

2. You can't randomly access the array holding the stack, because the array is a private member of the *Stack* class and can be accessed only via the stack operations defined for the class.

3. With our array implementation of a stack, a *Push()* operation requires that the stack pointer be *preincremented*.

4. The statement "With our array implementation of a stack, the stack is full when the value of *Top* becomes equal to *MAX*, where *MAX* is the maximum number of elements that the array can hold" is false, because the array begins at 0. Thus, *Top* must equal $MAX - 1$ when the stack is full.

5. With our array implementation of a stack, the stack is empty when the value of *Top* is -1.

6. The functional difference between the *Pop()* function and the *TopElement()* function is that the value of *Top* is not changed with the *TopElement()* function and it is with the *Pop()* function.

7. We had to include a *FullStack()* function in our implementation of a stack because of the finite storage capacity of an array.

SECTION 12-3

1. If the user filled a queue using the application test program in this section and a call was made to the *Insert()* function after the queue was full, *FullQ()* would return a value of true, and the message "The queue is full!" would be displayed on the screen.

2. The statement "With our array implementation of a queue, an *Insert()* operation requires that *Front* be advanced prior to placing the element in the array" is false, because *Rear* must be advanced not *Front*.

3. The pseudocode to advance *Front* for the circular array implementation of a queue is as follows:

If *Front == MAX* – 1
 Set *Front* = 0.
Else
 Set *Front = Front* + 1.

4. The statement "With the circular array implementation of a queue, *Front* can never have a higher value than *Rear*" is false because, for example, after the last element is removed, the value of *Front* can be greater than the value of *Rear*.

5. By using the circular array implementation of a queue, *Front == Rear* when there is only one element in the queue.

6. We had to include a *FullQ()* function in our implementation of a queue because of the finite storage capacity of the array used to hold the queue.

7. By using our array implementation of a queue, the element counter is equal to 0 when the queue is empty, and the element counter is equal to *MaxQ* when the queue is full.

SECTION 12-4

1. The statement "In a linked list, the sequencing of the nodes is implicit" is false. The sequencing of nodes in a linked list is explicit, because the location of the successor of any given node must be clearly specified in the node.

2. The two parts of a linked list node are the *element* and *locator* or *pointer*.

3. If *Node(P)* is the last node in the list, the value of *Next(P)* is *NULL*.

4. The statement "In a pointer implementation of a linked list, we know that the list is empty when the value of *First* is zero" is false because the list is empty when the value of *First* is NULL.

5. If you reverse the order of steps 3 and 4 in the insertion process illustrated in Figure 15-15, the linked list will be lost because the pointer to it will be reassigned to the single new node.

6. The list search algorithm given in this section will not detect multiple occurrences of the same item in a linked list. It could be made to detect multiple occurrences by placing the search in a **while** loop and searching for the item until the end of the linked list is reached.

7. If the statements *Set PredP = P* and *Set P = Next(P)* are reversed in the linked list search algorithm, *P* and *PredP* would be pointing to the same node.

8. An algorithm for the list destructor function, *~List()*, is

~List() **Algorithm**
BEGIN
 Set P = First

    While P ≠ NULL
        Set Temp = Next(P).
        Delete P.
        Set P = Temp.
END.

CHAPTER *13*

SECTION 13-1

1. The statement "A file is a random access data structure" is false because a file is a sequential-access data structure.

2. The two basic types of files that are possible in C++ are *character*, or *text*, files and *binary* files.

3. A channel where data can flow between your C++ program and the outside world is called a *file stream*.

4. Standard output in C++ is written to the *cout* file stream.

5. The *ifstream* class is used in C++ to perform input, or read, operations from disk files.

6. True: The *iostream* class provides an example of multiple inheritance.

7. A statement to define *MyFile* as an output file stream object is

    ofstream MyFile;

8. A statement to define *YourFile* as an input/output file stream object is

    fstream YourFile;

9. A statement that will open the file stream in question 7 for a text file called *ASCII.dat* is

    MyFile.open ("ASCII.dat");

10. To add information to the end of a file, you must use the *ios :: app* file mode.

SECTION 13-2

1. The statement "File operations in C++ are the same as those in C" is false because file operations in C++ are centered around classes and classes are not available in the C language.

2. The major operations that are required to create a new file if it does not already exist are as follows:

- Define an output file stream object.
- Open the file stream in the output mode, and attach it to a disk file name.
- Get the new file components from the user, and write them to the file.
- Close the file stream.

3. The major operations that are required to read an existing file are as follows:
   - Define an input file stream object.
   - Open the file stream in the input mode and attach it to a disk file name.
   - Read the file components and display them to the user.
   - Close the file stream.

4. The difference, relative to the position of the file window, between using the *ios :: out* versus the *ios :: app* file modes when opening a file is that the *ios :: out* mode positions the file window at the beginning of the file and the *ios :: app* positions the file window at the end of the file.

5. The *change.cpp* program in this section inherits the *tellg()* function from the *fstream* class..

6. The *tellg()* function returns the current position of the file window to the calling program.

7. True: The *tellg()* function should be used with input files, whereas the *tellp()* function should be used with output files.

8. The standard function, *seekp()*, must be used to position the file window for an output file.

9. The three predefined starting points available to the *seekg()* and *seekp()* functions are as follows:
   - *ios :: beg* (for the beginning of a file)
   - *ios :: end* (for the end of a file)
   - *ios :: cur* (for the current position of the file window)

10. The distance to move the file window from the specified starting point when using *seekg()* or *seekp()* must be expressed in *byte* units.

CHAPTER 14

SECTION 14-1

1. Given the two-dimensional array definition float Sample [10][15];, the maximum row index is 9, and the maximum column index is 14.

2. The statement cout << sizeof(Sample)/sizeof(float) << endl; will display the number of array positions in the array *Sample[ ]*, or 150.

3. A statement that will read a value from the keyboard and place it in the first row and last column of the array defined in question 1 is

    cin >> Sample [0] [14];

4. A statement that will display the value stored in the second row and third column of the array defined in question 1 is

    cout << Sample [1] [2];

5. The code, using **for** loops, that will display the elements of the array defined in question 1 is:

    ```
    for (int Row = 0; Row < 10; ++Row)
    {
        for (int Col = 0; Col < 15; ++Col)
            cout << Sample [Row] [Col];
        cout << endl;
    }//END OUTER FOR
    ```

6. A prototype for a function called *Display()* that will display the contents of the array defined in question 1 is

    void Display (float Sample [10] [15]);

7. A statement to call the *Display()* function in question 6 is

    Display (Sample);

8. A two-dimensional array in C++ is *row* major order.

SECTION 14-2

1. A problem that might be encountered when defining large multidimensional arrays is the "array size too big" error. This means that you are attempting to set aside more memory for the array than a particular computer system can allocate.

2. A three-dimensional array in C++ is *plane* major order.

3. A definition for a three-dimensional array of integers that has 10 planes, 15 rows, and 3 columns is

    int Integers [10] [15] [3];

4. To determine how many bytes of storage is occupied by the above array, you can use

    sizeof(Integers)

    If your compiler stores an integer in two bytes, this calculation becomes

    $(10 \times 15 \times 3) * 2 = 900$ bytes.

5. The code, using **for** loops, to display the contents of the array defined in question 3, one plane at a time is

```
for (int Plane = 0; Plane < 10; ++ Plane)
{
    for (int Row = 0; Row < 15; ++ Row)
    {
        for (int Col = 0; Col < 3; ++ Col)
            cout << Integers [Plane] [Row] [Col];
        cout << endl;
    } //END ROW FOR
} //END PLANE FOR
```

APPENDIX B
ASCII CHARACTER TABLE

Dec	Char		Dec	Char	Dec	Char	Dec	Char
0	^@	NUL	32	SPC	64	@	96	`
1	^A	SOH	33	!	65	A	97	a
2	^B	STX	34	"	66	B	98	b
3	^C	ETX	35	#	67	C	99	c
4	^D	EOT	36	$	68	D	100	d
5	^E	ENQ	37	%	69	E	101	e
6	^F	ACK	38	&	70	F	102	f
7	^G	BEL	39	'	71	G	103	g
8	^H	BS	40	(	72	H	104	h
9	^I	HT	41	)	73	I	105	i
10	^J	LF	42	*	74	J	106	j
11	^K	VT	43	+	75	K	107	k
12	^L	FF	44	,	76	L	108	l
13	^M	CR	45	-	77	M	109	m
14	^N	SO	46	.	78	N	110	n
15	^O	SI	47	/	79	O	111	o
16	^P	DLE	48	0	80	P	112	p
17	^Q	DC1	49	1	81	Q	113	q
18	^R	DC2	50	2	82	R	114	r
19	^S	DC3	51	3	83	S	115	s
20	^T	DC4	52	4	84	T	116	t
21	^U	NAK	53	5	85	U	117	u
22	^V	SYN	54	6	86	V	118	v

Dec	Char	Dec	Char	Dec	Char	Dec	Char
23	^W ETB	55	7	87	W	119	w
24	^X CAN	56	8	88	X	120	x
25	^Y EM	57	9	89	Y	121	y
26	^Z SUB	58	:	90	Z	122	z
27	^[ESC	59	;	91	[	123	{
28	^\ FS	60	<	92	\	124	|
29	^] GS	61	=	93	]	125	}
30	^^ RS	62	>	94	^	126	~
31	^-- US	63	?	95	--	127	DEL

GLOSSARY

Abstract data type (ADT)	A collection of data elements and related operations.
Access function	A function that returns only the values of the private members of an object.
Actual argument	A value passed to a function during a function call.
Address	A value that designates the memory location of a data element.
Algorithm	A series of step-by-step instructions that produce a solution to a problem.
Array	An indexed data structure that is used to store data elements of the same data class.
Base class	A class from which one or more other classes are derived. Also called a *parent class*.
Behavior	Used to describe how an ADT, or class, will act and react for a given operation.
Block scope	The accessibility, or visibility, of a local variable defined in a given block of code, such as a function.
Calling program	The program that calls, or invokes, a function.
Class (abstract level)	An *interface* that describes the attributes and behavior of its objects.
Class (implementation level)	A syntactical unit that describes a set of data and related operations that are common to its objects.
Compiling	The process of translating source code to machine, or object, code.
Components	Data elements in a file.

Compound statement   Several statements framed by curly braces.

Constructor   A special class function that is used to initialize the data members of an object automatically when the object is defined.

Control structure   A pattern for controlling the flow of a program module.

Data abstraction   That property of an ADT that allows you to work with the data elements without concern for how the data elements are stored inside the computer or how the data operations are performed inside the computer.

Data hiding   That property of a programming entity, such as a class object, that shields private data from operations that are not predefined to operate on the data.

Data type   A particular class of data elements.

Declaration   Specifies the name and attributes of a value, but does not reserve storage.

Default parameter   A function parameter that is assigned a default value in the function prototype or the function header, but not both.

Definition   Specifies the name and attributes of a variable and also reserves storage.

Delete operator   Deallocates memory created dynamically by the **new** operator.

Derived class   An inherited, or child, class that will include its own members and also include members inherited from its base classes.

Destructor   The counterpart of a constructor that is used to "clean up" an object after it is no longer needed. Normally used to deallocate memory allocated to an object by the object constructor.

Dynamic binding

Dynamic binding occurs when a polymorphic function is defined for several classes in a family, but the actual code for the function is not attached, or bound, until execution time. A polymorphic function that is dynamically bound is called a *virtual* function.

Encapsulation

To package data and/or operations into a single well-defined programming unit.

Enumerated data classs

A set of data elements that the programmer defines for a particular application.

Field

An item of meaningful data.

FIFO

First-in, first-out; FIFO is associated with queues.

File

A data structure that consists of a sequence of components of the same data class, usually associated with program I/O. A means by which the program communicates with the "outside world."

File scope

The scope of a global constant or variable created prior to *main()* that is accessible to any block in the same file.

File stream

A channel for data to flow between the program and the outside world.

File stream buffer

The link between a program and the file components.

File window

The means for a program to communicate with a file. The file window locates components within the file for processing.

Fixed repetition loop

A loop that will be executed a predetermined number of times.

Formal parameter

A variable used in a function header that receives the value of the respective actual argument in the function call.

Function	A subprogram that returns a single value, a set of values, or performs some specific task, such as I/O.
Function header	A statement that forms a common boundary, or interface, between the function and its calling program.
Function prototype	A model of the interface to the function that is used by the compiler to check calls to the function for the proper number of arguments and the correct data types of the arguments.
Global variable or constant	A variable or constant, defined prior to *main()*, that can be used by all functions of a given program, including *main()*. Global identifiers have file scope.
Identifier	A unique name associated with a constant, variable, function, data structure, class, object, and so on.
Information hiding	Information hiding is accomplished when there exists a binding relationship between the information, or data, and its related operations so that operations outside of an encapsulated unit cannot affect the information inside the unit.
Implementation	The definition of a function for a class that includes the function header and the body of the function.
Indirection	Indirection has to do with the levels of addressing it takes to access data.
Inheritance	That property of object-oriented programming that allows one class, called a *derived class*, to share the structure and behavior of another class, called a *base class*.
Instance	In object-oriented programming, an example, or specimen, of a class. We say that an object is an *instance* of a class.
IS-A	The link between a derived class and its base class.

Iteration	A control structure, also called looping, that causes the program flow to repeat a finite number of times.
LIFO	Last-in, first-out; LIFO is associated with stacks.
Linked list	A sequential data structure where, given any element in the list, the location of its successor element is specified by an *explicit* link, rather than by its natural position in the structure.
Linking	The process of combining object files needed for a program execution to form an executable file.
List	A *sequence* of data elements whose basic operations are insertion and deletion of elements to and from the list.
Local variable	A variable that is defined within a given block of code, such as a function. Local variables have block scope.
Manipulator	A function or special command that produces input or output formatting within a file stream.
Member	Any item declared in a structure or class.
Message	A call to a member function.
Method	A function that is a part of a structure or class.
Multiple inheritance	Multiple inheritance occurs when the inherited class members can be traced back to more than one parent class.
Nested looping	Looping structures that are located within other looping structures.
Nested structure	A structure within a structure.
new operator	The **new** operator is used to dynamically allocate memory.

Object

An instance, or specimen, of a given class. An object of a given class has the attributes and behavior described by the class that is common to all objects of the same class.

Object-oriented programming

A form of programming whereby data and related operations are specified as classes whose instances are objects. The data and related operations are so tightly bound so that only those operations defined for a class can affect the class data. This idea of encapsulation and information hiding allows the easy formation of ADTs.

Object program

The binary machine-language program generated by a compiler; usually has a file extension of *.obj*.

Overloaded function

A function that has different behavior depending on the number and/or class of arguments that it receives. An overloaded function is statically bound at compile time.

Parameter

A data item that is received by a function in order for it to perform its designated task.

Pointer

A pointer is used to represent an actual machine addresses.

Polymorphism

Polymorphism occurs when functions and/or objects have the same name for different classes of the same family but behave differently.

Posttest loops

Testing a condition *after* each loop iteration as in the **do/while** loop structure.

Preprocessor

The first part of a C++ program that acts as a smart text editor before any translation is performed.

Pretest loops

Testing a condition each time *before* a loop is executed, as in the **while** and **for** loop structures.

Primitive state

A known condition that terminates a recursive function call.

Private member

A member of a class that is accessible only to the public functions of the same class. Private members of a base class are *not* inherited by a derived class.

Problem abstraction

Provides for generalization in problem solving by allowing you to view a problem in general terms, without worrying about the details of the problem solution.

Protected member

A member of a class that is accessible to both the base class and any derived classes of the base class in which it is declared. Thus, a protected member of a base class is accessible to any class within the class family, but not accessible to things outside the class family.

Pseudocode

An informal set of English-like statements that is generally accepted within the computer industry to denote common computer programming operations. Pseudocode statements are used to describe the steps in a computer algorithm.

Public base class

A base class that allows all of its public members to be public in its derived classes.

Public member

A member of a class that is accessible outside the class within the scope of the class. A public member of a base class is inherited by a derived class if the base class is declared public in the derived class declaration.

Queue

A primary memory storage structure that consists of a list, or sequence, of data elements. All insertions of elements into the queue are made at one end of the queue, called the *rear* of the queue; and all deletions of elements from the queue are made at the other end of the queue, called the *front* of the queue. A queue operates on the *first-in*, *first-out*, or *FIFO*, principle.

Reading

Reading is obtaining data from something such as an input device or a data structure; a copy operation. A read operation is usually a nondestructive operation.

Recursion	A process whereby an operation calls itself until a primitive state is reached.
Recursive function	A function that calls itself.
Reference parameter	A function parameter that provides two-way communication between the calling program and the function.
Run-time error	An error that occurs when the program attempts to perform an illegal operation as defined by the laws of mathematics, logic, or the particular compiler in use.
Scope	Scope refers to the largest block in which a given constant, variable, data structure, or function is accessible, or visible.
Selection	A control structure where the program selects, or decides, between one of several routes depending on the conditions that are tested.
Sequence	A control structure where statements are executed sequentially, one after another, in a straight-line fashion.
Side effect	The process of altering the value of a global variable that is defined outside the block in which it is altered.
Single inheritance	Single inheritance occurs when all inherited class members can be traced back to a single parent class.
Source program	The program that you write in the C++ language that normally has a file extension of *.cpp*.
Stack	A primary memory storage structure that consists of a list, or sequence, of data elements where all the insertions and deletions of elements to and from the stack are made at one end of the stack called the ***top***. A stack operates on the ***last-in***, ***first-out***, or ***LIFO*** principle.

Standard function

A predefined operation that the C++ compiler will recognize and evaluate to return a result or perform a given task.

Star, *

In front of a pointer variable, the star denotes the contents of the memory location where the pointer is pointing.

Static binding

Static binding occurs when a polymorphic function is defined for several classes in a family and the actual code for the function is attached, or bound, at compile time. Overloaded functions are statically bound.

Static variable

A local function variable that will retain its value from one function call to the next.

Stepwise refinement

The process of gradually adding detail to a general problem solution until it can be easily coded in a computer language.

String

A collection of characters.

Structure

A collection of data members, or data fields, and function members. Also called a struct.

Structured design

A methodology that requires software to be designed using a top/down modular approach.

Structured programming

Structured programming allows programs to be written using well-defined control structures and independent program modules.

Syntax error

An error created by violating the required syntax, or grammar, of a programming language.

Value parameters

Parameters that allow for one-way communication of data from the calling program to the function.

Virtual function

Functions that have the same name but different implementations for various classes within a class family. A virtual function is a polymorphic function that is dynamically bound.

Visibility   That part of the program code in which a constant, variable, data structure, or function is accessible.

Whitespace   Blanks, tabs, new lines, form feeds, and so on, are all forms of whitespace.

Writing   Writing is often associated with the output of data to a display monitor, printer, or file. In addition, data can be "written" to data structures such as arrays, structs, or objects. A write operation is usually a destructive operation.

INDEX

+, addition operator, 164
+=, addition/assignment operator, 169
=, assignment operator, 61
\\, backslash escape sequence, 105
\b, backspace escape sequence, 105
\a, bell escape sequence, 105
{, begin block, 73
//, comment, 70, 75
\r, CR escape sequence, 105
\n, CRLF escape sequence, 102
−−, decrement operator, 167
#, directive, 70
#define directive, 510, 522
#endif directive, 522
#ifndef directive, 522
#include directive, 71
/, division operator, 164
., dot operator, 115, 437–38, 484
}, end block, 73
==, equal operator, 179
>>, stream extraction operator, 119, 655
\f, formfeed escape sequence, 105
{}, framing, 148
>, greater than operator, 179
>=, greater than or equal operator, 179
++, increment operator, 167
<<, stream insertion operator, 98, 653
<, less than operator, 179
<=, less than or equal operator, 179
%, modulus operator, 164
%=, modulus/assignment operator, 169
*, multiplication operator, 164
*=, multiplication/assignment operator, 169
!=, not equal operator, 179
\0, null terminator, 51
−>, pointer operator, 555, 557–58, 565–67
*, pointer contents operator, 533
\?, question mark escape sequence, 105

\'', double quote escape sequence, 105
\', single quote escape sequence, 105
−, subtraction operator, 164
−=, subtraction/assignment operator, 169
\t, horizontal tab escape sequence, 105
\v, vertical tab escape sequence, 105

A

\a, bell escape sequence, 105
abs(), absolute value function, 189
Abstract class, 510
Abstract data type (ADT), 37–39, 581–84
    data, 582
    encapsulation, 583
    function interface, 584
    information hiding, 583
    interface, 583
    linked list, 617–36, 620
        implementation, 620–36
        operations, 620–29
    operations, 582
    queue, 601–16
        implementation, 639
        operations, 603–10
    stack, 587–601
        implementation, 587–601
        operations, 586–87
Abstraction, 454, 581
    data, 38
    problem, 13, 25
Access function, 482
acos(), arc cosine function, 189
Ada, 464
Algorithm, 2
    effective, 12
    elegance, 415
    pseudocode operations, 12
    well-defined, 12

Alias, 534
Ambiguity of overloaded constructors, 477
Amplitude modulation, 192
AND, && operator, 182
use of to control loops, 270, 273
ANSI, 35
app, *ios* flag, 646
AppendFile() function, 657
Application file, 492
Argument, 84, 132
pointer, 547–52
Arithmetic operators, 163–68
order of precedence, 165
Array, 51, 378
access, 382–89, 675–88
circular, 603
definition format, 381, 672
dimension, 380
elements, 380
extracting elements from, 386–90, 676
using loops, 388, 677–88
holding a queue, 603
holding a stack, 588–89
indices, 380, 384
initialization of, 416–22
inserting elements into, 383–86, 675
using loops, 384, 677–88
more than two dimensions, 688–91
one-dimensional, 380–90
passing single elements to functions, 392
plane major order, 689
ragged edge, 577
reading elements into, 384, 677
row major order, 672
searching:
binary search, 409–22, 426
sequential search, 400–403
size of, 675
sorting:
bubble sort, 426
insertion sort, 403–9
selection sort, 427
static, 420
structure of, 378–79, 671, 688
two-dimensional, 671–88
two-dimensional array of strings, 686
wrap-around, 603
writing of elements, 387, 677
ASCII:
files, 647
table of values, 49, 744
asin(), arc sine function, 189
Assembler, 32
Assembly language, 31–32
Assignment, 61
of array elements, 383, 386
operators, 169
of pointers, 532
of structure member data, 557
of variable objects, 169
atan(), arc tangent function, 189
ate, *ios* flag, 646
atoi(), string to integer function, 188
Attribute, 29

B

\b, backspace escape sequence, 105
Bank account class, 508
Base class, 505
ios, 521
public, 511–14
BCD, binary coded decimal, 705
Behavior, 29, 38, 331, 454–55
Binary files, 647
Binary search, 409–22, 426
binary, *ios* flag, 646
Binding, 524
dynamic, 524
static, 524, 525
BinSearch() function, 412
Block-structure, 325
bool, 53, 64
Boolean flag for loop control, 258
Boolean object, 64
Boolean operations, 170–83
logical, 181–83
relational, 179–81
break statement:
in loops, 284–86
as part of **switch**, 229, 230
Bubble sort, 426
Buffer, file stream, 649

C

C language, history of, 35
C++ language, history of, 35–36
Calling program, 77, 304–05
case statement, as part of **switch**, 229
Central processing unit, 31
cerr object, 653
ChangeFile() function, 658
char, 50
Character, 48–53
  class ranges, 50
Chart, layout, 108
Checking account class, 508
Child class, 505
cin object, 118–35
Class, 29, 30, 37, 86, 429, 452–67
  abstract, 510
  abstract level, 454–57
  abstraction, 454
  attribute, 29
  bank account, 508
  base, 505
    public, 511–14
  behavior, 29, 38, 331, 454–55
  Boolean, 52, 64
  character, 48–53
  checking account, 508
  child, 505
  construct, 40
  constructor, 472–81
    format of header, 474
  declaration format, 457
  derived, 505
    declaration format, 508
  destructor, 567–69
    format of header, 569
  encapsulation, 458–67
  enumerated, 39, 65–69
  family, 505
  file, 650
  file hierarchy, 644
  floating-point, 44–47
  friend functions, 456
  fstream, 643–48
  function implementation, 470

hierarchy, 505–7
  IS-A relationship, 507
hierarchy in C++, 39
ifstream, 643–48
implementation level, 456–58
inheritance, 504–28
inside view of, 456–57
integer, 38, 41–44
interface, 454, 455
ios, 521, 655
iostream, 521
istream, 521
linked list, 629
member data, 456
member function, 456
  access, 482
  implementation format, 470
  naming of, 467
ofstream, 643–48
ostream, 521
outside view of, 455–56
parent, 505
pointer, 39, 40
private member, 456–58
protected member, 511–14
public, 511–14
public member, 456
queue, 610
savings account, 509
scalar, 39
stack, 594
standard, 39, 41–52
structured, 39, 40
super-now checking account, 509
as a syntactical unit, 457
ClearStack() function, 502
close() function, 654
Code:
  assembly, 31
  high level, 31
  machine, 31
Coding, 5
Commenting, 75
Compiler, 33
Compiling, 7
Component, file, 642, 649
Compound assignment operators, 169
Compound statement, 213

Computer efficiency, 360
Computer program, 31
const, 55
Constant, 52–58
  declaration format, 55
  global, 73, 351
  pointer, 530
  scope of, 351
  string, 57
    declaration format, 57
Constructor, 472–81
  default parameters, 474
  format of header, 474
  overloaded, 475
continue statement, in loops, 286–87
Control structure, 13, 211
  decision, 13, 211–12
  iteration, 13, 251
  sequence, 13, 211
cos( ), cosine function, 189, 202
Coupling via a function interface, 583
cout object, 91, 97–105
cpp file extension, 33
CPU. *See* Central Processing Unit
Cramer's rule, 696–97
CreateList( ), linked list function, 621
CRLF, carriage return/line feed, 102, 105,
  653
ctype header file, 188
Currency output using *showpoint*, 159, 160

D

Dangling **else**, 219
Data:
  abstraction, 38
  character, 37
  class member, 456
  numeric, 37
  object, 36
  within an ADT, 582
Data communications unit prefixes, 46
Data hiding, *See* Information hiding
Data input. *See* Input
Data structure, 378
Debugger, use of, 8
Debugging, 5–9

Decision control structure, 13
  if, 212–16
  if/else, 217–19
  switch, 227–34
Declaration, 55, 432
Decrement operator, − −, 167
Default parameter, 329–31
default statement as part of **switch**, 232
Defining a problem, 3
Definition, 55, 432
delete, pointer operator, 536, 564
DeleteNode( ), linked list function, 624, 627
Derived class, 505
  declaration format, 508
Design, structured, 76
Desk-checking, 6
Destructor, 567–69
  format of header, 569
Determinant, 692
  order three, 693
    expansion, 694
  order two, 692
    expansion, 693
Diagram, structure, 19, 80, 152, 268, 335, 362
Directive, 70
Directory:
  system, 72
  working, 72
Disk file. *See* File
Display freeze, 129
do/while loop, 262–70
  data entry using, 265–70
  flow of, 262
  format of, 263
Documentation, 9–10
  function, 346
Dot notation, *See* Dot operator
Dot, **.** operator, 115, 437–38, 484
double, 45
Dynamic binding, 524
Dynamic memory allocation, 535
  delete operator, 536, 564
  new operator, 536, 564
Dynamic pointer, 533
  initialization, 536
  for an object, 564
  for a structure, 556

E

Efficiency, computer, 360
Elegance of an algorithm, 415
Element of an array, 380
else. *See* **if/else**
    dangling/misplaced, 219
EmptyList(), linked list function, 628
EmptyStack() function, 502, 578, 598
Encapsulation, 458–67, 596
    within an ADT, 583
    with information hiding, 462–67
    without information hiding, 459–62
endl, end-of-line manipulator, 102
enum, 66
Enumerated class, 39, 65–69
    definition format, 66
    element ordering, 67
    use of to create Boolean data, 69
eof(), end-of-file function, 655
EOF, end-of-file marker, 148, 655
Equal, == operator, 179
Error:
    link, 7
    logic, 8
    of-by-one in loops, 296
    overflow, 43
    run-time, 8
    syntax, 7
    type mismatch, 7, 123, 190
Escape sequence, 102
    \\, backslash, 105
    \b, backspace, 105
    \a, bell, 105
    \r, CR, 105
    \n, CRLF, 102
    \f, formfeed, 105
    \?, question mark, 105
    \'', double quote, 105
    \', single quote, 105
    \t, horizontal tab, 105
    \v, vertical tab, 105
    table of, 105
Exchange() function, 323, 409
exe file extension, 33
exit(), function, 653
Explicit list, 617

Exponential format for a floating-point
    number, 44
Extraction, >> operator, 119, 655

F

\f, formfeed escape sequence, 105
Factorial, 361
false, 53
Family of classes, 505
fgets(), string input function, 138–41
Fibonacci sequence, 376
Field width, 109
FIFO, 586, 602
File:
    <<, stream insertion operator, 653
    >>, stream extraction operator, 655
    access, 648–66
    AppendFile() function, 657
    appending, 656–58
    application, 492
    ASCII, 647
    binary, 647
    ChangeFile() function, 658
    changing, 658–64
    class, 650
    close() function, 654
    closing, 654
    component, 642, 649
    copying, 148
    defining file objects, 142, 644–48
    eof(), end-of-file function, 148, 655
    EOF, end-of-file marker, 148, 655
    executable, *exe*, 33
    GetName() function, 651
    header, 490
    implementation, 491
    object, 644–48
    object, *obj*, 33
    open() function, 645
    opening, 143–45
        open mode designators, 645
        protection mode designators, 646
    operations, 649–66
    pointer, 649
    project, 490
    ReadFile() function, 654

reading, 654–56
reading and writing, 142–49
reading and writing using loops, 148–49
seekg( ) file window function, 661
seekp( ) file window function, 663
source, *cpp*, 33
stream, 142–45, 644–48
   cin, 118–35
   cout, 97–105
   named, 644
stream buffer, 649
tellg( ) function, 661
tellp( ) function, 661
window, 649
window functions, 663
window position, 661
WriteFile( ) function, 651
writing, 651–54
files header file, 650
Fixed decimal-point format of a floating-point
   number, 44
Fixed repetition loop, 251, 274. *See also*
   for loop
fixed, ios flag, 115
Flag:
   app, 646
   ate, 646
   beg, 662
   binary, 646
   cur, 662
   end, 662
   fixed, 114
   in, 646
   left, 116
   nocreate, 646
   noreplace, 646
   out, 646
   right, 116
   showpoint, 160
   trunc, 646
   use of for loop control, 258
Flat implementation, 84, 239
float, 45
Floating-point, 44–47
   class ranges, 45
   exponential format, 44
   fixed decimal format, 44
   output, 114

for loop, 274–83
   counter increment/decrement, 276
   counter initialization, 276
   down to, 282–83
   flow of, 275
   format of, 275
   test expression, 276, 281
Formatting:
   currency output, 159
   flags, 114
      setting of, 114
      unsetting of, 116
   left justification, 116
   of loops, 276
   output, 107–17
   table of functions and flags, 117
Framing:
   of **if** statement, 213
   of **if/else** statement, 218
   of loops, 253, 263
   using curly braces, 148
Freezing the display, 129
FrontElement( ), queue function, 610
fstream:
   class, 643–48
   header file, 643–48
FullStack( ) function, 502, 578, 598
Function, 20, 72, 304
   access, 482
   actual argument, 314
   ADT interface, 583
   argument, 84, 132
   behavior, 331
   calling, 77, 312–14
   calling using the dot operator, 115, 484
   class member, 456
   constructor, 472–81
   destructor, 567–69
   documentation, 346
   dynamic binding of, 524
   file window, 663
   formal parameter, 314
   format, 305
   friend, 456
   header, 306
   implementation, 458, 466, 470
   interface, 306

Function (*continued*)
    local variable, 310
    location in a program, 324–25
    member, 115
    message, 483
    name, 307–8
    naming of in classes, 467
    non-void, 305–15
    overloaded, 331–33
    parameter, 308–9, 337
        default, 329–31
        reference, 324, 353–61
        value, 318–20
    passing array elements to/from, 392–94
    passing arrays to/from, 390–99
    pointer, 552–55
    pointer arguments, 547–52
    pointer parameters, 547–52
    polymorphic, 523
    polymorphism, 333
    prototype, 326–29
    recursive, 353–61, 409–16
        calling of, 356
        when to use, 360
    return class, 306–7, 337
    return statement, 342
    scoping within, 478
    standard, 47, 184–92
        conversion, 188
        mathematical, 189
        string, 189
    statement section, 309–11
    static binding of, 525
    user-defined, 77, 304
    virtual, 524
    void, 316–24

G

Generality, 583
get(), character input function, 128, 260
getline(), string input function, 132–37
GetName(), file function, 651
gets(), string input function, 138–41
giga, 46
Global:
    constant, 73, 351
    variable, 347

Greater than or equal, >= operator, 179
Greater than, > operator, 179

H

Header file, 71
    bank account, 510
    class, 490
    ctype, 188
    files, 650
    fstream, 644
    iomanip, 110
    iostream, 92, 97, 521, 643–48
    istream, 521, 643–48
    list, 629
    math, 189
    ostream, 521, 643–48
    queue, 610
    stack, 594
    stdio, 138
    stdlib, 188, 189
Hierarchy:
    of classes, 505–7
    of file classes, 643–44
High-level language, 32–36
hypot(), hypotenuse function, 189

I

Identifier, 54, 60
    multiword, 56
    rules of, 56
if statement, 23–24, 212–16
    flow of, 212
    format of, 213
    framing of, 213
    nesting of, 221
if/else statement, 217–19
    flow of, 217
    format of, 218
    framing of, 218
    nesting of, 221
Imaginary number, 198
Implementation:
    file, 491
    of a class function, 458, 466, 470

Implicit list, 617
in, *ios* flag, 646
Include file, 71
Increment, ++ operator, 167
Indentation, 24
Index of an array, 380, 384
Indirection, 544–47
Infinite loop, 8, 257, 278
Information hiding, 458, 596
   within an ADT, 583
Inheritance, 429, 504–28
   base class, 505
     public, 511–14
   derived class, 505
   IS-A relationship, 507
   multiple, 521
   single, 521
   Venn diagram, 518
Initialization:
   of arrays, 416–22
   of dynamic pointers, 536
   of static pointers, 534
   of variable objects, 59
Input, 118–41
   character, 125–30
     using *cin*, 125–30
     using *get()*, 128, 690
   file streams, 142
   string, 130–41
     using *cin*, 130–32
     using *getline()*, 132, 662
     using *gets()* and *fgets()*, 138–41
   using a **do/while** loop, 265–70
   using a **while** loop, 258–61
   using *cin*, 118–35
Insert(), queue function, 606, 607
Insertion sort, 403–9
Insertion, << operator, 98, 653
InsertNode(), linked list function, 623
InsertSort() function, 404
Instance, 468
Instruction set, 31
int, 42
Integer, 41–44
   class ranges, 42
Integral data class, 229

Interface:
   ADT, 583
   class, 454–55, 583
   function, 306
Interpreter, 33
iomanip header file, 110
ios class, 521, 643–48, 655
ios flag:
   app, 646
   ate, 646
   beg, 662
   binary, 646
   cur, 662
   end, 662
   fixed, 115
   in, 646
   left, 116
   nocreate, 646
   noreplace, 646
   out, 646
   right, 116
   setting of, 114
   showpoint, 117, 159, 160
   trunc, 646
   unsetting of, 116
iostream:
   class, 97, 521, 643–48
   header file, 92, 521, 643–48
IS-A relationship, 507
istream:
   class, 521, 643–48
   header file, 521, 643–48
Iteration control structure, 13, 251
   break option, 284–86
   continue option, 286–87
   do/while, 262–70
   for, 274–83
   while, 251–61
itoa(), integer to string function, 188

K

Kernighan, Brian, 35
Keyword, 44
kilo, 46

L

Language:
    assembly, 32
    block-structured, 325
    high-level, 32
    history of C, 35
    history of C++, 35–36
    machine, 31
    midlevel, 36
    portability, 35
Late binding. *See* Dynamic binding
Law of sines, 208
Layout chart, 108
left, *ios* flag, 116
Less than or equal, <= operator, 179
Less than, < operator, 179
Lifetime of a variable, 351
LIFO, 358, 577, 585–86
Link error, 7
Linked list, 617–36
    ADT, 620
    application file, 634
    class, 629
    definition of, 617
    empty, 621
    header file, 629
    implementation, 620–36
    implementation file, 631
    implementation for a queue, 640
    implementation for a stack, 639
    node, 618
    node insertion, 622
    notation, 619
    operations, 620–29
    ordered, 623, 640
    pointer notation, 634
    searching, 624–26
    traversing, 619, 628
Linking, 7, 33–34
List, 616–36
    one-dimensional array, 380–90
List() constructor function, 630
Local:
    constant, 310
    variable, 73, 310, 347
log(), natural log function, 189
log10(), log base 10 function, 189

Logic error, 8
long double, 45
long int, or **long**, 42
Loop:
    boundaries, 296
    control variable, 253
    do/while, 262–70
    flag controlled, 258
    for, 274–83
    infinite, 8, 257, 278
    posttest, 251, 262
    pretest, 251
    sentinel controlled, 259, 266
    while, 251–61
Looping. *See* Iteration

M

Machine code, 31
Machine language, 31
main(), 72–75, 73
Manipulator, 102
    endl, end-of-line, 102
    setw(), set field width, 110–11
    table of, 110
    ws, whitespace, 138
math header file, 189
Mean, 300
mega, 46
Member function, 115
Memory allocation:
    dynamic, 535, 564
    static, 535
Menu-driven programs, 234–42, 267–73
Message, 483
    using the dot operator, 484
    using the pointer operator, 565, 571
Method, 456
micro, 46
Mid-level language, 36
milli, 46
Misplaced **else**, 219
Mnemonic, 32
Modula II, 464
Modularity, 211, 347–49, 583
Multifile programs, 488–95
Multiple inheritance, 521

N

\n, CRLF escape sequence, 102
NAND, Boolean operation, 184
nano, 46
Nesting:
   if's, 221
   if/else:
      if-else-if-else form, 224
      if-if-else-else form, 224
   loops, 281–83
   structures, 445–52
new, pointer operator, 536, 564
nocreate, *ios* flag, 646
Node, in a linked list, 618
Non-void function, 305–15
   calling of, 312
NOR, Boolean operation, 206
noreplace, *ios* flag, 646
Not equal, != operator, 179
NOT, ! operator, 182
Noun, within a problem statement, 4, 21
NULL pointer, 546
Null terminator, 51

O

obj file extension, 33
Object, 29, 36, 429, 454
   behavior, 454–55
   Boolean, 64
   cerr, 653
   cin, 118–35
   constant, 53–58
   constant string, 57
   cout, 91, 97–105
   file, 142, 644–48
   of a class, 467–69
      definition of, 468
   of a structure, 432
   pointer:
      dynamic, 564
      static, 564
   polymorphic, 523
   static definition format, 468
   variable, 58–64
   variable string, 62

Object program, 33
Object-oriented programming, 29, 35, 106, 429, 456, 467–70, 502, 505, 526, 593
   inheritance, 429
Off-by-one errors
   in loops, 296
Ohm's law, 26
open(), file stream function, 645
Operations within an ADT, 582
Operator:
   +, addition, 164
   +=, addition/assignment, 169
   =, assignment, 169
   /, division, 164
   ., dot, 115, 437–38, 484
   ==, equal, 179
   >>, stream extraction, 119, 655
   >, greater than, 179
   >=, greater than or equal, 179
   <<, stream insertion, 98, 653
   <, less than, 179
   <=, less than or equal, 179
   %, modulus, 164
   *, multiplication, 164
   *=, multiplication/assignment, 169
   !=, not equal, 179
   –>, pointer, 555, 557–58, 565–67
   *, pointer, 533
   –, subtraction, 164
   –=, subtraction/assignment, 169
   AND, &&, 182
   arithmetic, 163–68
   arithmetic order of precedence, 165
   Boolean logic, 181–83
   Boolean relational, 179–81
   delete, pointer, 536, 564
   new, pointer, 536, 564
   NOT, !, 182
   OR, ||, 182
   scoping, 479
   XOR, ^, 204
OR, || operator, 182
   use of to control loops, 270
Ordered linked list, 623, 640
ostream:
   class, 521, 643–48
   header file, 521, 643–48
out, *ios* flag, 646

Output, 97–117
    character, using *put( )*, 129
    currency using *showpoint*, 159, 160
    file streams, 142
    fixed character information, 99
    fixed decimal, 114
    fixed numeric information, 98
    floating-point, 114
    floating-point precision, 115
    formatting, 107–17
    printer, 105–7
    using *cout*, 91, 97–105
    variable information, 100
Overflow, 43
Overloaded:
    constructor, 475
        ambiguity, 477
    function, 331–33
        binding of, 525

P

Palindrome, 578, 639
Parallel circuit analysis, 288–96
Parameter, 308
    default, 329–31
    passing of, 319
    pointer, 547–52
    reference, 353–61
    value, 318–20
Parent class, 505
Parentheses within arithmetic
    expressions, 166
Passing of function parameters, 319
pico, 46
Planning a problem solution, 4
Pointer, 530
    alias, 534
    argument, 547–52
    arithmetic, 540–42
    arrays of, 544–47
    assignment, 532
    constant, 530
    definition format, 533
    dynamic, 533
        initialization, 536
    file, 649

    function, 552–55
    incorrect assignment, 535
    indirection, 544–47
    NULL, 546
    object:
        dynamic, 564
        static, 564
    parameter, 547–52
    scaling, 541
    static, 533–35
        initialization, 534
    string, 540, 545
    structure, 555–64
        dynamic, 556
        static, 556
    this, 479–81
    variable, 530
Polar coordinate, 197
Polymorphism, 333, 523–25
    function, 523
    object, 523
Pop( ), stack function, 503, 578, 591
Portability, 35
Postincrement operation, 168
Posttest loop, 251. *See also* **do/while** loop
Power, electrical, 247
precision( ), output precision function, 114
Preincrement operation, 168
Preprocessor directive, 71–72
    #define, 510, 522
    #endif, 510, 522
    #ifndef, 510, 522
    #include, 71–72
Pretest loop, 251, 255. *See also* **while** loop
Primitive state, 355
Printer output, 105–7
private. *See* Private member
Private member of a class, 456–58
Problem:
    abstraction, 2, 13, 25
    definition, 3–4
    refinement, 18
    solution planning, 4
Procedural programming, 29
Product over sum rule. *See* Parallel circuit
    analysis

Program, 30, 31
 calling, 77
 coding, 5
 compiling, 33
 description message, 101
 flat implementation, 84
 linking, 33, 34
 menu driven, 234–42, 267–73
 object, 33
 source, 33
 structure, 70–75
 testing and debugging, 5
 user-friendly, 151
Programmer's algorithm, 3
Programming:
 object-oriented, 29, 35, 429, 456, 505, 526
 procedural, 29
 structured, 29, 76
 top-down, 77
Project file, 490
Project manager, 490
Prompt, 19, 122
Protected class member, 511–14
Protection. *See* Information hiding
Prototype, 326–29
Pseudocode, 5
 operations used in this text, 12
public. *See* Public member
Public base class, 511–14
Public member of a class, 456–58
Push(), stack function, 503, 577, 590
put(), character output function, 129
Pythagorean theorem, 16

Q

Queue, 601–16
 ADT, 602
 application file, 614
 class, 610
 header file, 610
 implementation, 603–16, 639–40
 implementation file, 612
 implementation using a linked list, 640
 implementation using an array, 603
 operations, 603–10
Queue() constructor function, 611

R

\r, CR escape sequence, 105
Radians, 197, 202
Ragged edge array, 577
rand(), random number generator function, 189, 425
Random number generation, 425
Read operation, 19
ReadFile() function, 654
Record. *See* Structure
Rectangular coordinate, 198
Recursion, 353–61
 as used in binary search, 409–22
 when to use, 360
Reference parameter, 353–61
Remove(), queue function, 609
Repetition. *See* Iteration
Return class
 table of, 337
return statement, 310, 342
right, *ios* flag, 116
Ritchie, Dennis, 35
Running a program, 8
Run-time error, 8

S

Savings account class, 509
Scaling of pointer data, 541
Scope:
 block, 349
 file, 349
 of constants, 351
 of variables, 349–51
Scoping:
 inside of functions, 478
 operator, 471, 479
 this pointer, 479–81
Searching:
 binary search, 409–22, 426
 a linked list, 624–26
 sequential search, 400–403
seekg() file window function, 661
seekp() file window function, 663

Selection control structure:
    if, 212–16
    if/else, 217–19
    switch, 227–34
Selection sort, 427
Selector variable, 230
    in a **switch** statement, 227
Sentinel, 259, 266
SeqSearch( ) function, 400
Sequence, 616, 642
    explicit, 617
    Fibonacci, 376
    implicit, 617
Sequence control structure, 13
Sequential search, 400–403
Serial search. *See* Sequential search
setf( ), *ios* flag set function, 114
setw( ), set width manipulator, 110
short int, or **short**, 42
showpoint, *ios* flag, 117
Side effect, 350
Simultaneous equation solution, 692–703
sin( ), sine function, 189, 202
Single inheritance, 521
sizeof( ) function, 675
Software, 30
Solution planning, 4
Sorting:
    bubble sort, 426
    insertion sort, 403–9
    selection sort, 427
Source program, 33
sqrt( ), square root function, 189
srand( ), rand initializer function, 189, 425
Stack, 502–3, 577–78, 587–601
    ADT, 587
    application file, 599
    class, 594
    header file, 594
    implementation, 587–601, 639
    implementation file, 596
    implementation using a linked list, 639
    implementation using an array, 588–89
    operations, 586–87
    use of in recursion, 358
Stack( ), constructor function, 503
Standard classes, 39
Standard deviation, 300

Standard function, 47
    conversion, 188
    mathematical, 189
    string, 189
Statement, compound, 213
Static array, 420
Static binding, 525
Static memory allocation, 535
Static pointer, 533–35
    for a structure, 556
    for an object, 564
    initialization, 534
stdio header file, 138
stdlib header file, 188–89
Stepwise refinement, 14, 18, 25
strcat( ), string concatenation function, 190
strcmp( ), string compare function, 190–91
strcpy( ), string copy function, 190
Stream, 98
    <<, insertion operator, 98, 653
    >>, extraction operator, 119, 655
    cin, 118–35, 643
    classes, 142
    cout, 97–105, 643
    defining file objects, 142
    file, 142–45, 644–48
    file buffer, 649
    flushing output buffer, 102
    input buffer, 142
    output, 98
    output buffer, 142
    print object, 106
String, 51–52
    arrays of, 545
    functions, 189
    pointer, 540, 545
    strcat( ), string concatenation function, 190
    strcmp( ), string compare function, 190
    strcpy( ), string copy function, 189–90
    strlen( ), string length function, 190, 663
    two-dimensional array of, 686
strlen( ), string length function, 190, 663
Stroustrup, Bjarne, 35
struct, 30, 40. *See also* Structure
Structure, 430–52
    access, 437–45
        direct assignment, 437, 557
        dot operator, 437–38

path, 437
    reading information into, 438, 558
    retrieving information from, 439, 558
    using pointers, 555–64
declaration format, 431
defining objects for, 432
encapsulation, 459–62
initialization of, 434–36
members, 430–31
nested, 445–52
pointer:
    dynamic, 556
    static, 556
Structure diagram, 19, 80, 152, 236, 268, 335, 362
Structured design, 76
Structured programming, 29, 76, 325, 399
Super-now checking account class, 509
Swap( ) function, 372, 548
switch statement, 227–34
    break option, 230
    default option, 232–34
    flow of, 228
    format of, 229
    in menu-driven programs, 234–42, 267–73
Syntax error, 7
System directory, 72

T

\t, horizontal tab escape sequence, 105
Table. *See* Two-dimensional array
tan( ), tangent function, 189
tellg( ) function, 661
tellp( ) function, 661
Testing and debugging, 5–9
Thompson, Ken, 35
toascii( ), character to ASCII function, 188
tolower( ), character to lowercase function, 188
Top-down design, 78, 304–05, 349
TopElement( ), stack function, 594
toupper( ), character to uppercase function, 664
Translator:
    assembler, 32

compiler, 33
    interpreter, 33
TraverseList( ), linked list function, 628
Triangulation, 209
true, 53
trunc, *ios* flag, 646
Truth table, 182
Two-dimensional array, 671–88
Type mismatch error, 7, 123, 190

U

unsetf( ), *ios* flag unset function, 116
unsigned char, 50
unsigned int, 42
unsigned long, 42
User-defined function, 77, 304–05

V

\v, vertical tab escape sequence, 105
Value parameter, 318–20
Variable, 58–64
    Boolean, 64
    definition format, 58
    global, 347
    initialization, 254
    lifetime, 351
    local, 73, 347
    pointer, 530
    scope of, 349–51
    selector in a **switch** statement, 227
    static, 351
    string, 62
        definition format, 62
Variable parameter. *See* Reference parameter
Venn diagram, 518
Verb, within a problem statement, 4, 21
Virtual function, 524
    binding of, 524
Visibility. *See* Scope
void function, 316–24
    calling of, 317

W

Wheatstone bridge, 708
while loop, 251–61
   data entry using, 258–61
   flow of, 252
   format of, 252
Whitespace, 119, 125
   extraction using a trash variable, 137
   extraction using *ws*, 138

Window file functions, 663
Working directory, 72
Write operation, 19
WriteFile( ) function, 651
ws, whitespace manipulator, 138

X

XOR, ^ Boolean operator, 204